FOURTH EDITION

Concepts of Programming Languages

FOURTH EDITION

Concepts of Programming Languages

Robert W. Sebesta

University of Colorado, Colorado Springs

ADDISON-WESLEY

An imprint of Addison Wesley Longman, Inc.

Reading, Massachusetts • Harlow, England • Menlo Park, California
Berkeley, California • Don Mills, Ontario • Sydney • Bonn • Amsterdam
Tokyo • Mexico City

Acquisitions Editor: Maite Suarez-Rivas
Assistant Editor: Molly Taylor
Production Editor: Patricia A. O. Unubun
Cover Design: Alwyn R. Velásquez
Interior Design and Composition: Greg Johnson, Art Directions
Photo Credits: Photos reprinted with permission from *History of Programming Languages,* ACM Monograph Series, edited by Richard L. Wexelblat.

To Al and Violet

This book was typeset in QuarkXpress 3.32 on a Power Macintosh 8600. The fonts used were ITC Veljovic, Franklin Gothic, Courier 10 Pitch, and ITC Stone Sans for display. It was printed on New Era Matte.

Reprinted with corrections, February 1999.

Library of Congress Cataloging-in-Publication Data

Sebesta, Robert W.
    Concepts of programming languages / by Robert W. Sebesta. -- 4th ed.
        p.   cm.
    Includes bibliographical references and index.
    ISBN 0-201-38596-1
    1. Programming languages (Electronic computers) I. Title.
QA76.7.S43 1999
005.13--dc21   98-27193
                                                 CIP

4 5 6 7 8 9 10 MA 02010099

Preface

The goals, overall structure, and approach of this fourth edition of *Concepts of Programming Languages* remain the same as those of the three earlier editions. The principal goal is to provide the reader with the tools necessary for the critical evaluation of existing and future programming languages and constructs. An additional goal is to prepare the reader for the study of compiler design and construction.

The book should also answer a myriad of questions that may have occurred to the reader who may know only one high-level programming language. For example, why are there so many different programming languages? How and why were they developed? In what ways are they similar? What are their differences? What kinds of programming languages may be developed and used in the future? Why wouldn't we simply continue to use what we have now?

There are two ways in which a book on the concepts of programming languages can be organized: a horizontal approach and a vertical approach. With the horizontal approach, each language selected is presented in some depth. With the vertical approach, the general concepts and constructs of programming languages are described in some particular sequence. For each construct, design issues are explored and examples from a variety of languages are presented. Both methods have merit. In order to accurately describe individual language concepts it is important to focus on the concepts and consider their impact on programming and the evolution of languages. However, a chronological analysis of language developments necessitates the study of specific languages and their origins and development. Furthermore, the design of a specific facility of a particular language is often influenced by other characteristics of the language. Because of these considerations, this book uses the vertical approach for the majority of the material, but uses the horizontal approach when it is advantageous.

In this book I describe the fundamental concepts of programming languages by defining the design issues of the various language constructs, examining the design choices for these constructs in some of the most common languages, and critically comparing the design alternatives.

Taking this approach requires studying a collection of closely related topics. To discuss languages and language constructs, descriptive tools are vital. I discuss in detail the most effective and widely used methods of syntax description. I also introduce the most common methods for describing the semantics of programming languages. To understand some of the reasons why the particular design choices for existing languages were made, I describe the historical context and specific needs that spawned them. Because difficulty of implementation is often a significant influence on language design, discussions of implementation methods and issues are integrated throughout the book.

The following paragraphs outline the contents of the fourth edition.

Chapter 1 begins with a rationale for studying programming languages. It then discusses the criteria for evaluating programming languages. I recognize that defining these criteria is risky; however, evaluation principles are essential to any serious study of the design of programming languages. The primary influences on language design, common design trade-offs, and the basic approaches to implementation are also examined in the chapter.

Chapter 2 uses the horizontal approach to chart the chronological evolution of most of the important languages discussed in this book. Although no language is described completely, the origins, purposes, and contributions of each are discussed. This historical overview is valuable because it provides the background necessary to understanding the practical and theoretical basis for contemporary language design. It also motivates the further study of language design and evaluation. However, because none of the remainder of the book depends on Chapter 2, it can be skipped in its entirety.

Chapter 3 describes the primary formal methods for describing the syntax of programming languages: EBNF and syntax graphs. This is followed by a description of attribute grammars, which play a prominent role in compiler design. The difficult task of semantic description is then explored, including brief introductions to the three most common methods: operational, axiomatic, and denotational semantics.

Chapters 4 through 13 use the vertical approach to describe in detail the design issues for the primary constructs of the imperative languages. In each case, the design choices for several example languages are presented and evaluated. Specifically, the many characteristics of variables are covered in Chapter 4; more complicated data types in Chapter 5; expressions and assignment statements in Chapter 6; control statements in Chapter 7; subprograms and their implementation in Chapters 8 and 9; data abstraction facilities in Chapter 10; language features that support object-oriented programming (inheritance and dynamic method binding) in Chapter 11; concurrent program units in Chapter 12; and exception handling in Chapter 13. I use the vertical approach because it is inappropriate to describe and evaluate the details of a particular construct in several different parts of the book, as the horizontal approach would require for these topics. Discussing in a single chapter the various methods for providing concurrency, for example, allows for a concise comparison and evaluation of those methods.

The last two chapters (14 and 15) describe two of the most important alternative programming paradigms: functional programming and logic programming. Each is discussed as a programming methodology, and then exemplified through a brief introduction to a specific language.

Specifically, Chapter 14 begins by discussing simple mathematical functions, functional forms, and functional programming languages. It then presents an introduction to Scheme, including descriptions of some of its primitive functions, special forms, functional forms, and some examples of simple functions written in Scheme. Brief introductions to COMMON LISP, ML, and Haskell are given to illustrate some different kinds of functional languages. The chapter concludes with a comparison of functional and imperative languages.

The topic of Chapter 15 is logic programming and logic programming languages. I begin by introducing predicate calculus and explaining how it is used to prove theorems. This is followed by an overview of logic programming. The bulk of the chapter is an introduction to Prolog, including descriptions of resolution and unification, and some example programs and descriptions of their behavior.

Changes for the Fourth Edition

The fourth edition of this book is a significant revision of the third edition. Most of the changes result from the growing dominance of the object-oriented programming paradigm. The following paragraphs list the most important of these changes.

In a clear break from the earlier editions, and with most other books on programming languages, the fourth edition does *not* include a chapter on object-oriented languages. It *does* include a chapter on language support for object-oriented programming, specifically inheritance and dynamic method binding. This chapter, which is a greatly revised version of Chapter 15 in the third edition, has been moved to its more logical position as Chapter 11, immediately following the chapter on data abstraction. It has been significantly expanded to include an extensive discussion of a collection of design issues, which provides a framework for the descriptions and evaluations of the various language designs for inheritance and dynamic method binding.

There are two reasons for this new approach: First, the great majority of object-oriented software that is now written is authored in languages that are similar to the imperative languages of the past four decades. The expressions, assignment statements, data structures, and control structures of these languages are very similar to those of C and Pascal. Therefore, there is no reason to treat these features of these languages separately. By our definition of an imperative language, C++, Ada 95, and Java are imperative languages. I regard their support for object-oriented programming as being the next stage of development of the imperative languages. While the object-oriented software development paradigm is very different from the procedural paradigm, the languages in which these two approaches are used are not that different. The difference between a language that supports data-oriented programming, such as Ada 83, and one that supports object-oriented programming is even less significant. The second reason for the change in attitude about object-oriented languages is that object-oriented programming is no longer the new and experimental paradigm it was not too many years ago. It is now the dominant approach to software development and the languages used for it are the most widely used languages around today. Therefore, a book such as this should not relegate the discussions of language features for it to a single late chapter, such as we still do with logic programming languages. It clearly should be integrated into most of the chapters of the book, which is what we have done in the fourth edition.

Other changes include the following: The appearance of Java and its rapid rise in popularity requires added coverage of several of its interesting features. Specifically, its support for object-oriented programming has been added to Chapter 11, its concurrency to Chapter 12, and its exception handling to Chapter 13. In addition, some of its other features appear in earlier chapters.

Because Miranda is proprietary and Haskell is in the public domain, we have replaced the discussion or Miranda in Chapter 14 with one on Haskell.

The sections in Chapter 3 on axiomatic and denotational semantics have been again strengthened in the fourth edition.

Besides adding coverage of new languages and new features of older languages, we have deleted some discussion of older languages. For example, Modula-2 coroutines and its support for abstract data types have been dropped.

Numerous smaller changes ensure that the fourth edition correctly reflects the current state of programming language evolution.

To the Instructor

In the junior-level programming language course at the University of Colorado at Colorado Springs, the book is used as follows: We typically cover Chapters 1 and 3 in detail. Chapter 2 requires little lecture time because of its lack of hard technical content. Students find it interesting and beneficial reading, however. Because no material in subsequent chapters depends on Chapter 2, it can, as noted earlier, be skipped entirely.

Chapters 4 through 8 and 10 should be relatively easy for students with extensive programming experience in Pascal, C, C++, or Ada. Chapters 9, 11, 12, and 13 are more challenging and require more detailed lectures.

Chapters 14 and 15 are entirely new to most students at the junior level. Ideally, language processors for Scheme and Prolog should be available for Chapters 14 and 15. Sufficient material is included in these chapters to allow students to dabble with some simple programs.

Undergraduate courses will probably not be able to cover all of the last two chapters in detail. Graduate courses, however, by skipping over parts of the early chapters on imperative languages will be able to completely discuss the nonimperative languages.

Supplements

Two important and useful supplements are available for this book. An online solutions manual that includes answers to many of the problems in the chapter problem sets can be obtained upon request from an Addison-Wesley Publishing sales representative. A set of lecture notes slides is also available. These slides are in the form of Microsoft Powerpoint source files, one for each of the first 13 chapters of the book. I developed them over the past few years in teaching a course based on the book. The Powerpoint files are available through an anonymous ftp account on ftp.aw.com in directory/cseng/authors/sebesta/concepts4e. Please check the README or .message files at this site for further details and information on this and other supplements.

Language Processor Availability

Processors for and information about some of the programming languages discussed in this book can be found currently at the following Web sites:

Java	`http://java.sun.com`
Haskell	`http://haskell.org`
Scheme	`http://www-swiss.ai.mit/ftpdir/scheme-7.4/`

For updates, please refer to the home page for this book at `http://www.awl.com/cseng/titles/0-201-38596-1/`

Acknowledgments

The quality of this book was significantly improved as a result of the extensive suggestions, corrections, and comments provided by its reviewers.

The first three editions were reviewed by Vicki Allan, Henry Bauer, Peter Brouwer, Paosheng Chang, John Crenshaw, Barbara Ann Griem, Mary Lou Haag, Jon Mauney, Robert McCoard, Michael G. Murphy, Andrew Oldroyd, Jeffery Popyack, Steven Rapkin, Hamilton Richard, Tom Sager, Joseph Schell, and Mary Louise Soffa. The fourth edition was reviewed by:

- Mary Lou Haag, University of Colorado at Colorado Springs
- Hikyoo Koh, Lamar University
- Bruce Maxim, University of Michigan at Dearborn
- L. Andrew Oldroyd, Washington University
- Rebecca Parsons, University of Central Florida
- Don Bagert, Texas Technical University

Maite Suarez-Rivas, editor, Molly Taylor, assistant editor, and Pat Unubun, production editor, all deserve my gratitude for their efforts to produce the fourth edition quickly, as well as helping to make it be significantly better than the third.

Finally, I thank my children, Jake and Darcie, for their patience in enduring my absence from them throughout the endless hours of effort I invested in writing the four editions of this book.

About the Author

Robert Sebesta is an Associate Professor and Chairman of the Computer Science Department at the University of Colorado, Colorado Springs. Professor Sebesta received a B.S. in applied mathematics from the University of Colorado in Boulder and his M.S. and Ph.D. degrees in Computer Science from the Pennsylvania State University. He has been teaching computer science for over 25 years. His professional interests are the design and evaluation of programming languages, compiler design, and software testing methods and tools. He is a member of the ACM and the IEEE Computer Society.

Contents

FOURTH EDITION

Concepts of Programming Languages

1 Preliminaries

Konrad Zuse

Konrad Zuse designed a series of electromechanical computers between 1936 and 1944 in Germany. In 1945, he designed a complete algorithmic programming language, Plankalkül, which was never implemented, and its complete description was not even published until 1972.

Before we begin our exposition of the concepts of programming languages, we must consider a few preliminaries. First we discuss some reasons why computer science students and professional software developers should study general language-design and evaluation concepts. This discussion is valuable for those who believe that a working knowledge of one or two programming languages is sufficient for computer scientists. The major programming domains are then briefly described. Next, because the book evaluates language features, we present a list of criteria by which judgments can be made. The two major influences on language design, machine architecture and program design methodologies, are then discussed. Next we describe a few of the major trade-offs that must be considered during language design.

Because this book is also about the implementation of programming languages, this chapter includes an overview of the most common approaches to implementation. Finally, we briefly describe a few examples of programming environments and discuss their impact on software production.

1.1 Reasons for Studying Concepts of Programming Languages

It is natural for students to wonder how they will benefit from the study of programming language concepts. After all, an abundance of other topics in computer science are worthy of serious study. The following is what we believe to be a compelling list of potential benefits of studying language concepts.

- *Increased capacity to express ideas*. It is widely believed that the depth at which we can think is influenced by the expressive power of the language in which we communicate our thoughts. Those with a limited grasp of natural language are limited in the complexity of their thoughts, particularly in depth of abstraction. In other words, it is difficult for people to conceptualize structures they cannot describe, verbally or in writing. Programmers in the process of developing software are similarly constrained. The language in which they develop software places limits on the kinds of control structures, data structures, and abstractions they can use; thus the forms of algorithms they can construct are also limited.

  Awareness of a wider variety of programming language features can reduce such limitations in software development. Programmers can increase the range of their software-development thought processes by learning new language constructs.

  It might be argued that learning the capabilities of other languages does not help a programmer who is forced to use a language that lacks those capabilities. That argument does not hold up, however, because often language facilities can be simulated in other languages that do not support those features directly.

For example, having learned of the string manipulation functions of FORTRAN 90 (ANSI, 1992), such as the substring search function, INDEX, a Pascal (Ledgard, 1984) programmer would naturally be led to building subprograms to provide those operations. The same is true for many other more complex constructs that are discussed in this book.

The study of programming language concepts builds an appreciation for valuable language features and encourages programmers to use them.

The fact that many features of languages can be simulated in other languages does not lessen significantly the importance of designing languages with the best collection of features. It is always better to use a feature whose design has been integrated into a language than to use a simulation of that feature, which is often less elegant and more cumbersome in a language that does not support it.

- *Improved background for choosing appropriate languages*. Many professional programmers have had little formal education in computer science; rather, they have learned programming on their own or through in-house training programs. Such training programs often teach one or two languages that are directly relevant to the current work of the organization. Many other programmers received their formal training in the distant past. The languages they learned then are no longer used, and many features now available in programming languages were not widely known. The result of this background is that many programmers, when given a choice of languages for a new project, continue to use the language with which they are most familiar, even if it is poorly suited to the new project. If these programmers were familiar with the other languages available, and especially the particular features in those languages, they would be in a better position to make informed language choices.

- *Increased ability to learn new languages*. Computer programming is a young discipline, and design methodologies, software development tools, and programming languages are still in a state of continuous evolution. This makes software development an exciting profession, but it also means that continuous learning is essential. The process of learning a new programming language can be lengthy and difficult, especially for someone who is comfortable with only one or two languages and has never examined programming language concepts in general. Once a thorough understanding of the fundamental concepts of languages is acquired, it becomes far easier to see how these concepts are incorporated into the design of the language being learned.

For example, programmers who understand the concept of data abstraction will have a much easier time learning how to construct abstract data types in Java (Gosling et al., 1996) than those who are not at all familiar with data abstraction. The same phenomenon occurs in natural languages. The better you know the grammar of your native language, the easier you will find it to learn a second natural language. Furthermore, learning a second language also has the beneficial side effect of teaching you more about your first language.

Finally, it is essential that practicing programmers know the vocabulary and fundamental concepts of programming languages so they can read and understand programming language manuals and sales literature for languages and compilers.

- *Better understanding of the significance of implementation.* In learning the concepts of programming languages, it is both interesting and necessary to touch on the implementation issues that affect those concepts. In some cases, an understanding of implementation issues leads to an understanding of why languages are designed the way they are. This in turn leads to the ability to use a language more intelligently, as it was designed to be used. We can become better programmers by understanding the choices among programming language constructs and the consequences of those choices.

  Certain kinds of program bugs can only be found and fixed by a programmer who knows some related implementation details. Another benefit of understanding implementation issues is that it allows us to visualize how a computer executes various language constructs. This in turn fosters an understanding of the relative efficiency of alternative constructs that may be chosen for a program. For example, programmers who know little about how recursion is implemented often do not know that a recursive algorithm is typically far slower than an equivalent iterative algorithm.

- *Increased ability to design new languages.* To a student, the possibility of being required at some future time to design a new programming language may seem remote. However, most professional programmers occasionally do design languages of one sort or another. For example, most software systems require the user to interact in some way, even if only to enter data and commands. In simple situations, only a few data values are entered, and the input format language is trivial. On the other hand, the user might be required to traverse several levels of menus and enter a variety of commands, as in the case of a word processor. In such systems, the user interface is a complex design problem. The form of that interface is designed by the system developer and the criteria for judging it are similar to criteria used to judge the design of a programming language. A critical examination of programming languages, therefore, will help in the design of such complex systems, and more commonly, it will help users examine and evaluate such products.

■ *Overall advancement of computing.* Finally, there is a global view of computing that can justify the study of programming language concepts. Although it is usually possible to determine why a particular programming language became popular, it is not always clear, at least in retrospect, that the most popular languages are the best available. In some cases, it might be concluded, a language became widely used, at least in part, because those in positions to choose languages were not sufficiently familiar with programming language concepts.

For example, many people believe it would have been better if ALGOL 60 (Backus et al., 1962) had displaced FORTRAN in the early 1960s, because it was more elegant and had much better control statements than FORTRAN, among other reasons. That it did not is due partly to the programmers and software development managers of that time, many of whom did not clearly understand the conceptual design of ALGOL 60. They found its description difficult to read (which it was) and even more difficult to understand. They did not appreciate the benefits of block structure, recursion, and well-structured control statements, so they failed to see the benefits of ALGOL 60 over FORTRAN.

Of course, many other factors contributed to the lack of acceptance of ALGOL 60, as we will see in Chapter 2. However, the fact that computer users were generally unaware of the benefits of the language played a significant role.

In general, if those who choose languages are better informed, perhaps better languages would more quickly squeeze out poorer ones.

1.2 Programming Domains

Computers have been applied to a myriad of different areas, from controlling nuclear power plants to storing the records of personal checkbooks. Because of this great diversity in computer use, programming languages with very different goals have been developed. In this section, we briefly discuss a few of the areas of computer applications and their associated languages.

1.2.1 Scientific Applications

The first digital computers, which appeared in the 1940s, were used and in fact invented for scientific applications. Typically, scientific applications have simple data structures but require large numbers of floating-point arithmetic computations. The most common data structures are arrays and matrices; the most common control structures are counting loops and selections. The high-level programming languages invented for scientific applications were designed to provide for those needs. Their competition was assembly language, so efficiency was a primary concern. The first language for scientific applications was FORTRAN. ALGOL 60 and most of its descendants were also intended for use in this area, though they were designed to be used in other related areas also. For some scientific applications where efficiency is the primary concern, like those that were common in the 1950s and 1960s, no subsequent language is significantly better than FORTRAN.

1.2.2 Business Applications

The use of computers for business applications began in the 1950s. Special computers were developed for this purpose, along with special languages. The first successful high-level language for business was COBOL (ANSI, 1985), which appeared in 1960. It is still the most commonly used language for these applications. Business languages are characterized by facilities for producing elaborate reports, precise ways of describing and storing decimal numbers and character data, and the ability to specify decimal arithmetic operations.

With the advent of microcomputers came new ways for businesses, especially small businesses, to use computers. Two specific tools that can be used on small computers, spreadsheet systems and database systems, were developed for business and now are widely used.

There have been only limited developments in business application languages other than COBOL. Therefore, this book does not discuss business application languages other than to provide a history of the development of COBOL in Chapter 2.

1.2.3 Artificial Intelligence

Artificial intelligence (AI) is a broad area of computer applications characterized by the use of symbolic rather than numeric computations. Symbolic computation means that symbols, consisting of names rather than numbers, are manipulated. Also, symbolic computation is more conveniently done with linked lists of data rather than arrays. This kind of programming sometimes requires more flexibility than other programming domains. For example, in some AI applications the ability to create and execute code segments during execution is convenient.

The first widely used programming language developed for AI applications was the functional language LISP (McCarthy et al., 1965), which appeared in 1959. Most AI applications have been written in LISP or one of its close relatives. During the early 1970s, however, an alternative approach to these applications appeared—logic programming using the Prolog (Clocksin and Mellish, 1997) language. Scheme, a dialect of LISP, and Prolog are introduced in Chapters 14 and 15, respectively.

1.2.4 Systems Programming

The operating system and all of the programming support tools of a computer system are collectively known as its **systems software.** Systems software is used almost continuously and therefore must have execution efficiency. Therefore, a language for this domain must provide fast execution. Furthermore, it must have low-level features that allow the software interfaces to external devices to be written.

In the 1960s and 1970s, some computer manufacturers, such as IBM, Digital, and Burroughs (now UNISYS), developed special machine-oriented high-level languages for systems software on their machines. For IBM mainframe computers, the language was PL/S, a dialect of PL/I; for Digital, it was BLISS, a language at a level just above assembly language; for Burroughs, it was Extended ALGOL.

The UNIX operating system is written almost entirely in C (ANSI, 1989), which has made it relatively easy to port, or move, to different machines. Some of the characteristics of C make it nicely applicable to systems programming. It is low-level, it is execution efficient, and it does not burden the user with many safety restrictions. Systems programmers are often excellent programmers and do not believe they need such restrictions. Some, however, find C to be too dangerous to use on large, important software systems.

1.2.5 Scripting Languages

Scripting languages evolved slowly over the past 25 years. A scripting language is used by putting a list of commands, called a script, in a file to be executed. The first of these languages, named `sh` (for shell), began as a small collection of commands that were interpreted as calls to system subprograms that performed utility functions, such as file management and simple file filtering. To this basis were added variables, control flow statements, functions, and various other capabilities, and the result is a complete programming language. One of the most powerful and widely known of these is `ksh` (Bolsky and Korn, 1995), which was developed by David Korn at Bell Laboratories.

`awk` is another scripting language, developed by Al Aho, Brian Kernighan, and Peter Wienberger at Bell Laboratories (Aho et al., 1988). `awk` began as a report-generation language but later became a more general-purpose language. `tcl` is an extensible scripting language developed by John Ousterhout at the University of California at Berkeley (Ousterhout,

1994). `tcl` is now combined with `tk`, a language that provides a method of building X Window applications. The Perl language, developed by Larry Wall, was originally a combination of `sh` and `awk` (Wall et al., 1996). Perl has grown significantly since its beginnings, and is now a powerful though somewhat primitive programming language. Although it is still often called a scripting language, we prefer to think of it as an odd but full-fledged programming language. Since the advent of the World Wide Web, the popularity of Perl has risen dramatically, primarily because it is a nearly ideal language for Common Gateway Interface (CGI) programming.

Scripting languages in general have contributed little to the development of more conventional programming languages. However, Perl has several interesting features that we will discuss later in this book.

1.2.6   Special-Purpose Languages

A host of special-purpose languages have appeared over the past 40 years. They range from RPG, which is used to produce business reports, to APT, which is used for instructing programmable machine tools, to GPSS, which is used for systems simulation. This book does not discuss special-purpose languages, primarily because of their narrow applicability and the difficulty of comparing them with other languages.

1.3 Language Evaluation Criteria

As noted previously, the purpose of this book is to examine carefully the underlying concepts of the various constructs and capabilities of programming languages. We will also evaluate these features, focusing on their impact on the software development (including maintenance) process. To accomplish this, we need a set of evaluation criteria. However, a list of such criteria is necessarily controversial, because it is virtually impossible to get even two computer scientists to agree on the value of some given language characteristic relative to others. In spite of these differences, most computer scientists would agree that the criteria discussed in the following subsections are important.

Some of the characteristics that influence the most important of these criteria are shown in Table 1.1 on page 9, and the criteria themselves are discussed in the following sections.

1.3.1   Readability

One of the most important criteria for judging a programming language is the ease with which programs can be read and understood. Before 1970,

Table 1.1
Language evaluation criteria and the characteristics that affect them.

	Criteria		
Characteristic	*Readability*	*Writability*	*Reliability*
Simplicity/orthogonality	•	•	•
Control structures	•	•	•
Data types & structures	•	•	•
Syntax design	•	•	•
Support for abstraction		•	•
Expressivity		•	•
Type checking			•
Exception handling			•
Restricted aliasing			•

software development was largely thought of in terms of writing code. In the 1970s, however, the software life cycle concept (Booch, 1987) was developed; coding was relegated to a much smaller role, and maintenance was recognized as a major part of the cycle, particularly in terms of cost. Because ease of maintenance is determined in large part by the readability of programs, readability became an important measure of the quality of programs and programming languages.

Readability must be considered in the context of the problem domain. For example, if a program that describes a computation was written in a language not designed for such use, the program may be unnatural and convoluted, making it unusually difficult to read.

The following subsections describe characteristics that contribute to the readability of a programming language.

1.3.1.1 Overall Simplicity

The overall simplicity of a programming language strongly affects its readability. First of all, a language that has a large number of basic components is more difficult to learn than one with a small number of basic components. Programmers who must use a large language tend to learn a subset of the language and ignore its other features. This learning pattern is sometimes used to excuse the large number of language components, but that argument is not valid. Readability problems occur whenever the program's author has learned a different subset from that subset with which the reader is familiar.

A second complicating characteristic of a programming language is feature multiplicity—that is, having more than one way to accomplish a particular operation. For example, in C, a user can increment a simple integer variable in four different ways:

```
count = count + 1
count += 1
count++
++count
```

Although the last two statements have slightly different meaning from each other and from the others in some uses, all four have the same meaning when used as stand-alone expressions. These variations are discussed in Chapter 6.

A third potential problem is operator overloading, in which a single operator symbol has more than one meaning. Although this is a useful feature, it can lead to reduced readability if users are allowed to create their own overloading and do not do it sensibly. For example, it is clearly acceptable to overload + to use it for both integer and floating-point addition. In fact, this overloading simplifies a language by reducing the number of operators. However, suppose the programmer defined + used between single-dimensioned array operands to mean the sum of all elements of both arrays. Because the usual meaning of vector addition is quite different from this, it would make the program more confusing for both the author and its readers. An even more extreme example of program confusion would be a user defining + between two vector operands to mean the difference between their respective first elements. Operator overloading is further discussed in Chapter 6.

Simplicity in languages can, of course, be carried too far. For example, the form and meaning of most assembly language statements are models of simplicity, as you can see when you consider the statements that appear in the next section. This very simplicity, however, makes assembly language programs less readable. Because they lack more complex control statements, their structure is less obvious; because their statements are simple, far more of them are required than equivalent programs in a high-level language. These same arguments apply to the less extreme case of high-level languages with inadequate control and data structuring constructs.

1.3.1.2 Orthogonality

Orthogonality in a programming language means that a relatively small set of primitive constructs can be combined in a relatively small number of ways to build the control and data structures of the language. Furthermore, every possible combination of primitives is legal and meaningful. For example, consider data types. Suppose a language has four primitive data types, integer, float, double, and character, and two type operators, array and pointer. If the two type operators can be applied to themselves and the four primitive data types, a large number of data structures can be defined. However, if pointers were not allowed to point to arrays, many of those possibilities would be eliminated.

The meaning of an orthogonal language feature is independent of the context of its appearance in a program. (The name orthogonal comes from the mathematical concept of orthogonal vectors, which are independent of each other.) Orthogonality follows from a symmetry of relationships among primitives. Pointers should be able to point to any type of variable or data structure. The lack of orthogonality leads to exceptions to the rules of the language.

We can illustrate the use of orthogonality as a design concept by comparing one aspect of the assembly languages of the IBM mainframe computers and the VAX series of superminicomputers. We consider a single simple situation: adding two 32-bit integer values that reside in either memory or registers and replacing one of the two values with the sum. The IBM mainframes have two instructions for this purpose, which have the forms

```
A    Reg1, memory_cell
AR   Reg1, Reg2
```

where Reg1 and Reg2 represent registers. The semantics of these are

$$Reg1 \leftarrow contents(Reg1) + contents(memory\_cell)$$
$$Reg1 \leftarrow contents(Reg1) + contents(Reg2)$$

The VAX addition instruction for 32-bit integer values is

```
ADDL operand_1, operand_2
```

whose semantics is

$$operand\_2 \leftarrow contents(operand\_1) + contents(operand\_2)$$

In this case, either operand can be a register or a memory cell.

The VAX instruction design is orthogonal in that a single instruction can use either registers or memory cells as the operands. There are two ways to specify operands, which can be combined in all possible ways. The IBM design is not orthogonal. Only two operand combinations are legal out of four possibilities, and the two require different instructions, A and AR. The IBM design is more restricted and therefore less writable. For example, you cannot add two values and store the sum in a memory location. Furthermore, the IBM design is more difficult to learn because of the restrictions and the additional instruction.

Orthogonality is closely related to simplicity: The more orthogonal the design of a language, the fewer exceptions the language rules require. Fewer exceptions mean a higher degree of regularity in the design, which makes the language easier to learn, read, and understand. Anyone who has learned a significant part of the English language can testify to the difficulty of learning its many rule exceptions (for example, *i* before *e* except after *c*).

As examples of the lack of orthogonality in a high-level language, manifested as rule exceptions, consider the following rules in C. Although C has two kinds of structured data types, arrays and records (**struct**s), records can be returned from functions but arrays cannot. A member of a structure can be any data type except **void** or a structure of the same type. An array element can be any data type except **void** or a function. Parameters are passed by value, unless they are arrays, in which case they are, in effect, passed by reference (because the appearance of an array name without a subscript in a C program is interpreted to be the address of the array's first element). A simple addition expression, such as

```
a + b
```

usually means the values of a and b are fetched from memory and added. However, if a happens to be a pointer, the fetched value of b may be changed before the addition takes place. For example, if a points at a value that is two bytes long, b's value is multiplied by 2 before the addition takes place. The type of a, which is the left context of

```
+ b
```

forces the value of b to be modified before it is added to a.

Too much orthogonality can also cause problems. Perhaps the most orthogonal programming language is ALGOL 68 (van Wijngaarden et al., 1969). Every language construct in ALGOL 68 has a type, and there are no restrictions on those types. In addition, most constructs produce values. This combinational freedom allows extremely complex constructs. For example, a conditional can appear as the left side of an assignment, along with declarations and other assorted statements, as long as the result is a location. This extreme form of orthogonality leads to unnecessary complexity. Furthermore, because languages require a large number of primitives, a high degree of orthogonality results in an explosion of combinations. So, even if the combinations are simple, their sheer numbers lead to complexity.

Simplicity in a language, therefore, is at least in part the result of a combination of a relatively small number of primitive constructs and a limited use of the concept of orthogonality.

Some believe that functional languages offer a good combination of simplicity and orthogonality. A functional language, such as LISP, is one in which computations are made primarily by applying functions to given parameters. In contrast, in imperative languages such as C, Pascal, and Java, computations are usually specified with variables and assignment statements. Functional languages offer potentially the greatest overall simplicity because they can accomplish everything with a single construct, the function call, which can be combined with other function calls in simple ways. This simple elegance is the reason why some language researchers are attracted to functional languages as the primary alternative to complex nonfunctional languages such as C++ (Ellis and Stroustrup, 1990). Other factors, such as efficiency, however, have prevented functional languages from becoming more widely used.

1.3.1.3 Control Statements

The structured programming revolution of the 1970s was in part a reaction to the poor readability caused by the limited control statements of some of the languages of the 1950s and 1960s. In particular, it became

widely recognized that indiscriminate use of goto statements severely reduces program readability. A program that can be read from top to bottom is much easier to understand than a program that requires the reader to jump from one statement to some nonadjacent statement in order to follow the execution order. In certain languages, however, gotos that branch upward are sometimes necessary; for example, they are required to construct WHILE loops in FORTRAN 77. Restricting gotos in the following ways can make programs far more readable:

- They must precede their targets, except when used to form loops.
- Their targets must never be too distant.
- Their numbers must be limited.

The versions of BASIC and FORTRAN that were available in the early 1970s lacked the control statements that allow strong restrictions on the use of gotos, so writing highly readable programs in those languages was difficult. Most programming languages designed since the late 1960s, however, have included sufficient control statements, so the need for the goto statement has been nearly eliminated. Therefore, the control statement design of a language is now a less important factor in readability than it was in the past.

1.3.1.4 Data Types and Structures

The presence of adequate facilities for defining data types and data structures in a language is another significant aid to readability. For example, suppose a numeric type is used for an indicator flag because there are no Boolean types in the language. In such a language, we might have an assignment such as

```
sum_is_too_big = 1
```

whose meaning is unclear, whereas in a language that includes Boolean types, we would have

```
sum_is_too_big = true
```

whose meaning is perfectly clear. Similarly, record data types provide a method for representing employee records that is more readable than using a collection of similar arrays, one for each data item in an employee record, which is the required method in a language without records. For example, in FORTRAN 77, an array of employee records might be stored in the following arrays:

```
CHARACTER (LEN = 30) NAME (100)
INTEGER AGE (100), EMPLOYEE_NUMBER (100)
REAL SALARY (100)
```

Then a particular employee is represented by the elements of these four arrays with the same subscript value.

1.3.1.5 Syntax Considerations

The syntax, or form, of the elements of a language has a significant effect on the readability of programs. The following are three examples of syntactic design choices that affect readability:

- *Identifier forms*. Restricting identifiers to very short lengths detracts from readability. If identifiers can have six characters at most, as in FORTRAN 77, it is often not possible to use connotative names for variables. A more extreme example is the original American National Standards Institute (ANSI) BASIC (ANSI, 1978b), in which an identifier could consist only of a single letter or a single letter followed by a single digit.

  Other design issues concerning identifier forms are discussed in Chapter 4.

- *Special words*. Program appearance and thus program readability are strongly influenced by the forms of a language's special words (for example, **begin**, **end**, and **for**). Especially important is the method of forming compound statements, or statement groups, primarily in control constructs. Several languages use matching pairs of special words or symbols to form groups. Pascal requires **begin–end** pairs to form groups for all control constructs except the **repeat** statement, where they can be omitted (an example of Pascal's lack of orthogonality). C uses braces for the same purpose. Both languages suffer because statement groups are always terminated in the same way, which makes it difficult to determine which group is being ended when an **end** or } appears. FORTRAN 90 and Ada make this clearer by using a distinct closing syntax for each type of statement group. For example, Ada uses **end if** to terminate a selection construct, and **end loop** to terminate a loop construct. This is an example of the conflict between simplicity that results in fewer reserved words, as in Pascal, and the greater readability that can result from using more reserved words, as in Ada.

  Another important issue is whether the special words of a language can be used as names for program variables. If so, the resulting programs can be very confusing. For example, in FORTRAN 90, special words such as DO and END are legal variable names, so the appearance of these words in a program may or may not connote something special.

- *Form and meaning*. Designing statements so that their appearance at least partially indicates their purpose is an obvious aid to readability. Semantics, or meaning, should follow directly from syntax, or form. In some cases, this principle is violated by two language constructs that are identical or similar in appearance but have different meanings, depending perhaps on context. In C, for example, the meaning of the reserved word **static** depends on the context of its appearance. If used on the definition of a variable inside a function, it means the variable is created at compile time. If used on the definition of a variable that is outside all functions, it means the variable is visible only in the file in which its definition appears; that is, it is not exported from that file.

One of the primary complaints about the shell commands of UNIX (Kernighan and Pike, 1984) is that their appearance does not always suggest their function. For example, the UNIX command `grep` can be deciphered only through prior knowledge, or perhaps cleverness and familiarity with the UNIX editor, `ed`. Its appearance connotes nothing to UNIX beginners. (In `ed`, the command /regular_expression/ searches for a substring that matches the regular expression. Preceding this with `g` makes it a global command, specifying that the scope of the search is the whole file being edited. Following the command with `p` specifies that lines with the matching substring are to be printed. So `g`/regular_expression/`p`, which can obviously be abbreviated as `grep`, prints all lines in a file that contain substrings that match the regular expression.)

1.3.2 Writability

Writability is a measure of how easily a language can be used to create programs for a chosen problem domain. Most of the language characteristics that affect readability also affect writability. This follows directly from the fact that the process of writing a program requires the programmer frequently to reread the part of the program that is already written.

As is the case with readability, writability must be considered in the context of the target problem domain of a language. It is simply not reasonable to compare the writability of two languages in the realm of a particular application when one was designed for that application and the other was not. For example, the writabilities of COBOL (ANSI, 1985) and APL (Gilman and Rose, 1976) are dramatically different for creating a program to deal with two-dimensional data structures, for which APL is ideal. Their writabilities are also quite different for producing financial reports with complex formats, for which COBOL was designed.

The following subsections describe the most important factors influencing the writability of a language.

1.3.2.1 Simplicity and Orthogonality

If a language has a large number of different constructs, some programmers may not be familiar with all of them. This can lead to a misuse of some features and a disuse of others that may be either more elegant or more efficient, or both, than those that are used. It may even be possible, as noted by Hoare (1973), to use unknown features accidentally, with bizarre results. Therefore, a smaller number of primitive constructs and a consistent set of rules for combining them (that is, orthogonality) is much better than simply having a large number of primitives. A programmer can design a solution to a complex problem after learning only a simple set of primitive constructs.

On the other hand, too much orthogonality can be a detriment to writability. Errors in writing programs can go undetected when nearly any combination of primitives is legal. This can lead to absurdities in code that cannot be discovered by the compiler.

1.3.2.2 Support for Abstraction

Briefly, **abstraction** means the ability to define and then use complicated structures or operations in ways that allow many of the details to be ignored. Abstraction is a key concept in contemporary programming language design. This is a reflection of the central role that abstraction plays in modern program design methodologies. The degree of abstraction allowed by a programming language and the naturalness of its expression are therefore very important to its writability. Programming languages can support two distinct categories of abstraction, process and data.

A simple example of process abstraction is the use of a subprogram to implement a sort algorithm that is required several times in a program. Without the subprogram, the sort code would have to be replicated in all places where it was needed, which would make the program much longer and more tedious to write. More importantly, if the subprogram were not used, the code that used the sort subprogram would be cluttered with the sort algorithm details, greatly obscuring the flow and overall intent of that code.

As an example of data abstraction, consider a binary tree that stores integer data in its nodes. Such a binary tree would usually be implemented in FORTRAN 77 as three parallel integer arrays, where two of the integers are used as subscripts to specify offspring nodes. In C++ and Java, these trees can be implemented by using an abstraction of a tree node in the form of a simple class with two pointers and an integer. The naturalness of the latter representation makes it much easier to write a program that uses binary trees in these languages than to write one in FORTRAN 77. It is a simple matter of the problem solution domain of the language being closer to the problem domain.

The overall support for abstraction is clearly an important factor in the writability of a language.

1.3.2.3 Expressivity

Expressivity in a language can refer to several different characteristics. In a language like APL, it means that there are very powerful operators that allow a great deal of computation to be accomplished with a very small program. It more commonly means that a language has relatively convenient, rather than cumbersome, ways of specifying computations. For example, in C, the notation `count++` is more convenient and shorter than count = count + 1. Also, the **and then** Boolean operator in Ada is a convenient way of specifying short-circuit evaluation of a Boolean expression. The inclusion of the **for** statement in Pascal makes writing counting loops easier than with the use of **while**, which is also possible. All of these increase the writability of a language.

1.3.3 Reliability

A program is said to be **reliable** if it performs to its specifications under all conditions. The following subsections describe several language features that have a significant effect on the reliability of programs in a given language.

1.3.3.1 Type Checking

Type checking is simply testing for type errors in a given program, either by the compiler or during program execution. Type checking is an important factor in language reliability. Because run-time type checking is expensive, compile-time checking is more desirable. Furthermore, the earlier errors in programs are detected, the less expensive it is to make the required repairs. The design of Ada requires checks of the types of nearly all variables and expressions at compile time, except when the user explicitly states that type checking is to be suspended. This virtually eliminates type errors at run time in Ada programs. Types and type checking are discussed in depth in Chapters 4 and 5.

One example of how failure to type check, at either compile time or run time, has led to countless program errors is the use of subprogram parameters in the original C language (Kernighan and Ritchie, 1978). In this language, the type of an actual parameter in a function call is not checked to determine whether its type matches that of the corresponding formal parameter in the function. An **int** type variable can be used as an actual parameter in a call to a function that expects a **float** type as its formal parameter, and neither the compiler nor the run-time system will detect the inconsistency. This naturally leads to problems, the source of which is often difficult to determine. (In response to this and other similar problems, UNIX systems include a utility program named lint that checks C programs for such problems.) Subprograms and parameter-passing methods are discussed in Chapter 8.

In Pascal, the subscript range of an array variable is part of the variable's type. Therefore, subscript range checking is part of type checking, although it must be done at run time. Because most types are checked in Pascal, subscript ranges are also checked. Such checking is extremely important to program reliability because out-of-range subscripts often cause errors that do not appear until long after the actual violations. Ada and Java also require all subscripts to be range checked.

1.3.3.2 Exception Handling

The ability of a program to intercept run-time errors (as well as other unusual conditions detected by the program), take corrective measures, and then continue is a great aid to reliability. This language facility is called **exception handling.** Ada, C++, and Java include extensive capabilities for exception handling, but such facilities are practically nonexistent in many widely used languages, such as C and FORTRAN. Exception handling is discussed in Chapter 13.

1.3.3.3 Aliasing

Loosely defined, **aliasing** is having two or more distinct referencing methods, or names, for the same memory cell. It is now widely accepted that aliasing is a dangerous feature in a programming language. Most programming languages allow some kind of aliasing—for example, union members and pointers set to point to the same variable in C. In both cases, two different program variables can refer to the same memory cell. Some kinds of aliasing, as described in Chapters 4 and 8, can be prohibited by the design of a language.

In some languages, aliasing is used to overcome deficiencies in the language's data abstraction facilities. Other languages greatly restrict aliasing to increase their reliability.

1.3.3.4 Readability and Writability

Both readability and writability influence reliability. A program written in a language that does not support natural ways to express the required algorithms will necessarily use unnatural methods. Unnatural methods will be less likely to be correct for all possible situations. The easier a program is to write, the more likely it is to be correct.

Readability affects reliability in both the writing and maintenance phases of the life cycle. Programs that are difficult to read are difficult both to write and to modify.

1.3.4 Cost

The ultimate total cost of a programming language is a function of many of its characteristics.

First, there is the cost of training programmers to use the language. This is a function of the simplicity and orthogonality of the language and the experience of the programmers. Though more powerful languages need not be harder to learn, they often are.

Second is the cost of writing programs in the language. This is a function of the writability of the language, which depends on its closeness in purpose to the particular application. The original efforts to design and implement high-level languages were driven by the desire to lower the costs of creating software.

Both the cost of training programmers and the cost of writing programs in a language can be significantly reduced in a good programming environment. Programming environments are discussed in Section 1.7.

Third is the cost of compiling programs in the language. A major impediment to the early use of Ada was the prohibitively high cost of running the first-generation Ada compilers. This problem was diminished by the appearance of better Ada compilers.

Fourth, the cost of executing programs written in a language is greatly influenced by that language's design. A language that requires many run-time type checks will prohibit fast code execution, regardless of the quality of the compiler. Although execution efficiency was the foremost concern in the design of early languages, it is now considered to be less important.

A simple trade-off can be made between compilation cost and execution speed of the compiled code. Optimization is the name given to the collection of methods that compilers may use to decrease the size and/or increase the execution speed of the code they produce. If little or no optimization is done, compilation can be done much faster than if a significant effort is made to produce optimized code. The extra compilation effort results in faster code execution. The choice between the two alternatives is determined by the environment in which the compiler will be used. In a laboratory for beginning programming students, who use a great deal of compiling time but little code execution time (their programs are small and they must execute correctly only once), little or no optimization should be done. In a production environment, where completed programs are executed many times, it is better to pay the extra cost to optimize the code.

The fifth factor in the cost of a language is the cost of the language implementation system. One of the factors that explains the rapid acceptance of Java is that free compiler/interpreter systems have been available for it since soon after its design was first released. A language whose implementation system is either expensive or runs only on expensive hardware will have a much smaller chance of ever becoming widely used.

Sixth is the cost of poor reliability. If the software fails in a critical system, such as a nuclear power plant or an X-ray machine, the cost could be very high. The failures of noncritical systems can also be very expensive in terms of lost future business or lawsuits over defective software systems.

The final consideration is the cost of maintaining programs, which includes both corrections and modifications to add new capabilities. The cost of software maintenance depends on a number of language characteristics but primarily readability. Because maintenance is often done by individuals other than the original author of the software, poor readability can make the task extremely challenging.

The importance of maintainability of software cannot be overstated. It has been estimated that, for large software systems with relatively long lifetimes, maintenance costs can be as high as two to four times as much as development costs (Sommerville, 1992).

Of all the contributors to language costs, three are most important: program development, maintenance, and reliability. Because these are functions of writability and readability, these two evaluation criteria are, in turn, the most important.

Of course, a number of other criteria are available for evaluating programming languages. One, for example, is portability, or the ease with which programs can be moved from one implementation to another. Portability is most strongly influenced by the degree of standardization of the language. Some languages, such as BASIC, are not standardized at all, making BASIC programs very difficult to move from one implementation to another. Standardization is a time-consuming and difficult process. A committee began work on producing a standard version of C++ in 1989. As of early 1998, that standard had not yet been completed.

Generality (the applicability to a wide range of applications) and well-definedness (the completeness and precision of the language's official defining document) are two other criteria.

Most criteria, particularly readability, writability, and reliability, are neither precisely defined nor exactly measurable. They are useful concepts, however, and they provide valuable insight into the design and evaluation of programming languages.

A final note on evaluation criteria: Language design criteria are weighed differently from different perspectives. Language implementors are concerned primarily about the difficulty of implementing the constructs and features of the language. Language users are worried about writability first and readability later. Language designers are likely to emphasize elegance and the ability to attract widespread use. These characteristics are sometimes in conflict with one another.

1.4 Influences on Language Design

In addition to those factors described in Section 1.3, several other factors influence the basic design of programming languages. The most important of these are computer architecture and program design methodologies.

1.4.1 Computer Architecture

The basic architecture of computers has had a crucial effect on language design. Most of the popular languages of the past 35 years have been designed around the prevalent computer architecture, called the von Neumann architecture, after one of its originators, John von Neumann (pronounced "von Noyman"). These languages are called **imperative** languages. In a von Neumann computer, both data and programs are stored in the same memory. The central processing unit (CPU), which actually executes instructions, is separate from the memory. Therefore, instructions and data must be piped, or transmitted, from memory to the CPU. Results of operations in the CPU must be moved back to memory. Nearly all digital computers built since the 1940s have been based on the von Neumann architecture. The overall structure of a von Neumann computer is shown in Figure 1.1.

Because of the von Neumann architecture, the central features of imperative languages are variables, which model the memory cells; assignment statements, which are based on the piping operation; and the iterative form of repetition, which is the most efficient method on this architecture. Operands in expressions are piped from memory to the CPU, and the result of evaluating the expression is piped back to the memory cell represented by the left side of the assignment. Iteration is fast on von Neumann computers because instructions are stored in adjacent cells of memory. This efficiency discourages the use of recursion for repetition, although recursion is often more natural.

As stated earlier, a functional, or applicative, language is one in which the primary means of making computations is by applying functions to given parameters. Programming can be done in a functional language without the kind of variables that are used in imperative languages, without assignment statements, and without iteration. Although many computer scientists have expounded on the myriad benefits of functional languages, such

Figure 1.1
The von Neumann
computer architecture

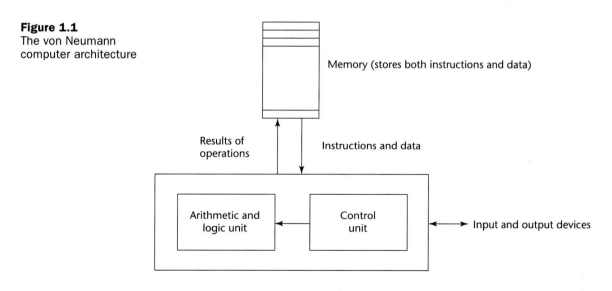

Memory (stores both instructions and data)

Results of operations

Instructions and data

Arithmetic and logic unit

Control unit

Input and output devices

Central processing unit

as LISP, it is unlikely that they will displace the imperative languages until a non-von Neumann computer is designed that will allow efficient execution of programs in functional languages. Among those bemoaning this fact, the most eloquent has been John Backus, the principal designer of the original version of FORTRAN (Backus, 1978).

The parallel architecture machines that appeared in the past 15 years hold some promise for speeding the execution of functional programs, but so far it has not been enough to make them competitive with imperative programs. In fact, although there are elegant ways of using parallel architectures to execute functional programs, most parallel machines are used for imperative programs, particularly those written in dialects of FORTRAN.

1.4.2 Programming Methodologies

The late 1960s and early 1970s brought an intense analysis, begun in large part by the structured programming movement, of both the software development process and programming language design.

An important reason for this research was the shift in the major cost of computing from hardware to software, as hardware costs decreased and programmer costs increased. Increases in programmer productivity were relatively small. In addition, progressively larger and more complex problems were being solved by computers. Rather than simply solving sets of equations to simulate satellite tracks, as in the early 1960s, programs were being written for large and complex tasks, such as controlling large petroleum refining facilities and providing worldwide airline reservation systems.

The new software development methodologies that emerged as a result of the research of the 1970s were called top-down design and stepwise refinement. The primary programming language deficiencies that were discovered were incompleteness of type checking and inadequacy of control statements (requiring the extensive use of gotos).

In the late 1970s, a shift from process-oriented to data-oriented program design methodologies began. Simply put, data-oriented methods emphasize data design, concentrating on the use of abstract data types to solve problems.

For data abstraction to be used effectively in software system design, it must be supported by the languages used for implementation. The first language to provide even limited support for data abstraction was SIMULA 67 (Birtwistle et al., 1973), although that language certainly was not propelled to popularity because of it. The benefits of data abstraction were not widely recognized until the early 1970s. However, most languages designed since the late 1970s support data abstraction. Data abstraction is discussed in detail in Chapter 10.

The latest step in the evolution of data-oriented software development, which began in the early 1980s, is object-oriented design. Object-oriented methodology begins with data abstraction, which encapsulates processing with data objects and hides access to data, and adds inheritance and dynamic type binding. Inheritance is a powerful concept that greatly enhances the potential reuse of existing software, thereby providing the possibility of significant increases in software development productivity. This is an important factor in the increase in popularity of object-oriented languages. Dynamic (run-time) type binding allows more flexible use of inheritance.

Object-oriented programming developed along with a language that supported its concepts: Smalltalk (Goldberg and Robson, 1983). Although Smalltalk never became as widely used as some other languages, support for object-oriented programming is now part of most popular imperative languages, including Ada 95 (AARM, 1995), Java, and C++. Object-oriented concepts have also found their way into functional programming in CLOS (Bobrow et al., 1988) and logic programming in Prolog++. Language support for object-oriented programming is discussed in detail in Chapter 11.

Process-oriented programming is, in a sense, the opposite of data-oriented programming. Although data-oriented methods now dominate software development, process-oriented methods have not been abandoned. On the contrary, a good deal of research has occurred in process-oriented programming in recent years, especially in the area of concurrency. These research efforts brought with them the need for language facilities for creating and controlling concurrent program units. Ada and Java include such capabilities. So programming evolution is again requiring new language capabilities. Concurrency is discussed in detail in Chapter 12.

1.5 Language Categories

Programming languages are often categorized into four bins: imperative, functional, logic, and object oriented. We have already discussed the characteristics of imperative and functional languages. We have also described how the most popular object-oriented languages grew out of imperative languages. Although the object-oriented software development paradigm differs greatly from the procedure-oriented paradigm usually used with imperative languages, the extensions to an imperative language required to support object-oriented programming are not overwhelming. For example, the expressions, assignment statements, and control statements of C and Java are nearly identical. (On the other hand, the arrays, subprograms, and semantics of Java are very different from those of C.)

A logic programming language is an example of a rule-based language. In an imperative language, an algorithm is specified in great detail and the specific order of execution of the instructions or statements must be included. In a rule-based language, rules are specified in no particular order, and the language implementation system must choose an execution order that produces the desired result. This approach to software development is radically different from those used with the other three kinds of languages, and clearly requires a completely different kind of language. Prolog, the most popular used logic programming language, and logic programming are discussed in Chapter 15.

Markup languages, such as HTML, are sometimes confused with programming languages. However, markup languages do not specify computations; rather, they describe the general appearance of documents. However, many of the design and evaluation criteria described in this chapter also apply to markup languages. After all, it is obviously important that markup code is easy to write and read.

1.6 Language Design Trade-Offs

The programming language evaluation criteria described in Section 1.3 provide a framework for language design. Unfortunately, that framework is self-contradictory. In his insightful paper on language design, Hoare (1973) states that "there are so many important but conflicting criteria, that their reconciliation and satisfaction is a major engineering task."

Two criteria that conflict are reliability and cost of execution. For example, the Ada language definition demands that all references to array elements be checked to ensure that the index or indices are in their legal ranges. This adds a great deal to the cost of execution of Ada programs that contain large numbers of references to array elements. C does not require index range checking, so C programs execute faster than semantically equivalent Ada programs, although Ada programs are more reliable. The designers of Ada traded execution efficiency for reliability.

As another example of conflicting criteria that leads directly to design trade-offs, consider the case of APL. APL includes a powerful set of operators for array operands. Because of the large number of operators, a significant number of new symbols had to be included in APL to represent the operators. Also, many APL operators can be used in a single long, complex expression. One result of this high degree of expressivity is that, for applications involving many array operations, APL is very writable. Indeed, a huge amount of computation can be specified in a very compact program. Another result is that APL programs have very poor readability. A compact and concise expression has a certain mathematical beauty but is difficult for anyone other than the person who wrote it to understand. The well-known author Daniel McCracken once noted that it took him four hours to read and understand a four-line APL program (McCracken, 1970). The designers of APL traded readability for writability.

The conflict between flexibility and safety is a common one in language design. Pascal variant records allow a memory cell to contain different type values at different times. For example, a cell may contain either a pointer or an integer. So a pointer value put in such a cell can be operated on as if it were an integer, using any operation defined for integer values. This provides a loophole in Pascal's type checking that allows a program to do arithmetic on pointers, which is sometimes convenient. However, this unchecked use of memory cells is, in general, a dangerous practice.

Examples of conflicts among language design (and evaluation) criteria abound; some are subtle, others are obvious. It is therefore clear that the task of choosing constructs and features when designing a programming language involves a collection of compromises and trade-offs.

1.7 Implementation Methods

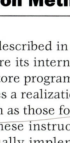

As described in Section 1.4.1, two of the primary components of a computer are its internal memory and its processor. The internal memory is used to store programs and data. The processor is a collection of circuits that provides a realization of a set of primitive operations, or machine instructions, such as those for arithmetic and logic operations. In most computers, some of these instructions, which are sometimes called macroinstructions, are actually implemented with an even lower-level set of instructions called microinstructions. Because microinstructions are never seen by software or programmers, they are usually not included in any discussion of software. Therefore, they will not be discussed further here.

The machine language of the computer is its set of macroinstructions. In the absence of other supporting software, its own machine language is the only language that most hardware computers "understand." Theoretically, a computer could be designed and built with a particular high-level language as its machine language, but it would be very complex and expensive. Furthermore, it would be highly inflexible, because it would be difficult (though not impossible) to use it with other high-level languages. The more practical machine design choice implements in hardware a very low-level language that provides the most commonly needed primitive operations and requires system software to create an interface to programs in higher-level languages.

A language implementation system cannot be the only software on a computer. Also required is a large collection of programs, called the operating system, which supplies higher-level primitives than those of the machine language. These primitives provide system resource management, input and output operations, a file management system, text and/or program editors, and a variety of other commonly needed functions. Because language implementation systems need many of the operating system facilities, they interface to the operating system rather than directly to the processor (in machine language).

The operating system and language implementations are layered over the machine language interface of a computer. These layers can be thought of as virtual computers, providing interfaces to the user at higher levels. For example, an operating system and a C compiler provide a virtual C computer. With other compilers, a machine can become other kinds of virtual computers. Most computer systems provide several different virtual computers. User programs form another layer over the top of the layer of virtual computers.

The layered view of a computer is shown in Figure 1.2.

The implementation systems of the first high-level programming languages, constructed in the late 1950s, were among the most complex software systems of that time. In the 1960s, intensive research efforts were made to understand and formalize the process of constructing these high-level language implementations. The greatest success of those efforts was in the area of syntax analysis, primarily because that part of the implementation process is an application of parts of automata theory and formal language theory that were then well understood.

Figure 1.2
Layered interface of virtual computers, provided by a typical computer system

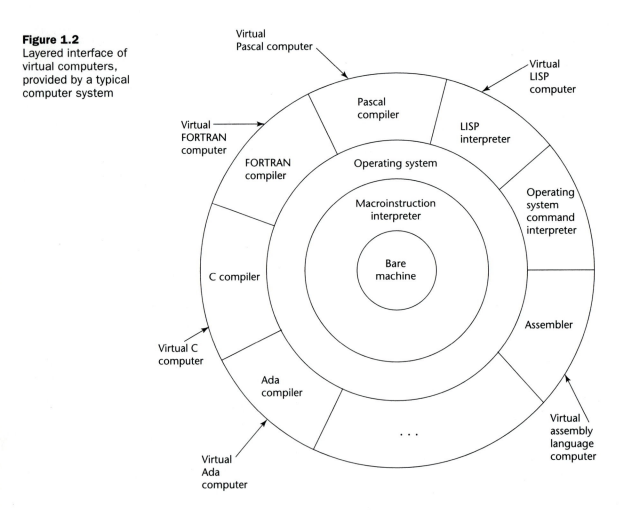

1.7.1 Compilation

Programming languages can be implemented by any of three general methods. At one extreme, programs can be translated to machine language, which can be executed directly on the computer. This is called a **compiler** implementation. This method has the advantage of very fast program execution, once the translation process is complete. Most production implementations of languages such as C, COBOL, and Ada are by compilers.

The language that a compiler translates is called the source language. The process of compilation takes place in several phases, the most important of which are shown in Figure 1.3.

The lexical analyzer gathers the characters of the source program into lexical units. The lexical units of a program are identifiers, special words, operators, and punctuation symbols. The lexical analyzer ignores comments in the source program, because the compiler has no use for them.

The syntax analyzer takes the lexical units from the lexical analyzer and uses them to construct hierarchical structures called parse trees. These parse trees represent the syntactic structure of the program. In many cases, no actual parse tree structure is constructed; rather, the information that would be required to build a tree is generated and used. Both lexical units and parse trees are further discussed in Chapter 3.

The intermediate code generator produces a program in a different language, at an intermediate level between the source program and the final output of the compiler, the machine language program. (Note that the words *language* and *code* are often used interchangeably.) Intermediate languages sometimes look very much like assembly languages and in fact sometimes are actual assembly languages. In other cases, the intermediate code is at a level somewhat higher than an assembly language. The semantic analyzer is an integral part of the intermediate code generator. The semantic analyzer checks for errors that are difficult if not impossible to detect during syntax analysis, such as type errors.

Simple examples of syntax analysis and intermediate code generation are provided in Chapter 3.

Optimization, which improves programs by making them smaller or faster or both, is often an optional part of compilation. In fact, some compilers are incapable of doing any significant optimization. This type of compiler would be used in situations where execution speed of the translated program is far less important than compilation speed. An example of such a situation is a computing laboratory for beginning programmers. In most commercial and industrial situations, execution speed is more important than compilation speed, so optimization is routinely desirable. Because many kinds of optimization cannot be done on machine language, most optimization is done on the intermediate code.

The code generator translates the optimized intermediate code version of the program into an equivalent machine language program.

Figure 1.3
The compilation
process

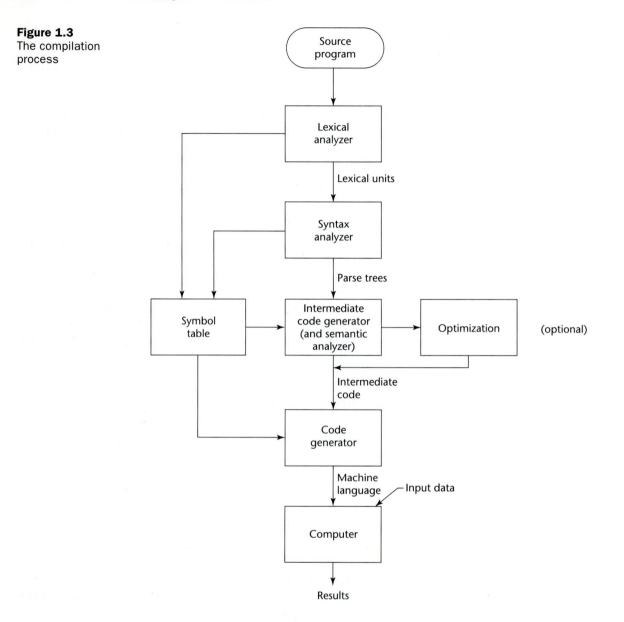

The symbol table serves as a database for the compilation process. The primary contents of the symbol table are the type and attribute information of each user-defined name in the program. This information is placed in the symbol table by the lexical and syntax analyzers and is used by the semantic analyzer and the code generator.

As stated above, although the machine language generated by a compiler can be executed directly on the hardware, it must nearly always be run along with some other code. Most user programs also require programs from the operating system. Among the most common of these are programs for input and output. The compiler builds calls to required system programs when they are needed by the user program. Before the machine language programs produced by a compiler can be executed, the required programs from the operating system must be found and linked to the user program. The linking operation connects the user program to the system programs by placing the addresses of the entry points of the system programs in the calls to them in the user program. The user and system code together are sometimes called a load module, or executable image. The process of collecting system programs and linking them to user programs is called linking and loading, or sometimes just linking. It is accomplished by a systems program called the linker.

In addition to systems programs, user programs must often be linked to previously compiled user programs that reside in libraries. So the linker not only links a given program to system programs, it may also link it to other user programs.

The execution of a machine code program on a von Neumann architecture computer occurs in a process called the **fetch-execute cycle.** As stated in Section 1.4.1, programs reside in memory but are executed in the CPU. Each instruction to be executed must be moved from memory to the processor. The address of the next instruction to be executed is maintained in a register named the program counter. The fetch-execute cycle can be simply described by the following algorithm:

> initialize the program counter
> **repeat** forever
> > fetch the instruction pointed to by the program counter
> > increment the program counter to point at the next instruction
> > decode the instruction
> > execute the instruction
> **end repeat**

The "decode the instruction" step in the process above means the instruction is examined to determine what action it specifies. Program execution terminates when a stop instruction is encountered, although on an actual computer a stop instruction is rarely executed. Rather, control transfers from the operating system to a user program for its execution and then back to the operating system when the user program execution is completed. In a computer system in which more than one user program may be in memory at a given time, this process is far more complex.

The speed of the connection between a computer's memory and its processor usually determines the speed of the computer, because instructions often can be executed faster than they can be moved to the processor for execution. This connection is called the von Neumann bottleneck; it is the primary limiting factor in the speed of von Neumann architecture computers. The von Neumann bottleneck has been one of the primary motivations for the research and development of parallel computers.

1.7.2 Pure Interpretation

At the opposite extreme of implementation methods, programs can be interpreted by another program called an interpreter, with no translation whatever. The interpreter program acts as a software simulation of a machine whose fetch-execute cycle deals with high-level language program statements rather than machine instructions. This software simulation obviously provides a virtual machine for the language.

This technique, called **pure interpretation,** or simply interpretation, has the advantage of allowing easy implementation of many source-level debugging operations, because all run-time error messages can refer to source-level units. For example, if an array index is found to be out of range, the error message can easily indicate the source line and the name of the array. On the other hand, this method has the serious disadvantage that execution is 10 to 100 times slower than in compiled systems. The primary source of this slowness is the decoding of the high-level language statements, which are far more complex than machine language instructions (although there may be fewer statements than instructions in equivalent machine code). Therefore, statement decoding, rather than the connection between the processor and memory, is the bottleneck of a pure interpreter.

Another disadvantage of pure interpretation is that it often requires more space. In addition to the source program, the symbol table must be present during interpretation. Furthermore, the source program may be stored in a form designed for easy access and modification rather than one that provides for minimal size.

Interpretation is a difficult process on programs written in a complicated language, because the meaning of each expression and statement must be determined directly from the source program at run time. Languages with simpler structure lend themselves to pure interpretation. For example, APL and LISP are sometimes implemented as pure interpretive systems. Most operation systems commands, such as the contents of UNIX shell scripts and DOS `.BAT` files, are implemented with pure interpreters. More complex languages such as FORTRAN and C are rarely implemented with pure interpreters.

The process of pure interpretation is shown in Figure 1.4.

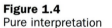

Figure 1.4
Pure interpretation

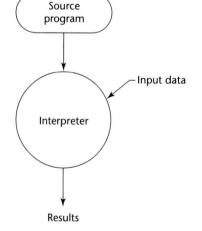

1.7.3 Hybrid Implementation Systems

Figure 1.5
Hybrid implementation system

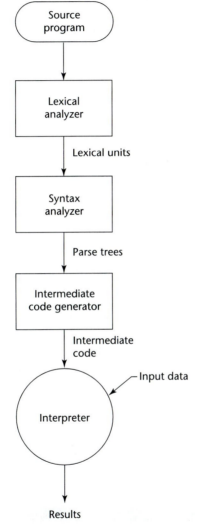

Some language implementation systems are a compromise between compilers and pure interpreters; they translate high-level language programs to an intermediate language designed to allow easy interpretation. This method is faster than pure interpretation because the source language statements are decoded only once. Such implementations are called **hybrid implementation systems.**

The process used in a hybrid implementation system is shown in Figure 1.5. Instead of translating intermediate language code to machine code, it simply interprets the intermediate code.

Perl is implemented with a hybrid system. It evolved from the interpretive languages sh and awk, but is partially compiled to detect errors before interpretation and to simplify the interpreter.

Initial implementations of Java were all hybrid. Its intermediate form, called byte code, provides portability to any machine that has a byte code interpreter and an associated run-time system. Together, these are called the Java Virtual Machine. There are now systems that translate Java byte code into machine code for faster execution. However, Java applets are always downloaded from the Web server in the form of byte code.

Sometimes an implementor may provide both compiled and interpreted implementations for a language. In these cases, the interpreter is used to develop and debug programs. Then, after a (relatively) bug-free state is reached, the programs are compiled to increase their execution speed.

1.8 Programming Environments

A programming environment is the collection of tools used in the development of software. This collection may consist of only a file system, a text editor, a linker, and a compiler. Or it may include a large collection of integrated tools, each accessed through a uniform user interface. In the latter case, the development and maintenance of software is greatly enhanced. Therefore, the characteristics of a programming language are not the only measure of the software development capability of a system. We now briefly describe several programming environments.

UNIX is an older programming environment, first distributed in the middle 1970s, built around a portable time-sharing operating system. It provides a wide array of powerful support tools for software production and maintenance in a variety of languages. In the past, the most important feature absent from UNIX was a uniform interface among its tools. This made it more difficult to learn and to use. However, UNIX is now often used through a graphical interface that runs on top of UNIX. In many cases, this interface is the Common Desktop Environment (CDE).

Borland C++ is a programming environment that runs on IBM-PC microcomputer systems and compatible clones. It provides an integrated compiler, editor, debugger, and file system, where all four are accessed through a graphical interface. One convenient feature of this kind of environment is that when the compiler encounters a syntax error, it stops and switches to the editor, leaving the cursor at the point in the source program where the error was detected.

Smalltalk is a language and an integrated programming environment, but it is more elaborate, complex, and powerful than Borland C++. Smalltalk was the first system to make use of a windowing system and a mouse pointing device to provide the user with a uniform interface to all tools. Smalltalk is discussed in Chapter 11.

The latest step in the evolution of software development environments is represented by Microsoft Visual C++. This is a large and elaborate collection of software development tools, all used through a windowed interface. This system, along with other similar systems such as Visual BASIC, Delphi, and the Java Development Kit from Sun Microsystems, provide simple ways of constructing graphical user interfaces to programs.

It is clear that most software development, at least in the near future, will make use of powerful programming environments. This will undoubtedly increase software productivity and perhaps also raise the quality of the software produced.

SUMMARY

The study of programming languages is valuable for a number of important reasons: It increases our capacity to use different constructs in writing programs, enables us to choose languages for projects more intelligently, and makes learning new languages easier.

Computers are used in a wide variety of problem-solving domains. The design and evaluation of a particular programming language is highly dependent on the domain in which it is to be used.

Among the most important criteria for evaluating languages are readability, writability, reliability, and overall cost. These will be the basis on which we examine and judge the various language features discussed in the remainder of the book.

The major influences on language design have been machine architecture and software design methodologies.

Designing a programming language is primarily an engineering feat, in which a long list of trade-offs must be made among features, constructs, and capabilities.

The major methods of implementing programming languages are compilation, pure interpretation, and hybrid implementation.

Programming environments have become important parts of software development systems, in which the language is just one of the components.

REVIEW QUESTIONS

1. Why is it useful for a programmer to have some background in language design, even though he or she may never actually design a programming language?

2. How can knowledge of programming language characteristics benefit the whole computing community?

3. What programming language has dominated scientific computing over the past 35 years?

4. What programming language has dominated business applications over the past 35 years?

5. What programming language has dominated artificial intelligence over the past 35 years?

6. In what language is UNIX written?

7. What is the disadvantage of having too many features in a language?

8. How can user-defined operator overloading harm the readability of a program?

9. What is one example of a lack of orthogonality in the design of C?

10. What language used orthogonality as a primary design criterion?

11. What primitive control statement is used to build more complicated control statements in languages that lack them?

12. What readability problem is caused by using the same closing reserved word for more than one kind of control statement?

13. What construct of a programming language provides process abstraction?

14. What does it mean for a program to be reliable?

15. Why is type checking the parameters of a subprogram important?

16. What is aliasing?

17. What is exception handling?

18. Why is readability important to writability?

19. How is the cost of compilers for a given language related to the design of that language?

20. What has been the strongest influence on programming language design over the past 40 years?

21. What is the name of the category of programming languages whose structure is dictated by the von Neumann computer architecture?

22. What two programming language deficiencies were discovered as a result of the research in software development in the 1970s?

23. What are three fundamental features of an object-oriented programming language?

24. What language was the first to support the three fundamental features of object-oriented programming?

25. What is an example of two language design criteria that are in direct conflict with each other?

26. What are the three general methods of implementing a programming language?

27. Which produces faster program execution, a compiler or a pure interpreter?

28. What role does the symbol table play in a compiler?

29. What does a linker do?

30. Why is the von Neumann bottleneck important?

31. What are the advantages in implementing a language with a pure interpreter?

32. What disadvantage does UNIX have as a software development environment?

PROBLEM SET

1. Do you believe our thinking capabilities are influenced by our language? Support your opinion.

2. What are some features of specific programming languages you know whose rationales are a mystery to you?

3. What arguments can you make for the idea of a single language for all programming domains?

4. What arguments can you make against the idea of a single language for all programming domains?

5. Name and explain another criterion by which languages can be judged (in addition to those in this chapter).

6. What common programming language statement, in your opinion, is most detrimental to readability?

7. Modula-2 uses **END** to mark the end of all compound statements. What are the arguments for and against this design?

8. Some languages, notably C and Java, distinguish between uppercase and lowercase in identifiers. What are the pros and cons of this design decision?

9. Explain the different aspects of the cost of a programming language.

10. What are the arguments for writing efficient programs even though hardware is relatively inexpensive?

11. Describe some design trade-offs between efficiency and safety in some language you know.

12. What major features would a perfect programming language include, in your opinion?

13. Was the first high-level programming language you learned implemented with a pure interpreter, a hybrid implementation system, or a compiler? (You would not necessarily know this without research.)

14. Describe the advantages and disadvantages of some programming environment you have used.

15. How do type declaration statements for simple variables affect the readability of a language, considering that some languages do not require them?

16. Write an evaluation of some programming language you know, using the criteria described in this chapter.

17. Pascal uses the semicolon to separate statements, while C uses it to terminate statements. Which of these, in your opinion, is most natural and least likely to result in syntax errors? Support your answer.

18. Some languages such as Pascal and C use delimiters on both ends of comments. Other languages, such as FORTRAN and Ada, use a symbol or symbol pair to indicate the beginning of a comment and the end of the line to terminate it. Discuss the advantages and disadvantages of each design choice with respect to our criteria.

2 Evolution of the Major Programming Languages

John Backus

John Backus, employed by IBM, designed the Speed-coding pseudocode system for IBM's 701 computer in the early 1950s. Between 1954 and 1957, he led the design team that produced FORTRAN, from which nearly all imperative languages evolved. In the 1958–1960 period, he was a member of the ALGOL design team.

CHAPTER OUTLINE

This chapter follows chronologically the development of a collection of programming languages, exploring the environment in which each was designed and focusing on the contributions of the language and the motivation for its development. Overall language descriptions are not included; rather, we discuss only the new features introduced by each language. Of particular interest are the features that most influenced subsequent languages or the field of computer science.

This chapter does not include an in-depth discussion of any language feature or concept; that is left for later chapters. Brief, informal explanations of features will suffice for our trek through the development of these languages.

The choice as to which languages to discuss here was subjective, and many readers will unhappily note the absence of one or more of their favorites. However, to keep this historical coverage to a reasonable size, it was necessary to leave out several languages that some regard highly. The choices were based on our estimate of each language's importance to language development and the computing world as a whole. We also include brief discussions of some other languages that are referenced later in the book.

This chapter includes listings of 11 complete example programs, each in a different language. None of these programs are described in this chapter; they are meant simply to illustrate the appearance of programs in these languages. Readers familiar with any of the common imperative languages should be able to read and understand most of the code in these programs, except those in LISP, COBOL, and Smalltalk. The LISP example is discussed in Chapter 14; the Smalltalk example is discussed in Chapter 11. The same problem is solved by the FORTRAN, ALGOL 60, PL/I, BASIC, Pascal, C, Ada, and Java programs.

Figure 2.1 is a chart of the genealogy of the high-level languages discussed in this chapter.

2.1 Zuse's Plankalkül

The first programming language discussed in this chapter is highly unusual in several respects. For one thing, it was never implemented. Furthermore, although developed in 1945, its description was not published until 1972. As a result of the general ignorance of the language, some of its capabilities did not appear in other languages until 15 years after Plankalkül's development.

2.1.1 Historical Background

Between 1936 and 1945, the German scientist Konrad Zuse (pronounced "Tsoo-zuh") built a series of complex and sophisticated computers from

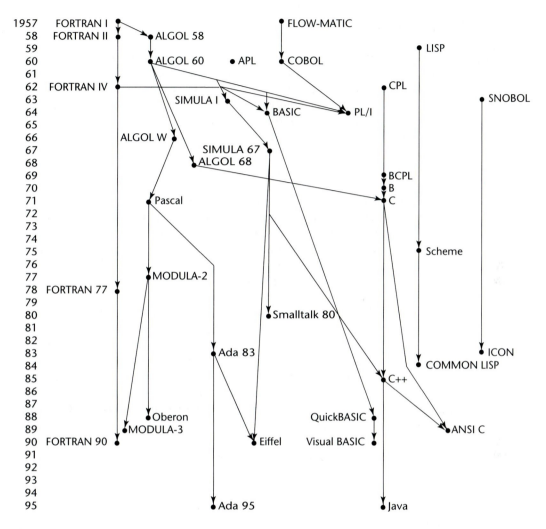

Figure 2.1
Genealogy of common high-level programming languages

electromechanical relays. By 1945, the war had destroyed all but one of his latest models, the Z4, so he moved to a remote Bavarian village, Hinterstein, and his research group members went their separate ways.

Working alone, Zuse embarked on an effort to develop a language for expressing computations, a project he had begun in 1943 as a proposal for his Ph.D. dissertation. He named this language Plankalkül, which means program calculus. In a lengthy manuscript dated 1945 but not published until 1972 (Zuse, 1972), Zuse defined Plankalkül and wrote algorithms in the language for a wide variety of problems.

2.1.2   Language Overview

Plankalkül was remarkably complete, with some of its most advanced features in the area of data structures. The simplest type in Plankalkül was the single bit. From the bit type were built types for integer and floating-point numeric types. The floating-point type used twos-complement notation and the "hidden bit" scheme currently used to avoid storing the most significant bit of the normalized fraction part of a value.

In addition to these usual scalar types, Plankalkül included arrays and records. The records could use recursion to include other records as elements.

Although the language had no explicit goto, it did include an iterative statement similar to the Pascal **for**. It also had the command Fin with a superscript that indicated a jump out of a specified number of iteration loop nestings or to the beginning of a new iteration cycle. Plankalkül included a selection statement, but it did not allow an else clause.

One of the most interesting features of Zuse's programs was the inclusion of mathematical expressions showing the relationships between program variables. These expressions stated what would be true during execution at the points in the code where they appeared. These are very similar to the assertions used today in the Eiffel programming language (Meyer, 1992) and in axiomatic semantics, which is discussed in Chapter 3.

Zuse's manuscript contained programs of far greater complexity than any written prior to 1945. Included were programs to sort arrays of numbers; test the connectivity of a given graph; carry out integer and floating-point operations, including square root; and perform syntax analysis on logic formulas that had parentheses and operators in six different levels of precedence. Perhaps most remarkable were his 49 pages of algorithms for playing chess, a game in which he was not an expert.

If a computer scientist had found Zuse's description of Plankalkül in the early 1950s, the single aspect of the language that would have hindered its implementation as defined would have been the notation. Each statement consisted of either two or three lines of code. The first line was most like the statements of contemporary languages. The second line, which was optional, contained the subscripts of the array references in the first line. It is interesting to note that the same method of indicating subscripts was used by Charles Babbage in programs for his Analytical Engine in the mid-19th century. The last line of each Plankalkül statement contained the type names for the variables mentioned in the first line. This notation is quite intimidating when first seen.

The following example assignment statement, which assigns the value of the expression `A(4)+1` to `A(5)`, illustrates this notation. The row labeled `v` is for subscripts, and the row labeled `s` is for the data types. In this example, `1.n` means an integer of n bits:

```
     |  A + 1  =>  A
  V  |  4          5
  S  |  1.n        1.n
```

We can only speculate on the direction that programming language design and computer development might have taken if Zuse's work had been widely known in 1945 or even 1950. It is also interesting to consider how his work might have been different had he done it in a peaceful environment surrounded by other scientists, rather than in Germany in 1945 in virtual isolation.

2.2 Minimal Hardware Programming: Pseudocodes

The computers that became available in the late 1940s and early 1950s were far less usable than those of today. In addition to being slow, unreliable, and expensive and having extremely small memories, the machines of that time were difficult to program because of the lack of supporting software.

There were no high-level programming languages or even assembly languages, so programming was done in machine code, which is both tedious and error-prone. Among its problems is the use of numeric codes for specifying instructions. For example, an ADD instruction might be specified by the code 14 rather than a connotative textual name, even if only a single letter. This makes programs very difficult to read. A more serious problem is absolute addressing, which makes programs very difficult to modify. For example, suppose we have a machine language program that is stored in memory. Many of the instructions in such a program refer to other locations within the program, usually to reference data or to indicate the targets of branch instructions. Inserting an instruction at any position in the program other than at the end invalidates the correctness of all instructions that refer to addresses beyond the insertion point, because those addresses must be increased to make room for the new instruction. To make the addition correctly, all those instructions that refer to addresses that follow the addition must be found and modified. A similar problem occurs with deletion of an instruction. In this case, however, machine languages often include a "no operation" instruction that can replace deleted instructions, thereby avoiding the problem.

These are standard problems with all machine languages and were the primary motivations for inventing assemblers and assembly languages. In addition, most programming problems of that time were numerical and required floating-point arithmetic operations and indexing of some sort to allow the convenient use of arrays. Neither of these capabilities, however, was included in the architecture of the computers of the late 1940s and early 1950s. These deficiencies naturally led to the development of somewhat higher-level languages.

2.2.1 Short Code

The first of these new languages, named Short Code, was developed by John Mauchly in 1949 for the BINAC computer. Short Code was later transferred to a UNIVAC I computer and, for a number of years, was one of the primary means of programming those machines. Although little is known of the original Short Code because its complete description was never published, a programming manual for the UNIVAC I version did survive (Remington-Rand, 1952). It is safe to assume that the two versions were very similar.

The UNIVAC I had words that consisted of 72 bits, grouped as 12 six-bit bytes. Short Code consisted of coded versions of mathematical expressions that were to be evaluated. The codes were byte-pair values, and most equations fit into a word. Some of the codes were

```
01  –       06  abs value    1n  (n+2)nd power
02  )       07  +            2n  (n+2)nd root
03  =       08  pause        4n  if <= n
04  /       09  (            58  print and tab
```

Variables, or memory locations, were named with byte-pair codes, as were locations to be used as constants. For example, `X0` and `Y0` could be variables. The statement

```
X0 = SQRT(ABS(Y0))
```

would be coded in a word as `00 X0 03 20 06 Y0`. The initial `00` was used as padding to fill the word. Interestingly, there was no multiplication code; multiplication was indicated by simply placing the two operands next to each other, as in algebra.

Short Code was not translated to machine code; rather, it was implemented with a pure interpreter. At the time, this process was called automatic programming. It clearly simplified the programming process but at the expense of execution time. Short Code interpretation was approximately 50 times slower than machine code.

2.2.2 Speedcoding

In other places, interpretive systems were being developed that extended machine languages to include floating-point operations. The

Speedcoding system developed by John Backus for the IBM 701 is an example of such a system (Backus, 1954). The Speedcoding interpreter effectively converted the 701 to a virtual three-address floating-point calculator. The system included pseudoinstructions for the four arithmetic operations on floating-point data, as well as operations such as square root, sine, arc tangent, exponent, and logarithm. Conditional and unconditional branches and input/output conversions were also part of the virtual architecture. To get an idea of the limitations of such systems, consider that the remaining usable memory after loading the interpreter was only 700 words and that the add instruction took 4.2 milliseconds to execute. On the other hand, Speedcoding included the novel facility of automatically incrementing address registers. This facility did not appear in hardware until the UNIVAC 1107 computers of 1962. Because of such features, matrix multiplication could be done in 12 Speedcoding instructions. Backus claimed that problems that could take two weeks to program in machine code could be programmed in a few hours using Speedcoding.

2.2.3 The UNIVAC "Compiling" System

Between 1951 and 1953, a team led by Grace Hopper at UNIVAC developed a series of "compiling" systems named A-0, A-1, and A-2 that expanded a pseudocode into machine code in the same way as macros are expanded into assembly language. The pseudocode source for these "compilers" was still quite primitive, although even this was a great improvement over machine code because it made source programs much shorter. Wilkes (1952) independently suggested a similar process.

2.2.4 Related Work

Other means of easing the task of programming were being developed at about the same time. At Cambridge University, David J. Wheeler developed a method of using blocks of relocatable addresses to partially solve the problem of absolute addressing (Wheeler, 1950), and later, Maurice V. Wilkes (also at Cambridge) extended the idea to design an assembly program that could combine chosen subroutines and allocate storage (Wilkes et al., 1951, 1957). This was indeed an important and fundamental advance.

We should also mention that assembly languages, which are quite different from the pseudocodes mentioned, evolved during the early 1950s. However, they had little impact on the design of high-level languages.

2.3 The IBM 704 and FORTRAN

Certainly one of the greatest single advances in computing came with the introduction of the IBM 704 in 1954, in large measure because its capabilities prompted the development of FORTRAN. One could argue that if it had not been IBM with the 704 and FORTRAN, it would soon thereafter have been some other organization with a similar computer and related high-level language. However, IBM was the first with both the foresight and the resources to undertake these developments.

2.3.1 Historical Background

One of the primary reasons why interpretive systems were tolerated from the late 1940s to the mid-1950s was the lack of floating-point hardware in the available computers. All floating-point operations had to be simulated in software, a very time-consuming process. Because so much processor time was spent in software floating-point processing, the overhead of interpretation and the simulation of indexing were relatively insignificant. As long as floating-point had to be done by software, interpretation was an acceptable expense. However, many programmers of that time never used interpretive systems, preferring the efficiency of hand-coded machine language. The announcement of the IBM 704 system, with both indexing and floating-point instructions in hardware, heralded the end of the interpretive era, at least for scientific computation.

Although FORTRAN is often credited with being the first compiled high-level language, the question of who deserves credit for implementing the first such language is somewhat open. Knuth and Pardo (1977) give the credit to Alick E. Glennie for his Autocode compiler for the Manchester Mark I computer. Glennie developed the compiler at Fort Halstead, Royal Armaments Research Establishment, in England. The compiler was operational by September 1952. However, according to John Backus (Wexelblat, 1981, p. 26), Glennie's Autocode was so low level and machine oriented that it should not be considered a compiled system. Backus gives the credit to Laning and Zierler at Massachusetts Institute of Technology.

The Laning and Zierler system (Laning and Zierler, 1954) was the first algebraic translation system to be implemented. By algebraic we mean that it translated arithmetic expressions, used function calls for mathematical functions, and included subscripted variable references. The system was implemented on the MIT Whirlwind computer, in experimental prototype form, in the summer of 1952, and in a more usable form by May 1953. The translator generated a subroutine call to code each formula, or expression, in the program. The source language was easy to read, and the only actual machine instructions included were for branching. Although this work preceded the work on FORTRAN, it never escaped MIT.

In spite of these earlier works, the first widely accepted compiled high-level language was FORTRAN. The following subsections chronicle this important development.

2.3.2 Design Process

Even before the 704 system was announced in May 1954, plans were begun for FORTRAN. By November 1954, John Backus and his group at IBM had produced the report entitled "The IBM Mathematical FORmula TRANslating System: FORTRAN" (IBM, 1954). This document described the first version of FORTRAN, which we refer to as FORTRAN 0, prior to its implementation. It also boldly stated that FORTRAN would provide the efficiency of hand-coded programs and the ease of programming of the interpretive pseudocode systems. In another burst of optimism, the document stated that FORTRAN would eliminate coding errors and the debugging process. Based on this premise, the first FORTRAN compiler included little syntax error checking.

The environment in which FORTRAN was developed was as follows: (1) Computers were still small, slow, and relatively unreliable. (2) The primary use of computers was for scientific computations. (3) There were no existing efficient ways to program computers. (4) Because of the high cost of computers compared to the cost of programmers, speed of the generated object code was the primary goal of the first FORTRAN compilers. The characteristics of the early versions of FORTRAN follow directly from this environment.

2.3.3 FORTRAN I Overview

FORTRAN 0 was modified during the implementation period, which began in January 1955 and continued until the release of the compiler in April 1957. The implemented language, which we call FORTRAN I, is described in the first FORTRAN *Programmer's Reference Manual*, published in October 1956 (IBM, 1956). FORTRAN I included input/output formatting, variable names of up to six characters (it had been just two in FORTRAN 0), user-defined subroutines, although they could not be separately compiled, the IF selection statement, and the DO loop statement.

FORTRAN 0 included a logical IF statement whose Boolean expression used relational operators in their algebraic form—for example, > for greater than. The 704 character set did not include characters such as >, so these relational operators had to be dropped. Because the machine had a three-way branch instruction based on the comparison of the value in a storage location with the value in a register, the original logical IF was replaced with the arithmetic selection, which has the form

```
IF (arithmetic expression) N1, N2, N3
```

where N1, N2, and N3 are statement labels. If the value of the expression is negative, the branch is to N1; if zero, it is to N2; if greater than zero, to N3. This statement is still part of FORTRAN.

The form of the FORTRAN I iterative (loop) statement was

```
DO N1 variable = first_value, last_value
```

where N1 was the label of the last statement of the loop, and the statement on the line following the DO was the first.

As with the IF statement, the 704 had a single instruction to implement the DO. Because the instruction was designed for posttest loops, FORTRAN I's DO was designed in that way. A pretest loop could have been implemented on the 704, but that would have required one additional machine instruction, and because efficiency was the overriding concern in the design of FORTRAN, it was not done.

All of FORTRAN I's control statements were based on 704 instructions. It is not clear whether the 704 designers dictated the control statement design of FORTRAN I or whether the designers of FORTRAN I suggested these instructions to the 704 designers.

There were no data-typing statements in the FORTRAN I language. Variables whose names began with I, J, K, L, M, and N were implicitly integer type, and all others were implicitly floating-point. The choice of the letters for this convention was based on the fact that at that time integers were used primarily as subscripts, and scientists usually used i, j, and k for subscripts. To be generous, FORTRAN's designers threw in the three additional letters.

The most audacious claim made by the FORTRAN development group during the design of the language was that the machine code produced by the compiler would be about as efficient as what could be produced by hand. This, more than anything else, made skeptics of potential users and prevented a great deal of interest in FORTRAN before its actual release. To almost everyone's surprise, however, the FORTRAN development group nearly achieved its goal in efficiency. The largest part of the 18 worker-years of effort used to construct the first compiler had been spent on optimization, and the results were remarkably effective.

The early success of FORTRAN is shown by the results of a survey made in April 1958. At that time, roughly half of the code being written for 704s was being done in FORTRAN, in spite of the extreme skepticism of most of the programming world only a year earlier.

2.3.4 FORTRAN II Overview

The FORTRAN II compiler was distributed in the spring of 1958. It fixed many of the bugs in the FORTRAN I compilation system and added some significant features to the language, the most important being the independent compilation of subroutines. Without independent compilation, any change in a program requires that the entire program be recompiled. FORTRAN I's lack of independent compilation capability, coupled with the poor reliability of the 704, placed a practical restriction on the length of programs to about 300 to 400 lines (Wexelblat, 1981, p. 68). Longer programs had a poor chance of being compiled completely before a machine failure occurred. The capability of including precompiled machine language versions of subprograms shortened the compilation process considerably.

2.3.5 FORTRAN IV, FORTRAN 77, and FORTRAN 90

A FORTRAN III was developed, but it was never widely distributed. FORTRAN IV, however, became one of the most widely used programming languages of its time. It evolved over the period 1960 to 1962 and was the standard version until 1978, when the FORTRAN 77 report (ANSI, 1978a) was released. FORTRAN IV was an improvement over FORTRAN II in many ways. Among its most important additions were explicit type declarations for variables, a logical IF construct, and the capability of passing subprograms as parameters to other subprograms.

FORTRAN 77 retains most of the features of FORTRAN IV and adds character string handling, logical loop control statements, and an IF with an optional ELSE clause.

FORTRAN 90 is the name of the latest version of FORTRAN (ANSI, 1992). FORTRAN 90 is dramatically different from FORTRAN 77. The most significant changes are briefly described in the following paragraphs.

A collection of functions is built in for array operations. These include DOTPRODUCT, MATMUL, TRANSPOSE, MAXVAL, MINVAL, PRODUCT, and SUM, whose meanings are obvious from their names. These are just a few of the most useful functions available.

Arrays can be dynamically allocated and deallocated on command if they have been declared to be ALLOCATABLE. This is a radical departure from earlier FORTRANs, which all had only static data. A form of records, called derived types, is included. Pointers are also part of FORTRAN 90.

New control statements have been added: CASE is a multiple selection statement, EXIT is used to depart prematurely from a loop, and CYCLE is used to transfer control to the bottom of a loop but not out.

Subprograms can be recursive and also have optional and keyword parameters.

A module facility has been added that is similar to the packages of Ada. Modules can contain data declarations and subprograms, each of which can be either PRIVATE or PUBLIC to regulate external access.

One new concept that is included in the FORTRAN 90 definition is that of removing language features from earlier versions. While FORTRAN 90 includes all of the features of FORTRAN 77, it has two lists of features that may be eliminated in future versions of FORTRAN. The obsolescent features list has features that may be eliminated in the next version of FORTRAN after 90. Included in this list are such things as the arithmetic `IF` and the assigned `GOTO` statements. The deprecated features list has features that may be eliminated in the second subsequent version after 90. Included in this list are the `COMMON`, `EQUIVALENCE`, and computed `GOTO` statements as well as statement functions.

2.3.6 Evaluation

The original FORTRAN design team thought of language design only as a necessary prelude to the critical task of designing the translator. Further, it never occurred to them that FORTRAN would be used on computers not manufactured by IBM. Indeed, they were forced to consider building FORTRAN compilers for other IBM machines only because the successor to the 704, the 709, was announced before the 704 FORTRAN compiler was released. The effect that FORTRAN has had on the use of computers, along with the fact that all subsequent programming languages owe a debt to FORTRAN, are indeed impressive in light of the modest goals of its designers.

One of the features of FORTRAN I, and all of its successors except 90, that allows highly optimizing compilers is that the types and storage for all variables are fixed before run time. No new variables or space can be allocated during run time. This is a sacrifice of flexibility to simplicity and efficiency. It eliminates the possibility of recursive subprograms and makes it difficult to implement data structures that grow or change shape dynamically. Of course, the kinds of programs that were being built at the time of the development of the early versions of FORTRAN were primarily numerical in nature and were simple in comparison with recent software projects. Therefore, the sacrifice was not a great one.

The overall success of FORTRAN is difficult to overstate: It dramatically changed forever the way computers are used. This is, of course, in large part due to its being the first widely used high-level language. In comparison with concepts and languages developed later, early versions of FORTRAN suffer in a variety of ways, as should be expected. After all, 1910 Model T Ford automobiles are not to be compared across the board with 1998 Ford Mustangs. Nevertheless, in spite of the inadequacies of FORTRAN, the momentum of the huge investment in FORTRAN software, among other factors, has kept it among the most widely used of all high-level languages.

Alan Perlis, one of the designers of ALGOL 60, said of FORTRAN in 1978, "FORTRAN is the *lingua franca* of the computing world. It is the language of the streets in the best sense of the word, not in the prostitutional sense of the word. And it has survived and will survive because it has turned out to be a remarkably useful part of a very vital commerce" (Wexelblat, 1981, p. 161).

The following is an example of a FORTRAN 90 program:

```
C    FORTRAN 90 EXAMPLE PROGRAM
C    INPUT:   AN INTEGER, LIST_LEN, WHERE LIST_LEN IS LESS
C             THAN 100, FOLLOWED BY LIST_LEN-INTEGER VALUES
C    OUTPUT:  THE NUMBER OF INPUT VALUES THAT ARE GREATER
C             THAN THE AVERAGE OF ALL INPUT VALUES
     INTEGER INTLIST(99)
     INTEGER LIST_LEN, COUNTER, SUM, AVERAGE, RESULT
     RESULT = 0
     SUM = 0
     READ *, LIST_LEN
     IF ((LIST_LEN .GT. 0) .AND.
        (LIST_LEN .LT. 100)) THEN
C    READ INPUT DATA INTO AN ARRAY AND COMPUTE ITS SUM
        DO 10 COUNTER = 1, LIST_LEN
           READ *, INTLIST(COUNTER)
           SUM = SUM + INTLIST(COUNTER)
10      CONTINUE
C    COMPUTE THE AVERAGE
        AVERAGE = SUM / LIST_LEN
C    COUNT THE VALUES THAT ARE GREATER THAN THE AVERAGE
        DO 20 COUNTER = 1, LIST_LEN
           IF (INTLIST(COUNTER) .GT. AVERAGE) THEN
              RESULT = RESULT + 1
           END IF
20      CONTINUE
C    PRINT THE RESULT
        PRINT *, 'NUMBER OF VALUES > AVERAGE IS:', RESULT
     ELSE
        PRINT *, 'ERROR—LIST LENGTH VALUE IS NOT LEGAL'
     END IF
     STOP
     END
```

2.4 Functional Programming: LISP

The first functional programming language was invented to provide language features for list processing, the need for which grew out of the first applications in the area of artificial intelligence (AI).

2.4.1 The Beginnings of Artificial Intelligence and List Processing

Interest in AI began to appear in the mid-1950s in a number of places. Some of this interest grew out of linguistics, some from psychology, and some from mathematics. Linguists were concerned with natural language processing. Psychologists were interested in modeling human information storage and retrieval, along with other fundamental processes of the brain. Mathematicians were interested in mechanizing certain intelligent processes, such as theorem proving. All of these investigations arrived at the same conclusion: Some method must be developed to allow computers to process symbolic data in linked lists. At the time, nearly all computation was on numeric data in arrays.

The concept of list processing was developed by Allen Newell, J.C. Shaw, and Herbert Simon. It was first published in a classic paper that describes one of the first AI programs, the Logical Theorist, and a language in which it could be implemented (Newell and Simon, 1956). The language, named IPL-I (Information Processing Language I), was never implemented. The next version, IPL-II, was implemented on a Rand Corporation Johnniac computer. Development of IPL continued until 1960, when the description of IPL-V was published (Newell and Tonge, 1960). The low level of the IPL languages prevented their widespread use. They were actually assembly languages for a hypothetical computer, implemented by interpreters, in which list-processing instructions were included. The first implementation was on the obscure Johnniac machine, another factor that kept the IPL languages from becoming popular.

The contributions of the IPL languages were in their list design and their demonstration that list processing was feasible and useful.

IBM became interested in AI in the mid-1950s and chose theorem proving as a demonstration area. At the time, the FORTRAN project was still under way. The high cost of the FORTRAN I compiler convinced IBM that their list processing should be attached to FORTRAN, rather than in the form of a new language. Thus, the FORTRAN List Processing Language (FLPL) was designed and implemented as an extension to FORTRAN. FLPL was used to construct a theorem prover for plane geometry, which was then considered the easiest area for mechanical theorem proving.

2.4.2 LISP Design Process

John McCarthy of MIT took a summer position at the IBM Information Research Department in 1958. His goal for the summer was to investigate symbolic computations and develop a set of requirements for doing such computations. As a pilot example problem area, he chose differentiation of algebraic expressions. From this study came a list of language requirements. Among them were the control flow methods of mathematical functions: recursion and conditional expressions. The only available high-level language of the time, FORTRAN I, had neither of these.

Another requirement that grew from the symbolic differentiation investigation was the need for dynamically allocated linked lists and some kind of implicit deallocation of abandoned lists. McCarthy simply would not allow his elegant algorithm for differentiation to be cluttered with explicit deallocation statements.

Because FLPL did not support recursion, conditional expressions, dynamic storage allocation, or implicit deallocation, it was clear to McCarthy that a new language was required.

When McCarthy returned to MIT in the fall of 1958, he and Marvin Minsky formed the MIT AI Project, with funding from the Research Laboratory for Electronics. The first important effort of the project was to produce a system for list processing. It was to be used initially to implement a program proposed by McCarthy called the Advice Taker. This application became the impetus for the development of the list-processing language LISP. The first version of LISP is sometimes called pure LISP because it is a purely functional language. In the following section, we describe the development of pure LISP.

2.4.3 Language Overview

2.4.3.1 Data Structures

Pure LISP has only two kinds of data structures: atoms and lists. Atoms are either symbols, which have the form of identifiers, or numeric literals. The concept of storing symbolic information in linked lists is natural and was used in IPL-II. Such structures allow insertions and deletions at any point, operations which were then thought to be a necessary part of list processing. As it eventually developed, however, LISP rarely requires these operations.

Lists are specified by delimiting their elements with parentheses. Simple lists, in which elements are restricted to atoms, have the form of the example

    (A B C D)

Nested list structures are also specified by parentheses. For example, the list

    (A (B C) D (E (F G)))

is composed of four elements. The first is the atom A; the second is the sublist (B C); the third is the atom D; the fourth is the sublist (E (F G)), which has as its second element the sublist (F G).

Internally, lists are usually stored as single-linked list structures, in which each node has two pointers and represents a list element. A node for an atom has its first pointer pointing to some representation of the atom, such as its symbol or numeric value. A node for a sublist element has its first pointer pointing to the first node of the sublist. In both cases, the second pointer of a node points to the next element of the list. A list is referenced by a pointer to its first element.

Figure 2.2
Internal representation of two LISP lists

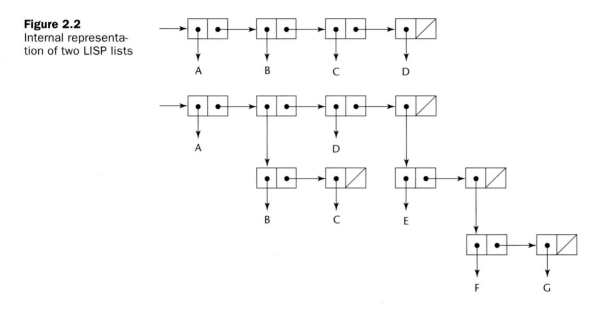

The internal representations of the two lists shown earlier are depicted in Figure 2.2. Note that the elements of a list are shown horizontally. The last element of a list has no successor, so its link is NIL. Sublists are shown with the same structure.

2.4.3.2 Processes in Functional Programming

LISP was designed as a functional programming language. All computation in a functional program is accomplished by applying functions to arguments. Neither the assignment statements nor the variables that abound in imperative language programs are necessary in functional language programs. Furthermore, iterative processes can be specified with recursive function calls, making loops unnecessary. These basic concepts of functional programming make it significantly different from programming in an imperative language.

2.4.3.3 The Syntax of LISP

LISP is very different from the imperative languages, both because it is a functional programming language and because LISP programs look so different from those in languages like FORTRAN or C. For example, the syntax of C is a complicated mixture of English and algebra, while LISP's syntax is a model of simplicity. Program code and data have exactly the same form: parenthesized lists. Consider again the list

    (A B C D)

When interpreted as data, it is a list of four elements. When viewed as code, it is the application of the function named A to the three parameters B, C, and D.

2.4.4   Evaluation

LISP totally dominated AI applications for a quarter of a century. It is still the most widely used language for AI. Much of the cause of LISP's reputation for being highly inefficient has been eliminated. Many contemporary implementations are compiled, and the resulting code is much faster than running the source code on an interpreter. In addition to its success in AI, LISP pioneered functional programming, which has proven to be a lively area of research in programming languages. As stated in Chapter 1, many programming language researchers believe functional programming is a much better approach to software development than the use of imperative languages.

During the 1970s and early 1980s, a large number of different dialects of LISP were developed and used. This led to the familiar problem of portability. To rectify this situation, a standard version named COMMON LISP was developed (Steele, 1984).

Scheme, a dialect of LISP, and functional programming are discussed at length in Chapter 14. The following is an example of a LISP program.

```
;   LISP Example function
;   The following code defines a LISP predicate function,
;   that  takes two lists as arguments and returns True
    if the two lists are equal, and NIL (false)
;   otherwise (DEFUN equal_lists (lis1 lis2)
    (COND
      ((ATOM lis1) (EQ lis1 lis2))
      ((ATOM lis2) NIL)
      ((equal (CAR lis1) (CAR lis2))
          (equal (CDR lis1) (CDR lis2)))
      (T NIL)
    )
)
```

2.4.5   Two Descendants of LISP

Two dialects of LISP are now widely used, COMMON LISP and Scheme. These are briefly discussed in the following subsections.

2.4.5.1   Scheme

The Scheme language emerged from MIT in the mid-1970s (Sussman and Steele, 1975). It is characterized by its small size, its exclusive use of static scoping (discussed in Chapter 4), and its treatment of functions as first-class entities. As first-class entities, Scheme functions can be the values of expressions and elements of lists; they can be assigned to variables, passed as parameters, and returned as the values of function applications. Early versions of LISP did not provide all of these capabilities, nor did they use static scoping.

As a small language with simple syntax and semantics, Scheme is well suited to educational applications, such as courses in functional programming and general introductions to programming. As mentioned before, Scheme is described in some detail in Chapter 14.

2.4.5.2 COMMON LISP

COMMON LISP (Steele, 1984) was created in an effort to combine the features of several dialects of LISP developed in the early 1980s, including Scheme, into a single language. Being such an amalgam, COMMON LISP is a large and complex language. Its basis, however, is pure LISP, so its syntax, primitive functions, and fundamental nature come from that language.

Recognizing the flexibility provided by dynamic scoping as well as the simplicity of static scoping, COMMON LISP allows both. The default scoping for variables is static, but by declaring a variable to be **special**, that variable becomes dynamically scoped.

COMMON LISP has a large number of data types and structures, including records, arrays, complex numbers, and character strings. It also has a form of packages for modularizing collections of functions and data providing access control.

COMMON LISP is further described in Chapter 14.

2.4.6 Related Languages

ML (*MetaLanguage*) was originally designed in the 1980s by Robin Milner at the University of Edinburgh as a metalanguage for a program verification system named Logic for Computable Functions (LCF) (Milner et al., 1990). ML is primarily a functional language, but it also supports imperative programming. In ML, functions are more general than in the imperative languages: They are routinely passed as parameters, and they can be polymorphic, meaning they can take parameters of different types at different calls. Unlike LISP and Scheme, the type of every variable and expression in ML can be determined at compile time. Types are associated with objects rather than names. Types of expressions are inferred from the context of the expression, as discussed in Chapter 6.

Unlike LISP and Scheme, ML does not use the parenthesized functional syntax that originated with lambda expressions. Rather, the syntax of ML resembles that of the imperative languages such as Pascal and C.

Miranda was developed by David Turner at the University of Kent in Canterbury, England, in the early 1980s (Turner, 1986). Miranda is based partly on the languages ML, SASL, and KRC. Haskell (Hudak and Fasel, 1992) is based in large part on Miranda. Like Miranda, it is a purely functional language, having no variables and no assignment statement. Another distinguishing characteristic of Haskell is its use of lazy evaluation. No expression is evaluated until its value is required. This leads to some surprising capabilities in the language.

Both ML and Haskell are briefly discussed in Chapter 14.

2.5 The First Step Toward Sophistication: ALGOL 60

ALGOL 60 has had a great influence on subsequent programming languages and is therefore of central importance in any historical review of languages.

2.5.1 Historical Background

ALGOL 60 came into being as a result of efforts to design a universal language. By late 1954, the Laning and Zierler algebraic system had been in operation for over a year, and the first report on FORTRAN had been published. FORTRAN became a reality in 1957, and several other high-level languages were being developed. Most notable among them were IT, which was designed by Alan Perlis at Carnegie Tech, and two languages for the UNIVAC computers, MATH-MATIC and UNICODE. The proliferation of languages made communication among users difficult. Furthermore, the new languages were all growing up around single architectures, some for UNIVAC computers and some for IBM 700-series machines. In response to this language proliferation, several major computer-user groups in the United States, including SHARE (the IBM scientific user group) and USE (UNIVAC Scientific Exchange, the large-scale UNIVAC scientific user group), submitted a petition to the Association for Computing Machinery (ACM) on May 10, 1957, to form a committee to study and recommend action to create a universal programming language. Although FORTRAN might have been a candidate, it could not become a universal language, because at the time it was solely owned by IBM.

Previously, in 1955, GAMM (a German acronym for Society for Applied Mathematics and Mechanics) had also formed a committee to design one universal, machine-independent, algorithmic language for use on all kinds of computers. The desire for this new language was in part due to the Europeans' fear of being dominated by IBM. By late 1957, however, the appearance of several high-level languages in the United States convinced the GAMM subcommittee that their effort had to be widened to include the

Americans, and a letter of invitation was sent to ACM. In April 1958, after Fritz Bauer of GAMM presented the formal proposal to ACM, the two groups officially agreed to a joint language-design project.

2.5.2 Early Design Process

GAMM and ACM decided that the joint design effort should be made at a meeting to which each group would send four members. The meeting, which was held in Zurich from May 27 to June 1, 1958, began with the following goals for the new language:

- The syntax of the language should be as close as possible to standard mathematical notation, and programs written in it should be readable with little further explanation.
- It should be possible to use the language for the description of computing processes in publications.
- Programs in the new language must be mechanically translatable into machine language.

The first goal indicates that the new language was to be used for scientific programming, which was the primary computer application area at that time. The second was something entirely new to the computing business. The last goal is an obvious necessity for any programming language.

Depending on how it is viewed, the Zurich meeting either produced momentous results or endless arguments. Actually, it did both. The meeting itself involved innumerable compromises, both among individuals and between the two sides of the Atlantic. In some cases, the compromises were not so much over great issues as they were over spheres of influence. The question of whether to use a comma (the European method) or a period (the American method) for a decimal point is one example.

2.5.3 ALGOL 58 Overview

The language designed at the Zurich meeting was named the International Algorithmic Language (IAL). It was suggested during the design that the language be named ALGOL, for ALGOrithmic Language, but the name was rejected because it did not reflect the international scope of the committee. During the following year, however, the name was changed to ALGOL, and the language subsequently became known as ALGOL 58.

In many ways, ALGOL 58 was a descendant of FORTRAN, which is quite natural. It generalized many of FORTRAN's features and added several new constructs and concepts. Some of the generalizations had to do with the goal of not tying the language to any particular machine, and others were attempts to make the language more flexible and powerful. A rare combination of simplicity and elegance emerged from the effort.

ALGOL 58 formalized the concept of data type, although only variables that were not floating-point required explicit declaration. It added the idea of compound statements, which most subsequent languages incorporated. Some features of FORTRAN that were generalized were the following: Identifiers were allowed to have any length, as opposed to FORTRAN's restriction to six or fewer characters; any number of array dimensions was allowed, unlike FORTRAN's limitation to no more than three; the lower bound of arrays could be specified by the programmer, whereas in FORTRAN it was implicitly 1; nested selection statements were allowed, which was not the case in FORTRAN.

ALGOL 58 acquired the assignment operator in a rather unusual way. Zuse used the form

    expression => variable

for the assignment statement in Plankalkül. Although Plankalkül had not yet been published, some of the European members of the ALGOL 58 committee were familiar with the language. The committee dabbled with the Plankalkül assignment form but, because of arguments about character limitations, the greater-than symbol was changed to a colon. Then, largely at the insistence of the Americans, the whole statement was turned around to the form

    variable := expression

The Europeans preferred the opposite form.

2.5.4 Reception of the ALGOL 58 Report

Publication of the ALGOL 58 report (Perlis and Samelson, 1958) in December 1958 was greeted with a good deal of enthusiasm. In the United States, the new language was viewed more as a collection of ideas for programming language design than as a universal standard language. Actually, the ALGOL 58 report was not meant to be a finished product but rather a preliminary document for international discussion. Nevertheless, three major design and implementation efforts used the report as their basis. At the University of Michigan, the MAD language was born (Arden et al., 1961). The U.S. Naval Electronics Group produced the NELIAC language (Huskey et al., 1963). At System Development Corporation, JOVIAL was designed and implemented (Shaw, 1963). JOVIAL, an acronym for Jules' Own Version of the International Algebraic Language, represents the only language based on ALGOL 58 to achieve widespread use (Jules was Jules I. Schwartz, one of JOVIAL's designers). JOVIAL became widely used because it was the official scientific language for the U.S. Air Force for a quarter of a century.

The rest of the U.S. computing community was not so kind to the new language. At first, both IBM and its major scientific user group, SHARE, seemed to embrace ALGOL 58. IBM began an implementation shortly after the report was published, and SHARE formed a subcommittee, SHARE IAL, to study the language. The subcommittee subsequently recommended that ACM standardize ALGOL 58 and that IBM implement it for all of the 700 series computers. The enthusiasm was short-lived, however. By spring 1959, both IBM and SHARE, through their FORTRAN experience, had had enough of the pain and expense of getting a new language started, both in terms of developing and using the first-generation compilers and in terms of training users in the new language and persuading them to use it. By the middle of 1959, both IBM and SHARE had developed such a vested interest in FORTRAN that they decided to retain it as *the* scientific language for the IBM 700 series machines, thereby abandoning ALGOL 58.

2.5.5   ALGOL 60 Design Process

During 1959, ALGOL 58 was furiously debated in both Europe and the United States. Large numbers of suggested modifications and additions were published in the European *ALGOL Bulletin* and in *Communications of the ACM*. One of the most important events of 1959 was the presentation of the work of the Zurich committee to the International Conference on Information Processing, for there Backus introduced his new notation for describing the syntax of programming languages, which later became known as BNF (for Backus-Naur form). BNF is described in detail in Chapter 3.

In January 1960, the second ALGOL meeting was held, this time in Paris. The work of this meeting was to debate the 80 suggestions that had been formally submitted for consideration. Peter Naur of Denmark had become heavily involved in the development of ALGOL, even though he had not been a member of the Zurich group. It was Naur who created and published the *ALGOL Bulletin*. He spent a good deal of time studying Backus's paper that introduced BNF and decided that BNF should be used to describe formally the results of the 1960 meeting. After making a few relatively minor changes to BNF, he wrote a description of the new proposed language in BNF and handed it out to the members of the 1960 group at the beginning of the meeting.

2.5.6   ALGOL 60 Overview

Although the 1960 meeting lasted only six days, the modifications made to ALGOL 58 were dramatic. Among the most important new developments were the following:

- The concept of block structure was introduced. This allowed the programmer to localize parts of programs by introducing new data environments, or scopes.

- Two different means of passing parameters to subprograms were allowed: pass by value and pass by name.

- Procedures were allowed to be recursive. The ALGOL 58 description was unclear on this issue. Note that although this recursion is new for the imperative languages, LISP had already provided recursive functions in 1959.

- Stack-dynamic arrays were allowed. A stack-dynamic array is one for which the subscript range or ranges are specified by variables, so that the size of the array is set at the time storage is allocated to the array, which happens when the declaration is reached during execution. Stack-dynamic arrays are described in detail in Chapter 5.

Several features that might have had a dramatic impact on the success or failure of the language were proposed but rejected. Most important among these were input and output statements with formatting, which were omitted because they were thought to be too machine dependent.

The ALGOL 60 report was published in May 1960 (Naur, 1960). A number of ambiguities still remained in the language description, and a third meeting was scheduled for April 1962 in Rome to address the problems. At this meeting the group dealt only with problems; no additions to the language were allowed. The results of this meeting were published under the title "Revised Report on the Algorithmic Language ALGOL 60" (Backus et al., 1962).

2.5.7 ALGOL 60 Evaluation

In some ways, ALGOL 60 was a great success; in other ways, it was a dismal failure. It succeeded in becoming, almost immediately, the only acceptable formal means of communicating algorithms in the literature, and it remained for over 20 years the sole language for publishing algorithms. Every imperative programming language designed since 1960 owes something to ALGOL 60. In fact, most are direct or indirect descendants; examples are PL/I, SIMULA 67, ALGOL 68, C, Pascal, Ada, C++, and Java.

The ALGOL 58/ALGOL 60 design effort included a long list of firsts. It was the first time that an international group attempted to design a programming language. It was the first language that was designed to be machine independent. It was also the first language whose syntax was formally described. This successful use of the BNF formalism initiated several important fields of computer science: formal languages, parsing theory, and compiler design. Finally, the structure of ALGOL 60 affected machine architecture. In the most striking example of this, an extension of the language was used as the systems language of a series of large-scale computers, the Burroughs B5000, B6000, and B7000 machines, which were designed with a hardware stack to implement efficiently the block structure and recursive procedures of the language.

On the other side of the coin, ALGOL 60 never achieved widespread or even significant use in the United States. Even in Europe, it never became the dominant language. There are a number of reasons for its lack of acceptance. For one thing, some of the features of ALGOL 60 turned out to be too flexible; they made understanding difficult and implementation inefficient. The best example of this is the pass-by-name method of passing parameters to subprograms, which is explained in Chapter 8. The difficulties of implementing ALGOL 60 are evidenced by Rutishauser's statement in 1967 that few if any implementations included the full ALGOL 60 language (Rutishauser, 1967, p. 8).

The lack of input and output statements in the language was another major reason for its lack of acceptance. Implementation-dependent input/output made programs difficult to port to other computers.

One of the most important contributions to computer science that is associated with ALGOL 60, BNF, was also a factor in its lack of acceptance. Although BNF is now considered a simple and elegant means of syntax description, to the world of 1960 it seemed strange and complicated.

Finally, although there were many other problems, the entrenchment of FORTRAN among users and the lack of support by IBM were probably the most important factors in ALGOL 60's failure to gain widespread use.

The ALGOL 60 effort was never really complete, in the sense that ambiguities and obscurities were always a part of the language description (Knuth, 1967).

The following is an example of an ALGOL 60 program:

```
comment ALGOL 60 Example Program
  Input:  An integer, listlen, where listlen is less than
          100, followed by listlen-integer values
  Output: The number of input values that are greater than
          the average of all the input values  ;
begin
  integer array intlist [1:99];
  integer listlen, counter, sum, average, result;
  sum := 0;
  result := 0;
  readint (listlen);
  if (listlen > 0) & (listlen < 100) then
    begin
comment Read input into an array and compute the average;
    for counter := 1 step 1 until listlen do
      begin
      readint (intlist[counter]);
      sum := sum + intlist[counter]
      end;
comment Compute the average;
    average := sum / listlen;
comment Count the input values that are > average;
    for counter := 1 step 1 until listlen do
      if intlist[counter] > average
        then result := result + 1;
```

```
comment Print result;
    printstring("The number of values > average is:");
    printint (result)
    end
  else
    printstring ("Error—input list length is not legal");
end
```

The ancestry of ALGOL 60 is shown in Figure 2.3.

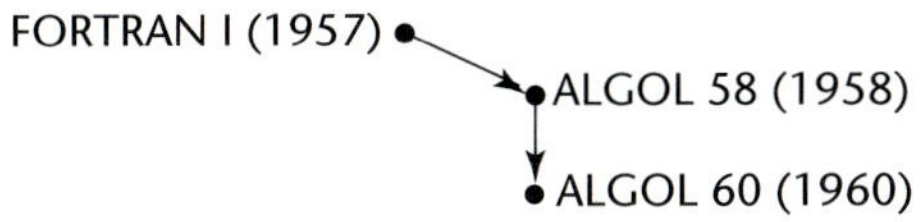

Figure 2.3
Genealogy of
ALGOL 60

FORTRAN I (1957) ●
              ●ALGOL 58 (1958)
              ●ALGOL 60 (1960)

2.6 Computerizing Business Records: COBOL

The story of COBOL is strange indeed. Although it has been used more than any other programming language, COBOL has had little effect on the design of subsequent languages, except for PL/I. It may still be the most widely used language, although it is difficult to be sure one way or the other. Perhaps the most important reason why COBOL has had little influence is that few have attempted to design a new language for business applications since it appeared. That may be a tribute to how well COBOL's capabilities meet the needs of its application area. Another reason is that a great deal of growth in business computing over the past 15 years has occurred in small businesses. In these businesses, very little software development has taken place. Instead, most of the software used is purchased as off-the-shelf packages for various general business applications.

2.6.1 Historical Background

The beginning of COBOL is somewhat similar to that of ALGOL 60, in the sense that the language was designed by a committee of people meeting for relatively short periods of time. The state of business computing at the time, which was 1959, was similar to the state of scientific computing several years earlier, when FORTRAN was being designed. One compiled language for business applications, FLOW-MATIC, had been implemented in 1957, but it belonged to one manufacturer, UNIVAC, and was designed for that company's computers. Another language, AIMACO, was being used by the U.S. Air Force, but it was only a minor variation of FLOW-MATIC.

IBM had designed a programming language for business applications, COMTRAN (COMmercial TRANslator), but it had not yet been implemented. Several other language design projects were being planned.

2.6.2 FLOW-MATIC

The origins of FLOW-MATIC are worth at least a brief discussion, because it was the primary progenitor of COBOL. In December 1953, Grace Hopper at Remington-Rand UNIVAC produced a proposal that was indeed prophetic. It suggested that "mathematical programs should be written in mathematical notation, data processing programs should be written in English statements" (Wexelblat, 1981, p. 16). Unfortunately, it was impossible in 1953 to convince nonprogrammers that a computer could be made to understand English words. It was not until 1955 that a similar proposal had some hope of being funded by UNIVAC management, and even then it took a prototype system to do the final convincing. Part of this selling process involved compiling and running a small program, first using English keywords, then using French keywords, and then using German keywords. This demonstration was considered remarkable by UNIVAC management and was a prime factor in their acceptance of Hopper's proposal.

2.6.3 COBOL Design Process

The first formal meeting on the subject of a common language for business applications, which was sponsored by the Department of Defense, was held at the Pentagon on May 28 and 29, 1959 (exactly one year after the Zurich ALGOL meeting). The consensus of the group was that the language, then named CBL (for Common Business Language) should have the following general characteristics. Most agreed that it should use English as much as possible, although a few argued for a more mathematical notation. The language must be easy to use, even at the expense of being less powerful, in order to broaden the base of those who could program computers. In addition to making the language easy to use, it was believed that the use of English would allow managers to read programs. Finally, the design should not be overly restricted by the problems of its implementation.

One of the overriding concerns at the meeting was that steps to create this universal language should be taken quickly, as a lot of work was already being done to create new business languages. In addition to the existing languages, RCA and Sylvania were working on their own business applications languages. If a universal language was not designed soon, its later acceptance would be far more difficult. On this basis, it was decided that there should be a quick study of existing languages. For this task, the Short Range Committee was formed.

There were early decisions to separate the statements of the language into two categories—data description and executable operations—and to have statements in these two categories reside in different parts of programs. One of the great debates of the Short Range Committee was over the inclusion of subscripts. Many committee members argued that subscripts were too complex for the people in data processing, who were thought to be mathematically naive. Similar arguments revolved around whether arithmetic expressions should be included. The final report of the Short Range Committee, which was completed in December 1959, described a language that was later named COBOL 60.

The language specifications for COBOL 60, published by the Government Printing Office in April 1960 (Department of Defense, 1960), were described as "initial." Revised versions were published in 1961 and 1962 (Department of Defense, 1961, 1962). The language was standardized by the American National Standards Institute (ANSI) group in 1968. The next two revisions were standardized by ANSI in 1974 and 1985. The language continues to evolve today.

2.6.4 Evaluation

The COBOL language originated a number of novel concepts, some of which eventually appeared in other languages. For example, the DEFINE verb of COBOL 60 was the first high-level language construct for macros. More important, hierarchical data structures, which first appeared in Plankalkül, were first implemented in COBOL. They have been included in virtually every imperative language designed since then. COBOL was also the first language that allowed names to be truly connotative, because it allowed both long names (up to 30 characters) and word-connector characters (dashes).

Overall, the data division is the strong part of COBOL's design, whereas the procedure division is relatively weak. Every variable is defined in detail in the data division, including the number of decimal digits and the location of the implied decimal point. File records are also described with this level of detail, as are lines to be output to a printer, which makes COBOL ideal for printing accounting reports. Perhaps the most important weakness of the procedure division lies in its lack of functions. Versions of COBOL prior to the 1974 standard also did not allow subprograms with parameters.

Our final comment on COBOL: It was the first programming language whose use was mandated by the Department of Defense (DoD). This mandate came after its initial development, because COBOL was not designed specifically for the DoD. In spite of its merits, COBOL probably would not have survived without that mandate. The poor performance of the early compilers simply made it far too expensive to use. Eventually, of course, people learned more about designing compilers, and computers became much faster, cheaper, and had much larger memories. Together, these factors have made COBOL a great success, inside and outside DoD. Its appearance led to the electronic mechanization of accounting, an important revolution by any measure.

The following is an example of a COBOL program. This program reads a file named `BAL-FWD-FILE` that contains inventory information about a certain collection of items. Among other things, each item record includes the number currently on hand (`BAL-ON-HAND`) and the item's reorder point (`BAL-REORDER-POINT`). The reorder point is the threshold number of items on hand at which more must be ordered. The program produces a list of items that must be reordered as a file named `REORDER-LISTING`.

```
IDENTIFICATION DIVISION.
PROGRAM-ID. PRODUCE-REORDER-LISTING.

ENVIRONMENT DIVISION.
CONFIGURATION SECTION.
SOURCE-COMPUTER. DEC-VAX.
OBJECT-COMPUTER. DEC-VAX.
INPUT-OUTPUT SECTION.
FILE-CONTROL.
    SELECT BAL-FWD-FILE   ASSIGN TO READER.
    SELECT REORDER-LISTING  ASSIGN TO LOCAL-PRINTER.

DATA DIVISION.
FILE SECTION.
FD  BAL-FWD-FILE
    LABEL RECORDS ARE STANDARD
    RECORD CONTAINS 80 CHARACTERS.

01  BAL-FWD-CARD.
    02 BAL-ITEM-NO        PICTURE IS 9(5).
    02 BAL-ITEM-DESC      PICTURE IS X(20).
    02 FILLER             PICTURE IS X(5).
    02 BAL-UNIT-PRICE     PICTURE IS 999V99.
    02 BAL-REORDER-POINT  PICTURE IS 9(5).
    02 BAL-ON-HAND        PICTURE IS 9(5).
    02 BAL-ON-ORDER       PICTURE IS 9(5).
    02 FILLER             PICTURE IS X(30).

FD  REORDER-LISTING
    LABEL RECORDS ARE STANDARD
    RECORD CONTAINS 132 CHARACTERS.

01  REORDER-LINE.
    02 RL-ITEM-NO         PICTURE IS Z(5).
    02 FILLER             PICTURE IS X(5).
    02 RL-ITEM-DESC       PICTURE IS X(20).
    02 FILLER             PICTURE IS X(5).
```

```
    02 RL-UNIT-PRICE        PICTURE IS ZZZ.99.
    02 FILLER               PICTURE IS X(5).
    02 RL-AVAILABLE-STOCK   PICTURE IS Z(5).
    02 FILLER               PICTURE IS X(5).
    02 RL-REORDER-POINT     PICTURE IS Z(5).
    02 FILLER               PICTURE IS X(71).

WORKING-STORAGE SECTION.
01  SWITCHES.
    02 CARD-EOF-SWITCH      PICTURE IS X.
01  WORK-FIELDS.
    02 AVAILABLE-STOCK      PICTURE IS 9(5).

PROCEDURE DIVISION.
000-PRODUCE-REORDER-LISTING.
    OPEN INPUT BAL-FWD-FILE.
    OPEN OUTPUT REORDER-LISTING.
    MOVE "N" TO CARD-EOF-SWITCH.
    PERFORM 100-PRODUCE-REORDER-LINE
        UNTIL CARD-EOF-SWITCH IS EQUAL TO "Y".
    CLOSE BAL-FWD-FILE.
    CLOSE REORDER-LISTING.
    STOP RUN.

100-PRODUCE-REORDER-LINE.
    PERFORM 110-READ-INVENTORY-RECORD.
    IF CARD-EOF-SWITCH IS NOT EQUAL TO "Y"
        PERFORM 120-CALCULATE-AVAILABLE-STOCK
        IF AVAILABLE-STOCK IS LESS THAN BAL-REORDER-POINT
            PERFORM 130-PRINT-REORDER-LINE.

110-READ-INVENTORY-RECORD.
    READ BAL-FWD-FILE RECORD
        AT END
            MOVE "Y" TO CARD-EOF-SWITCH.

120-CALCULATE-AVAILABLE-STOCK.
    ADD BAL-ON-HAND BAL-ON-ORDER
        GIVING AVAILABLE-STOCK.

130-PRINT-REORDER-LINE.
    MOVE SPACE             TO REORDER-LINE.
    MOVE BAL-ITEM-NO       TO RL-ITEM-NO.
    MOVE BAL-ITEM-DESC     TO RL-ITEM-DESC.
    MOVE BAL-UNIT-PRICE    TO RL-UNIT-PRICE.
    MOVE AVAILABLE-STOCK   TO RL-AVAILABLE-STOCK.
    MOVE BAL-REORDER-POINT TO RL-REORDER-POINT.
    WRITE REORDER-LINE.
```

The ancestry of COBOL is shown in Figure 2.4.

Figure 2.4
Genealogy of COBOL

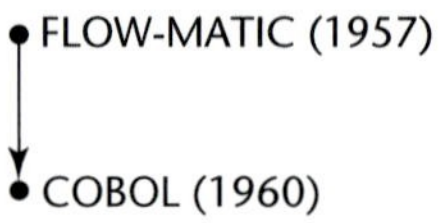

● FLOW-MATIC (1957)

● COBOL (1960)

2.7 The Beginnings of Timesharing: BASIC

BASIC (Mather and Waite, 1971) is another programming language that has enjoyed widespread use but has gotten little respect. Like COBOL, it has largely been ignored by computer scientists. Also, like COBOL, in its earliest versions it was inelegant and included only a meager set of control statements.

BASIC was very popular on microcomputers in the late 1970s and early 1980s. This followed directly from two of the main characteristics of BASIC: It is easy for beginners to learn, especially those who are not science oriented, and its smaller dialects can be implemented on computers with very small memories. There has been a resurgence in the use of BASIC with the appearance of Visual BASIC (Microsoft, 1991) in the early 1990s.

2.7.1 Design Process

BASIC (Beginner's All-purpose Symbolic Instruction Code) was designed at Dartmouth College (now Dartmouth University) in New Hampshire by two mathematicians, John Kemeny and Thomas Kurtz, who were involved in the early 1960s in producing compilers for a variety of dialects of FORTRAN and ALGOL 60. Their science students had little trouble learning or using those languages in their work.

However, Dartmouth was primarily a liberal arts institution, where science and engineering students made up only about 25 percent of the student body. It was decided in the spring of 1963 to design a new language especially for liberal arts students. This new language would use terminals as the method of computer access. The goals of the system were

1. It must be easy for nonscience students to learn and use.

2. It must be pleasant and friendly.

3. It must provide fast turnaround for homework.

4. It must allow free and private access.

5. It must consider user time more important than computer time.

The last goal was indeed a revolutionary concept. It was based at least partly on the belief that computers would become significantly cheaper as time went on, which, of course, they did.

The combination of the second, third, and fourth goals led to the time-shared aspect of BASIC. Only with individual access through terminals by numerous simultaneous users could these goals be met in the early 1960s.

In the summer of 1963, Kemeny began work on the compiler for the first version of BASIC, using remote access to a GE 225 computer. Design and coding of the operating system for BASIC began in the fall of 1963. At 4 a.m. on May 1, 1964, the first program using the time-shared BASIC was typed in and run. In June, the number of terminals on the system grew to 11, and by fall it had ballooned to 20.

2.7.2   Language Overview

The original version of BASIC was very small and, oddly, was not interactive: There was no means of getting input data from the terminal. Programs were typed in, compiled, and run, in a sort of batch-oriented way. The original BASIC had only 14 different statement types and a single data type, floating-point. Because it was believed that few of the targeted users would appreciate the difference between integer and floating-point types, the type was referred to as "numbers." Overall, it was a very limited language, though quite easy to learn.

2.7.3   Evaluation

The most important aspect of the original BASIC was that it was the first widely used method of remote terminal access to a computer. Terminals had just begun to be available at that time. Before then, most programs were entered into computers through either punched cards or paper tape.

Much of the design of BASIC came from FORTRAN, with some minor influence from the syntax of ALGOL 60. Later it grew in a variety of ways, with little or no effort made to standardize it. The American National Standards Institute issued a Minimal BASIC standard (ANSI, 1978b), but this represented only the bare minimum of language features. In fact, the original BASIC was very similar to Minimal BASIC.

Although it may seem surprising, Digital Equipment Corporation used a rather elaborate version of BASIC named BASIC-PLUS to write significant portions of their largest operating system for the PDP-11 minicomputers, RSTS, in the 1970s.

BASIC has been criticized for the poor structure of programs written in it, among other things. By our evaluation criteria, the language does indeed fare very poorly. Clearly, the early versions of the language were not meant for and should not have been used for serious programs of any significant size. Later versions are much better suited to such tasks.

The most probable reasons for BASIC's success are the ease with which it can be learned and the ease with which it can be implemented, even on very small computers.

Two of the contemporary versions of BASIC that are now being widely used are QuickBASIC (Bradley, 1989) and Visual BASIC. Both of these run on PCs. Visual BASIC is based on QuickBASIC but is designed for developing software systems that have windowed user interfaces. Visual BASIC has also been used as a scripting language for CGI programming.

The following is an example of a QuickBASIC program:

```
REM   QuickBASIC Example Program
REM   Input:   An integer, listlen, where listlen is less
REM            than 100, followed by listlen-integer values
REM   Output:  The number of input values that are greater
REM            than the average of all input values
  DIM intlist(99)
  result = 0
  sum = 0
  INPUT listlen
  IF listlen > 0 AND listlen < 100 THEN
REM   Read input into an array and compute the sum
    FOR counter = 1 TO listlen
      INPUT intlist(counter)
      sum = sum + intlist(counter)
    NEXT counter
REM   Compute the average
    average = sum / listlen
REM   Count the number of input values that are > average
    FOR counter = 1 TO listlen
      IF intlist(counter) > average
        THEN result = result + 1
    NEXT counter
REM   Print the result
    PRINT "The number of values that are > average is:";
          result
  ELSE
    PRINT "Error—input list length is not legal"
  END IF
END
```

The ancestry of BASIC is shown in Figure 2.5.

2.8 Everything for Everybody: PL/I

PL/I represents the first large-scale attempt to design a language that could be used for a broad spectrum of application areas. All previous and most subsequent languages have focused on one particular application area, such as science, artificial intelligence, or business.

Figure 2.5
Genealogy of BASIC

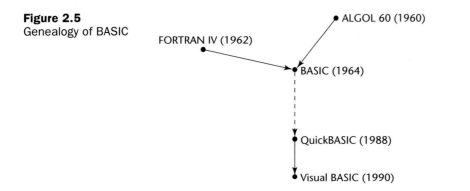

2.8.1 Historical Background

Like FORTRAN, PL/I was developed as an IBM product. By the early 1960s, the users of computers in industry had settled into two separate and quite different camps. From the IBM point of view, scientific programmers could use either the large-scale 7090 or the small-scale 1620 IBM computers. This group used the floating-point data type and arrays extensively. FORTRAN was the primary language, although some assembly language was also used. They had their own user group, SHARE, and had little contact with anyone who worked on business applications.

For business applications, people used the large 7080 or the small 1401 IBM computers. They needed the decimal and character string data types as well as elaborate and efficient input and output facilities. They used COBOL, although in early 1963 when the PL/I story begins, the conversion from assembly language to COBOL was far from complete. This category of users also had its own user group, GUIDE, and seldom had contact with scientific users.

In early 1963, IBM planners perceived the beginnings of a change in this situation. The two widely separated groups were moving toward each other in ways that were thought certain to create problems. Scientists began to gather large files of data to be processed. This data required more sophisticated and more efficient input and output facilities. Business applications people began to use regression analysis to build management information systems, which required floating-point data and arrays. It began to appear that computing installations would soon require two separate computers, supporting two very different programming languages.

These perceptions quite naturally led to the concept of designing a single universal computer that would be capable of doing both floating-point and decimal arithmetic, and therefore both scientific and business applications. Thus was born the concept of the IBM System/360 line of computers. Along with this came the idea of a programming language that could be used for both business and scientific applications. For good measure, systems programming and list processing were thrown in as capabilities. Therefore, the new language was to replace FORTRAN, COBOL, LISP, and the systems applications of assembly language.

2.8.2 Design Process

The design effort began when IBM and SHARE formed the Advanced Language Development Committee of the SHARE FORTRAN Project in October 1963. This new committee quickly met and formed a subcommittee called the 3 ↔ 3 Committee, so named because it had three members from IBM and three from SHARE. The 3 ↔ 3 Committee met for three or four days every other week to design the language.

As with the Short Range Committee for COBOL, the initial design was scheduled for completion in a remarkably short time. Apparently, regardless of the scope of a language design effort, in the early 1960s the prevailing belief was that it could be done in three months. The first version of PL/I, which was then named FORTRAN VI, was supposed to be completed by December, less than three months after the committee was formed. The committee pleaded successfully on two different occasions for extensions, moving the due date back to January and then to late February 1964.

The initial design concept was that the new language would be an extension of FORTRAN IV, maintaining compatibility, but that goal was dropped quickly along with the name FORTRAN VI. Until 1965, the language was known as NPL, an acronym for New Programming Language. The first published report on NPL was given at the SHARE meeting of March 1964. A more complete description followed in April, and the version that would actually be implemented was published in December 1964 (IBM, 1964) by the compiler group at the IBM Hursley Laboratory in England, which was chosen to do the implementation. In 1965, the name was changed to PL/I to avoid the confusion of the name NPL with the National Physical Laboratory in England. If the compiler had been developed outside the United Kingdom, the name might have remained NPL.

2.8.3 Language Overview

Perhaps the best single-sentence description of PL/I is that it included what were then considered the best parts of ALGOL 60 (recursion and block structure), FORTRAN IV (separate compilation with communication through global data), and COBOL 60 (data structures, input/output, and report-generating facilities), along with a few new constructs, all somehow blended together. We will not attempt, even in an abbreviated way, to discuss all the features of the language, or even its most controversial constructs. Instead, we will mention briefly some of the language's contributions to the pool of knowledge of programming languages.

PL/I was the first programming language to have the following facilities:

- Programs were allowed to create concurrently executing tasks. Although this was a good idea, it was poorly developed in PL/I.

- It was possible to detect and handle 23 different types of exceptions, or run-time errors.

- Procedures were allowed to be used recursively, but the capability could be disabled, allowing more efficient code for nonrecursive procedures.

- Pointers were included as a data type.

- Cross sections of arrays could be referenced. For example, the third row of a matrix could be referenced as if it were a vector.

2.8.4 Evaluation

Any evaluation of PL/I must begin by recognizing the ambitiousness of the design effort. In retrospect, it appears naive to think that so many constructs could have been combined successfully. However, that judgment must be tempered by acknowledging that there was little language design experience at the time. Overall, the design of PL/I was based on the premise that any construct that was useful and could be implemented should be included, with insufficient concern about how the many features would behave when thrown together. Edsger Dijkstra, in his Turing Award Lecture (Dijkstra, 1972), made one of the strongest criticisms of the complexity of PL/I: "I absolutely fail to see how we can keep our growing programs firmly within our intellectual grip when by its sheer baroqueness the programming language—our basic tool, mind you!—already escapes our intellectual control."

In addition to the problem with the complexity due to its large size, PL/I suffered from a number of what are now considered to be poorly designed constructs. Among these were pointers, exception handling, and concurrency, although we must point out that in each of these cases the construct was something new.

In terms of usage, PL/I must be considered at least a partial success. In the 1970s, it enjoyed significant use in both business and scientific applications. It was also widely used during that time as an instructional vehicle, primarily in several subset forms, such as PL/C (Cornell, 1977) and PL/CS (Conway and Constable, 1976).

The following is an example of a PL/I program:

```
/* PL/I PROGRAM EXAMPLE
   INPUT:   AN INTEGER, LISTLEN, WHERE LISTLEN IS LESS THAN
              100, FOLLOWED BY LISTLEN-INTEGER VALUES
   OUTPUT: THE NUMBER OF INPUT VALUES THAT ARE GREATER THAN
              THE AVERAGE OF ALL INPUT VALUES     */
PLIEX: PROCEDURE OPTIONS (MAIN);
  DECLARE INTLIST (1:99) FIXED.
  DECLARE (LISTLEN, COUNTER, SUM, AVERAGE, RESULT) FIXED;
  SUM = 0;
  RESULT = 0;
  GET LIST (LISTLEN);
  IF (LISTLEN > 0) & (LISTLEN < 100) THEN
    DO;
/* READ INPUT DATA INTO AN ARRAY AND COMPUTE THE SUM */
    DO COUNTER = 1 TO LISTLEN;
      GET LIST (INTLIST (COUNTER));
      SUM = SUM + INTLIST (COUNTER);
    END;
/* COMPUTE THE AVERAGE */
    AVERAGE = SUM / LISTLEN;
/* COUNT THE NUMBER OF VALUES THAT ARE > AVERAGE */
    DO COUNTER = 1 TO LISTLEN;
      IF INTLIST (COUNTER) > AVERAGE THEN
        RESULT = RESULT + 1;
    END;
/* PRINT RESULT */
    PUT SKIP LIST ('THE NUMBER OF VALUES > AVERAGE IS:');
    PUT LIST (RESULT);
    END;
  ELSE
    PUT SKIP LIST ('ERROR—INPUT LIST LENGTH IS ILLEGAL');
  END PLIEX;
```

The ancestry of PL/I is shown in Figure 2.6.

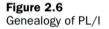
Figure 2.6
Genealogy of PL/I

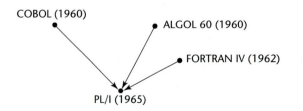

2.9 Two Early Dynamic Languages: APL and SNOBOL

The structure of this section is different from that shared by the other sections of the chapter because the languages discussed here are so different. Neither APL nor SNOBOL were based on any previous language, and neither had much influence on later mainstream languages (although the J language is based on APL, and ICON (Griswold and Griswold, 1983) is based on SNOBOL). Both APL and SNOBOL are used later in the book to illustrate and contrast some of their features with those of more conventional languages. This is why they are briefly discussed here.

In appearance and in purpose, APL and SNOBOL are very different. They share two common characteristics, however: dynamic typing and dynamic storage allocation. Variables in both languages are essentially untyped. A variable acquires a type when it is assigned a value, at which time it assumes the type of the value assigned. Storage is allocated to a variable only when it is assigned a value, because before that there is no way to know the amount of storage that will be needed.

2.9.1 Origins and Characteristics of APL

APL (Polinka and Pakin, 1975) was designed around 1960 by Kenneth E. Iverson at IBM. It was not originally designed to be an implemented programming language, but rather was intended to be a vehicle for describing computer architecture. APL was first described in the book from which it gets its name, *A Programming Language* (Iverson, 1962). In the mid-1960s, the first implementation of APL was developed at IBM.

APL has a large number of powerful operators, which created a problem for implementors. The first means of using APL was through IBM printing terminals. These terminals had special print balls that provided the odd character set required by the language. One reason APL has so many operators is that it allows arrays to be manipulated as if they were scalar variables. For example, the transpose of any matrix is done with a single operator. The large collection of operators provides very high expressivity but also makes APL programs difficult to read. Many people think of APL as a language that is best used for "throw-away" programming. Although programs can be written quickly, they should be discarded after being used because they will be difficult to maintain.

APL has been around for over 30 years and is still used today, though not widely. Furthermore, it has not changed a great deal over its lifetime.

2..9.2 Origins and Characteristics of SNOBOL

SNOBOL (pronounced "snowball") (Griswold et al., 1971) was designed in the early 1960s by three people at Bell Laboratories: D.J. Farber, R.E.

Griswold, and F.P. Polensky (Farber et al., 1964). It was designed specifically for text processing. The heart of SNOBOL is a collection of powerful operations for string pattern matching. One of the early applications of SNOBOL was for writing text editors. Because the dynamic nature of SNOBOL makes it slower than some other languages, it is now rarely used for such programs. However, SNOBOL is still a live and supported language that is used for a variety of text processing tasks in a number of different application areas.

2.10 The Beginnings of Data Abstraction: SIMULA 67

Although SIMULA 67 never achieved widespread use and had little impact on the programmers and computing of its time, some of the concepts it introduced make it important.

2.10.1 Design Process

Two Norwegians, Kristen Nygaard and Ole-Johan Dahl, developed the language SIMULA I between 1962 and 1964 at the Norwegian Computing Center (NCC). They were primarily interested in using computers for simulation, but also worked in operations research. SIMULA I was designed exclusively for system simulation and was first implemented in late 1964 on a UNIVAC 1107 computer.

As soon as the SIMULA I implementation was completed, Nygaard and Dahl began efforts to extend the language by adding entirely new features and modifying some existing constructs in order to make the language useful for more general-purpose applications. The result of this work was SIMULA 67, whose design was first presented publicly in March 1967 (Dahl and Nygaard, 1967). We will discuss only SIMULA 67, although some of the features of interest in SIMULA 67 are also in SIMULA I.

2.10.2 Language Overview

SIMULA 67 is an extension of ALGOL 60, taking both block structure and the control statement structure from that language. The primary deficiency of ALGOL 60 (and other languages at that time) for simulation applications is the design of its subprograms. Simulation requires subprograms that are allowed to restart at the position where they previously stopped. Subprograms with this kind of control are known as coroutines because the caller and called subprograms have a somewhat equal relationship with each other, rather than the rigid hierarchical relationship they usually have in imperative languages.

Figure 2.7
Genealogy of
SIMULA 67

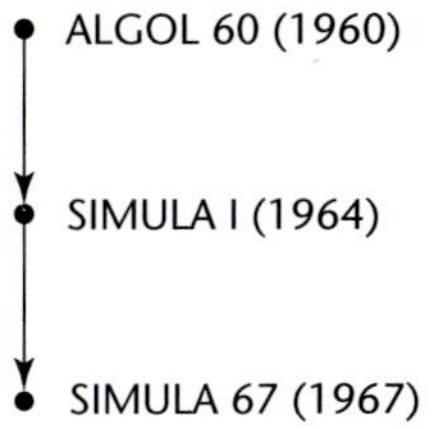

- ALGOL 60 (1960)

- SIMULA I (1964)

- SIMULA 67 (1967)

To provide support for coroutines in SIMULA 67, the class construct was developed. This was an important development because our ideas of data abstraction began with it. The basic idea of a class is that a data structure and the routines that manipulate that data structure are packaged together. Furthermore, a class definition is only a template for a data structure and as such is distinct from a class instance, so a program can create and use any number of instances of a particular class. Class instances can contain local data. They can also include code that is executed at creation time, which can initialize some data structure of the class instance.

A more thorough discussion of classes and class instances is presented in Chapter 10. It is interesting to note that the important concept of data abstraction was not developed and attributed to the class construct until 1972, when Hoare (1972) recognized the connection.

The ancestry of SIMULA 67 is shown in Figure 2.7.

2.11 Orthogonal Design: ALGOL 68

ALGOL 68 was the source of several new ideas in language design, some of which were subsequently adopted by other languages. We include it here for that reason, even though it never achieved widespread use in either Europe or the United States. Because some ALGOL 68 constructs are discussed in later chapters, we discuss in this chapter only two of its most important contributions.

2.11.1 Design Process

The development of the ALGOL family did not end when the revised report appeared in 1962, although it was six years until the next design iteration was published. The resulting language, ALGOL 68 (van Wijngaarden et al., 1969), was dramatically different from its predecessor.

One of the most interesting innovations of ALGOL 68 is one of its primary design criteria: orthogonality. Recall our discussion of orthogonality in Chapter 1. The use of orthogonality resulted in several innovative features of ALGOL 68, two of which are described in the following section.

2.11.2 Language Overview

One important result of orthogonality in ALGOL 68 was its inclusion of user-defined data types. Earlier languages, such as FORTRAN, included only a few basic data structures. PL/I included a large number of data structures, which made it harder to learn and difficult to implement, but it obviously could not provide an appropriate data structure for every application.

The approach of ALGOL 68 to data structures was to provide a few primitive types and structures and allow the user to combine those primitives into a large number of different structures. This provision for user-defined data types was carried over to some extent into all of the major imperative languages designed since then. User-defined data types are valuable because they allow the user to design data abstractions that fit particular problems very closely. All aspects of data typing are discussed in Chapter 5.

As another first in the area of data types, ALGOL 68 introduced the kind of dynamic arrays that will be termed implicit heap-dynamic in Chapter 4. A dynamic array is one in which the declaration does not specify subscript bounds. Assignments to a dynamic array cause allocation of required storage. In ALGOL 68, dynamic arrays are called **flex** arrays. For example, the declaration

```
flex [1:0] int list
```

states that `list` is a dynamic array of integers with a single subscript whose lower bound is 1, but it allocates no storage. The aggregate assignment

```
list := (3, 5, 6, 2)
```

causes `list` to be allocated sufficient storage for four integers, effectively changing its bounds to [1:4].

2.11.3 Evaluation

ALGOL 68 includes a significant number of features that had not been previously used. Its use of orthogonality, which some may argue was overdone, was nevertheless revolutionary. Many of the features that were introduced in ALGOL 68 became part of subsequent languages.

ALGOL 68 repeated one of the sins of ALGOL 60, however, and it was an important factor in its lack of widespread acceptance. The language was described using an elegant and concise but also unknown metalanguage. Before one could read the language-describing document (van Wijngaarden et al., 1969), he or she had to learn the new metalanguage, called van Wijngaarden grammars. To make matters worse, the designers invented a collection of words to explain the grammar and the language.

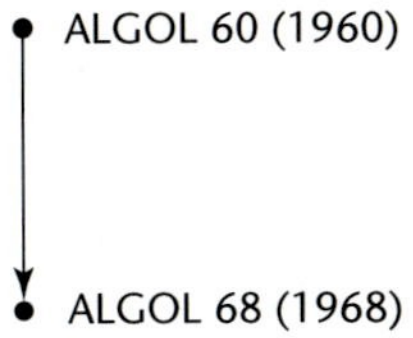

Figure 2.8
Genealogy of
ALGOL 68

- ALGOL 60 (1960)

- ALGOL 68 (1968)

For example, keywords are called indicants, substring extraction is called trimming, and the process of procedure execution is called a coercion of deproceduring, which might be meek, firm, or something else.

It is natural to contrast the design of PL/I with that of ALGOL 68. ALGOL 68 achieved writability by the principle of orthogonality: a few primitive concepts and the unrestricted use of a few combining mechanisms. PL/I achieved writability by including a large number of fixed constructs. ALGOL 68 extended the elegant simplicity of ALGOL 60, whereas PL/I simply threw together the features of several languages to attain its goals. Of course, it must be kept in mind that the goal of PL/I was to provide a unified tool for a broad class of problems; on the other hand, ALGOL 68 was targeted to a single class: scientific applications.

PL/I achieved far greater acceptance than ALGOL 68, due largely to IBM's promotional efforts and the problems of understanding and implementing ALGOL 68. Implementation was a difficult problem for both, but PL/I had the resources of IBM to apply to constructing a compiler. ALGOL 68 enjoyed no such benefactor.

The ancestry of ALGOL 68 is shown in Figure 2.8.

2.12 Some Important Descendants of the ALGOLs

All imperative languages, including the imperative/object-oriented languages such as C++ and Java, designed since 1960 owe some of their design to ALGOL 60 and/or ALGOL 68. This section discusses some of these languages. Notably missing from this section are Ada, which is discussed in Section 2.14, C++, which is discussed in Section 2.16, and Java, which is discussed in Section 2.17.

2.12.1 Simplicity by Design: Pascal

2.12.1.1 Historical Background

Niklaus Wirth (Wirth is pronounced "Virt") was a member of the International Federation of Information Processing (IFIP) Working Group 2.1, which was created to continue the development of ALGOL in the mid-1960s. In August 1965, Wirth and C.A.R. Hoare contributed to that effort by presenting to the group a somewhat modest proposal for additions and modifications to ALGOL 60 (Wirth and Hoare, 1966). The majority of the group rejected the proposal as being too small an advance over ALGOL 60. Instead, a much more complex proposed revision was developed, which eventually became ALGOL 68. Wirth, along with a few other group members, did not believe that the ALGOL 68 report should have been released, based on the complexity of both the language and the metalanguage used to describe it. This position later proved to have some validity because the ALGOL 68 documents, and therefore the language, were indeed found by the computing community to be very difficult to understand.

The Wirth and Hoare version of ALGOL 60 was named ALGOL-W. It was implemented at Stanford University and was used primarily as an instructional vehicle, but only at a few universities. The primary contributions of ALGOL-W were the value-result method of passing parameters and the **case** statement for multiple selection. The value-result method is an alternative to ALGOL 60's pass-by-name method. Both are discussed in Chapter 8. The **case** statement is discussed in Chapter 7.

Wirth's next major design effort, again based on ALGOL 60, was his most successful: Pascal. The original published definition of Pascal appeared in 1971 (Wirth, 1971). This version was modified somewhat in the implementation process and is described in Wirth (1973). The features that are often ascribed to Pascal in fact came from earlier languages. For example, user-defined data types were introduced in ALGOL 68, the **case** statement in ALGOL-W, and Pascal's records are similar to the structured variables of COBOL and PL/I.

2.12.1.2 Evaluation

The largest impact of Pascal has been on the teaching of programming. In 1970, most students of computer science, engineering, and science were introduced to programming with FORTRAN, although some universities used PL/I, languages based on PL/I, and ALGOL-W. By the mid-1970s, Pascal had become the most widely used language for this purpose. This was quite natural, although perhaps not predictable, because Pascal had, in fact, been designed specifically for teaching programming.

Because Pascal was designed as a teaching language, it lacks several features that are essential for many kinds of applications. The best example of this is the impossibility of writing a subprogram that takes as a parameter an array of variable length. Another example is the lack of any separate compilation capability. These deficiencies naturally led to many nonstandard dialects, such as Turbo Pascal.

Pascal's popularity, for both teaching programming and other applications, is based primarily on its remarkable combination of simplicity and expressivity. Although there are some insecurities in Pascal, as we discuss in later chapters, it is still a relatively safe language, particularly when compared with FORTRAN or C. By the mid-1990s, the popularity of Pascal was on the decline, both in industry and in universities.

The following is an example of a Pascal program:

```
{Pascal Example Program
  Input:  An integer, listlen, where listlen is less than
          100, followed by listlen-integer values
  Output: The number of input values that are greater than
          the average of all input values }
program pasex (input, output);
  type intlisttype = array [1..99] of integer;
  var
    intlist : intlisttype;
    listlen, counter, sum, average, result : integer;
  begin
  result := 0;
  sum := 0;
  readln (listlen);
  if ((listlen > 0) and (listlen < 100)) then
    begin
{ Read input into an array and compute the sum }
    for counter := 1 to listlen do
      begin
      readln (intlist[counter]);
      sum := sum + intlist[counter]
      end;
{ Compute the average }
    average := sum / listlen;
{ Count the number of input values that are > average }
    for counter := 1 to listlen do
      if (intlist[counter] > average) then
        result := result + 1;
{ Print the result }
    writeln ('The number of values > average is:',
             result)
    end { of the then clause of if (( listlen > 0 ... }
  else
    writeln ('Error—input list length is not legal')
end.
```

The ancestry of Pascal is shown in Figure 2.9.

2.12.2 A Portable Systems Language: C

Like Pascal, C contributed little to the previously known collection of language features, but it has been very widely used. Although originally designed for systems programming, C is well suited for a wide variety of applications.

Figure 2.9
Genealogy of Pascal

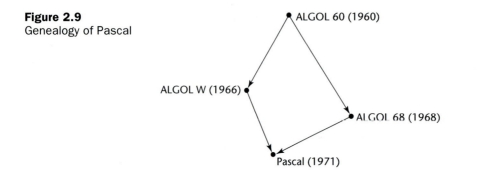

2.12.2.1 Historical Background

C's ancestors include CPL, BCPL, B, and ALGOL 68. CPL was developed at Cambridge University in the early 1960s. BCPL is a simple systems language developed by Martin Richards in 1967 (Richards, 1969).

The first work on the UNIX operating system was done in the late 1960s by Ken Thompson at Bell Laboratories. The first version was written in assembly language. The first high-level language implemented under UNIX was B, which was based on BCPL. B was designed and implemented by Thompson in 1970.

Neither BCPL nor B is a typed language, which is an oddity among high-level languages, although both are much lower level than a language such as Pascal. Being untyped means that all data are considered machine words, which, although extremely simple, leads to many complications and insecurities. For example, there is the problem of specifying floating-point rather than integer arithmetic in an expression. In one implementation of BCPL, the operands of a floating-point operation were preceded by periods. Operands not preceded by periods were considered to be integers. An alternative to this would have been to use different symbols for the floating-point operations.

This problem, along with several others, led to the development of a new typed language based on B. Originally called NB but later named C, it was designed and implemented by Dennis Ritchie at Bell Laboratories in 1972 (Kernighan and Ritchie, 1978). In some cases through BCPL, and in other cases directly, C was influenced by ALGOL 68. This is seen in its **for** and **switch** statements, in its assigning operators, and in its treatment of pointers.

The only "standard" for C in its first decade and a half was the book by Kernighan and Ritchie (1978). Over that time span the language slowly evolved, with different implementors adding different features. In 1989, ANSI produced an official description of C (ANSI, 1989), which included many of the features that implementors had already incorporated into the language.

A new version of C named C++ was developed in the middle and late 1980s (Ellis and Stroustrup, 1990). Its history and some of its most significant features are described in Section 2.16. Details of C++ support for data abstraction are discussed in Chapter 10. Details of C++ support for object-oriented programming are discussed in Chapter 11.

2.12.2.2 Evaluation

C has adequate control statements and data-structuring facilities to allow its use in many application areas. It also has a rich set of operators that allow a high degree of expressiveness.

One of the most important reasons why C is both liked and disliked is its lack of complete type checking. For example, functions can be written for which parameters are not type checked. Those who like C appreciate the flexibility; those who do not like it find it too insecure. A major reason for its great increase in popularity in the 1980s is that it is part of the widely used UNIX operating system. This inclusion in UNIX provides an inexpensive (often free with UNIX) and quite good compiler that is available to programmers on many different kinds of computers.

The following is an example of a C program:

```
/* C Example Program
   Input:  An integer, listlen, where listlen is less than
           100, followed by listlen-integer values
   Output: The number of input values that are greater than
           the average of all input values */
void main (){
  int intlist[98], listlen, counter, sum, average, result;
  sum = 0;
  result = 0;
  scanf("%d", &listlen);
  if ((listlen > 0) && (listlen < 100)) {
/* Read input into an array and compute the sum */
    for (counter = 0; counter < listlen; counter++) {
      scanf("%d", &intlist[counter]);
      sum = sum + intlist[counter];
    }
/* Compute the average */
    average = sum / listlen;
/* Count the input values that are > average */
    for (counter = 0; counter < listlen; counter++)
      if (intlist[counter] > average) result++;
/* Print result */
    printf("Number of values > average is:%d\n", result);
  }
  else
    printf("Error—input list length is not legal\n");
}
```

The ancestry of C is shown in Figure 2.10.

Figure 2.10
Genealogy of C

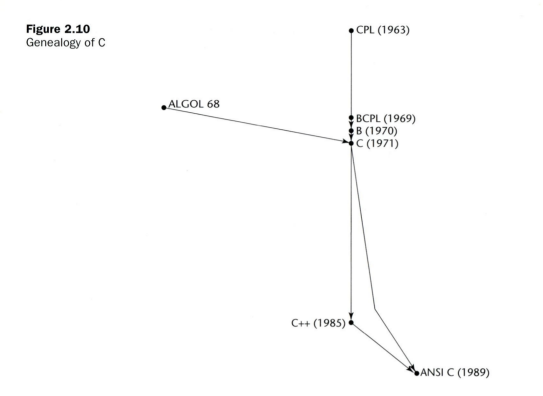

2.12.3   Other ALGOL Descendants

This section briefly discusses the origins and characteristics of some of the other ALGOL descendants that are referenced later in the book.

2.12.3.1   Modula-2

After Pascal, Niklaus Wirth designed Modula, which resulted from his experimentation with concurrency (Wirth, 1976). No compiler for Modula was ever released, and its development was discontinued soon after its publication. Wirth, however, did not abandon language design. His focus changed to building a language that was meant to be the single language for a new computer system that later was called Lilith. While the computer itself was never a commercial success, the language, Modula-2, was (Wirth, 1985).

The primary distinguishing features of Modula-2, whose design was based on Pascal and Modula, were modules, which provide support for abstract data types, procedures as types, low-level facilities for systems programming and coroutines, and some syntactic features that were improvements over that of Pascal.

Modula-2 achieved widespread use in the late 1980s and early 1990s as a teaching language in universities. It also was used, at least for a few years, in various industrial application areas.

2.12.3.2 Modula-3

Modula-3 was jointly designed by the Systems Research Center of Digital Equipment Corporation in Palo Alto and the Olivetti Research Center in Menlo Park in the late 1980s (Cardelli et al., 1989). It is based on Modula-2, Mesa (Mitchell et al., 1979), Cedar (Lampson, 1983), and Modula-2+ (Rovner, 1986). To Modula-2, it adds classes and objects for support of object-oriented programming, exception handling, garbage collection, and support for concurrency. Although it is a well-designed and powerful language, Modula-3's prospects for widespread use are dim. Although Digital supports it, the Modula-2 user base on which it could have grown has mostly disappeared.

2.12.3.3 Oberon

Oberon, which is loosely based on Modula-2, is the most recent language designed by Niklaus Wirth. The latest version of Oberon is named Oberon-2 (Mössenbock, 1993).

Wirth's passion for simplicity in programming languages is stunningly evident in the design of Oberon. Although some features were added to Modula-2 to get Oberon, a larger number of features were subtracted, putting Oberon in stark contrast to C++ and Ada 95. Oberon is, in terms of complexity and size, the opposite of those two languages.

The main feature added to Modula-2 to get Oberon is type extension, which supports object-oriented programming. Among the removed features are variant records, opaque types, enumeration types, subrange types, the `CARDINAL` type, noninteger array indexes, the **with** statement, and the **for** statement. It is remarkable to find a new language that is significantly smaller and less complex than its predecessor, but Oberon is exactly that.

2.12.3.4 Delphi

Delphi is a hybrid language, similar to C++ in that it was created by adding object-oriented support, among other things, to an existing imperative language. Delphi is derived from Pascal. Many of the differences between C++ and Delphi are a result of the languages and the surrounding programming cultures from which they are derived. Because C is a powerful but potentially unsafe language, C++ also fits that description, at least in the areas of array subscript range checking, pointer arithmetic, and its numerous type coercions. Likewise, because Pascal is more elegant and safe than C, Delphi is more elegant and safe than C++. Delphi is also less complex than C++. For example, Delphi does not allow user-defined operator overloading, generic subprograms, and parameterized classes, all of which are part of C++.

Delphi, like Visual C++, provides a graphical user interface (GUI) to the developer and simple ways to create GUI interfaces to applications written in Delphi. Delphi was designed, supported, and sold by Borland, the same company that developed Turbo Pascal.

2.13 Programming Based on Logic: Prolog

Simply put, logic programming is the use of a formal logic notation to communicate computational processes to a computer. Predicate calculus is the notation used in current logic programming languages.

Programming in logic programming languages is nonprocedural. Programs in such languages do not state exactly *how* a result is to be computed but rather describe the form of the result. What is needed to provide this capability for logic programming languages is a concise means of supplying the computer with both the relevant information and an inferencing process for computing desirable results. Predicate calculus supplies the basic form of communication to the computer, and the proof method named resolution, developed first by Robinson (1965), supplies the inference technique.

2.13.1 Design Process

During the very early 1970s, Alain Colmerauer and Phillippe Roussel in the Artificial Intelligence Group at the University of Aix-Marseille, together with Robert Kowalski of the Department of Artificial Intelligence at the University of Edinburgh, developed the fundamental design of Prolog. The primary components of Prolog are a method for specifying predicate calculus propositions and an implementation of a restricted form of resolution. Both predicate calculus and resolution are described in Chapter 15. The first Prolog interpreter was developed at Marseille in 1972. The version of the language that was implemented is described in Roussel (1975). The name Prolog is from *programming logic.*

2.13.2 Language Overview

Prolog programs consist of collections of statements. Prolog has only a few kinds of statements, but they can be complex.

One common use of Prolog is as a kind of intelligent database. This application provides a simple framework for discussing the Prolog language.

The database of a Prolog program consists of two kinds of statements, facts and rules. Examples of fact statement are

```
mother(joanne, jake).
father(vern, joanne).
```

which state that `joanne` is the `mother` of `jake`, and `vern` is the `father` of `joanne`.

An example of a rule statement is

```
grandparent(X, Z) :- parent(X, Y), parent(Y, Z).
```

which states that it can be deduced that `X` is the `grandparent` of `Z` if it is true that `X` is the `parent` of `Y` and `Y` is the parent of `Z`, for some specific values for the variables `X`, `Y`, and `Z`.

The Prolog database can be interactively queried with goal statements, an example of which is

```
father(bob, darcie).
```

which asks if `bob` is the `father` of `darcie`. When such a query, or goal, is presented to the Prolog system, it uses its resolution process to attempt to determine the truth of the statement. If it can conclude that the goal is true, it displays "true." If it cannot prove it, it displays "false."

2.13.3 Evaluation

There is a relatively small group of computer scientists who believe that logic programming provides the best hope for escape from the imperative languages, and also from the enormous problem of producing the large amount of reliable software that is currently needed. So far, however, there are two major reasons why logic programming has not become more widely used. First, as with some other nonimperative approaches, logic programming thus far has proven to be highly inefficient. Second, it has been shown to be an effective method for only a few relatively small areas of application: certain kinds of database management systems and some areas of AI.

Logic programming and Prolog are described in greater detail in Chapter 15.

2.14 History's Largest Design Effort: Ada

The Ada language is the result of the most extensive and most expensive language design effort ever undertaken. The Ada language was developed for the Department of Defense (DoD), so the state of their computing environment was instrumental in determining its form.

2.14.1 Historical Background

By 1974, over half of the applications of computers in DoD were embedded systems. An embedded system is one in which the computer hardware is embedded in the device it controls or for which it provides services. Software costs were rising rapidly, primarily because of the increasing complexity of systems. More than 450 different programming languages were in use for DoD projects, and none of them were standardized by DoD. Every defense contractor could define a new and different language for every contract. Because of this language proliferation, application software was rarely reused. Furthermore, no software development tools were created (because they are usually language dependent). A great many languages were in use, but none was actually suitable for embedded systems applications. For these reasons, the Army, Navy, and Air Force each independently proposed in 1974 the development of a high-level language for embedded systems.

2.14.2 Design Process

Noting this widespread interest, Malcolm Currie, Director of Defense Research and Engineering, in January 1975, formed the High-Order Language Working Group (HOLWG), initially headed by Lt. Col. William Whitaker of the Air Force. The HOLWG had representatives from all of the military services and liaisons with England, France, and West Germany. Its initial charter was to

- Identify the requirements for a new DoD high-level language.
- Evaluate existing languages to determine whether there was a viable candidate.
- Recommend adoption or implementation of a minimal set of programming languages.

In April 1975, the HOLWG produced the Strawman requirements document for the new language (Department of Defense, 1975a). This was distributed to military branches, federal agencies, selected industrial and university representatives, and interested parties in Europe.

The Strawman document was followed by Woodenman (Department of Defense, 1975b) in August 1975 and Tinman (Department of Defense, 1976) in January 1976. The Tinman document was considered a complete set of requirements for a language with the desired characteristics. The principal author of these documents was David Fisher of the Institute for Defense Analysis. The group of participants in the effort was large, numbering over 200, with representatives from over 40 organizations outside DoD. In January 1977, the Tinman document was replaced by the Ironman requirements document (Department of Defense, 1977), which was nearly equivalent in content but had a somewhat different format.

In April 1977, the Ironman document was used as the basis for an unrestricted request for proposals, which was then made public, thereby making Ada the first language to be designed by competitive contract. In July 1977, four of the proposing contractors—Softech, SRI International, Cii Honeywell/Bull, and Intermetrics—were chosen to produce, independently and in parallel, Phase 1 of the language design. All four of the resulting design proposals were based on Pascal.

When the six-month Phase 1 was completed in February 1978, there was a two-month evaluation by 400 volunteers in 80 review teams scattered around the world. The result of this evaluation was that two finalists—Intermetrics and Cii Honeywell/Bull—were chosen to go on to Phase 2 of the development.

In June 1978, the next iteration of the requirements document, Steelman, was released (Department of Defense, 1978).

At the end of Phase 2, another two-month evaluation was done, and in May 1979 the Cii Honeywell/Bull language design was chosen as the winner. Interestingly, the winner was the only foreign competitor among the final four. The Cii Honeywell/Bull design team in France was led by Jean Ichbiah.

In the spring of 1979, Jack Cooper of the Navy Materiel Command recommended the name for the new language, Ada, which was then adopted. Augusta Ada Byron (1815–1851), Countess of Lovelace, mathematician and daughter of poet Lord Byron, is generally recognized as being the world's first programmer. She worked with Charles Babbage on his mechanical computers, the Difference and Analytical Engines, writing programs for several numerical processes.

Phase 3 of the Ada design project began with the selection of the winning design. The design and the rationale for it were published by ACM in its *SIGPLAN Notices* (ACM, 1979) and distributed to a readership of over 10,000 people. A public test and evaluation conference was held in October 1979 in Boston, with representatives from over 100 organizations from the United States and Europe. By November, more than 500 language reports had been received from 15 different countries. Most of the reports suggested small modifications rather than drastic changes and outright rejections. Based on the language reports, the next version of the requirements specification, the Stoneman document (Department of Defense, 1980a), was released in February 1980.

A revised version of the language design was completed in July 1980 and was accepted as MIL-STD 1815, the standard *Ada Language Reference Manual*. The number 1815 was chosen because it was the year of the birth of Augusta Ada Lovelace. Another revised version of the *Ada Language Reference Manual* was released in July 1982. In 1983, the American National Standards Institute standardized Ada. This "final" official version is described in Goos and Hartmanis (1983). The Ada language design was then frozen for at least five years.

2.14.3 Language Overview

This section briefly describes four of the major features of the Ada language. Because we use the language in many examples throughout the remainder of the book, other features will be described along the way.

Packages in the Ada language provide the means for encapsulating data objects, specifications for data types, and procedures. This, in turn, provides the support for the use of data abstraction in program design, as described in Chapter 10.

The Ada language includes extensive facilities for exception handling, which allows the programmer to gain control after any one of a wide variety of exceptions, or run-time errors, has been detected. Exception handling is discussed in Chapter 13.

Program units can be generic in Ada. For example, it is possible to write a sort procedure that uses an unspecified type for the data to be sorted. Such a generic procedure must be instantiated for a specified type before it can be used. This is done with a statement that causes the compiler to generate a version of the procedure with the given type. The availability of such generic units increases the range of program units that might be reused, rather than duplicated, by programmers. Generics are discussed in Chapters 8 and 10.

The Ada language also provides for concurrent execution of special program units, named tasks, using the rendezvous mechanism. Rendezvous is the name of a method of intertask communication and synchronization. Concurrency is discussed in Chapter 12.

2.14.4 Evaluation

Perhaps the most important aspects of the design of the Ada language to consider are the following:

- Because the design was competitive, there was no limit on participation.
- The Ada language embodies most of the concepts of software engineering and language design of the late 1970s. Although one can question the actual methods used to include these features, as well as the wisdom of including such a large number of features in a language, most agree that the features are valuable.
- Although many people did not initially realize it, the development of a compiler for the Ada language was a difficult task. Only in 1985, almost four years after the language design was completed, did truly usable Ada compilers begin to appear.

The most serious criticism of Ada in its first few years was that it was too large and too complex. In particular, Hoare has stated that it should not be used for any application where reliability is critical (Hoare, 1981), which is precisely the type of applications for which it was designed. On the other hand, others have praised it as the epitome of language design.

The following is an example of an Ada program:

```
-- Ada Example Program
-- Input:  An integer, LIST_LEN, where LIST_LEN is less
--             than 100, followed by LIST_LEN-integer values
-- Output: The number of input values that are greater
--             than the average of all input values
with TEXT_IO; use TEXT_IO;
procedure ADA_EX is
   package INT_IO is new INTEGER_IO (INTEGER);
   use INT_IO;
   type INT_LIST_TYPE is array (1..99) of INTEGER;
   INT_LIST : INT_LIST_TYPE;
   LIST_LEN, SUM, AVERAGE, RESULT : INTEGER;
   begin
   RESULT := 0;
   SUM := 0;
   GET (LIST_LEN);
   if (LIST_LEN > 0) and (LIST_LEN < 100) then
-- Read input data into an array and compute the sum
      for COUNTER := 1 .. LIST_LEN loop
        GET (INT_LIST(COUNTER));
        SUM := SUM + INT_LIST(COUNTER);
      end loop;
-- Compute the average
      AVERAGE := SUM / LIST_LEN;
-- Count the number of values that are > average
      for COUNTER := 1 .. LIST_LEN loop
        if INT_LIST(COUNTER) > AVERAGE then
          RESULT := RESULT + 1;
        end if;
      end loop;
-- Print result
      PUT ("The number of values > average is:");
      PUT (RESULT);
      NEW_LINE;
    else
      PUT_LINE ("Error—input list length is not legal");
    end if;
end ADA_EX;
```

2.14.5 Ada 95

A revision effort for Ada began in 1988 with the establishment of the Ada 9X project by the Ada Joint Program Office. The Ada 9X project had three phases: the determination of the requirements for the revised language, the actual development of the definition of the revised language, and the transition into use of the revised language. The requirements were published in Department of Defense (1990).

The requirements focused on four areas of the language: interfacing (especially into graphical user interfaces), support for object-oriented programming, more flexible libraries, and better control mechanisms for shared data.

Two of the most important new features of the new version of Ada, named Ada 95, are described briefly in the following paragraphs. In the remainder of the book, we will use the named Ada 83 for the original version and Ada 95 (its actual name) for the later version when it is important to distinguish between the two versions. In discussions of language features common to both versions, we will use the name Ada. The Ada 95 standard language is defined in AARM (1995).

The type derivation mechanism of Ada 83 is extended to allow the adding of new components to those derived from a tagged parent type. This provides for inheritance, a key ingredient in object-oriented programming languages. Dynamic binding of subprogram calls to subprogram definitions is accomplished through subprogram dispatching, which is based on the tag value of derived types through classwide types. This feature provides for polymorphism, another principal feature of object-oriented programming. These features of Ada 95 are discussed in Chapter 11.

The rendezvous mechanism of Ada 83 provided only cumbersome means of sharing data among concurrent processes. It was necessary to introduce a new task to control access to the shared data. The protected objects of Ada 95 offer an attractive alternative to this. The shared data is encapsulated in a syntactic structure that controls all access to the data, either by rendezvous or by subprogram call. The new features of Ada 95 for concurrency and shared data are discussed in Chapter 12.

It is widely believed that the popularity of Ada 95 will suffer because the Department of Defense no longer requires its use in military software systems. There are, of course, other factors that hinder its growth in popularity.

The ancestry of Ada is shown in Figure 2.11.

Figure 2.11
Genealogy of Ada

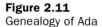

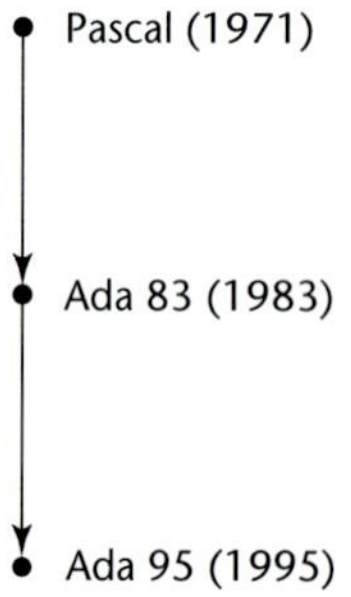

Pascal (1971)

Ada 83 (1983)

Ada 95 (1995)

2.15 Object-Oriented Programming: Smalltalk

As discussed in Chapter 1, object-oriented programming includes data abstraction as one of its three fundamental characteristics, the other two being inheritance and dynamic binding.

Inheritance appeared in a limited form in SIMULA 67, whose classes can be defined in hierarchies. Inheritance provides an effective method of code reuse.

The unit control concept of object-oriented programming is loosely modeled on the idea that programs simulate the real world, a legacy of its origins in SIMULA 67. Because much of the real world is populated by objects, a simulation of such a world must include simulated objects. In fact, a language based on the concepts of real-world simulation need only include a model of objects that can send and receive messages and react to the messages it receives.

The essence of object-oriented programming is solving problems by identifying the real-world objects of the problem and the processing required of those objects, and then creating simulations of those objects, their processes, and the required communications between the objects. Abstract data types, dynamic binding, and inheritance are the concepts that make object-oriented problem solving not only possible but also convenient and effective.

2.15.1 Design Process

The concepts that led to the development of Smalltalk originated in the Ph.D. dissertation work of Alan Kay in the late 1960s at the University of Utah (Kay, 1969). Kay had remarkable foresight in predicting the future availability of powerful desktop computers. Recall that the first microcomputer systems were not marketed until the mid-1970s, and they were only remotely related to the machines envisioned by Kay, which were seen to execute a million or more instructions per second and contain several megabytes of memory. Such machines, in the form of workstations, became widely available only in the early 1980s.

Kay believed that desktop computers would be used by nonprogrammers and thus would need very powerful human interfacing capabilities. The computers of the late 1960s were largely batch-oriented and were used exclusively by professional programmers and scientists. For use by nonprogrammers, Kay determined, a computer would have to be highly interactive and use sophisticated graphics in its interface to users. Some of the graphics concepts came from the LOGO experience of Seymour Papert, in which graphics was used to aid children in the use of computers (Papert, 1980).

Kay originally envisioned a system he called Dynabook, which was meant to be a general information processor. It was based in part on the

Flex language, which he had helped design. Flex was based primarily on SIMULA 67. Dynabook was based on the paradigm of the typical desk, on which there are a number of papers, some partially covered. The top sheet is often the focus of attention, with the others temporarily out of focus. The display of Dynabook would model this scene, using screen windows. The user would interact with such a display both through a keyboard and by touching the screen with his or her fingers. After the preliminary design of Dynabook earned him a Ph.D., Kay's goal became to see such a machine constructed.

Kay found his way to the Xerox Palo Alto Research Center (Xerox PARC) and presented his ideas on Dynabook. This led to his employment there and the subsequent birth of the Learning Research Group at Xerox. The first charge of the group was to design a language to support Kay's programming paradigm and implement it on the best personal computer then available. These efforts resulted in an "Interim" Dynabook, consisting of the Xerox Alto hardware and the Smalltalk-72 software. Together, they formed a research tool for further development. A number of research projects were conducted with this system, including several experiments to teach programming to children. Along with the experiments came further developments, leading to a sequence of languages that ended with Smalltalk-80, which is the version discussed in this book. As the language grew, so did the power of the hardware on which it resided. By 1980, both the language and the Xerox hardware nearly matched the early vision of Alan Kay.

2.15.2   Language Overview

The program units of Smalltalk are objects. Objects are structures that encapsulate local data and a collection of operations called methods that is available to other objects. A method specifies the reaction of the object when it receives a particular message that corresponds to that method. The Smalltalk world is populated by nothing but objects, from integer constants to large complex software systems.

All computing in Smalltalk is done by the same uniform technique: sending a message to an object to invoke one of its methods. A reply to a message is an object, which returns the requested information or simply notifies the sender that the requested processing has been completed. The fundamental difference between a message and a subprogram call is this: A message is sent to a data object, which then is processed by code associated with the object; a subprogram call usually sends the data to be processed to a subprogram code unit.

From the simulation point of view, which is never far away, Smalltalk is a simulation of a collection of computers (objects) that communicate with each other (through messages). Each object is an abstraction of a computer in the sense that it stores data and provides processing capability for manipulating that data. In addition, objects can send and receive messages. In essence, those are the fundamental capabilities of computers: to store and manipulate data and to communicate.

In Smalltalk, object abstractions are classes, which are very similar to the classes of SIMULA 67. Instances of the class can be created and are then the objects of the program. Each object has its own local data and represents a different instance of its class. The only difference between two objects of the same class is the state of their local variables.

As in SIMULA 67, class hierarchies can be formed in Smalltalk. Subclasses of a given class are refinements of it, inheriting the functionality and local variables of the parent class, or superclass. Subclasses can add new local memory and functionality and modify or hide inherited functionality.

As briefly discussed in Chapter 1, Smalltalk is not just a language, it is also a complete software development environment. The interface to the environment is highly graphical, making heavy use of multiple overlaid windows and pop-up menus and a mouse input device.

2.15.3 Evaluation

Smalltalk has done a great deal to promote two separate aspects of computing. The windowing systems that are now the dominant method of user interfaces to software systems grew out of Smalltalk. Today, the most significant software design methodologies and programming languages are object oriented. Although the origin of some of the ideas of object-oriented languages came from SIMULA 67, they reached maturation only in Smalltalk. It is clear that Smalltalk's impact on the computing world is extensive and will be long-lived.

The following is an example of a Smalltalk class definition:

```
"Smalltalk Example Program"
"The following is a class definition, instantiations of which
can draw equilateral polygons of any number of sides"
class name                 Polygon
superclass                 Object
instance variable names    ourPen
                           numSides
                           sideLength

"Class methods"
  "Create an instance"
  new
      ^ super new getPen

  "Get a pen for drawing polygons"
  getPen
     ourPen <- Pen new defaultNib: 2
```

```
"Instance methods"
"Draw a polygon"
draw
    numSides timesRepeat: [ourPen go: sideLength;
                           turn: 360 // numSides]

"Set length of sides"
length: len
    sideLength <- len

"Set number of sides"
sides: num
    numSides <- num
```

The ancestry of Smalltalk is shown in Figure 2.12.

Figure 2.12
Genealogy of Smalltalk

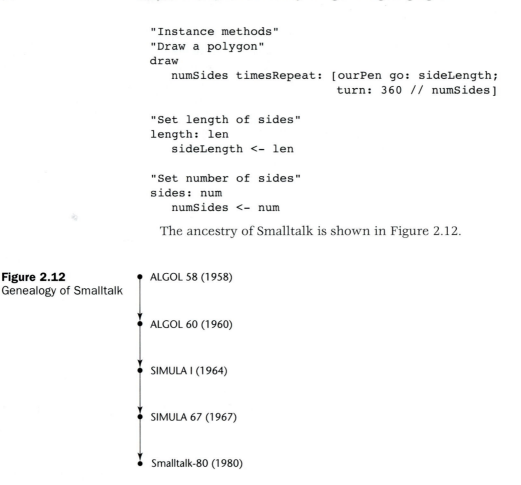

ALGOL 58 (1958)

ALGOL 60 (1960)

SIMULA I (1964)

SIMULA 67 (1967)

Smalltalk-80 (1980)

2.16 Combining Imperative and Object-Oriented Features: C++

The origins of C were discussed in Section 2.12; the origins of Smalltalk were discussed in Section 2.15. C++ builds language facilities on top of C to support much of what Smalltalk pioneered. C++ has evolved from C through a sequence of modifications to improve its imperative features and additions to support object-oriented programming.

2.16.1 Design Process

The first step from C toward C++ was made by Bjarne Stroustrup at Bell Laboratories in 1980. Modifications included the addition of function parameter type checking and conversion and, more significantly, classes, which are related to those of SIMULA 67 and Smalltalk. Also included were derived classes, public/private access control of inherited components, constructor and destructor functions, and friend classes. During 1981, inline functions, default parameters, and overloading of the assignment operator were added. The resulting language was called C with Classes and is described in Stroustrup (1983).

It is useful to consider some goals of C with Classes. The primary goal was to provide a language in which programs could be organized as they could be organized in SIMULA 67; that is, with classes and inheritance. Another important goal was that there should be no performance penalty, relative to C. So that C with Classes could be used for every application for which C could be used, but virtually none of the insecure features of C would be removed. For example, array index range checking was not even considered because a significant performance disadvantage, relative to C, would result.

By 1984, this language was extended by the inclusion of virtual functions, which provide dynamic binding of function calls to specific function definitions; function name and operator overloading; and reference types. This version of the language was called C++. It is described in Stroustrup (1984).

In 1985, the first available implementation appeared, a system named Cfront, which translates C++ programs into C programs. This version of Cfront and the version of C++ it implemented were named Release 1.0. It is described in Stroustrup (1986).

Between 1985 and 1989, C++ continued to evolve, based largely on user reaction to the first distributed implementation. This next version was named Release 2.0. Its Cfront implementation was released in June 1989. The most important features added to C++ Release 2.0 were support for multiple inheritance (classes with more than one parent class) and abstract classes, along with some other enhancements. Abstract classes are described in Chapter 11.

Release 3.0 of C++ evolved between 1989 and 1990. It added templates, which provide parameterized types, and exception handling. Both Release 2.0 and 3.0 are described in Ellis and Stroustrup (1990).

2.16.2 Language Overview

The most essential part of support for object-oriented programming is the class/object mechanism, which originated in SIMULA 67 and is the central feature of Smalltalk. C++ provides a collection of predefined classes, along with the possibility of user-defined classes. The classes of C++ are data types, which, like Smalltalk classes, can be instantiated any number of times. Such instantiations in C++ are merely object, or data, declarations. Class definitions specify data objects (called data members) and functions (called member functions). Classes can name one or more parent classes, providing inheritance and multiple inheritance, respectively. Classes inherit the data members and member functions of the parent class that are specified to be inheritable.

Operators in C++ can be overloaded, meaning the user can create operators for existing operators on user-defined types. C++ functions can also be overloaded, meaning the user can define more than one function with the same name, provided either the numbers or types of their parameters are different.

Dynamic binding in C++ is provided by virtual class functions. These functions define type-dependent operations, using overloaded functions, within a collection of classes that are related through inheritance. A pointer to an object of class A can also point to objects of classes that inherit class A. When this pointer points to an overloaded virtual function, the function of the current type is chosen dynamically.

Both functions and classes can be templated, which means that they can be parameterized. For example, a function can be written as a templated function to allow it to have versions for a variety of parameter types. Classes enjoy the same flexibility.

C++ includes exception handling that is significantly different from that of Ada. One difference is that hardware-detectable exceptions cannot be handled. The exception handling of C++ is discussed in Chapter 13.

2.16.3 Evaluation

C++ rapidly became and remains a very popular language. One factor in its popularity is the availability of good and inexpensive compilers. Another factor in favor of the popularity of C++ is that it is almost completely downward compatible with C (meaning that C programs can be, for the most part, compiled as C++ programs), and in most implementations it is possible to link C++ code with C code. Finally, programmers are now intensely interested in object-oriented programming. C++ is the vehicle by which many programmers use object-oriented programming methodology.

On the negative side, because C++ is a very large and complex language, it clearly suffers drawbacks similar to those of PL/I. It inherited most of the insecurities of C, which make it less safe than languages such as Delphi, Ada, and Java. Finally, in part because of its basis in C, C++ is more like PL/I than ALGOL 68, in that it is more of a collection of ideas thrown together than the result of an overall language design plan.

The object-oriented features of C++ are described in far more detail in Chapter 11.

The ancestry of C++ is shown in Figure 2.10.

2.16.4 A Related Language: Eiffel

Eiffel is another hybrid language with both imperative and object-oriented features (Meyer, 1992). Eiffel was designed by a single person, Bertrand Meyer, who is French but lives in California. The language includes features to support abstract data types, inheritance, and dynamic binding, so it fully supports object-oriented programming. Perhaps the most distinguishing feature of Eiffel is the integrated use of assertions to enforce the "contract" between subprograms and their callers. It is an idea that was born in Plankalkül but ignored by most other languages designed since then. It is natural to compare Eiffel to C++. Eiffel is smaller and simpler than C++ but has nearly equal expressivity and writability. The reasons for the soaring popularity of C++, while Eiffel is still seeing only limited use, are not difficult to determine. C++ is clearly the easiest way for software development organizations to move to object-oriented programming, because in many cases their developers already know C. Eiffel enjoys no such easy path to adoption. Also, for the first few years that use of C++ spread, the Cfront system was available and inexpensive. During its early years, Eiffel compilers were less available and more expensive. C++ had the backing of the prestigious Bell Laboratories, whereas Eiffel was backed by Bertrand Meyer and his relatively small software company, Interactive Software Engineering.

2.17 Programming the World Wide Web: Java

Java's designers started with C++, removed numerous constructs, changed some, and added a few others. The resulting language provides much of the power and flexibility of C++, but in a smaller, simpler, and safer language.

2.17.1 Design Process

Java, like many programming languages, was designed for an application for which there appeared to be no satisfactory existing language. In the case of Java, however, it was actually a sequence of applications, the first of which was the programming of embedded consumer electronic devices, such as toasters, microwave ovens, and interactive TV systems. It may not seem that reliability would be an important factor in the software for a microwave oven. If an oven had malfunctioning software, it probably would not pose a grave danger to anyone and probably would not lead to large legal settlements. However, if the software in a particular model was found to be erroneous after a million units had been manufactured and sold, their recall would entail significant cost. Therefore, reliability *is* an important characteristic of the software in consumer electronic products.

In 1990, Sun Microsystems decided that neither of the two programming languages they considered, C and C++, would be satisfactory for developing software for consumer electronic devices. Although C was relatively small, it did not provide support for object-oriented programming, which they deemed a necessity. C++ supported object-oriented programming, but its size and complexity were perceived to be significant liabilities. It was also believed that neither C nor C++ provided the necessary level of reliability. The design of Java was guided by the fundamental concept of providing greater simplicity and reliability than they believed were provided by C++.

Although the initial impetus for Java was consumer electronics, none of the products with which it was used in its early years were ever marketed. When the World Wide Web became widely used, starting in 1993, largely because of the new graphical browsers, Java was found to be a useful tool for Web programming. In its first few years in public use, the Web has been Java's most common application.

The Java design team was headed by James Gosling, who had previously designed the Unix emacs editor and the NeWS windowing system.

2.17.2 Language Overview

As we stated earlier, Java is based on C++ but was specifically designed to be smaller, simpler, and more reliable. Java has both types and classes. The primitive types are not objects based on classes. These include all of its scalar types, including those for integer, floating-point, Boolean, and character data. Objects are accessed through reference variables, but primitive type values are accessed exactly as the scalar values in purely imperative languages like C and Ada. Java arrays are instances of a predefined class, whereas in C++ they are not, although many C++ users build wrapper classes for arrays to add features like index range checking, which is implicit in Java.

Java does not have pointers, but its reference types provide some of the capabilities of pointers. These references are used to point to class instances—in fact, that is the only way class instances can be referenced. While pointers and references may seem a great deal alike, there are some important semantic differences. Pointers point to memory locations, but references point at objects. This makes any kind of arithmetic on references nonsense, eliminating that error-prone practice. The distinction between a pointer's value and the value to which it points is the responsibility of the programmer in many languages, in which pointers sometimes must be explicitly dereferenced. References are always implicitly dereferenced, when necessary. So they behave more like ordinary scalar variables.

Java has a primitive Boolean type, used mainly for the control expressions of its control statements (such as **if** and **while**). Unlike C and C++, arithmetic expressions cannot be used for control expressions. Java has no record, union, or enumeration types.

One significant difference between Java and many of its contemporaries that support object-oriented programming, including Ada 95 and C++, is that it is not possible to write stand-alone subprograms in Java. All Java subprograms are methods and are defined in classes. There is no construct in Java that is called a function or a subprogram. Furthermore, methods can only be called through a class or object.

Another important difference between C++ and Java is that C++ supports multiple inheritance directly in its class definitions. Some feel multiple inheritance leads to more complexity and confusion than it is worth. Java supports only single inheritance, although some of the benefits of multiple inheritance can be gained by using its interface construct.

Java includes a relatively simple form of concurrency control through its **synchronize** modifier, which can appear on methods and blocks. In either case, it causes a lock to be attached. The lock insures mutually exclusive access or execution. In Java it is relatively easy to create concurrent processes, which in Java are called threads. These threads can be started, suspended, resumed, and stopped, all with methods inherited from the parent class of all threads, Thread.

Java uses implicit storage deallocation for its heap-allocated objects (all Java class instances, or objects, are heap allocated), often called *garbage collection*. This frees the programmer from being concerned with putting storage back in the heap when it is no longer needed. Programs written in languages that require explicit deallocation often suffer from what is sometimes called memory leakage, which means that storage is allocated but never deallocated. This can obviously lead to eventual depletion of all available storage.

Unlike C and C++, Java includes type coercions (implicit type conversions) only if they are widening (from a "smaller" type to a "larger" type). So, **int** to **float** coercions are done, but **float** to **int** coercions are not.

2.17.3 Evaluation

The designers of Java did well at trimming out excess and/or unsafe features of C++. For example, the elimination of half of the coercions that are done in C++ was clearly a step toward higher reliability. Index range checking of array accesses also makes the language safer. The addition of concurrency enhances the scope of applications that can be written in the language, as do the class libraries for applets, graphical user interfaces, and networking.

On the other hand, Java is still a complex language. Its lack of multiple inheritance leads to some peculiar designs. For example, to run an applet as a task that can run concurrently with other tasks, it is necessary to put together the attributes of both applets and threads. This marriage is not necessarily a pretty one.

Java's portability, at least in intermediate form, has often been attributed to the design of the language, but it is not. Any language could be translated to an intermediate form and "run" on any platform that had a virtual machine for that intermediate form. The price of this kind of portability is the cost of interpretation, which is usually about an order of magnitude more than execution of machine code. Clearly, many applications must run faster, and therefore require compilers that translate source programs to machine code. However, such compilers have been slow to appear for Java. Because of this, for now at least, most large applications are still being written in other languages, such as C++, Delphi, and Ada.

Java is now widely used for programming World Wide Web pages. Before Java appeared, any significant computation required by a Web page was done through the Common Gateway Interface (CGI), using some application running on the Web server. Java applets are small programs that run on the Web client when it finds an applet call in the HTML of a page it is displaying. When called, the intermediate code form of the applet is downloaded from the server to the client, where it is interpreted. The output of an applet is displayed in the Web page.

The use of Java has increased faster than that of any other programming language. One of the reasons for this is its value in programming elaborate Web pages. Another is that the compiler/interpreter system for Java has been free and easy to obtain on the Web. It is clear that one of the reasons for Java's rapid rise to prominence is simply that programmers like its design. Finally, there have been for some time a collection of C++ programmers who objected to what they perceived as problems with the C++ language. Java offers them an alternative that has much of the power of C++, but fewer of the problems.

The following is an example of a Java program:

```
// Java Example Program
//   Input: An integer, listlen, where listlen is less
//          than 100, followed by length-integer values
// Output: The number of input data that are greater than
//          the average of all input values

import java.io.*;
class IntSort {
public static void main(String args[]) throws IOException {
  DataInputStream in = new DataInputStream(System.in);
   int listlen,
       counter,
       sum = 0,
```

```
            average,
            result = 0;
        int[] intlist = int[99];
        listlen = Integer.parseInt(in.readLine());
        if ((listlen > 0) && (listlen < 100)) {
    /* Read input into an array and compute the sum  */
            for (counter = 0; counter < listlen; counter++) {
                intlist[counter] =
                        Integer.valueOf(in.readLine()).intValue();
                sum += intlist[counter];
            }
    /* Compute the average */
            average = sum / listlen;
    /* Count the input values that are > average */
            for (counter = 0; counter < listlen; counter++)
                if (intlist[counter] > average) result++;
    /* Print result */
            System.out.println(
                "\nNumber of values > average is:" + result);
        }  //** end of then clause of if ((listlen > 0) ...
        else System.out.println(
                "Error—input list length is not legal\n");
    }  //** end of method main
}  //** end of class IntSort
```

SUMMARY

We have investigated the development and the development environments of a number of the most important programming languages. This chapter should have given the reader a good perspective on current issues in language design. We hope to have set the stage for an in-depth discussion of the important features of contemporary languages.

BIBLIOGRAPHIC NOTES

Perhaps the most important source of historical information about the development of programming languages is *History of Programming Languages*, edited by Richard Wexelblat (Wexelblat, 1981). It contains the developmental background and environment of 13 important programming languages, as told by the designers themselves. A similar work resulted from a second "history" conference, this time published as a special issue of *ACM SIGPLAN Notices* (ACM, 1993a). In this work, the history and evolution of 13 more programming languages are discussed.

The paper "Early Development of Programming Languages" (Knuth and Pardo, 1977), which is part of the *Encyclopedia of Computer Science and Technology*, is an excellent 85-page work that details the development of languages up to and including FORTRAN. The paper includes example programs to demonstrate the features of many of those languages.

Another book of great historical interest is *Programming Languages: History and Fundamentals*, by Jean Sammet (Sammet, 1969). It is a 785-page work filled with details of 80 programming languages of the 1950s and 1960s. Sammet has also published several updates to her book, such as Sammet (1976).

REVIEW QUESTIONS

1. In what year was Plankalkül designed? In what year was that design published?

2. What two common data structures were included in Plankalkül?

3. How were the pseudocodes of the early 1950s implemented?

4. Speedcoding was invented to overcome two significant shortcomings of the computer hardware of the early 1950s. What were these two?

5. Why was the slowness of interpretation of programs acceptable in the early 1950s?

6. What two important hardware features first appeared in the IBM 704 computer?

7. In what year was the FORTRAN design project begun?

8. What was the primary application area of computers at the time FORTRAN was designed?

9. What was the source of all of the control flow statements of FORTRAN I?

10. What was the most significant feature added to FORTRAN I to get FORTRAN II?

11. What control flow statements were added to FORTRAN IV to get FORTRAN 77?

12. Which version of FORTRAN was the first to have any sort of dynamic variables?

13. Which version of FORTRAN was the first to have character string handling?

14. Why were linguists interested in artificial intelligence in the late 1950s?

15. Where was LISP developed? By whom?

16. In what way are Scheme and COMMON LISP opposites of each other?

17. What dialect of LISP is used for introductory programming courses at some universities?

18. What two professional organizations together designed ALGOL 60?

19. In what version of ALGOL did block structure appear?

20. What missing language element of ALGOL 60 damaged its chances for widespread use?

21. What language was designed to describe the syntax of ALGOL 60?

22. On what language was COBOL based?

23. In what year did the COBOL design process begin?

24. What data structure appeared in COBOL that originated with Plankalkül?

25. What organization was most responsible for the early success of COBOL (in terms of extent of use)?

26. What user group was the target of the first version of BASIC?

27. Why was BASIC an important language in the early 1980s?

28. PL/I was designed to replace what two languages?

29. For what new line of computers was PL/I designed?

30. What features of SIMULA 67 are now important parts of some object-oriented languages?

31. What innovation of data structuring was introduced in ALGOL 68 but is often credited to Pascal?

32. What design criterion was used extensively in ALGOL 68?

33. What language introduced the **case** statement?

34. What operators in C were modeled on similar operators in ALGOL 68?

35. What are two characteristics of C that make it less safe than Pascal?

36. What is a nonprocedural language?

37. What are the two kinds of statements that populate a Prolog database?

38. What is the primary application area for which Ada was designed?

39. What are the concurrent program units of Ada called?

40. What Ada construct provides support for abstract data types?

41. What populates the Smalltalk world?

42. What three concepts are the basis for object-oriented programming?

43. Why does C++ include the features of C that are known to be unsafe?

44. What do the Ada and COBOL languages have in common?

45. What was the first application for Java?

46. What are two reasons why Java is safer than C++?

PROBLEM SET

1. What features of Plankalkül do you think would have had the greatest influence on FORTRAN 0 if the FORTRAN designers had been familiar with Plankalkül?

2. Determine the capabilities of Backus's 701 Speedcoding system, and compare them with those of a contemporary programmable hand calculator.

3. Write a short history of the A-0, A-1, and A-2 systems designed by Grace Hopper and her associates.

4. As a research project, compare the facilities of FORTRAN 0 with those of the Laning and Zierler system.

5. Which of the three original goals of the ALGOL design committee, in your opinion, was most difficult to achieve at that time?

6. Make an educated guess as to the most common syntax error in LISP programs.

7. LISP began as a pure functional language but gradually acquired more and more imperative features. Why?

8. Describe in detail the three most important reasons, in your opinion, why AL-GOL 60 did not become a very widely used language.

9. Why, in your opinion, did COBOL allow long identifiers when FORTRAN and ALGOL did not?

10. What is the primary reason you have heard why computer scientists seldom use BASIC?

11. Outline the major motivation of IBM in developing PL/I.

12. Was IBM's major motivation for developing PL/I correct, given the history of computers and language developments since 1964?

13. Describe, in your own words, the concept of orthogonality in programming language design.

14. What is the primary reason, in your opinion, why PL/I became more widely used than ALGOL 68?

15. What are the arguments both for and against the idea of a typeless language?

16. Are there any logic programming languages, other than Prolog?

17. What is your opinion of the argument that languages that are too complex are too dangerous to use and we should therefore keep all languages small and simple?

18. Do you think language design by committee is a good idea? Support your opinion.

19. Languages continually evolve. What sort of restrictions do you think are appropriate for changes in programming languages? Compare your answers with the evolution of FORTRAN.

20. Build a table identifying all of the major language developments, together with when they occurred, in what language they first appeared, and the identities of the developers.

3 Describing Syntax and Semantics

Grace M. Hopper

Grace M. Hopper, a naval officer and formerly employed by UNIVAC, designed a series of "compiler" systems in the early to mid-50s that were used for business applications programming. By 1958, these systems evolved to the first high-level programming language for business applications, FLOW-MATIC, on which COBOL was, to a large degree, based. She was also involved with the COBOL design effort, serving as an advisor to the executive committee of CODASYL.

This chapter covers the following topics. First, the terms *syntax* and *semantics* are defined. Then a detailed discussion of the most common method of describing syntax, context-free grammars (also known as Backus-Naur Form), is presented. This is followed by a description of syntax graphs and a brief introduction to recursive descent parsing, which is a common syntax analysis technique based directly on context-free grammars. Attribute grammars, which can be used to describe both the syntax and static semantics of programming languages, are discussed next. Finally, three formal methods of describing semantics—operational, axiomatic, and denotational semantics—are introduced. Because of the inherent complexity of the semantics description methods, our discussion of them will be brief. One could easily write an entire book on just one of the three (and several authors have).

3.1 Introduction

The task of providing a concise yet understandable description of a programming language is difficult but essential to the language's success. ALGOL 60 and ALGOL 68 were first presented using concise formal descriptions; in both cases, however, the descriptions were not easily understandable, partly because each used a new notation. The levels of acceptance of both languages suffered as a result. On the other hand, some languages have suffered the problem of having many slightly different dialects, a result of an understandable but informal and imprecise definition.

One of the problems in describing a language is the diversity of the people who must understand the description. Most new programming languages are subjected to a period of scrutiny by potential users before their designs are completed. The success of this feedback cycle depends heavily on the clarity of the description.

Programming language implementors obviously must be able to determine how the expressions, statements, and program units of a language are formed, and also their intended effect when executed. The difficulty of the job of implementors is in part determined by the clarity and precision of the language description.

Finally, language users must be able to determine how to encode software systems by referring to a language reference manual. Textbooks and courses enter into this process, but language manuals are usually the only authoritative printed information source about a language.

The study of programming languages, like the study of natural languages, can be divided into examinations of syntax and semantics. The

syntax of a programming language is the form of its expressions, statements, and program units. Its **semantics** is the meaning of those expressions, statements, and program units. For example, the syntax of a C **if** statement is

```
if (<expr>) <statement>
```

The semantics of this statement form is that if the current value of the expression is true, the embedded statement is selected for execution.

Although they are often separated for discussion purposes, syntax and semantics are closely related. In a well-designed programming language, semantics should follow directly from syntax; that is, the form of a statement should strongly suggest what the statement is meant to accomplish.

Describing syntax is easier than describing semantics, partly because a concise and universally accepted notation is available for syntax description, but none has yet been developed for semantics.

3.2 The General Problem of Describing Syntax

Languages, whether natural (such as English) or artificial (such as Java), are sets of strings of characters from some alphabet. The strings of a language are called **sentences** or statements. The syntax rules of a language specify which strings of characters from the language's alphabet are in the language. English, for example, has a large and complex collection of rules for specifying the syntax of its sentences. By comparison, even the largest and most complex programming languages are syntactically very simple.

Formal descriptions of the syntax of programming languages, for simplicity's sake, often do not include descriptions of the lowest level syntactic units. These small units are called **lexemes**. The description of lexemes can be given by a lexical specification, which can be separate from the syntactic description of the language. The lexemes of a programming language include its identifiers, literals, operators, and special words. One can think of programs as strings of lexemes rather than of characters.

A **token** of a language is a category of its lexemes. For example, an identifier is a token that can have lexemes, or instances, such as sum and total. In some cases, a token has only a single possible lexeme. For example, the token for the arithmetic operator symbol +, which may have the name plus_op, has just one possible lexeme. Consider the following example C statement.

```
index = 2 * count + 17;
```

The lexemes and tokens of this statement are

Lexemes	Tokens
index	identifier
=	equal_sign
2	int_literal
*	mult_op
count	identifier
+	plus_op
17	int_ literal
;	semicolon

The example language descriptions in this chapter are very simple, and most include lexeme descriptions.

3.2.1 Language Recognizers

In general, languages can be formally defined in two distinct ways: by **recognition** and by **generation.** (Although neither provides a definition that is practical by itself for people trying to learn or even use a programming language.) Suppose we have a language L that uses the alphabet Σ of characters. To formally define L using the recognition method, we would need to construct a mechanism R, called a recognition device, capable of reading strings of characters from the alphabet Σ. R would need to be designed so that it indicated that a given input string was or was not in L. In effect, R would either accept or reject the given string. Such devices are like filters, separating correct sentences from those that are incorrectly formed. If R, when fed any string of characters over Σ, accepts it only if it is in L, then R is a description of L. Because most useful languages are, for all practical purposes, infinite, this might seem like a lengthy and ineffective process. Recognition devices, however, are not used to enumerate all of the sentences of a language.

The syntax analysis part of a compiler is a recognizer for the language the compiler translates. In this role, the recognizer need not test all possible strings of characters from some set to determine whether each is in the language. Rather, it need only determine whether given programs are in the language. In effect then, the syntax analyzer determines whether the given programs are syntactically correct.

3.2.2 Language Generators

A language generator is a device that can be used to generate the sentences of a language. We can think of the generator as having a button that, when pushed, produces a sentence of the language. Because the particular sentence that is produced by a generator when its button is pushed is unpredictable, a generator seems to be a device of limited usefulness as a language descriptor. However, people prefer certain forms of generators over recognizers because they can more easily read and understand them. By contrast, the syntax-checking portion of a compiler (a language recognizer) is not as useful a language description for a programmer because it can only be used in trial-and-error mode. For example, to determine the correct syntax of a particular statement using a compiler, the programmer can only submit a guessed-at version and see if the compiler accepts it. On the other hand, it is often possible to determine whether the syntax of a particular statement is correct by comparing it with the structure of the generator.

There is a close connection between formal generation and recognition devices for the same language. This was one of the seminal discoveries in computer science, and it led to much of what is now known about formal languages and compiler design theory. We return to the relationship of generators and recognizers in the next section.

3.3 Formal Methods of Describing Syntax

This section discusses the formal language generation mechanisms that are commonly used to describe the syntax of programming languages. These mechanisms are often called grammars.

3.3.1 Backus-Naur Form and Context-Free Grammars

In the middle to late 1950s, two men, John Backus and Noam Chomsky, in unrelated research efforts, invented the same notation, which has since become the most widely used method for formally describing programming language syntax.

3.3.1.1 Context-Free Grammars

In the mid-1950s, Chomsky, a noted linguist, described four classes of generative devices or grammars that define four classes of languages (Chomsky, 1956, 1959). Two of these grammar classes, named context-free and regular, turned out to be useful for describing the syntax of programming languages. The tokens of programming languages can be described by regular grammars. Whole programming languages, with minor exceptions, can be described by context-free grammars. Because Chomsky was a linguist, his primary interest was the theoretical nature of natural languages. He had no interest at the time in the artificial languages used to communicate with computers. So it was not until later that his work was applied to programming languages.

3.3.1.2 Origins of Backus-Naur Form

Shortly after Chomsky's work on language classes, the ACM-GAMM group began designing ALGOL 58. A landmark paper describing ALGOL 58 was presented by John Backus, a prominent member of the ACM-GAMM group, at an international conference in 1959 (Backus, 1959). This paper introduced a new formal notation for specifying programming language syntax. The new notation was later modified slightly by Peter Naur for the description of ALGOL 60 (Naur, 1960). This revised method of syntax description became known as **Backus-Naur form,** or simply **BNF.**

BNF is a very natural notation for describing syntax. In fact, something similar to BNF was used by Panini to describe the syntax of Sanskrit several hundred years before Christ (Ingerman, 1967).

Although the use of BNF in the ALGOL 60 report was not readily accepted by computer users, it soon became and still remains the most popular method of concisely describing programming language syntax.

It is remarkable that BNF is nearly identical to Chomsky's generative devices for context-free languages, called **context-free grammars.** In the remainder of the chapter, we refer to context-free grammars simply as grammars. Furthermore, the terms BNF and grammar are used interchangeably.

3.3.1.3 Fundamentals

A **metalanguage** is a language that is used to describe another language. BNF is a metalanguage for programming languages.

BNF uses abstractions for syntactic structures. A simple C assignment statement, for example, might be represented by the abstraction < assign >. (Pointed brackets are often used to delimit names of abstractions.) The actual definition of < assign > may be given by

> < assign > → < var > = < expression >

The symbol on the left side of the arrow, which is aptly called the left-hand side (LHS), is the abstraction being defined. The text to the right of the arrow is the definition of the LHS. It is called the right-hand side (RHS) and consists of some mixture of tokens, lexemes, and references to other abstractions. (Actually, tokens are also abstractions.) Altogether, the definition is called a **rule,** or **production.** In the example rule just given, the abstractions < var > and < expression > obviously must be defined before the < assign > definition becomes useful.

This particular rule specifies that the abstraction < assign > is defined as an instance of the abstraction < var >, followed by the lexeme =, followed by an instance of the abstraction < expression >. One example sentence whose syntactic structure is described by the rule is

```
total = sub1 + sub2
```

The abstractions in a BNF description, or grammar, are often called **nonterminal symbols,** or simply **nonterminals,** and the lexemes and tokens of the rules are called **terminal symbols,** or simply **terminals.** A BNF description, or **grammar,** is simply a collection of rules.

Nonterminal symbols can have two or more distinct definitions, representing two or more possible syntactic forms in the language. Multiple definitions can be written as a single rule, with the different definitions separated by the symbol |, meaning logical OR. For example, a Pascal **if** statement can be described with the rules

< if_stmt > → **if** < logic_expr > **then** < stmt >
< if_stmt > → **if** < logic_expr > **then** < stmt > **else** < stmt >

or with the rule

< if_stmt > → **if** < logic_expr > **then** < stmt >
      | **if** < logic_expr > **then** < stmt > **else** < stmt >

Although BNF is simple, it is sufficiently powerful to describe the great majority of the syntax of programming languages. In particular, it can describe lists of similar constructs, the order in which different constructs must appear, nested structures to any depth, operator precedence, and operator associativity.

3.3.1.4 Describing Lists

Variable-length lists in mathematics are often written using an ellipsis (...); 1, 2, ... is an example. BNF does not include the ellipsis, so an alternative method is required for describing lists of syntactic elements in programming languages (for example, a list of identifiers appearing on a data declaration statement). The most common alternative is recursion. A rule is **recursive** if its LHS appears in its RHS. The following rules illustrate how recursion is used to describe lists:

< ident_list > → identifier
      | identifier , < ident_list >

This defines < ident_list > as either a single token (identifier) or an identifier followed by a comma followed by another instance of < ident_list >. Recursion is used to describe lists in many of the example grammars in the remainder of this chapter.

3.3.1.5 Grammars and Derivations

BNF is a generative device for defining languages. The sentences of the language are generated through a sequence of applications of the rules, beginning with a special nonterminal of the grammar called the **start symbol.** A sentence generation is called a **derivation.** In a grammar for a complete language, the start symbol represents a complete program and is usually named < program >. The simple grammar shown in Example 3.1 is used to illustrate derivations:

Example 3.1   **A Grammar for a Small Language**

```
<program>  →  begin <stmt_list> end
< stmt_list >  →  < stmt >
              |  < stmt > ; < stmt_list >
< stmt >  →  < var >  :=  < expression >
< var >  →  A | B | C
< expression >  →  < var > + < var >
              |  < var > – < var >
              |  < var >
```

The language in Example 3.1 has only one statement form: assignment. A program consists of the special word **begin**, followed by a list of statements separated by semicolons, followed by the special word **end**. An expression is either a single variable, or two variables separated by either a + or – operator. The only variable names in this language are A, B, and C.

A derivation of a program in this language follows:

```
< program >  = > begin < stmt_list > end
             = > begin < stmt > ; < stmt_list > end
             = > begin < var > := < expression > ; < stmt_list > end
             = > begin A := < expression > ; < stmt_list > end
             = > begin A := < var > + < var > ; < stmt_list > end
             = > begin A := B + < var > ; < stmt_list > end
             = > begin A := B + C ; < stmt_list > end
             = > begin A := B + C ; < stmt > end
             = > begin A := B + C ; < var > := < expression > end
             = > begin A := B + C ; B := < expression > end
             = > begin A := B + C ; B := < var > end
             = > begin A := B + C ; B := C end
```

This derivation, like all derivations, begins with the start symbol, in this case < program >. The symbol = > is read "derives." Each successive string in the sequence is derived from the previous string by replacing one of the nonterminals with one of that nonterminal's definitions. Each of the strings in the derivation, including < program >, is called a **sentential form.** In this derivation, the replaced nonterminal is always the leftmost nonterminal in the previous sentential form. Derivations that use this order of replacement are called **leftmost derivations.** The derivation continues until the sentential form contains no nonterminals. That sentential form, consisting of only terminals, or lexemes, is the generated sentence.

In addition to leftmost, a derivation may be rightmost or in an order that is neither leftmost nor rightmost. Derivation order has no effect on the language generated by a grammar.

By choosing alternative RHSs of rules with which to replace nonterminals in the derivation, different sentences in the language can be generated. By exhaustively choosing all combinations of choices, the entire language can be generated. This language, like most others, is infinite, so one cannot generate *all* the sentences in the language in finite time.

Example 3.2 is another example of a grammar for part of a typical programming language:

Example 3.2   **A Grammar for Simple Assignment Statements**

$$< assign > \rightarrow < id > := < expr >$$
$$< id > \rightarrow A \mid B \mid C$$
$$< expr > \rightarrow < id > + < expr >$$
$$\mid < id > * < expr >$$
$$\mid (< expr >)$$
$$\mid < id >$$

The grammar of Example 3.2 describes assignment statements whose right sides are arithmetic expressions with multiplication and addition operators and parentheses. For example, the statement

```
A := B * ( A + C )
```

is generated by the leftmost derivation:

$$< assign > \Rightarrow < id > := < expr >$$
$$\Rightarrow A := < expr >$$
$$\Rightarrow A := < id > * < expr >$$
$$\Rightarrow A := B * < expr >$$
$$\Rightarrow A := B * (< expr >)$$
$$\Rightarrow A := B * (< id > + < expr >)$$
$$\Rightarrow A := B * (A + < expr >)$$
$$\Rightarrow A := B * (A + < id >)$$
$$\Rightarrow A := B * (A + C)$$

3.3.1.6 Parse Trees

One of the most attractive features of grammars is that they naturally describe the hierarchical syntactic structure of the sentences of the languages they define. These hierarchical structures are called **parse trees.** For example, the parse tree in Figure 3.1 shows the structure of the assignment statement derived above.

Figure 3.1
A parse tree for the
simple statement
A := B * (A + C)

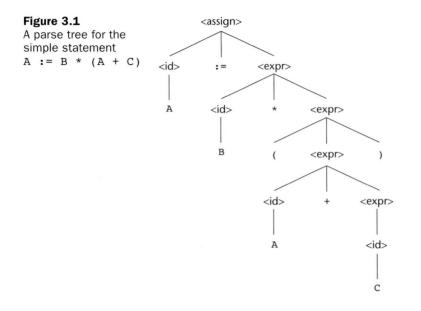

Every internal node of a parse tree is labeled with a nonterminal symbol; every leaf is labeled with a terminal symbol. Every subtree of a parse tree describes one instance of an abstraction in the statement.

3.3.1.7 Ambiguity

A grammar that generates a sentence for which there are two or more distinct parse trees is said to be **ambiguous.** Consider the grammar shown in Example 3.3, which is a minor variation of the grammar in Example 3.2.

Example 3.3   **An Ambiguous Grammar for Simple Assignment Statements**

$$
\begin{aligned}
&<assign> \rightarrow <id> := <expr> \\
&<id> \rightarrow A \mid B \mid C \\
&<expr> \rightarrow <expr> + <expr> \\
&\qquad\quad \mid <expr> * <expr> \\
&\qquad\quad \mid (<expr>) \\
&\qquad\quad \mid <id>
\end{aligned}
$$

The grammar of Example 3.3 is ambiguous because the sentence

    A := B + C * A

has two distinct parse trees, as shown in Figure 3.2.

Figure 3.2
Two distinct parse
trees for the same
sentence,

A := B + C * A

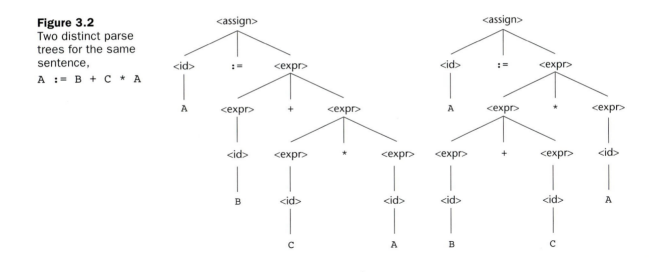

The ambiguity occurs because the grammar specifies slightly less syntactic structure than does the grammar of Example 3.2. Rather than allowing the parse tree of an expression to grow only on the right, this grammar allows growth on both the left and the right.

Syntactic ambiguity of language structures is a problem because compilers often base the semantics of those structures on their syntactic form. In particular, the compiler decides what code to generate for a statement by examining its parse tree. If a language structure has more than one parse tree, then the meaning of the structure cannot be determined uniquely. This problem is discussed in two specific examples in the following three sections.

3.3.1.8 Operator Precedence

As stated earlier, a grammar can describe a certain syntactic structure so that part of the meaning of the structure can follow from its parse tree. In particular, the fact that an operator in an arithmetic expression is generated lower in the parse tree (and therefore must be evaluated first) can be used to indicate that it has precedence over an operator produced higher up in the tree. In the first parse tree of Figure 3.2, for example, the multiplication operator is generated lower in the tree, which could indicate that it has precedence over the addition operator in the expression. The second parse tree, however, indicates just the opposite. It appears, therefore, that the two parse trees indicate conflicting precedence information.

Notice that although the grammar of Example 3.2 is not ambiguous, the precedence order of its operators is not the usual one. In this grammar, a parse tree of a sentence with multiple operators, regardless of the particular operators involved, has the rightmost operator in the expression at the lowest point in the parse tree, with the other operators in the tree moving progressively higher as one moves to the left in the expression. For example, in the parse tree in Figure 3.1, the plus operator is the rightmost operator in the expression and the lowest in the tree, giving it precedence over the multiplication operator to its left.

A grammar can be written to separate the addition and multiplication operators so they are consistently in a higher to lower ordering, respectively, in the parse tree. This ordering can be maintained regardless of the order in which the operators appear in an expression. The correct ordering is specified by using separate abstractions for the operands of the operators that have different precedence. This requires additional nonterminals and some new rules. The grammar of Example 3.4 is such a grammar.

Example 3.4	**An Unambiguous Grammar for Expressions**

$$< assign > \rightarrow < id > := < expr >$$
$$< id > \rightarrow A \mid B \mid C$$
$$< expr > \rightarrow < expr > + < term >$$
$$\mid < term >$$
$$< term > \rightarrow < term > * < factor >$$
$$\mid < factor >$$
$$< factor > \rightarrow (< expr >)$$
$$\mid < id >$$

The grammar in Example 3.4 generates the same language as the grammars of Examples 3.2 and 3.3, but it indicates the usual precedence order of multiplication and addition operators. The following derivation of the sentence A := B + C * A uses the grammar of Example 3.4:

$$< assign > => < id > := < expr >$$
$$=> A := < expr >$$
$$=> A := < expr > + < term >$$
$$=> A := < term > + < term >$$
$$=> A := < factor > + < term >$$
$$=> A := < id > + < term >$$
$$=> A := B + < term >$$
$$=> A := B + < term > * < factor >$$
$$=> A := B + < factor > * < factor >$$
$$=> A := B + < id > * < factor >$$
$$=> A := B + C * < factor >$$
$$=> A := B + C * < id >$$
$$=> A := B + C * A$$

The unique parse tree for this sentence, using the grammar of Example 3.4, is shown in Figure 3.3.

Figure 3.3
The unique parse tree for A := B + C * A using an unambiguous grammar

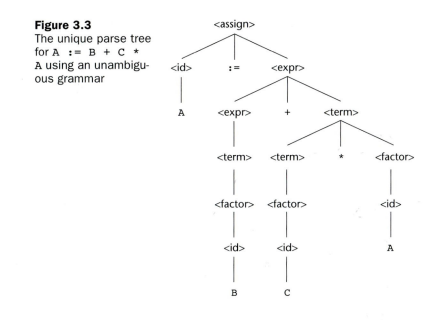

The connection between parse trees and derivations is very close: Either can easily be constructed from the other. Every derivation with an unambiguous grammar has a unique parse tree, although that tree can be represented by different derivations. For example, the following derivation of the sentence A := B + C * A is different from the derivation of the same sentence given previously. This is a rightmost derivation, whereas the previous one is leftmost. Both of these derivations, however, are represented by the same parse tree.

$$
\begin{aligned}
<assign> &=> <id> := <expr> \\
&=> <id> := <expr> + <term> \\
&=> <id> := <expr> + <term> * <factor> \\
&=> <id> := <expr> + <term> * <id> \\
&=> <id> := <expr> + <term> * A \\
&=> <id> := <expr> + <factor> * A \\
&=> <id> := <expr> + <id> * A \\
&=> <id> := <expr> + C * A \\
&=> <id> := <term> + C * A \\
&=> <id> := <factor> + C * A \\
&=> <id> := <id> + C * A \\
&=> <id> := B + C * A \\
&=> A := B + C * A
\end{aligned}
$$

3.3.1.9 Associativity of Operators

Another interesting question concerning grammars for expressions is whether operator associativity is also correctly described; that is, do the parse trees for expressions with two or more adjacent occurrences of operators with equal precedence have those occurrences in proper hierarchical order? An example of an assignment statement with such an expression is

    A := B + C + A

The parse tree for this sentence, as defined with the grammar of Example 3.4, is shown in Figure 3.4.

The parse tree of Figure 3.4 shows the left addition operator lower than the right addition operator. This is the correct order if addition is meant to be left associative, which is typical. In most cases, the associativity of addition in a computer is irrelevant. (In mathematics, addition is associative, which means that left and right associative orders of evaluation mean the same thing. That is, $(A + B) + C = A + (B + C)$.) Integer computer arithmetic is also associative. In some situations, however, floating-point addition is not associative. For example, suppose floating-point values store seven digits of accuracy. Consider the problem of adding eleven numbers together, where one of the numbers is 10^7 and the other ten are 1. If the small numbers (the 1s) are each added to the large number, one at a time, there is no effect on that number, because the small numbers occur in the eighth digit of the large number. However, if the small numbers are first added together and the result is added to the large number, the result in seven-digit accuracy is $1.000001 * 10^7$. Subtraction and division are not

Figure 3.4
A parse tree for A := B + C + A illustrating the associativity of addition

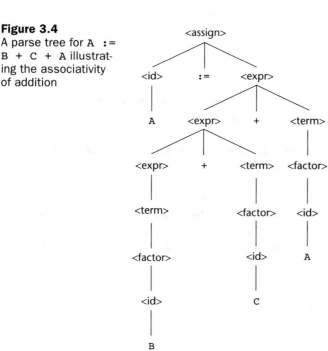

associative, whether in mathematics or in a computer. Therefore, correct associativity may be essential for an expression that contains either of them.

When a BNF rule has its LHS also appearing at the beginning of its RHS, the rule is said to be **left recursive.** This left recursion specifies left associativity. For example, the left recursion of the rules of the grammar of Example 3.4 causes it to make both addition and multiplication left associative.

In most languages that provide it, the exponentiation operator is right associative. To indicate right associativity, right recursion can be used. A grammar rule is **right recursive** if the LHS appears at the right end of the RHS. Rules such as

$$
\begin{aligned}
< \text{factor} > &\rightarrow\ < \text{exp} >\ \texttt{**}\ < \text{factor} > \\
&\mid\ < \text{exp} > \\
< \text{exp} > &\rightarrow\ (\ < \text{expr} >\ ) \\
&\mid\ < \text{id} >
\end{aligned}
$$

could be used to describe exponentiation as a right-associative operator.

3.3.1.10 An Unambiguous Grammar for `if-then-else`

The BNF rules given in Section 3.3.1.3 for one particular form of **if-then-else** statement are repeated here:

$$
\begin{aligned}
< \text{if\_stmt} > &\rightarrow\ \textbf{if}\ < \text{logic\_expr} >\ \textbf{then}\ < \text{stmt} > \\
&\mid\ \textbf{if}\ < \text{logic\_expr} >\ \textbf{then}\ < \text{stmt} >\ \textbf{else}\ < \text{stmt} >
\end{aligned}
$$

If we also have $< \text{stmt} > \rightarrow < \text{if\_stmt} >$, this grammar is ambiguous. The simplest sentential form that illustrates this ambiguity is

if $< \text{logic\_expr} >$ **then if** $< \text{logic\_expr} >$ **then** $< \text{stmt} >$ **else** $< \text{stmt} >$

The two parse trees in Figure 3.5 show the ambiguity of this sentential form. We will examine the practical problems associated with this else-association problem in Chapter 7.

We will now develop an unambiguous grammar that describes this **if** statement. The rule for **if** constructs in most languages is that an **else** clause, when present, is matched with the nearest previous unmatched **then**. Therefore, between a **then** and its matching **else**, there cannot be an **if** statement without an **else**. So, for this situation, statements must be distinguished between those that are matched and those that are unmatched, where unmatched statements are **else** less **if**s and all other statements are matched. The problem with the grammar above is that it treats all statements as if they had equal syntactic significance; that is, as if they were all matched.

To reflect the different categories of statements, different abstractions, or nonterminals, must be used. The unambiguous grammar based on these ideas follows:

< stmt > → < matched > | < unmatched >
< matched > → **if** < logic_expr > **then** < matched > **else** < matched >
        | any non-if statement
< unmatched > → **if** < logic_expr > **then** < stmt >
        | **if** < logic_expr > **then** < matched > **else** < unmatched >

There is just one possible parse tree, using this grammar, for the sentence shown in Figure 3.5.

3.3.2 Extended BNF

Because of a few minor inconveniences in BNF, it has been extended in several ways. Most extended versions are called Extended BNF, or simply EBNF, even though they are not all exactly the same. The extensions do not enhance the descriptive power of BNF; they only increase its readability and writability.

Three extensions are commonly included in the various versions of EBNF. The first of these denotes an optional part of an RHS, which is

Figure 3.5
Two distinct parse trees for the same sentential form

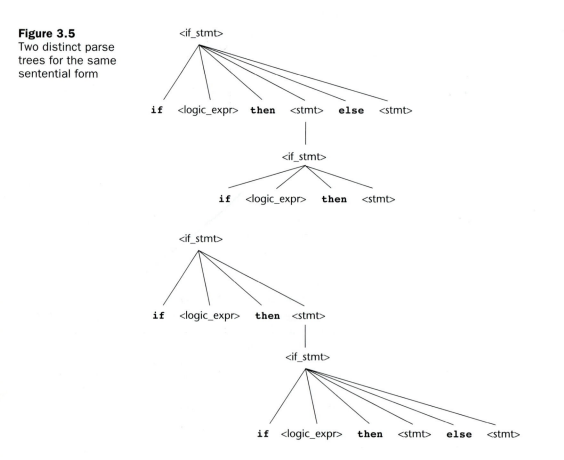

delimited by brackets. For example, a C selection statement can be described as

< selection > → **if** (< expression >) < statement > [**else** < statement >];

Without the use of the brackets, the syntactic description of this statement would require two rules.

The second extension is the use of braces in an RHS to indicate that the enclosed part can be repeated indefinitely, or left out altogether. This extension allows lists to be built with a single rule, instead of using recursion and two rules. For example, lists of identifiers separated by commas can be described by the following rule:

< ident_list > → < identifier > {, < identifier >}

This is a replacement of the recursion by a form of implied iteration; the part enclosed within braces can be iterated any number of times.

The third common extension deals with multiple-choice options. When a single element must be chosen from a group, the options are placed in parentheses and separated by the OR operator, |. For example, the following rule describes a Pascal **for** statement:

< for_stmt > → **for** < var > := < expr > (**to** | **downto**) < expr > **do** < stmt >

Once again, it would require two BNF rules to describe this structure. The brackets, braces, and parentheses in the EBNF extensions are metasymbols, which means they are notational tools and not terminal symbols in the syntactic entities they help describe. In cases where these metasymbols are also terminal symbols in the language being described, the instances that are terminal symbols can be underlined.

| **Example 3.5** | **BNF and EBNF Versions of an Expression Grammar** |

BNF: < expr > → < expr > + < term >
$\qquad$ | < expr > – < term >
$\qquad$ | < term >
$\qquad$ < term > → < term > * < factor >
$\qquad$ | < term > / < factor >
$\qquad$ | < factor >
EBNF: < expr > → < term > {(+ | –) < term >}
$\qquad$ < term > → < factor > {(* | /) < factor >}

Some versions of EBNF allow a numeric superscript to be attached to the right brace to indicate an upper limit to the number of times the enclosed part can be repeated. Also, some versions use a plus (+) superscript to indicate one or more repetitions. For example,

< compound > → **begin** < stmt > { < stmt >} **end**

and

$$< \text{compound} > \rightarrow \textbf{begin} \ \{ < \text{stmt} > \}^{+} \ \textbf{end}$$

are equivalent.

3.3.3   Syntax Graphs

A **graph** is a collection of nodes, some of which are connected by lines, called edges. A **directed graph** is one in which the edges are directional; that is, they have arrowheads on one end to indicate a direction. A parse tree is a restricted form of directed graph.

The information in BNF and EBNF rules can be represented in a directed graph. Such graphs are called **syntax graphs,** syntax diagrams, or syntax charts. A separate graph is used for each syntactic unit, in the same way a nonterminal symbol in a grammar represents such a unit.

Syntax graphs use different kinds of nodes to represent the terminal and nonterminal symbols of the right sides of a grammar's rules. Rectangle nodes contain the names of syntactic units (nonterminals). Circles or ellipses contain terminal symbols.

The Ada **if** statement syntax is described both in EBNF and with a syntax graph in Figure 3.6. Note that both the brackets and braces in the EBNF description are metasymbols rather than the terminal symbols used in the Ada language.

Using graphics to describe syntax offers the same advantage as using graphics to describe anything: It increases readability by allowing us to visualize it in two dimensions.

Figure 3.6
The syntax graph and
EBNF descriptions of
the Ada **if** statement

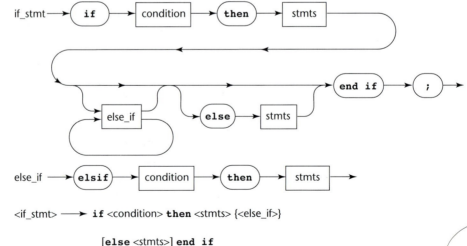

3.3.4   **Grammars and Recognizers**

Earlier in this chapter, we suggested that there was a close relationship between generation and recognition devices for a given language. In fact, given a context-free grammar, a recognizer for the language generated by the grammar can be algorithmically constructed. A number of software systems have been developed that perform this construction. Such systems allow the quick creation of the syntax analysis part of a compiler for a new language and are therefore quite valuable. One of the most widely used of these syntax analyzer generators is named yacc (yet another compiler-compiler) (Johnson, 1975).

Syntax analyzers for programming languages, which are often called parsers, construct parse trees for given programs. In some cases, the parse tree is only implicitly constructed, but in all cases, the information contained in the parse tree is created during the parse.

Parsers are categorized according to the direction in which they build parse trees. The two broad classes of parsers are top-down, in which the tree is built from the root downward to the leaves, and bottom-up, in which the parse tree is built from the leaves upward to the root. A simple top-down parsing algorithm is briefly introduced in Section 3.4.

3.4 **Recursive Descent Parsing**

As is stated in Section 3.3.1.7, a context-free grammar can serve as the basis for the syntax analyzer, or parser, of a compiler. To illustrate this use of grammars, we now introduce a simple kind of grammar-based top-down parser appropriately named recursive descent.

Parsing is the process of tracing or constructing a parse tree for a given input string. The basic idea of a recursive descent parser is that there is a subprogram for each nonterminal in the grammar. The responsibility of the subprogram for a particular nonterminal is as follows: When given an input string, it traces out the parse tree that can be rooted at that nonterminal and whose leaves match the input string. In effect, a recursive descent parsing subprogram is a parser for the language (set of strings) that can be generated by its nonterminal. In many cases, the language being parsed has nested syntactic units (expressions and statements, for example), so the parsing subprograms are often recursive. In the following discussion, we assume that each nonterminal has a single rule, possibly with multiple RHSs separated by OR operators.

Consider the following EBNF description of simple arithmetic expressions:

$$< expr > \rightarrow < term > \{(+ \mid -) < term >\}$$
$$< term > \rightarrow < factor > \{(* \mid /) < factor >\}$$
$$< factor > \rightarrow < id > \mid (< expr >)$$

Recursive descent subprograms call a lexical analyzer subprogram to get the next token of input when they need to see what token is next in the input being parsed. Recall from Chapter 1 that the lexical analyzer serves as a front end for the parser. It collects input characters into lexemes and returns the tokens associated with those lexemes. In the following recursive descent function, `expr`, this function is appropriately called `lexical`. It gets the next token and puts it in the global variable `next_token`.

The recursive descent subprogram for the first rule in the example grammar above, written in C, is

```
void expr() {
  term();   /* parse the first term */
  while (next_token == plus_code || next_token == minus_code){
    lexical();   /* get the next token from the input */
    term();   /* parse the next term */
  }
}
```

The parsing function above is written with the convention that each recursive descent function leaves the next token of input in `next_token`. So, whenever a parsing function begins, it is assured that `next_token` has the leftmost token of the input that has not yet been used in the parsing process.

The part of the language that the `expr` function parses consists of one or more `terms`, separated by either plus or minus operators. This is the language generated by < expr >. Therefore, it first calls the function that parses terms. Then it continues to call that function as long as it finds plus_code or minus_code tokens (which it passes over by calling `lexical`). This recursive descent function is simpler than most, for its rule has but one RHS. Furthermore, it does not include any syntax error detection or recovery.

The general process of writing a recursive descent parsing subprogram for a given nonterminal begins with writing code to determine which RHS of that nonterminal's rule matches the string of input tokens. This decision is made on the basis of the first terminal symbol of the input that is generated by the nonterminal. The code for each RHS is relatively simple. For each terminal symbol, that terminal symbol is compared with the next token. If they do not match, it is a syntax error. If they match, the lexical analyzer is called to go on to the next input token. For each nonterminal, the parsing subprogram for that nonterminal is called.

The function for the < factor > nonterminal must choose between its two RHSs. It also includes error detection. In the function for < factor >, the reaction to detecting a syntax error is simply to call the `error` function. In a real parser, a diagnostic message must be produced when an error is detected. Furthermore, most compilers must recover from the error so that the parsing process can continue. Such compilers cannot simply stop when they detect the first syntax error in a program.

```
void factor() {
  if (next_token) == id_code){
    lexical();
    return;
  }
  else if (next_token == left_paren_code) {
    lexical();
    expr();
    if (next_token == right_paren_code) {
      lexical();
      return;
    }
    else error();  /* expecting right parenthesis */
  }
  else error(); /* it was neither an id nor a left
                     parenthesis */
}
```

The objective of this brief discussion of parsing is to convince you that a recursive descent parser can be easily written if an appropriate grammar is available for the language. *Appropriate* here means that the grammar must have a particular form to be usable for recursive descent. A discussion of all of the characteristics that allow or disallow a particular grammar to be used with recursive descent parsing is beyond the scope of this book. See Fischer and LeBlanc (1988) for details.

One simple characteristic that causes a catastrophic problem for recursive descent parsers is left recursion. For example, consider the following rule:

<A> → <A> + <B>

A recursive descent parser subprogram for <A> immediately calls itself. That activation of the <A> parser subprogram then immediately calls itself again, and again, and so forth. It is easy to see that this gets nowhere. So, no left recursion can be allowed in a grammer for which a recursive descent parser is to be written.

The intimate connection of grammars to compilers is a significant factor in the importance of grammars.

3.5 Attribute Grammars

An *attribute grammar* is a device used to describe more of the structure of a programming language than is possible with a context-free grammar. An attribute grammar is an extension to a context-free grammar. The extension allows certain language rules to be described, such as type compatibility.

Before we formally define the form of attribute grammars, we must clarify the concept of static semantics.

3.5.1 Static Semantics

There are some characteristics of the structure of programming languages that are difficult to describe with BNF, and some that are impossible. As an example of a language rule that is difficult to specify with BNF, consider type compatibility rules. In Java, for example, a floating-point value cannot be assigned to an integer type variable, although the opposite is legal. Although this restriction can be specified in BNF, it requires additional nonterminal symbols and rules. If all of the typing rules of Java were specified in BNF, the grammar would become too large to be useful because the size of the grammar determines the size of the parser.

As an example of a language rule that cannot be specified in BNF, consider the common rule that all variables must be declared before they are referenced. It can be proven that this rule cannot be specified in BNF. Another example is the rule that if the **end** of an Ada subprogram is followed by a name, that name must match the name of the subprogram.

These two problems exemplify the category of language rules called static semantics rules. The **static semantics** of a language is only indirectly related to the meaning of programs during execution; rather, it has to do with the legal forms of programs (syntax rather than semantics). In many cases, the static semantic rules of a language state its type constraints. Static semantics is so named because the analysis required to check these specifications can be done at compile time.

Because of the problems of describing static semantics with BNF, a variety of more powerful mechanisms has been devised for that task. One such mechanism, attribute grammars, was designed by Knuth (1968a) to describe both the syntax and the static semantics of programs.

Dynamic semantics is discussed in Section 3.6.

3.5.2 Basic Concepts

Attribute grammars are grammars to which have been added attributes, attribute computation functions, and predicate functions. **Attributes,** which are associated with grammar symbols, are similar to variables in the sense that they can have values assigned to them. **Attribute computation functions,** sometimes called semantic functions, are associated with grammar rules to specify how attribute values are computed. **Predicate functions,** which state some of the syntax and static semantic rules of the language, are associated with grammar rules.

These concepts will become clearer after we formally define attribute grammars and provide an example.

3.5.3 Attribute Grammars Defined

An attribute grammar is a grammar with the following additional features:

- Associated with each grammar symbol X is a set of attributes A(X). The set A(X) consists of two disjoint sets S(X) and I(X), called synthesized and inherited attributes, respectively. **Synthesized attributes** are used to pass semantic information up a parse tree, while **inherited attributes** pass semantic information down a tree.

- Associated with each grammar rule is a set of semantic functions and a possibly empty set of predicate functions over the attributes of the symbols in the grammar rule. For a rule $X_0 \rightarrow X_1...X_n$, the synthesized attributes of X_0 are computed with a semantic function of the form $S(X_0) = f(A(X_1),...,A(X_n))$. So the value of a synthesized attribute on a parse tree node depends only on the values of the attributes on that node's children nodes. Inherited attributes of symbols X_j, $1 \leq j \leq n$ (in the rule above), are computed with a semantic function of the form $I(X_j) = f(A(X_0), ..., A(X_n))$. So the value of an inherited attribute on a parse tree node depends on the attribute values of that node's parent node and those of its sibling nodes. Note that, to avoid circularity, inherited attributes are often restricted to functions of the form $I(X_j) = f(A(X_0), ..., A(X_{(j-1)}))$. This form prevents an inherited attribute from depending on itself or on attributes to the right in the parse tree.

  A predicate function has the form of a Boolean expression on the attribute set $\{A(X_0),...,A(X_n)\}$. The only derivations allowed with an attribute grammar are those in which every predicate associated with every nonterminal is true. A false predicate function value indicates a violation of the syntax or static semantics rules of the language.

A parse tree of an attribute grammar is the parse tree based on its underlying BNF grammar, with a possibly empty set of attribute values attached to each node. If all the attribute values in a parse tree have been computed, the tree is said to be **fully attributed.** Although in practice it is not always done this way, it is convenient to think of attribute values as being computed after the complete unattributed parse tree has been constructed.

3.5.4 Intrinsic Attributes

Intrinsic attributes are synthesized attributes of leaf nodes whose values are determined outside the parse tree. For example, the type of an instance of a variable in a program could come from the symbol table, which is used to store variable names and their types. The contents of the symbol table are determined from earlier declaration statements. Initially, assuming that an unattributed parse tree has been constructed and that attribute values are desired, the only attributes with values are the intrinsic attributes of the leaf nodes. Given the intrinsic attribute values on a parse tree, the semantic functions can be used to compute the remaining attribute values.

3.5.5 Examples of Attribute Grammars

As a very simple example of how attribute grammars can be used to describe static semantics, consider the following fragment of an attribute grammar that describes the rule that the name on the **end** of an Ada procedure must match the procedure's name. The string attribute of < proc_name >, denoted by < proc_name >.string, is the actual string of characters that were found by the lexical analyzer. Notice that when there is more than one occurrence of a nonterminal in a syntax rule in an attribute grammar, the nonterminals are subscripted with brackets to distinguish them. Neither the subscript nor the brackets are part of the described language.

> Syntax rule: < proc_def > → **procedure** < proc_name >[1]
> < proc_body > **end** < proc_name >[2];
> Semantic rule: < proc_name >[1].string = < proc_name >[2].string

Next, consider a larger example of an attribute grammar. In this case, it is used to show how an attribute grammar can be used to check the type rules of a simple assignment statement. The syntax and semantics of this assignment statement are as follows: The only variable names are A, B, and C. The right side of the assignments can either be a variable or an expression in the form of a variable added to another variable. The variables can be one of two types: int or real. When there are two variables on the right side of an assignment, they need not be the same type. The type of the expression when the operand types are not the same is always real. When they are the same, the expression type is that of the operands. The type of the left side of the assignment must match the type of the right side. So the types of operands in the right side can be mixed, but the assignment is valid only if the LHS and the value resulting from evaluating the RHS have the same type. The attribute grammar specifies these semantic rules.

The syntax portion of our example attribute grammar is

> < assign > → < var > := < expr >
> < expr > → < var > + < var >
> | < var >
> < var > → A | B | C

The attributes for the nonterminals in the example attribute grammar are described in the following paragraphs.

actual_type A synthesized attribute associated with the nonterminals <var> and <expr>. It is used to store the actual type, int or real in the example, of a variable or expression. In the case of a variable, the actual type is intrinsic. In the case of an expression, it is determined from the actual types of the child node or children nodes of the <expr> nonterminal.

expected_type An inherited attribute associated with the nonterminal <expr>. It is used to store the type, either int or real, that is expected for the expression, as determined by the type of the variable on the left side of the assignment statement.

The complete attribute grammar follows in Example 3.6.

| Example 3.6 | **An Attribute Grammar for Simple Assignment Statements** |

1. Syntax rule: <assign> → <var> := <expr>
Semantic rule: <expr>.expected_type ← <var>.actual_type

2. Syntax rule: <expr> → <var>[2] + <var>[3]
Semantic rule: <expr>.actual_type ←

$\qquad$ if (<var>[2].actual_type = int) and

$\qquad$ (<var>[3].actual_type = int)

$\qquad$ then int

$\qquad$ else real

$\qquad$ end if

Predicate: <expr>.actual_type = <expr>.expected_type

3. Syntax rule: <expr> → <var>
Semantic rule: <expr>.actual_type ← <var>.actual_type
Predicate: <expr>.actual_type = <expr>.expected_type

4. Syntax rule: <var> → A | B | C
Semantic rule: <var>.actual_type ← look-up(<var>.string)

The look-up function looks up a given variable name in the symbol table and returns the variable's type.

An example of a parse tree of the sentence A := A + B generated by the grammar in Example 3.6 is shown in Figure 3.7. As in the grammar, bracketed numbers are added after the repeated node labels in the tree so they can be referenced unambiguously.

Figure 3.7
A parse tree for `A := A + B`

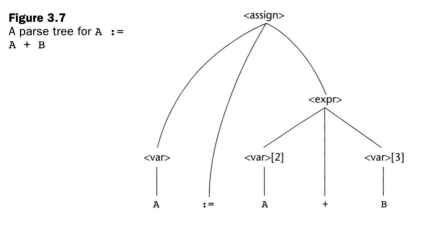

3.5.6 Computing Attribute Values

Now consider the process of decorating the parse tree with attributes. This could proceed in a completely top-down order, from the root to the leaves, if all attributes were inherited. Alternatively, it could proceed in a completely bottom-up order, from the leaves to the root, if all the attributes were synthesized. Because our grammar has both synthesized and inherited attributes, the evaluation process cannot be in any single direction. The following is an evaluation of the attributes, in an order in which they can be done. Determining attribute evaluation order for the general case of an attribute grammar is a complex problem, requiring the construction of a dependency graph to show all attribute dependencies.

1. $< var >$.actual_type $\leftarrow$ look-up(A) (Rule 4)
2. $< expr >$.expected_type $\leftarrow$ $< var >$.actual_type (Rule 1)
3. $< var >$[2].actual_type $\leftarrow$ look-up(A) (Rule 4)
    $< var >$[3].actual_type $\leftarrow$ look-up(B) (Rule 4)
4. $< expr >$.actual_type $\leftarrow$ either int or real (Rule 2)
5. $< expr >$.expected_type $=$ $< expr >$.actual_type is either
    TRUE or FALSE (Rule 2)

The tree in Figure 3.8 shows the flow of attribute values in the example of Figure 3.7. Solid lines are used for the parse tree; dashed lines show attribute flow in the tree.

The tree in Figure 3.9 shows the final attribute values on the nodes. In this example, A is defined as a real and B is defined as an int.

3.5.7 Evaluation

Attribute grammars have been used in a wide variety of applications. They have been used to provide complete descriptions of the syntax and static

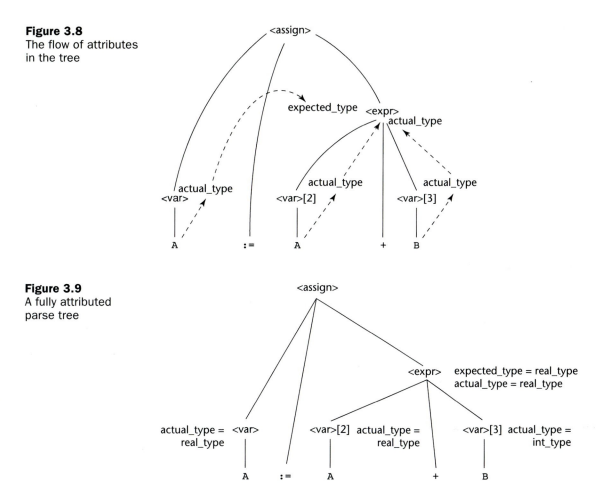

Figure 3.8
The flow of attributes
in the tree

Figure 3.9
A fully attributed
parse tree

semantics of programming languages (Watt, 1979); they have been used as
the formal definition of a language that can be input to a compiler generation system (Farrow, 1982); and they have been used as the basis of several
syntax-directed editing systems (Teitelbaum and Reps, 1981; Fischer et al.,
1984). In addition, attribute grammars have been used in natural language
processing systems (Correa, 1992).

One of the main difficulties in using an attribute grammar to describe
all of the syntax and static semantics of a real contemporary programming
language is its size and complexity. The large number of attributes and semantic rules required for a complete programming language make such
grammars difficult to write and read. Furthermore, the attribute values on
a large parse tree are costly to evaluate. On the other hand, less formal attribute grammars are a powerful and commonly used tool for compiler
writers, who are more interested in the process of producing a compiler
than they are in formalism.

3.6 Describing the Meanings of Programs: Dynamic Semantics

We now turn to the difficult task of describing the **dynamic semantics,** or meaning, of the expressions, statements, and program units. Because of the power and naturalness of the available notation, describing syntax is a relatively simple matter. On the other hand, no universally accepted notation has been devised for dynamic semantics. In this section, we briefly describe several of the methods that have been developed. For the remainder of this section, when we use the term *semantics,* we mean dynamic semantics; we will refer to static semantics as static semantics.

There are several different reasons why one may be concerned with describing semantics. First, programmers obviously need to know precisely what statements of a language do. But they usually find out by reading English explanations in language manuals. Such explanations are often imprecise and incomplete. Compiler writers also typically determine the semantics of the languages for which they are writing compilers from English descriptions. These informal descriptions are used because of the complexity of formal semantic descriptions. It is an obvious research goal to find a semantics formalism that could be used by programmers and compiler writers. Some experimental work has been done on the automatic generation of compilers for programming languages directly from their semantic descriptions. Finally, program correctness proofs rely on some formal description of the language semantics.

3.6.1 Operational Semantics

The idea behind **operational semantics** is to describe the meaning of a program by executing its statements on a machine, either real or simulated. The changes that occur in the machine's state when it executes a given statement define the meaning of that statement. To understand this concept further, consider a machine language instruction. Let the state of a computer be the values of all its registers and memory locations, including condition codes and status registers. If one simply records the state of the computer, executes the instruction for which the meaning is desired, and then examines the machine's new state, the semantics of that instruction are clear: It is represented by the change in the computer's state caused by the execution of the instruction.

3.6.1.1 The Basic Process

Describing the operational semantics of high-level language statements requires the construction of either a real or a virtual computer. Recall from Chapter 1 that the hardware of a computer is a pure interpreter for its machine language. A pure interpreter for any programming language can be constructed in software, which becomes a virtual computer for the language. The semantics of a high-level language can be described using a pure interpreter for the language. There are, however, two problems with this approach. First, the complexities and idiosyncrasies of the hardware computer and operating system that were used to run the pure interpreter would make the actions difficult to understand. Second, a semantic definition done this way would only be available to those with an identically configured computer.

These problems can be avoided by replacing the real computer with a low-level virtual computer, implemented as a software simulation. The registers, memory, status information, and execution process would all be simulated. The instruction set would be designed so that the semantics of each instruction was easy to describe and understand. In this way, the machine would be idealized and thus highly simplified, making its changes of state easy to understand.

Using the operational method to completely describe the semantics of a programming language L requires the construction of two components. First, a translator is needed to convert statements in L to the chosen low-level language. The other component is the virtual machine for that low-level language. The state changes in the virtual machine brought about by executing the code that results from translating a given statement in the high-level language defines the meaning of that statement.

This basic process of operational semantics is not unusual. In fact, the concept is frequently used in programming textbooks and programming language reference manuals. For example, the semantics of the C **for** construct can be described in terms of very simple instructions, as in

C Statement	*Operational Semantics*
```for (expr1; expr2; expr3) {```	expr1;
`...`	loop: **if** expr2 = 0 **goto** out
`}`	`...`
	expr3;
	goto loop
	out: `...`

The human reader of such a description is the virtual computer and is assumed to be able to correctly "execute" the instructions in the definition and recognize the effects of the "execution."

As an example of a low-level language that could be used for operational semantics, consider the following list of statements, which would be adequate for the simple control statements of a typical programming language.

```
ident := var
ident := ident + 1
ident := ident - 1
goto label
if var relop var goto label
```

In this list, relop is one of the relational operators from the set {=, <>, >, <, >=, <=}, ident is an identifier, and var is either an identifier or a constant. These statements are all simple and thus easy to understand and implement.

A slight generalization of the three assignment statements above allows more general arithmetic expressions and assignment statements to be described. The new statements are

```
ident := var bin_op var
ident := un_op var
```

where bin_op is a binary arithmetic operator and un_op is a unary operator. Multiple arithmetic data types and automatic type conversions, of course, complicate this generalization somewhat. Adding just a few more relatively simple instructions would allow the semantics of arrays, records, pointers, and subprograms to be described.

In Chapter 7, the semantics of various control statements are described using operational semantics.

3.6.1.2 Evaluation

The first and most significant use of formal operational semantics was to describe the semantics of PL/I (Wegner, 1972). That particular abstract machine and the translation rules for PL/I were together named the Vienna Definition Language (VDL), after the city where it was devised by IBM.

Operational semantics provides an effective means of describing semantics for language users and language implementors, as long as the descriptions are kept simple and informal. The VDL description of PL/I, unfortunately, is so complex that it serves virtually no practical purpose.

Operational semantics depends on algorithms, not mathematics. The statements of one programming language are described in terms of the statements of a lower-level programming language. This approach can lead to circularities, in which concepts are indirectly defined in terms of themselves. The methods described in the following two sections are much more formal, in the sense that they are based on logic and mathematics, not machines.

3.6.2 Axiomatic Semantics

Axiomatic semantics was defined in conjunction with the development of a method to prove the correctness of programs. Such correctness proofs, when they can be constructed, show that a program performs the computation described by its specification. In a proof, each statement of a program is both preceded and followed by a logical expression that specifies constraints on program variables. These, rather than the entire state of an abstract machine (as with operational semantics), are used to specify the meaning of the statement. The notation used to describe constraints, indeed the language of axiomatic semantics, is predicate calculus. Although simple Boolean expressions are often adequate to express constraints, in some cases they are not.

3.6.2.1 Assertions

Axiomatic semantics is based on mathematical logic. The logical expressions are called predicates, or **assertions.** An assertion immediately preceding a program statement describes the constraints on the program variables at that point in the program. An assertion immediately following a statement describes the new constraints on those variables (and possibly others) after execution of the statement. These assertions are called the **precondition** and **postcondition,** respectively, of the statement. Developing an axiomatic description or proof of a given program requires that every statement in the program have both a precondition and a postcondition.

In the following sections, we examine assertions from the point of view that preconditions for statements are computed from given postconditions, although it is possible to consider these in the opposite sense. We assume all variables are integer type. As a simple example, consider the following assignment statement and postcondition:

```
sum = 2 * x + 1 {sum > 1}
```

Precondition and postcondition assertions are presented in braces to distinguish them from program statements. One possible precondition for this statement is {x > 10}.

3.6.2.2 Weakest Preconditions

The **weakest precondition** is the least restrictive precondition that will guarantee the validity of the associated postcondition. For example, in the above statement and postcondition, {x > 10}, {x > 50}, and {x > 1000} are all valid preconditions. The weakest of all preconditions in this case is {x > 0}.

If the weakest precondition can be computed from the given postcondition for each statement of a language, then correctness proofs can be constructed for programs in that language. The proof is begun by using as the postcondition of the last statement of the program the desired results of the program's execution and by working backwards through the program, computing weakest preconditions for each statement until the beginning of the program is reached. At that point, the first precondition states the conditions under which the program will compute the desired results.

For some program statements, the computation of a weakest precondition from the statement and a postcondition is simple and can be specified by an axiom. In most cases, however, the weakest precondition can be computed only by an inference rule. An **axiom** is a logical statement that is assumed to be true; an **inference rule** is a method of inferring the truth of one assertion on the basis of the values of other assertions.

To use axiomatic semantics with a given programming language, whether for correctness proofs or for formal semantics specifications, either an axiom or an inference rule must be defined for each kind of statement in the language. In the following subsections, we present an axiom for assignment statements, and inference rules for statement sequences, selection statements, and logical pretest loops.

3.6.2.3 Assignment Statements

Let x = E be a general assignment statement and Q be its postcondition. Then its precondition, P, is defined by the axiom

$$P = Q_{x \to E}$$

which means that P is computed as Q with all instances of x replaced by E. For example, if we have the assignment statement and postcondition

```
a = b / 2 - 1 {a < 10}
```

the weakest precondition is computed by substituting `b / 2 - 1` in the assertion {a < 10}, as follows:

```
b / 2 - 1 < 10
b < 22
```

Thus the weakest precondition for the given assignment and postcondition is {b < 22}. Note that the assignment axiom is guaranteed to be true only in the absence of side effects. An assignment statement has a side effect if it changes some variable other than its left side.

The usual notation for specifying the axiomatic semantics of a given statement form is

$$\{P\}\ S\ \{Q\}$$

where P is the precondition, Q is the postcondition, and S is the statement form. In the case of the assignment statement, the notation is

$$\{Q_{x \to E}\}\ x = E\ \{Q\}$$

As another example of computing a precondition for an assignment statement, consider the following:

```
x = 2 * y - 3 {x > 25}
```

The precondition is computed as follows:

```
2 * y - 3 > 25
y > 14
```

So, {y > 14} is the weakest precondition for this assignment statement and postcondition.

Note that the appearance of the left side of the assignment statement in its right side does not affect the process of computing the weakest precondition. For example, for

```
x = x + y - 3 {x > 10}
```

the weakest precondition is

```
x + y - 3 > 10
y > 13 - x
```

At the beginning of our discussion, we stated that axiomatic semantics was developed to prove the correctness of programs. In light of that, it is natural at this point to wonder how the axiom for assignment statements can be used to prove anything. Here is how: A given assignment statement with both a precondition and a postcondition can be considered a theorem. If the assignment axiom, when applied to the postcondition and the assignment statement, produces the given precondition, the theorem is proved. For example, consider the logical statement

```
{x > 3} x = x - 3 {x > 0}
```

Using the assignment axiom on

```
x = x - 3 {x > 0}
```

produces {x > 3}, which is the given precondition. Therefore, we have proven the logical statement above.

Next, consider the logical statement

```
{x > 5} x = x - 3 {x > 0}
```

In this case, the given precondition, {x > 5}, is not the same as the assertion produced by the axiom. However, it is obvious that {x > 5} => {x > 3}. To use this in a proof, we need an inference rule, named the **rule of consequence.** The general form of an inference rule is

$$\frac{S1, S2, ..., Sn}{S}$$

which states that if S1, S2, ..., and Sn are true, then the truth of S can be inferred.

The form of the rule of consequence is

$$\frac{\{P\}\ S\ \{Q\}, P' => P,\ Q => Q'}{\{P'\}\ S\ \{Q\}}$$

The => symbol means "implies," and S can be any program statement. The rule can be stated as follows: If the logical statement {P} S {Q} is true, the assertion P' implies the assertion P, and the assertion Q implies the assertion Q', then it can be inferred that {P'} S {Q'}. In simpler language, the rule of consequence says that a postcondition can always be weakened and a precondition can always be strengthened. This is quite useful in program proofs. For example, it allows the completion of the proof of the last logical statement example above. If we let P be $\{x > 3\}$, Q and Q' be $\{x > 0\}$, P' be $\{x > 5\}$, we have

$$\frac{\{x > 3\}\ x = x - 3\ \{x > 0\},\ (x > 5)=>(x > 3),\ (x > 0)=>(x > 0)}{\{x > 5\}\ x = x - 3\ \{x > 0\}}$$

This completes the proof.

3.6.2.4 Sequences

The weakest precondition for a sequence of statements cannot be described by an axiom, because the precondition depends on the particular kinds of statements in the sequence. In this case, the precondition can only be described with an inference rule. Let S1 and S2 be adjacent program statements. If S1 and S2 have the following pre- and postconditions

$\{P1\}$ S1 $\{P2\}$
$\{P2\}$ S2 $\{P3\}$

the inference rule for such a two-statement sequence is

$$\frac{\{P1\}\ S1\ \{P2\},\{P2\}\ S2\ \{P3\}}{\{P1\}\ S1;S2\ \{P3\}}$$

So, for the above example, $\{P1\}$ S1; S2 $\{P3\}$ describes the axiomatic semantics of the sequence S1; S2. If S1 and S2 are the assignment statements

x1 = E1

and

x2 = E2

then we have

$\{P3_{x2 \to E2}\}$ x2 = E2 $\{P3\}$
$\{(P3_{x2 \to E2})_{x1 \to E1}\}$ x1 = E1 $\{P3_{x2 \to E2}\}$

Therefore, the weakest precondition for the sequence x1 = E1; x2 = E2 with postcondition P3 is $\{(P3_{x2 \to E2})_{x1 \to E1}\}$.

For example, consider the following sequence and postcondition:

y = 3 * x + 1;
x = y + 3;
{x < 10}

The precondition for the last assignment statement is

y < 7

This is then used as the postcondition for the first. The precondition for the first assignment statement can now be computed:

```
3 * x + 1 < 7
x < 2
```

3.6.2.5 Selection

We next consider the inference rule for selection statements. We consider only selections that include **else** clauses. The inference rule is

$$\frac{\{B \text{ and } P\} \ S1 \ \{Q\}, \ \{(\text{not } B) \text{ and } P\} \ S2 \ \{Q\}}{\{P\} \ \textbf{if } B \ \textbf{then} \ S1 \ \textbf{else} \ S2 \ \{Q\}}$$

This rule indicates that selection statements must be proven for both of their cases. The first logical statement above the line is the **then** clause; the second is the **else** clause.

Consider the following example of the computation using the selection inference rule. The example selection statement is

```
if (x > 0)
  y = y - 1
else y = y + 1
```

Suppose the postcondition for this selection statement is $\{y > 0\}$. We can use the axiom for assignment on the **then** clause

```
y = y - 1 {y > 0}
```

This produces $\{y - 1 > 0\}$ or $\{y > 1\}$. Now we apply the same axiom to the **else** clause

```
y = y + 1 {y > 0}
```

This produces the precondition $\{y + 1 > 0\}$ or $\{y > -1\}$. Because $\{y > 1\} => \{y > -1\}$, the rule of consequence allows us to use $\{y > 1\}$ for the precondition of the selection statement.

3.6.2.6 Logical Pretest Loops

Another essential construct of an imperative programming language is the logical pretest, or **while** loop. Computing the weakest precondition for a **while** loop is inherently more difficult than for a sequence because the number of iterations cannot in all cases be predetermined. In a case where the number of iterations is known, the loop can be treated as a sequence.

The problem of computing the weakest precondition for loops is similar to the problem of proving a theorem about all positive integers. In the latter case, induction is normally used, and the same inductive method can be used for loops. The principal step in induction is finding an inductive hypothesis. The corresponding step in the axiomatic semantics of a **while** loop is finding an assertion called a **loop invariant,** which is crucial to finding the weakest precondition.

The inference rule for computing the precondition for a **while** loop is

$$\frac{\text{(I and B) S } \{I\}}{\{I\} \text{ \textbf{while} B \textbf{do} S \textbf{end} } \{I \text{ and (not B)}\}}$$

where I is the loop invariant.

The axiomatic description of a **while** loop is written as

{P} **while** B **do** S **end** {Q}

The loop invariant must satisfy a number of requirements to be useful. First, the weakest precondition for the **while** must guarantee the truth of the loop invariant. In turn, the loop invariant must guarantee the truth of the postcondition upon loop termination. These constraints move us from the inference rule to the axiomatic description. During execution of the loop, the truth of the loop invariant must be unaffected by the evaluation of the loop-controlling Boolean expression and the loop body statements. Hence the name invariant.

Another complicating factor for **while** loops is the question of loop termination. If Q is the postcondition that holds immediately after loop exit, then a precondition P for the loop is one that guarantees Q at loop exit and also guarantees that the loop terminates.

The complete axiomatic description of a **while** construct requires all of the following to be true, in which I is the loop invariant:

```
P => I
{I} B {I}
{I and B} S {I}
(I and (not B)) => Q
the loop terminates
```

To find a loop invariant, we can use a method similar to that used for determining the inductive hypothesis in mathematical induction, which is as follows: The relationship for a few cases is computed, with the hope that a pattern emerges that will apply to the general case. It is helpful to treat the process of producing a weakest precondition as a function, wp. In general

wp(statement, postcondition) = precondition

To find I, we use the loop postcondition Q to compute preconditions for several numbers of iterations of the loop body, starting with none. If the loop body contains a single assignment statement, the axiom for assignment statements can be used to compute these cases. Consider the example loop

while y <> x **do** y = y + 1 **end** {y = x}

Be careful to remember that the equal sign is being used for two different purposes here. In assertions, it means mathematical equality; outside assertions, it means the assignment operator.

For zero iterations, the weakest precondition is, obviously,

{y = x}

For one iteration, it is

wp(y = y + 1, {y = x}) = {y + 1 = x}, or {y = x - 1}

For two iterations, it is

wp(y = y + 1, {y = x - 1}) = {y + 1 = x - 1},
              or {y = x - 2}

For three iterations, it is

wp(y = y + 1, {y = x - 2}) = {y + 1 = x - 2},
              or {y = x - 3}

It is now clear that {y < x} will suffice for cases of one or more iterations. Combining this with {y = x} for the zero iterations case, we get {y <= x}, which can be used for the loop invariant. A precondition for the **while** statement can be determined from the loop invariant. In this example, P = I can be used.

We must ensure that our choice satisfies the five criteria for I for our example loop. First, because P = I, P => I. The second requirement is that I be unaffected by the evaluation of the loop Boolean expression, which is y <> x. This expression changes nothing, so it cannot affect I. Next, it must be true that

{I and B} S {I}

In our example, we have

{y <= x and y <> x} y = y + 1 {y <= x}

Applying the assignment axiom to

y = y + 1 {y <= x}.

we get {y + 1 <= x}, which is equivalent to {y < x}, which is implied by {y <= x and y <> x}. So, the statement above is proven.

Next, we must have

{I and (not B)} => Q

In our example, we have

{(y <= x) and not (y <> x)} => {y = x}
{(y <= x) and (y = x)} => {y = x}
{y = x} => {y = x}

So this is obviously true. Next, loop termination must be considered. In this example, the question is whether the loop

$$\{y <= x\} \textbf{ while } y <> x \textbf{ do } y = y + 1 \textbf{ end } \{y = x\}$$

terminates. Recalling that x and y are assumed to be integer variables, we can easily see that this loop does terminate. The precondition guarantees that y initially is not larger than x. The loop body increases y with each iteration, until y is equal to x. No matter how much smaller y is than x initially, it will eventually become equal to x. So the loop will terminate. Because our choice of I satisfies all five criteria, it is adequate for the loop invariant and the loop precondition.

The process used above to compute the invariant for a loop does not always produce an assertion that is the weakest precondition (although it does in the example above).

As another example of finding a loop invariant, consider the following loop statement:

$$\textbf{while } s > 1 \textbf{ do } s = s / 2 \textbf{ end } \{s = 1\}$$

As above, we use the assignment axiom to try to find a loop invariant and a precondition for the loop. For zero iterations, the weakest precondition is $\{s = 1\}$. For one iteration, it is

$$wp(s = s / 2, \{s = 1\}) = \{s / 2 = 1\}, \text{ or } \{s = 2\}$$

For two iterations, it is

$$wp(s = s / 2, \{s = 2\}) = \{s / 2 = 2\}, \text{ or } \{s = 4\}$$

For three iterations, it is

$$wp(s = s / 2, \{s = 4\}) = \{s / 2 = 4\}, \text{ or } \{s = 8\}$$

From these cases, we can see clearly that the invariant is

$$\{s \text{ is a nonnegative power of } 2\}$$

Once again, the computed I can serve as P, and I passes the five requirements. Unlike our earlier example of finding a loop precondition, this one clearly is not a weakest precondition. Consider using the precondition $\{s > 1\}$. The logical statement

$$\{s > 1\} \textbf{ while } s > 1 \textbf{ do } s = s / 2 \textbf{ end } \{s = 1\}$$

can easily be proven, and this precondition is significantly broader than the one computed above. The loop and precondition are satisfied for any positive value for s, not just powers of 2 as the process indicates. Because of the rule of consequence, using a precondition that is stronger than the weakest precondition does not invalidate a proof.

Finding loop invariants is not always easy. It is helpful to understand the nature of these invariants. First, a loop invariant is a weakened version of the loop postcondition and also a precondition for the loop. So I must be weak enough to be satisfied prior to the beginning of loop execution, but when combined with the loop exit condition, it must be strong enough to force the truth of the postcondition.

Because of the difficulty of proving loop termination, that requirement is often ignored. If loop termination can be shown, the axiomatic description of the loop is called **total correctness.** If the other conditions can be met but termination is not guaranteed, it is called **partial correctness.**

In more complex loops, finding a suitable loop invariant, even for partial correctness, requires a good deal of ingenuity. Because computing the precondition for a **while** loop depends on finding a loop invariant, proving the correctness of programs with **while** loops using axiomatic semantics can be difficult.

The following is an example of a proof of correctness of a pseudocode program that computes the factorial function.

```
{n >= 0}
count = n;
fact = 1;
while count <> 0 do
    fact = fact * count;
    count = count - 1;
end
{fact = n!}
```

The method described earlier for finding the loop invariant does not work for the loop in this example. Some ingenuity is required here, which can be aided by a brief study of the code. The loop computes the factorial function in order of the last multiplication first; that is, $(n - 1) * n$ is done first, assuming n is greater than 1. So, part of the invariant can be

```
fact = (count + 1) * (count + 2) * … * (n - 1) * n
```

But we must also insure that `count` is always nonnegative, which we can do by adding that to the part above, to get

```
I = (fact = (count + 1) * … * n) AND (count >= 0)
```

Next, we must check that this I meets the requirements for invariants. We once again let I also be used for P, so P clearly implies I. Evaluation of the Boolean expression of the **while** statement, `count <> 0`, clearly does not affect I. The next question is

```
{I and B} S {I}
```

I and B is

```
((fact = (count + 1) * … * n) AND (count >= 0)) AND
    (count <> 0)
```

which reduces to

```
(fact = (count + 1) * … * n) AND (count > 0)
```

In our case, we must compute the precondition of the body of the loop, using the invariant for the postcondition. For

```
{P} count = count - 1 {I}
```

we compute P to be

```
{(fact = count * (count + 1) * … * n) AND (count >= 1)}
```

Using this as the postcondition for the first assignment in the loop body,

```
{P} fact = fact * count {(fact = count * (count + 1)
                          * … * n) AND (count >= 1)}
```

In this case, P is

```
{(fact = (count + 1) * … * n) AND (count >= 1)}
```

It is clear that I and B implies this P, so by the Rule of Consequence,

```
{I AND B} S {I}
```

is true. Finally, the last test of I is

I AND (NOT B) => Q

For our example, this is

```
((fact = (count + 1) * … * n) AND (count >= 0)) AND
    (count = 0)) => fact = n!
```

This is clearly true, for when `count = 0`, the first part is precisely the definition of factorial. So, our choice of I meets the requirements for a loop invariant. Now we can use our P (which is the same as I) from the **while** as the postcondition on the second assignment of the program.

```
{P} fact = 1 {(fact = (count + 1) * … * n) AND
              (count >= 0) }
```

which yields for P

```
(1 = (count + 1) * … * n) AND (count >= 0))
```

Using this as the postcondition for the first assignment in the code

```
{P} count = n {(1 = (count + 1) * … * n) AND
               (count >= 0)) }
```

produces for P

```
{(n + 1) * … * n = 1) AND (n >= 0) }
```

The left operand of the AND operator is true (because `1 = 1`) and the right operand is exactly the precondition of the whole code segment, `{n >= 0}`. Therefore, the program has been proven to be correct.

3.6.2.7 Evaluation

To define the semantics of a complete programming language using the axiomatic method, an axiom or an inference rule must be defined for each statement type in the language. Defining axioms and inference rules for some of the statements of programming languages has proven to be a difficult task. An obvious solution to this problem is to design the language with the axiomatic method in mind, so that only statements for which axioms or inference rules can be written are included. Unfortunately, such a language would be quite small and simple given the state of the science of axiomatic semantics.

Axiomatic semantics is a powerful tool for research into program correctness proofs, and it provides an excellent framework in which to reason about programs, both during their construction and later. Its usefulness in describing the meaning of programming languages to either language users or compiler writers is, however, highly limited.

3.6.3 Denotational Semantics

Denotational semantics is the most rigorous widely known method for describing the meaning of programs. It is solidly based on recursive function theory. A thorough discussion of the use of denotational semantics to describe the semantics of programming languages is long and complex. It is our intent to introduce just enough to make the reader aware of how denotational semantics works.

The fundamental concept of denotational semantics is to define for each language entity both a mathematical object and a function that maps instances of that entity onto instances of the mathematical object. Because the objects are rigorously defined, they represent the exact meaning of their corresponding entities. The idea is based on the fact that there are rigorous ways of manipulating mathematical objects but not for programming language constructs. The difficulty with this method lies in creating the objects and the mapping functions. The method is named denotational because the mathematical objects denote the meaning of their corresponding syntactic entities.

3.6.3.1 Two Simple Examples

We use a very simple language construct, binary numbers, to introduce the denotational method. The syntax of binary numbers can be described by the following grammar rules:

```
<bin_num> → 0
          | 1
          | <bin_num> 0
          | <bin_num> 1
```

A parse tree for the example binary number, 110, is shown in Figure 3.10.

To describe the meaning of binary numbers using denotational semantics and the grammar rules above, the actual meaning is associated with each rule that has a single terminal symbol as its RHS. The objects in this case are simple decimal numbers.

In our example, meaningful objects must be associated with the first two grammar rules. The other two grammar rules are, in a sense, computational rules because they combine a terminal symbol, to which an object can be associated, with a nonterminal, which can be expected to represent some construct. Presuming an evaluation that progresses upward in the parse tree, the nonterminal in the right side would already have its meaning attached. Then such a syntax rule would require a function that computed the meaning of the LHS, which must then represent the meaning of the complete RHS.

Let the domain of semantic values of the objects be N, the set of nonnegative decimal integer values. It is these objects that we wish to associate with binary numbers. The semantic function, named M_{bin}, maps the syntactic objects, as described in the grammar rules above, to the objects in N. The function M_{bin} is defined as follows:

$$M_{bin}('0') = 0$$
$$M_{bin}('1') = 1$$
$$M_{bin}(<bin\_num> \, '0') = 2 * M_{bin}(<bin\_num>)$$
$$M_{bin}(<bin\_num> \, '1') = 2 * M_{bin}(<bin\_num>) + 1$$

Notice that we put apostrophes around the syntactic digits to show they are not mathematical digits. This is similar to the relationship between ASCII coded digits and mathematical digits. When a program reads a number as a string, it must be converted to a mathematical number before it can be used as a number in the program.

The meanings, or denoted objects (which in this case are decimal numbers), can be attached to the nodes of the parse tree above, yielding

Figure 3.10
A parse tree of the binary number 110

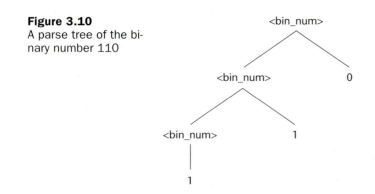

Figure 3.11
A parse tree with denoted objects for 110

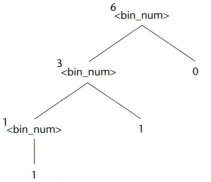

the tree in Figure 3.11. This is syntax-directed semantics. Syntactic entities are mapped to mathematical objects with concrete meaning.

In part because we need it later, we now show a similar example for describing the meaning of syntactic decimal literals.

$$<\text{dec\_num}> \rightarrow 0 \mid 1 \mid 2 \mid 3 \mid 4 \mid 5 \mid 6 \mid 7 \mid 8 \mid 9$$
$$\mid <\text{dec\_num}> (0 \mid 1 \mid 2 \mid 3 \mid 4 \mid 5 \mid 6 \mid 7 \mid 8 \mid 9)$$

The denotational mappings for these syntax rules are

$M_{dec}('0') = 0, M_{dec}('1') = 1, M_{dec}('2') = 2, ..., M_{dec}('9') = 9$
$M_{dec}(<\text{dec\_num}> '0') = 10 * M_{dec}(<\text{dec\_num}>)$
$M_{dec}(<\text{dec\_num}> '1') = 10 * M_{dec}(<\text{dec\_num}>) + 1$

...

$M_{dec}(<\text{dec\_num}> '9') = 10 * M_{dec}(<\text{dec\_num}>) + 9$

In the following sections, we present the denotational semantics of a few simple constructs. The most important simplifying assumption made here is that both the syntax and static semantics of the constructs are correct. In addition, we assume only two scalar types are included, integer and Boolean.

3.6.3.2 The State of a Program

The denotational semantics of a program could be defined in terms of state changes in an ideal computer. Operational semantics are defined in this way, and denotational semantics nearly are, too. In a further simplification, however, they are defined in terms of only the values of all of the program's variables. The key difference between operational semantics and denotational semantics is that state changes in operational semantics are defined by coded algorithms, whereas in denotational semantics, state changes are defined by rigorous mathematical functions.

Let the state s of a program be represented as a set of ordered pairs, as follows:

$$\{<i_1, v_1>, <i_2, v_2>, ..., <i_n, v_n>\}$$

Each i is the name of a variable, and the associated v's are the current values of those variables. Any of the v's can have the special value **undef,** which indicates that its associated variable is currently undefined. Let VARMAP be a function of two parameters, a variable name and the program state. The value of VARMAP(i_j, s) is v_j (the value paired with i_j in state s). Most semantics mapping functions for programs and program constructs map states to states. These state changes are used to define the meanings of programs and program constructs. Some language constructs, such as expressions, are mapped to values, not states.

3.6.3.3 Expressions

Expressions are fundamental to most programming languages. We assume here that expressions have no side effects. Furthermore, we deal with only very simple expressions: The only operators are + and * and an expression can have at most one operator; the only operands are scalar variables and integer literals; there are no parentheses; and the value of an expression is an integer. Following is the BNF description of these expressions:

> < expr > → < dec_num > | < var > | < binary_expr >
> < binary_expr > → < left_expr > < operator > < right_expr >
> < operator > → + | *

The only error we consider in expressions is that a variable has an undefined value. Obviously other errors can occur, but most of them are machine dependent. Let Z be the set of integers, and let **error** be the error value. Then Z ∪ {**error**} is the set of values to which an expression can evaluate.

The required mapping function for a given expression E and state s follows. To distinguish between mathematical function definitions and the assignment statements of programming languages, we use the symbol $\Delta=$ to define mathematical functions.

> M_e(< expr >, s) $\Delta=$
>   case < expr > of
>   < dec_num > => M_{dec}(< dec_num >, s)
>   < var > => if VARMAP(< var >, s) = **undef**
>   then **error**
>   else VARMAP(< var >, s)
>   < binary_expr > =>
>   if (M_e(< binary_expr >.< left_expr >, s) = **undef** OR
> M_e(< binary_expr >.< right_expr >, s) = **undef**)
>   then **error**
>   else if (< binary_expr >.< operator > = '+' then
> M_e(< binary_expr >.< left_expr >, s) +
> M_e(< binary_expr >.< right_expr >, s)
>   else M_e(< binary_expr >.< left_expr >, s) *
> M_e(< binary_expr >.< right_expr >, s)

3.6.3.4 Assignment Statements

An assignment statement is an expression evaluation plus the setting of the left-side variable to the expression's value. This can be described with the following function:

$$M_a(x = E, s) \; \Delta= \; \text{if } M_e(E, s) = \textbf{error}$$
$$\text{then } \textbf{error}$$
$$\text{else } s' = \{<i_1', v_1'>, <i_2', v_2'>, ..., <i_n', v_n'>\}, \text{where}$$
$$\text{for } j = 1, 2, ..., n, \; v_j' = \text{VARMAP}(i_j, s) \text{ if } i_j <> x;$$
$$M_e(E, s) \text{ if } i_j = x$$

Note that the two comparisons in the last two lines above, $i_j <> x$ and $i_j = x$, are of names, not values.

3.6.3.5 Logical Pretest Loops

The denotational semantics of a simple logical loop is deceptively simple. To expedite the discussion, we assume that there are two other existing mapping functions, M_{sl} and M_b, that map statement lists to states and Boolean expressions to Boolean values (or **error**), respectively. The function is

$$M_l(\textbf{while } B \textbf{ do } L, s) \; \Delta= \; \text{if } M_b(B, s) = \textbf{undef}$$
$$\text{then } \textbf{error}$$
$$\text{else if } M_b(B, s) = \text{false}$$
$$\text{then } s$$
$$\text{else if } M_{sl}(L, s) = \textbf{error}$$
$$\text{then } \textbf{error}$$
$$\text{else } M_l(\textbf{while } B \textbf{ do } L, M_{sl}(L, s))$$

The meaning of the loop is simply the value of the program variables after the statements in the loop have been executed the prescribed number of times, assuming there have been no errors. In essence, the loop has been converted from iteration to recursion, where the recursion control is mathematically defined by other recursive state mapping functions. Recursion is easier to describe with mathematical rigor than iteration.

One significant observation at this point is that this definition, like actual program loops, may compute nothing because of nontermination.

3.6.3.6 Evaluation

Objects and functions, such as those used in the statements above, can be defined for the other syntactic entities of programming languages. When a complete system has been defined for a given language, it can be used to determine the meaning of complete programs in that language. This provides a framework for thinking about programming in a highly rigorous way.

Denotational semantics can be used as an aid to language design. For example, statements for which the denotational semantic description is complex and difficult may indicate to the designer that such statements may also be difficult for language users to understand and that an alternative design may be in order.

A significant amount of work has been done on the possibility of using denotational language descriptions to generate compilers automatically (Jones, 1980; Milos et al., 1984; Bodwin et al., 1982). These efforts have shown that the method is feasible, but the work has never progressed to the point where it can be used to generate useful compilers.

Because of the complexity of denotational descriptions, they are of little use to language users. On the other hand, they provide an excellent method of concisely describing a language.

Although the use of denotational semantics is normally attributed to Scott and Strachey (1971), the general denotational approach to language description can be traced back to the nineteenth century (Frege, 1892).

SUMMARY

Backus-Naur form and context-free grammars are equivalent metalanguages that are almost ideally suited for the task of describing the syntax of programming languages. Not only are they concise descriptive methods, but the parse trees that can be associated with their generative actions give graphical evidence of the underlying syntactic structures. Furthermore, they are naturally related to recognition devices for the languages they generate, which leads to the relatively easy construction of syntax analyzers for compilers for these languages.

Syntax graphs are simply graphical representations of grammars.

An attribute grammar is a descriptive formalism that can describe both the syntax and static semantics of a language.

There are three primary methods of semantic description: operational, axiomatic, and denotational. Operational semantics is a method of describing the meaning of language constructs in terms of their effects on an ideal machine. Axiomatic semantics, which is based on formal logic, was devised as a tool for proving the correctness of programs. In denotational semantics, mathematical objects are used to represent the meanings of language constructs. Language entities are converted to these mathematical objects with recursive functions.

BIBLIOGRAPHIC NOTES

Syntax description using context-free grammars and BNF is thoroughly discussed in Cleaveland and Uzgalis (1976). Syntax graphs were developed at Burroughs for a compiler development project to use as a compact description of AL-

GOL 60 syntax (Taylor et al., 1961). They were later modified by A. Schai, director of the computer center at ETH in Zurich. This modified version first appeared in print in a book on ALGOL 60 by Rutishauser (1967).

Research in axiomatic semantics was begun by Floyd (1967) and further developed by Hoare (1969). The semantics of a large part of Pascal was described by Hoare and Wirth (1973) using this method. The parts they did not complete involved functional side effects and goto statements. These were found to be the most difficult to describe.

The technique of using preconditions and postconditions during the development of programs is described (and advocated) by Dijkstra (1976) and also discussed in detail in Gries (1981).

Good introductions to denotational semantics can be found in Gordon (1979) and Stoy (1977). Introductions to all three semantics description methods discussed in this chapter can be found in Marcotty et al. (1976). Another good reference for much of the material of this chapter is Pagan (1981). The form of the denotational semantic functions in this chapter is similar to that in Meyer (1990).

REVIEW QUESTIONS

1. Define syntax and semantics.
2. Who are language descriptions for?
3. Describe the operation of a general language generator.
4. Describe the operation of a general language recognizer.
5. What is the difference between a sentence and a sentential form?
6. Define a left recursive grammar rule.
7. What three extensions are common to most EBNFs?
8. Describe static and dynamic semantics.
9. What purpose do predicates serve in an attribute grammar?
10. What is the difference between a synthesized and an inherited attribute?
11. How is the order of evaluation of attributes determined for the trees of a given attribute grammar?
12. What is the primary use of attribute grammars?
13. What is the problem with using a software pure interpreter for operational semantics?
14. Explain what the preconditions and postconditions of a given statement mean in axiomatic semantics.
15. Describe the approach of using axiomatic semantics to prove the correctness of a given program.
16. Describe the basic concept of denotational semantics.
17. In what way do operational semantics and denotational semantics differ?

1. The two mathematical models of language description are generation and recognition. Describe how each can define the syntax of a programming language.

2. Write EBNF and syntax graph descriptions for the following:

   a. A Pascal **procedure** header statement

   b. A Pascal **procedure** call statement

   c. A C **switch** statement

   d. A C **union** definition

   e. C **float** literals

3. Using the grammar in Example 3.2, show a parse tree and a leftmost derivation for each of the following statements:

   a. A := A * (B + (C * A))

   b. B := C * (A * C + B)

   c. A := A * (B + (C))

4. Using the grammar in Example 3.4, show a parse tree and a leftmost derivation for each of the following statements:

   a. A := (A + B) * C

   b. A := B + C + A

   c. A := A * (B + C)

   d. A := B * (C * (A + B))

5. Prove that the following grammar is ambiguous:

   $<S> \rightarrow <A>$

   $<A> \rightarrow <A> + <A> \mid <id>$

   $<id> \rightarrow a \mid b \mid c$

6. Modify the grammar of Example 3.4 to add a unary minus operator that has higher precedence than either + or *.

7. Describe, in English, the language defined by the following grammar:

   $<S> \rightarrow <A> <B> <C>$

   $<A> \rightarrow a <A> \mid a$

   $<B> \rightarrow b <B> \mid b$

   $<C> \rightarrow c <C> \mid c$

8. Consider the following grammar:

   $<S> \rightarrow <A> a <B> b$

   $<A> \rightarrow <A> b \mid b$

   $<B> \rightarrow a <B> \mid a$

   Which of the following sentences are in the language generated by this grammar?

   a. baab

   b. bbbab

   c. bbaaaaa

   d. bbaab

9. Consider the following grammar:

<S> → a <S> c <B> | <A> | b
<A> → c <A> | c
<B> → d | <A>

Which of the following sentences are in the language generated by this grammar?

a. abcd

b. acccbd

c. acccbcc

d. acd

e. accc

10. Write a grammar for the language consisting of strings that have *n* copies of the letter a followed by the same number of copies of the letter b, where *n* > 0. For example, the strings ab, aaaabbbb, and aaaaaaaabbbbbbbb are in the language but a, abb, ba, and aaabb are not.

11. Draw parse trees for the sentences aabcc and aaabbbc, as derived from the grammar of Problem 10.

12. Using the virtual machine instructions given in Section 3.6.1.1, give an operational semantic definition of the following:

a. Pascal **repeat**

b. Pascal **for-downto**

c. FORTRAN DO of the form: DO N K = start, end, step

d. Pascal **if-then-else**

e. C **for**

f. C **switch**

13. Compute the weakest precondition for each of the following assignment statements and postconditions:

a. a := 2 * (b - 1) - 1 {a > 0}

b. b := (c + 10) / 3 {b > 6}

c. a := a + 2 * b - 1 {a > 1}

d. x := 2 * y + x - 1 {x > 11}

14. Compute the weakest precondition for each of the following sequences of assignment statements and their postconditions:

a. a := 2 * b + 1;
   b := a - 3
   {b < 0}

b. a := 3 * (2 * b + a);
   b := 2 * a - 1
   {b > 5}

15. Write a denotational semantics mapping function for the following statements:

    a. Pascal **for**

    b. Pascal **repeat**

    c. Pascal Boolean expressions

    d. C **for**

    e. C **switch**

16. What is the difference between an intrinsic attribute and a nonintrinsic synthesized attribute?

17. Write an attribute grammar whose BNF basis is that of Example 3.6 in Section 3.5.5, but whose language rules are as follows: Data types cannot be mixed in expressions, but assignment statements need not have the same types on both sides of the assignment operator.

18. Write an attribute grammar whose base BNF is that of Example 3.2 and whose type rules are the same as for the assignment statement example of Section 3.5.5.

19. Prove the following program is correct:

```
{x = Vx and y = Vy}
temp = x;
x = y;
y = temp;
{x = Vy and y = Vx}
```

20. Prove the following program is correct:

```
{n > 0}
count = n;
sum = 0;
while count <> 0 do
  sum = sum + count;
  count = count - 1;
end
{sum = 1 + 2 + … + n}
```

4 Names, Bindings, Type Checking, and Scopes

Bjarne Stroustrup

Bjarne Stroustrup, a member of the Technical Staff at AT&T Bell Labs since 1979, designed C++. C++ made object-oriented programming accessible and affordable to real-world software developers. Largely due to the popularity of C++, object-oriented programming became the pervasive development paradigm by the early 1990s. Stroustrup is the author of *The C++ Programming Language* and *The Design and Evolution of C++*.

This chapter introduces the fundamental semantic issues of variables. The most basic of these topics is covered first, the nature of names and special words in programming languages. The attributes of variables, including type, address, and value, are then discussed. The issue of aliases is included in that discussion. The important concepts of binding and binding times are then introduced. The different possible binding times for variable attributes define four different categories of variables. Their descriptions are followed by a thorough investigation of type checking, strong typing, and type compatibility rules. The two very different scoping rules for names, static and dynamic, are then discussed, along with the concept of a referencing environment of a statement. Finally, named constants and variable initialization techniques are described.

4.1 Introduction

Imperative programming languages are, to varying degrees, abstractions of the underlying von Neumann computer architecture. The architecture's two primary components are its memory, which stores both instructions and data, and its processor, which provides operations for modifying the contents of the memory. The abstractions in a language for the memory cells of the machine are variables. In some cases, the characteristics of the abstractions are very close to the characteristics of the cells; an example of this is an integer variable, which is usually represented exactly as in an individual hardware memory word. In other cases, the abstractions are far removed from the cells, as with a three-dimensional array, which requires a software mapping function to support the abstraction.

A variable can be characterized by a collection of properties, or attributes, the most important of which is type, a fundamental concept in programming languages. The design of the data types of a language requires that a variety of issues be considered. Among the most important of these are the scope and lifetime of variables. Related to these are the issues of type checking and initialization. A knowledge of all these concepts is requisite to understanding the imperative languages. Type compatibility is another important part of the data type design of a language.

In the remainder of this book, we will often refer to families of languages as if they were a single language. For example, when we refer to FORTRAN, we mean all of the versions of FORTRAN. This is also the case for Pascal and Ada. References to C include the original version of C and ANSI C. When we refer to a specific version of a language, it is because it is different from the other family members.

4.2 Names

Before we can begin our discussion of variables, we must discuss one of the fundamental attributes of variables—names, which have broader use than simply for variables. Names are also associated with labels, subprograms, formal parameters, and other program constructs. The term *identifier* is often used interchangeably with *name*.

4.2.1 Design Issues

The following are the primary design issues for names:

- What is the maximum length of a name?
- Can connector characters be used in names?
- Are names case sensitive?
- Are the special words reserved words or keywords?

These issues are discussed in the following two sections, which also include examples of several design choices.

4.2.2 Name Forms

A **name** is a string of characters used to identify some entity in a program. The earliest programming languages used single-character names. This was natural because early programming was primarily mathematical, and mathematicians have long used single-character names for unknowns in their formal notations.

FORTRAN I broke with the tradition of the single-character name, allowing up to 6 characters in its names. FORTRAN 77 still restricts names to six characters, but FORTRAN 90 and C allow up to 31 characters; Ada names have no length limit, and all are significant. Some languages, such as C++, do not specify a length limit on names, although implementors of those languages sometimes do. They do this so the symbol table in which identifiers are stored during compilation need not be too large, and also to simplify the maintenance of that table.

The commonly acceptable name form is a string with a reasonably long length limit, if any, with some connector character such as the underscore (_) included. The underscore serves the same purpose as a space in English text but without terminating the name string in which it is placed. Most contemporary languages allow connector characters in names.

In some languages, notably C, C++, and Java, uppercase and lowercase letters in names are distinct; that is, names in these languages are **case sensitive.** For example, the following three names are distinct in

C++: `rose`, `ROSE`, and `Rose`. To some, this is a serious detriment to readability because names that look very similar in fact denote different entities. In that sense, case sensitivity violates the design principle that language constructs that look the same should have the same meaning.

Obviously, not everyone agrees that case sensitivity is bad for names. In C, the problems of case sensitivity can be avoided by exclusive use of lowercase for names. In Java, however, the problem cannot be escaped because many of the predefined names include both uppercase and lowercase letters. For example, the Java method for converting a string to an integer value is `parseInt`, and spellings such as `ParseInt` and `parseint` are not recognized. This is a problem of writability rather than readability, because the need to remember odd spellings makes it more difficult to write correct programs. It is a kind of intolerance on the part of the language designer, which is enforced by the compiler.

In versions of FORTRAN prior to 90, only uppercase letters could be used in names, a needless restriction. Like FORTRAN 90, many implementations of FORTRAN 77 allow lowercase letters; they simply translate them to uppercase for internal use during compilation.

4.2.3 Special Words

Special words in programming languages are used to make programs more readable by naming actions to be performed. They also are used to separate the syntactic entities of programs. In most languages, these words are classified as reserved words, but in some they are only keywords.

A **keyword** is a word of a programming language that is special only in certain contexts. FORTRAN is one of the languages whose special words are keywords. In FORTRAN, the word `REAL`, when found at the beginning of a statement and followed by a name, is considered a keyword that indicates the statement is a declarative statement. However, if the word `REAL` is followed by the assignment operator, it is considered a variable name. These two uses are illustrated in the following:

```
REAL APPLE
REAL = 3.4
```

FORTRAN compilers and FORTRAN program readers must recognize the difference between names and special words by context.

A **reserved word** is a special word of a programming language that cannot be used as a name. As a language design choice, reserved words are better than keywords because the ability to redefine keywords can lead to readability problems. For example, in FORTRAN, one could have the statements

```
INTEGER REAL
REAL INTEGER
```

which declare the program variable REAL to be of INTEGER type and the variable INTEGER to be of REAL type. In addition to the strange appearance of these declaration statements, the appearance of REAL and INTEGER as variable names elsewhere in the program could be misleading to program readers.

In program code examples in this book, reserved words are presented in boldface.

Many languages include predefined names, which are in a sense between reserved words and user-defined names. They have predefined meanings but can be redefined by the user. For example, the built-in data type names in Ada, such as INTEGER and FLOAT, are predefined. These names are not reserved; they can be redefined by any Ada program. In Pascal, the predefined names are sometimes called standard identifiers. In that language, the normal input and output subprogram names, including readln and writeln, are predefined.

The definitions of the predefined names in Pascal and Ada must be visible to the compilers for those languages because of their compile-time type checking. In both languages, the examples of predefined names above are implicitly visible to the compiler. In Ada, other predefined names, such as the standard input and output subprograms GET and PUT, are made visible explicitly by **with** statements written by the user.

In C and C++, many names are predefined in libraries that user programs use. For example, the C input and output function names, printf and scanf, are defined in the library stdio. Access to names that are predefined in libraries are made available to the compiler through header files, which contain declarations for names that are defined in libraries.

4.3 Variables

A program variable is an abstraction of a computer memory cell or collection of cells. Programmers often think of variables as names for memory locations, but there is much more to a variable than just a name. The move from machine languages to assembly languages was largely one of replacing absolute numeric memory addresses with names, making programs far more readable and thus easier to write and maintain. That step also provided an escape from the problem of absolute addressing, because the translator that converted the names to actual addresses also chose those addresses.

A variable can be characterized as a sextuple of attributes: (name, address, value, type, lifetime, scope). Although this may seem too complicated for such a seemingly simple concept, it provides the clearest way to explain the various aspects of variables.

Our discussion of variable attributes will lead to examinations of the important related concepts of aliases, binding, binding times, declarations, type checking, strong typing, scoping rules, and referencing environments.

The name, address, type, and value attributes of variables are discussed in the following subsections. The lifetime and scope attributes are discussed in Sections 4.4.3 and 4.8, respectively.

4.3.1 Name

Variable names are the most common names in programs. They were discussed at length in Section 4.2 in the general context of entity names in programs. Most variables have names. The ones that do not are discussed in Section 4.4.3.3. Names are often referred to as identifiers.

4.3.2 Address

The **address** of a variable is the memory address with which it is associated. This association is not as simple as it may at first appear. In many languages, it is possible for the same name to be associated with different addresses at different places and at different times in the program. For example, a program can have two subprograms, `sub1` and `sub2`, each of which defines a variable that uses the same name, say `sum`. Because these two variables are independent of each other, a reference to `sum` in `sub1` is unrelated to a reference to `sum` in `sub2`. Similarly, most languages allow the same name to be associated with different addresses at different times during program execution. For example, a recursively called subprogram has multiple versions of each locally declared variable, one for each activation. The process of associating variables with addresses is further discussed in Section 4.4.3. An implementation model for subprograms and their activations for ALGOL-like languages is discussed in Chapter 9.

The address of a variable is sometimes called its **l-value,** because that is what is required when a variable appears in the left side of an assignment statement.

4.3.2.1 Aliases

It is possible to have multiple identifiers reference the same address. When more than one variable name can be used to access a single memory location, the names are called **aliases.** Aliasing is a hindrance to readability because it allows a variable to have its value changed by an assignment to a different variable. For example, if variables A and B are aliases, any change to A also changes B and vice versa. A reader of the program must always remember that A and B are different names for the same memory cell. Because there can be any number of aliases in a program, this is very difficult in practice. Aliasing also makes program verification more difficult.

Aliases can be created in programs in several different ways. In FOR-TRAN, aliases can be explicitly created with the `EQUIVALENCE` statement. Aliases can be created using the variant record structures of some languages, including Pascal and Ada, and using the union types of C and C++. The aliases created by these data types are meant to save storage by allowing the same locations to be used by different types of data at different times. They can also be used to circumvent the type rules of some of the languages in which they are provided. Variant records and unions are discussed at length in Chapter 5.

Two pointer variables are aliases when they point to the same memory location. The same is true for reference variables. This kind of aliasing is not meant to conserve storage but is simply a side effect of the nature of pointers and references. When a C++ pointer is set to point at a named variable, the pointer, when dereferenced, and the variable's name are aliases. This and other characteristics of pointers and references are discussed in Chapter 5.

Aliasing can be created in many languages through subprogram parameters. These kinds of aliases are discussed in Chapter 8.

Some of the justifications for aliases no longer exist. When a language construct creates aliases for the purpose of reusing storage, it can be replaced by a dynamic storage management scheme, which allows reuse of storage but will not necessarily create aliases. Furthermore, computer memories are far larger now than when languages like FORTRAN were developed, so memory is now not such a scarce commodity.

The time when a variable becomes associated with an address is very important to an understanding of programming languages. This subject is discussed in Section 4.4.3.

4.3.3 Type

The **type** of a variable determines the range of values the variable can have and the set of operations that are defined for values of the type. For example, the type `INTEGER` in some FORTRAN implementations specifies a value range of –32,768 to 32,767, and arithmetic operations for addition, subtraction, multiplication, division, and exponentiation, along with some library functions for operations like absolute value.

4.3.4 Value

The value of a variable is the contents of the memory cell or cells associated with the variable. It is convenient to think of computer memory in terms of *abstract* cells, rather than physical cells. The cells, or individually addressable units, of most contemporary computer memories are byte-sized, with a byte usually being eight bits in length. This size is too small for most program variables. We define an abstract memory cell to have the size required by the variable with which it is associated. For example, although floating-point values may occupy four physical bytes in a particular implementation of a particular language, we think of a floating-point value as occupying a single abstract memory cell. We consider the value of each simple nonstructured type to occupy a single abstract cell. Henceforth, when we use the term *memory cell*, we mean abstract memory cell.

A variable's value is sometimes called its **r-value** because it is what is required when the variable is used on the right side of an assignment statement. To access the *r*-value, the *l*-value must be determined first. Such determinations are not always simple. For example, scoping rules can greatly complicate matters, as is discussed in Section 4.8.

4.4 The Concept of Binding

In a general sense, a **binding** is an association, such as between an attribute and an entity or between an operation and a symbol. The time at which a binding takes place is called **binding time.** Binding and binding times are prominent concepts in the semantics of programming languages. Bindings can take place at language design time, language implementation time, compile time, link time, load time, or run time. For example, the asterisk symbol (*) is usually bound to the multiplication operation at language design time. A data type, such as INTEGER in FORTRAN, is bound to a range of possible values at language implementation time. At compile time, a variable in a C or Pascal program is bound to a particular data type. A call to a library subprogram is bound to the subprogram code at link time. A variable may be bound to a storage cell when the program is loaded into memory. That same binding does not happen until run time in some cases, as with variables declared in Pascal subprograms and in C functions (if the definition does not include the **static** qualifier).

Consider the following C assignment statement, whose variable count has been defined as shown:

```
int count;
...
count = count + 5;
```

Some of the bindings and their binding times for the parts of this assignment statement are as follows:

- Set of possible types for count: bound at language design time.
- Type of count: bound at compile time.
- Set of possible values of count: bound at compiler design time.

- Value of `count`: bound at execution time with this statement.
- Set of possible meanings for the operator symbol +: bound at language definition time.
- Meaning of the operator symbol + in this statement: bound at compile time.
- Internal representation of the literal 5: bound at compiler design time.

A complete understanding of the binding times for the attributes of program entities is a prerequisite for understanding the semantics of a programming language. For example, to understand what a subprogram does, one must understand how the actual parameters in a call are bound to the formal parameters in its definition. To determine the current value of a variable, you may need to know when the variable was bound to storage.

4.4.1 Binding of Attributes to Variables

A binding is **static** if it occurs before run time and remains unchanged throughout program execution. If it occurs during run time or can change in the course of program execution, it is called **dynamic.** The physical binding of a variable to a storage cell in a virtual memory environment is complex, because the page or segment of the address space in which the cell resides may be moved in and out of memory many times during program execution. In a sense, such variables are bound and unbound repeatedly. These bindings, however, are maintained by computer hardware, and the changes are invisible to the program and the user. Because they are not important to the discussion, we are not concerned with these hardware bindings. The essential point is to distinguish between static and dynamic bindings.

4.4.2 Type Bindings

Before a variable can be referenced in a program, it must be bound to a data type. The two important aspects of this binding are how the type is specified and when the binding takes place. Types can be specified statically through some form of explicit or implicit declaration.

4.4.2.1 Variable Declarations

An **explicit declaration** is a statement in a program that lists variable names and specifies that they are a particular type. An **implicit declaration** is a means of associating variables with types through default conventions instead of declaration statements. In this case, the first appearance of a variable name in a program constitutes its implicit declaration. Both explicit and implicit declarations create static bindings to types.

Most programming languages designed since the mid-1960s require explicit declarations of all variables (Perl and ML are two exceptions). Several widely used languages whose initial designs were done before the late 1960s, notably FORTRAN, PL/I, and BASIC, have implicit declarations. For example, in FORTRAN, an identifier that appears in a program that is not explicitly declared is implicitly declared according to the following convention: If the identifier begins with one of the letters I, J, K, L, M, or N, it is implicitly declared to be INTEGER type; otherwise, it is implicitly declared to be REAL type.

Although they are a minor convenience to programmers, implicit declarations can be detrimental to reliability because they prevent the compilation process from detecting some typographical and programmer errors. Variables that are accidentally left undeclared by the programmer are given default types and unexpected attributes, which could cause subtle errors that are difficult to diagnose.

Some of the problems with implicit declarations can be avoided by requiring names for specific types to begin with particular special characters. For example, in Perl any name that begins with $ is a scalar, which can store either a string or a numeric value. If a name begins with @, it is an array; if it begins with a %, it is a hash structure. This creates different name spaces for different type variables. In this scenario, the names @apple and %apple are unrelated, because each is from a different name space. Furthermore, a program reader always knows the type of a variable when reading its name.

In C and C++, one must sometimes distinguish between declarations and definitions. Declarations specify types and other attributes but do not cause allocation of storage. Definitions specify attributes *and* cause storage allocation. For a specific name, a C program can have any number of compatible declarations, but only a single definition. One purpose of variable declarations in C is to provide the type of a variable defined external to a function that is used in the function. It tells the compiler the type of a variable and that it is defined elsewhere. This idea carries over to the functions in C and C++, where prototypes declare names and interfaces, but not the code of functions. Function definitions, on the other hand, are complete.

4.4.2.2 Dynamic Type Binding

With dynamic type binding, the type is not specified by a declaration statement. Instead, the variable is bound to a type when it is assigned a value in an assignment statement. When the assignment statement is executed, the variable being assigned is bound to the type of the value, variable, or expression on the right side of the assignment.

Languages in which types are dynamically bound are dramatically different from those in which types are statically bound. The primary advantage of dynamic binding of variables to types is that it provides a great deal of programming flexibility. For example, a program to process a list of data in a language that uses dynamic type binding can be written as a generic program, meaning that it is capable of dealing with data of any type. Whatever type data is input will be acceptable, because the variables in which the data is to be stored can be bound to the correct type when the data is assigned to the variables after input. By contrast, because of static binding of types, one cannot write a C or Pascal program to process a list of data without knowing the type of that data.

In APL and SNOBOL4, the binding of a variable to a type is dynamic. For example, an APL program may contain the following statement:

```
LIST ← 10.2 5.1 0.0
```

Regardless of the previous type of the variable named `LIST`, this assignment causes it to become a single-dimensioned array of floating-point elements of length 3. If the statement

```
LIST ← 47
```

followed the assignment above, `LIST` would become an integer scalar variable.

There are two disadvantages to dynamic type binding. First, the error detection capability of the compiler is diminished relative to a compiler for a language with static type bindings, because any two types can appear on opposite sides of the assignment operator. Incorrect types of right sides of assignments are not detected as errors; rather, the type of the left side is simply changed to the incorrect type. For example, suppose that in a particular program, `i` and `x` are integer variables, and `y` is a floating-point array. Further suppose that the program needs the assignment statement

```
i := x
```

but because of a keying error, it has the assignment statement

```
i := y
```

In a language with dynamic type binding, no error is detected by the compiler or run-time system. `i` is simply changed to a floating-point array type. But because `y` was used instead of the correct variable `x`, the results are erroneous. In a language with static type binding, the compiler would detect the error and the program would not get to execution.

Note that this disadvantage is also present to some extent in some languages that use static type binding, such as FORTRAN, C, and C++, which in many cases automatically convert the type of the RHS of an assignment to the type of the LHS.

The other disadvantage of dynamic type binding is cost. The cost of implementing dynamic attribute binding is considerable, particularly in execution time. Type checking must be done at run time. Furthermore, every variable must have a descriptor associated with it to maintain the current type. The storage used for the value of a variable must be of varying size, because different type values require different amounts of storage.

Languages that have dynamic type binding for variables are often implemented using interpreters rather than compilers. This is partially because it is difficult to change dynamically the types of variables in machine code. Furthermore, the time to do dynamic type binding is hidden by the overall time of interpretation, so it seems less costly in that environment. On the other hand, languages with static type bindings are seldom implemented by interpretation, because programs in these languages can be easily translated to very efficient machine code versions.

4.4.2.3 Type Inference

ML is a relatively recent programming language that supports both functional and imperative programming (Milner et al., 1990). ML employs an interesting type inference mechanism, in which the types of most expressions can be determined without requiring the programmer to specify the types of the variables. For example, the function declaration

```
fun circumf(r) = 3.14159 * r * r;
```

specifies a function that takes a real argument and produces a real result. The types are inferred from the type of the constant in the expression. Likewise, in the function

```
fun times10(x) = 10 * x;
```

the argument and functional value are inferred to be of type integer.

The ML system rejects the function

```
fun square(x) = x * x;
```

because the type for the * operator cannot be inferred. In such cases, the programmer can supply a hint, such as the following, in which the type returned by the function is specified to be int.

```
fun square(x) : int = x * x;
```

The fact that the functional value is typed as an integer is sufficient to infer that the argument is also an integer. The following definitions are also legal:

```
fun square(x : int) = x * x;
fun square(x) = (x : int) * x;
fun square(x) = x * (x : int);
```

Type inference is also used in the purely functional languages Miranda and Haskell.

4.4.3   Storage Bindings and Lifetime

The fundamental character of a programming language is in large part determined by the design of the storage bindings for its variables. It is therefore important to have a clear understanding of these bindings.

The memory cell to which a variable is bound somehow must be taken from a pool of available memory. This process is called **allocation.** **Deallocation** is the process of placing a memory cell that has been unbound from a variable back into the pool of available memory.

The **lifetime** of a variable is the time during which the variable is bound to a specific memory location. So the lifetime of a variable begins when it is bound to a specific cell and ends when it is unbound from that cell. To investigate storage bindings of variables, it is convenient to separate scalar (unstructured) variables into four categories, according to their lifetimes. We call these categories static, stack-dynamic, explicit heap-dynamic, and implicit heap-dynamic. In the following sections, we discuss the meanings of these four categories, along with their purposes, advantages, and disadvantages.

4.4.3.1 Static Variables

Static variables are those that are bound to memory cells before program execution begins and remain bound to those same memory cells until program execution terminates. Variables that are statically bound to storage have several valuable applications to programming. Obviously, globally accessible variables are often used throughout the execution of a program, thus making it necessary to have them bound to the same storage during that execution. Sometimes it is convenient to have variables that are declared in subprograms be **history sensitive;** that is, have them retain values between separate executions of the subprogram. This is a characteristic of a variable that is statically bound to storage.

Another advantage of static variables is efficiency. All addressing of static variables can be direct; other kinds of variables often require indirect addressing, which is slower. Furthermore, no run-time overhead is incurred for allocation and deallocation of static variables.

One disadvantage of static binding to storage is reduced flexibility; in particular, in a language that has only variables that are statically bound to storage, recursive subprograms are not supported. Another disadvantage is that storage cannot be shared among variables. For example, suppose a program has two subprograms, both of which require large unrelated arrays. If they are static, their storage cannot be shared.

In FORTRAN I, II, and IV, all variables were static. C, C++, and Java allow programmers to include the **static** specifier on a local variable definition, making the variables it defines static. Pascal does not provide static variables.

4.4.3.2 Stack-Dynamic Variables

Stack-dynamic variables are those whose storage bindings are created when their declaration statements are elaborated, but whose types are statically bound. **Elaboration** of such a declaration refers to the storage allocation and binding process indicated by the declaration, which takes place when execution reaches the code to which the declaration is attached. Therefore, elaboration occurs during run time. For example, a Pascal procedure consists of a declaration section and a code section. The declaration section is elaborated just before execution of the code section begins, which happens when the procedure is called. The storage for the variables in the declaration section is allocated at elaboration time and deallocated when the procedure returns control to its caller. As their name indicates, stack-dynamic variables are allocated from the run-time stack.

The design of ALGOL 60 and its successor languages allows recursive subprograms. To be useful, at least in most cases, recursive subprograms require some form of dynamic local storage so that each active copy of the recursive subprogram has its own version of the local variables. These needs are conveniently met by stack-dynamic variables. Even in the absence of recursion, having stack-dynamic local storage for subprograms is not without merit, because all subprograms share the same memory space for their locals. The disadvantages are the run-time overhead of allocation and deallocation and the fact that locals cannot be history sensitive.

FORTRAN 77 and FORTRAN 90 allow implementors to use stack-dynamic variables for locals, but include a statement

SAVE list

that allows the programmer to specify that some or all of the variables (those in list) in the subprogram in which SAVE is placed will be static.

In C and C++, local variables are by default stack-dynamic. In Pascal and Ada, all non-heap variables defined in subprograms are stack-dynamic.

All attributes other than storage are statically bound to stack-dynamic scalar variables. That is not the case for some structured types, as is discussed in Chapter 5. Implementation of allocation/deallocation processes for stack-dynamic variables is discussed in Chapter 9.

4.4.3.3 Explicit Heap-Dynamic Variables

Explicit heap-dynamic variables are nameless (abstract) memory cells that are allocated and deallocated by explicit run-time instructions specified by the programmer. These variables, which are allocated from and deallocated to the heap, can only be referenced through pointer or reference variables. The heap is a collection of storage cells whose organization is highly disorganized because of the unpredictability of its use. An explicit heap-dynamic variable is created either by an operator (for example, in Ada and C++) or a call to a system subprogram provided for that purpose (for example, in C).

In C++, the allocation operator, named **new**, uses a type name as its operand. When executed, an explicit heap-dynamic variable of the operand type is created and a pointer to it is returned. Because an explicit heap-dynamic variable is bound to a type at compile time, that binding is static. However, such variables are bound to storage at the time they are created, which is during run time.

In addition to a subprogram or operator for creating of explicit heap-dynamic variables, some languages include a means of destroying them.

As an example of explicit heap-dynamic variables, consider the following C++ code segment:

```
int *intnode;
...
intnode = new int;   /* allocates an int cell */
...
delete intnode;      /* deallocates the cell to which
                        intnode points */
```

In this example, an explicit heap-dynamic variable of **int** type is created by the **new** operator. This variable can then be referenced through the pointer, `intnode`. Later, the variable is deallocated by the **delete** operator.

In the object-oriented language Java, all data except the primitive scalars are objects. Java objects are explicit heap dynamic and are accessed through reference variables. Java has no way of explicitly destroying a heap-dynamic variable; rather, implicit garbage collection is used.

Explicit heap-dynamic variables are often used for dynamic structures, such as linked lists and trees, that need to grow and/or shrink during execution. Such structures can be built conveniently using pointers or references and explicit heap-dynamic variables.

The disadvantages of explicit heap-dynamic variables are the difficulty of using pointer and reference variables correctly, along with the cost of references to the variables, allocations, and deallocations. These considerations, pointer and reference data types, and implementation methods for explicit heap-dynamic variables are discussed at length in Chapter 5.

4.4.3.4 Implicit Heap-Dynamic Variables

Implicit heap-dynamic variables are bound to heap storage only when they are assigned values. In fact, all their attributes are bound every time they are assigned. In a sense, they are just names that adapt to whatever use they are asked to serve. The advantage of such variables is that they have the highest degree of flexibility, allowing highly generic code to be written. The disadvantage is the run-time overhead of maintaining all the dynamic attributes, which could include array subscript types and ranges, among others. Another disadvantage is the loss of some error detection by the compiler, as discussed in Section 4.2.2.2. Examples of implicit heap-dynamic variables in APL appear in Section 4.4.2.2. Examples of them in ALGOL 68, in which they are called **flex** arrays, appear in Chapter 2.

4.5 Type Checking

For our discussion of type checking, we generalize the concept of operands and operators to include subprograms and assignment statements. We will think of subprograms as operators whose operands are their parameters. The assignment symbol will be thought of as a binary operator, with its target variable and its expression being the operands.

Type checking is the activity of ensuring that the operands of an operator are of compatible types. A **compatible** type is one that is either legal for the operator or is allowed under language rules to be implicitly converted by compiler-generated code to a legal type. This automatic conversion is called a **coercion.** A **type error** is the application of an operator to an operand of an inappropriate type.

If all bindings of variables to types are static in a language, then type checking can nearly always be done statically. Dynamic type binding requires type checking at run time, which is called dynamic type checking.

Some languages, such as APL and SNOBOL4, because of their dynamic type binding, allow only dynamic type checking. It is much better to detect errors at compile time than at run time because the earlier correction is usually less costly. The penalty for static checking is reduced programmer flexibility. Fewer shortcuts and tricks are possible. Such techniques, though, are now generally held in low esteem.

Type checking is complicated when a language allows a memory cell to store values of different types at different times during execution. This can be done with Ada and Pascal variant records, FORTRAN `EQUIVALENCE`, and C and C++ unions. In these cases, type checking, if done, must be dynamic and requires the run-time system to maintain the type of the current value of such memory cells. So even though all variables are statically bound to types in languages such as C and Pascal, not all type errors can be detected by static type checking.

4.6 Strong Typing

One of the new ideas in language design that became prominent in the so-called structured programming revolution of the 1970s is **strong typing.** Strong typing is widely acknowledged as being a highly valuable concept. Unfortunately, it is often loosely defined, and it is sometimes used in computing literature without being defined at all.

The following is one simple but incomplete definition of a strongly typed language: A strongly typed language is one in which each name in a program in the language has a single type associated with it, and that type is known at compile time. The essence of this definition is that all types are statically bound. The weakness of this definition is that it ignores the possibility that, although a variable's type may be known, the storage location to which it is bound may store values of different types at different times. To take this possibility into account, we define a programming language to be **strongly typed** if type errors are always detected. This requires that the types of all operands can be determined, either at compile time or at run time. The importance of strong typing lies in its ability to detect all misuses of variables that result in type errors. A strongly typed language also allows the detection, at run time, of uses of the incorrect type values in variables that can store values of more than one type.

FORTRAN is not strongly typed because the relationship between actual and formal parameters is not type checked. Also, the use of EQUIVALENCE between variables of different types allows a variable of one type to refer to a value of a different type, without the system being able to check the type of the value when one of the EQUIVALENCEd variables is referenced or assigned. In fact, type checking of EQUIVALENCEd variables would eliminate most of their usefulness.

Pascal is nearly strongly typed, but it fails in its design of variant records because it allows omission of the tag that stores the current type of a variable, which provides the means of checking for the correct value types. We discuss variant records and their potential problems in Chapter 5.

Ada is nearly strongly typed. References to variables in variant records are dynamically checked for correct type values. This is much better than Pascal and Modula-2, in which checking is not even possible, much less required. However, Ada allows programmers to breach the Ada type-checking rules by specifically requesting that type checking be suspended for a particular type conversion. This temporary suspension of type checking can be done only when the library function UNCHECKED_CONVERSION is used. This function, of which there can be a version for every data type, takes a variable of its type as its parameter and returns the bit string that is the current value of that variable. No actual conversion takes place; it is merely a means of extracting the value of a variable of one type and using it as if it were of a different type. This can be useful for user-defined storage allocation and deallocation operations, in which addresses are manipulated as integers but must be used as pointers. Because no checking is done in UNCHECKED_CONVERSION, it is the programmer's responsibility to ensure that the use of a value gotten from it is meaningful.

Modula-3 has a predefined procedure named LOOPHOLE that serves the same purpose as Ada's UNCHECKED_CONVERSION.

C and C++ are not strongly typed languages because both allow functions for which parameters are not type checked. Furthermore, the union types of these languages are not type checked.

ML is strongly typed but in a slightly different sense than that of the imperative languages. ML has variables whose types are all statically known, either from declarations or from its type inference rules, as discussed in Section 4.4.2.3.

Java, although it is loosely based on C++, is strongly typed in the same sense as Ada. Types can be explicitly cast, which could result in a type error. However, there are no implicit ways type errors can go undetected.

The coercion rules of a language have an important effect on the value of type checking. For example, expressions are strongly typed in Pascal. However, an arithmetic operator with one floating-point (named **real** in Pascal) operand and one integer operand is legal. The value of the integer operand is coerced to floating-point, and a floating-point operation takes place. This is what is usually intended by the programmer. However, the coercion also results in a loss of part of the reason for strong typing—error detection. So, the value of strong typing is weakened by coercion. Languages with a great deal of coercion, like FORTRAN, C, and C++, are significantly less reliable than those with little coercion, such as Ada. Java has half as many kinds of type coercions as C++. The issue of coercion is examined in detail in Chapter 6.

4.7 Type Compatibility

The idea of type compatibility was defined when the issue of type checking was introduced. In this section, we investigate the various kinds of type compatibility rules of languages. The design of the type compatibility rules of a language is important, because it influences the design of the data types and the operations provided for values of those types. Perhaps the most important result of two variables being of compatible types is that either one can have its value assigned to the other.

There are two different type compatibility methods: name compatibility and structure compatibility. **Name type compatibility** means that two variables have compatible types only if they are in either the same declaration or in declarations that use the same type name. **Structure type compatibility** means that two variables have compatible types if their types have identical structures. There are some variations of these two methods, and most languages use combinations of the different techniques.

Name type compatibility is easy to implement but is highly restrictive. Under a strict interpretation, a variable that is a subrange of the integers would not be compatible with an integer type variable. For example, supposing Pascal used strict name type compatibility, consider the following:

```
type indextype = 1..100;  { a subrange type }
var
  count : integer;
  index : indextype;
```

The variables count and index would not be compatible; count could not be assigned to index or vice versa.

Another problem with name type compatibility arises when a structured type is passed among subprograms through parameters. Such a type must be defined only once, globally. A subprogram cannot state the type of such formal parameters in local terms. This is the case with the original version of Pascal.

Structure type compatibility is more flexible than name type compatibility, but it is more difficult to implement. Under name type compatibility, only the two type names must be compared to determine compatibility. Under structure type compatibility, however, the entire structures of the two types must be compared. This comparison is not always simple. (Consider a data structure that refers to its own type, such as a linked list.) Other questions can also arise. For example, are two record or structure types compatible if they have the same structure but different field names? Are two single-dimensioned array types in a Pascal or Ada program compatible if they have the same element type but have subscript ranges of `0..10` and `1..11`? Are two enumeration types compatible if they have the same number of components but spell the literals differently?

Another difficulty with structure type compatibility is that it disallows differentiating between types with the same structure. For example, consider the following Pascal-like declarations:

```
type celsius = real;
     fahrenheit = real;
```

Variables of these two types are considered compatible under structure type compatibility, allowing them to be mixed in expressions, which is surely undesirable in this case. In general, types with different names are likely to be abstractions of different categories of problem values and should not be considered equivalent.

The original definition of Pascal (Wirth, 1971) does not specify clearly when name or structure type compatibility is to be used. This is highly detrimental to portability, because a program that is correct in one implementation could be illegal in another. The ISO Standard Pascal (ISO, 1982) clearly states the type compatibility rules of the language, which are neither completely by name nor completely by structure. Structure is used in most cases, while name is used for formal parameters and a few other situations. For example, consider the following declarations:

```
type
  type1 = array [1..10] of integer;
  type2 = array [1..10] of integer;
  type3 = type2;
```

In this example, `type1` and `type2` are not compatible, demonstrating that structure type compatability is not used. Furthermore, `type2` *is* compatible with `type3`, illustrating that name equivalence is not strictly used either. This form of compatibility is sometimes called **declaration equivalence,** because when a type is defined with the name of another type, the two are compatible, even though they are not name type compatible.

Ada uses name type compatibility but provides two type constructs, subtypes and derived types, that avoid the problems with that method. A **derived type** is a new type that is based on some previously defined type, with which it is incompatible, although it may have identical structure. Derived types inherit all the properties of their parent types. Consider the following example:

```
type celsius is new FLOAT;
type fahrenheit is new FLOAT;
```

Variables of these two derived types are not compatible, although their structures are identical. Furthermore, variables of neither type are compatible with any other floating-point type. Literals are exempt from the rule. A literal such as 3.0 has the type universal real and is compatible with any floating-point type. Derived types can also include range constraints on the parent type, while still inheriting all of the parent's operations.

An Ada **subtype** is a possibly range-constrained version of an existing type. A subtype is compatible with its parent type. For example, consider the following declaration:

```
subtype SMALL_TYPE is INTEGER range 0..99;
```

Variables of type SMALL_TYPE are compatible with INTEGER variables.

Type compatibility rules for Ada are more important than those for languages that have many coercions among types. For example, the two operands of an addition operator in C can have virtually any combination of numeric types in the language. One of the operands will simply be coerced to the type of the other. But in Ada, there are no coercions of the operands of an arithmetic operator.

C uses structural equivalence for all types except structures (C's records) and unions, for which C uses declaration equivalence. This rule changes, however, when two structures or unions are defined in two different files. In that case, structural type equivalence is used.

C++ uses name equivalence. Note that **typedef** in C and C++ does not introduce a new type. It simply defines a new name for an existing type.

Variables can be declared in many languages without using type names, creating anonymous types. Consider the following Ada examples:

```
A : array (1..10) of INTEGER;
```

In this case, A has an anonymous but unique type. If we also had

```
B : array (1..10) of INTEGER;
```

A and B would be of anonymous but distinct and incompatible types, though they are structurally identical. The multiple declaration

```
C, D : array (1..10) of INTEGER;
```

creates two anonymous types, one for C and one for D, which are incompatible. This declaration is actually treated as if it were the following two declarations:

```
C : array (1..10) of INTEGER;
D : array (1..10) of INTEGER;
```

The result of this is that C and D are not compatible. If we had written instead

```
type LIST_10 is array (1..10) of INTEGER;
C, D : LIST_10;
```

then C and D would be compatible.

In languages that do not allow users to define and name types, such as FORTRAN and COBOL, name equivalence obviously cannot be used.

Object-oriented languages such as Java and C++ bring another kind of type compatibility issue with them. The issue is object compatibility and its relationship to the inheritance hierarchy. This is discussed in Chapter 11.

Type compatibility in expressions is discussed in Chapter 6; type compatibility for subprogram parameters is discussed in Chapter 8.

4.8 Scope

One of the most important factors having an effect on the understanding of variables is scope. The **scope** of a program variable is the range of statements in which the variable is visible. A variable is **visible** in a statement if it can be referenced in that statement.

The scope rules of a language determine how a particular occurrence of a name is associated with a variable. In particular, scope rules determine how references to variables declared outside the currently executing subprogram or block are associated with their declarations and thus their attributes (blocks are discussed in Section 4.8.2). A complete knowledge of these rules for a language is therefore essential to our ability to write or read programs in that language.

As defined in Section 4.4.3.2, a variable is local in a program unit or block if it is declared there. (For this chapter, we consider program units to be either main program units or subprograms. Units such as C++ and Java classes are discussed in Chapter 10.) The **nonlocal variables** of a program unit or block are those that are visible within the program unit or block but are not declared there.

4.8.1 Static Scope

ALGOL 60 introduced the method of binding names to nonlocal variables, called **static scoping,** which has been copied by most subsequent imperative languages, and many nonimperative languages as well. Static scoping is thus named because the scope of a variable can be statically determined, that is, prior to execution.

Most individual static scopes in imperative languages are associated with program unit definitions, and for now we assume that *all* scopes are associated with program units. In this chapter, we also assume that scoping is the only method of accessing nonlocal variables in the languages under discussion. This is not true for all languages. It is not even true for all languages that use static scoping, but the assumption simplifies the discussion here. Additional methods of accessing nonlocals are discussed in Chapter 8.

In many languages, subprograms create their own scopes. In all common static-scoped languages except C, C++, Java, and FORTRAN, subprograms can be nested inside other subprograms, which can create a hierarchy of scopes in a program.

When a reference to a variable is found by a compiler for a static-scoped language, the attributes of the variable are determined by finding the statement in which it is declared. In static scoped languages with nested subprograms, this process can be thought of in the following way. Suppose a reference is made to a variable x in subprogram sub1. The correct declaration is found by first searching the declarations of subprogram sub1. If no declaration is found for the variable there, the search continues in the declarations of the subprogram that declared subprogram sub1, which is called its **static parent.** If a declaration of x is not found there, the search continues to the next larger enclosing unit (the unit that declared sub1's parent), and so forth, until a declaration for x is found or the largest unit's declarations have been searched without success. In that case, an undeclared variable error has been detected. The static parent of subprogram sub1, and its static parent, and so forth up to and including the main program, are called the **static ancestors** of sub1. Note that implementation techniques for static scoping, which are discussed in Chapter 9, are much more efficient than the process just described.

Consider the following Pascal procedure:

```
procedure big;
  var x : integer;
  procedure sub1;
    begin   { sub1 }
    ...x...
    end;   { sub1 }
  procedure sub2;
    var x : integer;
    begin   { sub2 }
    ...
    end;   { sub2 }
  begin   { big }
  ...
  end;   { big }
```

Under static scoping, the reference to the variable x in sub1 is to the x declared in the procedure big. This is true because the search for x begins in the procedure in which the reference occurs, sub1, but no declaration for x is found there. The search thus continues in the static parent of sub1, big, where the declaration of x is found.

The presence of predefined names, which are discussed in Section 4.2.3, complicates this process somewhat. In some cases, a predefined name is like a keyword and can be redefined by the user. In such cases, a predefined name is used only if the user program does not contain a redefinition. In other cases, a predefined name may be reserved, which means the search for the meaning of a given name begins with the list of predefined names, even before the local scope declarations are checked.

In languages that use static scoping, some variable declarations can be hidden from some subprograms. For example, consider the following skeletal Pascal program:

```
program main;
  var x : integer;
  procedure sub1;
    var x : integer;
    begin   { sub1 }
    ...x...
    end;   { sub1 }
  begin   { main }
  ...
  end.   { main }
```

The reference to x in sub1 is to sub1's declared x. In this case, the x of the main program is hidden from the code of sub1. In general, a declaration for a variable effectively hides any declaration of a variable with the same name in a larger enclosing scope.

In Ada, hidden variables from ancestor scopes can be accessed with selective references, which include the ancestor scope's name. For example, in the preceding program, the x declared in the main program can be accessed in sub1 by the reference main.x.

Although C and C++ do not allow subprograms to be nested inside other subprogram definitions, they do have global variables. These variables are declared outside any subprogram definition. Local variables can hide these globals, as in Pascal. In C++, such hidden globals can be accessed using the scope operator (::). For example, if x is a global that is hidden in a subprogram by a local named x, the global could be referenced as ::x.

4.8.2 Blocks

Many languages allow new static scopes to be defined in the midst of executable code. This powerful concept, introduced in ALGOL 60, allows a section of code to have its own local variables whose scope is minimized. Such variables are typically stack dynamic, so they have their storage allocated when the section is entered and deallocated when the section is exited. Such a section of code is called a **block.**

In Ada, blocks are specified with **declare** clauses, as in

```
...
declare TEMP : integer;
  begin
  TEMP := FIRST;
  FIRST := SECOND;
  SECOND := TEMP;
  end;
...
```

Blocks provide the origin of the phrase **block-structured language.** Although Pascal and Modula-2 are called block-structured languages, they do not include nonprocedural blocks.

C, C++, and Java allow any compound statement (a statement sequence surrounded by matched braces) to have declarations and thus define a new scope. Such compound statements are blocks. For example, if list were an integer array, one could write

```
if (list[i] < list[j]) {
  int temp;
  temp = list[i];
  list[i] = list[j];
  list[j] = temp;
}
```

The scopes created by blocks are treated exactly like those created by subprograms. References to variables in a block that are not declared there are connected to declarations by searching enclosing scopes in order of increasing size.

C++ and Java allow variable definitions to appear anywhere in functions. When a definition appears at a position other than at the beginning of a function, that variable's scope is from its definition statement to the end of the function.

The **for** statements of C++ and Java allow variable definitions in their initialization expressions. In early versions of C++, the scope of such a variable was from its definition to the end of the smallest enclosing block. In the draft standard version, however, the scope is restricted to the **for** construct, as is the case with Java.

The class and method definitions in object-oriented languages also create nested static scopes. This is discussed in Chapter 11.

4.8.3   Evaluation of Static Scoping

Static scoping provides a method of nonlocal access that works well in many situations. However, it is not without its problems. Consider the program whose skeletal structure is shown in Figure 4.1. For this example,

Figure 4.1
The structure of a
program

Figure 4.2
The tree structure
of the program in
Figure 4.1

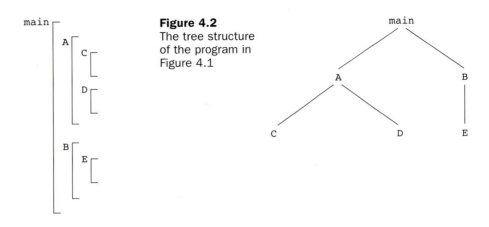

assume that all scopes are created by the definitions of the main program and the procedures.

This program contains an overall scope for `main`, with two procedures that define scopes inside `main`, A and B. Inside A are scopes for the procedures C and D. Inside B is the scope of procedure E. We assume that the necessary data and procedure access determined the structure of this program. The required procedure access is as follows: `main` can call A and B, A can call C and D, and B can call A and E.

It is convenient to view the structure of the program as a tree in which each node represents a procedure and thus a scope. A tree representation of the program of Figure 4.1 is shown in Figure 4.2. The structure of this program may appear to be a very natural program organization that clearly reflects the design needs. However, a graph of the potential procedure calls of this system, shown in Figure 4.3, shows that a great deal of calling opportunity beyond that required is possible.

Figure 4.4 shows the desired calls of the example program. The difference between Figures 4.3 and 4.4 illustrates the number of possible calls that are not necessary in this specific application.

Figure 4.3
The potential call
graph of the program
in Figure 4.1

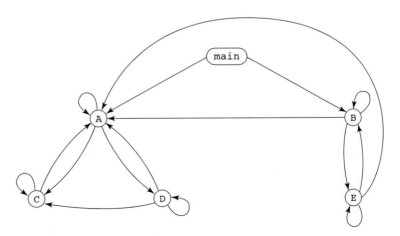

Figure 4.4
The graph of the de-
sirable calls in the
program in Figure 4.1

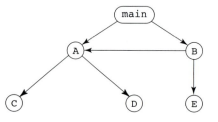

A programmer could mistakenly call a subprogram that should not have been callable, which would not be detected as an error by the compiler. That delays detection of the error until run time, which may make its correction more costly. Therefore, access to procedures should be restricted to those that are necessary.

Too much data access is a closely related problem. For example, all variables declared in the main program are visible to all of the procedures, whether or not that is desired, and there is no way to avoid it.

To illustrate another kind of problem with static scoping, consider the following scenario. Suppose that after the program has been developed and tested, a modification of its specification is required. In particular, suppose that procedure E must now gain access to some variables of the scope of D. One way to provide that access is to move E inside the scope of D. But then E can no longer access the scope of B, which it presumably needs (otherwise, why was it there?). Another solution is to move the variables defined in D that are needed by E into main. This would allow access by all the procedures, which would be more than is needed and thus creates the possibility of incorrect accesses. For example, a misspelled identifier in a procedure can be taken as a reference to an identifier in some enclosing scope, instead of being detected as an error. Furthermore, suppose the variable that is moved to main is named x, and x is needed by D and E. But suppose that there is a variable named x declared in A. That would hide the correct x from its original owner, D.

One final problem with moving the declaration of x to main is that it is harmful to readability to have the declaration of variables so far from their uses.

The problems associated with variable visibility with static scoping are also present for subprogram access. In the tree of Figure 4.2, suppose that, due to some specification change, procedure E needed to call procedure D. This could only be accomplished by moving D to nest directly in main, assuming that it was also needed by either A or C. It would then also lose access to the variables defined in A. This solution, when used repeatedly, results in programs that begin with long lists of low-level utility procedures.

Thus getting around the restrictions of static scoping can lead to program designs that bear little resemblance to the original, even in areas of the program in which changes have not been made. Designers are encouraged to use far more globals than are necessary. All procedures can end up being nested at the same level, in the main program, using globals instead of deeper levels of nesting. Moreover, the final design may be awkward and contrived, and it may not reflect the underlying conceptual design. These and other defects of static scoping are discussed in detail in Clarke, Wileden, and Wolf (1980). One solution to the problems of static scoping is an encapsulation construct, discussed in Chapter 8, which is included in many newer languages.

4.8.4 Dynamic Scope

The scope of variables in APL, SNOBOL4, and the early versions of LISP is dynamic. **Dynamic scoping** is based on the calling sequence of subprograms, not on their spatial relationship to each other. Thus the scope can be determined only at run time.

Consider again the procedure `big` from Section 4.8.1, which is shown again here:

```
procedure big;
  var x : integer;
  procedure sub1;
    begin  { sub1 }
    ... x ...
    end;  { sub1 }
  procedure sub2;
    var x : integer;
    begin  { sub2 }
    ...
    end;  { sub2 }
  begin  { big }
  ...
  end;  { big }
```

Assume that dynamic scoping rules apply to nonlocal references. The meaning of the identifier x referenced in `sub1` is dynamic—it cannot be determined at compile time. It may reference the variable from either declaration of x, depending on the calling sequence.

One way the correct meaning of x can be determined at run time is to begin the search with the local declarations. This is also the way static scoping began, but that is where the similarity between the two techniques ends. When the search of local declarations fails, the declarations of the dynamic parent, or calling procedure, are searched. If a declaration for x is not found there, the search continues in that procedure's dynamic parent, and so forth, until a declaration for x is found. If none is found in any dynamic ancestor, it is a run-time error.

Consider the two different call sequences for `sub1` in the example above. First, `big` calls `sub2`, which calls `sub1`. In this case, the search proceeds from the local procedure, `sub1`, to its caller, `sub2`, where a declaration for `x` is found. So the reference to `x` in `sub1` in this case is to the `x` declared in `sub2`. Next, `sub1` is called directly from `big`. In this case, the dynamic parent of `sub1` is `big`, and the reference is to the `x` declared in `big`.

4.8.5 Evaluation of Dynamic Scoping

The effect of dynamic scoping on programming is profound. The correct attributes of nonlocal variables visible to a program statement cannot be determined statically. Furthermore, such variables are not always the same. A statement in a subprogram that contains a reference to a nonlocal variable can refer to different nonlocal variables during different executions of the subprogam. Several kinds of programming problems follow directly from dynamic scoping.

First, during the time span beginning when a subprogram begins its execution and ending when that execution ends, the local variables of the subprogram are all visible to any other executing subprogram, regardless of its textual proximity. There is no way to protect local variables from this accessibility. Subprograms are *always* executed in the immediate environment of the caller; therefore, dynamic scoping results in less reliable programs than static scoping.

A second problem with dynamic scoping is the inability to statically type check references to nonlocals. This results from the inability to statically determine the declaration for a variable referenced as a nonlocal.

Dynamic scoping also makes programs much more difficult to read, because the calling sequence of subprograms must be known to determine the meaning of references to nonlocal variables. This can be virtually impossible for a human reader.

Finally, accesses to nonlocal variables in dynamic scoped languages take far longer than accesses to nonlocals when static scoping is used. The reason for this is explained in Chapter 9.

On the other hand, dynamic scoping is not without merit. In some cases, the parameters passed from one subprogram to another are simply variables that are defined in the caller. None of these need to be passed in a dynamically scoped language, because they are implicitly visible in the called subprogram.

It is not difficult to understand why dynamic scoping is not as widely used as static scoping. Programs in static scoped languages are easier to read, more reliable, and execute faster than equivalent programs in dynamic scoped languages. It was precisely for these reasons that dynamic scoping was replaced by static scoping in most current dialects of LISP. Implementation methods for both static and dynamic scoping are discussed in Chapter 9.

4.9 Scope and Lifetime

Sometimes the scope and lifetime of a variable appear to be related. For example, consider a variable that is declared in a Pascal procedure that contains no subprogram calls. The scope of such a variable is from its declaration to the **end** reserved word of the procedure. The lifetime of that variable is the period of time beginning when the procedure is entered and ending when execution of the procedure reaches the **end** (Pascal has no return statement). Although the scope and lifetime of the variable are clearly not the same because static scope is a textual, or spatial, concept whereas lifetime is a temporal concept, they at least appear to be related in this case.

This apparent relationship between scope and lifetime does not hold in other situations. In C and C++, for example, a variable that is declared in a function using the specifier **static** is statically bound to the scope of that function and is also statically bound to storage. So its scope is static and local to the function, but its lifetime extends over the entire execution of the program of which it is a part.

Scope and lifetime are also unrelated when subprogram calls are involved. Consider the following C++ functions:

```
void printheader() {
  ...
}  /* end of printheader */
void compute() {
  int sum;
  ...
  printheader();
}  /* end of compute */
```

The scope of the variable `sum` is completely contained within the `compute` function. It does not extend to the body of the function `printheader`, although `printheader` executes in the midst of the execution of `compute`. However, the lifetime of `sum` extends over the time during which `printheader` executes. Whatever storage location `sum` is bound to before the call to `printheader`, that binding will continue during and after the execution of `printheader`.

4.10 Referencing Environments

The **referencing environment** of a statement is the collection of all names that are visible in the statement. The referencing environment of a statement in a static-scoped language is the variables declared in its local scope plus the collection of all variables of its ancestor scopes that are visible. In such a language, the referencing environment of a statement is needed while that statement is being compiled, so code and data structures can be created to allow references to variables from other scopes during run time. Techniques for implementing references to nonlocal variables in both static- and dynamic-scoped languages are discussed in Chapter 9.

In Pascal, where scopes are created only by procedure definitions, the referencing environment of a statement includes the local variables, plus all of the variables declared in the procedures in which the statement is nested, plus the variables declared in the main program (excluding variables in nonlocal scopes that are hidden by declarations in nearer procedures). Each procedure definition creates a new scope and thus a new environment. Consider the following Pascal skeletal program:

```
program example;
  var a, b : integer;
  ...
  procedure sub1;
    var x, y : integer;
    begin  { sub1 }
    ...    ←——————————-1
    end;   { sub1 }
  procedure sub2;
    var x : integer;
    ...
    procedure sub3;
      var x : integer;
      begin  { sub3 }
      ...    ←——————————-2
      end;   { sub3 }
    begin  { sub2 }
    ...    ←——————————-3
    end;   { sub2 }
  begin  { example }
  ...    ←——————————-4
  end.   { example }
```

The referencing environments of the indicated program points are as follows:

Point	Referencing Environment
1	x and y of sub1, a and b of example
2	x of sub3, (x of sub2 is hidden), a and b of example
3	x of sub2, a and b of example
4	a and b of example

Now consider the variable declarations of this skeletal program. First note that, although the scope of sub1 is at a higher level (it is less deeply nested) than sub3, the scope of sub1 is not a static ancestor of sub3, so sub3 does not have access to the variables declared in sub1. There is a good reason for this. The variables declared in `sub1` are stack-dynamic, so they are not bound to storage if `sub1` is not in execution. Because `sub3` can be in execution when `sub1` is not, it cannot be allowed to access variables in `sub1`, which would not necessarily be bound to storage during the execution of `sub3`.

A subprogram is **active** if its execution has begun but has not yet terminated. The referencing environment of a statement in a dynamically scoped language is the locally declared variables, plus the variables of all other subprograms that are currently active. Once again, some variables in active subprograms can be hidden from the referencing environment. Recent subprogram activations can have declarations for variables that hide variables with the same names in previous subprogram activations.

Consider the following example program. Assume that the only function calls are the following: `main` calls `sub2`, which calls `sub1`.

```
void sub1() {
  int a, b;
  ... ←——————————-1
}  /* end of sub1 */
void sub2() {
  int b, c;
  ... ←——————————-2
  sub1;
}  /* end of sub2 */
void main() {
  int c, d;
  ... ←——————————-3
  sub2();
}  /* end of main */
```

The referencing environments of the indicated program points are as follows:

Point	Referencing Environment
1	a and b of `sub1` , c of `sub2`, d of `main`, , (c of `main` and b of `sub2` are hidden)
2	b and c of `sub2`, d of `main`, (c of `main` is hidden)
3	c and d of `main`

4.11 Named Constants

A **named constant** is a variable that is bound to a value only at the time it is bound to storage; its value cannot be changed by assignment or by an input statement. Named constants are useful as aids to readability and program reliability. Readability can be improved, for example, by using the name `pi` instead of the constant `3.14159`.

Another advantageous use of named constants is in programs that process a fixed number of data values, say 100. Such programs usually use the constant 100 in a number of locations for declaring array subscript ranges, for loop control limits, and other uses. Consider the following skeletal Pascal program segment:

```pascal
program example;
  type
    intarray = array [1..100] of integer;
    realarray = array [1..100] of real;
  ...
  begin  { example }
  ...
  for index := 1 to 100 do
    begin
    ...
    end;
  ...
  for count := 1 to 100 do
    begin
    ...
    end;
  ...
  average := sum div 100;
  ...
  end.  { example }
```

When this program must be modified to deal with a different number of data values, all occurrences of 100 must be found and changed. On a large program, this can be tedious and error-prone. An easier and more reliable method is to use a named constant, as in

```pascal
program example;
  const listlen = 100;
  type
    intarray = array [1..listlen] of integer;
    realarray = array [1..listlen] of real;
  ...
  begin  { example }
  ...
  for index := 1 to listlen do
    begin
    ...
    end;
  ...
  for count := 1 to listlen do
    begin
    ...
    end;
  ...
  average := sum div listlen;
  ...
  end.  { example }
```

Now when the length must be changed, only one line must be changed, regardless of the number of times it is used in the program. This is another example of the benefits of abstraction. The name listlen is an abstraction for the number of elements in some arrays and the number of iterations in some loops. This illustrates how named constants can aid modifiability.

Pascal named constant declarations require simple values on the right side of the = operator. However, Modula-2 and FORTRAN 90 allow constant expressions to be used. These constant expressions can contain previously declared named constants, constant values, and operators. The reason for the restriction to constants and constant expressions in Pascal and Modula-2, respectively, is that both use static binding of values to named constants. Named constants in languages that use static binding of values are sometimes called **manifest constants.**

Ada, C++, and Java allow dynamic binding of values to named constants. This allows expressions containing variables to be assigned to constants in the declarations. For example, the Ada statement

```
MAX : constant integer := 2 * WIDTH + 1;
```

declares MAX to be an integer type named constant whose value is set to the value of the expression 2 * WIDTH + 1, where the value of the variable WIDTH must be visible when MAX is allocated and bound to its value. Ada also allows named constants of enumeration and structured types, which are discussed in Chapter 5.

4.12 Variable Initialization

The discussion of binding values to named constants naturally leads to the topic of initialization of variables, because binding a value to a named constant is the same process, except it is permanent.

In many instances, it is convenient for variables to have values before the code of the program or subprogram in which they are declared begins executing. The binding of a variable to a value at the time it is bound to storage is called **initialization.** If the variable is statically bound to storage, binding and initialization occur before run time. If the storage binding is dynamic, initialization is also dynamic.

In FORTRAN, initial values of variables can be specified in a DATA statement, as in

```
REAL PI
INTEGER SUM
DATA SUM /0/, PI /3.14159/
```

which initializes SUM to zero and PI to 3.14159. The actual initializations take place at compile time, in this case. Once execution begins, SUM and PI are like any other variables.

In many languages, initial values of variables can be specified in the declaration statement, as in the Ada declaration

```
SUM : INTEGER := 0;
```

Neither Pascal nor Modula-2 provides a way to initialize variables, except at run time with assignment statements.

In general, initialization occurs only once for static variables, but it occurs with every allocation for dynamically allocated variables, such as the local variables in an Ada procedure.

SUMMARY

The form of the names of a language can impact both the readability and writability of the language. The relationship of names to special words, which are either reserved words or keywords, is also a significant design decision.

Variables can be characterized by the sextuple of attributes: name, address, value, type, lifetime, scope.

Aliases are two or more names bound to the same storage address. They are regarded as detrimental to reliability, but are difficult to eliminate entirely from a language.

Binding is the association of attributes with program entities. Knowledge of the binding times of attributes to entities is essential to understanding the semantics of programming languages. Binding can be static or dynamic. Declarations, either explicit or implicit, provide a means of specifying the static binding of variables to types. In general, dynamic binding allows greater flexibility but at the expense of readability, efficiency, and reliability.

Scalar variables can be separated into four categories by considering their lifetimes. These are static, stack-dynamic, explicit heap-dynamic, and implicit heap-dynamic.

Strong typing is the concept of requiring that all type errors be detected. The advantage of strong typing is increased reliability.

The type compatibility rules of a language have an important effect on the operations provided for the values in the language. Type compatibility is generally defined in terms of name compatibility or structure compatibility.

Static scoping is a central feature of ALGOL 60 and most of its descendants. It provides an efficient method of allowing visibility of nonlocal variables in subprograms. Dynamic scoping provides more flexibility than static scoping but, again, at the expense of readability, reliability, and efficiency.

The referencing environment of a statement is the collection of all of the variables that are visible to that statement.

Named constants are simply variables that are bound to values only when they are bound to storage. Initialization is the binding of a variable to a value at the time the variable is bound to storage.

1. What are the design issues for names?
2. What is the potential danger of case-sensitive names?
3. In what way are reserved words better than keywords?
4. What is an alias?
5. Which category of C++ reference variables are always aliases?
6. What is the *l*-value of a variable? What is the *r*-value?
7. Define *binding* and *binding time*.
8. After language design and implementation, what are the four times bindings can take place in a program?
9. Define *static binding* and *dynamic binding*.
10. What are the advantages and disadvantage of implicit declarations?
11. What are the advantages and disadvantages of dynamic type binding?
12. Define *static, stack-dynamic, explicit heap-dynamic,* and *implicit heap-dynamic variables.* What are the advantages and disadvantages of these?
13. Define *coercion, type error, type checking,* and *strong typing.*
14. Define *name type compatibility* and *structure type compatibility.* What are the relative merits of these two?
15. What is the difference between an Ada derived type and an Ada subtype?
16. Define *lifetime, scope, static scope,* and *dynamic scope.*
17. How is a reference to a nonlocal variable in a static-scoped program connected to its definition?
18. What is the general problem with static scoping?
19. What is the referencing environment of a statement?
20. What is a static ancestor of a subprogram? What is a dynamic ancestor of a subprogram?
21. What is a block?
22. What are the advantages and disadvantages of dynamic scoping?
23. What are the advantages of named constants?

1. Decide which of the following identifier forms is most readable, and then support that decision.

   ```
   SumOfSales
   sum_of_sales
   SUMOFSALES
   ```

2. Some programming languages are typeless. What are the obvious advantages and disadvantages of having no types in a language?

3. One common use of FORTRAN's **EQUIVALENCE** is the following: A large array of numeric values is made available to a subprogram as a parameter. The

array contains many different unrelated variables, rather than a collection of repetitions of the same variable. It is represented as an array to reduce the number of names that need to be passed as parameters. Within the subprogram, a lengthy **EQUIVALENCE** statement is used to create connotative names as aliases to the various array elements, which increases the readability of the code of the subprogram. Is this a good idea or not? What alternatives to aliasing are available?

4. Write a simple assignment statement with one arithmetic operator in some language you know. For each component of the statement, list the various bindings that are required to determine the semantics when the statement is executed. For each binding, indicate the binding time used for the language.

5. Dynamic type binding is closely related to implicit heap-dynamic variables. Explain this relationship.

6. Describe a situation when a history-sensitive variable in a subprogram is useful.

7. Look up the definition of *strongly typed* as given in Gehani (1983) and compare it with the definition given in this chapter. How do they differ?

8. Consider the following Pascal skeletal program.

```
program main;
   var x : integer;
   procedure sub3; forward;
   procedure sub1;
      var x : integer;
      procedure sub2;
        begin   { sub2 }
        ...
        end;   { sub2 }
      begin   { sub1 }
      ...
      end;   { sub1 }
   procedure sub3;
      begin   { sub3 }
      ...
      end;   { sub3 }
   begin   { main }
   ...
   end.   { main }
```

Assume that the execution of this program is in the following unit order:

main calls sub1
sub1 calls sub2
sub2 calls sub3

a. Assuming static scoping, which declaration of **x** is the correct one for a reference to **x** in:

   i. sub1
   ii. sub2
   iii. sub3

b. Repeat part a, but assume dynamic scoping.

9. Assume the following program was compiled and executed using static scoping rules. What value of **x** is printed in procedure **sub1**? Under dynamic scoping rules, what value of **x** is printed in procedure **sub1**?

```
program main;
  var x : integer;
  procedure sub1;
    begin   { sub1 }
    writeln('x =', x)
    end;   { sub1 }
  procedure sub2;
    var x : integer;
    begin   { sub2 }
    x := 10;
    sub1
    end;   { sub2 }
  begin   { main }
  x := 5;
  sub2
  end.   { main }
```

10. Consider the following program:

```
program main;
  var x, y, z : integer;
  procedure sub1;
    var a, y, z : integer;
    procedure sub2;
     var a, b, z : integer;
     begin   { sub2 }
     ...
     end;   { sub2 }
    begin   { sub1 }
    ...
    end;   { sub1 }
  procedure sub3;
    var a, x, w : integer;
    begin   { sub3 }
    ...
    end;   { sub3 }
  begin   { main }
  ...
  end.   { main }
```

List all the variables, along with the program units where they are declared, that are visible in the bodies of **sub1**, **sub2**, and **sub3**, assuming static scoping is used.

11. Consider the following program:

```
program main;
  var x, y, z : integer;
  procedure sub1;
    var a, y, z : integer;
    begin   { sub1 }
    ...
    end;   { sub1 }
  procedure sub2;
    var a, x, w : integer;
    procedure sub3;
      var a, b, z : integer;
      begin   { sub3 }
      ...
      end;   { sub3 }
    begin   { sub2 }
    ...
    end;   { sub2 }
  begin   { main }
  ...
  end.   { main }
```

List all the variables, along with the program units where they are declared, that are visible in the bodies of **sub1**, **sub2**, and **sub3**, assuming static scoping is used.

12. Consider the following C program:

```
void fun(void) {
  int a, b, c; /* definition 1 */
  ...
  while (...) {
    int b, c, d; /*definition 2 */
    ...  ←——————————1
    while (...) {
    int c, d, e; /* definition 3 */
      ...  ←——————————2
    }
    ...  ←——————————3
  }
  ...  ←——————————4
}
```

For each of the four marked points in this function, list each visible variable, along with the number of the definition statement that defines it.

13. Consider the following skeletal C program.

```
void fun1(void);   /* prototype */
void fun2(void);   /* prototype */
void fun3(void);   /* prototype */
void main() {
```

```
    int a, b, c;
    ...
  }
void fun1(void) {
  int b, c, d;
  ...
  }
void fun2(void) {
  int c, d, e;
  ...
  }
void fun3(void) {
  int d, e, f;
  ...
  }
```

Given the following calling sequences and assuming that dynamic scoping is used, what variables are visible during execution of the last function called? Include with each visible variable the name of the function in which it was defined.

a. main calls fun1; fun1 calls fun2; fun2 calls fun3.

b. main calls fun1; fun1 calls fun3.

c. main calls fun2; fun2 calls fun3; fun3 calls fun1.

d. main calls fun3; fun3 calls fun1.

e. main calls fun1; fun1 calls fun3; fun3 calls fun2.

f. main calls fun3; fun3 calls fun2; fun2 calls fun1.

14. Consider the following program:

```
program main;
  var x, y, z : integer;
  procedure sub1;
    var a, y, z : integer;
    begin  { sub1 }
    ...
    end;   { sub1 }
  procedure sub2;
    var a, b, z : integer;
    begin  { sub2 }
    ...
    end;   { sub2 }
  procedure sub3;
    var a, x, w : integer;
    begin  { sub3 }
    ...
    end;   { sub3 }
  begin  { main }
  ...
  end.   { main }
```

Given the following calling sequences and assuming that dynamic scoping is used, what variables are visible during execution of the last subprogram activated? Include with each visible variable the name of the unit where it is declared.

a. main calls sub1; sub1 calls sub2; sub2 calls sub3.

b. main calls sub1; sub1 calls sub3.

c. main calls sub2; sub2 calls sub3; sub3 calls sub1.

d. main calls sub3; sub3 calls sub1.

e. main calls sub1; sub1 calls sub3; sub3 calls sub2.

f. main calls sub3; sub3 calls sub2; sub2 calls sub1.

5 Data Types

James Gosling

James Gosling, a Vice President and Fellow at Sun Microsystems, developed the original design of Java and implemented the first compiler and virtual machine for it. Gosling also served as lead engineer of the NeWS window system and designed the EMACS text editor.

This chapter first introduces the concept of a data type and the characteristics of the common primitive data types. Then the designs of enumeration and subrange types are discussed. Next, structured data types, specifically arrays, records, and unions, are investigated. Set types are then discussed, followed by an in-depth look at pointers.

For each of the various categories of data types, the design issues are stated and the design choices made by the designers of the important languages are explained. These designs are then evaluated.

Implementation methods for data types often have a significant impact on their design. Therefore, implementation of the various data types is another important part of this chapter, especially for the implementation of arrays.

5.1 Introduction

Computer programs produce results by manipulating data. An important factor in determining the ease with which they can perform this task is how well the data types match the real-world problem space. It is therefore crucial that a language support an appropriate variety of data types and structures.

The contemporary concepts of data typing have evolved over the last 40 years. In the earliest languages, all problem space data structures had to be modeled with only a few basic language-supported data structures. For example, in pre-90 FORTRANs, linked lists and binary trees are commonly modeled with arrays.

The data structures of COBOL took the first step away from the FORTRAN I model by allowing programmers to specify the accuracy of decimal data values, and also by providing a structured data type for records of information. PL/I extended the capability of accuracy specification to integer and floating-point types. This has since been incorporated in Ada and FORTRAN 90. The designers of PL/I included many data types, with the intent of supporting a large range of applications. A better approach, introduced in ALGOL 68, is to provide a few basic types and a few flexible structure-defining operators that allow a programmer to tailor a structure to the problem at hand with user-defined data types. This was clearly one of the most important advances in the evolution of data type design. User-defined types provide improved readability through the use of meaningful names for types. They allow type checking of the variables of a special category of use, which would otherwise not be possible. User-defined types also aid modifiability: A programmer can change the type of a category of variables in a program by changing only a type declaration statement.

Ada 83 embodied the contemporary concepts in data type design of the late 1970s, which resulted from a natural extension to the idea of user-defined types. The philosophy of user-defined data types is that the user should be allowed to create a unique type for each unique class of variables in the problem space. Moreover, the language must enforce the uniqueness of the types, which are in fact abstractions of the problem space variables. This is a powerful concept, and it has a significant impact on the overall process of software design. Taking this concept a step farther, we arrive at abstract data types, which can be simulated in Ada 83. The fundamental idea of an abstract data type is that the use of a type is separated from the representation and set of operations on values of that type. All of the types provided by a high-level programming language are abstract data types. User-defined abstract data types are discussed in detail in Chapter 10.

The two most common structured (nonscalar) data types are arrays and records. These and a few other data types are specified by type operators, or constructors, which are used to form type expressions. For example, in C the type operators are brackets, parentheses, and asterisks, which are used to specify arrays, functions, and pointers.

It is convenient, both logically and concretely, to think of variables in terms of descriptors. A **descriptor** is the collection of the attributes of a variable. In an implementation, a descriptor is a collection of memory cells that store variable attributes. If the attributes are all static, descriptors are required only at compile time. They are built by the compiler, usually as a part of the symbol table, and are used during compilation. For dynamic attributes, however, part or all of the descriptor must be maintained during execution. In this case, the descriptor is used by the run-time system. In all cases, descriptors are used for type checking and by allocation and deallocation operations.

The word "object" is often associated with the value of a variable and the space it occupies. In this book, however, we reserve the word object exclusively for instances of user-defined abstract data types, rather than also using it for the values of variables of predefined types. In object-oriented languages, every instance of every class, whether predefined or user-defined, is called an object. Objects are discussed in detail in Chapters 10 and 11.

In the following sections all common data types are discussed. For most, design issues particular to the type are stated. For all, one or more example designs are described. One design issue is fundamental to all data types: What operations are provided for variables of the type and how are they specified?

5.2 Primitive Data Types

Data types that are not defined in terms of other types are called **primitive data types.** Nearly all programming languages provide a set of primitive data types. Some of the primitive types are merely reflections of the hardware; for example, integer types. Others require only a little non-hardware support for their implementation.

The primitive data types of a language are used, along with one or more type constructors, to provide the structured types.

5.2.1 Numeric Types

Many early programming languages had only numeric primitive types. These types still play a central role among the types supported by contemporary languages.

5.2.1.1 Integer

The most common primitive numeric data type is **integer.** Many computers now support several sizes of integers, and these capabilities are reflected in some programming languages. For example, Ada allows implementations to include up to three integer sizes: SHORT INTEGER, INTEGER, and LONG INTEGER. Some languages, such as C, include unsigned integer types, which are simply types for integer values without signs.

An integer value is represented in a computer by a string of bits, with one of the bits, typically the leftmost, representing the sign. Integer types are supported directly by the hardware.

A negative integer could be stored in sign-magnitude notation, in which the sign bit is set to indicate negative and the remainder of the bit string represents the absolute value of the number. Sign-magnitude notation, however, does not lend itself to computer arithmetic. Most computers now use a notation called twos complement to store negative integers, which is convenient for addition and subtraction. In twos complement notation, the representation of a negative integer is formed by taking the logical complement of the positive version of the number and adding one. Ones complement notation is still used by some computers. In ones complement notation, the negative of an integer is stored as the logical complement of its absolute value. Ones complement notation has the disadvantage that it has two representations of zero. See any book on assembly language programming for details of integer representations.

5.2.1.2 Floating-Point

Floating-point data types model real numbers, but the representations are only approximations for most real values. For example, neither of the fundamental numbers π or e (the base for the natural logarithms) can be correctly represented in floating-point notation. Of course, neither of these numbers can be accurately represented in any finite space. On most computers, floating-point numbers are stored in binary, which exacerbates the problem. For example, even the value 0.1 in decimal cannot be represented by a finite number of binary digits. Another problem with floating-point types is the loss of accuracy through arithmetic operations. For more information on the problems of floating-point notation, see Knuth (1981).

Floating-point values are represented as fractions and exponents, a form that is borrowed from scientific notation. Older computers used a variety of different representations for floating-point values. However, most newer machines use the IEEE Floating-Point Standard 754 format. Language implementers use whatever representation is supported by the hardware. Most languages include two floating-point types, often called **float** and **double.** The float type is the standard size, usually being stored in four bytes of memory. The double type is provided for situations where larger fractional parts are needed. Double-precision variables usually occupy twice as much storage as float variables and provide at least twice the number of bits of fraction.

The collection of values that can be represented by a floating-point type is defined in terms of precision and range. Precision is the accuracy of the fractional part of a value, measured as the number of bits. Range is a combination of the range of fractions, and, more importantly, the range of exponents.

Figure 5.1 shows the IEEE Floating-Point Standard 754 format for single- and double-precision representation (IEEE, 1985). Details of the IEEE formats can be found in Tanenbaum (1990).

Some smaller computers do not have hardware for floating-point operations. Instead, they emulate these operations in software, which can be 10 to 100 times slower than their hardware counterparts.

5.2.1.3 Decimal

Most larger computers that are designed to support business systems applications have hardware support for **decimal** data types. Decimal data types store a fixed number of decimal digits, with the decimal point at a

Figure 5.1
IEEE floating-point formats: (a) Single precision, (b) Double precision

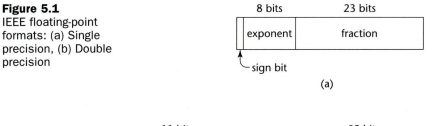

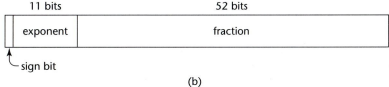

fixed position in the value. These are the primary data types for business data processing and are therefore essential to COBOL.

Decimal types have the advantage of being capable of precisely storing decimal values, at least those within a restricted range, which cannot be done in floating-point. The disadvantages of decimal types are that the range of values is restricted because no exponents are allowed, and their representation in memory is wasteful.

Decimal types are stored very much like character strings, using binary codes for the decimal digits. These representations are called binary coded decimal (BCD). In some cases, they are stored one digit per byte, but in others they are packed two digits per byte. Either way, they take more storage than binary representations. It takes at least 4 bits to code a decimal digit. Therefore, to store a six-digit coded decimal number requires 24 bits of memory. However, it takes only 20 bits to store the same number in binary. The operations on decimal values are done in hardware on machines that have such capabilities; otherwise, they are simulated in software.

5.2.2 Boolean Types

Boolean types are perhaps the simplest of all types. Their range of values has only two elements, one for true and one for false. They were introduced in ALGOL 60 and have been included in most general-purpose languages designed since 1960. One popular exception is C, in which numeric expressions can be used as conditionals. In such expressions, all operands with nonzero values are considered true, and zero is considered false. Although C++ has a Boolean type, it also allows numeric expressions to be used as if they were Boolean.

Boolean types are often used to represent switches or flags in programs. Although other types, such as integers, can be used for these purposes, the use of Boolean types is more readable.

A Boolean value could be represented by a single bit, but because a single bit of memory is difficult to access efficiently on many machines, they are often stored in the smallest efficiently addressable cell of memory, typically a byte.

5.2.3 Character Types

Character data are stored in computers as numeric codings. The most commonly used coding is ASCII (American Standard Code for Information Interchange), which uses the values 0..127 to code 128 different characters. To provide the means of processing codings of single characters, many programming languages include a primitive type for them.

Because of the globalization of business and the need for computers to communicate with other computers around the world, the ASCII character set is rapidly becoming inadequate. A new 16-bit character set named Unicode has recently been developed as an alternative. Unicode includes the characters from most of the world's natural languages. For example, Unicode includes the Cyrillic alphabet, as used in Serbia, and the Thai digits. Java is the first widely used language to use the Unicode character set, but it will surely find its way into other popular languages before long.

5.3 Character String Types

A **character string type** is one in which the values consist of sequences of characters. Character string constants are used to label output, and input and output of all kinds of data is often done in terms of strings. Of course, character strings also are an essential type for all programs that do character manipulation.

5.3.1 Design Issues

The two most important design issues that are specific to character string types are the following:

- Should strings be simply a special kind of character array or a primitive type (with no array-style subscripting operations)?
- Should strings have static or dynamic length?

5.3.2 Strings and Their Operations

If strings are not defined as a primitive type, string data is usually stored in arrays of single characters and referenced as such in the language. This is the approach taken by Pascal, C, C++, and Ada. In Pascal, although strings are not a primitive type, **char** arrays that have the **packed** attribute can be assigned and compared with the relational operators.

In Ada, STRING is a type that is predefined to be single-dimensioned arrays of CHARACTER elements. Substring reference, catenation, relational operators, and assignment are provided for STRING types. Substring reference allows any substring of a given string to be treated as a value in a reference or as a variable in an assignment. A substring reference is denoted by a parenthesized integer range, which indicates the desired substring by character position. For example,

```
NAME1(2:4)
```

specifies the substring consisting of the second, third, and fourth characters of the value in NAME1.

Character string catenation in Ada is an operation specified by the ampersand (`&`). The following statement catenates `NAME2` to the right end of `NAME1`:

```
NAME1 := NAME1 & NAME2;
```

For example, if `NAME1` has the string "`PEACE`" and `NAME2` has "`FUL`", then after the assignment statement is executed, `NAME1` will have the string "`PEACEFUL`".

C and C++ use **char** arrays to store character strings and provide a collection of string operations through a standard library whose header file is `string.h`. Most uses of strings and most of the library functions use the convention that character strings are terminated with a special character, null, which is represented with zero. This is an alternative to maintaining the length of string variables. The library operations simply carry out their operations until the null character appears in the string being operated on. Library functions that construct strings often supply the null character. The character string literals that are built by the compiler have the null character. For example, consider the following declaration:

```
char *str = "apples";
```

In this example, `str` is a **char** pointer set to point at the string of characters, `apples0`, where `0` is the null character. This initialization of `str` is legal because character string literals are represented by **char** pointers, rather than the string itself.

Some of the most commonly used library functions for character strings in C and C++ are `strcpy`, which moves strings; `strcat`, which catenates one given string onto another; `strcmp`, which lexicographically compares (by the order of their codes) two given strings; and `strlen`, which returns the number of characters, not counting the null, in the given string. The parameters and return values for most of the string manipulation functions are **char** pointers that point to arrays of **char**. Parameters can also be string literals.

FORTRAN 77, FORTRAN 90, and BASIC treat strings as a primitive type and provide assignment, relational operators, catenation, and substring reference operations for them.

In Java, strings are supported as a primitive type by the `String` class, whose values are constant strings, and the `StringBuffer` class, whose values are changeable and are more like arrays of single characters. Subscripting is allowed on `StringBuffer` variables.

In general, both assignment and comparison operations on character strings are complicated by the possibility of assigning and comparing operands of different lengths. For example, what happens when a longer string is assigned to a shorter string, or vice versa? Usually, simple and sensible choices are made for these situations, although users often have trouble remembering them.

Pattern matching is another fundamental character string operation. It is often provided by a library function rather than as an operation in the language. There are two important exceptions, one of which is SNOBOL4, which has an elaborate pattern-matching operation built into the language. SNOBOL4 is probably the ultimate string manipulation language.

String patterns in SNOBOL4 are expressions that can be assigned to variables. For example, consider the following:

```
LETTER = 'abcdefghijklmnopqrstuvwxyz'
WORDPAT = BREAK(LETTER) SPAN(LETTER) . WORD
```

`LETTER` is a variable with the value of a string of all lowercase letters. `WORDPAT` is a pattern that describes words as follows: First skip until a letter is found, then span those letters until a nonletter is found. This pattern also includes a "." operator, which specifies that the string that matches the pattern is to be assigned to the variable `WORD`.

This pattern can be used in the statement

```
TEXT WORDPAT
```

which attempts to find a string of letters in the string value of the variable, `TEXT`.

The second important language that includes built-in pattern matching operations is Perl. In this case, the pattern-matching expressions are somewhat loosely based on mathematical regular expressions. In fact, they are often called regular expressions. They evolved from the early UNIX line editor, `ed`, to become part of the UNIX shell languages. Eventually, they grew to their most complex form in Perl. It takes an entire chapter of a Perl book to explain these expressions. In fact, there is now a complete book on this kind of pattern-matching expressions (Friedl, 1997). In this section, we provide only a brief look at the style of these expressions through two relatively simple examples. Consider the following pattern expression:

```
/[A-Za-z][A-Za-z\d]+/
```

This pattern matches (or describes) the typical name form in programming languages. The brackets enclose character classes. The first class specifies all letters; the second specifies all letters and digits (a digit is specified with the abbreviation \d). If only the second class were included, we could not prevent a name from beginning with a digit. The plus operator following the second category specifies that there must be one or more of what is in the category. So, the whole pattern matches strings that begin with a letter, followed by one or more letters or digits.

Next consider the following pattern expression:

```
/\d+\.?\d*|\.\d+/
```

This pattern matches numeric literals. The \. specifies a literal decimal point. The question mark quantifies what it follows to have zero or one appearance. The vertical bar (|) separates two alternatives in the whole pattern. The first alternative matches strings of one or more digits, possibly followed by a decimal point, followed by zero or more digits; the second alternative matches strings that begin with a decimal point, followed by one or more digits.

5.3.3   String Length Options

There are several design choices regarding the length of string values. First, the length can be static and specified in the declaration. Such a string is called a **static length string.** This is the choice in the FORTRAN 77, FORTRAN 90, COBOL, Pascal, and Ada languages. For example, the following FORTRAN 90 statement declares `NAME1` and `NAME2` to be character strings of length 15:

```
CHARACTER(LEN = 15) NAME1, NAME2
```

Static length strings are always full; if a shorter string is assigned to a string variable, the empty characters are usually set to blanks. The second option is to allow strings to have varying length up to a declared and fixed maximum set by the variable's definition, as exemplified by the strings in C and C++. These are called **limited dynamic length strings.** Such string variables can store any number of characters between zero and the maximum. Recall that strings in C and C++ use a special character to indicate the end of the string's characters, rather than maintaining the string length.

The third option is to allow strings to have varying length with no maximum, as in SNOBOL4 and Perl. These are called **dynamic length strings.** This option requires the overhead of dynamic storage allocation and deallocation but provides maximum flexibility.

5.3.4   Evaluation

String types are important to the writability of a language. Dealing with strings as arrays can be more cumbersome than dealing with a primitive string type. The addition of strings as a primitive type to a language is not costly, in terms of either language or compiler complexity. Therefore, it is difficult to justify the omission of primitive string types in some contemporary languages. Of course, the availability of standard libraries of string manipulation subprograms can remove this deficiency when strings are not included as a primitive type.

String operations such as simple pattern matching and catenation are essential and should be included for string type values. Although dynamic length strings are obviously the most flexible, the overhead of their implementation must be weighed against that additional flexibility.

5.3.5 Implementation of Character String Types

Character string types are sometimes supported directly in hardware, but in most cases software is used to implement string storage, retrieval, and manipulation. When character string types are represented as character arrays, the language often supplies few operations.

A descriptor for a static character string type, which is only required during compilation, has three fields. The first field of every descriptor is the name of the type. In the case of static character strings, the second field is the type's length (in characters). The third field is the address of the first character. This descriptor is shown in Figure 5.2. Limited dynamic strings require a run-time descriptor to store both the fixed maximum length and the current length, as shown in Figure 5.3. Dynamic length strings require a simpler run-time descriptor because only the current length needs to be stored.

The limited dynamic strings of C and C++ do not require run-time descriptors because the end of a string is marked with the null character. They do not need the maximum length because index values in array references are not range-checked in these languages.

Static length and limited dynamic length strings require no special dynamic storage allocation. In the case of limited dynamic length strings, sufficient storage for the maximum length is allocated when the string variable is bound to storage, so only a single allocation process is involved. The maximum length is fixed at compile time.

Dynamic length strings require more complex storage management. The length of a string, and therefore the storage to which it is bound, must grow and shrink dynamically.

There are two possible approaches to the dynamic allocation problem. First, strings can be stored in a linked list, so that when a string grows, the newly required cells can come from anywhere in the heap. The drawback to this method is the large amount of storage occupied by the links in the list representation. The alternative is to store complete strings in adjacent storage cells. The problem with this method occurs when a string grows: How can storage that is adjacent to the existing cells continue to be allocated for the string variable? Frequently, such storage is not available. Instead, a new area of memory is found that can store the complete new string, and the old part is moved to this area. Then the memory cells used for the old string are deallocated.

Although the linked-list method requires more storage, the associated allocation and deallocation processes are simple.

Figure 5.2
Compile-time descriptor for static strings

Static string
Length
Address

Figure 5.3
Run-time descriptor for limited dynamic strings

Limited dynamic string
Maximum length
Current length
Address

However, some string operations are slowed by the required pointer chasing. On the other hand, using adjacent memory for complete strings results in faster string operations and requires significantly less storage. However, the allocation process is slower. The adjacency method involves the general problem of managing allocation and deallocation of variable-size segments. This problem is discussed in Section 5.10.10.3.

5.4 User-Defined Ordinal Types

An **ordinal type** is one in which the range of possible values can be easily associated with the set of positive integers. In Pascal and Ada, for example, the primitive ordinal types are integer, char, and Boolean. In many languages, users can define two kinds of ordinal types: enumeration and subrange.

5.4.1 Enumeration Types

An **enumeration type** is one in which all of the possible values, which become symbolic constants (in Ada, they could also be character literals), are enumerated in the definition. A typical enumeration type is shown in the following Ada example:

```
type DAYS is (Mon, Tue, Wed, Thu, Fri, Sat, Sun);
```

The primary design issue that is specific to enumeration types is the following: Is a literal constant allowed to appear in more than one type definition, and if so, how is the type of an occurrence of that literal in the program checked?

5.4.1.1 Designs

In Pascal, a literal constant is not allowed to be used in more than one enumeration type definition in a given referencing environment. Enumeration type variables can be used as array subscripts, **for** loop variables, and **case** selector expressions but can be neither input nor output. Two enumeration type variables and/or literals of the same type can be compared with the relational operators, with their relative positions in the declaration determining the result. For example, in

```
type colortype = (red, blue, green, yellow);
var color : colortype;
...
color := blue;
if color > red ...
```

the Boolean expression of the **if** will evaluate to true.

In ANSI C and C++, like Pascal, the same literal constant cannot appear in more than one enumeration type definition in a given referencing environment. Enumeration values in ANSI C and C++ are implicitly converted to integer, so they are subject only to the rules of use of integers.

The enumeration types of Ada are similar to those of Pascal, except that the literals are allowed to appear in more than one declaration in the same referencing environment. These are called **overloaded literals.** The rule for resolving the overloading—that is, deciding the type of an occurrence of such a literal—is that it must be determinable from the context of its appearance. For example, if an overloaded literal and an enumeration variable are compared, the literal's type is resolved to be that of the variable.

In some cases, the programmer must indicate some type specification for an occurrence of an overloaded literal. Suppose, for example, that a program has the following two enumeration types:

```
type LETTERS is ('A', 'B', 'C', 'D', 'E', 'F', 'G', 'H',
                 'I', 'J', 'K', 'L', 'M', 'N', 'O', 'P',
                 'Q', 'R', 'S', 'T', 'U', 'V', 'W', 'X',
                 'Y', 'Z');
type VOWELS is ('A', 'E', 'I', 'O', 'U');
```

Further suppose the program uses a **for** loop whose variable is to take on the values of the VOWELS type, as in

```
for LETTER in 'A'..'U' loop
```

The problem is that the compiler cannot determine the correct type for LETTER, so the discrete range (in this case, 'A'..'U') is ambiguous. (In Ada, the **for** variable is implicitly typed by the compiler. It has the type of the discrete range specified in the statement.) The solution is to use a type qualifier on the literals in the discrete range, as in

```
for LETTER in VOWELS'('A')..VOWELS'('U') loop
```

Enumeration variables can be output and enumeration literals can be input using Ada's TEXT_IO package. These operations require a generic instantiation of a built-in package for the specific enumeration type. Generic instantiations of packages are discussed in Chapter 10.

In Ada, both the BOOLEAN and CHARACTER types are actually predefined enumeration types. Common operations for enumeration types are for predecessor, successor, position in the list of values, and value for a given position number. In Pascal, these operations are provided by built-in functions. For example, pred(blue) is red. In Ada, they are attributes. For example, LETTER'PRED('B') is 'A'.

5.4.1.2 Evaluation

Enumeration types provide advantages in both readability and reliability. Readability is enhanced in a very direct way: Named values are easily recognized, whereas coded values are not. Codings are meaningless to everyone except the program's author. For example, suppose a program being written in FORTRAN required a variable to store ten different colors. Most likely, the names of the colors would be coded as integers, using the values 1, 2, ..., 10. The integer values used for codes are rarely connotative. If the constant 4, for example, denotes Blue and is assigned to a variable, that fact is not apparent to the reader of the program.

In the area of reliability, enumeration types provide two advantages. First, if an integer variable is used by the programmer for a coding that required only a very small subrange of the integer values, range errors could occur but would not be detected by the run-time system, for example, color 17. Second, any one of many arithmetic operations between the coded day and any integer would be legal, because their types would match. This eliminates compiler detection of many logic and typographical errors involving coded data. (Because ANSI C and C++ treat enumeration variables like integer variables, these languages do not provide this advantage either.)

So, using an enumerated type like the Ada **LETTERS** type defined above, rather than an integer, restricts the assignable values to a small range, is more readable, and provides type checking.

The **enum** types of C and C++ are not included in Java.

5.4.2 Subrange Types

A **subrange type** is a contiguous subsequence of an ordinal type. For example, **12..14** is a subrange of integer type. Subrange types were introduced by Pascal and are also included in Modula-2 and Ada. There are no design issues that are specific to subrange types.

5.4.2.1 Designs

In Pascal, typical subrange type declarations are

```
type
  uppercase = 'A'..'Z';
  index = 1..100;
```

The connection of a subrange type to its parent type is established by matching the values in the subrange definition to those in previously declared or built-in ordinal types. In the example above, the type **uppercase** is defined to be a subrange of the built-in type for single characters. The type **index** is defined to be a subrange of the integers.

In Ada, subranges are included in the class of types called subtypes. As was stated in Chapter 4, subtypes are not new types at all but rather only new names for possibly restricted, or constrained, versions of existing types. For example, assuming **DAYS** is defined as in Section 5.4.1, we could have the following:

```
subtype WEEKDAYS is DAYS range Mon..Fri;
subtype INDEX is INTEGER range 1..100;
```

In these examples, the restriction on the existing types is in the range of possible values. All of the operations defined for the parent type are also defined for the subtype, except assignment of values outside the specified range. For example, in the following,

```
DAY1 : DAYS;
DAY2 : WEEKDAYS;
...
DAY2 := DAY1;
```

the assignment is legal unless the value of DAY1 is Sat or Sun. As in Ada, the subrange types in Pascal and Modula-2 inherit all the operations of the parent.

One of the most common uses of user-defined ordinal types is for the indexes of arrays, as will be discussed in Section 5.5. They can also be used for loop variables. In fact, subranges of ordinal types are the only way the range of Ada **for** loop variables can be specified.

Note that subrange types are very different from Ada's derived types, which were discussed in Chapter 4. For example, consider the following type declarations:

```
type DERIVED_SMALL_INT is new INTEGER range 1..100;
subtype SUBRANGE_SMALL_INT is INTEGER range 1..100;
```

Variables of both types, DERIVED_SMALL_INT and SUBRANGE_SMALL_INT, inherit the value range and operations of INTEGER. However, variables of type DERIVED_SMALL_INT are not compatible with any INTEGER type. On the other hand, variables of type SUBRANGE_SMALL_INT are compatible with variables and constants of INTEGER type and any subtype of INTEGER.

5.4.2.2 Evaluation

Subrange types enhance readability by making it clear to readers that variables of subtypes can store only certain ranges of values. Reliability is increased with subrange types, because assigning a value to a subrange variable that is outside the specified range is detected as an error, either by the compiler (in the case of the assigned value being a literal value) or by the run-time system (in the case of a variable or expression).

5.4.3 Implementation of User-Defined Ordinal Types

Enumeration types are usually implemented by associating a nonnegative integer value with each symbolic constant in the type. Typically, the first enumeration value is represented as 0, the second as 1, and so forth. Of course, the operations allowed are dramatically different from those of integers, except for the relational operators, which are identical. As stated earlier, ANSI C and C++ enumeration types are often treated exactly like integers.

Subrange types are implemented in exactly the same way as their parent types, except that range checks must be implicitly included by the compiler in every assignment of a variable or expression to a subrange variable. This increases code size and execution time but is usually considered well worth the cost. Also, a good optimizing compiler can optimize some of the checking away.

5.5 Array Types

An **array** is a homogeneous aggregate of data elements in which an individual element is identified by its position in the aggregate, relative to the first element. A reference to an array element in a program often includes one or more non-constant subscripts. Such references require a run-time calculation to determine the memory location being referenced. The individual data elements of an array are of some previously defined type, either primitive or otherwise. A majority of computer programs need to model collections of values in which the values are of the same type and must be processed in the same way. Thus, the universal need for arrays is obvious.

5.5.1 Design Issues

The primary design issues specific to arrays are the following:

- What types are legal for subscripts?
- Are subscripting expressions in element references range checked?
- When are subscript ranges bound?
- When does array allocation take place?
- How many subscripts are allowed?
- Can arrays be initialized when they have their storage allocated?
- What kinds of slices are allowed, if any?

In the following sections, examples of the design choices made for the arrays of the most common programming languages are discussed.

5.5.2 Arrays and Indexes

Specific elements of an array are referenced by means of a two-level syntactic mechanism, where the first part is the aggregate name, and the second part is a possibly dynamic selector consisting of one or more items known as **subscripts** or **indexes.** If all of the indexes in a reference are constants, the selector is static; otherwise, it is dynamic. The selection operation can be thought of as a mapping from the array name and the set of index values to an element in the aggregate. Indeed, arrays are sometimes called finite mappings. Symbolically, this mapping can be shown as

array_name(index_value_list) → element

The syntax of array references is fairly universal: the array name is followed by the list of indexes, which is surrounded by either parentheses or brackets. A problem with using parentheses is that they often are also used to enclose the parameters in subprogram calls; this makes references to arrays appear exactly like those calls. For example, consider the following FORTRAN assignment statement:

```
SUM = SUM + B(I)
```

Because parentheses are used for both subprogram parameters and array subscripts in FORTRAN, both program readers and compilers are forced to use other information to determine whether B(I) in this assignment is a function call or a reference to an array element. This can be frustrating for the reader.

The designers of pre-90 FORTRANs and PL/I chose parentheses for array subscripts because no other suitable characters were available at the time. When an identifier followed by a parenthesized expression or list of expressions is found in a pre-90 FORTRAN or PL/I program, the compiler determines whether it is an array reference or a function call by matching the name against all arrays declared in the referencing environment. If no match is found, such a reference is assumed to be a function call. If it is not found to be a locally defined subprogram, it is assumed to be defined externally. If the reference was to an array whose declaration is missing, this fact cannot be determined by the compiler, because these languages have separate compilation, and subprograms that are used in a program but defined elsewhere need not be declared to be external.

In Ada, which also uses parentheses to enclose subprogram parameters and array indexes, the compiler can always determine whether a reference is to an array or a function, because it has access to information (from previously compiled programs) about all names that can be referenced in a program unit that is being compiled. This is in contrast to pre-90 FORTRANs and PL/I, in which the compiler has no access to information about previously compiled programs.

The designers of Ada specifically chose parentheses to enclose subscripts so there would be uniformity between array references and function calls in expressions, in spite of potential readability problems. They made this choice based on the fact that both array element references and function calls are mappings. Array element references map the subscripts to a particular element of the array. Function calls map the actual parameters to the function definition and, eventually, a functional value.

Pascal, C, C++, Modula-2, and Java use brackets to delimit their array indices.

Two distinct types are involved in an array type: the element type and the type of the subscripts. The type of the subscripts is often a subrange of integers, but Pascal, Modula-2, and Ada allow some other types to be used as subscripts, such as Boolean, character, and enumeration.

Early programming languages did not specify that subscript ranges be implicitly checked. Range errors in subscripts are common in programs, so requiring range checking is an important factor in the reliability of languages. Among contemporary languages, C, C++, and FORTRAN do not specify range checking of subscripts, but Pascal, Ada, and Java do.

5.5.3 Subscript Bindings and Array Categories

The binding of the subscript type to an array variable is usually static, but the subscript value ranges are sometimes dynamically bound.

In some languages, the lower bound of the subscript range is implicit. For example, in C, C++, and Java, the lower bound of all index ranges is fixed at zero; in FORTRAN I, II, and IV, it was fixed at 1; in FORTRAN 77 and FORTRAN 90, it defaults to 1. In most other languages, subscript ranges must be completely specified by the programmer.

As with scalar variables, arrays occur in four categories. In this case, the category definitions are based on the binding to subscript value ranges and the binding to storage. Once again, the category names indicate where and when storage is allocated.

A **static array** is one in which the subscript ranges are statically bound and storage allocation is static (done before run time). The advantage of static arrays is efficiency: No dynamic allocation or deallocation is required.

A **fixed stack-dynamic array** is one in which the subscript ranges are statically bound, but the allocation is done at declaration elaboration time during execution. The advantage of fixed stack-dynamic arrays over static arrays is space efficiency. A large array in one procedure can use the same space as a large array in a different procedure, as long as both procedures are not active at the same time.

A **stack-dynamic array** is one in which the subscript ranges are dynamically bound and the storage allocation is dynamic (done during run time). Once the subscript ranges are bound and the storage is allocated, however, they remain fixed during the lifetime of the variable. The advantage of stack-dynamic arrays over static and fixed stack-dynamic arrays is flexibility. The size of an array need not be known until the array is about to be used.

A **heap-dynamic array** is one in which the binding of subscript ranges and storage allocation is dynamic and can change any number of times during the array's lifetime. The advantage of heap-dynamic arrays over the others is flexibility: Arrays can grow and shrink during program execution as the need for space changes. Examples of the four categories are given in the following paragraphs.

In FORTRAN 77, the subscript type is bound to an array at language design time; all subscripts are integer type. The subscript ranges are statically bound, and all storage is statically allocated; therefore, FORTRAN 77's arrays are static.

Arrays that are declared in Pascal procedures and C functions (without the **static** specifier) are examples of fixed stack-dynamic arrays.

Ada arrays can be stack-dynamic, as in the following:

```
GET(LIST_LEN);
declare
  LIST : array (1..LIST_LEN) of INTEGER;
  begin
  ...
  end;
```

In this example, the user inputs the number of desired elements in the array list, which are then dynamically allocated when execution reaches the **declare** block. When execution reaches the end of the block, the LIST array is deallocated.

FORTRAN 90 provides dynamic arrays. They can be allocated and deallocated on demand. Their subscript ranges can be changed by any save, deallocate, or reallocate process.

For example, in FORTRAN 90 one can declare an array to be dynamic with

```
INTEGER, ALLOCATABLE, ARRAY (:,:) :: MAT
```

which declares that MAT is a matrix of INTEGER type elements that can be dynamically allocated. The allocation is specified with an ALLOCATE statement, such as

```
ALLOCATE (MAT(10, NUMBER_OF_COLS))
```

The subscript ranges can be specified by program variables, as well as literals. Lower bounds of subscript ranges default to 1.

Dynamic arrays can be destroyed by the DEALLOCATE statement, as in

```
DEALLOCATE (MAT)
```

To make an existing dynamic array larger or smaller, its elements must be saved temporarily in another array, and the array must be deallocated and then reallocated in the new size.

C and C++ also provide dynamic arrays. The standard library functions `malloc` and `free`, which are general heap allocation and deallocation operations, respectively, can be used for C arrays. C++ uses the operators **new** and **delete** to manage heap storage. Because there is no index range checking in C and C++, the length of an array is of no interest to the runtime system, so stretching or shrinking an array is easy. Arrays are treated as pointers to some collection of storage cells where the pointer can be indexed, as discussed in Section 5.10.6.

Perl has another kind of dynamic array. They implicitly grow whenever assignments are made to elements beyond the last current element. They can be made to shrink by assigning them an empty aggregate, specified with ().

In the original version of Pascal, the index range or ranges of an array were part of its type. This, along with the use of name equivalence for compatibility, disallowed the existence of a subprogram that processed arrays of different lengths. A procedure that sorted integer arrays, for example, could only be written for arrays with a single fixed subscript range. The ISO Standard Pascal (ISO, 1982) provides a loophole for this problem, **conformant arrays.** Conformant arrays are formal parameters that include the type definition of the array. Consider the following example:

```
procedure sumlist(var sum : integer;
                      list : array [lower .. upper :
                                       integer] of integer);
    var index : integer;
    begin
    sum := 0;
    for index := lower to upper do
      sum := sum + list[index]
    end;
```

An example call to this procedure is

```
var scores : array [1..100] of integer;
...
sumlist(sum, scores)
```

5.5.4 The Number of Subscripts in Arrays

FORTRAN I limited the number of array subscripts to three, because at the time of the design execution efficiency was a primary concern. FORTRAN I designers had developed a very fast method for accessing the elements of arrays of up to three dimensions, but not beyond three. From FORTRAN IV onward, the number of array dimensions was allowed to be up to seven, but most other contemporary languages enforce no such limits. There is no justification for FORTRAN's limitation. A programmer who wishes to use a variable with ten dimensions and is willing to pay for the cost of references to the elements of such an array should be allowed to do it.

Arrays in C can have only one subscript, but arrays can have arrays as elements, thus supporting multidimensional arrays. This is an example of orthogonality. For example, consider the following C declaration:

```
int mat[5][4];
```

It creates an integer variable, `mat`, which is an array of five elements, each of which is an array of four elements. The difference between this and a matrix in another language, say FORTRAN, is minimal. The user can nearly always ignore the fact that `mat` is not really a matrix, except that the syntax for references requires a set of brackets for each subscript.

5.5.5 Array Initialization

Some languages provide the means to initialize arrays at the time their storage is allocated. In FORTRAN 77, all data storage is statically allocated, so load-time initialization using the `DATA` statement is allowed. For example, in FORTRAN 77 we could have

```
INTEGER LIST(3)
DATA LIST /0, 5, 5/
```

The array `LIST` is initialized to the values from the list delimited by slashes.

ANSI C and C++ also allow initialization of their arrays, but with one new twist: In the declaration

```
int list [] = {4, 5, 7, 83};
```

the compiler sets the length of the array. This is meant to be a convenience but is not without cost. It effectively removes the possibility that the system could detect some kinds of programmer errors, such as mistakenly leaving a value out of the list.

Character strings in C and C++ are implemented as arrays of **char**. These arrays can be initialized to string constants, as in

```
char name [] = "freddie";
```

The array `name` will have eight elements because all strings are terminated with a null character (zero), which is implicitly supplied by the system for string constants.

Arrays of strings in C and C++ can also be initialized with string literals. In this case, the array is one of pointers to characters. For example,

```
char *names [] = {"Bob", "Jake", "Darcie"};
```

This example illustrates the nature of character literals in C and C++. In the previous example of a string literal being used to initialize the **char** array `name`, the literal is taken to be a **char** array. But in the latter example (`names`), the literals are taken to be pointers to characters, so the array is an array of pointers to characters. For example, `names[0]` is a pointer to the letter `'B'` in the literal character array that contains the characters `'B'`, `'o'`, `'b'`, and null.

Pascal and Modula-2 do not allow array initialization in the declaration sections of programs.

Ada provides two mechanisms for initializing arrays in the declaration statement: by listing them in the order in which they are to be stored, or by directly assigning them to an index position using the => operator, which in Ada is called an arrow. For example, consider the following:

```
LIST : array (1..5) of INTEGER := (1, 3, 5, 7, 9);
BUNCH : array (1..5) of INTEGER := (1 => 3, 3 => 4,
                                    others => 0);
```

In the first statement, all the elements of the array LIST have initializing values, which are assigned to the array element locations in the order in which they appear. In the second, the first and third array elements are initialized using direct assignment, and the **others** clause is used to initialize the remaining elements. These collections of values, delimited by parentheses, are called **aggregate values.**

5.5.6 Array Operations

An array operation is one that operates on an array as a unit. Some languages, such as FORTRAN 77, provide no array operations.

Ada allows array assignments, including those where the right side is an aggregate value rather than an array name. Ada also provides catenation, specified by the ampersand (&). Catenation is defined between two single-dimensioned arrays and between a single-dimensioned array and a scalar. Nearly all types in Ada have the built-in relational operators for equality and inequality.

FORTRAN 90 includes a number of array operations that are called **elemental** because they are operations between pairs of array elements. For example, the add operator (+) between two arrays results in an array of the sums of the element pairs of the two arrays. The assignment, arithmetic, relational, and logical operators are all overloaded for arrays of any size or shape. FORTRAN 90 also includes intrinsic, or library, functions for matrix multiplication, matrix transpose, and vector dot product.

Arrays and their operations are the heart of APL; it is the most powerful array-processing language ever devised. Because of its relative obscurity and its lack of effect on subsequent languages, however, we present here only a glimpse into its array operations.

In APL, the four basic arithmetic operations are defined for vectors (single-dimensioned arrays) and matrixes, as well as scalar operands. For example,

```
A + B
```

is a valid expression, whether A and B are scalar variables, vectors, or matrixes.

APL includes a collection of unary operators for vectors and matrixes, some of which are as follows (where V is a vector and M is a matrix):

ϕV   reverses the elements of V

ϕM   reverses the columns of M

θM   reverses the rows of M

⍉M   transposes M (its rows become its columns, and vice versa)

⊟M   inverts M

APL also includes several special operators that take other operators as operands. One of these is the inner product operator, which is specified with a period (.). It takes two operands, which are binary operators. For example,

```
+.×
```

is a new operator that takes two arguments, either vectors or matrixes. It first multiplies the corresponding elements of two arguments, and then it sums the results. For example, if A and B are vectors,

```
A × B
```

is the mathematical inner product of A and B (a vector of the products of the corresponding elements of A and B). The statement

```
A +.× B
```

is the sum of the inner product of A and B. If A and B are matrixes, this expression specifies the matrix multiplication of A and B.

The special operators of APL are actually functional forms, which are described in Chapter 14.

5.5.7 Slices

A **slice** of an array is some substructure of that array. For example, if A is a matrix, the first row of A is one possible slice, as are the last row and the first column. It is important to realize that a slice is not a new data type. Rather, it is a mechanism for referencing part of an array as a unit. If arrays cannot be manipulated as units in a language, that language has no use for slices.

One of the design questions for slices is the syntax of specifying a reference to a particular slice. A reference to a particular element of a complete array is the array name and an expression for each subscript. Because a slice is a substructure of an array, a slice reference requires fewer subscript expressions than a reference to the whole array. Somehow, however, the missing subscript expressions must be denoted, so that the present expressions are associated with the correct subscripts. The missing subscript or subscripts of slice references are sometimes specified by asterisks. For example, consider the following FORTRAN 90 declarations.

```
INTEGER VECTOR(1:10), MAT(1:3, 1:3), CUBE(1:3, 1:3, 1:4)
```

VECTOR(3:6) is a four-element array with the third through sixth elements of VECTOR; MAT(1:3, 2) refers to the second column of MAT; MAT(3, 1:3) refers to the third row of MAT. All of these references can be used as single-dimensioned arrays. References to all array slices are treated as if they were arrays of the remaining dimensionality. Thus a slice reference such as CUBE(1:3, 1:3, 2) could be legally assigned to MAT. Slices can also appear as the destinations of assignment statements. For example, a single-dimensioned array could be assigned to a slice of a matrix. Figure 5.4 shows several slices of MAT and CUBE.

More complex slices can also be specified in FORTRAN 90. For example, VECTOR(2:10:2) is a five-element array consisting of the second, fourth, sixth, eighth, and tenth elements of VECTOR. Slices can also have nonregular arrangements of elements of an existing array. For example VECTOR((/3, 2, 1, 8/)) is an array of the third, second, first, and eighth elements of VECTOR.

In Ada, only highly restricted slices are allowed: those that consist of consecutive elements of a single-dimensioned array. For example, if LIST is an array with index range (1..100), LIST(5..10) is a slice of LIST consisting of the six elements indexed from 5 to 10. As discussed in Section 5.3.2, a slice of a STRING type is called a substring reference.

Figure 5.4
Example slices in
FORTRAN 90

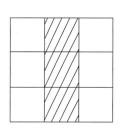

MAT (1:3, 2)

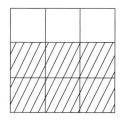

MAT (2:3, 1:3)

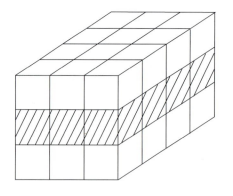

CUBE (2, 1:3, 1:4)

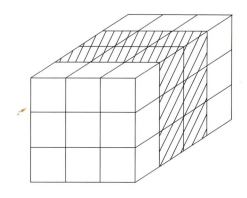

CUBE (1:3, 1:3, 2:3)

5.5.8 Evaluation

Arrays have been included in virtually all languages. They are simple and have been well developed. The only significant advance since their introduction in FORTRAN I has been the inclusion of all ordinal types as possible subscript types and, of course, dynamic arrays. Although arrays are essential and fundamental, there is little controversy involved in their design.

Although it is sometimes convenient to allow the programmer to specify a particular substructure of a multidimensional array, the increased difficulty of implementation and readability are not necessarily worth the convenience.

5.5.9 Implementation of Array Types

Implementing arrays requires more compile-time effort than does implementing simple types, such as integer. The code to allow accessing of array elements must be generated at compile time. At run time, this code must be executed to produce element addresses. Accesses to array elements, especially in arrays with several subscripts, are more expensive than necessary if the access code is not carefully designed. This is true regardless of whether the array is statically or dynamically bound to memory. There is no way to precompute the address to be accessed by a reference such as

```
list[k]
```

A single-dimensioned array is a list of adjacent memory cells. Suppose the array `list` is defined to have a subscript range lower bound of 1. The access function for `list` is often of the form

$$\text{address(list[k])} = \text{address(list[1])} + (k-1) * \text{element\_size}$$

This simplifies to

$$\text{address(list[k])} = (\text{address(list[1])} - \text{element\_size}) + (k * \text{element\_size})$$

where the first operand of the addition is the constant part of the access function, and the second is the variable part.

If the element type is statically bound and the array is statically bound to storage, then the value of the constant part can be computed before run time. Only the addition and multiplication operations remain to be done at run time. If the base, or beginning address, of the array is not known until run time, the subtraction must be done when the array is allocated.

The generalization of this access function for an arbitrary lower bound is

$$\text{address(list[k])} = \text{address(list[lower\_bound])} + ((k - \text{lower\_bound}) * \text{element\_size})$$

Figure 5.5
Compile-time descriptor for single-dimensioned arrays

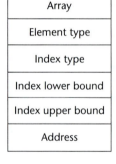

| Array |
| Element type |
| Index type |
| Index lower bound |
| Index upper bound |
| Address |

The compile-time descriptor for single-dimensioned arrays can have the form shown in Figure 5.5. The descriptor includes information required to construct the access function. If run-time checking of index ranges is not done and the attributes are all static, then only the access function is required during execution; no descriptor is needed. If run-time checking of index ranges is done, then those index ranges may need to be stored in a run-time descriptor. If the subscript ranges of a particular array type are static, the ranges may be incorporated into the code that does the checking, thus eliminating the need for the run-time descriptor. If any of the descriptor entries are dynamically bound, then those parts of the descriptor must be maintained at run time.

Multidimensional arrays are more complex to implement than single-dimensioned arrays, although the extension to more dimensions is fairly straightforward. Hardware memory is linear—it is usually a simple sequence of bytes. So values of data types that have two or more dimensions must be mapped onto the single-dimensioned memory. There are two common ways in which multidimensional arrays can be mapped to one dimension: row major order and column major order. In **row major order,** the elements of the array that have as their first subscript the lower bound value of that subscript are stored first, followed by the elements of the second value of the first subscript, and so forth. If the array is a matrix, it is stored by rows. For example, if the matrix had the values

```
3   4   7
6   2   5
1   3   8
```

it would be stored in row major order as

3, 4, 7, 6, 2, 5, 1, 3, 8

In **column major order,** the elements of an array that have as their last subscript the lower bound value of that subscript are stored first, followed by the elements of the second value of the last subscript, and so forth. If the array is a matrix, it is stored by columns. If the example matrix above were stored in column major order, it would have the following order in memory:

3, 6, 1, 4, 2, 3, 7, 5, 8

Column major order is used in FORTRAN, but the other languages use row major order.

It is sometimes essential to know the storage order of multidimensional arrays; for example, when such arrays are processed using pointers in C programs, and when an array is **EQUIVALENCE**d to another array with a different shape in a FORTRAN program. It is important in all languages when execution speed is a serious concern and the computer uses virtual memory (nearly all machines outside the world of PCs use virtual memory), sequential access to matrix elements will be faster if they are accessed in the order in which they are stored, because that will minimize paging. (Paging is the movement of blocks of information between disk and main memory.)

The access function for a multidimensional array is the mapping of its base address and a set of index values to the address in memory of the element specified by the index values. The access function for two-dimensional arrays stored in row major order can be developed as follows. In general, the address of an element is the base address of the structure plus the element size times the number of elements that precede it in the structure. For a matrix in row major order, the number of elements that precedes an element is the number of rows above the element times the size of a row, plus the number of elements to the left of the element. This is illustrated in Figure 5.6, in which we make the simplifying assumption that subscript lower bounds are all 1.

To get an actual address value, the number of elements that precede the desired element must be multiplied by the element size. Now, the access function can be written as

location(a[i,j]) = address of a[1, 1] +
                   ((((number of rows above the ith row) * (size of a row))
                        + (number of elements left of the jth column)) *
                            element size)

Because the number of rows above the ith row is (i - 1) and the number of elements to the left of the jth column is (j - 1), we have

location(a[i, j]) = address of a[1, 1] + ((((i - 1) * n) + (j - 1)) *
                    element_size)

Figure 5.6
The location of the [i,j] element in a matrix

	1	2	$\cdots$	$j-1$	j	$\cdots$	n
1							
2							
$\vdots$							
$i-1$							
i					$\otimes$		
$\vdots$							
m							

where n is the number of elements per row. This can be rearranged to the form

$$\text{location}(a[i, j]) = \text{address of } a[1, 1] - ((n + 1) * \text{element\_size}) + ((i * n + j) * \text{element\_size})$$

where the first two terms are the constant part and the last is the variable part.

The generalization to arbitrary lower bounds results in the following access function:

$$\text{location}(a[i, j]) = \text{address of } a[\text{row\_lb, col\_lb}] + (((i - \text{row\_lb}) * n) + (j - \text{col\_lb})) * \text{element\_size}$$

where row_lb is the lower bound of the rows, and col_lb is the lower bound of the columns. This can be rearranged to the form

$$\text{location}(a[i, j]) = \text{address of } a[\text{row\_lb, col\_lb}] - (((\text{row\_lb} * n) + \text{col\_lb}) * \text{element\_size}) + (((i * n) + j) * \text{element\_size})$$

where the first two terms are the constant part and the last is the variable part. This can be generalized relatively easily to an arbitrary number of dimensions.

For each dimension of an array, one add and one multiply instruction is required for the access function. Therefore, accesses to elements of arrays with several subscripts are costly. The compile-time descriptor for a multidimensional array is shown in Figure 5.7.

Slices add another layer of complexity to storage mapping functions. To illustrate this, consider a program in which there is a matrix and an array, and a column of the matrix is assigned to the array, as in

```
INTEGER MAT (1:10, 1:5), LIST (1:10)
...
LIST = MAT (1:3, 3)
```

Figure 5.7
A compile-time descriptor for a multidimensional array

Multidimensioned array
Element type
Index type
Number of dimensions
Index range 1
$\vdots$
Index range n
Address

The storage mapping function for the matrix, MAT, assuming row major order and an element size of 1, is

$$\text{location}(\text{MAT}[\texttt{i, j}]) = \text{address of } \text{MAT}[\texttt{1,1}] + ((i-1) * 5 + (j-1)) * 1$$
$$= (\text{address of } \text{MAT}[\texttt{1,1}] - 6) + ((5 * i) + j)$$

The storage mapping function for the slice reference MAT[1:3, 3] is

$$\text{location}(\text{MAT}[\texttt{i, 3}]) = \text{address of } \text{MAT}[\texttt{1,1}] + ((i-1) * 5 + (3-1)) * 1$$
$$= (\text{address of } \text{MAT}[\texttt{1,1}] - 3) + (5 * i)$$

Notice that this mapping has exactly the same form as any other one-dimensional array access function, although the form of the constant part is different because the basic array is two-dimensional.

The elements of MAT that are to be assigned to LIST are found by letting i take on the values in the subscript range of the first dimension of MAT.

5.6 Associative Arrays

An associative array is an unordered collection of data elements that are indexed by an equal number of values called keys. In the case of nonassociative arrays, the indices never need to be stored (because of their regularity). In an associative array, however, the user-defined keys must be stored in the structure. So, each element of an associative array is in fact a pair of entities, a key and a value. We use Perl's design of associative arrays to illustrate this data structure. Associative arrays are also supported by the standard class library of Java.

The design issues that are specific for associative arrays are

- What is the form of references to elements?
- Is the size of an associative array static or dynamic?

5.6.1 Structure and Operations

In Perl, associative arrays are often called hashes, because in the implementation their elements are stored and retrieved with hash functions. The name space for Perl hashes is distinct; every hash variable must begin with a percent sign (%). Hashes can be set to literal values with the assignment statement, as in

```
%salaries = ("Cedric" => 75000, "Perry" => 57000,
             "Mary" => 55750, "Gary" => 47850);
```

Individual element values are referenced using notation that is unique to Perl. The key value is placed in braces and the hash name is replaced by a scalar variable name that is the same except for the first character. Scalar variable names begin with dollar signs ($). For example,

```
$salaries{"Perry"} = 58850;
```

A new element is added using the same statement form. An element can be removed from the hash with the `delete` operator, as in

```
delete $salaries{"Gary"};
```

The entire hash can be emptied by assigning the empty literal to it, as in

```
@salaries = ();
```

The size of a Perl hash is dynamic: it grows when a new element is added and shrinks when an element is deleted, and also when it is emptied by assignment of the empty literal. The `exists` operator returns true or false, depending on whether its operand key is an element in the hash. For example,

```
if (exists $salaries{"Shelly"}) …
```

The `keys` operator, when applied to a hash, returns an array of the keys of the hash. The `values` operator does the same for the values of the hash. The `each` operator iterates over the element pairs of a hash.

A hash is much better than an array if searches of the elements are required, because the implicit hashing operation used to access hash element is very efficient. On the other hand, if every element of a list must be processed, it would be more efficient to use an array.

5.6.2 Implementing Associative Arrays

Perl associative arrays are implemented by providing some fixed amount of space initially. When the structure reaches some predetermined level of fullness, it is expanded. This expansion process is costly, for it requires that a new hash function be used and all existing elements be rehashed into the structure.

5.7 Record Types

A **record** is a possibly heterogeneous aggregate of data elements in which the individual elements are identified by names.

There is frequently a need in programs to model collections of data that are not homogeneous. For example, information about a college student might include name, student number, grade point average, and so forth. A data type for such a collection might use a character string for the name, an integer for the student number, a floating-point for the grade point average, and so forth. Records are designed to meet this kind of need.

Records have been part of all of the most popular programming languages, except pre-90 versions of FORTRAN, since the early 1960s when they were introduced by COBOL.

In object-oriented languages, the class construct supports records. C++ still includes C's `struct` for record structures, although it is redundant. Java does not have `struct`.

The following sections describe how records are declared or defined, how references to fields within records are made, and common record operations.

The design issues that are specific to records are

- What is the syntactic form of references to fields?

- Are elliptical references allowed?

5.7.1 Definitions of Records

The fundamental difference between a record and an array is the homogeneity of elements in arrays versus the possible heterogeneity of elements in records. One result of this difference is that record elements, or fields, are not usually referenced by indexes. Instead, the fields are named with identifiers, and references to the fields are made using these identifiers. One more important difference between arrays and records is that records in some languages are allowed to include unions, which are discussed in Section 5.8.

The COBOL form of a record declaration, which is part of the data division of a COBOL program, is illustrated in the following example:

```
01   EMPLOYEE-RECORD.
     02   EMPLOYEE-NAME.
          05   FIRST      PICTURE IS X(20).
          05   MIDDLE     PICTURE IS X(10).
          05   LAST       PICTURE IS X(20).
     02   HOURLY-RATE     PICTURE IS 99V99.
```

The `EMPLOYEE-RECORD` record consists of the `EMPLOYEE-NAME` record and the `HOURLY-RATE` field. The numerals `01`, `02`, and `05` that begin the lines of the record declaration are **level numbers,** which indicate by their relative values the hierarchical structure of the record. Any line that is followed by a line with a higher level number is itself a record. The `PICTURE` clauses show the formats of the field storage locations, with `X(20)` specifying 20 alphanumeric characters and `99V99` specifying four decimal digits with the decimal point in the middle.

Pascal, Modula-2, and Ada use a different syntax for records; rather than using the level numbers of COBOL, they indicate record structures in an orthogonal way by simply nesting record declarations inside record declarations. Consider the following Ada declaration:

```
EMPLOYEE_RECORD :
  record
    EMPLOYEE_NAME :
      record
        FIRST : STRING (1..20);
        MIDDLE : STRING (1..10);
        LAST : STRING (1..20);
      end record;
    HOURLY_RATE : FLOAT;
  end record;
```

C also provides records, which in C are called structures. They are very much like the records of Pascal, except that they do not include Pascal's record variants, or unions, which are described in Section 5.8.

FORTRAN 90 record declarations require that any nested records be previously defined as types. So, for the employee record above, the employee name record would need to be defined first, and then the employee record would simply name it as the type of its first field.

5.7.2 References to Record Fields

References to the individual fields of records are syntactically specified by several different methods, two of which name the desired field and its enclosing records. COBOL field references have the form

field_name OF record_name_1 OF ... OF record_name_n

where the first record named is the smallest or innermost record that contains the field. The next record name in the sequence is that of the record that contains the previous record, and so forth. For example, the MIDDLE field in the COBOL record example above can be referenced with

MIDDLE OF EMPLOYEE-NAME OF EMPLOYEE-RECORD

Most of the other languages use dot notation for field references, where the components of the reference are connected with periods. Names in dot notation have the opposite order of COBOL references: They use the name of the largest enclosing record first and the field name last. For example, the following is a reference to the field MIDDLE in the Ada record example above:

EMPLOYEE_RECORD.EMPLOYEE_NAME.MIDDLE

FORTRAN 90 field references have this form, except that percent signs (%) are used instead of periods.

A **fully qualified reference** to a record field is one in which all intermediate record names, from the largest enclosing record to the specific field, are named in the reference. Both the COBOL and the Ada field references above are fully qualified. As an alternative to fully qualified references, COBOL and PL/I allow **elliptical references** to record fields. In an elliptical reference, the field is named, but any or all of the enclosing record names can be omitted, as long as the resulting reference is unambiguous in the referencing environment. For example, FIRST, FIRST OF EMPLOYEE-NAME, and FIRST OF EMPLOYEE-RECORD are elliptical references to the employee's first name in the COBOL record declared above. Although elliptical references are a programmer convenience, they require a compiler to have elaborate data structures and procedures in order to correctly identify the referenced field. They are also somewhat detrimental to readability.

Pascal allows a kind of elliptical references within specific structures. A segment of code can be placed in a **with** clause, wherein a portion of the qualification is specified to be implicit. For example, consider the following two code segments; the first is written without a **with** clause and the second uses **with**.

```
employee.name := 'Bob';
employee.age := 42;
employee.sex := 'M';
employee.salary := 23750.0;

with employee do
  begin
  name := 'Bob';
  age := 42;
  sex := 'M';
  salary := 23750.0
  end; { end of with }
```

While a relatively small **with** clause is an aid to readability, a **with** clause that spans several pages of code can be a detriment to readability.

5.7.3 Operations on Records

Assignment is a common record operation. In most cases, the types of the two sides must be identical. Ada allows record comparisons for equality and inequality. Also, Ada records can be initialized with aggregate literals.

COBOL provides the MOVE CORRESPONDING statement for moving records. This statement copies a field of the specified source record to the destination record only if the destination record has a field with the same name. This is frequently a useful operation in data processing applications, where input records are moved to output files after some modifications. Because input records often have many fields that have the same names and purposes as fields in output records, but not necessarily in the same order, the `MOVE CORRESPONDING` operation can save many statements. For example, consider the following COBOL structures:

```
01   INPUT-RECORD.
     02  NAME.
         05  LAST        PICTURE IS X(20).
         05  MIDDLE      PICTURE IS X(15).
         05  FIRST       PICTURE IS X(20).
     02 EMPLOYEE-NUMBER  PICTURE IS 9(10).
     02 HOURS-WORKED     PICTURE IS 99.

01   OUTPUT-RECORD.
     02  NAME.
         05  FIRST       PICTURE IS X(20).
         05  MIDDLE      PICTURE IS X(15).
         05  LAST        PICTURE IS X(20).
     02  EMPLOYEE-NUMBER PICTURE IS 9(10).
     02  GROSS-PAY       PICTURE IS 999V99.
     02  NET-PAY         PICTURE IS 999V99.
```

The statement

```
MOVE CORRESPONDING INPUT-RECORD TO OUTPUT-RECORD.
```

copies the `FIRST`, `MIDDLE`, `LAST`, and `EMPLOYEE-NUMBER` fields from the input record to the output record.

5.7.4 Evaluation

Records are frequently valuable data types in programming languages. The design of record types is straightforward, and their use is safe. The only aspect of records that is not clearly readable is the elliptical references allowed by COBOL and PL/I.

Records and arrays are closely related structural forms, and it is therefore interesting to compare them. Arrays are used when all the data values have the same type and are processed in the same way. This processing is easily done when there is a systematic way of sequencing through the structure. Such processing is well supported by using dynamic subscripting as the addressing method.

Records are used when the collection of data values is heterogeneous and the different fields are not processed in the same way. Also, the fields of a record often need not be processed in a particular sequential order. Field names are like literal, or constant, subscripts. Because they are static, they provide very efficient access to the fields. Dynamic subscripts could be used to access record fields, but it would disallow type checking and would also be slower.

Records and arrays represent thoughtful and efficient methods of fulfilling two separate but related applications of data structures.

Figure 5.8
A compile-time descriptor for a record

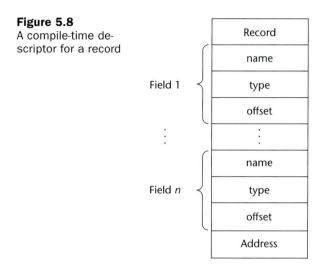

5.7.5 Implementation of Record Types

The fields of records are stored in adjacent memory locations. But because the sizes of the fields are not necessarily the same, the access method used for arrays is not used for records. Instead, the offset address, relative to the beginning of the record, is associated with each field. Field accesses are all handled using these offsets. The compile-time descriptor for a record has the general form shown in Figure 5.8. Run-time descriptors for records are unnecessary.

5.8 Union Types

A **union** is a type that may store different type values at different times during program execution. As an example of the need for a union type, consider a table of constants for a compiler, which is used to store the constants found in a program being compiled. One field of each table entry is for the value of the constant. Suppose that for a particular language being compiled, the types of constants were integer, floating point, and Boolean. In terms of table management, it would be convenient if the same location, a table field, could store a value of any of these three types. Then all constant values could be addressed in the same way. The type of such a location is, in a sense, the union of the three value types it can store.

5.8.1 Design Issues

The problem of type checking union types, which was discussed in Chapter 4, leads to one major design issue. The other fundamental question is how to syntactically represent a union. In some cases, unions are confined to be parts of record structures, but in others they are not. So the primary design issues that are particular to union types are the following:

- Should type checking be required? Note that any such type checking must be dynamic.
- Should unions be embedded in records?

5.8.2 Free Unions

FORTRAN, C, and C++ provide union constructs in which there is no language support for type checking. In FORTRAN, the **EQUIVALENCE** statement is used to specify unions; in C and C++, it is the **union** construct. The unions in these languages are called **free unions,** because programmers are allowed complete freedom from type checking in their use.

5.8.3 The Discriminated Unions of ALGOL 68

Type checking of unions requires that each union construct include a type indicator. Such an indicator is called a **tag,** or **discriminant,** and a union with a discriminant is called a **discriminated union.** The first language to provide discriminated unions was ALGOL 68. Consider the following example:

```
union (int, real) ir1, ir2
```

In this case, the two variables `ir1` and `ir2` are declared to be of a **union** type that can have either **int** or **real** type values. Although it is legal to assign values of either of the possible types to such a variable, it is not so simple to reference them. For example, in the following,

```
union (int, real) ir1;
int count;
...
ir1 := 33;
...
count := ir1;
```

the first assignment statement is legal, but the second is not because the system cannot statically check the type of `ir1`. The compiler cannot guarantee that `ir1` will actually contain an integer value. To alleviate this problem, ALGOL 68 provides **conformity clauses** for such references. For example, consider the following:

```
union (int, real) ir1;
int count;
real sum;
...
case ir1 in
  (int intval): count := intval,
  (real realval): sum := realval
esac
```

This **case** statement executes the assignment that is currently valid—that is, the one in which the value type of the union variable ir1 matches the type of the destination (count or sum). Therefore, the different types are handled individually. The correct choice is made by testing a type tag maintained by the run-time system for the variable. The parenthesized clauses that introduce the assignments specify the current type of ir1, and the following identifier is the means by which the value of ir1 is referenced. For example, **(int** intval**)** specifies that if the current type of the case variable (ir1) is **int**, the following statement is to be executed; the variable intval refers to the current value of ir1. intval and realval provide a means of referencing the union's values in a type-consistent way. This is a safe way of implementing discriminated union because it allows static type checking of user code and dynamic checking of system discriminants in order to disallow erroneous uses of values. The dummy variables, intval and realval, can be thought of as implicitly declared variables whose scope is the statement following their specifications.

5.8.4 Pascal Union Types

Pascal introduced the concept of integrating discriminated unions with a record structure. This design carried over into Modula-2 and Ada. In all of these, the discriminated union is called a **record variant**, or variant part of a record. The discriminant is a user-accessible variable in the record that stores the current type value in the variant. The following example illustrates a Pascal record with a variant part:

```
type shape = (circle, triangle, rectangle);
     colors = (red, green, blue);
     figure =
       record
         filled : boolean;
         color : colors;
         case form : shape of
           circle:  (diameter : real);
           triangle: (leftside : integer;
                        rightside : integer;
                        angle : real);
           rectangle: (side1 : integer;
                         side2 : integer)
               end;
var myfigure : figure;
```

Figure 5.9
A discriminated union of three shape variables (assume all variables are the same size)

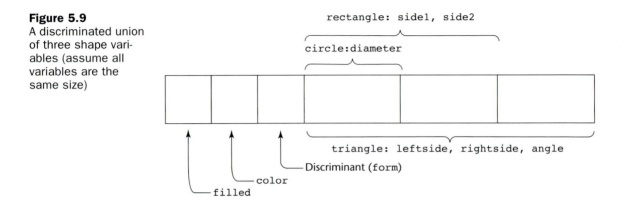

The structure of this variant record is shown in Figure 5.9, in which we assume that integers require half as much storage as reals. The variable **figure** consists of the tag, which is named **form**, and sufficient storage for its largest variant. In this case, the largest variant is for **triangle**, which consists of two integers and a real. At any time during execution, the tag should indicate which variant is currently stored. If the variant must be printed, we could use the following:

```
case myfigure.form of
  circle:  writeln('It is a circle; its diameter is:',
                 myfigure.diameter);
  triangle: begin
            writeln('It is a triangle');
            writeln(' its sides are:', myfigure.leftside,
                 myfigure.rightside);
            writeln(' the angle between the sides is:',
                 myfigure.angle);
          end;
  rectangle: begin
            writeln ('It is a rectangle');
            writeln (' its sides are:', myfigure.side1,
                 myfigure.side2)
          end
end
```

Although there was an attempt in Pascal to at least consider type checking in its variant records, there are two distinct problems in the design that make type checking virtually impossible. The first problem is that the user program can change the tag without making a corresponding change in the variant. Therefore, even if the run-time system checks the type of the variant by examining the tag before using the variant, it could not detect all type errors; the user program may have changed the tag so that its value is now inconsistent with the type of the current variant. This is one reason why implementors typically ignore type checking of variant record references in these languages.

The second problem is that the programmer can simply omit the tag from the variant record structure, making it a free union. For example, consider the following:

```
type
  figure =
    record
    ...
    case shape of
      circle : (diameter : real);
      triangle : (leftside : integer);
      ...
    end
```

With this structure, neither the user nor the system has any way to determine the current variant type. Suppose the value of `myfigure.diameter` is `2.73`. There is no way to guard against incorrect references such as

```
side := myfigure.leftside;
```

which is rarely useful because there is currently a floating-point value in that part of the variant where `leftside` resides. Both `myfigure.diameter` and `myfigure.leftside` can be assigned and referenced at any time.

Variant records in Pascal are sometimes used to get around some of the restrictions of the language. They provide a convenient loophole in the type-checking rules. For example, pointer arithmetic is not allowed in Pascal, although some applications need to manipulate pointer values. For example, the buddy system of dynamic storage management uses pointer arithmetic to compute the address of areas of memory to be allocated. To circumvent the restrictions against pointer arithmetic, a pointer can be placed in a variant with an integer, and the integer form can be manipulated as required. This particular application of variant records is not necessary in C, Modula-2, or Ada, as they all provide other methods for doing pointer, or address, arithmetic.

5.8.5 Ada Union Types

The Ada language extends the Pascal form of variant records to make them safer. Both of the problems associated with Pascal and Modula-2 variant records are avoided. The tag cannot be changed without the variant also being changed, and the tag is required on all variant records. Furthermore, Ada systems are required to check the tag for all references to variants.

The Ada design allows the user to specify variables of a variant record type that will store only one of the possible type values in the variant. In this way the user can tell the system when the type checking can be static. Such a restricted variable is called a **constrained variant variable.**

The tag of a constrained variant variable is treated like a named constant. Unconstrained variant records in Ada are more like their Pascal counterparts in that the values of their variants can change types during execution. However, the type of the variant can be changed only by assigning the entire record, including the discriminant. This disallows inconsistent records because if the newly assigned record is a constant data aggregate, the value of the tag and the type of the variant can be statically checked for consistency. If the assigned value is a variable, its consistency was guaranteed when it was assigned, so the new value of the variable now being assigned is sure to be consistent.

The following example shows the Ada version of the Pascal variant record defined above:

```
type SHAPE is (CIRCLE, TRIANGLE, RECTANGLE);
type COLORS is (RED, GREEN, BLUE);
type FIGURE (FORM : SHAPE) is
  record
    FILLED : BOOLEAN;
    COLOR : COLORS;
    case FORM is
      when CIRCLE =>
        DIAMETER : FLOAT;
      when TRIANGLE =>
        LEFT_SIDE : INTEGER;
        RIGHT_SIDE : INTEGER;
        ANGLE : FLOAT;
      when RECTANGLE =>
        SIDE_1 : INTEGER;
        SIDE_2 : INTEGER;
    end case;
  end record;
```

The following two statements declare variables of type `FIGURE`:

```
FIGURE_1 : FIGURE;
FIGURE_2 : FIGURE(FORM => TRIANGLE);
```

`FIGURE_1` is declared to be an unconstrained variant record that has no initial value. Its type can change by assignment of a whole record, including the discriminant, as in the following:

```
FIGURE_1 := (FILLED => true,
             COLOR => BLUE,
             FORM => RECTANGLE,
             SIDE_1 => 12,
             SIDE_2 => 3);
```

The right side of this assignment is a data aggregate.

The variable `FIGURE_2` declared above is constrained to be a triangle and cannot be changed to another variant.

This form of discriminated union is perfectly safe, because it always allows type checking, although the references to fields in unconstrained variants must be dynamically checked.

5.8.6 Evaluation

Unions are potentially unsafe constructs in many languages. They are one of the reasons why FORTRAN, Pascal, C, C++, and Modula-2 are not strongly typed: They do not allow type checking of references to their unions.

On the other hand, unions provide programming flexibility; for example, their presence in Pascal allows pointer arithmetic. Furthermore, they can be designed so that they can be safely used, as in Ada. In most other languages, unions must be used with care.

A number of recently designed languages do not include unions. Among these are Oberon, Modula-3, and Java. This may be reflective of the growing concern for safety in programming languages.

5.8.7 Implementation of Union Types

Discriminated unions are implemented by simply using the same address for every possible variant. Sufficient storage for the largest variant is allocated. In the case of constrained variants in the Ada language, the exact amount of storage can be used because there is no variation. The tag of a discriminated union is stored with the variant in a record-like structure.

At compile time, the complete description of each variant must be stored. This can be done by associating a case table with the tag entry in the descriptor. The case table has an entry for each variant, which points to a descriptor for that particular variant. To illustrate this arrangement, consider the following Ada example:

```
type NODE (TAG : BOOLEAN) is
  record
  case TAG is
      when true => COUNT : INTEGER;
      when false => SUM : FLOAT;
  end case;
  end record;
```

The descriptor for this type could have the form shown in Figure 5.10.

5.9 Set Types

A **set** type is one whose variables can store unordered collections of distinct values from some ordinal type called its **base type.** Set types are often used to model mathematical sets. For example, text analysis often requires that small sets of characters, such as punctuation characters or vowels, be stored and conveniently searched.

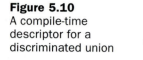

Figure 5.10
A compile-time
descriptor for a
discriminated union

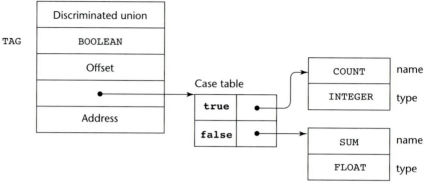

The only design issue that is particular to set types is, What should be the maximum number of elements in a set base type?

5.9.1 Sets in Pascal and Modula-2

Among the common imperative languages, only Pascal and Modula-2 include sets as a data type. We now briefly describe Pascal's set data type.

The maximum size of Pascal base sets is implementation dependent. Many implementations severely restrict it, often to much less than 100. They do so because sets and their operations are most efficiently implemented by representing set variables as bit strings that fit into a single machine word.

One problem with letting machine word size determine the maximum base set size is that users are restricted to modeling only very small sets. This is a deficiency in writability. Another problem is that different machines have different word sizes, so programs developed on machines with larger word sizes that use larger sets may not be portable to machines with smaller word sizes. Both these problems result from letting maximum base set size be chosen by implementors, rather than making it part of the language design.

Pascal includes a collection of set operations; for example, set union, set intersection, and set equality.

The following example shows the definition of a set type and some set type variables.

```
type colors = (red, blue, green, yellow, orange, white,
              black);
     colorset = set of colors;
var set1, set2 : colorset;
```

Constant values can be assigned to the set variables `set1` and `set2`, as in

```
set1 := [red, blue, yellow, white];
set2 := [black, blue];
```

Modula-2 and Modula-3 include the set type of Pascal, with a few minor changes in syntax and some additional operations. Set constants are enclosed in braces, ({}), and constants may be preceded by the type name, which clarifies the type of such occurrences of those constants. For example, consider the following set type declarations:

```
TYPE setype1 = SET OF [red, blue, green, yellow];
     setype2 = SET OF [blue, yellow];
VAR setvar1 : setype1;
```

In a program that includes these declarations, the constant {blue} may be ambiguous. However, the type of the constant, {blue}, in the statement

```
setvar1 := setype1 {blue};
```

is very clear. In Pascal, the constant would simply be [blue], which does not specify its type.

Modula-2, like Pascal, does not specify a minimum cardinality of sets, so it is again implementation dependent. Set type variables, like enumeration type variables, can be neither input nor output in Pascal or Modula-2.

Sets are commonly used to simplify and shorten compound Boolean OR expressions. For example,

```
if (ch = 'a') or (ch = 'e') or (ch = 'i') or (ch = 'o')
   or (ch = 'u') ...
```

can be replaced with

```
if ch in ['a', 'e', 'i', 'o', 'u'] ...
```

5.9.2 Evaluation

The Ada language does not include set types, although Ada was based on Pascal. Instead, Ada's designers added a set membership operator for its enumeration types. This provides for one of the most commonly needed set operations. Of course, the sets against which membership tests can be made are just enumeration values, which are constants.

In other languages without set types, set operations must be done with arrays, and the user must write the code to provide the operations. This is not difficult, although it is indeed more cumbersome and will most likely be far less efficient. For example, if the set of vowels were represented as a **char** array in Pascal, determining whether a given character variable stored a vowel would require a loop to search the vowel array. If the vowels were represented as a set, however, the same determination could be made with one application of the **in** operator. This is not only programmer efficient but also will probably be computer efficient. In both cases, it is better because the whole set can be dealt with as a unit, whereas the array must be searched one element at a time.

Arrays are, of course, far more flexible than sets; they allow many more operations, more complex shapes, and more options for element types. In fact, if arrays were restricted to a maximum length of 32, as are sets in many Pascal implementations, users would not consider them acceptable. Sets provide an alternative that trades flexibility for efficiency for a certain class of applications.

5.9.3   Implementation of Set Types

Sets are usually stored as bit strings in memory. For example, if a set has the ordinal base type

```
['a'..'p']
```

then variables of this set type can use the first 16 bits of a machine word, with each set bit (1) representing a present element, and each clear bit (0) representing an absent element. Using this scheme, the set value

```
['a', 'c', 'h', 'o']
```

would be represented as

```
1010000100000010
```

The payoff in this approach is that a typical operation such as set union can be computed as a single machine instruction, a logical OR. Set membership can also be done in a single instruction when the base set cardinality is less than or equal to the machine's word size. For example, if we had a set variable named `setchars`, and the membership test was

```
'g' in setchars
```

the process could be done with an AND operation between the bit string representations of the two operands.

5.10 Pointer Types

A **pointer** type is one in which the variables have a range of values that consists of memory addresses and a special value, nil. The value nil is not a valid address and is used to indicate that a pointer cannot currently be used to reference any memory cell.

Pointers have been designed for two distinct kinds of uses. First, pointers provide some of the power of indirect addressing, which is heavily used in assembly language programming. Second, pointers provide a method of dynamic storage management. A pointer can be used to access a location in the area where storage is dynamically allocated, which is usually called a **heap.**

Variables that are dynamically allocated from the heap are called **heap-dynamic variables.** They often do not have identifiers associated with them and thus can be referenced only by pointer or reference type variables. Variables without names are called **anonymous variables.** It is in this latter application area of pointers that the most important design issues arise.

Pointers, unlike arrays and records, are not structured types, although they are defined using a type operator (* in C and C++, **access** in Ada, and ^ in Pascal). Furthermore, they are also different from scalar variables because they are most often used to reference some other variable, rather than being used to store data of some sort.

Both kinds of uses of pointers add writability to a language. For example, suppose it is necessary to implement a dynamic structure like a binary tree in a language like FORTRAN 77, which does not have pointers. This would require the programmer to provide and maintain a pool of available tree nodes, which would probably be implemented in parallel arrays. Also, because of the lack of dynamic storage in FORTRAN 77, it would be necessary for the programmer to guess the maximum number of required nodes. This is clearly an awkward and cumbersome way to deal with binary trees.

5.10.1 Design Issues

The primary design issues particular to pointers are the following:

- What are the scope and lifetime of a pointer variable?
- What is the lifetime of a heap-dynamic variable?
- Are pointers restricted as to the type of value to which they can point?
- Are pointers used for dynamic storage management, indirect addressing, or both?
- Should the language support pointer types, reference types, or both?

5.10.2 Pointer Operations

Languages that provide a pointer type usually include two fundamental pointer operations, assignment and dereferencing. The first operation sets a pointer variable's value to some useful address. If pointer variables are used only to manage dynamic storage, the allocation mechanism, whether by operator or built-in subprogram, serves to initialize the pointer variable.

If pointers are used for indirect addressing to variables that are not heap-dynamic, then there must be an explicit operator or built-in subprogram for fetching the address of a variable, which can then be assigned to the pointer variable.

An occurrence of a pointer variable in an expression can be interpreted in two distinct ways. First, it could be interpreted as a reference to the contents of the memory cell to which the variable is bound, which in the case of a pointer is an address. This is exactly how a nonpointer variable in an expression would be interpreted, although in that case it would not be an address. However, the pointer could also be interpreted as a reference to the value in the memory cell whose address is in the memory cell to which the variable is bound. In this case, the pointer is interpreted as an indirect reference. The former case is a normal pointer reference; the latter is the result of **dereferencing** the pointer. Dereferencing, which takes a reference through one level of indirection, is the second fundamental pointer operation. To clarify dereferencing, consider a pointer variable, `ptr`, that is bound to a memory cell with the value 7080. Suppose that the memory cell whose address is 7080 has the value 206. A normal reference to `ptr` yields 7080, but a dereferenced reference to `ptr` yields 206.

Dereferencing can be either explicit or implicit. In ALGOL 68 and FORTRAN 90 it is implicit, but in most other contemporary languages, it occurs only when explicitly specified. In Pascal, it is explicitly specified with the circumflex (^) as a postfix unary operation. For example, if `ptr` is a pointer variable with the value 7080, as in the above example, and the cell whose address is 7080 has the value 206, then the assignment

        j := ptr^

sets j to 206. This process is shown in Figure 5.11.

When pointers point to records, the syntax of the references to the fields of these records varies among languages. In C and C++, there are two ways a pointer to a record can be used to reference a field in that record. If a pointer variable `p` points to a record with a field named `age`,

Figure 5.11
The assignment operation **j := ptr^**

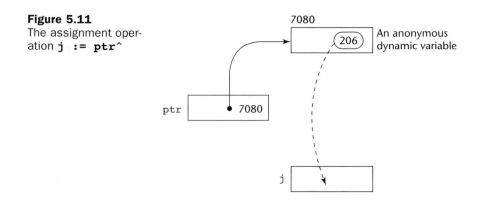

(`*p`)`.age` can be used to refer to that field. The operator, `->`, when used between a pointer to a record and a field of that record combines dereferencing and field reference. For example, the expression `p -> age` is equivalent to (`*p`)`.age`. In Pascal, the same reference is made with `p^.age`. In Ada, `p.age` can be used, because such uses of pointers are implicitly dereferenced.

Languages that provide pointers for the management of a heap must include an explicit allocation operation. Some also provide an explicit deallocation operation. These two operations are often in the form of built-in subprograms, although Ada, C++, and Java use an allocator operator.

5.10.3   Pointer Problems

The first high-level programming language to include pointer variables was PL/I, in which pointers can be used to refer to both heap-dynamic variables and other program variables. The pointers of PL/I are highly flexible, but their use can lead to several kinds of programming errors. Some of the problems of PL/I pointers are also present in the pointers of subsequent languages. Some recent languages, such as Java, have replaced pointers completely with reference types, which, along with implicit deallocation, eliminate the primary problems with pointers.

5.10.3.1 Dangling Pointers

A **dangling pointer,** or **dangling reference,** is a pointer that contains the address of a heap-dynamic variable that has been deallocated. Dangling pointers are dangerous for several reasons. First, the location being pointed to may have been reallocated to some new heap-dynamic variable. If the new variable is not the same type as the old one, type checks of uses of the dangling pointer are invalid. Even if the new one is the same type, its new value will bear no relationship to the old pointer's dereferenced value. Furthermore, if the dangling pointer is used to change the heap-dynamic variable, the value of the new heap-dynamic variable will be destroyed. Finally, it is possible that the location now is being temporarily used by the storage management system, possibly as a pointer in a chain of available blocks of storage, thereby allowing a change to the location to cause the storage manager to fail.

The following sequence of operations creates a dangling pointer in many languages:

1. Pointer `p1` is set to point at a new heap-dynamic variable.
2. Pointer `p2` is assigned `p1`'s value.
3. The heap-dynamic variable pointed to by `p1` is explicitly deallocated (setting p1 to nil), but `p2` is not changed by the operation. `P2` is now a dangling pointer.

5.10.3.2 Lost Heap-Dynamic Variables

A **lost heap-dynamic variable** is an allocated heap-dynamic variable that is no longer accessible to the user program. Such variables are often called **garbage** because they are not useful for their original purpose, and they also cannot be reallocated for some new use by the program. Lost heap-dynamic variables are most often created by the following sequence of operations:

1. Pointer `p1` is set to point to a newly created heap-dynamic variable.
2. `p1` is later set to point to another newly created heap-dynamic variable.

The first heap-dynamic variable is now inaccessible, or lost.

Languages that require explicit deallocation of dynamic variables share the problem of lost heap-dynamic variables. Sometimes this problem is called **memory leakage.** In the following sections, we investigate how language designers have dealt with the problems of dangling pointers and lost heap-dynamic variables.

5.10.4 Pointers in Pascal

In Pascal, pointers are used only to access dynamically allocated anonymous variables. Dangling pointers can be created easily in Pascal, because it includes an explicit deallocation operation. A Pascal programmer creates heap-dynamic variables with `new` and destroys them with `dispose`. To destroy heap-dynamic variables safely, the function `dispose` would be required to find and set all pointers pointing to the heap-dynamic variable being destroyed to `nil`. Unfortunately, this process is complex and costly, and as a result it is rarely implemented that way. This is a problem for all explicit deallocation processes in programming languages.

Pascal implementors choose among the following alternatives for explicit deallocation:

- Simply ignore `dispose`, in which case no deallocation is done, and none of the pointers that were pointing at the heap-dynamic object in question are changed.

- Do not include `dispose` in the language, making `dispose` an illegal statement.

- Actually deallocate the heap-dynamic variable in question and set the pointer that is the parameter to `dispose` to `nil`, thus creating dangling pointers from any other pointers that happen to be pointing at the object.

- Implement `dispose` completely and correctly, disallowing dangling pointers. (The author knows of no Pascal implementation that chose this alternative.)

5.10.5 Pointers in Ada

Ada provides pointers, called **access** types, that are similar to those of Pascal. In Ada, however, the dangling pointer problem is partially alleviated by the language's design. A heap-dynamic variable may be (at the implementor's option) implicitly deallocated at the end of the scope of its pointer type, thus dramatically lessening the need for explicit deallocation. Because heap-dynamic variables can only be accessed by variables of one type, when the end of the scope of that type declaration is reached, no pointers can be left pointing at the object. This lessens the problem because improperly implemented explicit deallocation is the major source of dangling pointers. Unfortunately, the Ada language also has an explicit deallocation, UNCHECKED_DEALLOCATION. Its name is meant to discourage its use, or at least warn the user of its potential problems.

The lost heap-dynamic variable problem is not eliminated by Ada's design of pointers.

One other small improvement in Ada pointers over those of Pascal and Modula-2 is the language's requirement that all pointers be implicitly initialized to **null** (Ada's version of nil). This prevents inadvertent accesses to random locations in memory because the user forgot to initialize a pointer before using it.

5.10.6 Pointers in C and C++

In C and C++, pointers can be used much as addresses are used in assembly languages. This means they are extremely flexible but must be used with great care. This design offers no solutions to the dangling pointer or lost heap-dynamic variable problems. However, the fact that pointer arithmetic is possible in C and C++ makes their pointers more interesting than those of the other programming languages.

Unlike the pointers of Pascal and Ada, which can only point into the heap, C and C++ pointers can point at virtually any variable anywhere in memory.

In C and C++, the asterisk (*) denotes the dereferencing operation, and the ampersand (&) denotes the operator for producing the address of a variable. For example, in the code

```
int *ptr;
int count, init;
...
ptr = &init;
count = *ptr;
```

the two assignment statements are equivalent to the single assignment:

```
count = init;
```

The assignment to the variable `ptr` sets `ptr` to the address of `init`. The first assignment to `count` dereferences `ptr` to produce the value at `init`, which is then assigned to `count`. So the effect of the first two assignment statements is to assign the value of `init` to `count`. Notice that the declaration of a pointer specifies its domain type.

Pointers can be assigned the address value of any object of the correct domain type, or they can be assigned the constant zero, which is used for nil.

Pointer arithmetic is also possible in some restricted forms. For example, if `ptr` is a pointer variable that is declared to point at some object of some data type, then

```
ptr + index
```

is a legal expression. The semantics of such an expression is as follows. Instead of simply adding the value of `index` to `ptr`, the value of `index` is first scaled by the size of the memory cell (in memory units) to which `ptr` is pointing. For example, if `ptr` points to a memory cell for a type that is four memory units in size, then `index` is multiplied by 4, and the result is added to `ptr`. The primary purpose of this sort of address arithmetic is array manipulation. The following discussion is related to single-dimensioned arrays only.

In C and C++, all arrays use zero as the lower bound of their subscript ranges, and array names without subscripts always refer to the address of the first element. In fact, an array name without a subscript is treated exactly like a pointer, except that it is a constant and therefore cannot be assigned. Consider the following declarations:

```
int list [10];
int *ptr;
```

Consider the initializing assignment

```
ptr = list;
```

which assigns the address of `list[0]` to `ptr`, because an array name without a subscript is interpreted as the base address of the array. Given this assignment, we can conclude that

```
*(ptr + 1) is equivalent to list[1],
*(ptr + index) is equivalent to list[index], and
ptr[index] is equivalent to list[index]
```

It is clear from these statements that the pointer operations include the same scaling that is used in indexing operations. Furthermore, pointers to arrays can be indexed as if they were array names.

Pointers can point to functions. This feature is used to pass functions as parameters to other functions. Pointers are also used for parameter passing, as discussed in Chapter 8.

C and C++ include pointers of type **void** *, which means they can point at values of any type. They are in effect generic pointers. However, type checking is not a problem with **void** * pointers, because they cannot be dereferenced. One common use of **void** * pointers is as parameters of functions that operate on memory. For example, suppose we wanted a function to move a sequence of bytes of data from one place in memory to another. It would be most general if it could be passed two pointers of any type. This would be legal if the corresponding formal parameters in the function were **void** * type. The function could then convert them to **char** * type and do the operation, regardless of what type pointers were sent as actual parameters.

5.10.7 Pointers in FORTRAN 90

Pointers in FORTRAN 90 are used to point to both heap-dynamic variables and static variables. For example, in

```
INTEGER, POINTER :: INT_PTR
INTEGER, POINTER, DIMENSION (:) :: INT_LIST_PTR
```

INT_PTR can point at any value of type INTEGER, and INT_LIST_PTR can point at any single dimensioned array of INTEGER elements.

FORTRAN 90 pointers are implicitly dereferenced in most uses. For example, when a pointer appears in a normal expression, it is always implicitly dereferenced. A special assignment statement form,

```
pointer => target
```

is used when dereferencing is not desired. This assignment is used both to set pointer variables to point at particular variables and to set them to have the address values of other pointer variables. Any variable that is to be pointed to by a pointer variable must have the **TARGET** attribute, which is set in its declaration. For example, in the following

```
INTEGER, TARGET :: APPLE
INTEGER ORANGE
```

APPLE can be pointed to by INT_PTR, but ORANGE cannot.

FORTRAN 90 pointers can easily become dangling, because the **DEALLOCATE** statement, which takes a pointer as an argument, makes no attempt to determine if other pointers are pointing at a heap-dynamic variable that is being deallocated.

5.10.8 Reference Types

C++ includes a special kind of pointer type, called a reference type, that is used primarily for the formal parameters in function definitions. A C++

reference type variable is a constant pointer that is always implicitly dereferenced. Because a C++ reference type variable is a constant, it must be initialized with the address of some variable in its definition, and after initialization a reference type variable can never be set to reference any other variable. The implicit dereference of course prevents assignment to the address value of a reference variable.

Reference type variables are specified in definitions by preceding their names with ampersands (`&`). For example,

```
int result = 0;
int &ref_result = result;
...
ref_result = 100;
```

In this code segment, `result` and `ref_result` are aliases.

When used as formal parameters in function definitions, reference types provide for two-way communication between the caller function and the called function. This is not possible with non-pointer parameter types, because C++ parameters are passed by value. Passing a pointer as a parameter accomplishes the same two-way communication, but pointer formal parameters require explicit dereferencing, making the code less readable and less safe. Reference parameters are referenced in the called function exactly as are other parameters. The calling function need not specify that a parameter whose corresponding formal parameter is a reference type is anything unusual. The compiler passes addresses, rather than values, to reference parameters.

In Java, reference variables are extended from their C++ form to one which allows them to replace pointers entirely. In their quest for increased safety over C++, the designers of Java removed C and C++ style pointers altogether. The fundamental difference between C++ pointers and Java references is that C++ pointers refer to memory addresses, whereas Java references refer to class instances. This immediately prevents arithmetic on references from being sensible. On the other hand, it does not disallow assignment. So, unlike C++ reference variables, Java reference variables can be assigned to refer to different class instances. All Java class instances are referenced by reference variables. That is in fact the only use of reference variables in Java. These issues are further discussed in Chapter 11. In the following, `String` is a standard Java class:

```
String str1;
...
str1 = "This is a Java literal string";
```

In this code, `str1` is defined to be a reference to a `String` class instance or object, but is initially set to null. The subsequent assignment sets `str1` to reference the `String` object, `"This is a Java literal string"`.

Because Java class instances are implicitly deallocated (there is no explicit deallocation operator), you cannot have a dangling reference.

5.10.9 Evaluation

The problems of dangling pointers and garbage have already been discussed at length. The problems of heap management are discussed in Section 5.10.l0.3.

Pointers have been compared with the goto. The goto statement widens the range of statements that can be executed next. Pointer variables widen the range of memory cells that can be referenced by a variable. Perhaps the most damning statement about pointers was made by Hoare (1973): "Their introduction into high-level languages has been a step backward from which we may never recover."

Java references provide some of the flexibility and the facilities of pointers, without the hazards. It remains to be seen if programmers will be willing to trade the full power of C and C++ pointers for the greater safety of Java references.

5.10.10 Implementation of Pointer and Reference Types

In most languages, pointers are used in heap management. The same is true for Java references. So, we cannot treat these two features separately. First we briefly describe how pointers and references are represented. We then discuss two possible solutions to the dangling pointer problem. Finally, we describe the major problems with heap management techniques.

5.10.10.1 Representations of Pointers and References

In most larger computers, pointers and references are single values stored in either two- or four-byte memory cells, depending on the size of the address space of the machine. However, most microcomputers are based on Intel microprocessors, which use addresses with two parts, a segment and an offset. So pointers and references are implemented in these systems as pairs of 16-bit words, one for each of the two parts of an address.

5.10.10.2 Solutions to the Dangling Pointer Problem

Dangling pointers are those that point to storage that has been deallocated. They are often created by explicit deallocation of heap-dynamic variables. Explicit deallocation creates dangling pointers because the deallocation statement names only one pointer to the heap-dynamic variable to be deallocated. Any other pointers to the disposed heap-dynamic variable are made dangling by the process, because the run-time system did not determine that other such pointers exist.

Two separate but related solutions to the dangling pointer problem have been either proposed or actually implemented. First, there is the proposal that uses extra heap cells, called tombstones.

Tombstones were proposed by Lomet (1975). The idea is to have all heap-dynamic variables include a special cell, called a tombstone, that is itself a pointer to the heap-dynamic variable. The actual pointer variable points only at tombstones and never to heap-dynamic variables. When a heap-dynamic variable is deallocated, the tombstone remains but is set to nil, indicating that the heap-dynamic variable no longer exists. This prevents a pointer from ever pointing to a deallocated variable. Any reference to any pointer that points to a nil tombstone can be detected as an error. The difference between the tombstone and nontombstone methods is shown in Figure 5.12.

Tombstones are costly in both time and space. Because tombstones are never deallocated, their storage is never reclaimed. Every access to a heap-dynamic variable through a tombstone requires one more level of indirection, which requires an additional machine cycle on most computers. Apparently none of the designers of the more popular languages have found the additional safety to be worth this additional cost, because no widely used language uses tombstones.

However, tombstones have been found to be valuable outside programming languages. They are used extensively by Macintosh system software to detect dangling pointer dereferences and to facilitate dynamic relocation of dynamically allocated memory cells.

An alternative to tombstones is the locks-and-keys approach used in the implementation of UW-Pascal (Fischer and LeBlanc, 1977, 1980). In

Figure 5.12
Implementing dynamic variables with and without tombstones

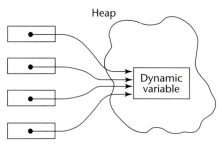

(a) Without tombstones

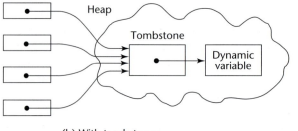

(b) With tombstones

this compiler, pointer values are represented as ordered pairs (key, address), where the key is an integer value. Heap-dynamic variables are represented as the storage for the variable plus a header cell that stores an integer lock value. When a heap-dynamic variable is allocated, a lock value is created and placed both in the lock cell of the heap-dynamic variable and in the key cell of the pointer that is specified in the call to `new`. Every access to the dereferenced pointer compares the key value of the pointer to the lock value in the heap-dynamic variable. If they match, the access is legal; otherwise, the access is treated as a run-time error. Any copies of the pointer value to other pointers must copy the key value. Therefore, any number of pointers can reference a given heap-dynamic variable. When a heap-dynamic variable is deallocated with `dispose`, its lock value is cleared to an illegal lock value. Then, if a pointer other than the one specified in the `dispose` is dereferenced, its address value will still be intact, but its key value will no longer match the lock, so the access will not be allowed.

As stated earlier, because Java does not have an explicit deallocation operation for heap memory, its references are never dangling.

5.10.10.3 Heap Management

Heap management can be a very complex run-time process. We examine the process in two separate situations: one in which all heap storage is allocated and deallocated in units of a single size, and one in which variable-size segments are allocated and deallocated. Our discussion will be brief and far from comprehensive, since a thorough analysis of these processes and their associated problems is not so much a language design issue as it is an implementation issue.

Single-Size Cells The simplest situation is when all allocation and deallocation is of a single-size cell. It is further simplified when every cell contains a pointer. This is the scenario of many implementations of LISP, where the problems of dynamic storage allocation were first encountered on a large scale. All LISP programs and most LISP data consist of cells connected into linked lists. Some string management processes are also involved, but we will ignore them here.

In a single-size allocation heap, all available cells are linked together using the pointers in the cells, forming a list of available space. Allocation is a simple matter of taking the required number of cells from this list when they are needed. Deallocation is a much more complex process. The basic problem with deallocation was discussed in Section 5.10.4, in connection with Pascal's `dispose` procedure. A heap-dynamic variable can be pointed to by more than one pointer, making it difficult to determine when the variable is no longer useful to the program. Simply because one pointer is disconnected from a cell obviously does not make it garbage; there could be several other pointers still pointing to the cell.

In LISP, several of the most frequent operations in programs create collections of cells that are no longer accessible to the program and therefore should be deallocated (put back on the list of available space). One of the fundamental design goals of LISP was to ensure that reclamation of unused cells would not be the task of the programmer but rather that of the run-time system. This left LISP implementors with the fundamental design question: When should deallocation be performed?

There are two distinct and in some ways opposite processes for reclaiming garbage: reference counters, in which reclamation is incremental and is done when inaccessible cells are created, and garbage collection, in which reclamation only occurs when the list of available space becomes empty. These two methods are sometimes called the **eager approach** and the **lazy approach,** respectively.

The **reference counter** method of storage reclamation accomplishes its goal by maintaining a counter in every cell, which stores the number of pointers that are currently pointing at the cell. Embedded in the decrement operation for the reference counters, which occurs when a pointer is disconnected from the cell, is a check for a zero value. If the reference counter reaches zero, it means that no program pointers are pointing at the cell, and it has thus become garbage and can be returned to the list of available space.

There are three distinct problems with the reference counter method. First, if storage cells are relatively small, the space required for the counters is significant. Second, some execution time is obviously required to maintain the counter values. Every time a pointer value is changed, the cell to which it was pointing must have its counter decremented, and the cell to which it is now pointing must have its counter incremented. In a language like LISP, in which nearly every action involves changing pointers, that can be a significant portion of the total execution time of a program. Of course, if pointer changes are not too frequent, this is obviously not a problem. Third, complications arise when a collection of cells is connected circularly. The problem here is that each cell in the circular list has a reference counter value of at least 1, which prevents it from being collected and placed back on the list of available space. A solution to this problem can be found in Friedman and Wise (1979).

The primary alternative to reference counters is called **garbage collection.** With this method, the run-time system allocates storage cells as requested and disconnects pointers from cells as necessary, without regard for storage reclamation (allowing garbage to accumulate), until it has allocated all available cells. At this point, a garbage collection process is begun to gather all the garbage left floating around in the heap. To facilitate the garbage collection process, every heap cell has an extra indicator bit or field that is used by the collection algorithm.

The collection process consists of three distinct phases. First, all cells in the heap have their indicators set to indicate they are garbage. This is, of course, a correct assumption for only some of the cells. The second part of the process is the most difficult. Every pointer in the program is traced into the heap, and all reachable cells are marked as not being garbage. After this, the third phase is executed: All cells in the heap that have not been specifically marked as still being used are returned to the list of available space.

To illustrate the flavor of algorithms used to mark the cells that are currently in use, we provide the following simple version of a marking algorithm. We assume that all heap-dynamic variables, or heap cells, consist of an information part, a part for the mark, named `tag`, and two pointers named `llink` and `rlink`. These cells are used to build directed graphs with at most two edges leading from any node. The marking algorithm traverses all spanning trees of the graphs, marking all cells that are found. Like other graph traversals, the marking algorithm uses recursion.

```
for every pointer r do
    mark(r)

procedure mark(ptr)
    if ptr <> null then
      if ptr^.tag is not marked then
        set ptr^.tag
        mark(ptr^.llink)
        mark(ptr^.rlink)
      end if
    end if
```

An example of the actions of this procedure on a given graph is shown in Figure 5.13. This simple marking algorithm suffers the problem of using a great deal of storage (for stack space to support recursion). A marking process that does not require additional stack space was developed by Schorr and Waite (1967). Their method reverses pointers as it traces out linked structures. Then, when the end of a list is reached, the process can follow the pointers back out of the structure.

The most serious problem with garbage collection can be summed up as follows: When you need it most, it works the worst. You need it most when the program actually needs most of the cells in the heap. Garbage collection in that situation takes a good deal of time, because most of the cells must be traced and marked as being useful. But in that case, the process yields only a small number of cells that can be placed on the list of available space. In addition to this problem, there is the cost of the additional space of the cell marks, which need be only a bit, and the execution time required to execute the collection process. However, these problems are not as serious as they sound, for two related reasons. First, memory is plentiful on most contemporary computers. Second, all larger computers use virtual memory, which makes their large memories appear much larger than they actually are.

Both the marking algorithms for the garbage collection method and the processes required by the reference counter method can be made more efficient by use of the pointer rotation and slide operations that are described by Suzuki (1982).

Figure 5.13
An example of the actions of the marking algorithm

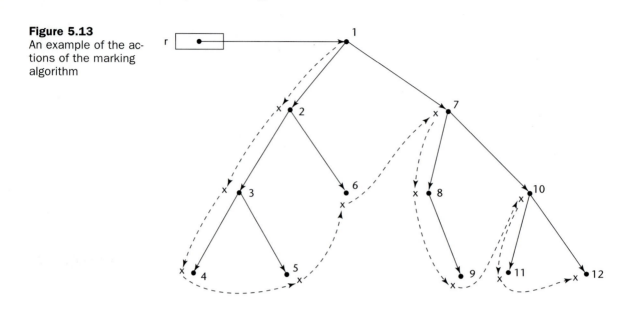

Dashed lines show the order of node_marking

Variable-Size Cells   Managing a heap from which variable-size cells are allocated has all the difficulties of managing one for single-size cells, but also has additional problems. Unfortunately, variable-size cells are required by most programming languages. The additional problems posed by variable-size cell management depend on the method used. If garbage collection is used, the following additional problems occur:

- The initial setting of the indicators of all cells in the heap to indicate that they are garbage is difficult. Because the cells are different sizes, scanning them becomes a problem. One solution to this is to require each cell to have the cell size as its first field. Then the scanning can be done, although it takes slightly more space and somewhat more time than its counterpart for fixed-size cells.

- The marking process is nontrivial. How can a chain be followed from a pointer if there is no predefined location for the pointer in the pointed-to cell? Cells that do not contain pointers at all are also a problem. Adding a system pointer to each cell will work, but it must be maintained in parallel with the user-defined pointers. This adds both space and execution time overhead to the cost of running the program.

- Maintaining the list of available space is another source of overhead. The list can begin with a single cell consisting of all available space. Requests for segments simply reduce the size of this block. Reclaimed cells are added to the list. The problem is that before long, the list becomes a long list of various-size segments, or blocks. This slows allocation because requests cause the list to be searched for sufficiently large blocks. Eventually, the list may consist of a large number of very small blocks, which are not large enough for most requests. At this point, adjacent blocks may need to be collapsed into larger blocks. Alternatives to using the first sufficiently large block on the list can shorten the search but require the list to be ordered by block size. In either case, maintaining the list is additional overhead.

If reference counters are used, the first two problems are avoided, but the available space list maintenance problem remains.

SUMMARY

The data types of a language are a large part of what determines that language's style and use. Along with control structures, they form the heart of a language.

The primitive data types of most imperative languages include numeric, character, and Boolean types. The numeric types are often directly supported by hardware.

The user-defined enumeration and subrange types are convenient and add to the readability and reliability of programs.

Arrays are part of most programming languages. The relationship between a reference to an array element and the address of that element is given in an access function, which is an implementation of a mapping. Arrays can be either static, as in FORTRAN 77; fixed stack-dynamic, as in Pascal procedures; stack-dynamic, as in Ada blocks; or heap-dynamic, as in FORTRAN 90's **ALLOCATABLE** arrays. Most languages allow only a few operations on complete arrays.

Records are now included in most languages. Fields of records are specified in a variety of ways. In the cases of COBOL and PL/I, they can be referenced without naming all of the enclosing records, although this is messy to implement and harmful to readability. In an object-oriented language such as Java, records are supported in the class construct.

Unions are locations that can store different type values at different times. Discriminated unions include a tag to record the current type value. A free union is one without the tag. Most languages with unions do not have safe designs for them, the exception being Ada.

Sets are sometimes convenient and are relatively easy to implement. The applications that usually use sets, however, can be done without too much difficulty using other data types.

Pointers are used for addressing flexibility and to control dynamic storage management. Pointers have some inherent dangers: Dangling pointers are difficult to avoid, and garbage is difficult to collect.

Reference types, such as those in Java, provide heap management without the dangers of pointers.

The level of difficulty in implementing a data type has a strong influence on whether the type will be included in a language. Enumeration types, subrange types, and record types are all relatively easy to implement. Arrays are also straightforward, although array element access is an expensive process when the array has several subscripts. The access function requires one addition and one multiplication for each subscript.

Pointers are costly to implement if they are used for dynamic storage management and if steps are taken to avoid dangling pointers. Heap management is relatively easy if all cells have the same size, but becomes more complicated with variable-size cell allocation and deallocation.

BIBLIOGRAPHIC NOTES

A wealth of computer science literature exists that is concerned with data type design, use, and implementation. Hoare gives one of the earliest systematic definitions of structured types in Dahl et al. (1972). Tenenbaum compares the type design of ALGOL 68 and Pascal (Tenenbaum, 1978). Feuer and Gehani (1982) compare C and Pascal, including their type structures. A discussion of the insecurities of the Pascal data type design is included in Welsh et al. (1977). A general discussion of a wide variety of data types is given in Cleaveland (1986).

Implementing run-time checks on the possible insecurities of Pascal data types is discussed in Fischer and LeBlanc (1980). Most compiler design books, such as Fischer and LeBlanc (1988) and Aho et al. (1986), describe implementation methods for data types, as do the other programming language texts, such as Pratt (1984) and Ghezzi and Jazayeri (1987). A detailed discussion of the problems of heap management can be found in Tenenbaum et al. (1990). Garbage collection methods are developed by Schorr and Waite (1967) and Deutsch and Bobrow (1976). A comprehensive discussion of garbage collection algorithms can be found in Cohen (1981).

REVIEW QUESTIONS

1. What is a descriptor?
2. What are the advantages and disadvantages of decimal data types?
3. What are the design issues for character string types?
4. Define the three string length options.
5. Define *ordinal*, *enumeration*, and *subrange types*.
6. What are the advantages of user-defined enumeration types?
7. What are the design issues for arrays?
8. Define *static*, *fixed stack-dynamic*, *stack-dynamic*, and *dynamic arrays*. What are the advantages of each?

9. What array initialization feature is available in Ada that is not available in other common imperative languages?

10. What is an aggregate constant?

11. What array operations are provided specifically for single-dimensioned arrays in Ada?

12. What are the differences between the slices of FORTRAN 90 and those of Ada?

13. Define *row major order* and *column major order*.

14. What is an access function for an array?

15. What are the required entries in a Pascal array descriptor, and when must they be stored (at compile time or run time)?

16. What is the purpose of level numbers in COBOL records?

17. Define *fully qualified* and *elliptical references* to fields in records.

18. Define *union, free union,* and *discriminated union*.

19. What are the design issues for unions?

20. What are the two problems with Pascal's unions?

21. In what ways are the unions of Ada safer than those of Pascal?

22. Why are there usually severe restrictions on the size of sets in Pascal implementations?

23. What are the design issues for pointer types?

24. What are the two common problems with pointers?

25. In what two ways are pointers in Ada safer than those of Pascal?

26. Why are the pointers of most languages restricted to pointing at a single type object?

27. What is a C++ reference type and what is its common use?

28. Why are reference variables in C++ better than pointers for formal parameters?

29. What advantages do Java reference type variables have over the pointers in other languages?

30. Describe the lazy and eager approaches to reclaiming garbage.

31. What are the differences between C++ and Java reference variables?

32. Why wouldn't arithmetic on Java references make sense?

PROBLEM SET

1. What are the arguments for and against representing Boolean values as single bits in memory?

2. Why does a decimal value waste memory space?

3. COBOL uses several different methods of storing decimal numbers. Explain the format and purpose of each.

4. VAX minicomputers use a format for floating-point numbers that is not the same as the IEEE standard. What is this format, and why was it chosen by the

designers of the VAX computers? A reference for VAX floating-point representations is Sebesta (1991).

5. Compare the tombstones and locks-and-keys methods of avoiding dangling pointers, from the points of view of safety and implementation cost.

6. Design a set of simple test programs to determine the type compatibility rules of a Pascal or C compiler to which you have access. Write a report of your findings.

7. What disadvantages are there in implicit dereferencing of pointers, but only in certain contexts? For example, consider the implicit dereference of a pointer to a record in Ada when it is used to reference a record field.

8. What significant justification is there for the -> operator in C and C++?

9. Determine which implementation option described in Section 5.9.4 is used by some Pascal compiler to which you have access.

10. The unions in C and C++ are separate from the records of those languages, rather than combined as they are in Pascal and Ada. What are the advantages and disadvantages to these two choices?

11. Determine whether some Pascal compiler to which you have access implements the **dispose** procedure.

12. Determine whether some C compiler to which you have access implements the **free** function.

13. Suppose that a language includes user-defined enumeration types and that the enumeration values could be overloaded; that is, the same literal value could appear in two different enumeration types, as in:

```
type
  colors = (red, blue, green);
  mood = (happy, angry, blue);
```

Use of the constant **blue** cannot be type checked. Propose a method of allowing such type checking without completely disallowing such overloading.

14. Multidimensional arrays can be stored in row major order, as in Pascal, or in column major order, as in FORTRAN. Develop the access functions for both of these arrangements for three-dimensional arrays.

15. In the Burroughs Extended ALGOL language, matrixes are stored as a single-dimensioned array of pointers to the rows of the matrix, which are treated as single-dimensioned arrays of values. What are the advantages and disadvantages of such a scheme?

16. Write a program that does matrix multiplication in some language that does subscript range checking and for which you can obtain an assembly language or machine language version from the compiler. Determine the number of instructions required for the subscript range checking and compare it with the total number of instructions for the matrix multiplication process.

17. Write a Pascal program that includes the following declarations:

```
var
  A, B : array [1..10] of integer;
  C : array [1..10] of integer;
  D : array [1..10] of integer;
```

Include code in the program that determines, for each array, which of the other three arrays are compatible with it.

18. If you have access to a compiler in which the user can specify whether subscript range checking is desired, write a program that does a large number of matrix accesses and times their execution. Run the program with subscript range checking and without it and compare the times.

19. Analyze and write a comparison of C's `malloc` and `free` functions with C++'s **new** and **delete** operators. Use safety as the primary consideration in the comparison.

20. Analyze and write a comparison of using C++ pointers and Java reference variables to refer to heap-dynamic variables. Use safety and convenience as the primary considerations in the comparison.

21. Write a short discussion of what was lost and what was gained in Java's designers decision to not include the pointers of C++.

22. What are the arguments for and against Java's implicit heap storage recovery, when compared with the explicit heap storage recovery required in C++?

6 Expressions and Assignment Statements

Friedrich (Fritz) L. Bauer

Fritz Bauer, whose home is Munich, along with Klaus Samelson in the early to mid-1950s, designed an algebraic language that could be directly implemented in hardware. Bauer's more significant contributions to language design, however, came as one of the principal members of the AL-GOL design team.

As the title indicates, the focus of this chapter is expressions and as-signment statements. The semantic rules that determine the order of evaluation of operators in expressions are discussed first. This is followed by the potential problems of implementation-defined operand evaluation order when expressions can have side effects. Overloaded operators, both predefined and user-defined, are then discussed, along with their effects on the expressions in programs. Next, mixed-mode expressions are dis-cussed and evaluated. This leads to the definition and evaluation of widen-ing and narrowing type conversions, both implicit and explicit. Relational and Boolean expressions are then discussed, including the idea of short-cir-cuit evaluation.

Finally, the assignment statement, from its simplest form to all of its variations, is covered, including assignments as expressions and mixed-mode assignments.

The material in this chapter is restricted to the conventional non-functional and non-logic programming languages, which use infix notation for arithmetic and logical expressions. Issues of expression specification and evaluation in functional and logic languages are discussed in Chapters 14 and 15, respectively.

Character string pattern-matching expressions were discussed as a part of the material on character strings in Chapter 5, so they are not men-tioned in this chapter.

6.1 Introduction

Expressions are the fundamental means of specifying computations in a programming language. It is crucial for a programmer to understand both the syntax and semantics of expressions. Methods of describing the syntax of expressions were described in Chapter 3. In this chapter, we focus on the semantics of expressions—that is, what they mean, which is deter-mined by how they are evaluated.

To understand expression evaluation, it is necessary to be familiar with the orders of operator and operand evaluation. The operator evalu-ation order of expressions is governed by the associativity and prece-dence rules of the language. Although the value of an expression sometimes depends on it, the order of operand evaluation in expressions is often unstated by language designers, a situation that allows programs to produce different results in different implementations. Other issues in expression semantics are type mismatches, coercions, and short-circuit evaluation.

The essence of the imperative programming languages is the domi-nant role of assignment statements. The purpose of an assignment state-ment is to change the value of a variable. So an integral part of all imperative languages is the concept of variables whose values change during program execution. (Nonimperative languages sometimes include variables of a different sort, such as the parameters of functions in functional languages.)

An assignment statement can simply cause a value to be copied from one memory cell to another. But in many cases, assignment statements include expressions with operators, which cause values to be copied to the processor and to be operated on, and the results to be copied back to memory.

Simple assignment statements specify an expression to be evaluated and a target location in which to place the result of the expression evaluation. As we shall see in this chapter, there are a number of variations on this basic form.

6.2 Arithmetic Expressions

Automatic evaluation of arithmetic expressions similar to those found in mathematics was one of the primary goals of the first high-level programming languages. Most of the characteristics of arithmetic expressions in programming languages were inherited from conventions that had evolved in mathematics. In programming languages, arithmetic expressions consist of operators, operands, parentheses, and function calls. The operators can be **unary,** meaning they have a single operand, or **binary,** meaning they have two operands. C, C++, and Java include a **ternary** operator, which has three operands, as discussed in Section 6.2.1.4.

In most imperative programming languages, binary operators are infix, which means they appear between their operands. One exception is Perl, which has some operators that are prefix, which means they precede their operands.

The purpose of an arithmetic expression is to specify an arithmetic computation. An implementation of such a computation must cause two actions: fetching the operands, usually from memory, and executing the arithmetic operations on those operands. In the following sections, we investigate the common design details of arithmetic expressions in the imperative languages.

Following are the primary design issues for arithmetic expressions, all of which are discussed in this section:

- What are the operator precedence rules?
- What are the operator associativity rules?
- What is the order of operand evaluation?
- Are there restrictions on operand evaluation side effects?

■ Does the language allow user-defined operator overloading?

■ What mode mixing is allowed in expressions?

6.2.1 Operator Evaluation Order

We first investigate the language rules that specify the order of evaluation of operators.

6.2.1.1 Precedence

The value of an expression depends, at least in part, on the order of evaluation of the operators in the expression. Consider the following expression:

```
A + B * C
```

Suppose the variables A, B, and C have the values 3, 4, and 5, respectively. If evaluated left to right (the addition first and then the multiplication), the result is 35. If evaluated right to left, the result is 23.

Instead of simply evaluating the order from left to right or right to left, mathematicians have developed the concept of placing operators in a hierarchy of evaluation priorities and basing the evaluation order of expressions partly on this hierarchy. For example, in mathematics, multiplication is considered to be of higher priority than addition. If we follow that convention in our example expression, the multiplication would be evaluated first.

The **operator precedence** rules for expression evaluation define the order in which the operators of different precedence levels are evaluated. The operator precedence rules for expressions are based on the hierarchy of operator priorities, as seen by the language designer. The operator precedence rules of the common imperative languages are nearly all the same, because they are all based on those of mathematics. In these languages, exponentiation has the highest precedence (when it is provided by the language), followed by multiplication and division on the same level, followed by binary addition and subtraction on the same level.

Many languages also include unary versions of addition and subtraction. Unary addition is called the **identity operator** because it usually has no associated operation and thus has no effect on its operand. Ellis and Stroustrup, speaking about C++, call it a historical accident and correctly label it useless (Ellis and Stroustrup, 1990, p. 56). In Java, unary plus actually does have an effect when its operand is **char**, **short**, or **byte**—it causes an implicit conversion of that operand to **int** type. Unary minus, of course, always changes its operand: It changes the sign of the operand's value.

In all of the common imperative languages, the unary minus operator can appear in an expression either at the beginning or anywhere inside the expression, as long as it is parenthesized to prevent it from being adjacent to another operator. For example,

```
A + (- B) * C
```

is legal, but

```
A + - B * C
```

usually is not.

As we shall see in Section 6.2.1.2, the precedence of the unary operators is rarely relevant in most languages.

The precedences of the arithmetic operators of a few common programming languages are as follows:

	FORTRAN	*Pascal*	*C*	*Ada*
Highest	**	*, /, **div**, **mod**	postfix ++, --	**, **abs**
	*, /	all +, -	prefix ++, --	*, /, **mod**
	all +, -		unary +, -	unary +, -
			*, /, %	binary +,-
Lowest			binary +, -	

The ** operator is exponentiation. The / and **div** operators of Pascal are described in Section 6.3. The % operator of C is exactly like the **mod** operator of Pascal and Ada: It takes two integer operands and yields the remainder of the first after division by the second. The ++ and -- operators of C are described in Section 6.7.5. The precedence rules of C++ and those of C are the same, except that in C++, all ++ and -- operators have equal precedence. Java's precedence rules are those of C++. The **abs** operator of Ada is a unary operator that yields the absolute value of its operand.

APL is odd among languages because it has a single level of precedence, as illustrated in the next section.

Precedence accounts for only some of the rules for the order of operator evaluation; associativity rules also affect it.

6.2.1.2 Associativity

Consider the following expression:

```
A - B + C - D
```

If the addition and subtraction operators have the same level of precedence, the precedence rules say nothing about the order of evaluation of the operators in this expression.

When an expression contains two adjacent occurrences of operators with the same level of precedence, the question of which operator is evaluated first is answered by the **associativity** rules of the language. An operator can either have left or right associativity, meaning that the leftmost occurrence is evaluated first or the rightmost occurrence is evaluated first, respectively.

Associativity in common imperative languages is left to right, except that the exponentiation operator (when provided) associates right to left. In the FORTRAN expression

```
A - B + C
```

the left operator is evaluated first. But exponentiation in FORTRAN is right associative, so in the expression

```
A ** B ** C
```

the right operator is evaluated first.

In Ada, exponentiation is nonassociative, which means that the expression

```
A ** B ** C
```

is illegal in Ada. Such an expression must be parenthesized to show the desired order, as in either

```
(A ** B) ** C
```

or

```
A ** (B ** C)
```

Now we can explain why the precedence of unary operators is most often not important. FORTRAN unary and binary minus operations have the same precedence, but in Ada (and most other common languages) unary minus has precedence over binary minus. However, consider the expression

```
- A - B
```

Because FORTRAN uses left associativity for both unary and binary minus, and because Ada gives precedence to unary minus over binary minus, this expression is equivalent to

```
(-A) - B
```

in both languages. Next consider the following expressions:

```
- A / B
- A * B
- A ** B
```

In the first two cases, the relative precedence of the unary minus operator and the binary operator is irrelevant—which is executed first has no effect on the value of the expression. In the last case, however, it does matter. Of the common programming languages, only FORTRAN and Ada have the exponentiation operator. In both cases, exponentiation has higher precedence than unary minus, so

```
- A ** B
```

is equivalent to

```
- (A ** B)
```

When unary operators appear at positions other than at the left end of expressions, they must be parenthesized in both languages, so in those situations those operators are forced to have the highest precedence (parentheses are discussed in Section 6.2.1.3).

The associativity rules for a few of the most common imperative languages are given below:

Language	Associativity Rule
FORTRAN	Left: *, /, +, –
	Right: **
Pascal	Left: all
C	Left: postfix ++, postfix --, *, /, %, binary +, binary –
	Right: prefix ++, prefix --, unary +, unary –
C++	Left: *, /, %, binary +, binary –
	Right: ++, --, unary –, unary +
Ada	Left: all except **
	Nonassociative: **

As stated in Section 6.2.1.1, in APL, all operators have the same level of precedence. Thus the order of evaluation of operators in APL expressions is determined entirely by the associativity rule, which is right to left for all operators. For example, in the expression

    A × B + C

the addition operator is evaluated first, followed by the multiplication operator (× is the APL multiplication operator). If A was 3, B was 4, and C was 5, the value of this APL expression would be 27.

Many compilers make use of the fact that some arithmetic operators are mathematically associative, meaning that the associativity rules have no impact on the value of an expression containing only those operators. For example, addition is mathematically associative, so in mathematics the value of the expression

    A + B + C

does not depend on the order of operator evaluation. If floating-point operations for mathematically associative operations were also associative, the compiler could use this fact to perform some simple optimizations. Specifically, if the compiler is allowed to reorder the evaluation of operators, it may be able to produce slightly faster code for expression evaluation. Compilers actually do these kinds of optimizations.

Unfortunately, both floating-point representations and floating-point arithmetic operations are only approximations of mathematics (because of size limitiations). The fact that a mathematical operator is associative does not necessarily imply that the corresponding floating-point operation is associative. In fact, only if all the operands and intermediate results can be exactly represented in floating-point notation will the process be precisely associative. For example, there are pathological situations in which integer addition on a computer is *not* associative. For example, suppose that a program must evaluate the expression

```
A + B + C + D
```

and that A and C are very large positive numbers, and B and D are negative numbers with very large absolute values. In this situation, adding B to A does not cause an overflow, but adding C to A does. Likewise, adding C to B does not cause overflow, but adding D to B does. Because of the limitations of computer arithmetic, addition is catastrophically unassociative in this case. Therefore, if the compiler reorders these addition operations, it affects the value of the expression. This is, of course, a problem that can be avoided by the programmer, assuming the approximate values of the variables are known. The programmer can simply parenthesize the expression (see Section 6.2.1.3) to ensure that only the safe order of evaluation is possible. However, this situation can arise in far more subtle ways, in which the programmer is less likely to notice the order dependence.

6.2.1.3 Parentheses

Programmers can alter the precedence and associativity rules by placing parentheses in expressions. A parenthesized part of an expression has precedence over its adjacent unparenthesized parts. For example, although multiplication has precedence over addition, in the expression

```
(A + B) * C
```

the addition will be evaluated first. Mathematically, this is perfectly natural. In this expression, the first operand of the multiplication operator is not available until the addition in the parenthesized subexpression is evaluated.

Languages that allow parentheses in arithmetic expressions could dispense with all precedence rules and simply associate all operators left to right or right to left. The programmer would specify the desired order of evaluation with parentheses. This would be simple because neither the author nor the readers of programs would need to remember any precedence or associativity rules. The disadvantage of this scheme is that it makes writing expressions more tedious, and it also seriously compromises the readability of the code. Yet this was the choice made by Ken Iverson, the designer of APL.

6.2.1.4 Conditional Expressions

We have now completed our discussion of unary and binary operators. Now we look at the ternary operator, **?:**, which is part of C, C++, and Java. This operator is used to form conditional expressions.

Sometimes **if-then-else** statements are used to perform a conditional expression assignment. For example, consider

```
if (count = 0)
  then average := 0
  else average := sum / count
```

In C, C++, and Java, this can be specified more conveniently in an assignment statement using a conditional expression, which has the form

```
expression_1 ? expression_2 : expression_3
```

where expression_1 is interpreted as a Boolean expression. If expression_1 evaluates to true, the value of the whole expression is the value of expression_2; otherwise, it is the value of expression_3. For example, the effect of the **if-then-else** above can be achieved with the following assignment statement, using a conditional expression:

```
average = (count == 0) ? 0 : sum / count;
```

In effect, the question mark denotes the beginning of the **then** clause, and the colon marks the beginning of the **else** clause. Both clauses are mandatory. Note that **?** is used in conditional expressions as a ternary operator.

Conditional expressions can be used anywhere in a C, C++, or Java program where any other expression can be used.

6.2.2   Operand Evaluation Order

A less commonly discussed design characteristic of expressions is the order of evaluation of operands. Variables in expressions are evaluated by fetching their values from memory. Constants are sometimes evaluated the same way. In other cases, a constant may be part of the machine language instruction and not require a memory fetch. If an operand is a parenthesized expression, then all operators it contains must be evaluated before its value can be used as an operand.

If neither of the operands of an operator has side effects, then operand evaluation order is irrelevant. Therefore, the only interesting case arises when the evaluation of an operand does have side effects.

6.2.2.1 Side Effects

A **side effect** of a function, called a **functional side effect,** occurs when the function changes either one of its parameters or a global variable. (A global variable is declared outside the function but is accessible in the function.)

Consider the expression

```
A + FUN(A)
```

If FUN does not have the side effect of changing A, then the order of evaluation of the two operands, A and FUN(A), has no effect on the value of the expression. However, if FUN changes A, there is an effect. Consider the following situation: FUN returns the value of its argument divided by 2 and changes its parameter to have the value 20. Suppose we have the following:

```
A := 10;
B := A + FUN(A)
```

Then, if the value of A is fetched first (in the expression evaluation process), its value is 10 and the value of the expression is 15. But if the second operand is evaluated first, then the value of the first operand is 20 and the value of the expression is 25.

The following C program illustrates the same problem when a function changes a global variable that appears in an expression:

```
int a = 5;
int fun1() {
  a = 17;
  return 3;
}  /* of fun1 */
void fun2() {
  a = a + fun1();
}  /* of fun2 */
void main() {
  fun2();
}  /* of main */
```

The value computed for a in fun2 depends on the order of evaluation of the operands in the expression a + fun1(). The value of a will be either 8 or 20.

There are two solutions to the problem of operand evaluation order. First, the language designer could disallow function evaluation from affecting the value of expressions by simply disallowing functional side effects. The second method of avoiding the problem is to state in the language definition that operands in expressions are to be evaluated in a particular order and demand that implementors guarantee that order.

Disallowing functional side effects is difficult, and it eliminates some flexibility for the programmer. Consider the case of C and C++, which have only functions. To eliminate the side effects of two-way parameters and still provide subprograms that return more than one value, a new subprogram type that is similar to the procedures of the other imperative languages would be required. Access to globals in functions would also have to be disallowed. However, when efficiency is important, using access to global variables to avoid parameter passing is an important method of increasing execution speed. In compilers, for example, global access to data such as the symbol table is commonplace.

The problem with having a strict evaluation order is that some code optimization techniques used by compilers involve reordering operand evaluations. A guaranteed order disallows those optimization methods when function calls are involved. There is, therefore, no perfect solution, as is borne out by actual language designs.

The designers of FORTRAN 77 envisioned a third solution. The FORTRAN 77 definition states that expressions that have function calls are legal only if the functions do not change the values of other operands in the expression. Unfortunately, it is not easy for the compiler to determine the exact effect a function can have on variables outside the function, especially in the presence of global variables provided by COMMON and the aliasing provided by EQUIVALENCE. This is a case where the language definition specifies the conditions under which a construct is legal but leaves it to the programmer to ensure that such constructs are legally specified in programs.

Pascal and Ada allow the operands of binary operators to be evaluated in any order chosen by the implementor. Furthermore, functions in these languages can have side effects, so the problems discussed above can occur. Functional side effects are further discussed in Chapter 8.

The Java language definition guarantees that operands appear to be evaluated in left-to-right order, eliminating the problem discussed in this section.

6.3 Overloaded Operators

Arithmetic operators are often used for more than one purpose. For example, + is frequently used for addition of any numeric type operands. Some languages, Java for example, also use it for string catenation. This multiple use of an operator is called **operator overloading** and is generally thought to be acceptable, as long as readability and/or reliability do not suffer. Some believe there is too much operator overloading in APL and SNOBOL, where most operators are used for both unary and binary operations.

As an example of the possible dangers of overloading, consider the use of the ampersand (&) in C. As a binary operator, it specifies a bitwise logical AND operation. As a unary operator, however, its meaning is totally different. As a unary operator with a variable as its operand, the expression value is the address of that variable. In this case, the ampersand is called the address-of operator. For example, the execution of

```
x = &y;
```

causes the address of y to be placed in x. There are two problems with this multiple use of the ampersand. First, using the same symbol for two completely unrelated operations is detrimental to readability. Second, the simple keying error of leaving out the first operand for a bitwise AND operation can go undetected by the compiler, because it is interpreted as an address-of operator. Such an error may be difficult to diagnose.

Virtually all programming languages have a less serious but similar problem, which is often due to the overloading of the minus operator. The problem is only that the compiler cannot tell if the operator is meant to be binary or unary. So once again, failure to include the first operand when the operator is meant to be binary cannot be detected as an error by the compiler. However, the meanings of the two operations, unary and binary, are at least closely related, so readability is not affected.

Distinct operator symbols not only increase readability, but they are sometimes convenient to use for common operations as well. The division operator is an example. Consider the problem of finding the floating-point average of a list of integers. Normally the sum of those integers is computed as an integer. Suppose this has been done in the variable `sum`, and the number of values is in `count`. Now, if the floating-point average is to be computed and placed in the floating-point variable `avg`, this computation could be specified in C++ as

```
avg = sum / count;
```

But this assignment produces an incorrect result in most cases. Because both operands of the division operator are integer type, an integer division operation takes place, in which the result is truncated to an integer. Then, in spite of the fact that the destination (`avg`) is floating-point type, its value from this assignment cannot have a fractional part. The integer result of division is converted to floating-point for the assignment *after* the truncation from the integer division.

When a distinct operator symbol for floating-point division is available, the situation is simplified. For example, in Pascal, where / means floating-point division, the following assignment can be used

```
avg := sum / count
```

where `avg` is floating-point type, and `sum` and `count` are integer type. Both operands will be implicitly converted to floating point, and a floating-point division operation is used. This kind of implicit conversion operation is further discussed in the following section. Integer division in Pascal is specified by the **div** operator, which takes integer operands and produces an integer result. When no distinct operator for floating-point division is provided, explicit conversions must be used. Such conversions are discussed in Section 6.4.2.

Some languages that support abstract data types (see Chapter 10), for example Ada, C++, and FORTRAN 90, allow the programmer to further overload operator symbols. For example, suppose a user wants to define the * operator between a scalar integer and an integer array to mean that each element of the array is to be multiplied by the scalar. This could be done by writing a function subprogram named * that performs this new operation. The compiler will choose the correct meaning when an overloaded operator is specified, based on the types of the operands, as with language-defined overloaded operators. For example, if this new definition for * is defined in an Ada program, an Ada compiler will use the new definition for * whenever the * operator appears with a simple integer as the left operand and an integer array as the right operand.

When sensibly used, user-defined operator overloading can aid readability. For example, if + and * are overloaded for a matrix abstract data type and A, B, C, and D are variables of that type, then

```
A * B + C * D
```

can be used instead of

```
MatrixAdd(MatrixMult(A, B), MatrixMult(C, D))
```

On the other hand, user-defined overloading can be harmful to readability. For one thing, nothing prevents a user from defining + to mean multiplication. Furthermore, seeing an * operator in a program, the reader must find both the types of the operands and the definition of the operator to determine its meaning. Any or all of these definitions could be in other files.

C++ has a few operators that cannot be overloaded. Among these are the class or structure member operator (.) and the scope resolution operator (::). Interestingly, operator overloading was one of the C++ features that was not copied into Java.

6.4 Type Conversions

Type conversions are either narrowing or widening. A **narrowing conversion** converts a value to a type that cannot store even approximations of all of the values of the original type. For example, converting a **double** to a **float** in C (the range of **double** is much larger than that of **float**). A **widening conversion** converts a value to a type that can include at least approximations of all of the values of the original type, for example, converting an **int** to a **float** in C. Widening conversions are nearly always safe, whereas narrowing conversions are not.

As an example of a potential problem with a widening conversion, consider the following. In many language implementations, although integer to float conversions are widening conversions, some accuracy may be lost. For example, in some implementations, integers are stored in 32 bits, which allows at least nine decimal digits of precision. But in many cases, floating-point values are also stored in 32 bits, with only about seven decimal digits of precision. So, integer to floating-point widening can result in the loss of two digits of precision.

Type conversions can be either explicit or implicit. The following two subsections discuss these two kinds of type conversions.

6.4.1 Coercion in Expressions

One of the design decisions concerning arithmetic expressions is whether an operator can have operands of different types. Languages that do allow such expressions, which are called **mixed-mode expressions,** must define conventions for implicit operand type conversions, called coercions, because computers usually do not have binary operations that take operands of different types. Recall that in Chapter 4 we defined coercion to be an implicit type conversion that is initiated by the compiler. We refer to type conversions explicitly requested by the programmer as explicit conversions, or casts, not coercions.

Although some operator symbols may be overloaded, we assume that a computer system, either in hardware or in some level of software simulation, has an operation for each operand type and operator defined in the language. For overloaded operators in a language that uses static type binding, the compiler chooses the correct type of operation on the basis of the types of the operands. When the two operands of an operator are not of the same type and that is legal in the language, the compiler must choose one of them to be coerced and supply the code for that coercion. In the following discussion, we examine the coercion design choices of several common languages.

Language designers are not in agreement on the issue of coercions in arithmetic expressions. Those against a broad range of coercions are concerned with the reliability problems that can result from such coercions, because they eliminate the benefits of type checking. Those who would rather include all these coercions are more concerned with the loss in flexibility that results from restrictions. The issue is whether programmers should be concerned with this category of errors or whether the compiler should detect them.

As a simple illustration of the problem, consider the following skeletal C program:

```
void main() {
  int a, b, c;
  float d;
  ...
  a = b * d;
  ...
}
```

Assume that the second operand of the multiplication operator was supposed to be c, but because of a keying error it was typed as d. Because mixed-mode expressions are legal in C, the compiler would not detect this as an error. It would simply insert code to coerce the value of the other operand, b, to **float**. If mixed-mode expressions were not legal in C, this keying error would have been detected by the compiler as a type error.

As a more extreme example of the dangers and costs of too much coercion, consider PL/I's efforts to achieve flexibility in expressions. In PL/I, a character string variable can be combined with an integer in an expression. At run time, the string is scanned for a numeric value. If the value happens to contain a decimal point, the value is assumed to be of floating-point type, the other operand is coerced to floating-point, and the resulting operation is floating-point. This coercion policy is very expensive because both the type check and the conversion must be done at run time. It also eliminates the possibility of detecting programmer errors in expressions, because a binary operator can combine an operand of any type with an operand of virtually any other type.

Because error detection is reduced when mixed-mode expressions are allowed, two languages, Ada and Modula-2, allow very few mixed type operands in expressions. Neither allows mixing of integer and floating-point operands in an expression, with one exception: In Ada, the exponentiation operator, `**`, can take either a floating-point or an integer type for the first operand and an integer type for the second operand. Both languages allow a few other kinds of operand type mixing, usually related to subrange types.

In most of the other common languages, there are no restrictions on mixed-mode arithmetic expressions.

C++ and Java have integer types that are smaller than the **int** type. In C++, these are **char** and **short int**; in Java, they are **byte**, **short**, and **char**. Operands of all of these types are coerced to **int** whenever virtually any operator is applied to them. So while data can be stored in variables of these types, it cannot be manipulated before conversion to a larger type. For example, consider the following Java code:

```
byte a, b, c;
...
a = b + c;
```

The values of b and c are coerced to **int** and an **int** addition is performed. Then the sum is converted to **byte** and put in a.

6.4.2 Explicit Type Conversion

Most languages provide some capability for doing explicit conversions, both widening and narrowing. In some cases, warning messages are produced when an explicit narrowing conversion results in a significant change to the value of the object being converted.

Both Modula-2 and Ada provide explicit conversion operations that have the syntax of function calls. For example, in Ada, we can have

```
AVG := FLOAT(SUM) / FLOAT(COUNT)
```

where AVG is floating-point type, and SUM and COUNT can be any numeric type.

In the C-based languages, explicit type conversions are called **casts.** The syntax of a cast is not that of a function call; rather, the desired type is placed in parentheses just before the expression to be converted, as shown in

```
(int) angle
```

One of the reasons for the parentheses in C conversions is that C has several two-word type names, such as **long int**.

6.4.3 Errors in Expressions

A number of errors can occur in expression evaluation. If the language requires type checking, then operand type errors cannot occur. We already discussed the errors that can occur because of coercions of operands in expressions. The other kinds of errors are due to limitations of computer arithmetic and the inherent limitations of arithmetic. The most common error is created when the result of an operation cannot be represented in the memory cell where it must be stored. This is called overflow or underflow, depending on whether the result was too large or too small. One limitation of arithmetic is that division by zero is disallowed. Of course, the fact that it is not mathematically allowed does not prevent a program from attempting to do it.

Floating-point overflow and underflow, and division by zero are examples of run-time errors, which are sometimes called exceptions. The ways language designers can deal with exceptions are discussed in Chapter 13.

6.5 Relational and Boolean Expressions

In addition to arithmetic expressions, programming languages have relational and Boolean, or logical, expressions.

6.5.1 Relational Expressions

A **relational operator** is an operator that compares the values of its two operands. A **relational expression** has two operands and one relational operator. The value of a relational expression is Boolean, except when Boolean is not a type in the language. The relational operators are usually overloaded for a variety of types. The operation that determines the truth or falsehood of a relational expression depends on the operand types. It can be simple, as for integer operands, or complex, as for character string operands. Typically, the types of the operands that can be used for relational operators are numeric types, strings, and ordinal types.

The syntax of the relational operators available in some common languages is as follows:

Operation	Pascal	Ada	C	FORTRAN 77
Equal	=	=	==	.EQ.
Not equal	<>	/=	!=	.NE.
Greater than	>	>	>	.GT.
Less than	<	<	<	.LT.
Greater than or equal	>=	>=	>=	.GE.
Less than or equal	<=	<=	<=	.LE.

The FORTRAN I designers used English abbreviations because the symbols > and < were not on the card punches at the time of FORTRAN I's design. FORTRAN 90 allows both the original FORTRAN relational operators and operators that are exactly like those of Pascal except that == is used for equality.

The relational operators always have lower precedence than the arithmetic operators, so that in expressions such as

```
a + 1 > 2 * b
```

the arithmetic expressions are evaluated first.

6.5.2 Boolean Expressions

Boolean expressions consist of Boolean variables, Boolean constants, relational expressions, and Boolean operators. The operators usually include those for the AND, OR, and NOT operations, and sometimes for exclusive OR and equivalence. Boolean operators usually take only Boolean operands (Boolean variables, Boolean literals, or relational expressions) and produce Boolean values.

In most languages, the Boolean operators, like the arithmetic operators, are evaluated in a hierarchical precedence order. In most of the common imperative languages, the unary NOT has the highest precedence, followed by AND at a separate level, and OR at the lowest level.

Because arithmetic expressions can be the operands of relational expressions, and relational expressions can be the operands of Boolean expressions, the three categories of operators must be placed in precedence levels relative to each other.

The precedence of all Ada operators is

Highest   ******, **abs**, **not**

          *, /, **mod**, **rem**

          +, − (unary)

          +, −, & (binary)

          =, /=, <, >, <=, >=, **in**, **not in**

Lowest   **and**, **or**, **xor**, **and then**, **or else**

Notice that Ada's Boolean operators, with the exception of **not**, share the same precedence level. All of these equal-precedence Boolean operators are nonassociative. If two or more different Boolean operators appear in an expression, parentheses must be used to show the order of evaluation. For example,

```
A > B and A < C or K = 0
```

is illegal in Ada. This expression can be legally written as either

```
(A > B and A < C) or K = 0
```

or

```
A > B and (A < C or K = 0)
```

The Ada Boolean operators **and then** and **or else** are discussed in the next section.

C is odd among the popular imperative languages in that it has no Boolean type and thus no Boolean values. Instead, numeric values are used to represent Boolean values. In place of Boolean operands, numeric variables and constants are used, with zero considered false and all nonzero values considered true. The result of evaluating such an expression is an integer, with the value 0 if false and 1 if true.

One odd result of C's design is that the expression

```
a > b > c
```

is legal. The leftmost relational operator is evaluated first because the relational operators of C are left associative, producing either 0 or 1. Then this result is compared with the variable **c**. There is never a comparison between **b** and **c**.

When the nonarithmetic operators of C and C++ are included, there are over 50 operators and 17 different levels of precedence. This is clear evidence of the richness of the collections of operators and the complexity of expressions possible in these languages.

Readability dictates that a language should include a Boolean type, as we stated in Chapter 5, rather than simply using numeric types in Boolean expressions, as in C. Some error detection is lost in C's use of numeric types, because any numeric expression, whether intended or not, is a legal operand to a Boolean operator. In the other imperative languages, any non-Boolean expression used as an operand of a Boolean operator is detected as an error.

In Pascal, the Boolean operators have higher precedence than the relational operators, so the expression

```
a > 5 or a < 0
```

is illegal (because 5 is not a legal Boolean operand). The correct version is

```
(a > 5) or (a < 0)
```

6.6 **Short-Circuit Evaluation**

A **short-circuit evaluation** of an expression is one in which the result is determined without evaluating all of the operands and/or operators. For example, the value of the arithmetic expression

```
(13 * A) * (B / 13 - 1)
```

is independent of the value of (B / 13 - 1) if A is 0, because 0 * x = 0 for any x. So when A is 0, there is no need to evaluate (B / 13 - 1) or perform the second multiplication. However, in arithmetic expressions this shortcut is not easily detected during execution, so it is never taken.

The value of the Boolean expression

```
(A >= 0) and (B < 10)
```

is independent of the second relational expression if A < 0, because (FALSE **and** x) is FALSE for all values of x. So when A < 0, there is no need to evaluate B, the constant 10, the second relational expression, or the **and** operation. Unlike the case of arithmetic expressions, this shortcut can be easily discovered during execution and taken.

Many Pascal programmers have encountered a problem when attempting to write a table look-up loop using the **while** statement. One simple version of Pascal code for such a look-up, assuming that list[1..listlen] is the array to be searched and key is the searched-for value, is

```
index := 1;
while (index <= listlen) and (list[index] <> key) do
    index := index + 1
```

The problem with this is that most (standard) Pascal implementations do not use short-circuit evaluation, so both relational expressions in the Boolean expression of the **while** statement are evaluated, regardless of the value of the first. Thus, if key is not in list, the program will terminate with a subscript out-of-range error. The same iteration that has index > listlen will reference list[listlen+1], which causes the indexing error because list is declared to have listlen as an upper bound subscript value.

If a language provides short-circuit evaluation of Boolean expressions and it is used, this is not a problem. In the preceding example, a short-circuit evaluation scheme would evaluate the first operand of the AND operator, but it would skip the second operand if the first operand is false.

Short-circuit evaluation of expressions exposes the problem of allowing side effects in expressions. Suppose that short-circuit evaluation is used on an expression and part of the expression that contains a side effect is not evaluated; then the side effect will only occur in complete evaluations of the whole expression. If program correctness depends on the side effect, short-circuit evaluation can result in a serious error. For example, consider the C expression

```
(a > b) || (b++ / 3)
```

In this expression, **b** is changed (in the second arithmetic expression) only when **a** **<=** **b**. If the programmer assumed **b** would be changed every time this expression is evaluated during execution, the program will fail.

In Modula-2, every evaluation of AND and OR expressions is short circuit.

The FORTRAN 77 definition recognizes this problem and simply states that the implementor may choose not to evaluate any more of an expression than is necessary to determine the result. The relevant caveat is that if the unevaluated part of the expression is a function call whose execution assigns a value to any variable declared outside the function, that variable must be set to "undefined" by the short-circuit evaluation. There are, however, problems in actually implementing the rule. The main problem is the difficulty of detecting any such relevant side effects of functions.

Ada allows the programmer to specify short-circuit evaluation of the Boolean operators AND and OR by using the two-word operators **and then** and **or else**. For example, again assuming that LIST is declared to have a subscript range of 1..LISTLEN, the Ada code

```
INDEX := 1;
while (INDEX <= LISTLEN) and then (LIST (INDEX) /= KEY)
  loop
  INDEX := INDEX + 1;
  end loop;
```

will not cause an error when KEY is not in LIST and INDEX becomes larger than LISTLEN.

In C, C++, and Java, the usual AND and OR operators, **&&** and **||**, respectively, are short circuit. However, these languages also have bitwise AND and OR operators, **&** and **|**, respectively, that can be used on Boolean-valued operands and are not short circuit.

The inclusion of both short-circuit and ordinary operators is clearly the best design because it provides the programmer the flexibility of choosing short-circuit evaluation for any or all Boolean expressions.

6.7 Assignment Statements

As we have previously stated, the assignment statement is one of the central constructs in imperative languages. It provides the mechanism by which the user can dynamically change the bindings of values to variables. In the following section, the simplest form of assignment is discussed. Subsequent sections describe a variety of alternatives.

6.7.1 Simple Assignments

The general syntax of the simple assignment statement is

< target_variable > < assignment_operator > < expression >

FORTRAN, BASIC, PL/I, C, C++, and Java use the equal sign for the assignment operator. This can lead to confusion if the equal sign is also used as a relational operator, as it is in PL/I and BASIC. For example, the PL/I assignment

```
A = B = C
```

sets `A` to the Boolean value of the relational expression `B = C`, although it looks as though these variables are being set equal to each other. In the cases of the other languages that use = for assignment, a different symbol is used for the relational operator for equality, which avoids the problem of overloading the assignment operator.

ALGOL 60 pioneered the use of `:=` as the assignment operator, and many later languages have followed that choice.

The assignment operator in C, C++, and Java is treated much like a binary operator, and as such it can appear embedded in expressions. This operator is discussed in Section 6.7.6.

The design choices of how assignments are used in a language have varied widely. In some languages, such as FORTRAN, Pascal, and Ada, it can only appear as a stand-alone statement and the destination is restricted to a single variable. There are, however, many alternatives.

6.7.2 Multiple Targets

One alternative to the simple assignment statement is to allow assignment of the expression value to more than one location. For example, in PL/I, the statement

```
SUM, TOTAL = 0
```

assigns the value zero to both `SUM` and `TOTAL`. Multiple target assignment statements are a convenience for programmers, but not a significant one.

The effects of multiple-target assignments can also be achieved using the assignment operator in C, C++, and Java, as discussed in Section 6.7.6.

6.7.3 Conditional Targets

C++ and Java allow conditional targets on assignment statements. For example, consider

```
flag ? count1 : count2 = 0;
```

This is equivalent to

```
if (flag) count1 = 0 ; else count2 = 0 ;
```

6.7.4 Compound Assignment Operators

A **compound assignment operator** is a shorthand method of specifying a commonly needed form of assignment. The form of assignment that can be abbreviated with this technique has the destination variable also appearing as the first operand in the expression on the right side, as in

```
a = a + b
```

Compound assignment operators were introduced by ALGOL 68 and later adopted in a slightly different form by C. The syntax of C's compound assignment operators is the catenation of the desired binary operator to the = operator. For example,

```
sum += value;
```

is equivalent to

```
sum = sum + value;
```

C, C++, and Java have versions of the compound assignment operators for most of their binary operators.

6.7.5 Unary Assignment Operators

C, C++, and Java include two special unary arithmetic operators that are actually abbreviated assignments. They combine increment and decrement operations with assignment. The operators, ++ for increment and -- for decrement, can be used either in expressions or to form stand-alone single-operator assignment statements. They can appear as either prefix operators, meaning they precede the operands, or as postfix operators, meaning they follow the operands. In the assignment statement

```
sum = ++ count;
```

the value of count is incremented by 1 and then assigned to sum. This could also be stated as

```
count = count + 1;
sum = count;
```

If the same operator is used as a postfix operator, as in

```
sum = count ++;
```

the assignment of the value of `count` to `sum` occurs first; then `count` is incremented. The effect is the same as that of the two statements

```
sum = count;
count = count + 1;
```

An example of the use of the unary increment operator to form a complete assignment statement is

```
count ++;
```

which simply increments `count`. It does not look like an assignment, but it certainly is one. It is equivalent to the statement

```
count = count + 1;
```

When two unary operators apply to the same operand, the association is right to left. For example, in

```
- count ++
```

`count` is first incremented and then negated. So it is

```
- (count ++)
```

not

```
(- count) ++
```

The increment and decrement operators of C, C++, and Java are frequently used to form array subscript expressions.

The PDP-11 computer, on which C was first implemented, has autoincrement and autodecrement addressing modes, which are hardware versions of the increment and decrement operators of C when they are used as array indexes. We might guess from this that the design of these C operators was based on the design of the PDP-11 architecture. That guess would be wrong, however, because the C operators were inherited from the B language, which was designed before the first PDP-11.

6.7.6 Assignment as an Expression

In C, C++, and Java, the assignment statement produces a result, which is the same as the value assigned to the target. It can therefore be used as an expression and as an operand in other expressions. This design treats the assignment operator much like any other binary operator, except that it has the side effect of changing its left operand. Although this may seem odd to those who have not used one of these languages, it is sometimes convenient. For example, in C, it is common to write statements such as

```
while ((ch = getchar()) != EOF) { ... }
```

In this statement, the next character from the standard input file, usually the keyboard, is gotten with `getchar` and assigned to the variable `ch`. The result, or value assigned, is then compared with the constant `EOF`. If `ch` is not equal to `EOF`, the compound statement { ... } is executed. Note that the assignment must be parenthesized—in these languages the precedence of the assignment operator is lower than that of the relational operators. Without the parentheses, the new character would be compared with `EOF` first. Then the result of that comparison, either 0 or 1, would be assigned to `ch`.

The disadvantage of allowing assignment statements to be operands in expressions is that it provides yet another kind of expression side effect. This type of side effect can lead to expressions that are difficult to read and understand. An expression with any kind of side effect has this disadvantage. Such an expression cannot be read as an expression, which in mathematics is a denotation of a value, but only as a list of instructions with an odd order of execution. For example, the expression

```
a = b + (c = d / b++) - 1
```

denotes the instructions

```
Assign b to temp
Assign b + 1 to b
Assign d / temp to c
Assign b + c to temp
Assign temp - 1 to a
```

Note that C's use of the assignment operator allows the effect of multiple-target assignments, such as

```
sum = count = 0;
```

in which `count` is first assigned the zero, and then `count`'s value is assigned to `sum`.

There is a loss of error detection in the C design of the assignment operation that frequently leads to program errors. In particular, if we type

```
if (x = y) ...
```

instead of

```
if (x == y) ...
```

which is an easy mistake to make, it is not detectable as an error by the compiler. Rather than testing a relational expression, the value that is assigned to `x` is tested (in this case, it is the value of `y` that reaches this statement). This is actually a result of three design decisions: allowing assignment to behave like an ordinary binary operator, using arithmetic expressions as Boolean operands, and using two very similar operators, = and ==, to have completely different meanings. This is another example of the safety deficiencies of C and C++ programs. Note that Java allows only **boolean** expressions in its **if** statements, disallowing this problem.

6.8 Mixed-Mode Assignment

We discussed mixed-mode expressions in Section 6.4.1. Frequently, assignment statements also are mixed-mode. The design question is, Does the type of the expression have to be the same as the type of the variable being assigned, or can coercion be used in some cases of type mismatch?

FORTRAN, C, and C++ use coercion rules for mixed-mode assignment that are similar to those they use for mixed-mode expressions; that is, many of the possible type mixes are legal, with coercion freely applied.

Pascal includes some assignment coercion; for example, `integer` values can be assigned to `real` variables, but not vice versa. Ada and Modula-2 do not allow mixed-mode assignment.

In a clear departure from C and C++, Java allows mixed-mode assignment only if the required coercion is widening. So, an **int** value can be assigned to a **float** variable, but not vice versa.

In all languages that allow mixed-mode assignment, the coercion takes place only after the right side expression has been evaluated. One alternative would be to coerce all operands in the right side to the type of the target before evaluation. For example, consider the following code:

```
int a, b;
float c;
...
c = a / b;
```

Because c is float, the values of a and b could be coerced to **float** before the division, which could produce a different value for c than if the coercion were delayed (for example, if a were 2 and b were 3).

SUMMARY

Expressions consist of constants, variables, parentheses, function calls, and operators. Assignment statements include target variables, assignment operators, and expressions.

The semantics of an expression is determined in large part by the order of evaluation of operators. The associativity and precedence rules for operators in the expressions of a language determine the order of operator evaluation in those expressions. Operand evaluation order is important if functional side effects are possible. Type conversions can be widening or narrowing. Some narrowing conversions produce erroneous values. Implicit type conversions, or coercions, in expressions are common, although they eliminate the error-detection benefit of type checking, which in turn lowers reliability. Explicit type conversions are often called casts.

Assignment statements have appeared in a wide variety of forms, including conditional targets, multiple targets, and assigning operators.

1. Define *operator precedence* and *operator associativity*.

2. Define *functional side effect*.

3. What is a coercion?

4. What is a conditional expression?

5. What is an overloaded operator?

6. Define *narrowing* and *widening conversions*.

7. What is a mixed-mode expression?

8. How does operand evaluation order interact with functional side effects?

9. What is short-circuit evaluation?

10. Name a language that always does short-circuit evaluation of Boolean expressions. Name one that never does it. Name one in which the programmer is allowed to choose.

11. How does C support relational and Boolean expressions?

12. What is the purpose of a compound assignment operator?

13. What is the associativity of C's unary arithmetic operators?

14. What is one possible disadvantage of treating the assignment operator as if it were an arithmetic operator?

15. What mixed-mode assignments are allowed in Ada?

16. What mixed-mode assignments are allowed in Java?

P R O B L E M   S E T

1. When might you want the compiler to ignore type differences in an expression?

2. State your own arguments for and against allowing mixed-mode arithmetic expressions.

3. Do you think the elimination of overloaded operators in your favorite language would be beneficial? Why or why not?

4. Would it be a good idea to eliminate all operator precedence rules and require parentheses to show the desired precedence in expressions? Why or why not?

5. Should C's assigning operations (for example, **+=**) be included in other languages? Why or why not?

6. Should C's single-operand assignment forms (for example, **++count**) be included in other languages? Why or why not?

7. Describe a situation in which the add operator in a programming language would not be commutative.

8. Describe a situation in which the add operator in a programming language would not be associative.

9. Write a Pascal program segment, using a **while** construct to search an array of integers for a particular integer, that would work even if short-circuit evaluation of Boolean expressions was not done.

10. Assume the following rules of associativity and precedence for expressions:

Precedence:	Highest	$*$, $/$, **not**
		$+$, $-$, &, **mod**
		$-$ (unary)
		$=$, $/=$, $<$, $<=$, $>=$, $>$
		and
	Lowest	**or**, **xor**
Associativity:	Left to right	

Show the order of evaluation of the following expressions by parenthesizing all subexpressions and placing a superscript on the right parenthesis to indicate order. For example, for the expression

a + b * c + d

the order of evaluation would be represented as

$((a + (b * c)^1)^2 + d)^3$

a. a * b - 1 + c
b. a * (b - 1) / c **mod** d
c. (a - b) / c & (d * e / a - 3)
d. -a **or** c = d **and** e
e. a > b **xor** c **or** d <= 17
f. -a + b

11. Show the order of evaluation of the expressions of Problem 10, assuming that there are no precedence rules and all operators associate right to left.

12. Write a BNF description of the precedence and associativity rules defined for the expressions in Problem 10. Assume the only operands are the names a, b, c, d, and e.

13. Using the grammar of Problem 12, draw parse trees for the expressions of Problem 10.

14. Let the function FUN be defined as

```
function FUN(var K : integer) : integer;
  begin
  K := K + 4;
  FUN := 3 * K - 1
  end;
```

Suppose FUN is used in a program as follows:

```
. . .
I := 10;
SUM1 := (I / 2) + FUN(I);
J := 10;
SUM2 := FUN(J) + (J / 2);
```

What are the values of SUM1 and SUM2

a. if the operands in the expressions are evaluated left to right?
b. if the operands in the expressions are evaluated right to left?

15. Let the C function **fun** be defined as

```
int fun(int *k) {
  *k += 4;
  return 3 * (*k) - 1;
}
```

Suppose fun is used in a program as follows:

```
void main() {
  int i = 10, j = 10, sum1, sum2;
  sum1 = (i / 2) + fun(&i);
  sum2 = fun(&j) + (j / 2);
}
```

Determine the values of **sum1** and **sum2** by running the program on a computer. Explain the results.

16. What is your primary argument against (or for) the operator precedence rules of APL?

17. For some language of your choice, make up a list of operator symbols that could be used to eliminate all operator overloading.

18. Determine whether the narrowing explicit type conversions in two languages you know provide error messages when a converted value loses its usefulness.

19. Should an optimizing compiler for C or C++ be allowed to change the order of subexpressions in a Boolean expression? Why or why not?

20. Answer the question in Problem 19 for Ada.

21. Consider the following C program:

```
int fun(int *i) {
  *i += 5;
  return 4;
}
void main() {
  int x = 3;
  x = x + fun(&x);
}
```

What is the value of **x** after the assignment statement in **main**, assuming

a. operands are evaluated left to right.

b. operands are evaluated right to left.

22. Write a test program in your favorite language that determines and outputs the precedence and associativity of its arithmetic and Boolean operators.

7 Statement-Level Control Structures

Peter Naur

Peter Naur, whose home is in Copenhagen, became heavily involved in language design after the first ALGOL report was issued in 1958. He became editor for the ALGOL Bulletin, a European discussion medium for people involved in the ALGOL development process. He modified the notation that Backus used in 1959 and used it to present the latest version of ALGOL at the Paris ALGOL meeting in 1960.

The flow of control, or execution sequence, in a program can be examined at several levels. In Chapter 6 we discussed the flow of control within expressions, which is governed by operator associativity and precedence rules. At the highest level is the flow of control among program units, which is discussed in Chapters 8 and 12. Between these two extremes is the important issue of the flow of control among statements, which is the subject of this chapter.

We begin by giving an overview of the evolution of control statements in the imperative programming languages. This is followed by a thorough examination of selection constructs, including those for single-way, two-way, and multiple selection. We then discuss the variety of looping constructs that have been developed and used in programming languages. Then we take a close look at the controversial unconditional branch statement. Finally, we describe the guarded command control constructs.

7.1 Introduction

Computations in imperative language programs are accomplished by evaluating expressions and assigning the resulting values to variables. There are, however, only a few useful programs that consist entirely of assignment statements. At least two additional linguistic mechanisms are necessary to make the computations in programs flexible and powerful: some means of selecting among alternative control flow paths (of statement execution) and some means of causing the repeated execution of certain collections of statements. Statements that provide these kinds of capabilities are called **control statements.**

The control statements of the first successful programming language, FORTRAN, were, in effect, designed by the architects of the IBM 704. All were directly related to machine language instructions, so their capabilities had more to do with instruction design than language design. At the time, little was known about the difficulty of programming, and as a result, the control statements of FORTRAN in the late 1950s were thought to be entirely acceptable. Subsequent sections of this chapter discuss FORTRAN's control statements and the reasons why they are now thought to be inadequate for software development.

A great deal of research and discussion was devoted to control statements in the ten years between the mid-1960s to the mid-1970s. One of the primary conclusions of these efforts was that, although a single control statement (a selectable goto) is obviously sufficient, a language that is designed *not* to include a goto needs only a small number of different control statements. In fact, it was proven that all algorithms that can be expressed by flowcharts can be coded in a programming language with only two control statements: one for choosing between two control flow paths and one for logically controlled iterations (Böhm and Jacopini, 1966). An important result of this is that unconditional branch statements are superfluous—possibly convenient but nonessential. This fact, combined with the problems of using the unconditional branches, or gotos, led to a great deal of debate about the goto, as will be discussed in Section 7.5.1.

Programmers care less about the results of theoretical research on control statements than they do about writability and readability. All languages that have become widely used contain more control statements than the two that are minimally required, because writability is enhanced by a larger number of control statements. For example, rather than requiring the use of a **while** for all loops, it is easier to write programs when a **for** can be used to build loops that are naturally controlled by a counter. The primary factor that restricts the number of control statements in a language is readability, because the presence of a large number of statement forms demands that program readers learn a larger language. Recall that few people learn all of a very large language; instead, they learn the subset they choose to use, which is often a different subset from that used by the programmer who wrote the program they are trying to read. On the other hand, too few control statements can require the use of lower-level statements, such as the goto, which makes programs less readable.

The question as to the best collection of control statements to provide the required capabilities and the desired writability has been widely debated for the past quarter century. It is essentially a question of how much a language should be expanded to increase its writability, at the expense of its simplicity, size, and readability.

A **control structure** is a control statement and the collection of statements whose execution it controls. The programming language research of the 1960s determined that control structures should have single entries and single exits. Multiple entries to iterative structures, in particular, make programs more difficult to read and understand.

7.2 Compound Statements

One of the auxiliary language features that helps make control statement design easier is a method of forming statement collections. The primary reason for the inadequacies of the control statements of the early versions of FORTRAN was the lack of such a construct.

ALGOL 60 introduced the first statement collection structure, the **compound statement,** whose form is

```
begin
statement_1;
...
statement_n
end
```

Compound statements allow a collection of statements to be abstracted to a single statement. This is a powerful concept, which can be used to great advantage in control statement design. Data declarations can be added to the beginning of a compound statement in several languages, making it a **block,** as discussed in Chapter 4.

Pascal followed ALGOL 60's design for compound statements but does not allow blocks. The C-based languages (C, C++, Java) use braces to delimit both compound statements and blocks. Some languages have eliminated the need for specially delimited compound statements by integrating compound statements into their control structures. These are discussed in the following section.

There is one design issue that is relevant to all of the selection and iteration control statements: whether the control structure can have multiple entries. All selection and iteration statements control the execution of code segments, and the question is whether the execution of those code segments always begins with the first statement in the segment. It is now generally believed that multiple entries add little to the flexibility of a control construct, relative to the decrease in readability caused by the increased complexity. Note that multiple entries are possible only in languages that include gotos and statement labels.

At this point the reader may wonder why multiple exits from control structures is not listed as a design issue here. Because there is no danger in multiple exits, they are included in all languages. Thus, they do not create much of an issue.

7.3 Selection Statements

A **selection statement** provides the means of choosing between two or more execution paths in a program. Such statements are fundamental and essential parts of all programming languages, as was proven by Böhm and Jacopini.

Selection statements fall into two general categories, two-way and *n*-way, or multiple selection. Within the category of two-way selectors, there is a degenerate form called single-way selectors. There is also a degenerate multiple selector, FORTRAN's arithmetic IF, which is a three-way selector.

7.3.1 Two-Way Selection Statements

Although the two-way selection statements of contemporary imperative languages are quite similar, the variations in the evolution of them has been based on a collection of design considerations.

7.3.1.1 Design Issues

Perhaps the simplest design issue for two-way selectors is the type of expression that controls the selector. A more interesting design issue is the question of whether single statements, compound statements, or statement sequences can be selected. A selector that can select only single statements is severely limited and usually leads to a heavy dependence on gotos. Allowing compound statements to be selected was a major step in the evolution of control statements. Allowing statement sequences to be selected requires that the selector include a syntactic entity to terminate such sequences. Another interesting and related issue is the question of how the meaning of nested selectors is specified—by syntax or a static semantic rule.

These design issues are summarized as follows:

- What is the form and type of the expression that controls the selection?
- Can a single statement, a sequence of statements, or a compound statement be selected?
- How should the meaning of nested selectors be specified?

7.3.1.2 Examples of Two-Way Selectors

All imperative languages include a single-way selector, in most cases as a subform of a two-way selector. One exception is FORTRAN IV, which did not include a two-way selector.

FORTRAN IV's single-way selector, called a logical IF statement, has the form

        IF (Boolean expression) statement

The semantics of this statement is that the selectable statement is executed only if the Boolean expression evaluates to true. The design choices for the FORTRAN IV logical IF statement are as follows: The selector control expression is Boolean type, and only a single statement is selectable. Nesting of logical IF statements is not allowed.

The single-way logical IF statement is very simple yet highly inflexible. The fact that only a single statement can be selected promotes the use of goto statements, because often more than one statement must be conditionally executed. The only reasonable way to conditionally execute a group of statements is to conditionally branch around the group. For example, suppose we wanted to initialize the two variables I and J to the values 1 and 2, but only if FLAG is 1. The typical way to do it in FORTRAN IV is

```
        IF(FLAG .NE. 1) GO TO 20
        I = 1
        J = 2
20      CONTINUE
```

The negative logic required by this form can be harmful to readability.

This structure can have multiple entries, because any of the segment statements can be labeled and thus be the target of a GO TO anywhere in the program.

The compound statement, introduced by ALGOL 60, provides the selection construct with a simple mechanism for conditionally executing groups of statements. It allows either a single statement or a compound statement to be selected, as in the following:

```
if (Boolean expression) then
  begin
  statement_1;
  . . .
  statement_n
  end
```

Most of the languages that followed ALGOL 60, including FORTRAN 77 and 90, provide single-way selectors that can select a compound statement or a sequence of statements.

ALGOL 60 introduced the first two-way selector, which had the general form

```
if (Boolean_expression) then
  statement
else
  statement
```

where either or both selectable statements could be compound. The statement following the **then** reserved word is called the **then clause,** and the statement following the **else** reserved word is called the **else clause.**

The semantics of a two-way selector is that the **then** clause is executed if the Boolean expression evaluates to true; otherwise, the **else** clause is executed. Under no circumstances are both clauses executed.

All of the imperative languages designed since the mid-1960s have incorporated two-way selection statements, although the syntax has varied.

The two-way selectors of ALGOL 60, C, and C++ can have more than one entry, but those of most other contemporary languages can have only one.

7.3.1.3 Nesting Selectors

An interesting problem arises when two-way selection constructs can be nested. Consider the following Pascal-like code:

```
if sum = 0 then
  if count = 0 then
    result := 0
else
  result := 1
```

This construct can be interpreted in two different ways, depending on whether the **else** clause is matched with the first **then** clause or the second. Notice that the indentation seems to indicate that the **else** clause belongs with the first **then** clause. However, indentation has no effect on semantics in most contemporary languages and is therefore ignored by their compilers.

The crux of the problem in this example is that the **else** clause follows two **then** clauses with no intervening **else** clause, and there is no syntactic indicator to specify a matching of the **else** clause to one of the **then** clauses. In Pascal, as in many other imperative languages, the static semantics of the language specify that the **else** clause is always paired with the most recent unpaired **then** clause. A rule, rather than a syntactic entity, is used to provide the disambiguation. So, if the above example were Pascal, the **else** clause would be the alternative to the second **then** clause. The disadvantage of using a rule rather than some syntactic entity is that although the programmer may have meant the **else** clause to be the alternative to the first **then** clause and the compiler found the structure syntactically correct, its semantics is the opposite. To force the alternative semantics in Pascal, a different syntactic form is required, in which the inner **if-then** is put in a compound.

The designers of ALGOL 60 chose to use syntax, rather than a rule, to connect **else** clauses to **then** clauses. Specifically, an **if** statement is not allowed to be nested directly in a **then** clause. If an **if** must be nested in a **then** clause, it must be placed in a compound statement. For example, if the selection construct above were to pair the **else** clause with the second **then** clause, in ALGOL 60 it would be written as

```
if sum = 0 then
  begin
  if count = 0 then
    result := 0
  else
    result := 1
  end
```

If the **else** clause were to be paired with the first **then** clause, it would be written as

```
if sum = 0 then
  begin
  if count = 0 then
    result := 0
  end
else
  result := 1
```

This is exactly what is necessary to get this meaning in Pascal. The difference between the two designs is that the Pascal version allows one to write the nested selector that looks like it pairs the **else** clause with the first

then clause but does not, whereas this same form is syntactically illegal in ALGOL 60, thereby disallowing Pascal's subtle problem.

C, C++, and Java have the same problem as Pascal with selection statement nesting. Perl requires that all **then** and **else** clauses be compound, thereby avoiding the problem altogether.

An alternative to ALGOL 60's design is to require special closing words for **then** and **else** clauses, as discussed in the following section.

7.3.1.4 Special Words and Selection Closure

Consider the syntactic structure of the Pascal **if** statement. The **then** clauses are introduced by the reserved word **then** and the **else** clauses are introduced by the reserved word **else**. When the **then** clause is a single statement and the **else** clause is present, although there is no need to mark the end, the **else** reserved word in fact marks the end of the **then** clause. When the **then** clause is a compound, it is terminated by an **end**. However, if the last clause in an **if**, whether **then** or **else**, is not a compound, there is no syntactic entity to mark the end of the whole selection construct. The use of a special word for this purpose would resolve the question of the semantics of nested selectors and also add to the readability of the construct. This is the design of the selection construct in ALGOL 68, FORTRAN 77 and 90, Modula-2, and Ada. For example, consider the following Ada construct:

```
if A > B then
   SUM := SUM + A;
   ACOUNT := ACOUNT + 1;
else
   SUM := SUM + B;
   BCOUNT := BCOUNT + 1;
end if;
```

The design of this construct is more regular than that of Pascal and ALGOL 60 selection constructs, because the form is the same regardless of the number of statements in the **then** and **else** clauses. These clauses consist of statement sequences rather than compound statements. The first interpretation of the selector example at the beginning of Section 7.3.1.3 can be written in Ada as follows:

```
if SUM = 0 then
   if COUNT = 0 then
     RESULT := 0;
   else
     RESULT := 1;
   end if;
end if;
```

Because the **end if** reserved words close the nested **if**, it is clear that the **else** clause is matched to the inner **then** clause.

The second interpretation of the selection construct in Section 7.3.1.3 can be written in Ada as follows:

```
if SUM = 0 then
  if COUNT = 0 then
    RESULT := 0;
  end if;
else
  RESULT := 1;
end if;
```

Modula-2 closes all control constructs with the same reserved word, **END.** Although Modula-2 accomplishes the same result as that of the Ada examples above, and does it with fewer special words, Modula-2 programs are less readable than the same programs in Ada, especially when different control constructs are embedded in one another. When used to close an **IF** control construct, **END** carries only part of the information that **END IF** connotes.

7.3.2 Multiple Selection Constructs

The **multiple selection** construct allows the selection of one of any number of statements or statement groups. It is, therefore, a generalization of a selector. In fact, single-way and two-way selectors can be built with a multiple selector. The original forms of multiple selector are from FORTRAN, as you might have suspected.

The need to choose among more than two control paths in a program is common. Although a multiple selector can be built from two-way selectors and gotos, the resulting structures are cumbersome, difficult to write and read, and unreliable. Therefore, the need for a special structure is clear.

7.3.2.1 Design Issues

Some of the design issues for multiple selectors are similar to some of those for two-way selectors. For example, one issue is whether single statements, compound statements, or statement sequences may be selected. If the entire multiple selection structure is encapsulated, then all of the selectable segments must be together. This restricts control flow from straying outside into statements that are not part of the multiple selection structure during its execution. Because this affects its readability, encapsulation is an issue. Another issue related to two-way selectors is the question of the type of expression on which the selector is based. In this case, the range of possibilities is larger, in part because the number of possible selections is larger. A two-way selector needs an expression with only two possible values. Next, there is the question of whether only a single selectable segment can be executed when the construct is executed. This is not an issue for two-way selectors because every design allows only one of the clauses to be on a control path during one execution. As we shall see, the resolution of this issue for multiple selectors is a trade-off between reliability and flexibility. Finally, there is the issue of what should result from the selector expression evaluating to a value that does not select one of the segments. The choice here is between simply disallowing the situation from arising and having a rule that describes what happens when it does arise. Unrepresented selector expression values will be discussed in Section 7.3.2.3.

The following is a summary of these design issues:

- What is the form and type of the expression that controls the selection?
- May single statements, sequences of statements, or compound statements be selected?
- Is the entire construct encapsulated in a syntactic structure?
- Is execution flow through the structure restricted to include just a single selectable segment?
- How should unrepresented selector expression values be handled, if at all?

7.3.2.2 Early Multiple Selectors

The multiple selectors that were introduced in FORTRAN I are included here for historical reasons and also because they are still part of the latest version of FORTRAN, FORTRAN 90. Like FORTRAN I's other control statements, its multiple selectors are based directly on IBM 704 instructions.

As stated earlier, FORTRAN's **three-way selector,** which is called an arithmetic IF, is a special degenerate case of a multiple selection statement. Because only three or fewer statement collections can be selected, however, it is not, strictly speaking, a multiple selection statement.

The arithmetic IF chooses among three branch target addresses based on the value of an expression. The branch is mathematically based on the trichotomy of numbers, which means that a given numeric value is either greater than zero, equal to zero, or less than zero. The arithmetic IF has the form

IF (arithmetic expression) N1, N2, N3

where N1, N2, and N3 are statement labels to which control is to transfer if the expression's value is negative, zero, or greater than zero, respectively. For example, if an arithmetic IF is used to select among three statement sequences, its general form is often the following:

```
        IF (expression) 10, 20, 30
   10   ...
        ...
        GO TO 40
```

```
20      . . .
        . . .
        GO TO 40
   30   . . .
        . . .
   40   . . .
```

Actually, this selector type could be much more harmful to readability than the example illustrates, because the statement sequences to be selected can literally be anywhere in the program unit that contains the GO TO. There is no syntactic encapsulation of the GO TO and its selectable sequences. Because the user is responsible for putting the GO TOs at the ends of the selectable segments, an execution of the construct can cause control flow to go through any number of selectable segments. The problem is that the mistake of leaving out one of these branches is not detected as an error by the compiler. Even when multiple segment execution is desired, the increase in complexity of the structure that results is highly detrimental to readability. This design is a trade-off of reliability for some added flexibility.

The arithmetic IF can be entered through any of its statements from anywhere in the program.

The first two actual multiple selection statements appeared in FORTRAN I. Like the arithmetic IF, these are part of all versions of FORTRAN. The FORTRAN computed GO TO has the form

GO TO (label 1, label 2, ..., label n), expression

where the expression has an integer value and the labels are all defined as statement labels in the program. The semantics of the statement is that the expression's value is used to choose a label to which control is to transfer. The first label is associated with the value 1, the second label with 2, and so forth. If the value is outside the range of 1 to n, the statement does nothing. There is no built-in error detection.

FORTRAN's other early multiple selector, the assigned GO TO, is similar in form to the computed GO TO. Both of these multiple selectors suffer the same deficiencies as the arithmetic IF—the lack of encapsulation and possibly multiple entries. Furthermore, neither restricts a control flow to a single selectable segment.

7.3.2.3 Modern Multiple Selectors

A better form of multiple selector, named case, was suggested by C.A.R. Hoare and included in ALGOL-W (Wirth and Hoare, 1966). This structure is encapsulated and has single entry. Implicit branches to a single point at the end of the whole construct are also provided for each selectable statement or compound statement. This restricts the control flow through the structure to a single selectable segment.

The general form of Hoare's multiple selector is

```
case integer_expression of
   begin
   statement_1;
   ...
   statement_n
   end
```

where the statements could be either single statements or compound statements. The executed statement is the one chosen by the value of the expression. A value of 1 chooses the first and so forth.

Pascal's **case** is very much like that of ALGOL-W, except that the selectable segments are labeled. It has the form

```
case expression of
   constant_list_1: statement_1;
   ...
   constant_list_n: statement_n
   end
```

where the expression is of ordinal type (integer, Boolean, character, or enumeration type). As is the case with most (but not all) of Pascal's control statements, the selectable statements can be either single statements or compound statements.

The semantics of the Pascal **case** is the following: The expression is evaluated, and the value is compared with the constants in the constant lists. If a match is found, control transfers to the statement attached to the matched constant. When statement execution is completed, control transfers to the first statement following the whole **case** construct.

The constant lists must be of the same type as the expression, of course. They must be mutually exclusive but need not be exhaustive; that is, a constant may not appear in more than one constant list, but not all values in the range of the expression type need be present in the lists.

Note that while the constant lists of the selectable segments have a form similar to that of labels, they are not the legal targets of branch statements.

Oddly, Pascal's first widely used definition (Jensen and Wirth, 1974) was not concerned with the possibility of unrepresented selector expression values (the expression taking on a value that did not appear in any of the constant lists). Such occurrences were said to cause undefined results. Such vagueness, however, meant that the problem was simply ignored. The later ANSI/IEEE Pascal Standard (Ledgard, 1984) is more concrete; it specifies that such occurrences are errors, presumably to be detected and reported during execution by the code generated by Pascal compilers.

Many dialects of Pascal now include an optional clause to be executed when the expression value does not appear in any constant list in the **case**, as in the following:

```
case index of
   1, 3: begin
           odd := odd + 1;
           sumodd := sumodd + index
           end;
   2, 4: begin
           even := even + 1;
           sumeven := sumeven + index
           end
      else writeln('Error in case, index =', index)
   end
```

Whenever **index** is not in the range of **1** to **4** when this **case** statement is executed, the error message will be displayed.

Note that the **else** clause need not be used exclusively for error conditions. Sometimes it is also convenient to use it for the normal condition and use the other cases for the unusual circumstances.

Operational semantics is an effective way to describe the semantics of some control constructs. For this purpose, we extend the operational semantics introduced in Chapter 3 to include assignment statements with general expressions as RHSs. We also allow English descriptions of some operations. Such descriptions will appear in brackets. Finally, we allow the inclusion of output statements from the language being described.

An operational semantics description of the preceding **case** statement is given below:

```
        if index = 1 goto one_three
        if index = 3 goto one_three
        if index = 2 goto two_four
        if index = 4 goto two_four
        writeln('Error in case, index = ', index)
        goto out
one_three:
        odd := odd + 1;
        sumodd := sumodd + index
        goto out
two_four:
        even := even + 1;
        sumeven := sumeven + index
out: ...
```

The C multiple selector construct, **switch**, which also appears in C++ and Java, is a relatively primitive design. Its general form is

```
switch (expression) {
   case constant_expression_1: statement_1;
   ...
   case constant_expression_n: statement_n;
   [default: statement_n+1]
   }
```

where the control expression and the constant expressions are integer type. The selectable statements can be statement sequences, compound statements, or blocks.

The **switch** encapsulates the selectable code segments, as does the Pascal **case**, but it does not disallow multiple entries, and it does not provide implicit branches at the end of those code segments. This allows control to flow through more than one selectable code segment on a single execution. Consider the following example, which is similar to the Pascal **case** construct above:

```
switch (index) {
  case 1:
  case 3: odd += 1;
          sumodd += index;
  case 2:
  case 4: even += 1;
          sumeven += index;
  default: printf("Error in switch, index = %d\n", index);
}
```

This code prints the error message on every execution. Likewise, the code for the 2 and 4 constants is executed every time the code at the 1 and 3 constants is executed. To logically separate these segments, an explicit branch must be used. C includes a **break** statement for exiting both **switch** and the bodies of C's loop structures. The **break** statement is actually a restricted goto.

The following C **switch** construct uses **break** and matches the semantics of the Pascal **case** example above:

```
switch (index) {
  case 1:
  case 3: odd += 1;
          sumodd += index;
          break;
  case 2:
  case 4: even += 1;
          sumeven += index;
          break;
  default: printf("Error in switch, index = %d\n", index);
}
```

Occasionally, it is convenient to allow control to flow from one selectable code segment to another. This is obviously the reason why there are no implicit branches in the **switch** construct. The reliability problem with this design arises when the mistaken absence of a **break** statement in a segment allows control to incorrectly flow to the next segment. The designers of C's **switch**, like those of FORTRAN's computed GO TO, chose to trade some decrease in reliability for some increase in flexibility. Studies have shown, however, that the ability to have control flow from one selectable segment to another is rarely used. C's **switch** is modeled on the multiple selection statement in ALGOL 68, which also does not have implicit branches from selectable segments.

The Ada **case** allows subranges, such as `10..15`, and also OR operators specified by the symbol `|`, as in `10 | 15 | 20` in the constant lists. An **others** clause is available for unrepresented values. The additional Ada restriction that the constant lists be exhaustive provides a bit more reliability because it disallows the error of inadvertent omission of one or more constant values. Only integer and enumerated types are allowed for the **case** expression. Most Ada **case** statements include an **others** clause because that is the best way to ensure that the constant list is exhaustive.

The FORTRAN 90 `CASE` is similar to that of Ada.

In many situations, a **case** construct is inadequate for multiple selection. For example, when selections must be made on the basis of a Boolean expression rather than some ordinal type, nested two-way selectors can be used to simulate a multiple selector. To alleviate the poor readability of deeply nested two-way selectors, some languages, such as FORTRAN 90 and Ada, have been extended specifically for this use. The extension allows some of the special words to be left out. In particular, **else-if** sequences are replaced with a single special word, and the closing special word on the nested **if** is dropped. The nested selector is then called an **elsif clause.** Consider the following Ada selector construct:

```
if COUNT < 10 then BAG1 := TRUE;
elsif COUNT < 100 then BAG2 := TRUE;
elsif COUNT < 1000 then BAG3 := TRUE;
end if;
```

which is equivalent to the following:

```
if COUNT < 10 then
  BAG1 := TRUE;
else
  if COUNT < 100 then
    BAG2 := TRUE;
  else
    if COUNT < 1000 then
      BAG3 := TRUE;
    end if;
  end if;
end if;
```

The **elsif** version is the more readable of the two. Notice that this example is not easily simulated with a **case** statement, because each selectable statement is chosen on the basis of a Boolean expression. Therefore, the **elsif** construct is not a redundant form of **case**. In fact, none of the multiple selectors in contemporary languages are as general as the **if-then-else** simulation. An operational semantics description of a general selector statement with **elsif** clauses, in which the E's are logic expressions and the S's are statements, is given below:

```
        if E1 goto 1
        if E2 goto 2
        ...
1: S1
        goto out
2: S2
        goto out
    ...
out: ...
```

From this description, we can see the difference between multiple selection structures and **elsif** constructs: In a multiple selection construct, all the E's would be restricted to comparisons between the value of a single expression and some other values.

Languages that do not include the **elsif** construct can use the same control structure, with only slightly more typing.

elsif constructs are based on the common mathematics construct, the conditional expression. Functional programming languages, which will be discussed in Chapter 14, often use conditional expressions as one of their basic control constructs.

7.4 Iterative Statements

An **iterative statement** is one that causes a statement or collection of statements to be executed zero, one, or more times. Every programming language from Plankalkül on has included some method of repeating the execution of segments of code. Iteration is the very essence of the power of the computer. If iteration were not possible, programmers would be required to state every action in sequence; useful programs would be huge and inflexible and take huge amounts of time to write.

The repeated execution of a statement is often accomplished in a functional language by recursion rather than by iterative constructs. Recursion in functional languages will be discussed in Chapter 14.

The first iterative constructs in programming languages were directly related to arrays. This resulted from the fact that in the early years of the computer era, computing was overwhelmingly numerical in nature, frequently using loops to process data in arrays.

Several categories of iteration control statements have been developed. The primary categories are defined by how designers answered two basic design questions:

- How is the iteration controlled?
- Where should the control mechanism appear in the loop?

The primary possibilities for iteration control are logical, counting, or a combination of the two. The main choices for the location of the control mechanism are the top of the loop or the bottom of the loop. Top and bottom here are logical, rather than physical, denotations. The issue is not the physical placement of the control mechanism; rather, it is whether the mechanism is executed and affects control before or after execution of the loop's body. A third option, which allows the user to decide where to put the control, is discussed in Section 7.4.3. The **body** of a loop is the collection of statements whose execution is controlled by the iteration statement. We use the term **pretest** to mean that the test for loop completion occurs before the loop body is executed and **posttest** to mean that it occurs after the loop body is executed. The iteration statement and the associated loop body together form an **iteration construct.**

In addition to the primary iteration statements, we discuss an alternative form that is in a class by itself: user-defined iteration control.

7.4.1   Counter-Controlled Loops

A counting iterative control statement has a variable, called the **loop variable,** in which the count value is maintained. It also includes some means of specifying the **initial** and **terminal** values of the loop variable and the difference between sequential loop variable values, often called the **stepsize**. The initial, terminal, and stepsize specifications of a loop are called the **loop parameters.**

Although logically controlled loops are more general than counter-controlled loops, they are not necessarily more commonly used. Because counter-controlled loops are more complex, their design is more demanding.

Counter-controlled loops are often supported by machine instructions. Unfortunately, machine architecture often outlives the prevailing approaches to programming at the time of the architecture design. For example, VAX computers have an instruction that is very convenient for the implementation of posttest counter-controlled loops, which FORTRAN had at the time of the design of the VAX. But FORTRAN no longer had such a loop by the time VAX computers became widely used.

It is, of course, also true that language constructs outlive machine architecture. For example, the author knows of no contemporary machine that has a three-way branch instruction to implement FORTRAN's arithmetic IF statement.

7.4.1.1   Design Issues

There are many design issues for iterative counter-controlled statements. The nature of the loop variable and the loop parameters provide a number of design issues. The type of the loop variable and that of the loop parameters obviously should be the same or at least compatible, but what types should be allowed? One apparent choice is integer, but what about enumeration, character, and floating-point types? Another question is whether the loop variable is a normal variable, in terms of scope, or whether it should have some special scope. Related to the scope issue is the question of the value of the loop variable after loop termination. Allowing the user to change the loop variable or the loop parameters within the loop can lead to code that is very difficult to understand, so another question is whether the additional flexibility that might be gained by allowing such changes is worth that additional complexity. A similar question arises about the number of times and the specific time when the loop parameters are evaluated: If they are evaluated just once, it results in simple but less flexible loops.

The following is a summary of these design issues:

- What is the type and scope of the loop variable?
- What value does the loop variable have at loop termination?
- Should it be legal for the loop variable or loop parameters to be changed in the loop, and if so, does the change affect loop control?
- Should the loop parameters be evaluated only once, or once for every iteration?

7.4.1.2 The DO Statement of FORTRAN 77 and FORTRAN 90

FORTRAN I included a DO counting iterative control statement, which remained the same in FORTRAN II and IV. The distinctive feature of this statement was that it was posttest, making it different from the counting iterative statements of all other programming languages. The general form of this statement is

DO label variable = initial, terminal [, stepsize]

where the label is that of the last statement in the loop body and the stepsize, when absent, defaults to 1. The loop parameters are restricted to unsigned integer constants or simple integer variables with positive values.

The form of the FORTRAN 77 DO statement is similar to that of FORTRAN IV, except it is pretest. The loop variable is allowed to be INTEGER, REAL, or DOUBLE-PRECISION type. The loop parameters are allowed to be expressions and can have positive or negative values. They are evaluated at the beginning of the execution of the DO statement, and the value is used to compute an **iteration count,** which then has the number of times the loop is to be executed. The loop is controlled by the iteration count, not the loop parameters, so even if the parameters are changed in the loop, which is legal, those changes cannot affect loop control. The iteration count is an internal variable that is inaccessible to the user code.

DO constructs can only be entered through the DO statement, thereby making the statement a single-entry structure. When a DO terminates—regardless of how it terminates—the loop variable has its most recently assigned value. Thus the usefulness of the loop variable is independent of the method by which the loop terminates. An operational semantics description of the FORTRAN 77 DO statement is given below:

```
      init_value := init_expression
      terminal_value := terminal_expression
      step_value := step_expression
      do_var := init_value
      iteration_count :=
      max(int((terminal_value - init_value + step_value) / step_value) , 0)
loop:
      if iteration_count ≤ 0 goto out
      [loop body]
      do_var := do_var + step_value
      iteration_count := iteration_count - 1
      goto loop
out: ...
```

FORTRAN 90 includes the FORTRAN 77 DO and adds a new form:

[name:] DO variable = initial, terminal [, stepsize]

  ...

END DO [name]

This DO restricts the loop variable type to INTEGER (like pre-77 FORTRANs). Another change is that it uses a specific closing special word (or phrase), END DO, instead of a labeled statement.

7.4.1.3 The ALGOL 60 for Statement

A description of the ALGOL 60 **for** statement is included here to show how the quest for flexibility can quickly lead to excessive complexity. ALGOL 60's **for** statement is a significant generalization of the FORTRAN DO, as is shown in its EBNF description:

```
< for_stmt > → for var := < list_element > {, < list_element >} do < statement >
< list_element > → < expression >
                 | < expression > step < expression > until < expression >
                 | < expression > while < Boolean_expr >
```

One significant difference between this and most other counter-controlled loops is that this construct can combine a counter and a Boolean expression for loop control. The three simplest forms are exemplified by the following:

```
for count := 1, 2, 3, 4, 5, 6, 7, 8, 9, 10 do
   list[count] := 0

for count := 1 step 1 until 10 do
   list[count] := 0

for count := 1, count + 1 while (count <= 10) do
   list[count] := 0
```

This statement is far more complex when its different simple forms are combined, as in the following:

```
for index := 1, 4, 13, 41
              step 2 until 47,
              3 * index while index < 1000,
              34, 2, -24 do
    sum := sum + index
```

The statement adds the following values to sum:

```
1, 4, 13, 41, 43, 45, 47, 147, 441, 34, 2, -24
```

Although there may be occasions when such a complicated statement is convenient, those occasions occur too rarely to justify the inclusion of such complexity in a language.

The ALGOL 60 **for** statement is even more difficult to understand than it first appears, because all the expressions in the **for** lists are evaluated for every iteration, or execution, of the loop statements. Thus, if a **step** expression includes a reference to the variable count, for example, and if the loop statements change the value of count, the stepsize will change with each iteration. For example, consider the loop

```
i := 1;
for count := 1 step count until 3 * i do
    i := i + 1
```

This **for** statement causes the assignment (i := i + 1) to be repeatedly executed while count doubles with each iteration (because the step is always the previous value of count). Because count is increasing faster than the **until** clause expression (3 * i), the loop is not infinite, although that is not obvious at first glance. The values of the variables and the control expressions for this loop are as follows:

i	count	step	until
1	1	1	3
2	2	2	6
3	4	4	9
4	8	8	12
5	16	16	15 - terminate loop

The design choices of the ALGOL 60 **for** are the following: The loop variable can be either integer or real type, and it is declared like any other variable, so its scope is that of its declaration. As is the case in FORTRAN 77, the loop variable has its most recently assigned value after loop termination, regardless of the cause of that termination. Loop parameters, but not the loop variable, can be changed in the loop body. It is illegal to branch into the loop body and the loop parameters are evaluated for every iteration.

It is not feasible to present an operational semantics description of the complete ALGOL 60 **for** statement with all of its options. Instead, we first present a description of a general **for** statement with only the **step-until** form:

```
        for_var := init_expr
    loop:
        until := until_expr
        step := step_expr
        temp := (for_var - until) * SIGN(step)
        if temp > 0 goto out
        [loop body]
        for_var := for_var + step
        goto loop
    out: ...
```

Below is an operational semantics description of a more complex example of a **for** statement:

```
for count := 10 step 2 * count until init * init,
                3 * count while sum <= 1000 do
    sum := sum + count

        count := 10
    loop1:
        if count > init * init goto loop2
        sum := sum + count
        count := count + (2 * count)
        goto loop1
    loop2:
        count := 3 * count
        if sum > 1000 goto out
        sum := sum + count
        goto loop2
    out: ...
```

7.4.1.4 The Pascal `for` Statement

The Pascal **for** statement is the model of simplicity. Its form is

> **for** variable := initial_value (**to** | **downto**) final_value **do** statement

The **to** | **downto** choice allows the value of the variable to grow or shrink in steps of 1. The design choices for Pascal's **for** are as follows: The loop variable must be an ordinal type, and it has the scope of its declaration. At normal loop termination, the loop variable is undefined. If the loop is terminated prematurely, it has its last value. The loop variable may not be changed in the loop body. The initial and final values, which can be expressions of any type that is compatible with that of the loop variable, can be changed in the loop, but because they are evaluated only once, it cannot affect loop control.

7.4.1.5 The Ada `for` Statement

The Ada **for** statement is similar to the Pascal version. It is a pretest loop with the form

```
for variable in [reverse] discrete_range loop
   ...
end loop
```

A discrete range is a subrange of an integer or enumeration type, such as 1..10.

The most interesting new feature of the Ada **for** statement is the scope of the loop variable, which is the range of the loop. The variable is implicitly declared at the **for** statement and implicitly undeclared after loop termination. For example, in

```
COUNT : FLOAT := 1.35;
for COUNT in 1..10 loop
   SUM := SUM + COUNT;
end loop
```

the FLOAT variable COUNT is unaffected by the **for** loop. Upon loop termination, the variable COUNT is still FLOAT type with the value of 1.35. Also, the FLOAT-type variable COUNT is hidden from the code in the body of the loop, being masked by the loop counter COUNT, which is implicitly declared to be the type of the discrete range, INTEGER.

The Ada loop variable cannot be assigned a value in the loop body. Variables used to specify the discrete range can be changed in the loop, but because the range is evaluated only once, these changes do not affect loop control. It is not legal to branch into the Ada **for** loop body. Below is an operational semantics description of the Ada **for** loop:

```
       [define for_var (its type is that of the discrete range)]
       [evaluate discrete range]
loop:
       if [there are no elements left in the discrete range] goto out
       for_var := [next element of discrete range]
       [loop body]
       goto loop
out:
       [undefine for_var]
```

7.4.1.6 The `for` Statement of C, C++, and Java

The general form of C's **for** statement is

```
for (expression_1; expression_2; expression_3)
   loop body
```

The loop body can be a single statement, a compound statement, or a null statement.

Because statements in C produce results and thus can be considered expressions, the expressions in a **for** statement are often statements. The first expression is for initialization and is evaluated only once, when **for** statement execution begins. The second expression is the loop control and is evaluated before each execution of the loop body. As is usual in C, a zero value means false and all nonzero values mean true. Therefore, if the value of the second expression is zero, the **for** is terminated; otherwise, the loop statements are executed. The last expression in the **for** is executed after each execution of the loop body. It is often used to increment the loop counter. An operational semantics description of the C **for** statement is shown below. Because C expressions are also statements, we show expression evaluations as statements.

```
        expression_1
loop:
        if expression_2 = 0 goto out
        [loop body]
        expression_3
        goto loop
out: ...
```

A typical C counting loop is

```
for (index = 0; index <= 10; index++)
  sum = sum + list[index];
```

All of the expressions of C's **for** are optional. An absent second expression is considered true, so a **for** without one is potentially an infinite loop. If the first and/or third expressions are absent, no assumptions are made. For example, if the first expression is absent, it simply means that no initialization takes place.

Note that C's **for** need not count. It can easily model counting *and* logical loop structures, as demonstrated in the next section.

The C **for** design choices are the following: There is no explicit loop variable or loop parameters. All involved variables can be changed in the loop body. The expressions are evaluated in the order stated above. Despite the fact that it can create havoc, it is legal to branch into a C **for** loop body.

C's **for** is more flexible than that of the other languages we have discussed because each of the expressions can comprise multiple statements, which in turn allows multiple loop variables that can be of any type. When multiple statements are used in a single expression of a **for** statement, they are separated by commas. All C statements have values, and this form of multiple statement is no exception. The value of such a multiple statement is the value of the last component.

Consider the following **for** statement:

```
for (count1 = 0, count2 = 0.0;
     count1 <= 10 && count2 <= 100.0;
     sum = ++count1 + count2, count2 *= 2.5);
```

The operational semantics description of this is

```
        count1 := 0
        count2 := 0.0
loop:
        if count1 > 10 goto out
        if count2 > 100.0 goto out
```

```
       count1 := count1 + 1
       sum := count1 + count2
       count2 := count2 * 2.5
       goto loop
out: ...
```

The C **for** statement above does not need and thus does not have a loop body. All the desired actions happen to be part of the **for** statement itself, rather than in its body. The first and third expressions are multiple statements. In both of these cases, the whole expression is evaluated, but the resulting value is not used in the loop control.

The C++ **for** statement differs from C's in two ways. First, in addition to arithmetic expression, it can use a **boolean** expression for loop control. Second, the first expression can include variable definitions. For example,

```
for (int count = 0; count < len; count++) { ... }
```

This may look like it accomplishes what Ada's **for** does, in terms of the scope of the loop counter variable. But in the case of C++, the scope of a variable defined in the **for** statement is from its definition to the end of the function in which it is defined. The **for** expressions are not part of the compound statement body of the **for**. Also, variable definitions in C functions must appear before any executable statements, so the **for** statement above is illegal in C.

Java's **for** statement is like that of C++, except that the loop control expression is restricted to **boolean**, and the scope of a variable defined in the first expression is that of the loop body, which is similar to Ada.

7.4.2 Logically Controlled Loops

In many cases, collections of statements must be repeatedly executed, but the repetition control is based on a Boolean expression rather than a counter. For these situations, a logically controlled loop is convenient. In fact, logically controlled loops are more general than counter-controlled loops. Every counting loop can be built with a logical loop, but the reverse is not true. Also, recall that only selection and logical loops are essential to express the control structure of any flowchart.

7.4.2.1 Design Issues

Because they are much simpler than counter-controlled loops, logically controlled loops have a relatively short list of design issues, one of which is also an issue for counter-controlled loops. There is little here that is either controversial or difficult.

- Should the control be pretest or posttest?
- Should the logically controlled loop be a special form of a counting loop or a separate statement?

7.4.2.2 Examples

Some imperative languages—for example Pascal, C, C++, and Java—include both pretest and posttest logically controlled loops that are not special forms of their counter-controlled iterative statements. In C++, the pretest and posttest logical loops have the following forms:

```
while (expression)
   loop body
```

and

```
do
   loop body
while (expression)
```

These two statement forms are exemplified by the following C++ code segments:

```
sum = 0;
cin >> indat;
while (indat >= 0) {
  sum += indat;
  cin >> indat;
}

cin >> value;
do {
  value /= 10;
  digits ++;
} while (value > 0);
```

Note that all variables in these examples are integer type. `cin` is the standard input stream (the keyboard) and `>>` is the input operator.

In the pretest version (**while**), the statement is executed as long as the expression evaluates to true (nonzero). In the C, C++, and Java posttest statement (**do**), the loop body is executed until the expression evaluates to false (zero). The only real difference between the **do** and the **while** is that the **do** always causes the loop body to be executed at least once. In both cases, the statement can be compound. The operational semantics descriptions of those two statements are given below:

while	**do-while**
loop:	loop:
if expression = 0 **goto** out	[loop body]
[loop body]	**if** expression ≠ 0 **goto** loop
goto loop	
out: **...**	

It is legal in both C and C++ to branch into both **while** and **do** loop bodies.

Java's **while** and **do** statements are similar to those of C and C++, except the control expression must be **boolean** type, and because Java does not have a goto, the loop bodies cannot be entered anywhere but their beginnings.

FORTRAN 77 has neither a pretest nor a posttest logical loop. The same is true for FORTRAN 90. Ada has a pretest logical loop but no posttest version of the logical loop.

Pascal's posttest logical loop statement, **repeat–until**, differs from the **do-while** of C, C++, and Java in that the logic of the control expression is reversed. The loop body is executed while the control expression evaluates to false, rather then true, as in the case of C, C++, and Java.

repeat-until is odd because its body can be either a compound statement or a statement sequence. It is the only control structure in Pascal with this flexibility. This is another example of the lack of orthogonality in the design of Pascal.

Posttest loops are infrequently useful and also can be somewhat dangerous in the sense that programmers sometimes forget that the loop body will *always* be executed at least once. The syntactic design of placing a posttest control after the loop body, where it has its semantic effect, helps avoid such problems by making the logic clear.

7.4.3   User-Located Loop Control Mechanisms

In some situations, it is convenient for a programmer to choose a location for loop control other than the top or bottom of the loop. As a result, some languages provide this capability. A syntactic mechanism for user-located loop control can be relatively simple, so its design is not difficult. Perhaps the most interesting question is whether a single loop or several nested loops can be exited. The design issues for such a mechanism are the following:

- Should the conditional mechanism be an integral part of the exit?
- Should the mechanism be allowed to appear in a controlled loop or only in one without any other control?
- Should only one loop body be exited, or can enclosing loops also be exited?

Several languages, including Ada, have loop statements that have no iteration control; they are infinite loops unless controls are added by the programmer. The form of the Ada infinite loop is

```
loop
  ...
end loop
```

The Ada **exit** can be either unconditional or conditional, and it can appear in any loop. Its general form is

```
exit [loop_label] [when condition]
```

With neither of the optional parts, **exit** causes the termination of only the loop in which it appears. For example, in

```
loop
  ...
  if SUM >= 10000 then exit;
  ...
end loop;
```

the **exit**, when executed, transfers control to the first statement after the end of the loop.

An **exit** with a **when** condition exits its loop only if the specified condition is true. For example, the loop above can be written as

```
loop
  ...
  exit when SUM >= 10000;
  ...
end loop;
```

Any loop can be labeled, and when a loop label is included on the **exit**, control is transferred to the statement immediately following the referenced loop. For example, consider the following code segment:

```
OUTER_LOOP:
  for ROW in 1 .. MAX_ROWS loop
INNER_LOOP:
    for COL in 1 .. MAX_COLS loop
      SUM := SUM + MAT(ROW, COL);
      exit OUTER_LOOP when SUM > 1000.0;
    end loop INNER_LOOP ;
  end loop OUTER_LOOP;
```

In this example, the **exit** is a conditional branch to the first statement after the outer loop. If the **exit** were instead

```
exit when SUM > 1000.0;
```

it would be a conditional branch to the first statement after the inner loop. Note that **exit** statements are often used for handling unusual or error conditions.

C, C++, and Modula-2 have unconditional unlabeled exits (**break** in C and C++ and **EXIT** in Modula-2); FORTRAN 90 and Java have unconditional labeled exits (**EXIT** in FORTRAN 90 and **break** in Java), like Ada, except that in the Java version the target can be any enclosing compound statement.

C and C++ include a control mechanism, **continue**, that transfers control to the control mechanism of the smallest enclosing loop. This is not an exit but rather a way to skip the rest of the loop statements on the current iteration without terminating the loop structure. For example, consider the following:

```
while (sum < 1000) {
  getnext(value);
  if (value < 0) continue;
  sum += value;
}
```

A negative value causes the assignment statement to be skipped, and control is transferred instead to the conditional at the top of the loop. On the other hand, in

```
while (sum < 1000) {
  getnext(value);
  if (value < 0) break;
  sum += value;
}
```

a negative value terminates the loop.

FORTRAN 90 and Java have statements similar to **continue**, except they can include labels that specify which loop is to be continued.

Both **exit** and **break** provide for multiple exits from loops, which is somewhat of a hindrance to readability. However, unusual conditions that require loop termination are so common that such a construct is justified. Furthermore, readability is not seriously harmed, because the target of all such loop exits is the first statement after the loop rather than just anywhere in the program. Java's **break** is the exception for, as stated above, its target can be any enclosing compound statement.

7.4.4 Iteration Based on Data Structures

Only one additional kind of looping structure remains to be considered here: iteration that depends on data structures. Rather than have a counter or Boolean expression control the iterations, these loops are controlled by the number of elements in a data structure. COMMON LISP and Perl have such statements.

In COMMON LISP, the `dolist` function iterates on simple lists, which are the most common data structure in LISP programs. Because of this restriction, `dolist` is automatic in the sense that it always implicitly iterates on list elements. It causes the execution of its body once for each element in the given list. Perl's `foreach` statement is similar; it iterates on the elements of lists or arrays. For example,

```
@names = ("Bob", "Carol", "Ted", "Beelzebub");
...
foreach $name (@names) {
  print $name;
}
```

A more general data-based iteration statement uses a user-defined data structure and a user-defined function to go through the structure's elements. This function is called an **iterator.** The iterator is called at the beginning of each iteration, and each time it is called, the iterator returns an element from a particular data structure in some specific order. For example, suppose a program has a binary tree of data nodes, and the data in each node must be processed in some particular order. A user-defined iteration statement for the tree would successively set the loop variable to point to the nodes in the tree, one for each iteration. The initial execution of the user-defined iteration statement needs to issue a special call to the iterator to get the first tree element. The iterator must always remember which node it presented last so that it visits all nodes without visiting any node more than once. So an iterator must be history sensitive. A user-defined iteration statement terminates when the iterator fails to find more elements.

The **for** construct of C, C++, and Java, because of its great flexibility, can be used to simulate a user-defined iteration statement. Once again, suppose the nodes of a binary tree are to be processed. If the tree root is pointed to by a variable named `root`, and if `traverse` is a function that sets its parameter to point to the next element of a tree in the desired order, the following could be used:

```
for (ptr = root; ptr == null; traverse(ptr)) {
  ...
}
```

In this statement, `traverse` is the iterator.

User-defined iteration statements are more important in object-oriented programming than they were in earlier software development paradigms. This results from the fact that users now routinely construct abstract data types for data structures. In such cases, a user-defined iteration statement and its iterator must be provided by the author of the data abstraction because the representation of the objects of the type is not known to the user. In C++, iterators for user-defined types, or classes, are often implemented either as friend functions to the class or as separate iterator classes.

7.5 Unconditional Branching

An **unconditional branch statement** transfers execution control to a specified place in the program.

7.5.1 Problems with Unconditional Branching

The most heated debate in language design of the late 1960s was over the issue of whether unconditional branching should be part of any high-level language, and if so, whether its use should be restricted.

The unconditional branch, or goto, is the most powerful statement for controlling the flow of execution of a program's statements. However, using the goto carelessly can lead to problems. The goto has stunning power and great flexibility (all other control structures can be built with goto and a selector), but this very power makes its use dangerous. Without restrictions on use, imposed either by language design or programming standards, goto statements can make programs virtually unreadable, and as a result, highly unreliable and difficult to maintain.

These problems follow directly from a goto's capability of forcing any program statement to follow any other in execution sequence, regardless of whether that statement precedes or follows the first in textual order. Readability is best when the execution order of statements is nearly the same as the order in which they appear—in our case, this would mean top to bottom, which is the order to which we are accustomed. Thus restricting gotos so they can transfer control only downward in a program partially alleviates the problem. It allows gotos to transfer control around code sections in response to errors or unusual conditions, but disallows their use to build any sort of loop.

Although several thoughtful people had suggested them earlier, it was Edsger Dijkstra who gave the computing world the first widely read exposè on the dangers of the goto. In his letter he noted, "The goto statement as it stands is just too primitive; it is too much an invitation to make a mess of one's program" (Dijkstra, 1968a). During the first few years after publication of Dijkstra's views on the goto, a large number of people argued publicly for either outright banishment or at least restriction of the goto. Among those who did not favor complete elimination was Donald Knuth, who argued that there were occasions when the efficiency of the goto outweighed its harm to readability (Knuth, 1974).

A few languages have been designed without a goto—for example, Modula-2 and Java. However, most currently popular languages include a goto statement. Kernighan and Ritchie (1978) call the goto infinitely abusable, but it is nevertheless included in Ritchie's language, C. The languages that have eliminated the goto have provided additional control statements, usually in the form of loop and subprogram exits, to replace many of the typical applications of the goto.

7.5.2 Label Forms

Some languages, such as ALGOL 60 and C, use their identifier forms for labels. FORTRAN and Pascal use unsigned integer constants for labels. Ada uses its identifier form as the target part of its goto statement, but when the label appears on a statement, it must be delimited by the symbols <<OUT>>. For example, consider the following:

```
goto FINISHED;
...
<<FINISHED>> SUM := SUM + NEXT;
```

The bracketing makes labels easier to find when the program is read. In most other languages, labels are attached to statements by colons, as in

```
finished: sum := sum + next
```

In its design of labels, PL/I once again takes a construct to its limit of flexibility and complexity. Instead of treating labels as mere constants, PL/I allows them to be variables. In their variable form, they can be assigned values and used as subprogram parameters. This allows a goto to be targeted to virtually anywhere in a program, and the target cannot be statically determined. Although this flexibility is sometimes useful, it is far too detrimental to readability to be worthwhile. Imagine trying to read and understand a program that has branches whose targets depend on values assigned at run time. Consider a subprogram that has several labels and a goto whose target label is a formal parameter. To determine the target of the goto, one must know the calling program unit and the actual parameter value used in the call. The implementation of variable labels is also complex, primarily because of all the possible ways label variables can be bound to values.

7.5.3 Restrictions on Branches

Recognizing the problem inherent with gotos, most languages restrict their use. As an example of how the unconditional branch can be restricted, consider Pascal. Pascal labels must be declared as if they were variables, but they cannot be passed as parameters, stored, or modified. The scope of a label is the same as that of the variables that are declared where the label is declared. As part of the **goto** statement, labels must be simple constants—not expressions or variables with labels as values.

Let a **statement group** be either a compound statement, including a complete subprogram, or the collection of statements in a **repeat** loop. A statement group is **active** it if has begun but not completed its execution. The Pascal restriction states that the target of a **goto** cannot be a statement in a statement group that is not active. Therefore, the target can never be in a statement group that is at the same level or is nested more deeply than that of the one of the **goto**. This prevents control structures from having more than one entry point.

An important problem with Pascal's restrictions is that it is still legal to branch into an enclosing subprogram. The target subprogram, because it is enclosing, must be active. Consider the following example:

```
procedure sub1;
  label 100;
  ...
  procedure sub2;
    ...
    goto 100;
    ...
```

```
        end;   { of sub2 }
    ...
100: ...
    ...
    end;   { of sub1 }
```

The **goto** in this example is legal. It transfers control to the parent subprogram, sub1, terminating sub2, the home of the **goto**. So a **goto** can terminate one or more procedure activations, or executions, but cannot start one by branching into it. Of course, a branch to a procedure call indirectly causes the start of execution of a procedure.

Branching from one procedure to another is highly detrimental to program readability and is therefore an unreliable programming practice. If Pascal's restrictions on **goto** limited targets to enclosing statement groups except those that define subprograms, it would be more in spirit with the motive of making programs safer.

On the positive side—in defense of Pascal's **goto** target rules—the ability to branch from a procedure to its parent or other ancestor can be a convenient method of propagating error conditions to ancestor procedures for possible corrective action. This process is, however, more properly done by an exception-handling mechanism designed into the language. Exception handling will be discussed in Chapter 13.

All of the loop exit statements discussed in Section 7.4.3 are actually camouflaged goto statements. They are, however, severely restricted gotos and are not harmful to readability. In fact, it can be argued that they improve readability because to avoid their use results in convoluted and unnatural code that would be much harder to understand.

7.6 Guarded Commands

Alternative and different forms of selection and loop structures were suggested by Dijkstra (1975). His motivation was to provide control statements that would support a program design methodology that ensured correctness during development rather than relying on verification or testing of completed programs to ensure their correctness. This methodology is described in Dijkstra (1976).

Guarded commands are covered in this chapter because they are the basis for two linguistic mechanisms developed later for concurrent programming in two languages, CSP (Hoare, 1978) and Ada. Concurrency in Ada is discussed in Chapter 12.

Dijkstra's selection construct has the form

```
if   < Boolean expression >  ->  < statement >
[]   < Boolean expression >  ->  < statement >
[]   ...
[]   < Boolean expression >  ->  < statement >
fi
```

The closing reserved word, **fi**, is the opening reserved word spelled backwards. This form of closing reserved word is taken from ALGOL 68. The small blocks, called fatbars, are used to separate the guarded clauses and allow the clauses to be statement sequences.

This selection construct has the appearance of a multiple selection, but its semantics is different. All of the Boolean expressions are evaluated each time the construct is reached during execution. If more than one expression is true, one of the corresponding statements is nondeterministically chosen for execution. If none is true, a run-time error occurs that causes program termination. This forces the programmer to consider and list all possibilities, as with Ada's **case** statement. Consider the following example:

```
if  i = 0 -> sum := sum + i
[]  i > j -> sum := sum + j
[]  j > i -> sum := sum + i
fi
```

If i = 0 and j > i, this construct chooses nondeterministically between the first and third assignment statements. If i is equal to j and is not zero, a run-time error occurs because none of the conditions is true.

This construct can be an elegant way of allowing the programmer to state that the order of execution, in some cases, is irrelevant. For example, to find the largest of two numbers, we can use

```
if  x >= y -> max := x
[]  y >= x -> max := y
fi
```

This computes the desired result without overspecifying the solution. In particular, if x and y are equal, it does not matter which we assign to max. This is a form of abstraction provided by the nondeterministic semantics of the statement.

Another situation in which Dijkstra's selection construct is valuable is the following: Suppose we are writing a program that services interrupts, and the interrupts have the same priority. For this, we need a construct that chooses among current interrupts in some random way.

The semantics of the guarded commands are difficult to describe precisely. Although flow diagrams are not good tools for program design, they are sometimes useful for semantics descriptions. Figure 7.1 is a flowgraph describing the approach used by Dijkstra's selector statement. Note that this flowgraph is relatively imprecise, reflecting the difficulty in capturing the semantics of the guarded commands.

The loop structure proposed by Dijkstra has the form

```
do  < Boolean expression >  ->  < statement >
[]  < Boolean expression >  ->  < statement >
[]  ...
[]  < Boolean expression >  ->  < statement >
od
```

Figure 7.1
Flowgraph of the
approach used with
Dijkstra's selector
statement

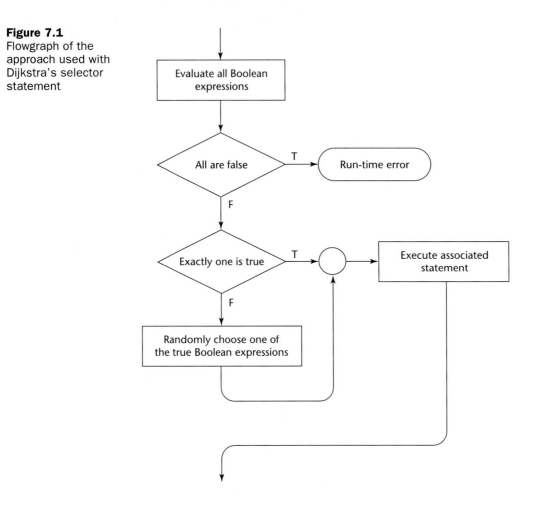

The semantics of this construct is that all Boolean expressions are evaluated on each iteration. If more than one is true, one of the associated statements is nondeterministically chosen for execution, after which the expressions are again evaluated. When all expressions are simultaneously false, the loop terminates.

Consider the following code, which appears in slightly different form in Dijkstra (1975). The four variables q1, q2, q3, and q4 are to have their values rearranged so that q1 ≤ q2 ≤ q3 ≤ q4.

```
do q1 > q2 -> temp := q1; q1 := q2; q2 := temp;
[] q2 > q3 -> temp := q2; q2 := q3; q3 := temp;
[] q3 > q4 -> temp := q3; q3 := q4; q4 := temp;
od
```

A flowgraph describing the approach used by Dijkstra's loop statement is shown in Figure 7.2. Once again, note that the control-flow semantics of this construct cannot be completely depicted in a flowgraph.

Figure 7.2
Flowgraph of the approach used with Dijkstra's loop statement

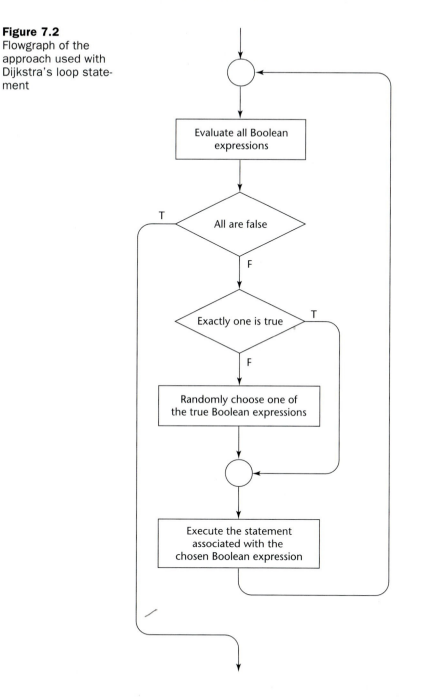

Dijkstra's guarded commands, as these two constructs are known, are interesting in part because they illustrate how the syntax and semantics of statements can have an impact on program verification, and vice versa. Program verification is virtually impossible when goto statements are used. Verification is greatly simplified if either only logical loops and selections, like those of Pascal, are used, or only guarded commands are used. The axiomatic semantics of guarded commands is conveniently specified (Gries, 1981). It should be obvious, however, that there is considerably increased complexity in the implementation of the guarded commands over their conventional deterministic counterparts.

7.7 Conclusions

We have described and discussed a variety of statement-level control structures. A brief evaluation now seems to be in order.

First, we have the theoretical result that only sequence, selection, and pretest logical loops are absolutely required to express computations (Böhm and Jacopini, 1966). This result has been widely used by those who wish to ban unconditional branching altogether. Of course, there are already sufficient practical problems with the goto to condemn it without also finding a theoretical reason. One application of goto that many feel is justified is its use to allow premature exits from loops in languages that do not have exit statements.

One obvious misuse of the Böhm and Jacopini result is to argue against the inclusion of *any* control structures beyond selection and pretest logical loops. No widely used language has yet taken that step; further, we doubt that any ever will because of the effect on writability and readability. Programs written with only selection and pretest logical loops are generally less natural in structure, more complex, and therefore harder to write and more difficult to read. For example, the Ada multiple selection structure is a great boost to Ada writability, with no clear negatives. Another example is the counting loop structure of many languages, especially when the statement is simple, as in Pascal and Ada.

It is not so clear that the utility of many of the other control structures that have been proposed is worth their inclusion in languages (Ledgard and Marcotty, 1975). This question rests to a large degree on the fundamental question of whether the size of languages must be minimized. Both Wirth (1975) and Hoare (1973) strongly endorse simplicity in language design. In the case of control structures, simplicity means that only a few control statements should be in a language, and they should all be simple.

The rich variety of statement-level control structures that have been invented shows the diversity of opinion among language designers. After all the invention, discussion, and evaluation there is still no unanimity of opinion on the precise set of control statements that should be in a language. Most contemporary languages do, of course, have similar control statements, but there is still some variation in the details of their syntax and semantics. Furthermore, there is still disagreement on whether a language should include a goto; C++ and Ada 95 do, but Modula-2 and Java do not.

One final note: The control structures of functional and logic programming languages and of Smalltalk are all quite different from those described in this chapter. These mechanisms are discussed in some detail in Chapters 14, 15, and 11, respectively.

SUMMARY

The control statements of the imperative languages occur in several categories: selection, multiple selection, iterative, and unconditional branching.

FORTRAN introduced a single-way statement selector, the logical IF. ALGOL 60's selector is more advanced, allowing selection of compound statements and including an optional **else** clause. Many control structures benefited from the compound statement that ALGOL 60 introduced.

FORTRAN's arithmetic IF is a three-way selector that usually requires other unconditional branches.

FORTRAN introduced two forms of multiple selection statements: the computed GO TO and the assigned GO TO. True to their names, both are actually multiple-way branches. The Pascal **case** is representative of modern multiple selection statements; it includes both encapsulation of the selectable segments and implicit branches at the end of each to the single exit point.

A large number of different loop statements have been invented for high-level languages, starting with FORTRAN's counting DO. The **for** statement of ALGOL 60 was far too complex, combining logic and counter controls in a single statement. Pascal's **for** statement is, in terms of complexity, the opposite. It elegantly implements only the most commonly needed counting loop forms. C's **for** statement is the most flexible iteration construct.

Modula-2, C, C++, FORTRAN 90, Java, and Ada have exit statements for their loops; these statements take the place of one of the most common uses of goto statements.

Data-based iterators are loop constructs for processing data structures, such as linked lists, hashes, and trees.

The unconditional branch, or goto, has been part of most imperative languages. Its problems have been widely discussed and debated. The current consensus is that it should remain in most languages but that its dangers should be minimized through programming discipline.

Dijkstra's guarded commands are alternative control constructs with positive theoretical characteristics. Although they have not been adopted as the control constructs of a language, part of the semantics appear in the concurrency mechanisms of CSP and Ada.

REVIEW QUESTIONS

1. What is the definition of *control structure?*
2. What is the definition of *block?*
3. What are the design issues for selection structures?
4. What are the common solutions to the nesting problem for two-way selectors? What is wrong with Modula-2's solution?
5. What are the design issues for multiple selection statements?
6. What is the basis for the control statements of FORTRAN I?
7. What is wrong with FORTRAN's arithmetic **IF** statement?
8. What is unusual about C's multiple selection statement? What design trade-off was made in this design?
9. What are the design issues for counter-controlled loop statements?
10. What is a pretest loop statement? What is a posttest loop statement?
11. What is the most significant change in the **DO** statement design between FORTRAN IV and FORTRAN 77?
12. What characteristic of ALGOL 60's **for** statement makes programs that use it difficult to read?
13. What is the difference between the **for** statement of C++ and that of Java?
14. What are the design issues for logically controlled loop statements?
15. What is the main reason user-located loop control statements were invented?
16. What advantage does Ada's **exit** statement have over C's **break** statement?
17. What are the differences between the **break** statement of C++ and that of Java?
18. What is a user-defined iteration control?
19. What are two disadvantages of PL/I's label variables?
20. What is the primary problem with Pascal's goto restrictions?
21. What common programming language borrows part of its design from Dijkstra's guarded commands?

PROBLEM SET

1. Write a defense of the claim that the three-way selection statement of FORTRAN I was the best choice, given the circumstances of the time.
2. Devise a situation in which the label variable of PL/I would be a great advantage.
3. Describe three situations where a combined counting and logical looping construct is needed.
4. Compare the FORTRAN-computed GO TO with the Pascal **case** statement, especially in terms of readability and reliability.
5. What are the possible reasons why Pascal has a logical posttest loop, while ALGOL 60 did not?

6. Study the iterator feature of CLU in Liskov et al. (1984) and determine its advantages and disadvantages.

7. Compare the set of Ada control statements with those of FORTRAN 77 and decide which are better and why.

8. What are the pros and cons of using unique closing reserved words on compound statements?

9. Analyze the potential readability problems with using closure reserved words for control statements that are the reverse of the corresponding initial reserved words, such as the **case-esac** reserved words of ALGOL 68. For example, consider common typing errors such as the reversal of two adjacent characters.

10. Rewrite the following code segment using a loop structure in the following languages:

```
k := (j + 13) / 27
loop:
    if k > 10 then goto out
    k := k + 1
    i := 3 * k - 1
    goto loop
out: ...
```

   a. Pascal

   b. FORTRAN 77

   c. Ada

   d. C, C++, or Java

   Assume all variables are integer type. Discuss which language, for this code, has the best writability, the best readability, and the best combination of the two.

11. Redo Problem 10, except this time make all the variables and constants floating-point type, and change the statement

```
k := k + 1
```

   to

```
k := k + 1.2
```

12. Rewrite the following code segment using a multiple selection statement in the following languages:

```
if (k = 1) or (k = 2) then j := 2 * k - 1
if (k = 3) or (k = 5) then j := 3 * k + 1
if (k = 4) then j := 4 * k - 1
if (k = 6) or (k = 7) or (k = 8) then j := k - 2
```

   a. Pascal

   b. FORTRAN 90 (you'll have to look this one up)

   c. Ada

   d. C, C++, or Java

   Assume all variables are integer type. Discuss the relative merits of the use of these languages for this particular code.

13. Consider the following ALGOL 60-style **for** statement:

    ```
    for i := j + 1 step i * j until 3 * j do j := j + 1
    ```

    Assume that the initial value of j is 1. List the sequence of values for the variable i used, assuming the following semantics:

    a. All expressions are evaluated once at the loop entry.

    b. All expressions are evaluated before each iteration.

    c. **step** expressions are evaluated once at loop entry, and **until** expressions are evaluated before each iteration.

    d. **until** expressions are evaluated once at loop entry, and **step** expressions are evaluated before each iteration, just after the loop counter is incremented.

    In all cases, when more than one expression is evaluated at the same time, they are evaluated in left-to-right order. Also, the assignment is always done as soon as its RHS is evaluated.

14. Use the *Science Citation Index* to find an article that refers to Knuth (1974). Read the article and Knuth's paper and write a paper that summarizes both sides of the goto argument.

15. In his paper on the goto issue, Knuth (1974) suggests a loop control construct that allows multiple exits. Read the paper and write an operational semantics description of the construct.

16. Consider the following Pascal **case** statement. Rewrite it using only two-way selection.

    ```
    case index - 1 of
       2, 4: even := even + 1;
       1, 3: odd := odd + 1;
       0: zero := zero + 1;
       else error := true
    end
    ```

17. Consider the following C program segment. Rewrite it using no **goto**s or **break**s.

    ```
    j = -3;
    for (i = 0; i < 3; i++) {
      switch (j + 2) {
        case 3:
        case 2: j--; break;
        case 0: j += 2; break;
        default: j = 0;
      }
      if (j > 0) break;
      j = 3 - i
    }
    ```

18. In a letter to the editor of CACM, Rubin (1987) uses the following code segment as evidence that the readability of some code with gotos is better than the equivalent code without gotos. This code finds the first row of an $n \times n$ integer matrix named **x** that has nothing but zero values.

```
for i := 1 to n do
  begin
  for j := 1 to n do
    if x[i, j] <> 0
      then goto reject;
    writeln('First all-zero row is:', i);
    break;
reject:
  end;
```

Rewrite this code without goto's in one of the following languages, C, C++, Pascal, Java, or Ada. Compare the readability of your code to that of the code above.

19. What are the arguments both for and against the exclusive use of Boolean expressions in the control statements in Java (as opposed to also allowing arithmetic expressions, as in C and C++)?

8 Subprograms

Dennis Ritchie

Dennis Ritchie of Bell Laboratories was on of the principals involved with the development of UNIX. He was the designer of the first version of C, which was then used to rewrite UNIX for PDP-11 computers

Subprograms are the fundamental building blocks of programs and are therefore among the most important concepts in programming language design. We now explore the design of subprograms, including parameter-passing methods, local and nonlocal referencing environments, overloaded subprograms, generic subprograms, separate and independent compilation, and the aliasing and side effects problems that are associated with subprograms. We also include a brief discussion of coroutines, which provide symmetric unit control.

Implementation methods for subprograms are discussed in Chapter 9.

8.1 Introduction

Two fundamental abstraction facilities can be included in a programming language: process abstraction and data abstraction. In the early history of high-level programming languages, only process abstraction was recognized and included. Process abstraction has been a central concept in all programming languages. In the 1980s, however, many people began to believe that data abstraction was equally important. Data abstraction is discussed in detail in Chapter 10.

The first programmable computer, Babbage's Analytical Engine, built in the 1840s, had the capability of reusing collections of instruction cards at several different places in a program when that was convenient. In a modern programming language, such a collection of statements is written as a subprogram. This reuse results in several different kinds of savings, from memory space to coding time. Such reuse is also an abstraction, for the details of the subprogram's computation are replaced in a program by a statement that calls the subprogram. Instead of explaining how some computation is to be done in a program, that explanation (the collection of statements in the subprogram) is enacted by a call statement, effectively abstracting away the details. This increases the readability of a program by exposing its logical structure while hiding the small-scale details.

8.2 Fundamentals of Subprograms

8.2.1 General Subprogram Characteristics

All subprograms discussed in this chapter, except the coroutines described in Section 8.13, have the following characteristics:

- Each subprogram has a single entry point.

- The calling program unit is suspended during the execution of the called subprogram, which implies that there is only one subprogram in execution at any given time.
- Control always returns to the caller when the subprogram execution terminates.

Although FORTRAN subprograms can have multiple entries, that particular kind of entry is relatively unimportant because it does not provide any fundamentally different capabilities. Therefore, in this chapter, we will ignore the possibility of multiple entries in FORTRAN subprograms.

Alternatives to the above assumptions result in coroutines (Section 8.13) and concurrent units, which are explored in Chapter 12.

The methods of object-oriented languages are closely related to the subprograms discussed in this chapter. The primary ways methods differ from subprograms is the way they are called and their association with classes and objects. Although these special characteristics of methods are discussed in Chapter 11, the features they share with subprograms, such as parameters and local variables, are included in this chapter.

8.2.2 Basic Definitions

A **subprogram definition** describes the interface to and the actions of the subprogram abstraction. A **subprogram call** is the explicit request that the subprogram be executed. A subprogram is said to be **active** if, after having been called, it has begun execution but has not yet completed that execution. The two fundamental kinds of subprograms, procedures and functions, are defined and discussed in Section 8.2.4.

A **subprogram header,** which is the first line of the definition, serves several purposes. First, it specifies that the following syntactic unit is a subprogram definition of some particular kind. This specification is often accomplished with a special word. Second, it provides a name for the subprogram. Third, it may optionally specify a list of parameters. They are optional because not all subprogram definitions have parameters.

Consider the following header examples:

```
SUBROUTINE ADDER(parameters)
```

This is the header of a FORTRAN subroutine subprogram named ADDER. In Ada, the header for ADDER would be

```
procedure ADDER(parameters)
```

No special word appears in the header of a C subprogram. C has only one kind of subprogram, the function, and the header of a function is recognized by context rather than by a special word. For example,

```
void adder(parameters)
```

would serve as the header of a function named adder, where **void** indicates that it does not return a value.

The **parameter profile** of a subprogram is the number, order, and types of its formal parameters. The **protocol** of a subprogram is its parameter profile plus, if it is a function, its return type. In languages in which subprograms have types, those types are defined by the subprogram's protocol.

Subprograms can have declarations as well as definitions. This parallels the variable declarations and definitions in C, in which the declarations can be used to provide type information but not to define variables. They are necessary when a variable must be referenced before the compiler has seen its definition. Subprogram declarations provide interface information, which is primarily parameter types, but do not include subprogram bodies. They are necessary when the compiler must translate a call to a subprogram before it has seen that subprogram's definition. In both the cases of variables and subprograms, declarations are needed for static type checking. Subprogram declarations are common in C programs, where they are called **prototypes.** They are also used in Ada and Pascal, where they are sometimes called forward or external declarations.

Java does not allow declarations of its methods, because forward references to them are implicitly allowed wherever they are visible.

8.2.3 Parameters

Subprograms typically describe computations. There are two ways that a subprogram can gain access to the data that it is to process: through direct access to nonlocal variables (declared elsewhere but visible in the subprogram) or through parameter passing. Data passed through parameters are accessed through names that are local to the subprogram. Parameter passing is more flexible than direct access to nonlocal variables. In essence, a subprogram with parameter access to the data it is to process is a parameterized computation. It can perform its computation on whatever data it receives through its parameters (presuming the types of the parameters are as expected by the subprogram). If data access is through nonlocal variables, the only way the computation can proceed on different data is to assign new values to those nonlocal variables between calls to the subprogram. Extensive access to nonlocals can cause reduced reliability. Variables that are visible to the subprogram where access is desired often end up also being visible where access to them is not needed. This problem was discussed in Chapter 4 and is reviewed in Section 8.11.

In some situations, it is convenient to be able to transmit computations, rather than data, as parameters to subprograms. In these cases, the name of the subprogram that implements that computation may be used as a parameter. This form of parameter is discussed in Section 8.6. Data parameters are discussed in Section 8.5.

The parameters in the subprogram header are called **formal parameters.** They are sometimes thought of as dummy variables because they are not variables in the usual sense: In some cases, they are bound to storage only when the subprogram is called, and that binding is often through some other program variables.

Subprogram call statements must include the name of the subprogram and a list of parameters to be bound to the formal parameters of the subprogram. These parameters are called **actual parameters.** They must be distinguished from formal parameters because the two can have different restrictions on their forms, and of course their uses are quite different.

In nearly all programming languages, the correspondence between actual and formal parameters—or the binding of actual parameters to formal parameters—is done by simple position: The first actual parameter is bound to the first formal parameter and so forth. Such parameters are called **positional parameters.** This is a good method for relatively short parameter lists.

When lists are long, however, it is easy for the program writer to make mistakes in the order of parameters in the list. One solution to this problem is to provide **keyword parameters,** in which the name of the formal parameter to which an actual parameter is to be bound is specified with the actual parameter. The advantage of keyword parameters is that they can appear in any order in the actual parameter list. Ada procedures can be called using this method, as in

```
SUMER(LENGTH => MY_LENGTH,
      LIST => MY_ARRAY,
      SUM => MY_SUM);
```

where the definition of SUMER has the formal parameters LENGTH, LIST, and SUM.

The chief disadvantage to keyword parameters is that the user of the subprogram must know the names of formal parameters.

In addition to keyword parameters, Ada and FORTRAN 90 allow positional parameters. The two can be mixed in a call, as in

```
SUMER(MY_LENGTH,
      SUM => MY_SUM,
      LIST => MY_ARRAY);
```

The only restriction with this is that after a keyword parameter appears in the list, all remaining parameters must be keyworded. This is necessary because position may no longer be well defined after a keyword parameter has appeared.

In C++, FORTRAN 90, and Ada, formal parameters can have default values. A default value is used if no actual parameter is passed to the formal parameter in the subprogram header. Consider the following Ada function header:

```
function COMPUTE_PAY(INCOME : FLOAT;
                     EXEMPTIONS : INTEGER := 1;
                     TAX_RATE : FLOAT) return FLOAT;
```

The EXEMPTIONS parameter can be absent in a call to COMPUTE_PAY; when it is, the value 1 is used. No comma is included for an absent actual parameter in an Ada call, because the only value of such a comma would be to indicate the position of the next parameter, which in this case is not necessary because all actual parameters after an absent actual parameter must be keyworded. For example, consider the following call:

```
PAY := COMPUTE_PAY(20000.0, TAX_RATE => 0.15);
```

In C++, which has no keyword parameters, the rules for default parameters are necessarily different. The default parameters must appear last, for parameters are positionally associated. Once a default parameter is omitted in a call, all remaining formal parameters must have default values. A C++ function header for COMPUTE_PAY can be written as follows:

```
float compute_pay(float income, float tax_rate,
                  int exemptions = 1)
```

Notice that the parameters are rearranged so that the one with the default value is last. An example call to the C++ compute_pay is

```
pay = compute_pay(20000.0, 0.15);
```

In most languages that do not have default values for formal parameters, the number of actual parameters in a call must match the number of formal parameters in the subprogram definition header. However, in C and C++ this is not required. When there are fewer actual parameters in a call than formal parameters in a function definition, it is the programmer's responsibility to ensure that the parameter correspondence, which is always positional, and the subprogram execution are sensible.

Although this design, which allows a variable number of parameters, is clearly prone to error, it is also sometimes convenient. For example, the printf function of C can print any number of items (data values and/or literal strings). Ada subprograms must have a fixed number of parameters, so a predefined Ada output procedure prints only a single value. Such output subprograms are more cumbersome to use.

8.2.4 Procedures and Functions

There are two distinct categories of subprograms: procedures and functions, both of which can be viewed as approaches to extending the language. Procedures are collections of statements that define parameterized computations. These computations are enacted by single call statements. In effect, procedures define new statements. For example, because Pascal does not have a sort statement, a user can build a procedure to sort arrays of data and use a call to that procedure in place of the unavailable sort statement.

Procedures can produce results in the calling program unit by two methods. First, if there are variables that are not formal parameters but are still visible in both the procedure and the calling program unit, the procedure can change them. Second, if the subprogram has formal parameters that allow the transfer of data to the caller, those parameters can be changed.

Functions structurally resemble procedures but are semantically modeled on mathematical functions. If a function is a faithful model, it produces no side effects; that is, it modifies neither its parameters nor any variables defined outside the function.

Functions are called by appearances of their names in expressions, along with the required actual parameters. The value produced by a function's execution is returned to the calling code, effectively replacing the call itself. For example, the value of the expression `f(x)` is whatever value `f` produces when called with the parameter `x`. For a function that does not produce side effects, the returned value is its only effect.

Functions define new user-defined operators. For example, if a language does not have an exponentiation operator, a function can be written that returns the value of one of its parameters raised to the power of another parameter. Its header in C could be

```
float power(float base, float exp)
```

which could be called with

```
result = 3.4 * power(10.0, x)
```

The standard C libraries already include a similar function named `pow`. Compare this with the same operation in FORTRAN, in which exponentiation is a built-in operation:

```
RESULT = 3.4 * 10.0 ** X
```

In Ada and C++, users are permitted to overload operators by defining new functions. In these languages, the user could define an exponentiation operator that could be used much like the built-in exponentiation operator in FORTRAN. User-defined operator overloading is discussed in Section 8.12.

Most common imperative languages provide both functions and procedures. C and C++ have only functions. However, these functions can behave like procedures. They can be defined to return no value by defining its return type to be **void**. Because expressions in these languages can be used as statements, a stand-alone call to a **void** function is legal. For example, consider the following function header and call:

```
void sort(int list[], int listlen);
...
sort(scores, 100);
```

The methods of Java and C++ are similar to the functions of C.

8.3 Design Issues for Subprograms

Subprograms are complex structures in programming languages, and it follows from this that a lengthy list of issues is involved in their design. One obvious issue is the choice of parameter-passing method or methods that will be used. The wide variety of methods that have been used in various languages is a reflection of the diversity of opinion on the subject. A closely related issue is whether the types of actual parameters will be type checked against the types of the corresponding formal parameters.

The nature of the local environment of a subprogram dictates to some degree the nature of the subprogram. The most important question here is whether local variables are statically or dynamically allocated.

As mentioned earlier, some languages allow subprogram names to be passed as parameters. One design issue is simply whether this is to be allowed in a language. If it is, that raises the question of what should be the referencing environment of a subprogram that has been passed as a parameter. Another related issue is whether the types of the parameters of subprograms, which are themselves passed as parameters, are checked.

Another issue is whether subprogram definitions can appear inside other subprogram definitions.

Next, there are the questions of whether subprograms can be overloaded or generic. An overloaded subprogram is one that has the same name as another subprogram in the same referencing environment. A generic subprogram is one whose computation can be done on data of different types with different calls.

Finally, a language that is meant to be useful for constructing significant software systems must allow the compilation of parts of programs (as opposed to being required to compile only complete programs). When some facility for this kind of compilation is provided, the next design issue is how flexible and reliable the mechanism should be. Two distinct approaches have been used, separate and independent compilation.

The following is a summary of these design issues for subprograms in general. Additional issues that are specifically associated with functions are discussed in Section 8.10.

- What parameter-passing method or methods are used?
- Are the types of the actual parameters checked against the types of the formal parameters?
- Are local variables statically or dynamically allocated?
- If subprograms can be passed as parameters, what is the referencing environment of such a subprogram?
- If subprograms can be passed as parameters, are the types of parameters checked in calls to the passed subprograms?

- Can subprogram definitions appear in other subprogram definitions?
- Can subprograms be overloaded?
- Can subprograms be generic?
- Is either separate or independent compilation possible?

These issues and example designs are discussed in the following sections.

8.4 Local Referencing Environments

Subprograms are generally allowed to define their own variables, thereby defining local referencing environments. Variables that are defined inside subprograms are called **local variables** because access to them is usually restricted to the subprogram in which they are defined.

In the terminology of Chapter 4, local variables can be either static or stack dynamic. If local variables are stack dynamic, they are bound to storage when the subprogram begins execution and unbound from storage when that execution terminates. There are several advantages of stack-dynamic local variables, the primary one being the flexibility they provide the subprogram. It is essential that recursive subprograms have stack-dynamic local variables. Another advantage of stack-dynamic locals is that some of the storage for local variables of all subprograms can be shared. Such sharing obviously cannot take place among subprograms that are active at the same time. This is not as great an advantage as it was when computers had smaller memories.

The main disadvantages of stack-dynamic local variables are the following: First there is the cost of the time required to allocate, initialize (when necessary), and deallocate such variables for each activation. Second, accesses to stack-dynamic local variables must be indirect, whereas accesses to static variables can be direct. This indirectness is required because the place in the stack where a particular local variable will reside can only be determined during execution (see Chapter 9). On most computers, indirect addressing is slower than direct addressing. Finally, with stack-dynamic local variables, subprograms cannot be history sensitive; that is, they cannot retain data values of local variables between calls. It is sometimes desirable to be able to write history-sensitive subprograms. A common example of a need for a history-sensitive subprogram is one whose task is to generate pseudorandom numbers. Each call to such a subprogram computes one pseudorandom number, using the last one it computed. It must, therefore, store the last one in a static local variable. Coroutines and the subprograms used in iterator loop constructs (discussed in Chapter 7) are other examples of the need to be history sensitive.

The primary advantage of static local variables is that they are very efficient—they usually can be accessed faster because there is no indirection. Furthermore, they require no run-time overhead for allocation and deallocation. And, of course, they allow subprograms to be history sensitive. The greatest disadvantage is the inability to support recursion.

In ALGOL 60 and its descendant languages, local variables in a subprogram are by default stack dynamic. In C and C++ functions, locals are stack dynamic unless specifically declared to be **static**. For example, in the following C (or C++) function, the variable `sum` is static and `count` is stack dynamic.

```
int adder(int list[], int listlen) {
  static int sum = 0;
  int count;
  for (count = 0; count < listlen; count ++)
    sum += list [count];
  return sum;
}
```

Pascal, Modula-2, and Ada subprograms have only stack-dynamic local variables. Java methods also have only stack-dynamic local variables.

As discussed in Chapter 4, FORTRAN 77 implementors can choose whether local variables are to be static or stack dynamic. Most implementors stay with the tradition of earlier FORTRANs and make them static. Actually, because pre-90 FORTRANs do not allow recursion, there is really no compelling reason to make them stack dynamic. The savings in storage is not usually thought to be worth the loss in efficiency. FORTRAN 77 users can force one or more local variables to be static regardless of the implementation by listing their names on a **SAVE** statement.

In FORTRAN 90, a subprogram can be explicitly specified to be recursive, in which case its local variables are stack dynamic. This idea of specifying that a particular subprogram can be recursively called originated with PL/I. The purpose of this explicit specification is to allow nonrecursive subprograms to be implemented in a more efficient way.

8.5 Parameter-Passing Methods

Parameter-passing methods are the ways in which parameters are transmitted to and/or from called subprograms. We first focus on the primary semantics models of parameter-passing methods. Then we discuss the various implementation models invented by language designers for these semantics models. Next we survey the design choices of the various imperative languages and discuss the actual methods used to implement the implementation models. We finally consider the design considerations that face a language designer in choosing among the methods.

8.5.1 Semantics Models of Parameter Passing

Formal parameters are characterized by one of three distinct semantics models: (1) They can receive data from the corresponding actual parameter, (2) they can transmit data to the actual parameter, or (3) they can do both. These three semantics models are called **in mode, out mode,** and **inout mode,** respectively.

There are two conceptual models of how data transfers take place in parameter transmission: Either an actual value is physically moved (to the caller, to the callee, or both ways), or an access path is transmitted. Most commonly, the access path is a simple pointer. Figure 8.1 illustrates the three semantics models of parameter passing when physical moves are used.

8.5.2 Implementation Models of Parameter Passing

A variety of models has been developed by language designers to guide the implementation of the three basic parameter transmission modes. In the following sections, we discuss several of these and evaluate their strengths and weaknesses.

8.5.2.1 Pass-By-Value

When a parameter is **passed by value,** the value of the actual parameter is used to initialize the corresponding formal parameter, which then acts as a local variable in the subprogram, thus implementing in-mode semantics.

Figure 8.1
The three semantics models of parameter passing when physical moves are used

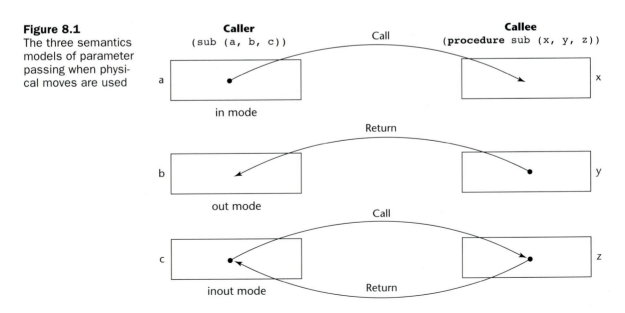

Pass-by-value is normally implemented by actual data transfer, because accesses are usually more efficient with this method. It could be implemented by transmitting an access path to the value of the actual parameter in the caller, but that would require that the value be in a write-protected cell (one that can only be read). Enforcing the write protection is not always a simple matter. For example, suppose the subprogram to which the parameter was passed passes it in turn to another subprogram. This is another reason to use physical transfer. As we will see in Section 8.5.3, C++ provides a convenient and effective method for enforcing write protection on pass-by-value parameters that are transmitted by access path.

The main disadvantage of the pass-by-value method if physical moves are done is that additional storage is required for the formal parameter, either in the called subprogram or in some area outside both the caller and the called subprogram. In addition, the actual parameter must be physically moved to the storage area for the corresponding formal parameter. The storage and the move operations can be costly if the parameter is large, such as a long array.

8.5.2.2 Pass-By-Result

Pass-by-result is an implementation model for out-mode parameters. When a parameter is passed by result, no value is transmitted to the subprogram. The corresponding formal parameter acts as a local variable, but just before control is transferred back to the caller, its value is passed back to the caller's actual parameter, which obviously must be a variable. (How would the caller reference the computed result if it were a literal or an expression?) If values are returned (as opposed to access paths), as they typically are, pass-by-result also requires the extra storage and the copy operations that are required by pass-by-value. As with pass-by-value, the difficulty of implementing pass-by-result by transmitting an access path usually results in it being implemented by data transfer. In this case, the problem is in ensuring that the initial value of the actual parameter is not used in the called subprogram.

One problem with the pass-by-result model is that there can be an actual parameter collision, such as the one created with the call

```
sub(p1, p1)
```

In sub, assuming the two formal parameters have different names, the two can obviously be assigned different values. Then whichever of the two is assigned to their corresponding actual parameter last becomes the value of p1. Thus the order in which the actual parameters are assigned determines their value. Because the order is usually implementation dependent, portability problems can occur that are difficult to diagnose.

Calling a procedure with two identical actual parameters can also lead to different kinds of problems when other parameter-passing methods are used, as discussed in Section 8.5.2.4.

Another problem that can occur with pass-by-result is that the implementor may be able to choose between two different times to evaluate the addresses of the actual parameters: at the time of the call or at the time of the return. For example, suppose a subprogram has the parameter `list[index]`. If `index` is changed by the subprogram, either through global access or as a formal parameter, then the address of `list[index]` will change between the call and the return. The implementor must choose the time at which the address to which to return the value will be determined, at the time of the call or at the time of the return. This makes programs unportable between implementations that choose differently in this issue.

8.5.2.3 Pass-By-Value-Result

Pass-by-value-result is an implementation model for inout-mode parameters in which actual values are moved. It is in effect a combination of pass-by-value and pass-by-result. The value of the actual parameter is used to initialize the corresponding formal parameter, which then acts as a local variable. In fact, pass-by-value-result formal parameters must have local storage associated with the called subprogram. At subprogram termination, the value of the formal parameter is transmitted back to the actual parameter.

Pass-by-value-result is sometimes called pass-by-copy because the actual parameter is copied to the formal parameter at subprogram entry and then copied back at subprogram termination.

Pass-by-value-result shares with pass-by-value and pass-by-result the disadvantages of requiring multiple storage for parameters and time for copying values. It shares with pass-by-result the problems associated with the order in which actual parameters are assigned.

8.5.2.4 Pass-By-Reference

Pass-by-reference is a second implementation model for inout-mode parameters. Rather than transmitting data values back and forth, however, as in pass-by-value-result, the pass-by-reference method transmits an access path, usually just an address, to the called subprogram. This provides the access path to the cell storing the actual parameter. Thus the called subprogram is allowed to access the actual parameter in the calling program unit. In effect, the actual parameter is shared with the called subprogram.

The advantage of pass-by-reference is that the passing process itself is efficient, in terms of both time and space. Duplicate space is not required, nor is any copying.

There are, however, several disadvantages to the pass-by-reference method. First, access to the formal parameters will most likely be slower because one more level of indirect addressing is needed than when data values are transmitted, as with pass-by-value-result. Second, if only one-way communication to the called subprogram is required, inadvertent and erroneous changes may be made to the actual parameter.

Another serious problem of pass-by-reference is that aliases can be created. This should be expected because pass-by-reference makes access paths available to the called subprograms, thereby broadening their access to nonlocal variables. There are several ways aliases can be created when parameters are passed by reference.

First, collisions can occur between actual parameters. Consider a C function procedure that has two parameters that are to be passed by reference, as in

```
void fun(int *first, int *second)
```

If the call to fun happens to pass the same variable twice, as in

```
fun(&total, &total)
```

then first and second in fun will be aliases.

Collisions between array elements can also cause aliases. For example, suppose the function fun is called with two array elements that are specified with variable subscripts, as in

```
fun(&list[i], &list[j])
```

If i happens to be equal to j, then first and second are again aliases.

Collisions between array-element parameters and elements of arrays passed as array-name parameters are another possible cause of aliases. If two of the formal parameters of a subprogram are a scalar and an array with elements of the same type, then a call such as

```
fun1(&list[i], &list)
```

could result in aliasing in fun1, because fun1 can access all elements of list through the second parameter and access a single element through its first parameter.

Still another way to get aliasing with pass-by-reference parameters is through collisions between formal parameters and nonlocal variables that are visible.

These aliases are possible when a language provides more nonlocal access than is necessary, such as sometimes happens with static scoping. For example, consider the following Pascal code:

```
procedure bigsub;
  var global : integer;
  procedure smallsub(var local : integer);
    begin
    ...
    end;  { of smallsub }
  begin
  ...
  smallsub(global);
  ...
  end;  { of bigsub }
```

Inside smallsub, local and global are aliases. As stated above, the main reason for this aliasing is that static scoping often provides too much access to nonlocal variables. If the variable `global` in `bigsub` were not implicitly visible in `smallsub`, `local` and `global` would not be aliases there. Obviously, because `global` is sent as a parameter to `smallsub`, the programmer probably forgot that it was already visible there.

The problem with these kinds of aliasing is the same as in other circumstances: It is harmful to readability and thus to reliability. It also makes program verification extremely difficult.

All these possible aliasing situations are eliminated if pass-by-value-result is used instead of pass-by-reference. However, in place of aliasing, other problems sometimes arise, as discussed in Section 8.5.2.3.

8.5.2.5 Pass-By-Name

Pass-by-name is an inout-mode parameter transmission method that does not correspond to a single implementation model, as explained below. When parameters are passed by name, the actual parameter is, in effect, textually substituted for the corresponding formal parameter in all its occurrences in the subprogram. This is quite different from the methods discussed thus far. In those cases, formal parameters are bound to actual values or addresses at the time of the subprogram call. A pass-by-name formal parameter is bound to an access method at the time of the subprogram call, but the actual binding to a value or an address is delayed until the formal parameter is assigned or referenced.

The objective of the late binding in pass-by-name parameters is flexibility. This is consistent with other situations in which we have encountered differences in binding time. For example, binding a variable to a type occurs at a later point in APL than it does in FORTRAN, thus yielding more flexible uses of variables.

The form of the actual parameter dictates the implementation model of pass-by-name parameters. This distinguishes pass-by-name parameters from those passed by other methods. If the actual parameter is a scalar variable, then pass-by-name is equivalent to pass-by-reference. If the actual parameter is a constant expression, then pass-by-name is equivalent to pass-by-value. If the actual parameter is an array element, pass-by-name may be different from any other method, because the value of the subscript expression can change during execution between the times of various references. This allows different appearances of the formal parameter in the called subprogram to refer to different array elements. This is discussed in greater detail later in this section.

If the actual parameter is an expression that contains a variable, pass-by-name is again different from any other method. It is different because the expression is evaluated for each access to the formal parameter at the time the variable is reached. If any of the variables in the expression are themselves accessible and are changed by the subprogram, the value of the expression can change with each reference to the formal parameter.

Consider the following example program, written in an ALGOL-like language:

```
procedure BIGSUB;
  integer GLOBAL;
  integer array LIST[1:2];
  procedure SUB(PARAM);
    integer PARAM;
    begin
    PARAM := 3;
    GLOBAL := GLOBAL + 1;
    PARAM := 5
    end;
  begin
  LIST[1] := 2;
  LIST[2] := 2;
  GLOBAL := 1;
  SUB(LIST[GLOBAL])
  end;
```

After execution, the array LIST has the values 3 and 5, both set in SUB. Access to LIST[2] is provided after GLOBAL is incremented to the value 2 in SUB.

The primary advantage of pass-by-name is the flexibility it affords the programmer. The main disadvantage is the slowness of the process, relative to other parameter-passing methods. The cost of pass-by-name parameters, in terms of execution efficiency, is discussed in Section 8.5.5. Besides their cost disadvantage, pass-by-name parameters are difficult to implement and can confuse both readers and writers of programs that use them. Furthermore, some simple operations are not possible with pass-by-name parameters. The classical example is having a subprogram swap its two parameter's values (see Problem 10).

The concept of late binding, on which pass-by-name is based, is by no means an odd or discredited one. The powerful mechanism of dynamic binding and polymorphism, which is an integral part of object-oriented programming, is simply a late binding of calls to subprograms or messages to objects. (Polymorphism is discussed in Section 8.8.) Lazy evaluation is another useful mechanism that is a form of late binding. It is, briefly, the process of only evaluating parts of functional code when it becomes certain that the evaluation of that code is necessary. In the imperative languages, short-circuit evaluation of Boolean expressions is an example of lazy evaluation. All expression evaluation in the functional language Haskell is lazy, as is discussed in Chapter 14.

8.5.3 Parameter-Passing Methods of the Major Languages

FORTRAN has always used the inout-mode semantics model of parameter passing, but the language does not specify whether pass-by-reference or pass-by-value-result should be used. In most FORTRAN implementations before FORTRAN 77, parameters were passed by reference. In later implementations, however, pass-by-value-result has been frequently used for simple variable parameters.

ALGOL 60 introduced the pass-by-name method. It also allows pass-by-value as an option. Primarily because of the difficulty in implementing them, pass-by-name parameters were not carried from ALGOL 60 to any subsequent languages that became popular, other than SIMULA-67.

C uses pass-by-value. Pass-by-reference semantics is achieved by using pointers as parameters. C copied this from ALGOL 68. In both C and C++, formal parameters can be typed as pointers to constants. The corresponding actual parameters need not be constants, for in such cases they are coerced to constants. This allows pointer parameters to provide the efficiency of pass-by-reference with the semantics of pass-by-value.

C++ includes a special pointer type, called a reference type, as discussed in Chapter 5, that is often used for parameters. Reference parameters are implicitly dereferenced, and their semantics are pass-by-reference. C++ also allows reference parameters to be defined to be constants. For example, we could have

```
void fun(const int &p1, int p2, int &p3) { ... }
```

where `p1` is pass-by-reference but cannot be changed in the function `fun`, parameter `p2` is pass-by-value, and `p3` is pass-by-reference. Neither `p1` nor `p3` need be explicitly dereferenced in `fun`.

Constant parameters and in-mode parameters are not exactly alike. Constant parameters clearly implement in mode. However, in all of the common imperative languages except Ada, in-mode parameters can be assigned in the subprogram even though those changes are never reflected in the values of the corresponding actual parameters. Constant parameters can never be assigned.

As with C and C++, all Java parameters are passed by value. However, because objects can only be accessed through reference variables, object parameters are in effect passed by reference. Likewise, because reference variables cannot point to scalar variables directly and Java does not have pointers, scalars cannot be passed by reference in Java (although an object that contains a scalar can).

ALGOL W (Wirth and Hoare, 1966) introduced the pass-by-value-result method of parameter passing as an alternative to the inefficiency of pass-by-name and the problems of pass-by-reference.

In Pascal and Modula-2, the default parameter-passing method is pass-by-value, and pass-by-reference can be specified by prefacing formal parameters with the reserved word **var**.

The designers of Ada defined versions of the three semantics modes of parameter transmission: in, out, and inout. The three modes are appropriately named with the reserved words **in**, **out**, and **in out**, where **in** is the default method. For example, consider the following Ada header:

```
procedure ADDER(A : in out INTEGER;
                B : in INTEGER;
                C : out FLOAT)
```

Ada formal parameters declared to be **out** mode can be assigned but not referenced. Parameters that are **in** mode can be referenced but not assigned. Quite naturally, **in out** mode parameters can be both referenced and assigned. The issue of how Ada **in out** mode parameters are implemented is interesting and is discussed in Section 8.5.5.

8.5.4 Type-Checking Parameters

It is now widely accepted that software reliability demands that the types of actual parameters be checked for consistency with the types of the corresponding formal parameters. Without such type checking, small typographical errors can lead to program errors that may be difficult to diagnose because they are not detected by the compiler or the run-time system. For example, in the function call

```
RESULT := SUB1(1)
```

the actual parameter is an integer constant. If the formal parameter of SUB1 is a floating-point type, no error will be detected without parameter type checking. Although an integer 1 and a floating-point 1 have the same value, the representations of these two are very different. SUB1 cannot produce a correct result given an integer actual parameter value when it expects a floating-point value.

FORTRAN 77 does not require parameter type checking; Pascal, Modula-2, FORTRAN 90, Java, and Ada do require it.

C and C++ require some special discussion in the matter of parameter type checking. In the original C, neither the number of parameters nor their types were checked. In ANSI C, the formal parameters of functions can be defined in two ways. First, they can be as in the original C; that is, the names of the parameters are listed in parentheses and the type declarations for them follow, as in

```
double sin(x)
  double x;
  { ... }
```

Using this method avoids type checking, thereby allowing calls such as

```
double value;
int count;
...
value = sin(count);
```

to be legal but nonsense.

The alternative is called the **prototype** method, in which the formal parameter types are included in the list, as in

```
double sin(double x)
  { ... }
```

If this version of `sin` is called with the same call as above, that is

```
value = sin(count);
```

it is also legal. The type of the actual parameter (**int**) is checked against that of the formal parameter (**double**). Although they do not match, **int** is coercible to **double**, so the conversion is done. If the conversion is not possible (for example, if the actual parameter had been an array) or if the number of parameters is wrong, then a syntax error is detected. So in ANSI C, the user chooses whether he or she wants parameters to be type checked.

In C++, all functions must have their formal parameters in prototype form. However, type checking can be avoided for some of the parameters by replacing the last part of the parameter list with an ellipsis, as in

```
printf(const char* ...);
```

A call to `printf` must include at least one parameter, a pointer to a constant character string. Beyond that, anything (including nothing) is legal. The way `printf` determines whether there are additional parameters is by the presence of special symbols in the string parameter. For example, the format code for integer output is %d. This appears as part of the string, as in

```
printf("The sum is %d\n", sum);
```

The % tells the compiler there is one more parameter.

8.5.5 Implementing Parameter-Passing Methods

We now address the question of how the various implementation models of parameter passing are actually implemented.

In ALGOL 60 and its descendant languages, parameter communication takes place through the run-time stack. The run-time stack is initialized and maintained by the run-time system, which is a system program that manages the execution of programs. The run-time stack is used extensively for subprogram control linkage and parameter passing, as is discussed in Chapter 9. In the following discussion, we assume that the stack is used for all parameter transmission.

Pass-by-value parameters have their values copied into stack locations. The stack locations then serve as storage for the corresponding formal parameters. Pass-by-result parameters are implemented as the opposite of pass-by-value. The values assigned to the pass-by-result actual parameters are placed in the stack, where they can be retrieved by the calling program unit upon termination of the called subprogram. Pass-by-value-result parameters can be implemented directly from their semantics as a combination of pass-by-value and pass-by-result. The stack location for the parameters is initialized by the call and is then used like a local variable in the called subprogram.

Pass-by-reference parameters are perhaps the simplest to implement. Regardless of the type of the actual parameter, only its address must be placed in the stack. In the case of literals, the address of the literal is transmitted. In the case of an expression, the compiler must build code to evaluate the expression just before the transfer of control to the called subprogram. The address of the memory cell in which the code places the result of its evaluation is then put in the stack. The compiler must be sure to prevent the called subprogram from changing parameters that are literals or expressions, as discussed below. Access to the formal parameters in the called subprogram is by indirect addressing from the stack location of the address. The implementation of pass-by-value, -result, -value-result, and -reference, where the run-time stack is used, is shown in Figure 8.2.

A subtle but fatal error can occur with pass-by-reference and pass-by-value-result parameters if care is not taken in their implementation. Suppose a program contains two references to the constant 10, the first as an actual parameter in a call to a subprogram. Further suppose that the subprogram mistakenly changes the formal parameter that corresponds to the 10 to the value 5. The compiler for this program may have built a single location for the value 10 during compilation, as compilers often do, and use that location for all references to the constant 10 in the program. But after the return from the subprogram, all subsequent occurrences of 10 will actually be references to the value 5. If this is allowed to happen, it creates a programming problem that is very difficult to diagnose. This did in fact happen with many implementations of FORTRAN IV.

Pass-by-name parameters are usually implemented with parameterless procedures or code segments called **thunks.** A thunk must be called for every reference to a pass-by-name parameter in the called subprogram. The thunk evaluates the reference in the proper referencing environment,

Figure 8.2
One possible stack implementation of the common parameter-passing methods

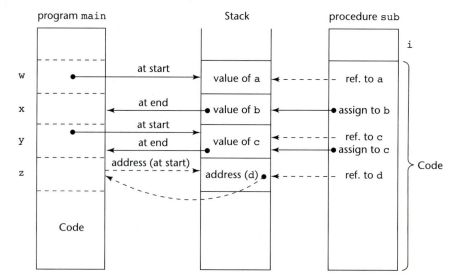

which is that of the subprogram that passed the actual parameter. Thunks are bound to their referencing environment at the time of the call that passed the pass-by-name parameter. A thunk returns the address of the actual parameter. If the parameter reference is in an expression, the code of the reference must include the necessary dereference to get the value from the cell whose address was returned by the thunk. Altogether, this is a costly process, relative to the simple indirect addressing used by pass-by-reference parameters. Recall that for actual parameters that are scalar variables, pass-by-name and pass-by-reference are semantically equivalent. The cost of implementing pass-by-reference is that of indirect addressing, whereas pass-by-name requires a subprogram call—albeit without parameters—and its execution to accomplish the same thing.

The Ada 83 language definition specifies that scalar (nonstructured) parameters are to be passed by copy; that is, **in** and **in out** mode parameters are to be local variables that are initialized by copying the value of the corresponding actual parameter. Simple parameters that are **out** or **in out** mode are to have their values copied back to the corresponding actual parameter at subprogram termination. The order of these copies, when there are more than one, is not defined by the language definition. The evaluation of **out** and **in out** mode parameters is done before the transfer of control to the called subprogram occurs. For example, suppose an **out** mode actual parameter has the form

```
LIST(INDEX)
```

The address value of this parameter is computed at the time of the call. If **INDEX** happened to be visible in the called subprogram and the subprogram changed it, the parameter address would not be affected.

In the case of formal parameters that are arrays or records, Ada 83 implementors are given the choice between pass-by-value-result and pass-by-reference. By failing to specify the implementation method for passing structured parameters, the Ada 83 designers left open the possibility of a subtle problem. The problem is that the two implementation methods can lead to different program results for certain programs. This difference can occur because the pass-by-reference method provides access to a location in the calling program that can also be provided if the actual parameter is also visible as a global, thereby creating an alias. If pass-by-value-result is used in place of pass-by-reference, this dual access to the actual parameter is not possible.

An additional problem is the following: Suppose the subprogram terminates abnormally (via an exception); the actual parameter in the pass-by-value-result implementation will be unchanged, whereas the pass-by-reference implementation may have changed the corresponding actual parameter before the error occurred. Once again, there can be a difference between the two implementation methods.

Ada 83 programs that produce different results depending on how the **in out** method is implemented are termed **erroneous.** Despite this label, however, there is no way the compiler can detect the erroneous condition.

So the error is usually detected only when the user moves the program from one implementation to another and realizes that it no longer produces the same result. The Ada 83 design philosophy in this situation is that programmers must guard against aliasing: If they create aliases, they must contend with the potential problems.

In recognition of this problem, the Ada 95 definition removed the implementor's choice of parameter passing methods for structured parameters. All structured parameters are passed by reference.

8.5.6 Multidimensional Arrays as Parameters

The storage-mapping functions that are used to map the index values of references to elements of multidimensional arrays to addresses in memory were discussed at length in Chapter 5. In some languages, such as C and C++, when a multidimensional array is passed as a parameter to a subprogram, the compiler must be able to build the mapping function for that array while seeing only the text of the subprogram. This is true because the subprograms can be compiled separately from the programs that call them. Consider the problem of passing a matrix to a function in C. Multidimensional arrays in C are really arrays of arrays and they are stored in row major order. The mapping function for row major order for two dimensions needs the number of columns but not the number of rows. Therefore, in C and C++, when a matrix is passed as a parameter, the formal parameter must include the number of columns in the second pair of brackets. This is illustrated in the following skeletal C program:

```
void fun(int matrix[][10]) {
  ... }
void main() {
  int mat[5][10];
  ...
  fun(mat);
  ...
}
```

The problem with this method of passing matrixes as parameters is that it does not allow the programmer to write a function that can accept matrixes with different numbers of columns; a new function must be written for every matrix with a different number of columns. This, in effect, disallows writing flexible functions that may be effectively reusable if the functions deal with multidimensional arrays. In C and C++, there is a way around the problem because of their inclusion of pointer arithmetic. The matrix can be passed as a pointer, and the actual dimensions of the matrix can be included as parameters. Then the function can evaluate the user-written storage-mapping function using pointer arithmetic each time an element of the matrix must be referenced. For example, consider the following function prototype:

```
void fun(float *mat_ptr, int num_rows, int num_cols);
```

The following statement can be used to move the value of the variable x to the [row][col] element of the parameter matrix in fun:

```
*(mat_ptr + (row * num_cols) + col) = x;
```

Although this works, it is obviously difficult to read, and because of its complexity, it is error prone. The difficulty with reading this can be alleviated by using a macro to define the storage-mapping function, such as

```
#define mat_ptr(r,c)
            (*(mat_ptr + ((r) * num_cols) + (c)))
```

With this, the assignment above can be written as

```
mat_ptr(row,col) = x;
```

Other languages deal differently with the problem of passing multidimensional arrays. Ada compilers are able to determine the defined size of dimensions of all arrays that are used as parameters at the time subprograms are compiled. In Ada, unconstrained array types can be formal parameters. An unconstrained array type is one in which the index ranges are not given in the array type definition. Definitions of variables of unconstrained array types must include index ranges. The code in a subprogram that is passed an unconstrained array can obtain the index range information of the actual parameter associated with such parameters. For example, consider the following definitions:

```
type MATRIX_TYPE is array (INTEGER range <>,
                           INTEGER range <>) of FLOAT;
MATRIX_1 : MATRIX_TYPE(1..100, 1..20);
```

A function that returns the sum the elements of arrays of MATRIX_TYPE type follows:

```
function SUMER(MAT : in MATRIX_TYPE) return FLOAT is
  SUM : FLOAT := 0.0;
  begin
  for ROW in MAT'range(1) loop
    for COL in MAT'range(2) loop
      SUM := SUM + MAT(ROW, COL);
    end loop;  — for COL ...
  end loop;  — for ROW ...
  return SUM;
  end SUMER;
```

The **range** attribute returns the subscript range of the named subscript of the actual parameter array, so this works regardless of the size or index ranges of the parameter.

In pre-90 versions of FORTRAN, the problem is addressed in the following way. Formal parameters that are arrays must have a declaration after the header. For single-dimensioned arrays, the subscripts in such declarations are irrelevant. But for multidimensional arrays, the subscripts in such declarations allow the compiler to build the storage-mapping function. Consider the following example skeletal FORTRAN subroutine:

```
SUBROUTINE SUB(MATRIX, ROWS, COLS, RESULT)
  INTEGER ROWS, COLS
  REAL MATRIX(ROWS, COLS), RESULT
  ...
  END
```

This works perfectly as long as the COLS actual parameter has the value used for the number of columns in the definition of the passed matrix. If the array to be passed is not currently filled with useful data to the defined size, then both the defined index sizes and the filled index sizes can be passed to the subprogram. Then the defined sizes are used in the local declaration of the array, and the filled index sizes are used to control the computation in which the array elements are referenced. For example, consider the following FORTRAN 90 subprogram:

```
SUBROUTINE MATSUM(MATRIX, ROWS, COLS, FILLED_ROWS,
                  FILLED_COLS, SUM)
  INTEGER ROWS, COLS, FILLED_ROWS, FILLED_COLS,
          ROW_INDEX, COL_INDEX
  REAL MATRIX(ROWS, COLS), SUM
  SUM = 0.0
  DO 20 ROW_INDEX = 1, FILLED_ROWS
    DO 10 COL_INDEX = 1, FILLED_COLS
      SUM = SUM + MATRIX(ROW_INDEX, COL_INDEX)
10    CONTINUE
20  CONTINUE
    RETURN
    END
```

Java uses a technique for passing multidimensional arrays as parameters that is similar to that of Ada. In Java, arrays are objects. They are all single-dimensioned, but the elements can be arrays. Each array inherits a named constant (length) that is set to the length of the array when the array object is created. The formal parameter for a matrix appears with two sets of empty brackets, as in the method below that does what the Ada example function SUMER does.

```
float sumer(float mat[][]) {
  float sum = 0.0f;
  for (int row = 0; row < mat.length; row++) {
    for (int col = 0; col < mat[row].length; col++) {
      sum += mat[row][col];
    } //** for (int row ~
  } //** for (int col ~
  return sum;
}
```

Because each array has its own length value, in a matrix the rows can have different lengths.

8.5.7 Design Considerations

Two important considerations are involved in choosing parameter-passing methods: efficiency and whether one-way or two-way data transfer is needed.

Contemporary software engineering principles dictate that access by subprogram code to data outside the subprogram be minimized. With this goal in mind, in-mode parameters should be used whenever no data are to be returned through parameters to the caller. Out-mode parameters should be used when no data are transferred to the called subprogram but the subprogram must transmit data back to the caller. Finally, inout-mode parameters should be used only when data must move in both directions between the caller and the called subprogram.

There is a practical consideration that is in conflict with this principle. Sometimes it is justifiable to pass access paths for one-way parameter transmission. For example, when a large array is to be passed to a subprogram that does not modify it, a one-way method may be preferred. However, pass-by-value would require that the entire array be moved to a local storage area of the subprogram. This would be costly in both time and space. Because of this, large arrays are often passed by reference. This is precisely the reason why the Ada 83 definition allows implementors to choose between the two methods for structured parameters. C++ constant reference parameters offer another solution. Another alternative approach would be to allow the user to choose between the methods.

The choice of a parameter-passing method for functions is related to another design issue: functional side effects. This issue is discussed in Section 8.10.

8.5.8 Examples of Parameter Passing

Consider the following C function:

```
void swap1(int a, int b) {
  int temp = a;
  a = b;
  b = temp;
}
```

Suppose this function is called with

```
swap1(c, d);
```

Recall that C uses pass-by-value. The actions of `swap1` can be described by the following pseudocode:

```
a = c          — Move first parameter value in
b = d          — Move second parameter value in
temp = a
```

```
a = b
b = temp
```

Although a ends up with d's value and b ends up with c's value, the values of c and d are unchanged because nothing is transmitted back to the caller.

In Pascal, swap1 can be written with the same in-mode semantics, as in

```
procedure swap1(a, b: integer)
  temp : integer;
  begin
  temp := a;
  a := b;
  b := temp
  end;
```

Now we modify the C swap function to deal with pointer parameters to achieve the effect of pass-by-reference:

```
void swap2(int *a, int *b) {
  int temp = *a;
  *a = *b;
  *b = temp;
}
```

swap2 can be called with

```
swap2(&c, &d);
```

The actions of swap2 can be described with

```
a = &c          — Move first parameter address in
b = &d          — Move second parameter address in
temp = *a
*a = *b
*b = temp
```

In this case, the swap operation is successful: The values of c and d are in fact interchanged.

swap2 can be written in C++ using reference parameters as follows:

```
void swap2(int &a, int &b) {
  int temp = a;
  a = b;
  b = temp;
}
```

This simple swap operation is not possible in Java, because it has neither pointers nor C++'s kind of references. In Java, a reference variable can only point to an object, not a scalar value.

In Pascal, swap2 would be written as

```
procedure swap2(var a, b: integer)
  temp : integer;
```

```
begin
temp := a;
a := b;
b := temp
end;
```

Suppose the Pascal version of `swap2` is called with

```
swap2(i, list[i]);
```

In this case, the actions are described by

```
a = &i            — Move first parameter address in
b = &list[i]      — Move second parameter address in
temp = *a
*a = *b
*b = temp
```

Although the value of `*a` (which is `i`) is changed before `*b` (which is `list[i]`), it does not affect the correctness of the interchange, because the address of `list[i]` is computed at the time of the call and does not change after that, regardless of what happens to `i`.

The semantics of pass-by-value-result is identical to those of pass-by-reference, except when aliasing is involved. Recall that Ada uses pass-by-value-result for in out mode scalar parameters. To explore pass-by-value-result, consider the following function, `swap3`, which we assume uses pass-by-value-result parameters. It is written in a syntax similar to that of Ada.

```
procedure swap3(a : integer, b : integer) is
  temp : integer;
  begin
  temp := a;
  a := b;
  b := temp;
  end swap3;
```

Suppose `swap3` is called with

```
swap3(c, d);
```

The actions of `swap3` with this call are

```
addr_c = &c       — Move first parameter address in
addr_d = &d       — Move second parameter address in
a = *addr_c       — Move first parameter value in
b = *addr_d       — Move second parameter value in
temp = a
a = b
b = temp
*addr_c = a       — Move first parameter value out
*addr_d = b       — Move second parameter value out
```

So once again, this swap subprogram operates correctly. Next, consider the call

```
swap3(i, list[i]);
```

In this case, the actions are

```
addr_i = &i                — Move first parameter address in
addr_listi = &list[i]      — Move second parameter address in
a = *addr_i                — Move first parameter value in
b = *addr_listi            — Move second parameter value in
temp = a
a = b
b = temp
*addr_i = a                — Move first parameter value out
*addr_listi = b            — Move second parameter value out
```

Again, the subprogram operates correctly, in this case because the addresses to which to return the values of the parameters are computed at the time of the call, rather than at the time of the return. If the addresses of the actual parameters were computed at the time of the return, the results would be wrong.

Finally, we must explore what happens when aliasing is involved with pass-by-value-result and pass-by-reference. Consider the following skeletal program written in C-like syntax:

```
int i = 3;   /* i is a global variable */
void fun(int a, int b) {
  i = b;
}
void main() {
  int list[10];
  list[i] = 5;
  fun(i, list[i]);
}
```

In fun, if pass-by-reference is used, i and a are aliases. If pass-by-value-result is used, i and a are not aliases. The actions of fun, assuming pass-by-value-result, are

```
addr_i = &i                — Move first parameter address in
addr_listi = &list[i]      — Move second parameter address in
a = *addr_i                — Move first parameter value in
b = *addr_listi            — Move second parameter value in
i = b                      — Sets i to 5
*addr_i = a                — Move first parameter value out
*addr_listi = b            — Move second parameter value out
```

In this case, the assignment to the global i in fun changes its value from 3 to 5, but the copy back of the first formal parameter (the second last line above) sets it back to 3. The important observation here is that if pass-by-reference is used, the result is that the copy back is not part of the semantics, and i remains 5. Also note that because the address of the second parameter is computed at the beginning of `fun`, any change to the global `i` has no effect on the address used at the end to return the value of `list[i]`.

8.6 Parameters That Are Subprogram Names

A number of situations occur in programming that are most conveniently handled if subprogram names can be sent as parameters to other subprograms. One of the more common of these occurs when a subprogram must sample some mathematical function. For example, a subprogram that does numerical integration estimates the area under the graph of a function by sampling the function at a number of different points. When such a subprogram is written, it should be usable for any given function; it should not need to be rewritten for every function that must be integrated. It is therefore natural that the name of a program function that evaluates the mathematical function to be integrated be sent to the integrating subprogram as a parameter.

Although the idea is natural and seemingly simple, the details of how it works can be confusing. If only the transmission of the subprogram code was necessary, it could be done by passing a single pointer. However, several complications arise.

First, there is the matter of type checking the parameters of the activations of the subprogram that was passed as a parameter. The original definition of Pascal (Jensen and Wirth, 1974) allowed subprograms to be passed as parameters without including their parameter type information. If independent compilation is possible (which it was not in the original Pascal), the compiler is not allowed even to check for the correct number of parameters. In the absence of independent compilation, checking for parameter consistency is possible but is a very complex task, and it usually is not done. FORTRAN 77 suffers the same problem, but because parameter type consistency is never checked in FORTRAN 77, it is not an additional problem.

When a subprogram name is passed as a parameter in ALGOL 68 or in the later versions of Pascal, the formal parameter types are included in the formal parameter list of the receiving subprogram, so parameter type consistency in the actual call to the passed subprogram can be statically checked. For example, consider the following Pascal code:

```
procedure integrate(function fun(x : real) : real;
                    lowerbd, upperbd : real;
                    var result : real);
    ...
    var funval : real;
    begin
    ...
```

```
funval := fun(lowerbd);
...
end;
```

The actual parameter in the call to `fun` in `integrate` can be statically checked for consistency with the type of `fun`'s formal parameter, which appears in the formal parameter list of `integrate`.

In C and C++, functions cannot be passed as parameters, but pointers to functions can. The type of a pointer to a function is the function's protocol. Because the protocol includes all parameter types, such parameters can be completely type checked.

In Modula-2, procedure types are used to pass procedures as if they were variables. This method allows consistency checking of the parameters of passed subprograms, because the types of the parameters are part of the procedure type. FORTRAN 90 has a mechanism for providing types of parameters for subprograms that are passed as parameters, and they must be checked. Ada does not allow subprograms to be passed as parameters. The functionality of passing subprograms as parameters is instead provided by Ada's generic facility, which is discussed in Section 8.8.

A more interesting aspect of subprogram names that are passed as parameters is the question regarding the correct referencing environment for executing the passed subprogram. The three choices are

1. The environment of the call statement that enacts the passed subprogram (**shallow binding**)

2. The environment of the definition of the passed subprogram (**deep binding**)

3. The environment of the call statement that passed the subprogram as an actual parameter (**ad hoc binding**)

The following example program illustrates these choices. Assume it is legal for SUB3 to call SUB4.

```
procedure SUB1;
  var x : integer;
  procedure SUB2;
    begin
    write('x =', x)
    end;  { of sub2 }
  procedure SUB3;
    var x : integer;
    begin
    x := 3;
    SUB4(SUB2)
    end; { of SUB3 }
  procedure SUB4(SUBX);
    var x : integer;
    begin
    x := 4;
```

```
      SUBX
    end; { of SUB4 }
  begin  { of SUB1}
  x := 1;
  SUB3
  end; { of SUB1 }
```

Consider the execution of SUB2 when it is called in SUB4. For shallow binding, the referencing environment of that execution is that of SUB4, so the reference to x in SUB2 is bound to the local x in SUB4, and the output of the program is x = 4. For deep binding, the referencing environment of SUB2's execution is that of SUB1, so the reference to x in SUB2 is bound to the local x in SUB1, and the output is x = 1. For ad hoc binding, the binding is to the local x in SUB3, and the output is x = 3.

In some cases, the subprogram that declares a subprogram also passes that subprogram as a parameter. In those cases, deep binding and ad hoc binding are the same. Ad hoc binding has never been used because, one can assume, the environment in which the procedure appears as a parameter has no natural connection to the passed subprogram.

Shallow binding is not appropriate for block-structured languages because of static binding of variables. For example, suppose the procedure SENDER passes the procedure SENT as a parameter to the procedure RECEIVER. The problem is that RECEIVER may not be in the static environment of SENT, thereby making it very unnatural for SENT to have access to RECEIVER's variables. On the other hand, it is perfectly normal in a static-scoped language for any subprogram, including one sent as a parameter, to have its referencing environment determined by the lexical position of its definition. It is therefore more logical for block-structured languages to use deep binding. Some dynamic-scoped languages like SNOBOL use shallow binding.

8.7 Overloaded Subprograms

An overloaded operator is one that has multiple meanings. The meaning of a particular instance of an overloaded operator is determined by the types of its operands. For example, if the * operator has two floating-point operands in a C program, it specifies floating-point multiplication. But if the same operator has two integer operands, it specifies integer multiplication.

An **overloaded subprogram** is a subprogram that has the same name as another subprogram in the same referencing environment. Every version of an overloaded subprogram must have a unique protocol; that is, it must be different from the others in the number, order, or types of its parameters, or in its return type if it is a function. The meaning of a call to an overloaded subprogram is determined by the actual parameter list (and/or possibly the type of the returned value, in the case of a function).

C++, Java, and Ada include predefined overloaded subprograms. For example, Ada has several versions of the output function PUT. The most common versions are those that accept string, integer, and floating-point type values as parameters. Because each version of PUT has a unique parameter type, the compiler can disambiguate occurrences of calls to PUT by the different type parameters.

In Ada, the return type of an overloaded function is used to disambiguate calls. Therefore, two overloaded functions can have the same parameter profile and differ only in their return types. This works because Ada does not allow mixed-mode expressions, so the context of a function call can specify the type that is returned from the function. C++ and Java allow mixed-mode expressions, and the return type is irrelevant to disambiguation of overloaded functions (or methods).

Users are also allowed to write multiple versions of subprograms with the same name in Ada, Java, and C++. Although it is not necessary for such subprograms to provide basically the same process, they usually do. For example, a particular program may require two sorting procedures, one for integer arrays and one for floating-point arrays. They both can be named SORT, as long as the types of their parameters are different. In the following skeletal Ada program, two procedures named SORT are included:

```
procedure MAIN is
  type FLOAT_VECTOR is array (INTEGER range <>) of FLOAT;
  type INT_VECTOR is array (INTEGER range <>) of INTEGER;
  ...
  procedure SORT(FLOAT_LIST : in out FLOAT_VECTOR;
                 LOWER_BOUND : in INTEGER;
                 UPPER_BOUND : in INTEGER) is
    ...
  end SORT;
  procedure SORT(INT_LIST    : in out INT_VECTOR;
                 LOWER_BOUND : in INTEGER;
                 UPPER_BOUND : in INTEGER) is
    ...
  end SORT;
  ...
end MAIN;
```

Overloaded subprograms that have default parameters can lead to ambiguous subprogram calls. For example, consider the following C++ code:

```
void fun(float b = 0.0);
void fun();
...
fun();
```

The call is ambiguous and will cause a compilation error.

8.8 Generic Subprograms

Software reuse can be an important contributor to software productivity increases. One way to increase the reusability of software is to lessen the need to create different subprograms that implement the same algorithm on different types of data. For example, a programmer should not need to write four different sort subprograms to sort four arrays that differ only in element type.

A **generic** or **polymorphic subprogram** takes parameters of different types on different activations. Overloaded subprograms provide a particular kind of polymorphism called **ad hoc polymorphism.** A more general kind of polymorphism is provided by the functions of APL. Because of the dynamic type binding of APL, the types of parameters can be left unspecified; they are simply bound to the type of the corresponding actual parameters.

Parametric polymorphism is provided by a subprogram that takes a generic parameter that is used in a type expression that describes the types of the parameters of the subprogram. Both Ada and C++ provide a kind of compile-time parametric polymorphism.

8.8.1 Generic Subprograms in Ada

Ada provides parametric polymorphism through a construct that supports the construction of multiple versions of program units to accept parameters of different data types. The different versions of the subprogram are instantiated, or constructed, by the compiler upon request from the user program. Because the versions of the subprogram all have the same name, this provides the illusion that a single subprogram can process data of different types on different calls. Because program units of this sort are generic in nature, they are sometimes called **generic units.**

The same mechanism can be used to allow different executions of a subprogram to call different instantiations of a generic subprogram. This is useful in providing the functionality of subprograms passed as parameters.

The following example illustrates a procedure that has three generic parameters, allowing the subprogram to take as a parameter a generic array. It is an exchange sort procedure that is designed to work on any array with elementary numeric type elements, using any ordinal type subscript range:

```
generic
  type INDEX_TYPE is (<>);
  type ELEMENT_TYPE is private;
  type VECTOR is array (INTEGER_TYPE range <>) of
      ELEMENT_TYPE;
  procedure GENERIC_SORT(LIST : in out VECTOR);
  procedure GENERIC_SORT(LIST : in out VECTOR) is
    TEMP : ELEMENT_TYPE;
```

```
      begin
      for TOP in LIST'FIRST..INDEX_TYPE'PRED(LIST'LAST) loop
        for BOTTOM in INDEX_TYPE'SUCC(TOP)..LIST'LAST loop
          if LIST(TOP) > LIST(BOTTOM) then
            TEMP := LIST(TOP);
            LIST(TOP) := LIST(BOTTOM);
            LIST(BOTTOM) := TEMP;
          end if;
        end loop; — for BOTTOM ...
      end loop; — for TOP ...
      end GENERIC_SORT;
```

Parts of this generic procedure may appear rather odd if you are not familiar with Ada. However, it is not important to understand all the details of the syntax. The array type and the type of its elements are the two generic parameters of this procedure. The array is declared to have any type subscript (that is, any type that is legal as a subscript) with any range.

This generic sort is nothing more than a template for a procedure; no code is generated for it by the compiler, and it has no effect on a program unless it is instantiated for some type. Instantiation is accomplished with a statement such as the following:

```
procedure INTEGER_SORT is new GENERIC_SORT(
                             INDEX_TYPE => INTEGER;
                             ELEMENT_TYPE => INTEGER;
                             VECTOR => INT_ARRAY);
```

The compiler reacts to this statement by building a version of GENERIC_SORT named INTEGER_SORT that sorts arrays of type INT_ARRAY with INTEGER type elements and INTEGER type subscripts.

GENERIC_SORT, as written, assumes that the operator > is defined for the elements of the array to be sorted. The genericity of GENERIC_SORT can be increased by including a comparison function among its generic parameters.

Recall that Ada does not allow subprograms to be passed as parameters to other subprograms. To provide that functionality, Ada uses generic formal subprograms. In a language such as Pascal, subprograms are passed as parameters so that a particular call of a subprogram can execute using the specific passed subprogram to compute its result. In Ada, the same result is achieved by allowing the user to instantiate a generic subprogram any number of times, each with a different subprogram that can be used. For example, the procedure integrate, as defined in Section 8.6, can be written in Ada as

```
generic
  with function FUN(X : FLOAT) return FLOAT;
  procedure INTEGRATE (LOWERBD : in FLOAT;
                       UPPERBD : in FLOAT;
                       RESULT : out FLOAT) is
```

```
            FUNVAL  : FLOAT;
            begin
            ...
            FUNVAL := FUN(LOWERBD);
            ...
            end;
```

This could be instantiated for a user-defined function `FUN1` with

```
    INTEGRATE_FUN1 is new INTEGRATE(FUN => FUN1);
```

Now, `INTEGRATE_FUN1` is a procedure for integrating the function `FUN1`.

8.8.2 Generic Functions in C++

Generic functions in C++ have the descriptive name of template functions. The definition of a template function has the general form

template < **class** parameters >
— a function definition that may include the class parameters

Each class parameter (there must be at least one) has the form

class identifier

As an example, consider the template function

```
template <class Type>
Type max(Type first, Type second) {
  return first > second ? first : second;
}
```

where `Type` is the parameter that specifies the type of data on which the function will operate. This template function can be instantiated for any type for which the operator > is defined. For example, if it were instantiated with **int** as the parameter, it would be

```
int max(int first, int second) {
  return first > second ? first : second;
}
```

Although this process could be defined as a macro, a macro would have the disadvantage of not operating correctly if the parameters were expressions with side effects. For example, suppose the macro was defined as

```
#define max(a, b) ((a) > (b)) ? (a) : (b)
```

This is generic in the sense that it works for any numeric type. However, it does not always work correctly if called with a parameter that has a side effect, such as

```
max(x++, y)
```

This produces

```
((x++) > (y) ? (x++) : (y))
```

Whenever the value of x is greater than that of y, x will be incremented twice.

C++ template functions are instantiated implicitly either when the function is named in a call or when its address is taken with the & operator. For example, the template function defined above would be instantiated twice by the following code segment, once for **int** type parameters and once for **char** type parameters:

```
int a, b, c;
char d, e, f;
...
c = max(a, b);
f = max(d, e);
```

The following is the C++ version of the generic sort subprogram given in Section 8.8.1. It is somewhat different because C++ array subscripts are restricted to being integers with the lower bound fixed at zero.

```
template <class Type>
void generic_sort(Type list[], int len) {
  int top, bottom;
  Type temp;
  for (top = 0; top < len - 2; top++)
    for (bottom = top + 1; bottom < len - 1; bottom++)
      if (list[top] > list[bottom]) {
        temp = list[top];
        list[top] = list[bottom];
        list[bottom] = temp;
      } //** end of for (bottom = ...
} //** end of generic_sort
```

An example instantiation of this template function is:

```
float flt_list[100];
...
generic_sort(flt_list, 100);
```

The generic subprograms of Ada and the templated functions of C++ are a kind of poor cousin to a subprogram in which the types of the formal parameters are dynamically bound to the types of the actual parameters in a call. In this case, only a single copy of the code is needed, whereas with the Ada and C++ approaches, a copy must be created at compile time for each different type that is required and the binding of subprogram calls to subprograms is static.

Smalltalk, Java, Ada 95, and C++ support methods in which the calls are dynamically bound to the correct version of the method, according to the types of the actual parameters. This is discussed in Chapter 11.

8.9 Separate and Independent Compilation

The capability of compiling parts of a program without compiling the whole program is essential to the construction of large software systems. Thus languages that are designed for such applications must allow this kind of compilation. With such a capability, only the modules of a system that are being changed need to be recompiled during development or maintenance. Newly compiled and previously compiled units are collected by a program called the linker, which is a part of the operating system. Without this capability, every change to a system would require a complete recompilation. In the case of a large system, this is costly.

In this section, we discuss two distinct approaches to compiling parts of programs, called separate compilation and independent compilation. The parts of programs that can be compiled are sometimes called compilation units.

The term **separate compilation** means that compilation units can be compiled at different times, but their compilations are not independent of each other if either accesses or uses any entities of the other. This interdependence is required if interface checking is to be done. We first discuss separate compilation in the context of Ada.

To provide reliable separate compilation of a unit, the compiler must have access to information about program entities (variables, types, and the protocols of subprograms) that the unit uses but that are declared elsewhere. Information about the entities of an Ada package that can be visible in other units, which are called the exported entities, forms the interface of the package. Recall that the protocol of a procedure includes the number, names, and types of its parameters, along with the order in which they appear. In the case of a function, the type of the returned value is also included. Ada implementations maintain these kinds of unit interface information in a library that is accessible to the compiler. Every compilation causes the interface information of that compilation to be placed in a library.

Libraries store library units, which are compiled compilation units. Compilation units in Ada are entities such as subprogram headers, package declarations (see Chapter 10), and subprogram bodies.

During compilation of an Ada program unit, all externally declared entities that are used are type checked against their local uses. In the case of subprograms, the whole protocol is type checked. Not all library information is available to a particular program unit compilation. The names of those units that provide required external entities are listed on a **with** statement at the beginning of the unit being compiled. Using **with**, the programmer specifies the external units that the code in the compilation must access. For example, the following procedure uses entities from two external units, GLOBALS and TEXT_IO, and thus specifies those two:

```
with GLOBALS, TEXT_IO;
procedure EXAMPLE is
  ...
  end EXAMPLE;
```

Modula-2 provides separate compilation that is similar to that of Ada. FORTRAN 90 also allows separate compilation of its subprograms and modules. Separate compilation in Ada is discussed in greater detail in Chapter 10, after we have discussed the data abstraction facilities of that language.

In some languages, most notably C and FORTRAN 77, independent compilation is allowed. With **independent compilation,** program units can be compiled without information about any other program units.

The most important characteristic of independent compilation is that the interfaces between the separately compiled units are not checked for type consistency. The interface of a FORTRAN 77 subroutine is its parameter list. When a subroutine is independently compiled, the types of its parameters are not stored with the compiled code or in a library. Therefore, when another program that calls that subroutine is compiled, the types of the actual parameters in the calls cannot be checked against the types of the formal parameters of the subroutine, even if the machine code for the called subroutine is available.

This is not surprising in FORTRAN 77. Even when the program that calls a subprogram and the subprogram itself are compiled from the same file, they are in effect, if not actually, compiled independently. So the parameter interface between FORTRAN 77 program units is never checked for type compatibility.

Some languages provide neither separate nor independent compilation, meaning that the only compilation unit is a complete program. FORTRAN II and the original version of Pascal are such languages. This is a severe restriction on the language, making it virtually unusable for industrial applications. It is clear that independent compilation, although it allows unchecked program unit interfaces, is better than having no means of compiling parts of programs. Later versions of both FORTRAN and Pascal recognized this.

8.10 Design Issues for Functions

The following two design issues are specific to functions:

- Are side effects allowed?
- What types of values can be returned?

8.10.1 Functional Side Effects

Because of the problems of side effects of functions that are called in expressions, as described in Chapter 4, parameters to functions should always be in mode. Some languages, in fact, require this; for example, Ada functions can have only in-mode formal parameters. This effectively prevents a function from causing side effects through its parameters or through aliasing of parameters and globals. In most other languages, however, functions can have either pass-by-value or pass-by-reference parameters, thus allowing functions that cause side effects and aliasing.

8.10.2 Types of Returned Values

Most imperative programming languages restrict the types that can be returned by their functions. FORTRAN 77, Pascal, and Modula-2 functions allow only unstructured types to be returned. C allows any type to be returned by its functions except arrays and functions. Both of these can be handled by pointer type return values. C++ is like C but also allows user-defined types, or classes, to be returned from its functions. The Ada language is alone among current imperative languages in that its functions can return values of any type.

8.11 Accessing Nonlocal Environments

Although much of the required communication among subprograms can be accomplished through parameters, most languages provide some other method of accessing variables from external environments.

The **nonlocal variables** of a subprogram are those that are visible within the subprogram but are not locally declared. **Global variables** are those that are visible in all program units. In Chapter 4, two methods of accessing nonlocal variables were discussed, static scoping and dynamic scoping. The problems with these designs are reviewed in the following paragraphs.

The primary problem of using static scoping as the means of nonlocal variable sharing is the following: A good deal of program structure may be dictated by the accessibility of subprograms and nonlocal variables to other subprograms, rather than by well-engineered problem solutions. Additionally, in all cases, more access to nonlocals is provided than is necessary. Recall our examples of this problem in Chapter 4.

Two kinds of programming problems follow directly from dynamic scoping. First, during the time span beginning when execution of a subprogram begins and ending when that execution ends, the local variables of the subprogram are visible to any other executing subprogram regardless of its textual proximity. There is no way to protect local variables from this accessibility. Subprograms are always executed in the immediate environment of the caller. Because of this, dynamic scoping results in less reliable programs than static scoping.

A second problem with dynamic scoping is the inability to statically type check references to nonlocals, because it is not possible to statically determine the declaration for a variable referenced as a nonlocal.

Implementation of accesses to nonlocal variables is discussed in detail in Chapter 9.

8.11.1 FORTRAN COMMON Blocks

FORTRAN provides access to blocks of global storage through its COMMON statement. There can be any number of these blocks, all but one of which must be named. (There can be one unnamed COMMON block, often called blank COMMON, which has some different properties from named COMMON blocks.) Any subprogram that wishes to access or create a common block has a COMMON statement that names the block and provides a list of the variables that it can use to access storage in the block. A common block is created when the first COMMON statement that mentions the block's name is found by the compiler.

Any number of subprograms can include a COMMON statement that specifies the same block. Further, each subprogram that specifies the block can specify a different list of variables, whose number and types can be unrelated to those in the other subprograms. For example, it is perfectly legal to have the declarations

Figure 8.3
Two views of a
COMMON block

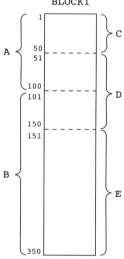

```
REAL A(100)
INTEGER B(250)
COMMON /BLOCK1/ A, B
```

in one subprogram, and the declarations

```
REAL C(50), D(100)
INTEGER E(200)
COMMON /BLOCK1/ C, D, E
```

in another subprogram. The identifier delimited by slashes, BLOCK1, is the block name. The two views of the variables in BLOCK1 are shown in Figure 8.3. Note that we assume that integer and real variables take the same amount of space.

This can make sense only if BLOCK1 is merely used as shared storage, not shared data. In fact, storage sharing is the main reason for allowing this. In most cases, data in a COMMON block are to be shared using the same variable names and types. A simple ordering error in the list of variables on a COMMON statement in this situation can cause inadvertent storage sharing between variables of different types, which can cause an error that is difficult to locate.

The FORTRAN 90 definition states that COMMON is one of the "deprecated features," which means that it may be included in only one more version of FORTRAN. EQUIVALENCE is also a deprecated feature of FORTRAN 90.

8.11.2 External Declarations and Modules

The Modula-2 and Ada languages use static scoping as a means of sharing data among program units. They both also provide an alternative method of data sharing by allowing units to specify the external modules to which access is required. Using this method, every module can specify exactly the other modules to which access is needed, no more and no less. In Modula-2, this access can be restricted to only specific procedures, variables, and data types from a given external module. Ada allows the user to specify only an external module's name, which then provides access to all of its types, variables, and procedures. This method is also possible in Modula-2. The approach of specifying each entity to which access is desired is certainly more tedious to use, because the lists of desired types, variables, and procedures can become long. It is, however, a safer method than simply specifying a module's name.

FORTRAN 90 also includes modules that can provide for selective and type-checked sharing of nonlocal data.

These language features are discussed more thoroughly in Chapter 10 in connection with data abstraction.

In object-oriented languages such as C++ and Java, a class can be used to encapsulate collections of data to be shared among other classes. Classes are discussed in detail in Chapter 11.

In C, there is no nesting of subprograms, so there is only a single level of subprogram scoping. Global variables can be created by placing their declarations outside function definitions. Access is provided to a variable in a function that declares the variable to be external with an **extern** statement. All functions whose definitions follow globally declared variables in a code file have access to those variables without declaring them to be external. This method is elegant, but insecure, and provides far more access than is usually needed.

Global variables that are defined in other files of C code that are included in a program can also be accessed by functions declaring them to be external. Thus separate, nonshared scopes can be introduced by separate compilation of modules. By this method, access to variables in those separately compiled modules is restricted to those other functions that declare the variables to be external.

8.12 User-Defined Overloaded Operators

Operators can be overloaded by the user in Ada and C++ programs. As an example of this, consider the following Ada function that overloads the multiplication operator (*) to compute the dot product of two arrays. The dot product of two arrays is the sum of the products of each of the corresponding pairs of elements of the two arrays. Suppose VECTOR_TYPE has been defined to be an array type with INTEGER elements.

```
function "*"(A, B : in VECTOR_TYPE) return INTEGER is
  SUM : INTEGER := 0;
  begin
  for INDEX in A'range loop
    SUM := SUM + A(INDEX) * B(INDEX);
  end loop;  — for INDEX ...
  return SUM;
  end "*";
```

The dot product, as specified in this function definition, will be computed whenever the asterisk appears with two operands of VECTOR_TYPE type. The asterisk can be further overloaded any number of times, as long as the defining functions have unique protocols.

The dot product function above could also be written in C++. The prototype of such a function could be

```
int operator *(const vector &a, const vector &b, int len);
```

The question naturally arises: How much operator overloading is good, or can you have too much? The answer is, to a large degree, a matter of taste. The argument against too much operator overloading is mainly one of readability. In many cases, it is more readable to call a function to carry out an operation than to use an operator that is more frequently used for other type operands. Even in the case of the dot product, it may be too easy to forget what is involved when a simple assignment statement, such as

```
C := A * B
```

is found in a program. It is easy to assume A, B, and C are simple scalars.

Another consideration is the process of building a software system from modules created by different groups. If the different groups overloaded the same operators in different ways, these differences would obviously need to be eliminated before putting the system together.

8.13 Coroutines

A coroutine is a special kind of subprogram. Rather than the master-slave relationship between a caller and a called subprogram that exists with conventional subprograms, caller and called coroutines are on a more equal basis. In fact, the coroutine control mechanism is often called the symmetric unit control model.

The actual origin of the concept of symmetric unit control is difficult to determine. One of the earliest published applications of coroutines was in the area of syntax analysis (Conway, 1963). The first high-level programming language to include facilities for coroutines was SIMULA 67. Recall that the original purpose of SIMULA was system simulation, which often requires the modeling of independent processes. This need was the motivation for the development of SIMULA 67's coroutines. Other languages that support coroutines are BLISS (Wulf et al., 1971), INTERLISP (Teitelman, 1975), and Modula-2 (Wirth, 1985).

Coroutines have multiple entry points, which are controlled by the coroutines themselves. They also have the means to maintain their status between activations. This means that coroutines must be history sensitive and thus have static local variables. Secondary executions of a coroutine often begin at points other than its beginning. Because of this, the invocation of a coroutine is called a **resume** rather than a call.

One of the usual characteristics of subprograms is maintained in coroutines: Only one coroutine actually executes at a given time. Rather than executing to their ends, however, coroutines often partially execute and then transfer control to some other coroutine. When restarted, a coroutine resumes execution just after the statement it used to transfer control elsewhere. This sort of execution sequence is related to the way multiprocessor operating systems work. Although there may be only one processor, all of the executing programs in such a system appear to run concurrently while sharing the processor. In the case of coroutines, this is sometimes called quasi-concurrency.

Typically, coroutines are created in an application by a program unit called the **master unit,** which is not a coroutine. When created, coroutines execute their initialization code and then return control to that master unit. When all of a family of coroutines are constructed, the master program resumes one of the coroutines, and the members of the family of coroutines then resume each other in some order until their work is completed, if in fact it can be completed. If the execution of a coroutine reaches the end of its code section, control is transferred to the master unit that created it. This is the mechanism for ending execution of the collection of coroutines, when that is desirable. In some programs, the coroutines run whenever the computer is running.

One example of a problem that can be solved with this sort of collection of coroutines is the simulation of a card game. Suppose the game has four players who all use the same strategy for playing. Such a game can be simulated by having a master program unit create a family of coroutines, each with a collection, or hand, of cards. The master program could then start the simulation by resuming one of the player coroutines, which, after it had played its turn, could resume the next player coroutine, and so forth until the game ended.

Figure 8.4
Two possible execution control sequences for two coroutines without loops

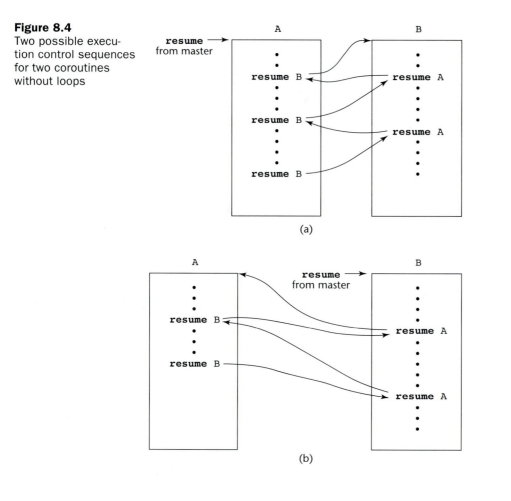

The same form of resume statement can be used both to start and to restart the execution of a coroutine.

Suppose program units A and B are coroutines. Figure 8.4 shows two ways an execution sequence involving A and B might proceed.

In Figure 8.4a, the execution of coroutine A is started by the master unit. After some execution, A starts B. When coroutine B in Figure 8.4a first causes control to return to coroutine A, the semantics is that A continues from where it ended its last execution. In particular, its local variables have the values left them by the previous activation. Figure 8.4b shows an alternative execution sequence of coroutines A and B. In this case, B is started by the master unit.

Rather than have the patterns shown in Figure 8.4, a coroutine often has a loop containing a resume. Figure 8.5 shows the execution sequence of this scenario. In this case, A is started by the master unit. Inside its main loop, A resumes B, which in turn resumes A in its main loop.

Figure 8.5
Coroutine execution
sequence with loops

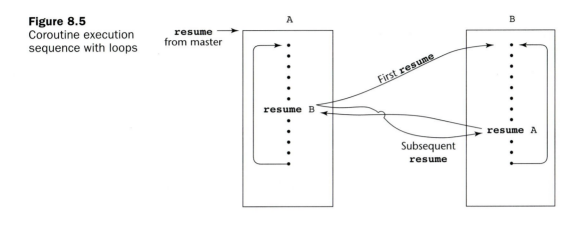

S U M M A R Y

Process abstractions are represented in programming languages by subprograms. A subprogram definition describes the actions represented by the subprogram. A subprogram call enacts those actions.

Formal parameters are the names that subprograms use to refer to the actual parameters given in subprogram calls.

Subprograms can be either functions, which model mathematical functions and are used to define new operations, or procedures, which define new statements.

Local variables in subprograms can be dynamically allocated from a stack, providing support for recursion, or statically allocated, providing efficiency and history-sensitive local variables.

There are three fundamental semantics models of parameter passing—in mode, out mode, and inout mode—and a number of approaches to implementation.

Aliasing can occur when pass-by-reference parameters are used, both among two or more parameters and between a parameter and an accessible nonlocal variable.

Access to nonlocal variables is provided in several different ways: through external declarations, global data blocks, external modules, and static and dynamic scoping.

Parameters that are subprogram names provide a necessary service but are sometimes difficult to understand. The opaqueness lies in the referencing environment that is available when a subprogram that has been passed as a parameter is executing.

Ada and C++ allow both subprogram and operator overloading. Subprograms can be overloaded as long as the various versions can be disambiguated by the types of their parameters or returned values. Function definitions can be used to build additional meanings for operators.

Subprograms in Ada and C++ can be generic, using parametric polymorphism, so the desired types of their data objects can be passed to the compiler, which then can construct units for the requested types.

A coroutine is a special subprogram that has multiple entries. They can be used to provide interleaved execution of subprograms.

REVIEW QUESTIONS

1. What are the three general characteristics of subprograms?
2. What does it mean for a subprogram to be active?
3. What is a parameter profile? What is a subprogram protocol?
4. What are formal parameters? What are actual parameters?
5. What are the advantages and disadvantages of keyword parameters?
6. What are the design issues for subprograms?
7. What are the advantages and disadvantages of dynamic local variables?
8. What are the three semantic models of parameter passing?
9. What are the modes, the conceptual models of transfer, the advantages and the disadvantages of pass-by-value, pass-by-result, pass-by-value-result, pass-by-reference, and pass-by-name parameter-passing methods?
10. In what ways can aliases occur with pass-by-reference parameters?
11. What is the difference in the way original C and ANSI C deal with an actual parameter whose type is not identical to that of the corresponding formal parameter?
12. What is the problem with Ada's policy of allowing implementors to decide which parameters to pass by reference and which to pass by value-result?
13. What are two fundamental design considerations for parameter-passing methods?
14. What are the two issues that arise when subprogram names are parameters?
15. Define *shallow* and *deep binding* for referencing environments of subprograms that have been passed as parameters.
16. What is an overloaded subprogram?
17. What is parametric polymorphism?
18. What causes a C++ template function to be instantiated?
19. Define *separate* and *independent compilation*.
20. What are the design issues for functions?
21. In what ways are coroutines different from conventional subprograms?

1. What are arguments for and against a user program building additional definitions for existing operators, as can be done in Ada and C++? Do you believe such user-defined operator overloading is good or bad? Support your answer.

2. In most FORTRAN IV implementations, parameters were passed by reference, using access path transmission only. State both the advantages and disadvantages of this design choice.

3. Argue in support of the Ada 83 designers' decision to allow the implementor to choose between implementing **in out** mode parameters by copy or by reference.

4. FORTRAN has two slightly different kinds of **COMMON**, blank and named. One difference between them is that blank **COMMON** cannot be initialized at compile time. See if you can determine the reason why blank **COMMON** was designed this way. *Hint*: This design decision was made early in the development of FORTRAN, when computer memories were quite small.

5. Suppose you wish to write a subprogram that prints a heading on a new output page, along with a page number that is 1 in the first activation and that increases by 1 with each subsequent activation. Can this be done without parameters and without reference to nonlocal variables in Pascal? Can it be done in FORTRAN? Can it be done in C?

6. FORTRAN allows a subprogram to have multiple entry points. Why is this sometimes a valuable capability?

7. Write a Pascal procedure **ADDER** that adds two integer arrays together. It must have only two parameters, which have the two arrays to be added. The second array also will hold the sum array on exit. Both parameters must be passed by reference. Test **ADDER** with the call

   ```
   ADDER(A, A)
   ```

   where A is an array to be added to itself. Explain the results of running this program.

8. Repeat Problem 7 using C.

9. Consider the procedure **BIGSUB** in Section 8.5.2.5. Change the two assignments to the **LIST** array to

   ```
   LIST[1] := 3
   LIST[2] := 1
   ```

   Hand execute the new program under the following assumptions, and compare the resulting values in the array **LIST** in **BIGSUB** after the return from **SUB**.

   a. Parameters are passed by value.

   b. Parameters are passed by reference.

   c. Parameters are passed by name.

   d. Parameters are passed by value-result.

10. Consider the following program written in C syntax:

```c
void main() {
  int value = 2, list[5] = {1, 3, 5, 7, 9};
  swap(value, list[0]);
  swap(list[0], list[1]);
  swap(value, list[value]);

}
void swap(int a, int b) {
  int temp;
  temp = a;
  a = b;
  b = temp;
}
```

For each of the following parameter-passing methods, what are all of the values of the variables `value` and `list` after each of the three calls to `swap`?

a. Passed by value

b. Passed by reference

c. Passed by name

d. Passed by value-result

11. Present one argument against providing both static and dynamic local variables in subprograms.

12. Argue against the C design of providing only function subprograms.

13. From a textbook on FORTRAN, learn the syntax and semantics of statement functions. Justify their existence in FORTRAN.

14. Study the methods of user-defined operator overloading in C++ and Ada, and write a report comparing the two using our criteria for evaluating languages.

15. Consider the following ALGOL 60 procedure, which is called Jensen's Device after, J. Jensen, of the Regnecentralen in Copenhagen, who designed it in 1960:

```
real procedure SUM(ADDER, INDEX, LENGTH);
  value LENGTH;
  real ADDER;
  integer INDEX, LENGTH;
  begin
  real TEMPSUM;
  TEMPSUM := 0.0;
  for INDEX := 1 step 1 until LENGTH do
    TEMPSUM := TEMPSUM + ADDER;
  SUM := TEMPSUM
  end;
```

What is returned by each of the following calls to `SUM`, recalling that parameters are passed by name and noting that the return value is set by assigning it to the subprogram's name?

a. `SUM(A, I, 100)`, where `A` is a scalar

b. `SUM(A[I]*A[I], I, 100)`, where `A` is an array of 100 elements

c. `SUM(A[I]*B[I], I, 100)`, where `A` and `B` are arrays of 100 elements

9 Implementing Subprograms

John Kemeny

John Kemeny and his colleague Thomas Kurtz developed compilers for several dialects of ALGOL and FORTRAN at Dartmouth in the early 1960s. In 1963, Kemeny began the design of BASIC, which became operational in 1964.

CHAPTER OUTLINE

The purpose of this chapter is to explore methods for implementing subprograms. The discussion will provide the reader with some insight into how such languages "work," and also why ALGOL 60 was a challenge to the unsuspecting compiler writers of the early 1960s. We begin with the simplest kind of subprograms—those in FORTRAN 77—and progress to the more complicated subprograms of the static-scoped languages, such as Pascal and Ada. The increased difficulty of implementing subprograms in these languages is caused by the need to include support for recursion and for mechanisms to access nonlocal variables.

Two methods of accessing nonlocals in static-scoped languages, static chains and displays, are discussed in detail and compared. Techniques for implementing blocks are covered briefly. Several methods of implementing nonlocal variable access in a dynamic-scoped language are discussed. Finally, a method is described for implementing parameters that are subprogram names.

9.1 The General Semantics of Calls and Returns

The subprogram call and return operations of a language are together called its **subprogram linkage.** Any implementation method for subprograms must be based on the semantics of subprogram linkage.

A subprogram call in a typical language has numerous actions associated with it. The call must include the mechanism for whatever parameter-passing method is used. If local variables are not static, the call must cause storage to be allocated for the locals declared in the called subprogram and bind those variables to that storage. It must save the execution status of the calling program unit. It must arrange to transfer control to the code of the subprogram and ensure that control can return to the proper place when the subprogram execution is completed. Finally, the call must cause some mechanism to be created to provide access to nonlocal variables that are visible to the called subprogram.

The required actions of a subprogram return are also complicated. If the subprogram has parameters that are out mode and are implemented by copy, the first action of the return process is to move the local values of the associated formal parameters to the actual parameters. Next, it must deallocate the storage used for local variables and restore the execution status of the calling program unit. Some action must then be taken to return the mechanism used for nonlocal references to the configuration it had before the call. Finally, control must be returned to the calling program unit.

9.2 Implementing FORTRAN 77 Subprograms

We begin with the relatively simple situation of FORTRAN 77 subprograms. All referencing of nonlocal variables in FORTRAN 77 is through COMMON. Because COMMON is not connected to the subprogram linkage mechanism, it is not discussed here. Another simplifying characteristic of FORTRAN 77 is that subprograms cannot be recursive. Furthermore, in most implementations, variables declared in subprograms are statically allocated.

The semantics of a FORTRAN 77 subprogram call requires the following actions:

1. Save the execution status of the current program unit.

2. Carry out the parameter-passing process.

3. Pass the return address to the callee.

4. Transfer control to the callee.

The semantics of a FORTRAN 77 subprogram return requires the following actions:

1. If pass-by-value-result parameters are used, the current values of those parameters are moved to the corresponding actual parameters.

2. If the subprogram is a function, the functional value is moved to a place accessible to the caller.

3. The execution status of the caller is restored.

4. Control is transferred back to the caller.

The call and return actions require storage for the following:

- Status information about the caller
- Parameters
- Return address
- Functional value for function subprograms

These, along with the local variables and the subprogram code, form the complete set of information a subprogram needs to execute and then return control to the caller.

A FORTRAN 77 subprogram consists of two separate parts: the actual code of the subprogram, which is constant, and the local variables and data listed above, which can change when the subprogram is executed. Both of these parts have fixed sizes.

The format, or layout, of the noncode part of a subprogram is called an **activation record,** because the data it describes are only relevant during

Figure 9.1
A FORTRAN 77
activation record

Functional value
Local variables
Parameters
Return address

the activation of the subprogram. The form of an activation record is static. An **activation record instance** is a concrete example of an activation record, a collection of data in the form of an activation record.

Because FORTRAN 77 does not support recursion, there can be only one active version of a given subprogram at a time. Therefore, there can be only a single instance of the activation record for a subprogram. One possible layout for FORTRAN 77 activation records is shown in Figure 9.1. The saved execution status of the caller is omitted here and in the remainder of this chapter simply because it is not relevant to the discussion.

Because an activation record instance for a FORTRAN 77 subprogram has fixed size, it can be statically allocated. In fact, it could be attached to the code part of the subprogram.

Figure 9.2 shows a FORTRAN 77 program consisting of COMMON storage, a main program, and three subprograms: A, B, and C. Although the figure shows all the code segments separated from all of the activation record instances, in some cases the activation record instances are attached to their associated code segments.

Figure 9.2
The code and activation records of a
FORTRAN 77 program

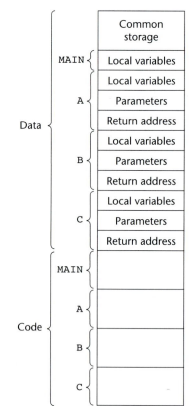

The construction of the complete FORTRAN 77 program shown in Figure 9.2 is not done entirely by the compiler. In fact, because of independent compilation, the four program units—MAIN, A, B, and C—may have been compiled on different days, or even in different years. At the time each unit is compiled, the machine code for it, along with a list of references to external subprograms and COMMON variables within the code, is written to a file. The executable program shown in Figure 9.2 is put together by the **linker,** which is part of the operating system. (Sometimes linkers are called loaders, linker/loaders, or link editors.) When the linker is called for a main program, its first task is to find the files that contain the translated subprograms referenced in that program, along with their activation record instances, and load them into memory. It also must determine the size of all COMMON blocks and allocate storage for them. Then the linker must set the target addresses of all calls to those subprograms in the main program to the entry addresses of those subprograms. The same must be done for all calls to subprograms in the loaded subprograms and all calls to FORTRAN library subprograms. In the example above, the linker was called for MAIN. The linker had to find the machine code programs for A, B, and C, along with their activation record instances, and load them into memory with the code for MAIN. Then it had to patch in the target addresses for all calls to A, B, C, and any library subprograms in A, B, C, and MAIN. Furthermore, all references to variables in COMMON had to be patched with the proper addresses. In many cases, references to COMMON variables are handled by offset addressing within the block, obviating the need for address patching.

FORTRAN 90 allows its subprograms to be both nested (using static scoping) and recursive, thereby requiring its implementation to be more like that of the ALGOL-like languages. Implementation methods for these languages are discussed at length in the following section.

9.3 Implementing Subprograms in ALGOL-Like Languages

We now examine the implementation of the subprogram linkage in ALGOL-like static-scoped languages, such as Pascal, Ada, FORTRAN 90, and Delphi, focusing on the call and return operations required for increasingly complicated situations. Two related but different approaches to implementing nonlocal variable accesses, called static chains and displays, are described in detail.

Although C, C++, and Java do not permit nested subprograms, their implementations are similar to those of the other static-scoped languages. The difference is the support for nonlocal variable references, which can be much simpler when subprograms cannot be nested.

9.3.1 More Complex Activation Records

Subprogram linkage in ALGOL-like languages is more complex than the linkage of FORTRAN 77 subprograms for the following reasons:

- Parameters can usually be passed by two different methods. For example, in many languages they are passed by value or by reference.

- Variables declared in subprograms are often dynamically allocated.

- Recursion adds the possibility of multiple simultaneous activations of a subprogram, which means there can be more than one instance (incomplete execution) of a subprogram at a given time, with one call from outside the subprogram and one or more recursive calls. Recursion, therefore, requires multiple instances of activation records, one for each subprogram activation that can exist at the same time. Each activation requires its own copy of the formal parameters and the dynamically allocated local variables, along with the return address.

■ Finally, ALGOL-like languages use static scoping to provide access to nonlocal variables. Support for these nonlocal accesses must be part of the linkage mechanism.

The format of an activation record for a given subprogram in a static-scoped language is known at compile time. In Pascal procedures, the size is also known for activation records because all data local to a Pascal procedure is of fixed size. That is not the case in some other languages, in which the size of a local array can depend on the value of an actual parameter. In those cases, the format is static, but the size can be dynamic. In the case of the ALGOL-like languages, activation record instances must be created dynamically. The typical activation record for an ALGOL-like language is shown in Figure 9.3.

Because the return address, static link, dynamic link, and parameters are placed in the activation record instance by the caller, these entries must appear first. We assume for this chapter that the stack grows upward. Therefore, the return address will be at the bottom of an activation record.

The return address often consists of a pointer to the code segment of the caller and an offset address in that code segment of the instruction following the call. The **static link,** which is sometimes called a static scope pointer, points to the bottom of the activation record instance of an activation of the static parent. It is used for accesses to nonlocal variables. Static links are discussed in detail in Section 9.3.4. The **dynamic link** is a pointer to the top of an instance of the activation record of the caller. In static-scoped languages, this link is used in the destruction of the current activation record instance when the procedure completes its execution. The dynamic link is required because in some cases there are other allocations from the stack by a subprogram beyond its activation record. For example, temporaries needed by the machine language version of the subprogram may be allocated there. So, although the size of the activation record may be known, the size cannot simply be subtracted from the stack top pointer to remove the activation record. The actual parameters in the activation record are the values or addresses provided by the caller.

Local scalar variables are bound to storage within an activation record

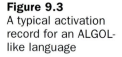

Figure 9.3
A typical activation record for an ALGOL-like language

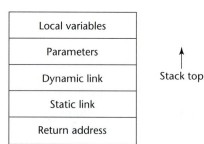

| Local variables |
| Parameters |
| Dynamic link |
| Static link |
| Return address |

Stack top ↑

instance. Local variables that are structures are sometimes allocated elsewhere, and only their descriptors and a pointer to that storage are part of the activation record. Local variables are allocated and possibly initialized in the called subprogram, so they appear last.

Consider the following skeletal Pascal procedure:

```
procedure sub(var total : real; part : integer);
  var list : array [1..5] of integer;
      sum : real;
  begin
  ...
  end;
```

The activation record for sub is shown in Figure 9.4.

Activating a procedure requires the dynamic creation of an instance of the activation record for the procedure. As stated earlier, the format of the activation record is fixed at compile time, although its size may depend on the call in some languages other than Pascal. Because the call and return semantics specify that the subprogram last called is the first to complete, it is reasonable to create instances of these activation records on a stack. This stack is part of the run-time system, and therefore is called the **run-time stack,** although we will usually just refer to it as the stack. Every procedure activation, whether recursive or nonrecursive, creates a new instance of an activation record on the stack. This provides the required separate copies of the parameters, local variables, and the return address.

Recall from Chapter 8 that a subprogram is **active** from the time it is called until the time that execution is completed. At the time it becomes inactive, its local scope ceases to exist and its referencing environment is no longer meaningful. So at that time, its activation record instance is destroyed.

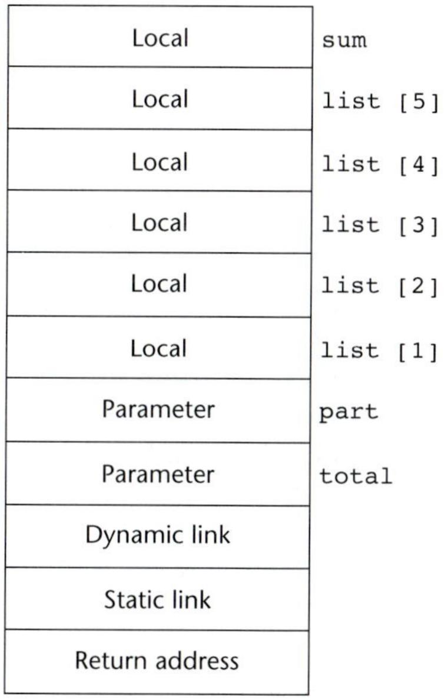

Figure 9.4
The activation record for procedure sub

Local	sum
Local	list [5]
Local	list [4]
Local	list [3]
Local	list [2]
Local	list [1]
Parameter	part
Parameter	total
Dynamic link	
Static link	
Return address	

9.3.2 An Example Without Recursion and Nonlocal References

Because of the complexity of implementing subprogram linkage, we consider it in several stages. First we examine an example program that does not reference nonlocal variables and has no recursive calls. For this example, the static link is not used. We later consider how recursion and nonlocal referencing can be implemented.

Consider the following skeletal example program:

```
program MAIN_1;
  var P : real;
  procedure A(X : integer);
    var Y : boolean;
    procedure C(Q : boolean);
      begin   { C }
      ...      <─────────────3
      end; { C }
    begin   { A }
    ...      <─────────────2
    C(Y);
    ...
    end;   { A }
  procedure B(R : real);
    var S, T : integer;
    begin   { B }
    ...      <─────────────1
    A(S);
    ...
    end;   { B }
  begin   { MAIN_1 }
  ...
  B(P);
  ...
  end.   { MAIN_1 }
```

The sequence of procedure calls in this program is

MAIN_1 calls B
B calls A
A calls C

The stack contents for the points labeled 1, 2, and 3 are shown in Figure 9.5.

At point 1, only the activation record instances for program MAIN_1 and procedure B are on the stack. When B calls A, an instance of A's activation record is created on the stack. When A calls C, an instance of C's activation record is created on the stack. When C's execution ends, the instance of its activation record is removed from the stack, and the dynamic link is used to reset the stack top pointer. A similar process takes place when procedures A and B terminate. After the return from the call to B from MAIN_1, the stack has only the instance of the activation record of MAIN_1. Note that some implementations do not actually use an activation record instance on the stack for main programs, such as the one shown in the figure. However, it can be done this way, and it simplifies both the implementation and our discussion. In this example and in all others in this chapter, we assume that the stack grows from lower addresses to higher addresses.

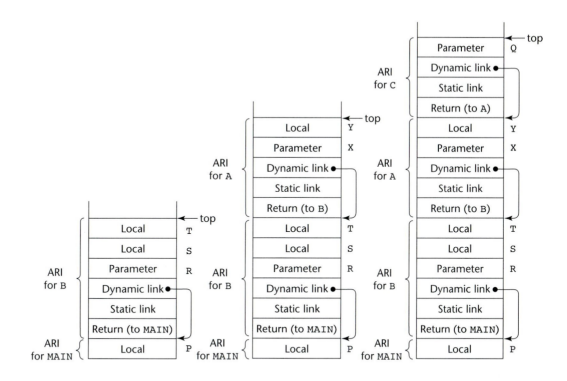

ARI = activation record instance

Figure 9.5
Stack contents for three points in a program

The collection of dynamic links present in the stack at a given time is called the **dynamic chain,** or **call chain.** It represents the dynamic history of how execution got to its current position, which is always in the procedure code whose activation record instance is on top of the stack. References to local variables can be represented in the code as offsets from the beginning of the activation record of the local scope. Such an offset is called a **local_offset.**

The local_offset of a variable in an activation record can be determined at compile time, using the order, types, and sizes of variables declared in the procedure associated with the activation record. To simplify the discussion, assume that all variables take one position in the activation record. The first local variable declared in a procedure would be allocated in the activation record three positions plus the number of parameters from the bottom (the first three positions are for the return address, the static link, and the dynamic link). The second local variable declared would be one position nearer the stack top and so forth. For example, consider the preceding example program. In A, the local_offset of Y is 4. Likewise, in B, the local_offset of S is 4; for T it is 5.

9.3.3 Recursion

Consider the following example C program, which uses recursion to compute the factorial function:

```
int factorial(int n) {
                    <──────────1
  if (n <= 1)
    return 1;
  else return (n * factorial(n - 1));
                  <──────────2
}
void main() {
  int value;
  value = factorial(3);
                <──────────3
}
```

The activation record format for the function `factorial` is shown in Figure 9.6. Notice that it has an additional entry for the returned value of the function.

Figure 9.7 shows the contents of the stack for the three times that execution reaches position 1 in the function `factorial`. Each shows one more activation of the function, with its functional value undefined. The first activation record instance has the return address to the calling function, `main`. The others have a return address to the function itself; these are for the recursive calls.

Figure 9.8 (on page 388) shows the stack contents for the three times that execution reaches position 2 in the function `factorial`. Position 2 is meant to be the time after the **return** is executed but before the activation record has been removed from the stack. Recall that the code for the function multiplies the current value of the parameter n by the value returned by the recursive call to the function. The first return from `factorial` returns the value 1. The activation record instance for that activation has a value of 1 for its version of the parameter n. The result from that multiplication, 1, is returned to the second activation of `factorial` to be multiplied by its parameter value for n, which is 2. This returns the value 2 to the first activation of `factorial` to be multiplied by its parameter value for n, which is 3, yielding the final functional value of 6, which is then returned to the first call to `factorial` in `main`.

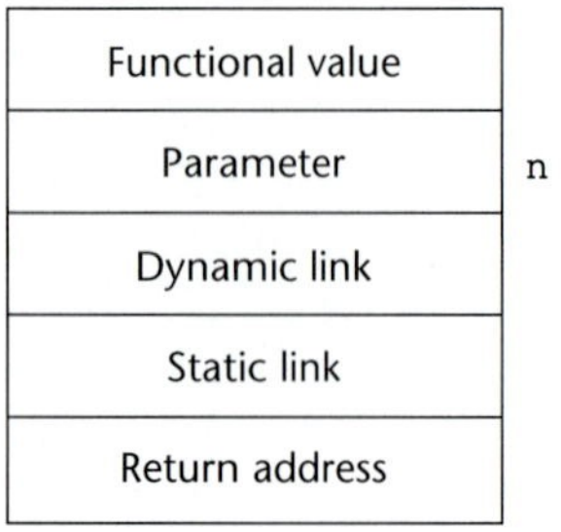

Figure 9.6
Stack contents for three points in a program

Functional value	
Parameter	n
Dynamic link	
Static link	
Return address	

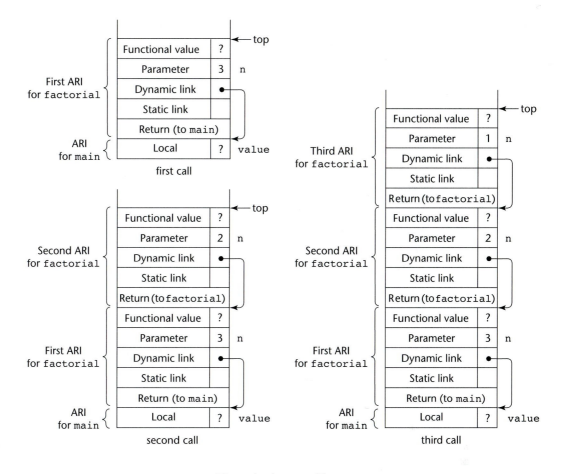

ARI = activation record instance

Figure 9.7
Stack contents at position 1 in factorial

9.3.4 Mechanisms for Implementing Nonlocal References

There are two major implementation techniques for creating accesses to nonlocal variables in a static-scoped language: static chains and displays. Both of these are examined in detail in the following sections.

A reference to a nonlocal variable requires a two-step access process. All variables that can be nonlocally accessed are in existing activation record instances and therefore are somewhere in the stack. The first step of the access process is to find the instance of the activation record in the stack in which the variable was allocated. The second part is to use the local_offset of the variable (within the activation record instance) to access it.

Figure 9.8
Stack contents during execution of `main` and `factorial`

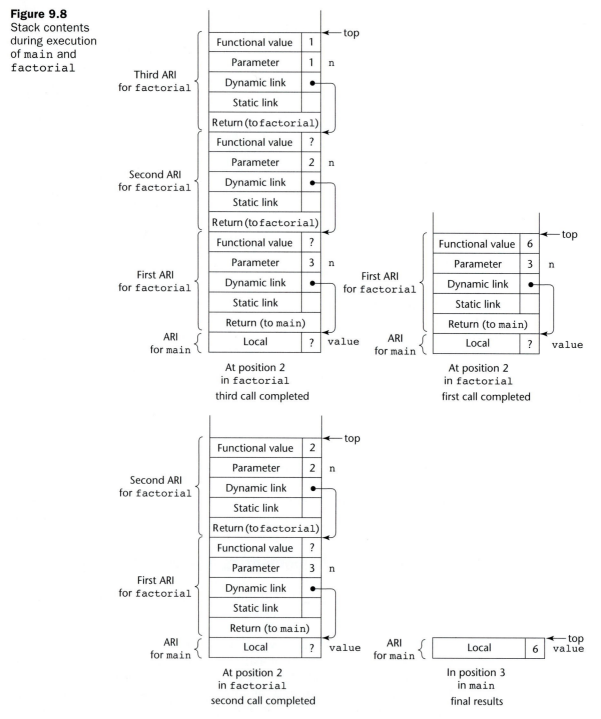

At position 2
in `factorial`
third call completed

At position 2
in `factorial`
first call completed

At position 2
in `factorial`
second call completed

In position 3
in `main`
final results

ARI = activation record instance

Finding the correct activation record instance is the more interesting and more difficult of the two steps. First note that in a given subprogram, only variables that are declared in static ancestor scopes are visible and can be accessed. Also, activation record instances of all of the static ancestors are guaranteed to exist on the stack when variables in them are referenced by a nested procedure. This is guaranteed by the static semantic rules of the static-scoped languages: A procedure is callable only when all of its static ancestor program units are active. If a particular static ancestor were not active, its local variables would not be bound to storage, so it would be nonsense to allow access to them.

Note that although the parent scope activation record must have an instance on the stack, it need not appear adjacent to the child's activation record instance. This is illustrated in an example in Section 9.3.4.1.

The semantics of nonlocal references dictates that the correct declaration is the first one found when looking through the enclosing scopes, most closely nested first. So to support nonlocal references, it must be possible to find all of the instances of activation records in the stack that correspond to those static ancestors. This observation leads to the two methods described in the following sections.

We do not address the issue of blocks until Section 9.4, so in the remainder of Section 9.3, all scopes are defined by subprograms. Because functions cannot be nested in C and C++ (the only static scopes are created with blocks), the discussions of this section do not apply to these languages.

9.3.4.1 Static Chains

A **static chain** is a chain of static links that connect certain activation record instances in the stack.

During the execution of a procedure P, the static link of its activation record instance points to an activation record instance of P's static parent program unit. That instance's static link points, in turn, to P's static grandparent program unit's activation record instance, if there is one. So the static chain links all the static ancestors of an executing subprogram, in order of static parent first. This chain can obviously be used to implement the accesses to nonlocal variables in static-scoped languages.

Finding the correct activation record instance of a nonlocal variable using static links is relatively straightforward. When a reference is made to a nonlocal variable, the activation record instance containing the variable can be found by searching the static chain until a static ancestor activation record instance is found that contains the variable. However, it is much easier than that. Because the nesting of scopes is known at compile time, the compiler can determine not only that a reference is nonlocal but also the length of the static chain needed to reach the activation record instance that contains the nonlocal object.

Let **static_depth** be an integer associated with a static scope that indicates how deeply it is nested in the outermost scope. A Pascal main program has a static_depth of 0. If procedure A is the only procedure defined in a main program, its static_depth is 1. If procedure A contains the definition of a nested procedure B, then B's static_depth is 2.

The length of the static chain needed to reach the correct activation record instance for a nonlocal reference to a variable X is exactly the difference between the static_depth of the procedure containing the reference to X and the static_depth of the procedure containing the declaration for X. This difference is called the **nesting_depth,** or **chain_offset,** of the reference. The actual reference can be represented by an ordered pair of integers (chain_offset, local_offset), where chain_offset is the number of links to the correct activation record instance (local_offset is described in Section 9.3.2). For example, consider the following skeletal program:

```
program A;
  procedure B;
    procedure C;
      ...
    end;  { C }
    ...
  end;  { B }
  ...
end;  { A }
```

The static_depths of A, B, and C are 0, 1, and 2, respectively. If procedure C references a variable declared in A, the chain_offset of that reference would be 2 (static_depth of C minus the static_depth of A). If procedure C references a variable declared in B, the chain_offset of that reference would be 1. References to locals can be handled using the same mechanism, with a chain_offset of zero.

To illustrate the complete process of nonlocal accesses, consider the following skeletal program in Pascal:

```
program MAIN_2;
  var X : integer;
  procedure BIGSUB;
    var A, B, C : integer;
    procedure SUB1;
      var A, D : integer;
      begin  { SUB1 }
      A := B + C;    <————————1
      ...
      end;  { SUB1 }
    procedure SUB2(X : integer);
      var B, E : integer;
      procedure SUB3;
        var C, E : integer;
        begin  { SUB3 }
        ...
```

```
          SUB1;
          ...
          E := B + A;    <——————————2
          end;   { SUB3 }
       begin   { SUB2 }
       ...
       SUB3;
       ...
       A := D + E;    <——————————3
       end;   { SUB2 }
    begin   { BIGSUB }
    ...
    SUB2(7);
    ...
    end;   { BIGSUB }
 begin   { MAIN_2 }
 ...
 BIGSUB;
 ...
 end.   { MAIN_2 }
```

The sequence of procedure calls is:

MAIN_2 calls BIGSUB
BIGSUB calls SUB2
SUB2 calls SUB3
SUB3 calls SUB1

The stack situation when execution first arrives at point 1 in this program is shown in Figure 9.9.

At position 1 in procedure SUB1, the reference is to the local variable, A, not to the nonlocal variable A from BIGSUB. This reference to A has the chain_offset/local_offset pair (0, 3). The reference to B is to the nonlocal B from BIGSUB. It can be represented by the pair (1, 4). The local_offset is 4, because a 3 offset would be the first local variable (BIGSUB has no parameters). Notice that if the dynamic link were used to do a simple search for an activation record instance with a declaration for the variable B, it would find the variable B declared in SUB2, which would be incorrect. If the (1, 4) pair were used with the dynamic chain, the variable E from SUB3 would be used. The static link, however, points to the activation record for BIGSUB, which has the correct version of B. The variable B in SUB2 is not in the referencing environment at this point and is (correctly) not accessible. The reference to C at point 1 is to the C defined in BIGSUB, which is represented by the pair (1, 5).

After SUB1 completes its execution, the activation record instance for SUB1 is removed from the stack, and control returns to SUB3. The reference to the variable E at position 2 in SUB3 is local and uses the pair (0, 4) for access. The reference to the variable B is to the one declared in SUB2, because that is the nearest static ancestor that contains such a declaration.

Figure 9.9
Stack contents at
position 1 in the
program MAIN_2

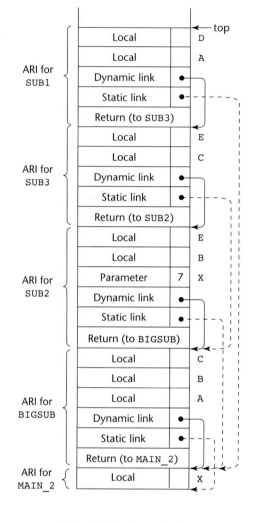

ARI = activation record instance

It is accessed with the pair (1, 4). The local_offset is 4 because B is the first variable declared in SUB1, and SUB2 has one parameter. The reference to the variable A is to the A declared in BIGSUB, because neither SUB3 nor its static parent SUB2 has a declaration for a variable named A. It is referenced with the pair (2, 3).

After SUB3 completes its execution, the activation record instance for SUB3 is removed from the stack, leaving only the activation record instances for MAIN_2, BIGSUB, and SUB2. At position 3 in SUB2, the reference to the variable A is to the A in BIGSUB, which has the only declaration of A among the active routines. This access is made with the pair (1, 3). At this position, there is no visible scope containing a declaration for the variable D, so this reference to D is a static semantics error. The error would be detected when the compiler attempted to compute the chain_offset/local_offset pair. The reference to E is to the local E in SUB2, which can be accessed with the pair (0, 5).

In summary, the references to the variable A at points 1, 2, and 3, would be represented by the following points:

(0, 3) (local)

(2, 3) (two levels away)

(1, 3) (one level away)

It is reasonable at this point to ask how the static chain is maintained during program execution. If its maintenance is too complex, the fact that it is simple and effective will be unimportant. In this section, we assume that pass-by-name parameters and parameters that are subprogram names are not implemented.

The static chain must be modified for each subprogram call and return. The return part is trivial: When the subprogram terminates, its activation record instance is removed from the stack. After this removal, the new top activation record instance is that of the unit that called the subprogram whose execution just terminated. Because the static chain from this activation record instance was never changed, it works correctly just as it did before the call to the other subprogram. Therefore, no other action is required.

The action required at a subprogram call is more complex. Although the correct parent scope is easily determined at compile time, the most recent activation record instance of the parent scope must be found at the time of the call. This can be done by looking at activation record instances on the dynamic chain until the first one of the parent scope is found. However, this search can be avoided by treating procedure declarations and references exactly like variable declarations and references. When the compiler encounters a procedure call, among other things, it determines the procedure that declared the called procedure, which must be a static ancestor of the calling routine. It then computes the nesting_depth, or number of enclosing scopes between the caller and the procedure that declared the called procedure. This information is stored and can be accessed by the procedure call during execution. At the time of the call, the static link of the called procedure's activation record instance is determined by moving down the static chain of the caller the number of links equal to the nesting depth computed at compile time.

Consider again the program MAIN_2 and the stack situation shown in Figure 9.9. At the call to SUB1 in SUB3, the compiler determines the nesting_depth of SUB3 (the caller) to be two levels inside the procedure that declared the called procedure SUB1, which is BIGSUB. When the call to SUB1 in SUB3 is executed, this information is used to set the static link of the activation record instance for SUB1. This static link is set to point to the activation record instance that is pointed to by the second static link in the static chain from the caller's activation record instance. In this case, the caller is SUB3, whose static link points to its parent's activation record instance (that of SUB2). The static link of the activation record instance for SUB2 points to the activation record instance for BIGSUB. So the static link for the new activation record instance for SUB1 is set to point to the activation record instance for BIGSUB.

This method works for all procedure linkage, except when parameters that are subprogram names are involved. That situation is discussed in Section 9.6.

One criticism of using the static chain to access nonlocal variables is that references to variables in scopes beyond the static parent are costly. The static chain must be followed, one link per enclosing scope from the reference to the declaration. Another criticism is that it is difficult for a programmer working on a time-critical program to estimate the costs of nonlocal references, because the cost of each reference depends on the depth of nesting between the reference and the scope of declaration. Further complicating this problem is that subsequent code modifications may change nesting depths, thereby changing the timing of some references, both in the changed code and possibly in code far from the changes.

9.3.4.2 Displays

The only widely used alternative to static chains is to use a display. For this approach, the static links are collected in a single array called a **display,** rather than being stored in the activation records. The contents of the display at any specific time is a list of addresses of the accessible activation record instances in the stack—one for each active scope—in the order in which they are nested.

Accesses to nonlocals using a display require exactly two steps for every access, regardless of the number of scope levels between the reference and the declaration of the variable being accessed. These two steps are accomplished as follows: The link to the correct activation record, which resides in the display, is found using a statically computed value called the display_offset, which is closely related to the static chain chain_offset. The local_offset within the activation record instance is computed and used exactly as with static chain implementations. A nonlocal reference is represented by an ordered pair of integers, (display_offset/ local_offset). A nonlocal variable can be addressed conveniently and quickly with two applications of an offset-indirect addressing mode, which many contemporary computers have.

Every subprogram call and return requires that the display be modified to reflect the new scope situation. We now investigate the actions required to maintain the display. Once again, we assume that parameters are not subprogram names and that pass-by-name parameters are not involved. The more complex case is considered in Section 9.6.

First, note that the display_offset depends only on the static_depth of the procedure in which the nonlocal reference appears. If the static_depth of procedure P is 2, then the link to P's activation record instance will always appear in position 2 in the display. Display entries begin at the subscript of 0, with the zeroth position being used for access to variables declared in the outermost scope (the main program).

In general, the pointer at position k of the display points to an activation record instance for a procedure with a static_depth of k. The display modification required for a call to procedure P, which has a static_depth of k, is

1. Save, in the new activation record instance, a copy of the pointer stored at position k in the display.
2. Place the link to the activation record instance for P at position k in the display.

Subprogram termination requires the saved pointer in the activation record instance of the terminating subprogram to be placed back in the display. Then the activation record instance is removed from the stack, as with the static chain implementation.

To verify that the two simple steps of display modification for procedure calls are always correct, we examine the three possible situations defined by considering a call to procedure P by procedure Q. Let Psd be the static_depth of P and Qsd be the static_depth of Q. The three cases are defined as follows:

1. Qsd = Psd
2. Qsd < Psd
3. Qsd > Psd

We use the following program, which is a skeletal version of the program of our earlier example, MAIN_2, to examine these three cases:

```
program MAIN_3;
  procedure BIGSUB;
    procedure SUB1;
      . . .
      end;   { SUB1 }
    procedure SUB2;
      procedure SUB3;
        . . .
        end;   { SUB3 }
      . . .
      end;   { SUB2 }
    . . .
    end;   { BIGSUB }
  end.   { MAIN_3 }
```

The first case would occur if SUB2 called SUB1, because they are both at a depth level of 2. The stack and display for the situation for just before and just after the call are shown in Figure 9.10.

Figure 9.10
Display modification for callers and callees with equal depth value (Qsd = Psd)

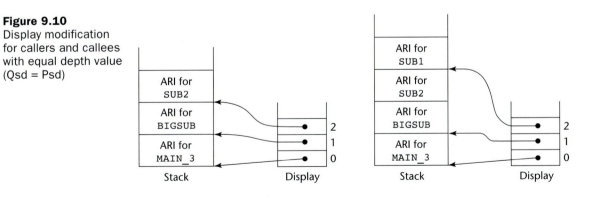

(a) MAIN_3 calls BIGSUB; BIGSUB calls SUB2   (b) SUB2 calls SUB1

ARI = activation record instance

Figure 9.11
Display modifications
for callers with smaller
depth values than the
callee (Qsd < Psd)

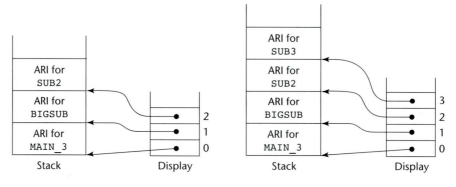

(a) MAIN calls BIGSUB; BIGSUB calls SUB2   (b) SUB2 calls SUB3

ARI = activation record instance

The call, as always, requires that the new activation record instance for
SUB1 be added to the stack. The new referencing environment includes
only SUB1, BIGSUB, and MAIN_3. Because the static_depth values of SUB1
and SUB2 are equal, their display links must occupy the same position in
the display; that is, their display offsets must be equal. Because the display
links are always saved in the new activation record instance, this is no problem. In this case, therefore, the display entry for SUB2 must be removed.
The new display entry for SUB1 is then inserted into its proper position,
which is position 2, the static_depth of SUB1. When SUB1 completes its execution and returns control to SUB2, the display entry for SUB2 must be restored. Just before the activation record instance for SUB1 is removed from
the stack, the saved display entry is moved from the instance to the display.

The second case would occur if SUB2 called SUB3. The static_depth
value of SUB2 is 2, and for SUB3 it is 3. The stack and display for the situations just before the call and just after the call are shown in Figure 9.11.

In this case, the new activation record instance is created on the stack,
as usual, but the referencing environment simply grows by one new scope,
that of the called subprogram. Thus the new pointer can be simply added
to the display. This particular example does not require that the existing
pointer in the display at the position of the new pointer be saved.
However, this is not true in general. Other situations of the same case do
require that the existing display pointer be saved. It is easier simply to save
the existing pointer each time than it is to determine at every subprogram
call whether it must be saved. As an example of a situation in which the
pointer must be saved, suppose there were a subprogram, SUB4, defined in
SUB1 in our example, as shown below:

```
program MAIN_4;
   procedure BIGSUB;
      procedure SUB1;
```

```
        procedure SUB4;
          ...
          end;  { SUB4 }
        ...
        end;  { SUB1 }
    procedure SUB2;
      procedure SUB3;
        ...
        end;  { SUB3 }
      ...
      end;  { SUB2 }
    ...
    end;  { BIGSUB }
end.  { MAIN_4 }
```

Suppose execution produced the following sequence of subprogram calls:

MAIN_4 calls BIGSUB
BIGSUB calls SUB2
SUB2 calls SUB3
SUB3 calls SUB1

The result would be the stack and display contents shown in Figure 9.12.

Now suppose SUB1 calls SUB4. This is an example of a subprogram calling a subprogram with a larger static_depth. In this case, the display pointer for SUB3 is at the position where SUB4's pointer must be placed in the display. They both have a static_depth of 3. Therefore, the existing display pointer must be saved before the new pointer is placed in the display. The correct stack and display for the execution of SUB4 are shown in Figure 9.13.

Figure 9.12
Stack and display before SUB1 calls SUB4 in MAIN_4; dashed lines indicate inactive pointers

Figure 9.13
Stack and display after SUB1 calls SUB4 in program MAIN_4 (Qsd < Psd)

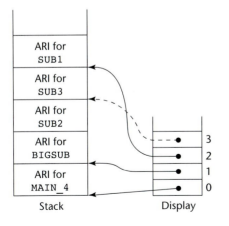

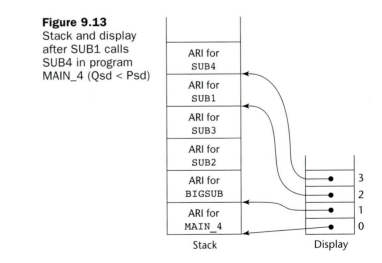

ARI = activation record instance

ARI = activation record instance

The third case (Qsd > Psd) is illustrated by a call to SUB1 from SUB3. The procedure SUB3 has a static_depth of 3, and that of SUB1 is 2. The stack and display values for just before the call and just after the call are shown in Figure 9.14.

In this case, it appears that two display elements must be temporarily removed: those for SUB2 and SUB3, which are not in the referencing environment of SUB1. However, only one must actually be removed, the one for SUB2. The pointer for SUB3 can remain in the display. Variable references in SUB1 will not use the SUB3 display pointer because the SUB3 variables are not visible to SUB1; thus it is safe to leave the pointer in the display. The compiler will not generate code that will access display entries above the entry for the current active subprogram.

The display can be stored as a static array in memory. The maximum size of the display, which is the maximum static_depth of any subprogram in the program, can be determined by the compiler. Storing the display in memory works reasonably well as long as the machine provides indirect addressing through memory locations. Nonlocal accesses, then, cost one more memory cycle than local accesses, which can use direct addressing. An alternative is to place the display in registers, assuming the machine has a sufficient number of spare registers. In this case, accesses do not require the extra memory cycle.

We can now compare the static chaining and display methods. In an implementation such as we have described, it may appear that references to local variables would be slower with a display than with static chains if the display is not stored in registers, because all references must go through display entries, a process that adds a level of indirection. This indirection can be avoided, however, so the cost of accessing locals is the same for the two methods.

Figure 9.14
Display modification for callers with larger depth values than their callees (Qsd > Psd)

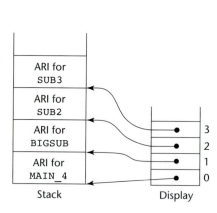
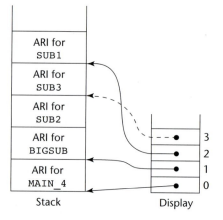

(a) MAIN_4 calls BIGSUB; BIGSUB calls SUB2; SUB2 calls SUB3

(b) SUB3 calls SUB1

ARI = activation record instance

References to nonlocals that are only one static level away take the same time for both methods, but if they are more than one static level away, they will be faster with a display because no chain must be followed. The task of estimating the time required for a nonlocal reference is trivial when a display is used—the time is equal for all nonlocal references. For time-critical code, this is an advantage of displays over static chains.

The maintenance at a subprogram call is faster with static chains, unless the called procedure is more than a few static levels away. In that case, extra time is required to follow the static chain of the caller to the activation record instance of the declarer of the called subprogram. The maintenance of a subprogram return has fixed cost with both methods, with static chaining always being slightly faster. The display must be restored when the subprogram terminates.

Overall, displays are better if there are many references to distant nonlocal variables. Static chaining is better if there are few references to distant nonlocal variables, which is the more common situation. Experiments indicate that nesting levels rarely exceed three in practice.

9.4 Blocks

Recall from Chapter 4 that several languages, including Ada, C, C++, and Java, provide for user-specified local scopes for variables called blocks. As an example of a block, consider the following C code segment:

```c
{ int temp;
  temp = list[upper];
  list[upper] = list[lower];
  list[lower] = temp;
}
```

A block is specified in C as a segment of code that begins with one or more data definitions and is enclosed in braces. The lifetime of the variable `temp` in the block above begins when control enters the block and ends when control exits the block. The advantage of using such a local is that it cannot interfere with any other variable with the same name that is declared elsewhere in the program.

Blocks can be implemented by using the process we described for implementing Pascal subprograms. Blocks are treated as parameterless subprograms that are always called from the same place in the program. If blocks are implemented this way using the display method, one disadvantage is that as maximum nesting grows, required display size grows along with it. A display must be limited in size if it is to be stored in registers. So requiring display cells for blocks can cause the display to be stored in memory rather than in registers, causing considerable slowing of references to nonlocal variables.

Blocks can also be implemented in a different and somewhat simpler way. The maximum amount of storage required for block variables at any time during the execution of a program can be statically determined, because blocks are entered and exited in strictly textual order. This amount of space can be allocated after the local variables in the activation record. Offsets for all block variables can be statically computed, so block variables can be addressed exactly as if they were local variables.

For example, consider the following skeletal program:

```
main_5() {
  int x, y, z;
  while ( ... ) {
    int a, b, c;
    ...
    while ( ... ) {
      int d, e;
      ...
    }
  }
  while ( ... ) {
    int f, g;
    ...
  }
  ...
}
```

For this program, the static memory layout shown in Figure 9.15 (on page 401) could be used. Note that f and g occupy the same memory locations as a and b, because a and b are popped off the stack when their block is exited (before f and g are allocated).

9.5 Implementing Dynamic Scoping

There are at least two distinct ways in which nonlocal references in a dynamic-scoped language can be implemented: deep access and shallow access. Note that deep access and shallow access are not concepts related to deep and shallow binding. The primary difference between binding and access here is that deep and shallow bindings result in different semantics; deep and shallow accesses do not.

9.5.1 Deep Access

When a program in a language that uses dynamic scoping refers to a non-local variable, the reference can be resolved by searching through the declarations in the other subprograms that are currently active, beginning with the one most recently activated. This concept is somewhat similar to

Figure 9.15
Block variable storage
when blocks are not
treated as parameter-
less procedures

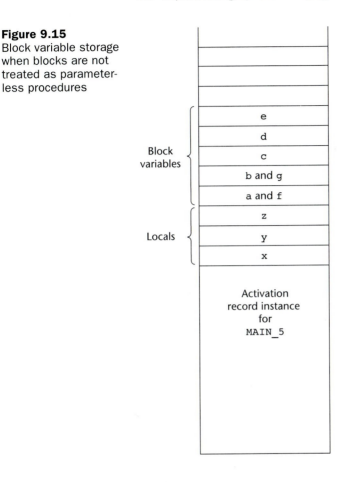

that of accessing nonlocal variables in a static-scoped language, except that
the dynamic—rather than the static—chain is followed. The dynamic chain
links together all subprogram activation record instances in the reverse of
the order in which they were activated. Therefore, the dynamic chain is
exactly what is needed to reference nonlocal variables in a dynamic-
scoped language. This method is called **deep access** because access may
require searches deep in the stack.

Consider the following example program:

```
procedure C;
   integer x, z;
   begin
   x := u + v;
   ...
   end;
procedure B;
   integer w, x;
   begin
```

```
    ...
    end;
  procedure A;
    integer v, w;
    begin
    ...
    end;
  program MAIN_6;
    integer v, u;
    begin
    ...
    end;
```

This program is written in a syntax that gives it the appearance of a program in an ALGOL-like language, but it is not meant to be in any particular language. Suppose the following sequence of procedure calls occurs:

MAIN_6 calls A
A calls A
A calls B
B calls C

Figure 9.16
Stack contents for a dynamic-scoped program

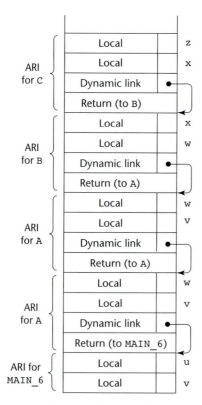

ARI = activation record instance

Figure 9.16 shows the stack during the execution of procedure C after this calling sequence. Notice that the activation record instances do not have static links, which would serve no purpose in a dynamic-scoped language.

Consider the references to the variables x, u, and v in procedure C. The reference to x is found in the activation record instance for C. The reference to u is found by searching *all* of the activation record instances on the stack, because the only existing variable with that name is in MAIN_6. This involves following four dynamic links and examining ten variable names. The reference to v is found in the most recent (nearest on the dynamic chain) activation record instance for the procedure A.

There are two important differences between the deep access method for nonlocal access in a dynamic-scoped language and the static chain method for static-scoped languages. First, in a dynamic-scoped language, there is no way to determine at compile time the length of the chain that must be searched. Every activation record instance in the chain must be searched until the first instance of the variable is found. This is one reason why dynamic-scoped languages typically have slower execution speeds than static-scoped languages. Second, activation records must store the names of variables for the search process, whereas in static-scoped language implementations, only the values are required. (Names are not required for static scoping because all variables are represented by the chain_offset/local_offset pairs.)

9.5.2 Shallow Access

Shallow access is an alternative implementation method, not an alternative semantics. As stated above, the semantics of deep access and shallow access are identical. In the shallow access method, variables declared in subprograms are not stored in the activation records of those subprograms. Because with dynamic scoping there is at most one visible version of a variable of any specific name at a given time, a very different approach can be taken. One variation of shallow access is to have a separate stack for each variable name in a complete program. Every time a new variable with a particular name is created by a declaration at the beginning of a subprogram activation, the variable is given a cell on the stack for its name. Every reference to the name is to the variable on top of the stack associated with that name, because the top one is the most recently created. When a subprogram terminates, the lifetime of its local variables ends, and the stacks for those variable names are popped. This method allows very fast references to variables, but maintaining the stacks at the entrances and exits of subprograms is costly.

Figure 9.17 shows the variable stacks for the above example program in the same situation as shown with the stack in Figure 9.16.

Another option for implementing shallow access is to use a central table that has a location for each different variable name in a program. Along with each entry, a bit called **active** is maintained that indicates whether the name has a current binding or variable association. Any access to any variable can then be to an offset into the central table. The offset is

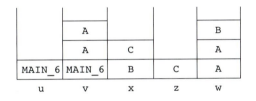

	A			B
	A	C		A
MAIN_6	MAIN_6	B	C	A
u	v	x	z	w

(The names in the stack cells indicate the program units of the variable declaration)

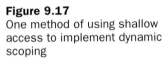

Figure 9.17
One method of using shallow access to implement dynamic scoping

static, so the access can be fast. SNOBOL implementations use the central table implementation technique.

Maintenance of a central table is straightforward. A subprogram call requires that all of its local variables be logically placed in the central table. If the position of the new variable in the central table is already active—that is, if it contains a variable whose lifetime has not yet ended (which is indicated by the active bit)—that value must be saved somewhere during the lifetime of the new variable. Whenever a variable begins its lifetime, the active bit in its central table position must be set.

There have been several variations in the design of the central table and in the way values are stored when they are temporarily replaced. One variation is to have a "hidden" stack on which all saved objects are stored. Because subprogram calls and returns, and thus the lifetimes of local variables, are nested, this works well.

The second variation is perhaps the cleanest and least expensive to implement. A central table of single cells is used, storing only the current version of each variable name. Replaced variables are stored in the activation record of the subprogram that created the replacement variable. This is a stack mechanism, but one that already exists, so the new overhead is minimal.

The choice between shallow and deep access to nonlocal variables depends on the relative frequencies of subprogram calls and nonlocal references. The deep access method provides fast subprogram linkage, but references to nonlocals, especially references to distant nonlocals (in terms of the call chain), are costly. The shallow access method provides much faster references to nonlocals, especially distant nonlocals, but is more costly in terms of subprogram linkage.

9.6 Implementing Parameters That Are Subprogram Names

Parameters that are subprogram names were discussed at length in Chapter 8. Recall that static-scoped languages use a method called deep binding to associate a referencing environment with the activation of a subprogram that was passed as a parameter. We now investigate how deep binding can be implemented using the static chain and display methods.

9.6.1 Static Chaining

Suppose static chaining is used in the implementation. A subprogram that passes a subprogram name as a parameter must have in its static ancestry the unit in which that subprogram was declared; if it does not, the name of the subprogram to be passed will not be visible, and the compiler will detect this as a syntax error. So, for syntactically correct calls, the compiler can simply pass the link to the static parent of the subprogram to be passed, along with the subprogram name. The activation record instance of the subprogram that is passed is then initialized with this link in its static link field, instead of a link derived in the usual way. Terminating the passed subprogram does not require any actions different from those for any other subprogram activation.

9.6.2 Displays

Now suppose a display, rather than static chaining, is used. Recall that we specifically stated that the display maintenance process described in Section 9.3.4.2 was correct only when there were no subprogram name parameters and no pass-by-name parameters. Display maintenance for subprogram calls without these requires only the replacement of a single display pointer. When the call is to a subprogram that has been passed as a parameter, pointers to all of the static ancestors of that subprogram must be placed in the display, thus requiring that that number of old display pointers be saved. Because the static environment of an activation of a subprogram that has been passed as a parameter may have little relationship to the static environment of the subprogram in which it is called, in many cases several display pointers must be replaced. In some implementations, the entire existing display is saved for every call to a subprogram that has been passed as a parameter, often in the activation record instance of the subprogram in execution. When the passed subprogram terminates, the complete saved display replaces the display used for the passed subprogram's execution.

9.6.3 Referencing Environment Confusion Revisited

We can now expand our discussion of a problem introduced in Chapter 8: the possible misunderstanding concerning which referencing environment is correct when a subprogram that was passed as a parameter is executed. For example, consider the following skeletal program, which is a variation of one found in Ghezzi and Jazayeri (1987):

```
program MAIN_7;
  procedure SUB1;
    begin   { SUB1 }
    ...
    end;   { SUB1 }
  procedure SUB2(procedure SUBX);
    var SUM : real;
```

```
procedure SUB3;
  begin  { SUB3}
  SUM := 0.0;
  ...
  end;  { SUB3 }
begin  { SUB2 }
SUBX;
SUB2 (SUB3);
...
  end;  { SUB2 }
begin { MAIN_7 }
...
SUB2(SUB1);
...
end.  { MAIN_7 }
```

MAIN_7 calls SUB2, sending SUB1 as a parameter. SUB2 then calls the passed procedure, SUB1. Upon return from SUB1, SUB2 calls itself, sending its own procedure, SUB3, as a parameter. There are now two instances of the activation record for SUB2 on the stack, with the topmost being for the recursive call. The topmost activation of SUB2 then calls SUB3. When SUB3 uses the variable SUM, there are two versions of it, one for each activation of SUB2, where it is declared. Because the referencing environment of SUB3 is that of the caller that sent SUB3 as a parameter, it is the first activation of SUB2, not the most recent. This is indeed not apparent to the casual reader of the program.

This is admittedly a contrived example. However, the same kind of situation could occur in more realistic programs. The problem is that, although intuitively it may seem that the most recent activation should be the referencing environment, that is not always the case.

Figure 9.18 shows the stack during the execution of SUB3 of the preceding example program.

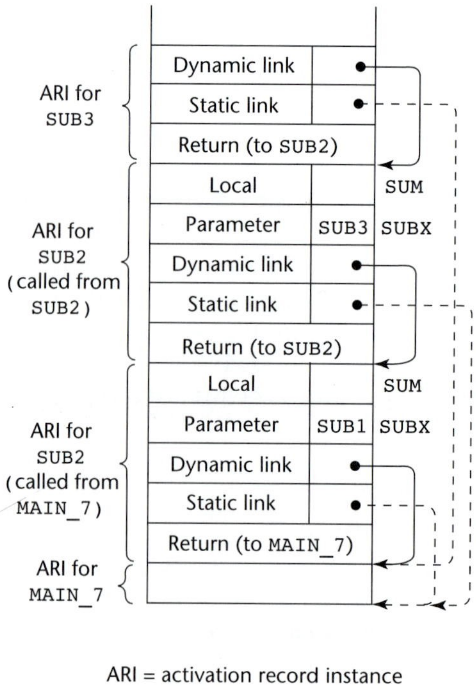

Figure 9.18
Stack contents for the example program MAIN_7, with a parameter that is a subprogram (SUB1 was called, but has completed its execution)

ARI = activation record instance

SUMMARY

Subprogram linkage semantics requires many actions by the implementation. In the case of FORTRAN 77, these actions are relatively simple for the following reasons: the lack of nonlocal references, other than through COMMON; the fact that local variables are usually static; and the absence of recursion. In the ALGOL-like languages, subprogram linkage is far more complex. This follows from the requirements of nonlocal accesses through static scoping, stack-dynamic local variables, and recursion.

Subprograms in ALGOL-like languages have two components: the actual code, which is static, and the activation record, which is stack-dynamic. Activation record instances contain the formal parameters and local variables, among other things.

Static chains and displays are the two primary methods of implementing accesses to nonlocal variables in static-scoped languages. In both methods, access paths can be statically established to variables in all static ancestor scopes.

Access to nonlocal variables in a dynamic-scoped language can be implemented by use of the dynamic chain or through some central variable table method. Dynamic chains provide slow accesses but fast calls and returns. The central table methods provide fast accesses but slow calls and returns.

Parameters that are subprograms provide a useful service but are sometimes difficult to understand. The opaqueness lies in the referencing environment that is available when a subprogram that has been passed as a parameter is executing. Subprograms that are passed as parameters can be implemented with either static chains or displays.

BIBLIOGRAPHIC NOTES

Implementation of both static and dynamic scoping is covered in Pratt (1984) and Ghezzi and Jazayeri (1987), but it is discussed more thoroughly in books on compiler design, such as Fischer and LeBlanc (1988).

REVIEW QUESTIONS

1. What are the four reasons why implementing subprograms in ALGOL-like languages is more difficult than implementing subprograms in a language like FORTRAN 77?

2. What is the difference between an activation record and an activation record instance?

3. Why are the return address, static link, dynamic link, and parameters placed in the bottom of the activation record?

4. What are the two steps in locating a nonlocal variable in a static scoped language, regardless of what method is used?

5. Define *static chain*, *static_depth*, *nesting_depth*, and *chain_offset*.

6. Explain how a reference to a nonlocal variable is found when static chains are used.

7. What are the two potential problems with the static chain method?

8. What is a display?

9. Explain how a reference to a nonlocal variable is found when a display is used.

10. How are references to variables represented in the static chain method? How are they represented in the display method?

11. What changes are required to the display when a subprogram is called (assume there are no pass-by-name parameters and no parameters that are subprograms)?

12. Compare the efficiency of the static chain and display methods for local accesses, nonlocal accesses, returns, and overall.

13. Explain the two methods of implementing blocks.

14. Describe the deep access method of implementing dynamic scoping.

15. Describe the shallow access method of implementing dynamic scoping.

16. What are the two differences between the deep access method for nonlocal access in dynamic-scoped languages and the static chain method for static-scoped languages?

17. Compare the efficiency of the deep access method to that of the shallow access method, in terms of both calls and nonlocal accesses.

18. Describe a method of implementing parameters that are subprograms when the static chaining implementation technique is used.

19. Describe a method of implementing parameters that are subprograms when the display implementation technique is used.

20. In a language that allows parameters that are subprogram names, is the correct activation record instance of a static parent always the nearest instance of the parent that is currently in the stack?

PROBLEM SET

1. Write an algorithm to perform the display maintenance required upon entry to a subprogram in a language that uses static scoping and also allows subprogram names as parameters.

2. Write an algorithm to perform the display maintenance required upon exit from a subprogram in a language that uses static scoping and also allows subprogram names as parameters.

3. Show the stack with all activation record instances, including static and dynamic chains, when execution reaches position 1 in the following skeletal program. Assume BIGSUB is at level 1.

```
procedure BIGSUB;
  procedure A;
    procedure B;
      begin   { B }
      ... <——————————1
      end;   { B }
    procedure C;
      begin   { C }
      ...
      B;
      ...
      end;   { C }
    begin   { A }
    ...
    C;
    ...
    end;   { A }
  begin   { BIGSUB }
  ...
  A;
  ...
  end;   { BIGSUB }
```

4. For the skeletal program in Problem 3, show the display that would be active at position 1, along with the activation record instances on the stack.

5. Show the stack with all activation record instances, including static and dynamic chains, when execution reaches position 1 in the following skeletal program. Assume BIGSUB is at level 1.

```
procedure BIGSUB;
  procedure C; forward;
  procedure A(flag: boolean);
    procedure B;
      ...
      A(false)
      end;   { B }
    begin   { A }
    if flag
      then B
      else C
    ...
    end;   { A }
  procedure C;
    procedure D;
      ... <——————————1
      end;   { D }
    ...
    D
    end;   { C }
  A(true);
  ...
  end;   { BIGSUB }
```

The calling sequence for this program for execution to reach D is

BIGSUB calls A

A calls B

B calls A

A calls C

C calls D

6. For the skeletal program in Problem 5, show the display that would be active at position 1, along with the activation record instances on the stack.

7. Although local variables in Pascal procedures are dynamically allocated at the beginning of each activation, under what circumstances could the value of a local in a particular activation retain the value of the previous activation?

8. It is stated in this chapter that when nonlocal variables are accessed in a dynamic-scoped language using the dynamic chain, variable names must be stored in the activation records with the values. If this were actually done, every nonlocal access would require a sequence of costly string comparisons on names. Design an alternative to these string comparisons that would be faster.

9. Pascal allows gotos with nonlocal targets. How could such statements be handled if static chains were used for nonlocal variable access? *Hint:* Consider the way the correct activation record instance of the static parent of a newly enacted procedure is found (see Section 9.3.4.1).

10. Repeat Problem 9, using a display instead of static chains.

11. How could the display mechanism described in this chapter be modified to make local variables accessible without indirect addressing?

12. The static chain method could be expanded slightly by using two static links in each activation record instance, where the second points to the static grandparent activation record instance. How would this affect the time required for subprogram linkage and nonlocal references?

10 Abstract Data Types

Ole-Johan Dahl

Ole-Johan Dahl and Kristen Nygaard, then both at the Norwegian Computing Center, were primarily interested in computer simulation. Driven by their needs in simulation, they designed and implemented the simulation languages SIMULA in 1964, and SIMULA 67 in 1967.

In this chapter, we explore programming language support for data abstraction, from its origins in SIMULA 67 to its form in contemporary languages. Among the new ideas of the last 25 years in programming methodologies and programming language design, data abstraction is one of the most profound.

We begin by discussing the general concept of abstraction in programming and programming languages. Next we introduce and discuss encapsulation in programming languages. Data abstraction is then defined and illustrated with an example. This is followed by a brief description of the partial support for data abstraction in SIMULA 67. Full linguistic support for data abstraction is discussed in terms of two specific languages: Ada and C++. An implementation of the same example data abstraction is shown in each of these languages. This illuminates the similarities and differences in the design of the language facilities that support data abstraction. Modula-2 support for data abstraction is briefly discussed as an alternative to Ada. Likewise, Java support for data abstraction is briefly discussed as an alternative to C++. Finally, the capabilities in Ada and C++ to build parameterized abstract data types are discussed.

Note that in this book, the phrases *data abstraction* and *abstract data types* refer to the same concept.

10.1 The Concept of Abstraction

An abstraction is a view or representation of an entity that includes only the attributes of significance in a particular context. Abstraction allows one to collect instances of entities into groups in which their common attributes need not be considered. These common attributes are abstracted away. Within the groups, only the attributes that distinguish the individual elements need be considered. This results in significant simplification of the elements in the group. Less abstract views of these entities must be considered when it is necessary to see a higher level of detail. Abstraction is a weapon against the complexity of programming; its purpose is to simplify the programming process. It is an effective weapon because it allows programmers to focus on essential attributes and ignore subordinate attributes.

The two fundamental kinds of abstraction in contemporary programming languages are process abstraction and data abstraction.

The concept of **process abstraction** is among the oldest in programming language design. Even Plankalkül supported process abstraction. All subprograms are process abstractions because they provide a way for a program to specify that some process is to be done, without providing the details of how it is to be done (at least in the calling program). For example, when a program needs to sort an array of numeric data objects of some type, it usually uses a subprogram for the sorting process. At the point where the sorting process is required, a statement such as

```
sort_int(list, list_len)
```

is placed in the program. This call is an abstraction of the actual sorting process, whose algorithm is not specified. The call is independent of the algorithm implemented in the called subprogram.

In the case of the subprogram `sort_int`, the only essential attributes are the name of the array to be sorted, the type of its elements, the array's length, and the fact that the call to `sort_int` will result in the array being sorted. The particular algorithm that `sort_int` implements is an attribute that is not essential to the user.

Process abstraction is crucial to the programming process. The ability to abstract away many of the details of algorithms in subprograms makes it possible to construct, read, and understand large programs. Remember that to be considered a large program now, the program must have at least several hundred thousand lines of code.

All subprograms, including concurrent subprograms (discussed in Chapter 12) and exception handlers (discussed in Chapter 13), are process abstractions.

The evolution of data abstraction necessarily followed that of process abstraction, because an integral and central part of every data abstraction is its operations, which are defined as process abstractions.

10.2 Encapsulation

Preliminary to introducing abstract data types, we must discuss encapsulation, a precursor of and support mechanism for abstract data types.

When the size of a program reaches beyond a few thousand lines, two practical problems appear. From the programmer's point of view, having such a program appear as a single collection of subprograms does not impose an adequate level of organization on the program to keep it intellectually manageable. One solution is to organize the program into syntactic containers that include groups of logically related subprograms and data. These syntactic containers are often called **modules,** and the process of designing them is called **modularization.** The second practical problem for larger programs is recompilation. In the case of a small program, recompiling the whole program after each modification is not costly. But when programs grow beyond a few thousand lines, the cost of recompilation ceases to be insignificant. So there is an obvious need to find ways to avoid recompilation of the parts of a program that are not affected by a change. This can be provided by organizing programs into collections of subprograms and data, each of which can be compiled without recompilation of the rest of the program. Such a collection is called a **compilation unit.**

An **encapsulation** is a grouping of subprograms and the data they manipulate. An encapsulation, which is either separately or independently compilable, provides an abstracted system and a logical organization for a collection of related computations. Therefore, an encapsulation solves both of the practical problems described above.

Encapsulations are often placed in libraries and made available for reuse in programs other than those for which they were written.

People have been writing programs with more than a few thousand lines for over 40 years, so techniques for providing encapsulations have been evolving for some time.

In many of the ALGOL-like languages, programs can be organized by nesting subprogram definitions inside the logically larger subprograms that use them. As discussed in Chapter 4, this method of organizing programs, which uses static scoping, is far from ideal. Furthermore, in some languages subprograms are not compilation units. Therefore, subprograms do not make good encapsulation constructs.

In FORTRAN 77, subprograms can be collected into files and be independently compiled and placed in libraries. Collections of COMMON block definitions can also be handled this way. This is an effective organization technique, but no interface checking is done when these encapsulations are used, so this approach is inherently unsafe.

In C, a collection of related functions and data definitions can be placed in a file, which can be independently compiled. Although C compilation systems now check the correctness of the interfaces of properly defined functions, they still do not type check data definitions from different files. (By "properly defined" we mean that the pre-ANSI C function headers are not used.) So C files also do not make safe encapsulations.

Many contemporary languages, including FORTRAN 90 and Ada, provide the ability to gather collections of subprograms, types, and data into units that can be compiled separately, meaning that their interface information is saved by the compiler and used for interface type checking when used by another unit. These languages also include access control mechanisms for the entities in these units. This allows the unit to have some type names that are visible to outside units, while having the representation of those types visible only to other entities in the unit. These units make perfect encapsulations. They not only support a concise and logical program organization, but they also make that organization obvious to readers of the program.

The characteristics of the encapsulation facilities in SIMULA 67, Ada, and C++ are discussed in conjunction with abstract data types in Section 10.5.

10.3 Introduction to Data Abstraction

An abstract data type, simply put, is an encapsulation that includes only the data representation of one specific data type and the subprograms that provide the operations for that type. Through access control, unnecessary details of the type can be hidden from units outside the encapsulation that use the type. Program units that use an abstract data type can declare variables of that type, even though the actual representation is hidden from them. An instance of an abstract data type is called an **object.**

One of the motivations for data abstraction is similar to that of process abstraction. It is a weapon against complexity, a means of making large and/or complicated programs more manageable. Other motivations for and advantages of abstract data types are discussed later in this section. Just as the presence of process abstraction allows a very different program design methodology, the availability of data abstraction does also.

In the last few years, a new methodology for software development has become increasingly popular—object-oriented programming. Object-oriented programming, which is described in Chapter 11, is an outgrowth of the use of data abstraction in software development, and data abstraction is one of its most important components.

10.3.1 Floating-Point as an Abstract Data Type

The concept of abstract data types, at least in terms of built-in types, is not a recent development. All built-in data types, even those of FORTRAN I, are abstract data types, although they are rarely called that. For example, consider a floating-point data type. Most languages include at least one of these, which provides a means of creating variables for floating-point data and also provides a set of arithmetic operations for manipulating objects of the type.

Floating-point types in high-level languages employ a key concept in data abstraction: information hiding. The actual format of the data value in a floating-point memory cell is hidden from the user. The only operations available are those provided by the language. The user is not allowed to create new operations on data of the type, except those that can be constructed using the built-in operations. The user cannot directly manipulate the parts of the actual representation of floating-point objects because that representation is hidden. It is this feature that allows program portability between implementations of a particular language, even though the implementations may use different representations of floating-point values.

10.3.2 User-Defined Abstract Data Types

The concept of user-defined abstract data types *is* a relatively recent one. A user-defined abstract data type should provide the same characteristics provided by floating-point types: (1) a type definition that allows program units to declare variables of the type but hides the representation of these variables, and (2) a set of operations for manipulating objects of the type.

We now formally define an abstract data type in the context of user-defined types. An **abstract data type** is a data type that satisfies the following two conditions:

- The representation, or definition, of the type and the operations on objects of the type are contained in a single syntactic unit. Also, other program units may be allowed to create variables of the defined type.

- The representation of objects of the type is hidden from the program units that use the type, so the only direct operations possible on those objects are those provided in the type's definition.

Program units that use a specific abstract data type are called **clients** of that type.

The primary advantages of packaging the representation and operations in a single syntactic unit are the same as those of encapsulation. It provides a method of organizing a program into logical units that can be compiled separately. Furthermore, it allows modifications on the representations or operations of the type to be done in a single area of the program. There are several advantages to hiding representation details. The most important of these is clients are not able to "see" the representation details, and thus their code cannot depend on that representation. This results in representations that can be changed at any time without requiring changes to the clients. The interface for the abstraction represents some, but not all, of its attributes.

Another distinct and important benefit of information hiding is increased reliability. Clients cannot change the underlying representations of objects directly, either intentionally or by accident, thus increasing the integrity of such objects. Objects can be changed only through the provided operations. It is difficult to overstate the importance of hiding the representation details of an abstract data type.

10.3.3 An Example

Suppose an abstract data type is to be constructed for a stack that has the following abstract operations:

create(stack)	Creates and possibly initializes a stack object
destroy(stack)	Deallocates the storage for the stack
empty(stack)	A predicate (or Boolean) function that returns true if the specified stack is empty and false if otherwise
push(stack, element)	Pushes the specified element on the specified stack
pop(stack)	Removes the top element from the specified stack

top(stack)   Returns a copy of the top element from the specified stack

Note that some implementation designs of abstract data types do not require the create and destroy operations. For example, simply defining a variable to be of an abstract data type may implicitly create the underlying data structure and initialize it.

A client of the stack type could have a code sequence such as the following:

```
...
create(STK1);
push(STK1, COLOR1);
push(STK1, COLOR2);
if(not empty(STK1))
  then TEMP := top(STK1);
...
```

Suppose that the original implementation of the stack abstraction uses an adjacency representation (one that implements stacks in arrays). At a later time, because of memory management problems with the adjacency representation, it is changed to a linked list representation. Because data abstraction was used, this change can be made in the code that defines the stack type, but no changes will be required in any of the clients of the stack abstraction. In particular, the code sequence above does not need to be changed. Of course, a change in protocol of any of the operations would require changes in the clients.

If the stack were not implemented as an abstract data type, such a change would require clients of the stack type be modified to conform to the new representation. Suppose, for example, that the stack operations had been implemented in Ada to operate on arrays. The change to linked list representation would require that clients be modified to send pointers instead of array names as parameters to the stack operation procedures. In this case, the protocol of some of the operations *must* be changed, thereby forcing changes in the clients.

In summary, the goal of data abstraction is to allow programs to define data types that have the characteristics and behavior of built-in types.

10.4 Design Issues

A facility for defining abstract data types in a language must provide a syntactic unit that can encapsulate the type definition and subprogram definitions of the abstraction operations. It must be possible to make the type name and subprogram headers visible to clients of the abstraction. This allows clients to declare variables of the abstract type and manipulate their values. Although the type name must have external visibility, the type definition must be hidden. The same is often true for subprogram definitions—the headers must be visible but the bodies may be hidden.

Few, if any, general built-in operations should be provided for objects of abstract data types, other than those provided with the type definition. There simply are not many operations that apply to a broad range of possible abstract data types. Among these are assignment and comparisons for equality and inequality. If the language does not allow users to overload assignment, it must be built in. Comparisons for equality and inequality should be predefined in some cases but not in others. For example, if the type is a pointer, equality may mean pointer equality, but the user may want it to mean equality of the structures pointed to by the pointers.

Some operations are required by most abstract data types, but because they are not universal they must be provided by the designer of the type. Among these are iterators, constructors, and destructors. Iterators were discussed in Chapter 7. Constructors are used to initialize parts of newly created objects. Destructors are used to reclaim heap storage that may be used by parts of abstract data type objects.

As stated earlier, an abstract data type encapsulates a single data type and its operations. Concurrent Pascal (Brinch Hansen, 1975), Smalltalk (Goldberg and Robson, 1983), C++, and Java directly support abstract data types. The alternative to this is to provide a more generalized construct that can define any number of entities, any of which can be selectively specified to be visible outside the enclosing unit. This is the approach of Modula-2 and Ada. We have called these constructs encapsulations. Encapsulations are not abstract data types, but rather are generalizations of abstract data types. As such, they can be used to define abstract data types.

The primary design issues beyond encapsulation include the following: The first is whether the kinds of types that can be abstract should be restricted. Restricting them can have some advantages. In particular, if only pointers can be abstract, a great deal of recompilation can be avoided in the software development process. On the other hand, some consider this a severe restriction because of its disadvantages. Another design issue is whether abstract data types can be parameterized. For example, if the language supports parameterized abstract data types, one could design an abstract data type for queues that could store elements of any scalar type. Parameterized abstract data types are discussed in Section 10.6. Finally, there is the issue of what access controls are provided, and how such controls are specified.

10.5 Language Examples

In this section, we describe the support for data abstraction provided by SIMULA 67, Ada, C++, and Java.

10.5.1 SIMULA 67 Classes

The first language facilities for the direct support of data abstraction, although incomplete by our definition, appeared in the class construct in SIMULA 67.

10.5.1.1 Encapsulation

A SIMULA 67 class definition is a description of a type. Instances, or objects of a class, are created dynamically on the heap at the request of the user program and can be referenced only with pointer variables. Class objects are therefore heap-dynamic.

The general syntactic form of a SIMULA 67 class definition is

```
class class_name;
  begin
  -- class variable declarations --
  -- class subprogram definitions --
  -- class code section --
  end class_name;
```

The code section of a class definition is executed only once, at object creation time. It serves as the constructor for the class and as such is used for initialization of the variables defined in the class.

SIMULA 67's contribution to data abstraction is the encapsulation capability of the class construct. Interestingly, the significance of this aspect of classes was not recognized until several years after the design of SIMULA 67 was completed. The importance of data abstraction was not generally understood until the early 1970s.

10.5.1.2 Information Hiding

The variables that are declared in a SIMULA 67 class are not hidden from the clients that create objects of that class. These variables can be accessed through the operations provided by the class subprograms or directly through their names. This violates the information hiding requirement of the definition of an abstract data type because multiple access paths to class entities are possible. The impact of this is that a SIMULA 67 class is far less reliable than a true abstract data type. Furthermore, because clients of the class can be designed to depend on the variable definitions in the class, changes to those variable definitions may require changes in the clients. This makes such programs more difficult to maintain.

10.5.1.3 Evaluation

The SIMULA 67 class construct provides encapsulation, but it does not provide information hiding, which allows representation details to be kept from the clients of the class.

SIMULA 67 was revolutionary in its development of the class construct. However, because the language never enjoyed widespread use, we included it here only for its historic interest. We now turn our attention to two contemporary languages that provide a complete support for data abstraction: Ada and C++.

10.5.2   Abstract Data Types in Ada

Ada provides encapsulation facilities that can be used to simulate abstract data types, including the ability to hide their representations.

10.5.2.1 Encapsulation

The encapsulating constructs in Ada are called **packages.** Packages can have two parts, each of which is also called a package. These are called the **specification package,** which provides the interface of the encapsulation, and the **body package,** which provides the implementation of the entities named in the specification. Not all packages have a body part (packages that encapsulate only data do not have or need bodies).

A specification package and its associated body package share the same name. The reserved word **body** in a package header identifies it as being a body package. Specification and body packages may be compiled separately, provided the specification package is compiled first.

10.5.2.2 Information Hiding

There are no restrictions on the kinds of types that can be defined in and exported from a specification package. The user can choose to make an entity entirely visible to clients or provide only the interface information. This is done by providing two sections of the specification package—one in which entities are visible to clients and one that hides its contents. For example, if a type is to be exported but have its representation hidden, an abbreviated declaration appears in the visible part of the specification, providing only the name of the type and the fact that its representation is hidden. The representation of the type appears in a part of the specification called the **private** part, which is introduced by the reserved word **private**. The private clause is always at the end of the specification.

Suppose a type named NODE_TYPE is to be exported by a package but its representation is to be hidden. NODE_TYPE is declared in the visible part of the specification package without its representation details, as in

```
type NODE_TYPE is private;
```

In the private clause, the declaration of NODE_TYPE is repeated, but this time with the complete type definition, as in

```
package LINKED_LIST_TYPE is
  type NODE_TYPE is private;
  ...
  private
    type NODE_TYPE;
    type PTR is access NODE_TYPE;
    type NODE_TYPE is
      record
      INFO : INTEGER;
      LINK : PTR;
      end record;
  end LINKED_LIST_TYPE;
```

If none of the entities in a package are to be hidden, there is no purpose or need for the private part of the specification.

The reason why a type's representation appears in the specification package at all has to do with compilation issues. A client can only see the specification package (not the body package), but the compiler must be able to allocate objects of the exported type when compiling the client. Furthermore, the client is compilable when only the specification package for the abstract data type is present. Therefore, the compiler must be able to determine the size of an object from the specification package. So the representation of the type must be visible to the compiler but not to the client code. This is exactly the situation specified by the private clause in a specification package.

Types that are declared to be private are called **private types.** Private data types have built-in operations for assignment and comparisons for equality and inequality. Any other operation must be declared in the specification package that defined the type.

An alternative to private types is a more restricted form, **limited private types.** Limited private types are described in the private section of a specification package, as are private types. The only syntactic difference is that limited private types are declared to be **limited private** in the visible part of the package specification. Objects of a type that is declared limited private have no built-in operations. Such a type is useful when the usual predefined operations of assignment and comparison are not meaningful or useful. For example, assignment and comparison are rarely used for stacks. If assignment or equality comparisons are required but the built-in versions are not useful, these operations must be provided by the specification package. The assignment operation must be in the form of a normal procedure, whereas the equal and not-equal operators can be provided by overloading those operators for the new type.

10.5.2.3 An Example

The following is the specification package for a stack abstract data type:

```
package STACKPACK is
-- The visible entities, or public interface
  type STACKTYPE is limited private;
  MAX_SIZE : constant := 100;
  function EMPTY(STK : in STACKTYPE) return BOOLEAN;
  procedure PUSH(STK : in out STACKTYPE;
 ELEMENT : in INTEGER);
  procedure POP(STK : in out STACKTYPE);
  function TOP(STK : in STACKTYPE) return INTEGER;
-- The part that is hidden from clients
  private
    type LIST_TYPE is array (1..MAX_SIZE) of INTEGER;
    type STACKTYPE is
      record
      LIST  : LIST_TYPE;
      TOPSUB : INTEGER range 0..MAX_SIZE := 0;
      end record;
  end STACKPACK;
```

Notice that no create or destroy operations are included because they are not necessary.

The body package for STACKPACK is

```
with TEXT_IO; use TEXT_IO;
package body STACKPACK is
  function EMPTY(STK: in STACKTYPE) return BOOLEAN is
    begin
    return STK.TOPSUB = 0
    end EMPTY;

  procedure PUSH(STK : in out STACKTYPE;
                 ELEMENT : in INTEGER) is
    begin
    if STK.TOPSUB >= MAX_SIZE then
      PUT_LINE("ERROR - Stack overflow");
    else
      STK.TOPSUB := STK.TOPSUB + 1;
      STK.LIST(TOPSUB) := ELEMENT;
    end if;
  end PUSH;

  procedure POP(STK : in out STACKTYPE) is
    begin
    if STK.TOPSUB = 0
      then PUT_LINE("ERROR - Stack underflow");
      else STK.TOPSUB := STK.TOPSUB - 1;
    end if;
    end POP;
```

```
      function TOP(STK : in STACKTYPE) return INTEGER is
        begin
        if STK.TOPSUB = 0
          then PUT_LINE("ERROR - Stack is empty");
          else return STK.LIST(STK.TOPSUB);
        end if;
        end TOP;
    end STACKPACK;
```

The first line of the code of this body package contains two statements: a **with** and a **use**. The **with** statement imports external packages, in this case TEXT_IO, which provides functions for input and output of text. The **use** statement eliminates the need for explicit qualification of the references to entities from the named package. This allows the use of the procedure PUT_LINE from TEXT_IO without explicit qualification (the code would have to use TEXT_IO.PUT_LINE() if the **use** were not included).

The body package must have subprogram definitions with headings that match the subprogram headings in the associated specification package. The specification package promises that these subprograms will be defined in the associated body package.

The following procedure, USE_STACKS, is a client of package STACK-PACK. It illustrates how the package might be used.

```
    with STACKPACK, TEXT_IO;
    use STACKPACK, TEXT_IO;
    procedure USE_STACKS is
      TOPONE : INTEGER;
      STACK : STACKTYPE;    -- Creates a STACKTYPE object
      begin
      PUSH(STACK, 42);
      PUSH(STACK, 17);
      TOPONE := TOP(STACK);
      POP(STACK);
      ...
      end USE_STACKS;
```

10.5.2.4 A Related Language: Modula-2

The modules of Modula-2 are similar to the packages of Ada, so they provide a similar level of support for abstract data types. The primary difference between the two languages in their support for abstract data types is that in Modula-2, all types whose representations are hidden in modules must be pointers. This restriction provides an alternative to the two-part specification packages of Ada. The size of all pointers is the same, so the compiler need not see a type's representation definition to allow creation of objects of the type in clients. Another advantage of this restriction is that client code never needs to be recompiled after modifications to the abstract type definition. The same is true for pointer abstract data types in

Ada. If an Ada abstract data type is not a pointer, however, client code must be recompiled when the type definition is modified. One disadvantage of Modula-2's restriction to pointers is the forced used of pointers, which introduce their own batch of insecurities. Compounding this problem is the fact that in Modula-2 pointers are not implicitly initialized to nil. This allows clients to declare a variable of an abstract data type and use it before it is set to point to an allocated cell in the heap.

10.5.3   Abstract Data Types in C++

C++ was created by adding features to C. The first important additions were those to support object-oriented programming. Because one of the primary components of object-oriented programming is abstract data types, C++ obviously must support them.

While Ada and Modula-2 provide encapsulation that can be used to simulate abstract data types, C++ provides the class, which more directly supports abstract data types. C++ classes are types; Ada packages and Modula-2 modules are not. Packages and modules are imported, allowing the importing unit to declare variables of any type defined in the package or module. In a C++ program, variables are declared to be of class types. So classes are much more like the built-in types than either packages or modules. A program unit that gains visibility to an Ada package or a Modula-2 module can access any of its public entities directly by their names. A C++ program unit that declares an instance of a class can also access any of the public entities in that class, but only through an instance of the class.

10.5.3.1 Encapsulation

The classes of C++ are based on the classes of SIMULA 67 and are an extension to the **struct** types of C. Because of its SIMULA 67 heritage, a C++ class is a description of a data type.

The data defined in a class are called **data members;** the functions defined in a class are called **member functions.** All of the instances of a class share a single set of member functions, but each instance gets its own set of the class's data members. Although class instances can also be static and heap-dynamic, we consider only stack-dynamic classes here. The instances of such classes are always created by elaboration of an object declaration. Furthermore, the lifetime of such a class instance ends when the end of the scope of its declaration is reached. Classes can have heap-dynamic data members, so that even though a class instance is stack-dynamic, it can include data members that are heap-dynamic and allocated from the heap. C++ provides the **new** and **delete** operators to manage the heap.

A member function of a class can be defined in two distinct ways: The complete definition can appear in the class, or only in its header. When both the header and the body of a member function appear in the class definition, the member function is implicitly inlined. Recall that this means that its code is placed in the caller's code, rather than requiring the usual call and return linkage process. If only the header of a member function appears in the class definition, its complete definition appears outside the class and is separately compiled. It is a good idea to have small member functions inlined, because they will not occupy much space in the client and the linkage time is saved.

10.5.3.2 Information Hiding

A C++ class can contain both hidden and visible entities. Entities that are to be hidden are placed in a **private** clause, and visible, or public, entities are written in a **public** clause. The **public** clause therefore describes the interface to class objects. There is also a third category of visibility, **protected**, which is discussed in the context of inheritance in Chapter 11.

C++ allows the user to include **constructor** functions in class definitions, which are used to initialize the data members of newly created objects. A constructor may also allocate the heap-dynamic data members of the new object. Constructors are implicitly called when an object of the class type is created. A constructor has the same name as the class of which it is a part, which looks odd but is harmless. There can be more than one constructor for a class, in which case they are obviously overloaded. Of course, each must have a unique parameter profile.

A C++ class can also include a function called a **destructor,** which is implicitly called when the lifetime of an instance of the class ends. All heap-dynamic objects live until explicitly deallocated with the **delete** operator. As stated above, stack-dynamic class instances can contain heap-dynamic data members. The destructor function for such an instance can include a **delete** operator on the heap-dynamic members to deallocate their heap space. Destructors are often used as a debugging aid, in which case they simply display or print the values of some or all of the object's data members before those members are deallocated. The name of a destructor is the class's name, preceded by a tilde (~).

Neither constructors nor destructors have return types, and neither use **return** statements. Both constructors and destructors can be explicitly called.

10.5.3.3 An Example

Our example of a C++ abstract data type is, once again, a stack:

```
#include <iostream.h>
class stack {
  private:  //** These members are visible only to other
            //** members and friends (see Section 10.5.3.4)
    int *stack_ptr;
```

```
       int max_len;
       int top_ptr;
    public:    //** These members are visible to clients
       stack() {
         stack_ptr = new int [100];   //** A constructor
         max_len = 99;
         top_ptr = -1;
       }
       ~stack() {delete [] stack_ptr;};   //** A destructor
       void push(int number) {
         if (top_ptr == max_len)
           cout << "Error in push—stack is full\n";
         else stack_ptr[++top_ptr] = number;
       }
       void pop() {
         if (top_ptr == -1)
           cout << "Error in pop—stack is empty\n";
         else top_ptr--;
       }
       int top() {return (stack_ptr[top_ptr]);}
       int empty() {return (top_ptr == -1);}
  }
```

We will discuss only a few of the aspects of this class definition, because it is not necessary to understand all of the details of the code. The #include is used to provide visibility to a standard input and output package, iostream, which includes the simple output stream used by the code, cout. The stack class has three data members—stack_ptr, max_len, and top_ptr—all of which are private. It also has four public member functions—push, pop, top, and empty—a constructor, and a destructor. The constructor uses the allocator operator **new** to allocate an array of 100 **int** elements from the heap. It also initializes max_len and top_ptr. The purpose of the destructor function is to deallocate the storage for the array used to implement the stack when the lifetime of a stack object ends. This array was allocated by the constructor. Because the bodies of the member functions are included, they are all implicitly inlined.

An example program that uses the C++ stack abstract data type is

```
  void main() {
    int top_one;
    stack stk;  //** Creates an instance of the stack class
    stk.push(42);
    stk.push(17);
    top_one = stk.top();
    stk.pop();
    ...
  }
```

When the end of this function is reached during execution, the lifetimes of the variables top_one and stk end, which results in the destructor for stk being implicitly called. This causes the array part of `stack` to be deallocated.

10.5.3.4 Evaluation

C++ support for abstract data types, through its class construct, is similar in expressive power to that of Ada, through its packages. Both provide effective mechanisms for encapsulation and information hiding of general types. The primary difference is that classes are types, whereas Ada packages are encapsulations. Furthermore, the class was designed for more than data abstraction, as discussed in Chapter 11.

One language design problem that results from having classes but no generalized encapsulation construct is that it is not always natural to associate object operations with single objects. For example, suppose we have an abstract data type for matrices and one for vectors and need a multiplication operation between a vector and a matrix. In which class should this operation appear? In the case of C++, these kinds of situations can be handled by allowing nonmember functions to be "friends" of a class. Friend functions have access to the private entities of the class where they are declared to be friends. For the matrix/vector multiplication operation, one C++ solution is to define the operation outside both the matrix and the vector classes, but define it to be a friend of both. The following skeletal code illustrates this scenario:

```
class Matrix;  //** A class declaration
class Vector {
  friend Vector multiply(const Matrix&, const Vector&);
  ...
};
class Matrix {  //** The class definition
  friend Vector multiply(const Matrix&, const Vector&);
  ...
};
//** The function that uses both Matrix and Vector objects
Vector multiply(const Matrix& m1, const Vector& v1) {
  ...
}
```

Both the matrix and the vector could be defined in an Ada package, thereby avoiding the problem.

In addition to functions, whole classes can be defined to be friends of a class; then all the private members of the class are visible to all of the members of the friend class.

10.5.3.5 A Related Language: Java

Java support for abstract data types is very similar to that of C++. There are, however, a few important differences. All user-defined data types in

Java are classes and all objects are allocated from the heap and accessed through reference variables. Another difference between the support for abstract data types in Java and that of C++ is that subprograms (methods) in Java can *only* be defined in classes. So one cannot have just function headers in Java classes.

Rather than having private and public clauses in its class definitions, in Java **private** and **public** are modifiers that can be attached to method and variable definitions.

While C++ depends on classes as their only encapsulation construct, Java includes a second one at a level above classes, the package. Packages can contain more than one class definition, and the classes in a package are partial friends of one another. Partial here means that the entities defined in a class in a package that either are public or protected (see Chapter 11) or have no access specifier are visible to all other classes in the package. Entities without access modifiers are said to have **package scope,** because they are visible throughout the package. Java therefore has less need for explicit friend declarations and does not include the friend functions or friend classes of C++. Packages, which often contain libraries, can be defined in hierarchies. The standard class libraries of Java are defined in a hierarchy of packages. Package scope is further discussed in Chapter 11.

The following is a Java class definition for our stack example:

```java
import java.io.*;
class Stack_class {
  private int [] stack_ref;
  private int max_len,
              top_index;
  public Stack_class() {  // A constructor
    stack_ref = new int [100];
    max_len = 99;
    top_index = -1;
  }
  public void push(int number) {
    if (top_index == max_len)
      System.out.println("Error in push—stack is full");
    else stack_ref[++top_index] = number;
  }
  public void pop() {
    if (top_index == -1)
      System.out.println("Error in pop—stack is empty");
    else --top_index;
  }
  public int top() {return (stack_ref[top_index]);}
  public boolean empty() {return (top_index == -1);}
}
```

An example class that uses `Stack_class` follows:

```
public class Tst_Stack {
  public static void main(String[] args) {
    Stack_class myStack = new Stack_class();
    myStack.push(42);
    myStack.push(29);
    System.out.println("29 is: " + myStack.top());
    myStack.pop();
    System.out.println("42 is: " + myStack.top());
    myStack.pop();
    myStack.pop();  // Produces an error message
  }
}
```

A stack is a silly example for Java because the Java library includes a class definition for stacks. However, our class definition for stacks allows us to compare a Java implementation with the C++ implementation in Section 10.5.3. One obvious difference is the lack of a destructor in the Java version, obviated by Java's implicit garbage collection. Another significant difference is the use of a reference variable, rather than a pointer, to refer to stack objects.

10.6 Parameterized Abstract Data Types

It is often convenient to parameterize abstract data types. For example, we should be able to design a stack abstract data type that can store any scalar type elements rather than be required to write a separate stack abstraction for every different scalar type. In the following two subsections, the capabilities of Ada and C++ to construct parameterized abstract data types are discussed.

10.6.1 Ada

Generic procedures in Ada were discussed and illustrated in Chapter 8. Packages can also be generic, so we can also construct generic, or parameterized, abstract data types.

The Ada stack abstract data type example shown in Section 10.5.2 suffers two restrictions: (1) Stacks of its type can store only integer type elements, and (2) the stacks can have only up to 100 elements. Both of these restrictions can be eliminated by using a generic package, which can be instantiated for other element types and any desirable size. (This is a generic instantiation, which is very different from the instantiation of a class to create an object.) The following specification package describes the interface of a generic stack abstract data type with these features:

```
generic
  MAX_SIZE : POSITIVE;   -- A generic parameter for stack size
  type ELEMENT_TYPE is private;   -- A generic parameter for
                                  -- element type
package GENERIC_STACK is
-- The visible entities, or public interface
  type STACKTYPE is limited private;
  function EMPTY(STK : in STACKTYPE) return BOOLEAN;
  procedure PUSH(STK : in out STACKTYPE;
                 ELEMENT : in ELEMENT_TYPE);
  procedure POP(STK : in out STACKTYPE);
  function TOP(STK : in STACKTYPE) return ELEMENT_TYPE;
-- The hidden part
private
  type LIST_TYPE is array (1..MAX_SIZE) of ELEMENT_TYPE;
  type STACKTYPE is
   record
   LIST : LIST_TYPE;
   TOPSUB : INTEGER range 0..MAX_SIZE := 0;
   end record;
  end GENERIC_STACK;
```

The body package for GENERIC_STACK is the same as the body package for
STACKPACK in the previous section except that the type of the ELEMENT formal parameter in PUSH and TOP is ELEMENT_TYPE instead of INTEGER.

The following statement instantiates GENERIC_STACK for a stack of 100
elements of INTEGER type:

```
package INTEGER_STACK is new GENERIC_STACK(100, INTEGER);
```

One could also build an abstract data type for a stack of length 500 for
FLOAT elements, as in

```
package FLOAT_STACK is new GENERIC_STACK(500, FLOAT);
```

These instantiations build two different source code versions of
GENERIC_STACK at compile time.

10.6.2 C++

C++ also supports parameterized, or generic, abstract data types. To make
the example C++ stack class of Section 10.5.3 generic in the stack size,
only the constructor function needs to be changed, as in

```
stack(int size) {
  stk_ptr = new int [size];
  max_len = size - 1;
  top = -1;
}
```

The declaration for a stack object now may appear as

```
stack(150) stk;
```

The class definition for **stack** can include both constructors, so users can use the default size stack or specify some other size.

The element type of the stack can be made a parameter by making the class a templated class. Then the element type can be a template parameter. The definition of the templated class for a stack type is

```
#include <iostream.h>
template <class Type>  // Type is the template parameter
class stack {
  private:
    Type *stack_ptr;
    int max_len;
    int top_ptr;
  public:
// A constructor for 100 element stacks
    stack() {
      stack_ptr = new Type [100];
      max_len = 99;
      top_ptr = -1;
    }
// A constructor for a given number of elements
    stack(int size) {
      stack_ptr = new Type [size];
      max_len = size - 1;
      top = -1;
    }
    ~stack() {delete stack_ptr;};   // A destructor
    void push(Type number) {
      if (top_ptr == max_len)
        cout << "Error in push—stack is full\n";
      else stack_ptr[++top_ptr] = number;
    }
    void pop() {
      if (top_ptr == -1)
        cout << "Error in pop—stack is empty\n";
      else top_ptr--;
    }
    Type top() {return (stack_ptr[top_ptr]);}
    int empty() {return (top_ptr == -1);}
}
```

As in Ada, C++ templated classes are instantiated at compile time. The difference is that in C++ the instantiations are implicit: A new instantiation is created whenever an object is created that requires a version of the templated class that does not yet exist.

S U M M A R Y

The concept of abstract data types and their use in program design was a milestone in the development of programming as an engineering discipline. Although the concept is relatively simple, its use did not become convenient and safe until languages were designed to support it.

An encapsulation is a compilation unit that can include a collection of logically related types, objects, and subprograms. An encapsulation may also provide access control to its entities. Encapsulations provide the programmer with a method of organizing programs that also limits recompilation.

The two primary features of abstract data types are the packaging of data objects with their associated operations and information hiding. A language may support abstract data types directly or simulate them with more general encapsulations.

SIMULA 67 provided the first construct for encapsulating data objects with their operations—the class. However, the class construct of SIMULA 67 does not provide for information hiding.

Ada and Modula-2 provide encapsulations that can be used to simulate abstract data types. The main difference between the two designs is Modula-2's restriction of exported types with hidden representations to pointers. This restriction allows changes to representations that do not require recompilation of definition modules and their client units. The Ada language allows any type to be exported. When nonpointer types are exported, client units must be recompiled when the representation is changed.

C++ data abstraction is provided by classes, which are loosely modeled on the classes of SIMULA 67. Classes are types, and instances can be created in all of the ways object instances of other types can be created. Java data abstractions are similar to those of C++, except all Java objects are allocated from the heap and are accessed through reference variables. Also, Java has a higher-level encapsulation construct than classes, called packages. Partially because of the availability of packages, Java does not have friend functions or friend classes.

Both Ada and C++ allow their abstract data types to be parameterized, Ada through its generic packages and C++ through its templated classes.

R E V I E W   Q U E S T I O N S

1. Define *abstract data type*.

2. What are the advantages of the two parts of the definition of *abstract data type?*

3. What are the language design requirements for a language that supports abstract data types?

4. What are the language design issues for abstract data types?

5. What is missing in the SIMULA 67 support for abstract data types?

6. What feature of SIMULA 67 classes later became a foundation part of object-oriented languages?

7. What are the two reasons why Modula-2 abstract data types are restricted to being pointers?

8. Explain how information hiding is provided in an Ada package.

9. What is the difference between **private** and **limited private** types in Ada?

10. How are C++ class objects created?

11. Where are Java class objects created?

12. Why does Java not have destructors?

13. What is a constructor? What is a destructor?

14. What is a friend function? What is a friend class?

15. What is one reason Java does not have friend functions or friend classes?

16. How are instances of C++ template classes created?

P R O B L E M   S E T

1. Design the example abstract stack type in Pascal, assuming that the stack definition, its operations, and the code that use it are all in the same program.

2. What critical part or parts of the definition of an abstract data type are missing from a Pascal implementation of the stack type, such as the one in Problem 1?

3. Design the example abstract stack type in FORTRAN 77, using a single subprogram with multiple entries for the type definition and the operations.

4. How does the FORTRAN implementation of Problem 3 compare with the Ada implementation in this chapter in terms of reliability and flexibility?

5. Modify the C++ class for the abstract stack type to use a linked list representation, and test it with the same code that appears in this chapter.

6. Some software engineers believe that all imported entities should be qualified by the name of the exporting program unit. Do you agree? Support your answer.

7. Design an abstract data type for a matrix abstraction in a language that you know, including operations for addition, subtraction, and matrix multiplication.

8. Design a queue abstract data type in a language you know, including operations for enqueue, dequeue, and empty.

9. Suppose someone designed a stack abstract data type in which the function, top, returned an access path (or pointer) rather than returning a copy of the top element. This is not a true data abstraction. Why? Give an example that illustrates the problem.

10. Write an abstract data type for complex numbers, including operations for addition, subtraction, multiplication, division, extraction of each of the parts of a complex number, and construction of a complex number from two floating-point constants, variables, or expressions. Use either Modula-2, Ada, C++, or Java.

11. Write an abstract data type for queues whose elements store 10-character names. The queue elements must be dynamically allocated from the heap. Queue operations are enqueue, dequeue, and empty. Use either Modula-2, Ada, C++, or Java.

11 Support for Object-Oriented Programming

Adele Goldberg

Adele Goldberg spent 14 years at Xerox's Palo Alto Research Center, leading the design team for Smalltalk and its implementation. She was instrumental in the development not only of Smalltalk, but of the window- and icon-based user interface paradigm.

This chapter begins with an introduction to object-oriented programming. This is followed by a discussion of the primary design issues for inheritance and dynamic binding. Next, we provide an overview of Smalltalk, followed by a detailed description of a subset of Smalltalk, which is illustrated with two complete Smalltalk programs. Brief descriptions of the support for object-oriented programming in C++, Java, Ada 95, and Eiffel follow.

11.1 Introduction

Languages that support object-oriented programming now are firmly entrenched in the mainstream. From COBOL to LISP, including virtually every language in between, dialects that support object-oriented programming have been created. Among these are C++, Ada 95, and CLOS, an object-oriented version of LISP (Bobrow et al., 1988). C++ and Ada 95 support procedural- and data-oriented programming, in addition to object-oriented programming. CLOS also supports functional programming. Some of the newer languages that were designed to support object-oriented programming do not support other programming paradigms, but still employ some of the basic structures and have the appearance of the older imperative languages. Among these are Eiffel and Java. Finally, there is one purely object-oriented language that is quite unconventional, Smalltalk. Smalltalk was the first language to offer complete support for object-oriented programming. The specific support for object-oriented programming varies widely among languages, and that is an important topic of this chapter.

This chapter relies heavily on Chapter 10. It is in fact a continuation of that chapter. This reflects the reality that object-oriented programming is in essence an application of the principle of abstraction to abstract data types. Specifically, in object-oriented programming the commonality of a collection of similar abstract data types is factored out and put in a new type. The members of the collection inherit the common parts from that new type. This is inheritance, which is at the center of object-oriented programming and the languages that support it.

11.2 Object-Oriented Programming

11.2.1 Introduction

The concept of **object-oriented programming** has its roots in SIMULA 67 but was not fully developed until the evolution of Smalltalk resulted in producing Smalltalk 80 (in 1980, of course). Indeed, some consider Smalltalk to be the only purely object-oriented programming language. A language that is object oriented must provide support for three key language features: abstract data types, inheritance, and a particular kind of dynamic binding.

Procedure-oriented programming, which was the most popular software development paradigm in the 1970s, focuses on subprograms and subprogram libraries. Data are sent to subprograms for computations. For example, an array of integer values that needs to be sorted is sent as a parameter to a subprogram that sorts such arrays.

Data-oriented programming focuses on abstract data types, which are discussed in detail in Chapter 10. In this paradigm, computation on a data object is specified by calling subprograms associated with the data object. If an array object needs to be sorted, the sorting operation is defined in the abstract data type for the array. The sorting process is enacted by calling that operation on the specific array object. The data-oriented programming paradigm was popular in the 1980s, and it is well served by the data abstraction facilities of Modula-2, Ada, and several more recent languages. Languages that support data-oriented programming are often called **object-based** languages.

11.2.2 Inheritance

By the middle to late 1980s, it became apparent to many software developers that one of the best opportunities for increased productivity in their profession was in software reuse. Abstract data types, with their encapsulation and access controls, were obviously the units to be reused. The problem with the reuse of abstract data types is that, in nearly all cases, the features and capabilities of the existing type are not quite right for the new use. The old type requires at least some minor modification. Such modifications can be difficult, for they require the person doing the modification to understand part, if not all, of the existing code. Furthermore, in many cases the modifications require changes to all client programs.

A second problem with data-oriented programming is that all abstract data type definitions are independent and are at the same level. This often makes it impossible to structure a program to fit the problem space being addressed by the program. In many cases, the underlying problem has categories of objects that are related, both as siblings (being similar to each other) and as parents and children (having some kind of subordinate relationship).

Inheritance offers a solution to both the modification problem posed by abstract data type reuse and the program organization problem. If a new abstract data type can inherit the data and functionality of some existing type, and is also allowed to modify some of those entities and add new entities, reuse is greatly facilitated without requiring changes to the reused abstract data type. Programmers can take an existing abstract data type and mold it to fit a new problem requirement. For example, suppose a program already has an abstract data type for integer arrays that includes a sort operation. After some period of use, the program is upgraded and requires an abstract data type for integer arrays with the sort operation, but also needs an operation to compute the median of the elements of the array objects. Because the array structure is hidden in an abstract data type, without inheritance that type must be modified to add the new operation in that structure. With inheritance, there is no need to modify the existing type; one can define a subclass of the existing type that retains the sort operation but adds an operation for the median computation.

The abstract data types in object-oriented languages, following the lead of SIMULA 67, are usually called classes. As with instances of abstract data types, class instances are called **objects.** A class that is defined through inheritance from another class is a **derived class** or **subclass.** A class from which the new class is derived is its **parent class** or **superclass.** The subprograms that define the operations on objects of a class are called **methods.** The calls to methods are often called **messages.** The entire collection of methods of an object is called the **message protocol,** or **message interface,** of the object. A message must have at least two parts, the specific object to which it is being sent and the name of a method that defines the requested action on the object. So computations in an object-oriented program are specified by messages sent from objects to other objects.

In the simplest case, a class inherits all of the entities (variables and methods) of its parent class. This can be complicated by access controls on the entities in a parent class. For example, as we saw in the abstract data type definitions in Chapter 10, some of the entities are classified as being public and others are private. These access controls allow the program designer to hide parts of the abstract data type from clients. These same controls are usually present in the classes in object-oriented languages. Derived classes are another kind of client to which access may be granted or withheld. To take this into account, some object-oriented languages include a third category of access control, often called **protected,** that is used to provide access to derived classes while withholding it from other classes.

In addition to inheriting entities from its parent class, a derived class can add new entities and modify inherited methods. A modified method has the same name, and often the same protocol, as the one of which it is a modification. The new method is said to **override** the inherited version, which is then called an **overriden** method. The most common purpose of an overriding method is to provide an operation that is specific for objects of the derived class but is not appropriate for objects of the parent class. For example, consider a class hierarchy in which the root class describes the general architectural characteristics of French Gothic cathedrals. This root class, `French_Gothic`, has a method to draw the facade of a generic French Gothic cathedral. Next, suppose the `French_Gothic` class has three derived classes, `Reims`, `Amien`, and `Chartres`, each of which includes a method to draw its particular facade. These versions of `draw` must override the inherited `draw` method from the parent class.

Classes can have two kinds of methods and two kinds of variables. The most commonly used methods and variables are called **instance** methods and variables. Every object of a class has its own set of instance variables, which store the object's state. The only difference between two objects of the same class is the state of their instance variables. Instance methods operate only on the objects of the class. **Class variables** belong to the class, rather than its object, so there is only one copy for the class. **Class methods** can perform operations on the class, and possibly also on the objects of the class. In most of the remainder of this chapter, we will ignore class methods and class variables.

If a class created by inheritance has a single parent class, then the process is called **single inheritance.** If a class has more than one parent class, the process is called **multiple inheritance.** When a number of classes are related through single inheritance, their relationships to each other can be shown in a derivation tree. The class relationships in a multiple inheritance can be shown in a derivation graph.

Program design for an object-oriented system begins with defining a hierarchy of classes that describe the relationships of the objects that will populate the solution program. The better this class hierarchy matches the problem space the more natural the complete solution will be.

One disadvantage of inheritance as a means of increasing the possibility of reuse is that it creates a dependency among the classes in an inheritance hierarchy. This works against one of the advantages of abstract data types, which is that they are independent of each other. Of course, not all abstract data types must be completely independent. But in general the independence of abstract data types is one of their strongest positive characteristics. However, it may be difficult, if not impossible to increase the reusability of abstract data types without creating dependencies among some of them.

11.2.3 Polymorphism and Dynamic Binding

The third characteristic of object-oriented programming languages is a kind of polymorphism provided by the dynamic binding of messages to method definitions. This is supported by allowing one to define polymorphic variables of the type of the parent class that are also able to reference objects of any of the subclasses of that class. The parent class can define a method that is overriden by its subclasses. The operations defined by these methods are similar, but must be customized for each class in the hierarchy. When such a method is called through the polymorphic variable, that call is bound to the method in the proper class dynamically. One purpose of this dynamic binding is to allow software systems to be more easily extended during both development and maintenance. Such programs can be written to perform operations on generic class objects. These operations are generic in that they can apply to objects of any class related through derivation from the same base class. As an example of dynamic binding, consider the cathedral example. If a program that uses the French_Gothic class has a polymorphic variable, cathedral, of the type of the French_Gothic class, that variable could reference objects of French_Gothic, and also objects of any of the derived classes. Now, when cathedral is used to call draw (which is defined in French_Gothic and all its descendants), that call is dynamically bound to the correct version of draw, chosen by the type to which the polymorphic variable is then referencing.

Dynamic binding through polymorphic variables is a powerful concept. Suppose our cathedrals example is written in C. The three examples of French Gothic cathedrals could be stored in variables of a **struct** type. There could be a single draw function that used a **switch** statement to call the correct drawing function, based on the specific cathedral. However, in this kind of implementation it is the programmer's responsibility to call the proper version of the drawing function. Maintenance is much easier with the object-oriented implementation. For example, suppose we need to add a new cathedral to the collection, say Paris. This would force us to modify the **switch** construct in the general drawing function, along with any similarly constructed functions for cathedrals. In the object-oriented case, however, adding a new cathedral has no affect on the existing code.

In many cases the design of an inheritance hierarchy results in one or more classes that are so high in the hierarchy that an instantiation of them does not make sense. For example, suppose that there was a building class as the parent or ancestor class of the French_Gothic class. It probably would not make sense to have an implemented draw method in building. But because all of its descendant classes should have such an implemented method, the protocol (but not the body) of that method is included in building. This abstract method is often called a **virtual method.** Furthermore, any class that includes at least one virtual method is called a **virtual class.** Such a class cannot be instantiated, because not all of its methods have bodies. Any subclass of a virtual class that is to be instantiated must provide implementations of all of the inherited virtual methods.

11.2.4 Computing with an Object-Oriented Language

All computing in a pure object-oriented language is done by the same uniform technique: sending a message to an object to invoke one of its methods. A reply to a message is an object that returns the value of the computation of the method.

An executing program in an object-oriented language can be described as a simulation of a collection of computers (objects) that communicate with each other through messages. Each object is an abstraction of a computer in the sense that it stores data and provides processing capability for manipulating that data. In addition, objects can send and receive messages. In essence, those are the fundamental capabilities of computers: to store and manipulate data and to communicate.

The essence of object-oriented programming is solving problems by identifying the real-world objects of the problem and the processing required of those objects, and then creating simulations of those objects, their processes, and the required communications between the objects.

11.3 Design Issues for Object-Oriented Languages

A number of issues must be considered when designing the programming language features to support inheritance and dynamic binding. Those that we consider most important are discussed in this section.

11.3.1 The Exclusivity of Objects

A language designer who is totally committed to the object model of computation designs an object system that absorbs all other concepts of type. Everything, from the smallest integer to a complete software system, is an object in this scenario. The advantage of this choice is the elegant and pure uniformity of the language and its use. The primary disadvantage is that simple operations must be done through the message-passing process, which often makes them slower than similar operations in an imperative model, where simple and fast machine instructions implement such simple operations.

In this purest model of object-oriented computation, all types are classes. There is no distinction between predefined and user-defined classes. In fact, all classes are treated the same way and all computation is accomplished through message passing.

One alternative to the exclusive use of objects that is common in imperative languages to which support for object-oriented programming has been added is to retain a complete imperative typing model and simply add the object model. This results in a larger language whose type structure is confusing to all but expert users.

Another alternative to the exclusive use of objects is to have an imperative-style type structure for the primitive scalar types. This provides the speed of operations on primitive values that is comparable to those expected in the imperative model. Unfortunately, this alternative also leads to complications in the language. Invariably, non-object values must be mixed with objects. This creates a need for so-called wrapper classes for the non-object types, so that some commonly needed operations can be sent to objects with non-object type values. In Section 11.6, we will discuss an example of this in Java.

11.3.2 Are Subclasses Subtypes?

The issue here is relatively simple: Does an "is-a" relationship hold between a parent class and its derived classes? An is-a relationship would guarantee that a variable of the derived class type could appear anywhere a variable of the parent class type was legal.

The subtypes of Ada are examples of this simple form of inheritance. For example,

```
subtype SMALL_INT is INTEGER range –100..100;
```

Variables of SMALL_INT type have all of the operations of INTEGER variables but can store only a subset of the values possible in INTEGER. Furthermore, every SMALL_INT variable can be used anywhere an INTEGER variable can be used. That is, every SMALL_INT variable is, in a sense, an INTEGER variable.

A derived class is called a **subtype** if it has an is-a relationship with its parent class. The characteristics of a subclass that ensures that it is a subtype are as follows: The subclass can only add variables and methods and override inherited methods in "compatible" ways. Compatible here means that the overriding method can replace the overriden method without causing type errors. Having an identical number of parameters and identical parameter types and return type would, of course, guarantee compliance. Less severe restrictions are possible, depending on the type compatibility rules of the language.

Our definition of subtype clearly disallows having entities in the parent class that are not inherited to the subclass.

11.3.3 Implementation and Interface Inheritance

The concept of information hiding in an abstract data type provides the interface of its facilities to clients, but hides their implementation. Yet what about subclasses? Should they see only the interface of their parent class, or should they also be granted access to the implementation details of the facilities of the parent? If only the interface of the parent class is visible to the subclass, it is called **interface inheritance.** If the implementation details are also visible, it is called **implementation inheritance.**

This issue presents the language designer with a design trade-off in which there are advantages and disadvantages to be considered. Granting subclasses access to the "hidden" part of the parent class makes the subclass dependent on those details. Any change in the implementation of the parent class will require recompilation of the subclass, and in many cases, the change will require modification of the subclass. This defeats the advantage of information hiding to the subclass clients. On the other hand, keeping the implementation part of the parent class hidden from the subclasses can cause inefficiencies in the execution of the instances of those subclasses. This can be caused by the difference in efficiency of having direct access to data structures versus requiring access through the operations defined in the parent class. For example, consider a class that defines a stack and a subclass that must include an operation to return the second element from the top. If the language uses implementation inheritance, this operation can be defined to simply return the element at the position of the stack top minus one. However, if the language designer has chosen interface inheritance, this code would look something like

```
int second() {
  int temp = top();
  pop();
  int temp_result = top();
  push(temp);
  return temp_result;
}
```

This is clearly a slower process than the direct access to the second element from the top of the stack. However, if the implementation of the stack is changed, this method will also probably need to be changed.

The best solution for the language designer is to provide both implementation and interface inheritance options to the software designer and let him or her decide, on a case-by-case basis, which version is better.

11.3.4 Type Checking and Polymorphism

In Section 11.2, polymorphism in the object-oriented realm is defined to be the use of a polymorphic pointer or reference to access a method whose name is overridden in the class hierarchy that defines the object to which the pointer or reference is pointing. The polymorphic variable is the type of the parent class, and the parent class defines at least the protocol of a method that is overridden by the derived classes. The polymorphic variable can reference objects of the parent class and the derived classes, so the class of the object to which it points cannot always be statically determined. The binding of messages to methods that are sent through polymorphic variables must be dynamic. The issue here is when the type checking of this binding takes place.

This issue is an important one, for it aligns with the fundamental nature of the programming language. If the language design has strong typing as one of its basic goals, as many contemporary languages do, then this type checking should be statically done. This forces some serious restrictions on the relationship between polymorphic messages and methods.

There are two kinds of type checking that must be done between a message and a method in a strongly typed language: the message's parameter types must be checked against the method's formal parameters, and the return type of the method must be checked against the message's expected type. If these types must match exactly, then an overriding method must have the same number and types of parameters and return type as the overridden method. One relaxation of this rule could be to allow assignment compatibility between actual and formal parameters and between the returned type and the type expected by the message.

The obvious alternative to static type checking is to delay type checking until the polymorphic variable is used to call a method. As in other situations, this kind of dynamic type checking is more expensive and delays type error detection.

11.3.5 Single and Multiple Inheritance

Another simple issue is: Does the language allow multiple inheritance (in addition to single inheritance)? Well, maybe it's not so simple. The purpose of multiple inheritance is to allow a new class to inherit from two or more classes that describe distinct abstractions. For example, in Java it is common to write applets that include animation. Such animation is often run concurrently with the other parts of the applet. Applets are supported by the `Applet` class and concurrency is supported by the `Thread` class. It would be necessary for such an applet to inherit from both of these two classes. In Section 11.10.2, we discuss how Java supports this need.

Because multiple inheritance is sometimes very useful, why would a language designer not include it? The reasons fall in two categories, complexity and efficiency. The additional complexity is illustrated by several problems. One obvious problem is name collisions. For example, if a subclass named C inherits from both class A and class B and both A and B include an inheritable variable named `sum`, how can C refer to the two different `sum`s? A variation of this occurs if both A and B are derived from a common parent, z, in which case it is called **diamond** inheritance. In this case, both A and B have z's inheritable variables, and C inherits two versions of each of these (assuming they are inheritable) from A and B. Diamond inheritance is shown in Figure 11.1.

Figure 11.1
An example of
diamond inheritance

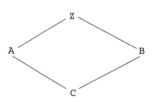

The question of efficiency may be more perceived than real. In C++, for example, supporting multiple inheritance requires just one extra addition operation for each dynamically bound method call (Stroustrup, 1994, p. 270). Although this is required even if the program does not use multiple inheritance, it is a small additional cost.

The use of multiple inheritance can easily lead to complex program organizations. Many who have attempted to use multiple inheritance have found that designing the classes to be used as multiple parents is difficult. Maintenance of systems that use multiple inheritance can be a more serious problem, for multiple inheritance leads to more complex dependencies among classes. It is not clear to some that the benefits of multiple inheritance are worth the added effort to design and maintain a system using it.

11.3.6 Allocation and Deallocation of Objects

There are two design questions concerning the allocation and deallocation of objects. The first of these is the place from which objects are allocated. If they behave like the abstract data types, then perhaps they can be allocated from anywhere. This means they could be statically allocated by the compiler, allocated as stack-dynamic objects from the run-time stack, or explicitly created on the heap with an operator or function, such as **new**. If they are all allocated from the heap, there is the advantage of having a uniform method of creation and access through pointer or reference variables. This simplifies the assignment operation for objects, making it in all cases only a pointer or reference value change. It also allows references to objects to be implicitly dereferenced, simplifying the access syntax.

The second question here is concerned with those cases where objects are allocated from the heap. The question is whether deallocation is implicit or explicit or both. If deallocation is implicit, some implicit method of storage reclamation is required, such as reference counters or garbage collection. If allocation can be explicit, that raises the issue of whether dangling pointers or references can be created.

11.3.7 Dynamic and Static Binding

As we have already discussed, dynamic binding of messages to methods in an inheritance hierarchy is an essential part of object-oriented programming. The question here is whether all binding of messages to methods is dynamic. The alternative is to allow the user to specify whether a specific binding is to be dynamic or static. The advantage of this is that static bindings are faster. So if a binding need not be dynamic, why pay the price.

11.4 Overview of Smalltalk

Smalltalk is the definitive object-oriented programming language. This section introduces a few general characteristics of Smalltalk. Section 11.5 describes the specifics of a subset of the small-scale syntax and semantics of Smalltalk. Section 11.6 describes two complete Smalltalk example programs. Section 11.7 discusses several large-scale features of Smalltalk, specifically in terms of the design issues described in Section 11.3.

11.4.1 General Characteristics

A program in Smalltalk consists entirely of objects, and the concept of an object is truly universal. Virtually everything, from items as simple as the integer constant 2 to a complex file-handling system, is an object. As objects, they are treated uniformly. They all have local memory, inherent processing ability, the capability to communicate with other objects, and the possibility of inheriting methods and instance variables from ancestors.

Messages can be parameterized with variables that reference objects. Replies to messages have the form of objects and are used to return requested information or to confirm that the requested service has been completed.

All Smalltalk objects are allocated from the heap and are referenced through reference variables, which are implicitly dereferenced. There is no explicit deallocation statement or operation. All deallocation is implicit, using a garbage collection process for storage reclamation.

Unlike hybrid languages like C++ and Ada 95, Smalltalk was designed for just one software development paradigm, object oriented. Furthermore, it adopts none of the appearance of the imperative languages. Its purity of purpose is reflected in its simple elegance and uniformity of design.

11.4.2 The Smalltalk Environment

Smalltalk's environment is quite different from that used with most imperative languages. The Smalltalk system integrates a program editor, compiler, the usual features of an operating system, and a virtual machine into a single system. The interface to this system is the original graphical user interface.

An important aspect of the Smalltalk environment is that it is written almost entirely in Smalltalk, and the user can modify it to fit his or her particular needs. Therefore, the source version of the Smalltalk system must be available to a user.

To reiterate, Smalltalk is far more than just a programming language; it is also a programming methodology (object oriented) and a programming environment.

11.5 Introduction to the Smalltalk Language

This section introduces a subset of the Smalltalk language. The topics discussed here are sufficient to convey the flavor of programming in Smalltalk. The most important features that are not described are the large hierarchy of classes that are supplied with a Smalltalk system, which provide the basis for most Smalltalk programs, and the powerful windowed environment in which Smalltalk programs are developed.

11.5.1 Expressions

Smalltalk methods are constructed from expressions. An expression specifies an object, which happens to be the value of the expression. Smalltalk has four kinds of expressions: literals, variable names, message expressions, and block expressions. Literals, variables, and message expressions are discussed in the following three subsections. Block expressions are described in Section 11.5.4.1.

11.5.1.1 Literals

The most common literals are numbers, strings, and keywords. Numbers are literal objects that represent numeric values. They are quite different from the numeric literals of the common imperative languages, which act somewhat like named constants because they are associated with memory locations that contain their values. In Smalltalk, numeric literals are objects that are characterized by their message protocol and by the results that are produced when messages are received. The message protocol of numeric literals, as is the case with other objects, is defined in the class definition along with its inherited class definitions. In the case of an integer literal, the class is `Integer`; it provides methods for the usual arithmetic operators, among other things.

Syntactically, a string literal is a sequence of characters delimited by apostrophes. Semantically, a string literal is an object that is capable of responding to messages that access individual characters, replace substrings, and perform comparisons with other strings.

A keyword is an identifier, which may be user-defined, with a trailing colon. The use of keywords is discussed in Section 11.5.1.3.

11.5.1.2 Variables

A Smalltalk name is syntactically similar to those of other programming languages: a sequence of letters and/or digits that begins with a letter. Smalltalk variables come in two varieties: private, which means they are local to an object, and shared, which means they are visible outside the object in which they are "declared." Names of private variables must begin with lowercase letters. Names of shared variables must begin with uppercase letters.

All Smalltalk variables are references; they can only refer to objects or classes. They are typeless; any variable can point to any object. The only shared variables discussed here are those that refer to classes. All variables are implicitly dereferenced, which leads us frequently to refer to an object (in our discussion) by the name of its reference variable.

Instance variables are either named or indexed. Named variables correspond to pointers to nonarray types in an imperative language. Indexed instance variables are accessed not by name but by messages that have integers as parameters. Most indexed variables are used in a way that corresponds to arrays in other languages, although indexing itself is done through message passing. The integer parameter in a message to reference an indexed instance variable corresponds to the subscript in a reference to an array element in a conventional imperative language.

11.5.1.3 Message Expressions

Messages have the form of expressions. They provide the means of communication among objects and are the way the operations of an object are requested.

Message expressions have two parts, a specification of the object that is to receive the message and the message itself. The message itself specifies a selector entry, or method, in the receiver object and possibly one or more parameters. Parameters are, like other variables, pointers to other objects. When a message is evaluated, it is sent to the specified receiver object. Methods are discussed in Sections 11.5.2 and 11.5.6.

For the remainder of the chapter, we will refer to message expressions simply as messages. Replies to messages are objects. Messages correspond in many ways to function calls in languages like Pascal and C.

There are three categories of messages: unary, binary, and keyword. Unary messages are the simplest kind, having no parameters. They have only two parts, the object to which they are to be sent and the name of the method in that receiving object. The first symbol of a unary message specifies a receiver object; the last symbol specifies the method of that object that is to be executed. For example, the message

```
firstAngle sin
```

sends a parameterless message to the `sin` method of the object `firstAngle`. Recall that all objects are referenced by pointers, so `firstAngle` is really a pointer to an object. The `sin` method (probably) returns a number object that is the value of the sine of the value of `firstAngle`.

Binary messages have a single parameter, an object, which is passed to the specified method of the specified receiver object. Among the most common binary messages are those for arithmetic operations, such as

    21 + 2

and

    sum / count

In the first message, the receiver object is the number 21, to which is sent the message + 2. So the message 21 + 2 passes the parameter object 2 to the + method of the object 21. The code of that method uses the object 2 to build a new object, in this case, 23. If the system already contains the object 23, then the result is a reference to it rather than to a new object.

It may seem odd to consider the number 21 an object, but in Smalltalk it is perfectly natural for numbers to be objects with operations. The usual operations for integer objects are defined in the class `Integer`, of which they are instances.

In the second message above, the message / `count` is sent to the object referred to by `sum`, which results in the object referenced by the variable `count` being passed as a parameter to the / method of the object referenced by `sum`.

Keyword expressions specify one or more keywords to organize the correspondence between the actual parameters in the message and the formal parameters in the method. That is, the keywords act in concert to select the method to which the message is directed. The interspersion of keywords and parameters in messages enhances their readability. Methods that accept keyword messages are not named. Such methods instead are identified by the keywords themselves. Consider the following example:

    firstArray at: 1 put: 5

This message sends the objects 1 and 5 to a particular method, `at:put:`, of the object `firstArray`. The keywords `at:` and `put:` identify the formal parameters of the method to which 1 and 5, respectively, are to be sent. The method to which this message is sent includes the keywords of the message. As mentioned earlier, keyword methods do not have names; rather, they are identified by their keywords. This catenation—in this case, `at:put:`—is called a **selector.**

Message expressions can consist of any number of combinations of the three kinds of expressions, as in

    total - 3 * divisor.
    firstArray at: index - 1 put: 77

To determine how these are evaluated, the precedence and associativity of expression operators must be known. Unary expressions have the highest precedence, followed by binary expressions, followed by keyword expressions. Both unary and binary expressions associate left to right. Note that this is quite different from the precedence rules commonly used in languages such as Ada and C.

Expressions can be parenthesized to force any order of operator evaluation. The first expression above, parenthesized to illustrate but not alter its normal evaluation order, is

```
(total - 3) * divisor
```

This expression sends the 3 to the – method of the object `total`. The value of the variable `divisor` is then sent to the * method of the object that resulted from the first operation.

The expression

```
firstArray at: index - 1 put: 77
```

sends 1 to the – method of the object `index`. The result of this operation, along with 77, is then sent to the `at:put:` method of the object `firstArray`.

Messages can be cascaded—which means that multiple messages can be sent to the same object without duplicating the receiver object's name—by separating the selector-parameter groups, or messages, by semicolons. The messages are sent sequentially, as they appear, left to right. For example,

```
ourPen home; up; goto: 500@500; down; home
```

is equivalent to the following:

```
ourPen home.
ourPen up.
ourPen goto: 500@500.
ourPen down.
ourPen home
```

This sequence draws a line on the display, assuming that `ourPen` is an instance of the `Pen` class. An object of class `Pen` is illustrated in Section 11.6.2.

Notice that periods are used to separate messages that are sent to different methods and appear on adjacent lines. This is similar to the use of semicolons to separate statements in Pascal programs.

11.5.2 Methods

The general syntactic form of a Smalltalk method is

message_pattern [| temporary variables |] statements

where the brackets are metasymbols that indicate that what they enclose is optional. Because Smalltalk has no type declarations, temporary variables, when present, need only be named in a list. Temporary variables exist only during execution of the method in which they are listed. No punctuation appears at the end of a method.

The message pattern of a message corresponds to the function header in a language such as C. Message patterns, which are prototypes for messages, can be in one of two basic forms. For unary or binary messages, only the method's name is included. For keyword messages, the keywords and the names of the formal parameters form the message pattern.

A value to be returned by a method is indicated by preceding the expression that describes it with an up arrow (^). In many cases, this is the last expression that appears in the method. If no return value is specified in a method, the receiver object itself is the return value.

A message pattern for a unary message is simply the method name. An example of a unary method is

```
currentTotal
  ^(oldTotal + newValue)
```

This method, named `currentTotal`, returns the value of the expression

```
oldTotal + newValue.
```

Binary methods are used primarily for arithmetic operations, which are predefined, so they are not discussed here.

The general form of the message pattern for keyword message methods is

```
key_1: parameter_1 key_2: parameter_2 ... key_n: parameter_n
```

Consider the following example keyword method, which does not specify a value to be returned:

```
x: xCoord y: yCoord
  ourPen up; goto xCoord@yCoord; down.
```

In this method, which matches the `x:y:` message selector, the object `ourPen` is sent the messages `up`, `goto` (which uses the two parameters `xCoord` and `yCoord`), and `down`. The message pattern is simply a list of the keyword/formal parameter name pairs in the method.

An example message for this method is

```
ourPen x: 300 y: 400
```

Additional features of methods, including temporary variables, are discussed in Section 11.5.6.

11.5.3 Assignment Statements

Smalltalk has assignment statements that are similar, at least in appearance, to those of languages such as Pascal and C. Any message expression, literal object, or variable name can be the right side of an assignment statement. The left side is a variable name, and the operator is specified with a left arrow, as in

```
total <- 22.
sum <- total
```

The particular object referenced by a variable is changed when that variable's name appears on the left side of an assignment. In this example, the variable `total` is set to refer to the object `22`. Then the variable `sum` is set to refer to the same object. This operation is closely related to the assignment of pointer variables in Pascal or Ada.

Recall that all methods transmit information back to the senders that sent the messages. To save that returned information, the message expression is placed on the right side of an assignment to a variable. The variable is then set to refer to the returned information, as in the following examples:

```
index <- index + 1.
netPay <- deducts grossPay: 350.0 dependents: 4
```

In the first assignment, the message `+ 1` is sent to the object referenced by `index`. The variable `index` is set to reference the new object that results from executing the `+` method. In the second, the keyword message `grossPay: 350.0 dependents: 4` is sent to the `grossPay:dependents:` method of the object `deducts`. The variable `netPay` is set to refer to the object returned by `deducts`.

It should be obvious that Smalltalk is, by our definition, an imperative language because computation is through expression evaluation and assignment statements, and results are stored in variables.

11.5.4 Blocks and Control Structures

One of the most unusual aspects of Smalltalk is that statements in the language do not provide the control structures. Instead, they are formed with the fundamental object-oriented paradigm: message passing.

Blocks provide a way to collect expressions into groups. These groups can be used to build execution control constructs.

11.5.4.1 Blocks

A block is an unnamed literal object that contains a sequence of expressions. Blocks are instances of the class `Block`. A message can be sent to a block by placing the message immediately after the block.

A block is specified in brackets, with its expression components separated by periods, as in

```
[index <- index + 1. sum <- sum + index]
```

The expressions in a block are deferred actions because they are not executed when encountered; rather they are executed only when the block is sent the unary message **value**, which is defined in class `Block`. For example,

```
[sum <- sum + index] value
```

sends the message **value** to the block, causing its execution. When a block execution is completed, the value of the last expression in the block is returned.

Blocks can be assigned to variables and executed by sending the **value** message to the variable, given the expression

```
addIndex <- [sum <- sum + index]
```

The message expression

```
addIndex value
```

causes `index` to be added to `sum`. This message expression could also be assigned to a variable, as follows:

```
addIndex <- [sum + index]
sum <- addIndex value
```

Blocks are always executed in the context of their definition, even when they are sent as parameters to a different object. Thus, they are semantically related to the pass-by-name parameters of ALGOL 60.

Blocks can be thought of as procedure declarations that may appear anywhere. Like procedures, blocks can have parameters. Block parameters are specified in a section at the beginning of the block that is separated from the remainder of the block by a vertical bar (`|`). The formal parameter specifications require a colon to be attached to the left end of each parameter. Because there are no declared types, the specifications include only the formal parameter names, which are listed without any separating punctuation. As an example of a block with parameters, consider the following:

```
[:x :y | sum <- x + 10. total <- sum * y]
```

Blocks provide a means of collecting expressions, so they are a natural way to form control structures in Smalltalk.

11.5.4.2 Iteration

Blocks can contain relational expressions, in which case they return one of the predefined Boolean objects, **true** or **false**. Such blocks are sometimes called conditional blocks. The two objects, **true** and **false**, have methods that provide some of the facilities for building control structures.

Logical pretest loops can be formed by using the keyword method `whileTrue:`, which the class `Block` provides, to send the block to be controlled to a second block that contains the loop condition. This method is defined for all blocks that return Boolean objects. The `whileTrue:` method is defined to send **value** to the object that contains the method (either **true** or **false**), thereby causing its parameter block to be executed, as in the following:

```
count <- 1.
sum <- 0.
[count <= 20]      "The block with the loop condition"
   whileTrue: [sum <- sum + count.
               count <- count + 1] "The loop body"
```

Although this code may have a somewhat conventional appearance and it does accomplish a rather conventional operation, the process by which it does it is significantly different from that used by imperative languages.

The loop control is realized as follows: The block containing the code to add `count` to `sum` and increment `count`, which is the code segment whose execution is to be controlled, is sent as the parameter to the `whileTrue:` method of the conditional block `[count <= 20]`. The `whileTrue:` method sends **value** to the conditional block, thus causing that block to be evaluated. The result of this evaluation is a Boolean object. If the result is **true**, the `whileTrue:` method causes the parameter sent by the `whileTrue:` message to be evaluated. Its parameter is the block that contains the expressions of the iteration. After they are evaluated, the process is repeated by sending the block of expressions to `[count <= 20]` again. The repetition stops when an evaluation of `[count <= 20]` produces **false** as a result object.

Suppose the control block in the above example were `[count <= 2]`, rather than `[count <= 20]`. The following is a trace of the actions that occur when the modified code is executed. Note that → indicates a message being sent, and comments are delimited by quotes.

```
count <- 1
sum <- 0
[sum <- sum + count. count <- count + 1] → [count <= 2] whileTrue
value → [count <= 2]   "value sent by whileTrue"
[count <= 2] returns true
whileTrue evaluates [sum <- sum + count. count <- count + 1]
   (sum <- 1; count <- 2)  "results of the evaluation"
[sum <- sum + count. count <- count + 1] → [count <= 2] whileTrue
value → [count <= 2]    "value sent by whileTrue"
[count <= 2] returns true
whileTrue evaluates [sum <- sum + count. count <- count + 1]
    (sum <- 3; count <- 3)  "results of the evaluation"
[sum <- sum + count. count <- count + 1] → [count <= 2] whileTrue
value → [count <= 2]
[count <= 2] returns false
```

Another common loop control structure is simple repetition with a counter control. For this, there is a method for integers named `timesRepeat:`. When `timesRepeat:` is sent to an integer with a block as the parameter, the block is executed the number of times equal to the value of the integer. For example,

```
xCube <- 1.
3 timesRepeat: [xCube <- xCube * x]
```

computes the cube of **x** by a rather lengthy process.

Control structures similar to ALGOL 68's **for** loops can be built with some of the methods of integers. The two most useful of these are to:do: and to:by:do:. First consider the method to:do:. The to: parameter is an integer expression whose value serves as the terminal value. The do: parameter is a block that is to be executed by the integer method. The to:do: method generates, internally, a sequence of values, beginning with the integer literal to which the message is sent and ending with the to: parameter value. For example, consider the following message:

```
1 to: 5 do: [sum <- sum + x]
```

The block is executed five times. The internal values produced and returned by the object 1 are 1, 2, 3, 4, and 5.

The block that forms a loop body can have a parameter. Such a parameter is implicitly assigned the internal values created by the message. The internal values are those returned by the numeric object to which the whole message is sent. For example, consider the following message:

```
2 to: 10 by: 2 do: [:even | sum <- sum + even]
```

This message causes the block to be executed five times, but in this case **even**, the block parameter, takes on the internal values, which are 2, 4, 6, 8, and 10.

11.5.4.3 Selection

Selection constructs also have a conventional appearance but operate in an unconventional way. The method ifTrue:ifFalse: is provided for the **true** and **false** objects. The two arguments of the ifTrue:ifFalse: message represent the then and else clauses of the selection construct. The message is sent to a Boolean expression. If the expression evaluates to **true**, then the message is sent to **true**. In this case, the ifTrue:ifFalse: method sends **value** to its first argument and ignores its second argument. If sent to **false**, the opposite takes place. For example, consider the following message:

```
total = 0
  ifTrue: [average <- 0]
  ifFalse: [average <- sum // total]
```

The Boolean expression total = 0, causes the message = 0 to be sent to the object total, which returns either **true** or **false**. The resulting object (either **true** or **false**) is then used as the receiver for the message, which is sent to the ifTrue:ifFalse: method. The two parameters to this method are the then and else blocks, one of which is to be executed. The `//` operator specifies integer division.

Four different messages can be sent to the **true** and **false** objects. In addition to `ifTrue:ifFalse:`, there are `ifTrue:`, `ifFalse:`, and `ifFalse:ifTrue:`.

The semantics of the control structures we have just discussed may seem rather odd, but they are really quite natural to experienced Smalltalk users. Furthermore, the ability to handle control structures within this framework is a tribute to the power and flexibility of the message-passing model. It also simplifies Smalltalk by obviating the need for any structure outside the world of objects and message passing.

11.5.5 Classes

A Smalltalk class has four parts:

- A class name
- The superclass name
- Declarations of the instance variables
- Declarations of the instance and class methods

Instance variables are not visible to other objects. Each instance variable refers to one object, called its value. The values of all of an instance's variables together represent that instance's current state.

In Smalltalk, all classes are themselves objects. This allows classes to receive messages. Class definitions may include both class methods and instance methods, where class methods respond to messages that are sent to the class and instance methods respond to messages sent to instances of the class.

Sending the message **new** to a class in an assignment creates an instance of the class. This also sets the left-side variable to reference the newly created object. For example,

```
ourPen <- Pen new
```

creates an instance of the class `Pen` (by sending the message **new** to the class `Pen`) and sets the variable `ourPen` to reference it.

11.5.6 More About Methods

In this section, we examine some features of methods that were not covered in Section 11.5.2.

The following method illustrates the use of temporary variables:

```
first: x second: y | temp |
  temp <- x + y.
```

```
temp > 1000
  ifTrue: [y <- 1000].
^ y
```

This method adds the values of its two parameters together and places the sum in the temporary variable `temp`. If the value of `temp` is greater than 1000, the second parameter, `y`, is set to 1000. The value of `y` is the returned object.

The pseudovariable **self** is an object name that refers to the object in which it appears. Therefore, **self** is used for recursive messages, or messages to the object itself. The object name **self** is often used for error message display, as in

```
total = 0
  ifTrue: [self error: 'Error- cannot compute average']
  ifFalse: [^ sum // total]
```

If `total` is equal to zero, this code sends the message `error: 'Error - cannot compute average'` to the object in which the code resides. Otherwise, it returns the value of the expression `sum // total`.

The message `error`, like other messages, is directed to a superclass of the object to which it is sent if that object does not include a method for it. If no other ancestor class has a method for the `error` message, the system object, `Object`, which does include an `error` method, receives the message. `Object`'s method for `error` prints the message parameter and terminates the program.

For a somewhat more familiar example of recursion, consider the following method, which is understood by integers. It is taken from Goldberg and Robson (1983).

```
factorial
  self = 0
    ifTrue: [^1].
  self < 0
    ifTrue: [self error 'Factorial not defined']
    ifFalse: [^ self * (self - 1) factorial]
```

This is a binary method for integer objects. It can be invoked by a message such as

```
5 factorial
```

The first Boolean expression, **self** = 0, sends the parameter 0 to the = method of the integer to which the factorial message was sent. The message `ifTrue: [^1]` is then sent to the result of the = method execution. If the result is the object **true**, as it would be for the message 0 `factorial`, the value 1 is returned to the sender of `factorial`. If the result of the = method execution is **false**, no action is taken because the `ifTrue:` method in **false** is defined to do nothing.

The next Boolean expression, **self** < 0, sends the parameter 0 to the < method of the integer to which `factorial` was sent. The rest of the factorial message (the entire `ifTrue:ifFalse:` message) is then sent to the result of the < method execution. If the resulting object is **true**, the error message is sent to the object to which `factorial` was sent. If the result of the < method is **false**, then the block on the `ifFalse:` part of the `ifTrue:ifFalse:` method is executed, and the result is returned to the sender of `factorial`.

To understand the `ifFalse:` message, you must understand the precedence rules of message evaluation. In this expression, there are two binary expressions (those with * and -) and one unary expression (`factorial`). Recall that unary expressions take precedence over binary expressions unless the binary expression is parenthesized. Also, all expressions have left associativity. Now the order of evaluation is clear: First, - 1 is sent to **self**, producing an object that is smaller by 1 than the object to which the message was sent. Then `factorial` is sent to this new object. The final result of this message, after all recursion, is sent with * to **self**, which is the original object to which `factorial` was sent. The result of this message is the factorial value.

This example illustrates the similarity in recursion across widely differing language semantics.

11.6 Smalltalk Example Programs

11.6.1 A Simple Table Handler

The example class of this section demonstrates that simple table management problems typically implemented in common imperative languages can also be implemented easily in Smalltalk. The problem is to build a program that creates and does look-ups in a table of department names and their code numbers. Because of the lack of static typing, the resulting system could be used for any table consisting of two parallel arrays of data, where the look-ups are based on the data elements in the first array.

One of the interesting features used in the program is the dynamic binding of index range to array. The two arrays are always exactly the size of the stored data. Each addition to the table simply increases the size of the table. Note that while this may be interesting and space efficient, it is highly inefficient in terms of execution time. Each addition causes the creation of two new arrays and a move of the contents of the old arrays to the new arrays—a very time-consuming process.

One of the omissions of the program is the lack of a method for removing an entry.

```
class name                     DeptCodes
superclass                     Object
instance variable names          names
                                 codes
```

```
"Class methods"
"Create an instance"
  new
    ^ super new

"Instance methods"
"Number of table entries"
  size
    ^ names size

"Fetch the code for a department"
  at: name | index |
    index <- self indexOf: name.
    index = 0
    ifTrue: [self error: 'Error—Name not in table']
    ifFalse: [^codes at: index]

"Install a new code; create entry if necessary"
  at: name put: code |index|
    index <- self indexOf: name.
    index = 0
    ifTrue: [index <- self newIndexOf: name].
    ^ codes at: index put: code

"Look-up index of a given department name"
  indexOf: name
     1 to: names size do:
       [:index | (names at: index) = name ifTrue:
                                   [^index]].
     ^ 0

"Create a new entry with the given name and return index"
  newIndexOf: name
    self grow.
    names at: names size put: name.
    ^ names size

"Stretch table by one element and put in new name"
  grow | oldNames oldCodes|
    oldNames <- names.
    oldCodes <- codes.
    names <- Array new: names size + 1.
    codes <- Array new: codes size + 1.
    names replaceFrom: 1 to: oldNames size with: oldNames.
    codes replaceFrom: 1 to: oldNames size with: oldCodes

"Test for inclusion of a given name"
  includes: name
    ^ (self indexOf: name) ~= 0

"Test for empty"
  isEmpty
    ^ names isEmpty
```

```
"Create initial empty arrays"
  initialize
    names <- Array new: 0.
    codes <- Array new: 0
```

We now briefly describe the action of the `replaceFrom:` method. The first `replaceFrom:` method used in the `grow` method operates by moving the elements of the array `oldNames` indexed with the range 1 to the size of `oldNames` to the array named `names`.

The following expressions and the computed results illustrate how an instance of `DeptCodes` behaves. Note that `isEmpty:` is a unary method inherited from `Object`.

Expression	*Result*
`dCodes <- DeptCodes new`	Creates a new instance
`dCodes initialize`	Creates empty arrays
`dCodes isEmpty`	true
`dCodes at: 'Physics' put: 100`	100
`dCodes at: 'Chemistry' put: 110`	110
`dCodes at: 'Biology' put: 120`	120
`dCodes isEmpty`	false
`dCodes size`	3
`dCodes at: 'Chemistry'`	110
`dCodes includes 'Physics'`	true
`dCodes includes 'Computing'`	false

11.6.2 LOGO-Style Graphics

In this section, an example program is presented that illustrates the Smalltalk class that provides the kind of drawing that originated in the turtle graphics of LOGO. This class, named `Pen`, is a subclass of another system class, `BitBlt`, which we will not discuss.

An instance of `Pen` is very much like a ballpoint pen under computer control, writing on a screen rather than paper. A `Pen` object has three primary parameters: direction, position, and frame. The position is either up or down, where up means it does not write when moved, and down means it does. Direction is measured clockwise in degrees from the direction of 0, with 0 being toward the right on the screen. The frame of a `Pen` object is the region of the screen in which it can draw, measured in bits. When a `Pen` instance is outside its frame, it cannot draw.

The initial condition of an instance of `Pen` is that it is pointing at 270 degrees, which by convention is straight up on the screen; it is located at the coordinates (300,400) and is in the up position. The (300,400) position is the center of the assumed screen size, which is 600 bits wide and 800 bits high.

The current parameters of a `Pen` instance can be gotten from the methods direction, location, and frame. The frame method returns the upper-left corner and the lower-right corner coordinates of the area in which the pen can draw.

The frame can be set by a second frame message

```
frame: (aPoint extent: aPoint)
```

where `aPoint` is a pair of bit positions separated by an "at" sign (@). The parentheses are required to force the desired precedence in the message expression. The first occurrence of `aPoint` in this message indicates the upper-left corner of the frame. The second indicates the distance the frame will extend in the *x* and *y* directions from the upper-left corner. For example, the message

```
frame: (50@50 extent: 300@300)
```

sets the frame to have an upper-left corner at (50,50) and a lower-right corner at (350,350).

The message protocol for moving and drawing with objects of the class `Pen` is as follows:

`down`	Sets the pen in the drawing position.
`up`	Sets the pen in the non-drawing position.
`turn: degrees`	Changes the direction of the pen by the number of degrees specified in the parameter.
`go: distance`	Moves the pen in its current direction by the number of bits specified in the parameter.
`goto: aPoint`	Moves the pen to the position specified by the parameter point. If the pen is currently down, it draws a line.
`place: aPoint`	Sets the pen at the position specified in the parameter. No lines are drawn.
`home`	Sets the pen at the center of the frame.
`north`	Sets the direction of the pen to 270, which is straight up on the screen.

The color of the lines drawn by instances of `Pen` has default value of black. The shape of the pen tip defaults to 1 bit by 1 bit. Both can be changed.

Simple geometric shapes can easily be drawn with instances of `Pen`. First, an instance of `Pen` must be created:

```
ourPen <- Pen new defaultNib: 2.
ourPen up; goto: 800@300; down
```

Now a triangle can be drawn with

```
ourPen go: 100; turn: 120; go: 100; turn: 120; go: 100
```

Figure 11.2
Smalltalk screen with
output of a triangle

Figure 11.2 shows the result of executing this code. It also shows the rest of the screen at the time, which illustrates the flavor of the Smalltalk user interface.

The message above can be simplified somewhat with a block, as in

```
3 timesRepeat: [ourPen go: 100. ourPen turn: 120]
```

This message can be generalized to draw any equilateral polygon by repeating the block a number of times equal to the number of sides and turning by an amount equal to 360 divided by the number of sides, as in the following:

```
numSides timesRepeat: [ourPen go: 100.
                       ourPen turn: 360 // numSides]
```

Using this method, a general equilateral polygon-drawing class can be built. The following example is similar to one in Goldberg and Robson (1983):

```
class name                       Polygon
superclass                       Object
instance variable names           ourPen
                                 numSides
                                 sideLength
                                   -

"Class methods"
"Create an instance"
  new
    ^ super new getPen
```

```
"Instance methods"
"Get a pen for drawing polygons"
  getPen
    ourPen <- Pen new defaultNib: 2

"Draw a polygon"
  draw
    numSides timesRepeat: [ourPen go: sideLength;
                                  turn: 360 // numSides]

"Set length of sides"
  length: len
    sideLength <- len

"Set number of sides"
  sides: num
    numSides <- num
```

Notice that the variable `ourPen` in the class definition above does not begin with an uppercase letter, as it did when it was used outside a class. This is the case because it is a local, private variable here, but it had to be a global variable when it was used outside the class definition.

With this class, a sequence of polygons with various numbers of sides can be drawn, as with

```
| MyPoly |
MyPoly <- Polygon new.
MyPoly length: 60.
3 to: 8 do: [:sides | MyPoly sides: sides. MyPoly draw]
```

This code draws the figure shown in Figure 11.3 on page 464. The lines in the figure can be made wider by changing the shape of the pen tip, which is done by sending the message inside the class definition:

```
ourPen defaultNib: 4
```

This changes the shape of the tip to 4 bits by 4 bits. The result of drawing the same polygons as above with this new tip is shown in Figure 11.4 on page 464.

11.7 Large-Scale Features of Smalltalk

11.7.1 Type Checking and Polymorphism

The dynamic binding of messages to methods in Smalltalk operates as follows: A message to an object causes the class to which the object belongs to be searched for a corresponding method. If the search fails, it is continued in the superclass of that class, and so forth, up to the system class, `Object`,

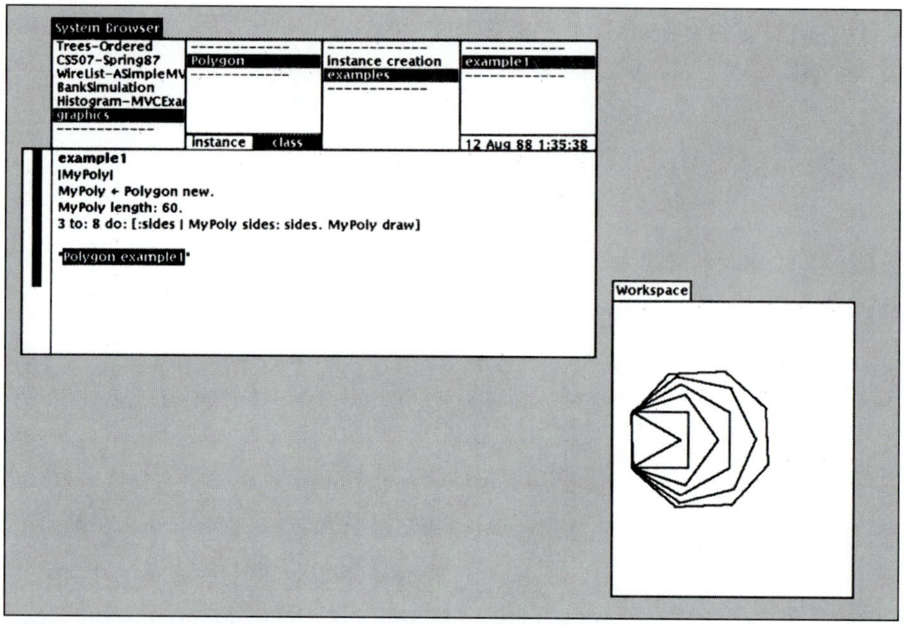

Figure 11.3
Concentric polygons
from the object
`Polygon`

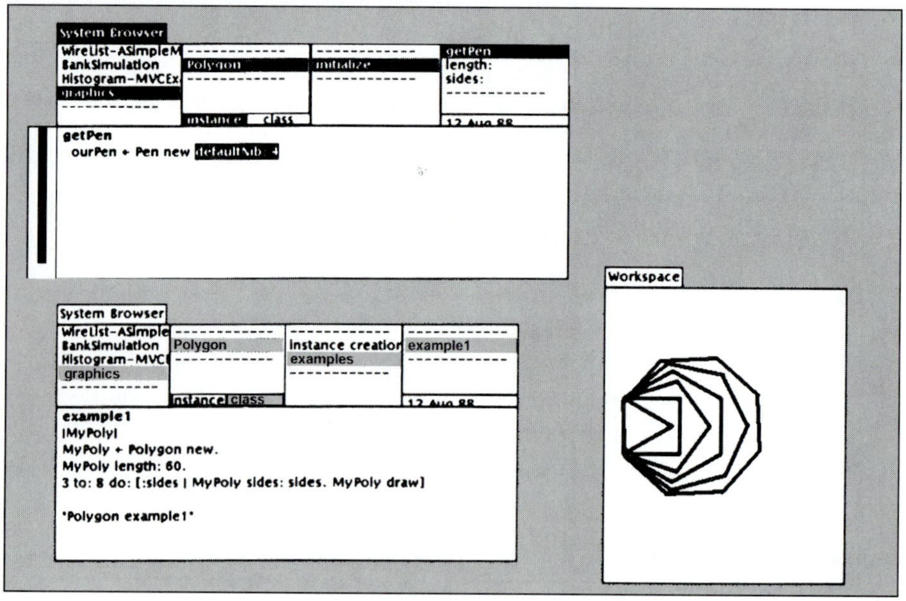

Figure 11.4
Concentric polygons
with `nib` set to 4

which has no superclass. `Object` is the root of the class derivation tree on which every class is a node. If no method is found anywhere in that chain, an error occurs. It is important to remember that this method search is dynamic—it takes place when the message is sent. Smalltalk does not, under any circumstances, bind messages to methods statically.

The only type checking in Smalltalk is dynamic, and the only type error occurs when a message is sent to an object that has no matching method, either locally or through inheritance. This is a different concept of type checking than that of most other languages. Smalltalk type checking has the simple goal of ensuring that a message matches a method.

Smalltalk variables are not typed; any name can be bound to any object. As a direct result, Smalltalk supports dynamic polymorphism. All Smalltalk code is generic in the sense that the types of the variables are irrelevant, as long as they are consistent. The meaning of an operation (method or operator) on a variable is determined by the class of the variable to which the variable is currently bound.

The point of this discussion is that as long as the objects referenced in an expression have methods for the messages of the expression, the types of the objects are irrelevant. This means that all code is generic; none is tied to a particular type.

11.7.2 Inheritance

A Smalltalk subclass inherits all of the instance variables, instance methods, and class methods of its superclass. The subclass can also have its own instance variables, which must have different names than the variable names in its ancestor classes. Finally, the subclass can define new methods and redefine methods that already exist in an ancestor class. When a subclass has a method whose name and protocol are the same as an ancestor class, the subclass method hides that of the ancestor class. Access to such a hidden method is provided by prefixing the message with the pseudovariable **super**. This causes the method search to begin in the superclass rather than locally.

Because entities in a parent class cannot be hidden from subclasses, all subclasses are subtypes. Furthermore, all inheritance is implementation inheritance.

Smalltalk supports single inheritance; it does not allow multiple inheritance.

11.8 Evaluation of Smalltalk

Smalltalk is a small language, although the Smalltalk system is large. The syntax of the language is simple and very regular. It is a good example of the power that can be provided by a small language if that language is built around a simple but powerful concept. In the case of Smalltalk, that concept is that all programming can be done using only a class hierarchy built using inheritance, objects, and message passing.

In comparison with conventional compiled imperative language programs, equivalent Smalltalk programs are significantly slower. Although it is theoretically interesting that array indexing and loops can be provided within the message-passing model, efficiency is an important factor in the evaluation of programming languages. Therefore, efficiency will clearly be an issue in most discussions of the practical applicability of Smalltalk.

Smalltalk's dynamic binding allows type errors to go undetected until run time. A program can be written and compiled that includes messages to nonexistent methods. This causes a great deal more error repair later in the development than would occur in a static-typed language.

The Smalltalk user interface has had an important impact on computing: The integrated use of windows, mouse-pointing devices, and pop-up or pull-down menus dominate contemporary software systems.

Perhaps the greatest impact of Smalltalk is the advancement of object-oriented programming, now the most widely used design and coding methodology.

11.9 Support for Object-Oriented Programming in C++

Chapter 2 describes how C++ evolved from C and SIMULA 67, with the design goal of support for object-oriented programming. C++ classes, as they are used to support abstract data types, are discussed in Chapter 10. C++ support for the other essentials of object-oriented programming is explored in this section. The whole collection of details of C++ classes, inheritance, and dynamic binding is large and complex. This section discusses only the most important among these topics, specifically those directly related to the design issues discussed in Section 11.3.

11.9.1 General Characteristics

Because one of the primary design considerations of C++ was that it be almost completely backward compatible with C, it retains the type system of C and adds classes to it. Therefore, C++ has both traditional imperative language types and the class structure of an object-oriented language. This makes it a hybrid language, supporting both procedural programming and object-oriented programming.

The objects of C++ can be allocated from all of the same places variables can be allocated in C: They can be statically allocated by the compiler, stack-dynamically allocated, or heap allocated using the **new** operator. Explicit deallocation is required using the **delete** operator. There is no implicit storage reclamation.

All C++ classes include at least one constructor method, which is used to initialize the data members of the new object. Constructor methods are implicitly called when an object is created. If any of the data members are heap-allocated, the constructor does that allocation. If no constructor is included in a class definition, the compiler includes a trivial constructor. This default constructor calls the constructor of the parent class, if there is a parent class (see Section 11.9.2).

Most class definitions include a destructor method, which is implicitly called when an object of the class ceases to exist. The destructor is used to delete heap-allocated data members. It may also be used to record part or all of the state of the object just before it dies, usually for debugging purposes.

While Smalltalk does not allow the user to exercise any access control on the instance variables and methods in a class, C++ provides a variety of such access controls. Some of these are for controlling what a client can see and not see in the class definition. Others are to control access by subclasses. C++ access controls for class entities are discussed in Section 11.9.2.

11.9.2 Inheritance

A C++ class can be derived from an existing class, which is then its parent, or base, class. Unlike Smalltalk, a C++ class can also be stand-alone, without a superclass.

Recall that the data defined in a class definition are called data members of that class, and the functions defined in a class definition are called member functions of that class. Some or all of the data members and member functions of the base class may be inherited by the derived class, which can also add new data members and member functions and modify inherited members. Accessibility to the members of subclasses can be different than that of the corresponding members of the base class. This is how derived classes in C++ can be prevented from being subtypes.

Recall from Chapter 10 that class members can be private, protected, or public. Private members are accessible only by member functions and friends of the class. Both functions and classes can be declared to be friends of a class and thereby be given access to its private members. Public members are accessible by any function. Protected members are like private members, except in derived classes, whose access is described below. Derived classes can modify accessibility for their inherited members. The syntactic form of a derived class is

    class derived_class_name : access_mode base_class_name
      {data member and member function declarations};

The access_mode can be either **public** or **private**. The public and protected members of a base class are also public and protected, respectively, in a public derived class. In a private derived class, both the public and protected members of the base class are private. So in a class hierarchy, a private derived class cuts off access to all members of all ancestor classes to all successor classes, and protected members may or may not be accessible to subsequent subclasses (past the first). Private members of a base class are inherited by a derived class, but they are not visible to the members of that derived class and are therefore of no use there. Consider the following example:

```
class base_class {
  private:
    int a;
    float x;
  protected:
    int b;
    float y;
  public:
    int c;
    float z;
};

class subclass_1 : public base_class { ... };
class subclass_2 : private base_class { ... };
```

In subclass_1, b and y are protected, and c and z are public. In subclass_2, b, y, c, and z are private. No derived class of subclass_2 can have members with access to any member of base_class. The data members a and x in base_class are not accessible in either subclass_1 or subclass_2.

Under private class derivation, no member of the parent class is implicitly visible to the instances of the derived class. Any member that must be made visible must be reexported in the derived class. This reexportation in effect exempts a member from being hidden even though the derivation was private. For example, consider the following class definition:

```
class subclass_3 : private base_class {
  base_class :: c;
  ...
}
```

Now, instances of subclass_3 can access c. As far as c is concerned, it is as if the derivation had been public. The double colon (::) in this class definition is a scope resolution operator. It specifies the class where its following entity is defined.

Consider the following example of C++ inheritance, in which a general linked list class is defined and then used to define two useful subclasses:

```
class single_linked_list {
  class node {
    friend class single_linked_list;
    private:
      node *link;
      int contents;
```

```
    };
    private:
      node *head;
    public:
      single_linked_list() {head = 0};
      void insert_at_head(int);
      void insert_at_tail(int);
      int remove_at_head();
      int empty();
  };
```

The nested class, **node**, defines a cell of the linked list to consist of an integer location and a pointer to a cell. It lists **single_linked_list** as a **friend**, thus granting objects of class **single_linked_list** access to its two data members, **link** and **contents**. This is necessary because enclosing classes have no special access rights to members of their nested classes.

The enclosing class, **single_linked_list**, has just a single data member, a pointer to act as the list's header. It contains a constructor function, which simply sets **head** to the null pointer value. The four member functions allow nodes to be inserted at either end of a list object, nodes to be removed from one end of a list, and lists to be tested for empty.

The following definitions provide stack and queue classes, both based on the **single_linked_list** class:

```
class stack : public single_linked_list {
  public:
    stack() {}
    void push(int value) {
      single_linked_list :: insert_at_head(int value);
    }
    int pop() {
      return single_linked_list :: remove_at_head();
    }
};
class queue : public single_linked_list {
  public:
    queue() {}
    void enqueue(int value) {
      single_linked_list :: insert_at_tail(int value);
    }
    int dequeue() {
      single_linked_list :: remove_at_head();
    }
};
```

Note that objects of both the **stack** and **queue** subclasses can access the **empty** function defined in the base class, **single_linked_list** (because it is a public derivation). Both subclasses define constructor functions that do nothing. When an object of a subclass is created, the proper constructor in the subclass is implicitly called. Then any applicable constructor in the base class is called. So in our example, when an object of type `stack` is created, the `stack` constructor is called, which does nothing. Then the constructor in `single_linked_list` is called, which does the necessary initialization.

The classes `stack` and `queue` both suffer from the same serious problem: Objects of both can access all of the public members of the parent class, `single_linked_list`. Therefore, a `stack` object could access `insert_at_tail`, thereby destroying the integrity of its stack. Likewise, a `queue` object could access `insert_at_head`. These unwanted accesses are allowed because both `stack` and `queue` are subtypes of `single_linked_list`. These two derived classes can be written to make them not subtypes of their parent class by using **private**, rather than **public** derivation. Then both will also need to reexport `empty`, because it will become hidden to their instances. The new definitions of the stack and queue types, named `stack_2` and `queue_2`, are shown in the following:

```
class stack_2 : private single_linked_list {
  public:
    stack_2() {}
    void push(int value) {
      single_linked_list :: insert_at_head(int value);
    }
    int pop() {
      return single_linked_list :: remove_at_head();
    }
    single_linked_list:: empty;
};
class queue_2 : private single_linked_list {
  public:
    queue_2() {}
    void enqueue(int value) {
      single_linked_list :: insert_at_tail(int value);
    }
    int dequeue() {
      single_linked_list :: remove_at_head();
    }
    single_linked_list:: empty;
};
```

The two versions of stack and queue illustrate the difference between subtypes and derived types that are not subtypes.

One of the reasons why friends are necessary is that sometimes a subprogram must be written that must access the members of two different classes. For example, suppose a program uses a class for vectors and one for matrices, and a subprogram is needed to multiply objects of these two classes. In C++, the multiply function is simply made a friend of both classes.

C++ provides the option of multiple inheritance by allowing more than one class to be named as the parent of a new class. For example,

```
class A { ... };
class B { ... };
class C : public A, public B { ... };
```

Class C inherits all of the members of both A and B. If both A and B happen to include members with the same name, they can be unambiguously referenced in objects of class C by using the scope resolution operator.

Overriding methods in C++ must have exactly the same protocol as the overridden method. If there is any difference in the protocols, the method in the subclass is considered a new method that is unrelated to the method with the same name in the ancestor class.

11.9.3 Dynamic Binding

All of the member functions we have defined thus far are statically bound; that is, a call to one of them is statically bound to a function definition. In C++, a pointer or reference variable that has the type of a base class can be used to point to objects of any class derived from that base class, making it a polymorphic variable. When this polymorphic variable is used to call a function defined in one of the derived classes, the call must be dynamically bound to the correct function definition. Member functions that must be dynamically bound must be declared to be virtual functions by preceding their headers with the reserved word **virtual**, which can only appear in a class body.

Consider the situation of having a base class named shape, along with a collection of derived classes for different kinds of shapes, such as circles, rectangles, and so forth. If these shapes need to be displayed, then the displaying member function, draw, must be unique for each subclass, or kind of shape. These versions of draw must be defined to be virtual. When a call to draw is made with a pointer to the base class of the derived classes, that call must be dynamically bound to the member function of the correct derived class. The following has the definitions of the example situation just described:

```
class shape {
  public:
    virtual void draw() = 0;
    ...
}
class circle : public shape {
  public:
    virtual void draw() { ... }
    ...
}
class rectangle : public shape {
  public:
    virtual void draw() { ... }
    ...
```

```
      }
      class square : public rectangle {
        public:
          virtual void draw() { ... }
        ...
      }
```

Given these definitions, the following has examples of both statically and dynamically bound calls:

```
square s;
rectangle r;
shape &ref_shape = s;   // a reference to the square s
ref_shape.draw();       // dynamically bound to draw in
                        // square
r.draw();               // statically bound to draw in
                        // rectangle
```

Notice that the draw function in the definition of the base class shape above is set to zero. This peculiar syntax is used to indicate that this member function is a **pure virtual function,** meaning it has no body and it cannot be called. It must be redefined in derived classes. The purpose of a pure virtual function is to provide the interface of a function without revealing any of its implementation. This is a new form of information hiding, or encapsulation.

Any class that includes a pure virtual function is an **abstract class.** No object of an abstract class can be created. In a strict sense, an abstract data type is one that cannot have concrete objects but rather is used only to represent the concepts of a type. Subclasses of such a type can, of course, have objects. C++ provides abstract classes to model these truly abstract types. If a subclass of an abstract class does not redefine a pure virtual function of its parent class, that function remains as a pure virtual function.

Abstract classes and inheritance together support a powerful technique for software development. They allow types to be hierarchically defined, so that related types can be subclasses of truly abstract types that define their common abstract characteristics.

Dynamic binding allows the code that uses members like draw to be written before all or even any of the versions of draw are written. New derived classes could be added years later, without requiring any change to the code that uses such dynamically bound members. This is a powerful feature of object-oriented languages.

11.9.4 Evaluation

It is natural to compare the object-oriented features of C++ with those of Smalltalk, which is what is done in this section.

The inheritance of C++ is more intricate than that of Smalltalk in terms of access control. By using both the access controls within the class definition and the derivation access controls, and also the possibility of friend functions and classes, the C++ programmer has highly detailed control over the access to class members. Furthermore, although there is some debate over its real value, C++ provides multiple inheritance, whereas Smalltalk allows only single inheritance.

In C++, the programmer can specify whether static binding or dynamic binding is to be used. Because static binding is faster, this is an advantage for those situations where dynamic binding is not necessary. Furthermore, even the dynamic binding in C++ is fast when compared with that of Smalltalk. Binding a virtual member function call in C++ to a function definition has a fixed cost, regardless of how distant in the inheritance hierarchy the definition appears. Calls to virtual functions require only five more memory references than statically bound calls (Stroustrup, 1988). In Smalltalk, however, messages are always dynamically bound to methods, and the farther away in the inheritance hierarchy the correct method is, the longer it takes. The disadvantage of allowing the user to decide which bindings are static and which are dynamic is that the original design must include these decisions, which may have to be changed later.

The static type checking of C++ is a significant advantage over Smalltalk, where all type checking is dynamic. A Smalltalk program can be compiled with messages to nonexistent methods, which are then discovered in dynamic testing. A C++ compiler finds such errors. Compiler-detected errors are less expensive to repair than those found in execution.

Smalltalk is essentially typeless, meaning that all code is effectively generic. This provides a great deal of flexibility, but static type checking is sacrificed. C++ provides generic classes through its template facility (as described in Chapter 10), which retains the benefits of static type checking.

The primary advantage of Smalltalk lies in the elegance and simplicity of the language that results from the single philosophy of its design. It is purely and completely devoted to the object-oriented paradigm, devoid of compromises necessitated by the whims of an entrenched user base. C++, on the other hand, is a large and complex language with no single philosophy as its foundation, except to include the C user base. One of its most significant goals was to preserve the efficiency and flavor of C while providing the advantages of object-oriented programming. Some people feel that the features of this language do not always fit well together and that much of the complexity is unnecessary.

According to Chambers and Ungar (1991), Smalltalk ran a particular set of small C-style benchmarks at only 10 percent of the speed of optimized C. C++ programs require only slightly more time than equivalent C programs (Stroustrup, 1988). Given the great efficiency gap between Smalltalk and C++, it is little wonder that the commercial use of C++ is far more widespread than that of Smalltalk. Of course, there are other factors in this difference, but efficiency is clearly a strong argument in favor of C++.

11.10 Support for Object-Oriented Programming in Java

Because Java's design of classes, inheritance, and methods is similar to that of C++, we focus in this section only on those areas in which Java differs from C++.

11.10.1 General Characteristics

As with C++, Java does not use objects exclusively. However, in Java only values of the primitive scalar types (Boolean, character, and the numeric types) are not objects. Java has no enumeration or record types, and its arrays are objects. The reason to have non-objects is efficiency. However, as discussed in Section 11.3.1, having two type systems leads to some cumbersome situations. One of these in Java is that the predefined data structure `Vector` can only contain objects. So if you want to put a primitive type value into a `Vector` object, the value must first be placed in an object. This can be done by creating a new object of the wrapper class for the primitive type. Such a class has an instance variable of that primitive type and a constructor that takes a value of the primitive type as a parameter and assigns it to its instance variable. For example, to put 10 into the `Vector` object referenced by the variable `myVector`, we could use the following statement:

```
myVector.addElement(new Integer(10));
```

where `addElement` is a method of `Vector` that inserts a new element and `Integer` is the wrapper class for **int**.

Whereas C++ classes can be defined to have no parent, that is not possible in Java. All Java classes must be subclasses of the root class, `Object`, or some class that is a descendant of `Object`. One reason to have a single root class is that there are some operations that are universally needed. Among these is a method for comparing objects for equality.

All Java objects are explicit heap dynamic. Most are allocated with the **new** operator, but there is no explicit deallocation operator. Garbage collection is used for storage reclamation.

11.10.2 Inheritance

Java directly supports only single inheritance. However, it includes a kind of virtual class, called an interface, which provides a version of multiple inheritance. An interface definition is similar to a class definition, except that it can contain only named constants and method declarations (not definitions). So an interface is no more than what its name indicates—it defines only the specification of a class. (Recall that a C++ abstract class can have instance variables and all but one of the methods can be completely defined.) The typical use of an interface is to define a class that inherits both some of the methods and variables from its parent class, and also implements a parent interface.

We now return to an inheritance scenario involving Java applets discussed briefly in Section 11.3.5. Applets are programs that are interpreted by a World Wide Web browser after being downloaded from a Web server. Calls to applets are embedded in the HTML code that describes a Web page. These applets all need certain capabilities, which they can inherit from the predefined class, `Applet`. When an applet is used to implement animation, it is often defined to run in its own thread of control. This concurrency is supported by a predefined class named `Thread`. However, an applet class being designed to use concurrency cannot inherit from both `Applet` and `Thread`. But Java includes a predefined interface named `Runnable` that supplies the interface (but not the implementation) to one of the methods of `Thread`. The syntax of the header of such an applet is exemplified by

public class Clock **extends** Applet **implements** Runnable

Although this appears to provide multiple inheritance, in this case it requires a further complication. For an object of the `Clock` class to run concurrently, a `Thread` object must be created and connected to the `Clock` object. The messages that control the concurrent execution of the `Clock` object must be sent to the corresponding `Thread` object. This is surely an inelegant and potentially confusing necessity. Concurrency and Java threads are discussed in Chapter 12.

In Java, a method can be defined to be **final**, which means that it cannot be overriden in any descendant class. When the **final** reserved word is specified on a class definition, it means the class cannot be the parent of any subclass.

11.10.3 Dynamic Binding

In C++, a method must be defined to be virtual to allow dynamic binding. In Java, all method calls are dynamically bound unless the called method has been defined to be **final**, in which case it cannot be overriden and all bindings are static.

11.10.4 Encapsulation

Java has two kinds of encapsulation constructs, classes and packages. A package is a logical, rather than a physical, encapsulation: Any class definition can specify that it belongs in a particular package. A class that does not specify a package name is placed in an unnamed package. A package creates a new name space. Any method or variable that does not include an access modifier (**private**, **protected**, or **public**) has what is called

package scope. All methods and variables that are not declared private are visible throughout the package in which they are declared. This is an expansion of the definition of protected as used in C++, in which protected members are visible only in the class where they are defined and in subclasses of that class. Package scope is an alternative to the friends of C++, which are meant to provide access to private methods and instance variables in a class to other specified methods or classes. In the case of Java, when there are nonpublic methods or variables that we want to make visible to other classes, we define them to be protected. This hides them from non-subclasses outside the package, but puts their class in a package with the other classes to which we want to provide access. In effect, all non-private variables and methods of all of the classes in a package are friends.

As an example of a use of a package, suppose we have a class for matrices and one for vectors and need an operation that uses an object of each of those classes. Their instance variables can be defined to be protected and the two classes can be placed in the same package. Then an operation between objects of the two classes will have access to the variables, which is, of course, required in this scenario.

There remains the problem of where to put an operation between a matrix and a vector; dot product is an example. While package scope allows the operation, whether it is in the matrix or the vector class, to access the data of both, there still is no guidance about where it belongs. It could be in either of the two classes, or it could appear in a separate class in the package with the other two.

11.10.5 Evaluation

Java's design for supporting object-oriented programming is similar to that of C++, but differs from it in several significant ways. In keeping with its consistent adherence to object-oriented principles, as in its lack of functions, Java does not allow parentless classes. It also uses dynamic binding as the "normal" approach to bind method calls to method definitions. Access control for the contents of a class definition are rather simple when compared with the jungle of access controls of C++, ranging from derivation controls to friend functions.

11.11 Support for Object-Oriented Programming in Ada 95

Ada 95 was derived from Ada 83, with some significant extensions. This section presents a brief look at the extensions that were designed to support object-oriented programming. Because Ada 83 already included constructs for building abstract data types, which are discussed in Chapter 10, the remaining necessary features were those for supporting inheritance and dynamic binding. The design objectives for these features included the goals of requiring minimal changes to the type and package structures of Ada 83 and retaining as much static type checking as possible.

11.11.1 General Characteristics

Ada 95 classes are a new category of types called **tagged types,** which can be either records or private types. They are encapsulated in packages, which allows them to be separately compiled. Tagged types are so named because each object of a tagged type implicitly includes a system-maintained tag that indicates its type. The subprograms that define the operations on a tagged type appear in the same declaration list as the type declaration. Consider this example:

```
package PERSON_PKG is
  type PERSON is tagged private;
  procedure DISPLAY(P : in out PERSON);
  private
    type PERSON is tagged
      record
        NAME : STRING(1..30);
        ADDRESS : STRING(1..30);
        AGE : INTEGER;
      end record;
end PERSON_PKG;
```

This package defines the type PERSON that can be used on its own and as the parent class of other derived classes.

Unlike C++, there is no implicit calling of constructor or destructor subprograms in Ada 95. These subprograms can be written, but they must be explicitly called by the programmer.

11.11.2 Inheritance

Ada 83 has a restricted form of inheritance in its derived types and subtypes. In both of these, a new type can be defined on the basis of an existing type. But the only modification allowed is to restrict the range of values of the new type. Derived classes in Ada 95 are based on tagged types. New entities are added to the inherited entities by including a record definition. Consider this example:

```
with PERSON_PKG; use PERSON_PKG;
package STUDENT_PKG is
  type STUDENT is new PERSON with
    record
      GRADE_POINT_AVERAGE : FLOAT;
      GRADE_LEVEL : INTEGER;
```

```
        end record;
     procedure DISPLAY (ST : in STUDENT);
   end STUDENT_PKG;
```

In this example, the derived type STUDENT is defined to have the entities of its parent class, PERSON, along with the new entities GRADE_POINT_AVER-AGE and GRADE_LEVEL. It also redefines the procedure DISPLAY. This new class is defined in a separate package to allow it to be changed without requiring recompilation of the package containing the definition of the parent type.

Through this inheritance mechanism, there is no way to prevent entities of the parent class from being included in the derived class. Therefore, derived classes can only extend parent classes, and are therefore subtypes.

Suppose we have the following definitions:

```
P1 : PERSON;
S1 : STUDENT;
FRED : ("FRED", "321 Mulberry Lane", 35);
FREDDIE : ("FREDDIE", "725 Main St.", 20, 3.25, 3);
```

Because STUDENT is a subtype of PERSON, the assignment

```
P1 := FRED;
```

should be legal, and it is. The GRADE_POINT_AVERAGE and GRADE_LEVEL entities of FRED are simply ignored in the required coercion.

The obvious question now is whether an assignment in the opposite direction is legal; that is, can we assign a PERSON to a STUDENT. In Ada 95, this is legal in a form that includes the entities in the subclass. In our example, the following is legal:

```
S1 := (FRED, 3.05, 2);
```

To derive a class that does not include all of the parent class's entities, child library packages are used. A child library package is simply a package whose name is prefixed with that of a parent package. Child library packages can also be used in place of the friend definitions in C++. For example, if a subprogram must be written that must access the members of two different classes, the parent package can define one of the classes, and the child package can define the other. Then a subprogram in the child package can access the members of both.

Ada 95 does not provide for multiple inheritance. There is a way to achieve a similar effect by using generics, but it is not as elegant as the C++ method, and it is not discussed here.

11.11.3 Dynamic Binding

Ada 95 provides both static binding and dynamic binding of function calls to function definitions in tagged types. Dynamic binding is forced by using classwide types, which are types that in a sense represent all of the types in a class hierarchy. For a tagged type `T`, the classwide type is specified with `T'class`. If we wanted to write a procedure that could call either of the two `DISPLAY` procedures defined in `PERSON` and `STUDENT`, the following will work:

```
procedure DISPLAY_ANY_PERSON(P: in out PERSON'class) is
  begin
  DISPLAY (P);
  end DISPLAY_ANY_PERSON;
```

This procedure can be called with both of the following calls:

```
with PERSON_PKG; use PERSON_PKG;
with STUDENT_PKG; use STUDENT_PKG;
P : PERSON;
S : STUDENT;
DISPLAY_ANY_PERSON(P);  — call the DISPLAY in PERSON
DISPLAY_ANY_PERSON(S);  — call the DISPLAY in STUDENT
```

We can have polymorphic pointers by defining them to have the class-wide type, as in

```
type ANY_PERSON_PTR is access PERSON'class;
```

Purely abstract base types can be defined in Ada 95 by including the reserved word **abstract** in the type definitions and the subprogram definitions. Furthermore, the subprogram definitions cannot have bodies. Consider this example:

```
package BASE_PKG is
  type T is abstract tagged null record;
  procedure DO_IT (A : T) is abstract;
end BASE_PKG;
```

11.11.4 Evaluation

A detailed comparison of the object-oriented features of C++ and Ada 95 is not possible based only on the meager description of these features provided here. However, a few distinctions can be made between the two designs.

C++ classes have their own type system that is in addition to the usual type system, mainly inherited from C. In Ada 95, the class mechanism is built into the existing type system. One result of this is that there are no oddities in Ada 95 such as some that are possible in C++. For example, if class `B_CLASS` is derived from class `A_CLASS` in a C++ program and `B` is a pointer to `B_CLASS` objects, and `A` is a pointer to `A_CLASS` objects, we have

```
B = A;  // an illegal assignment
A = B;  // a legal assignment
```

C++ clearly offers a better form of multiple inheritance than Ada 95. However, the use of child library units to control access to the entities of the parent class seems to be a cleaner solution than the friend functions and classes of C++. For example, if the need for a friend is not known when a class is defined, it will need to be changed and recompiled when such a need is discovered. In Ada 95, new classes in new child packages can be defined without disturbing the parent package.

The design of C++ constructors and destructors for initialization of objects and the handling of heap allocation and deallocation is good, and Ada 95 includes no such capabilities.

Another difference between these two languages is that the designer of a C++ root class must decide whether a particular member function will be statically or dynamically bound. If the choice is made in favor of static binding, but a later change in the system requires dynamic binding, the root class must be changed. In Ada 95, this design decision need not be made with the design of the root class. Each call can itself specify whether it will be statically or dynamically bound, regardless of the design of the root class.

A more subtle difference is that dynamic binding in C++ is restricted to pointers and references to objects, rather than the objects themselves. Ada 95 has no such restriction, so in this case Ada 95 is more orthogonal.

11.12 Support for Object-Oriented Programming in Eiffel

Eiffel is a pure object-oriented language in the sense that it was designed specifically to support object-oriented programming only and it is not based on any existing language. Furthermore, subprograms can be enacted only through objects. Its syntax is similar to that of Pascal and Ada. It has several distinguishing characteristics, such as the inclusion of assertions. However, in this chapter we only discuss its support for object-oriented programming, specifically inheritance and dynamic binding.

11.12.1 General Characteristics

Eiffel is like Java because it has both basic types, for simple scalars, and objects defined in classes. In the original version of the language, all objects were allocated from the heap and accessed through references. Later versions added a second kind of objects, called expanded objects, which are allocated from the stack. There are three predefined operations for all objects: `copy`, `clone`, and `equal`. `copy` copies the entities of one allocated object to another allocated object. `clone` first creates storage for an object and then copies the entities from another object to this new space. `equal` tests two objects for equality, considering their entities, not just the reference values.

The methods of Eiffel are called **routines;** its instance variables are called **attributes.** The routines and attributes of a class together are called its **features.**

Reference variables are defined in the usual way, as in

```
stkl : stack;
```

However, a second statement is required to allocate an object. This is done with an operator, !!, as in

```
!!stkl;
```

Object creation implicitly includes initialization of attributes using standard default values. Constructor routines for classes can be defined by the user for initialization with nonstandard default values. Constructors are defined in a **creation** clause and are explicitly called in the object creation statement. For example, in the following, initComplex is a constructor:

```
class Complex
  creation
    initComplex
  feature
    real_part, imag_part : REAL
  feature
    initComplex(r, i : REAL) is
      do
      real_part := r;
      imag_part := i
      end;
    ...
```

Now, with the following we can create a reference to a Complex object, and create and initialize that object:

```
c1 : Complex;
!!c1.initComplex(2.4, -3.2);
```

There is no explicit deallocation operation in Eiffel. When an object can no longer be referenced, it is implicitly deallocated and a garbage collection process eventually reclaims its storage.

11.12.2 Inheritance

The parent of a class is specified with the **inherit** clause, as in

```
class square
inherit rectangle
...
```

A class definition can include one or more **feature** clauses. A **feature** clause with no qualifiers is visible to both subclasses and clients. If the {**none**} qualifier is attached to the **feature** reserved word, the features it defines are hidden from both subclasses and clients. If the name of the class is used as a qualifier, the features are hidden from clients but visible to subclasses. The following code segment illustrates these three levels of visibility:

```
class child
inherit parent
feature
— Features defined here are visible to clients and
—   subclasses
feature {child}
— Features defined here are hidden from clients but
—   visible to subclasses
feature {none}
— Features defined here are hidden from both clients and
—   subclasses
...
end;
```

Inherited features can be hidden within the subclass using **undefine**. This obviously prevents the subclass from being a subtype. To control access by clients to inherited features, an **export** clause can be used.

Abstract classes are defined by adding the **deferred** reserved word at the beginning of the class definition, as in

```
deferred class figure
```

Such a class includes one or more features that are also deferred. Any subclass of a deferred class that is not itself deferred must of course include definitions of the deferred features of the parent.

Eiffel supports multiple inheritance, which is specified by simply having more than one **inherit** clause.

11.12.3 Dynamic Binding

All bindings of messages to methods in Eiffel are dynamic. Routines in subclasses can override inherited routines. To be an overriding routine, the types of the formal parameters must be assignment compatible with those of the overridden routine. Furthermore, the return type of the overriding routine must be assignment compatible with that of the overridden routine. All overriding features must be defined in a **redefine** clause.

Access to overridden features can be maintained by putting their names in a **rename** clause.

11.12.4 Evaluation

Eiffel's support for object-oriented programming is similar to that of Java. In neither case is procedural programming supported, and in both cases nearly all bindings of messages to methods are dynamic. Before Java came along, the elegance and clean design of Eiffel's classes and inheritance were second only to those of Smalltalk.

11.13 Implementation of Object-Oriented Constructs

There are at least two parts of language support for object-oriented programming that pose interesting questions for language implementers, storage structures for instance variables and the dynamic bindings of messages to methods. In this section we take a brief look at these two.

11.13.1 Instance Data Storage

In C++, classes are defined as extensions of record structures. In fact, a C++ **struct** can include functions. The only difference between a **struct** and a class is that all of the members of a **struct** are by default public, whereas in a class all members are by default private. This similarity certainly suggests a storage structure for the instance variables of class instances—that of a record. We call this form of this structure a **class instance record** (CIR). The structure of a CIR is static, so it is built at compile time and used as a template for the creation of class instances. Subclasses of a class can simply extend the CIR of the parent class by adding the new instance variables.

Because the structure of the CIR is static, access to all instance variables can be done as it is in records, using constant offsets from the beginning of the CIR instance. This makes these accesses as efficient as those for the fields of records.

The CIR for a class that has a parent simply adds its new data to the parent CIR.

This approach to implementing instance data storage should work for all of the object-oriented languages discussed in this chapter.

11.13.2 Dynamic Binding of Messages to Methods

Methods in a class that are statically bound need not be involved in the CIR for the class. However, methods that will be dynamically bound must have entries in this structure. Such entries could simply have a pointer to the code of the method, which must be set at object creation time. Calls to a method could then be connected to the corresponding code through this pointer in the instance structure. The drawback to this technique is that every instance would need to store pointers to all dynamically bound methods that could be called from the instance.

Notice that the list of dynamically bound methods that can be called from an instance of a class is the same for all instances of that class. Therefore, the list of such methods must only be stored once. So the CIR needs only a single pointer to that list to enable it to find called methods. The storage structure for the list is sometimes called a **virtual method table** (VMT). Method calls can be represented as offsets in the VMT. Polymorphic variables of an ancestor class always reference the CIR of the correct type object, so getting to the correct version of a dynamically-bound method is assured. Consider the following example, in which all methods are assumed to be dynamically bound:

```
class Small {
  public int a, b, c;
  public void draw() { ... }
}
class Large extends Small {
  public int d, e;
  public void draw() { ... }
  public void sift() { ... }
}
```

The CIRs for the `Small` and `Large` classes, along with their VMTs, are shown in Figure 11.5.

Figure 11.5
Class instance records and virtual methods tables

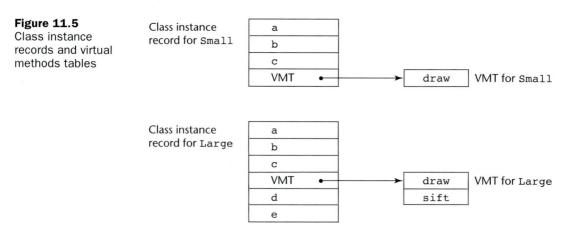

SUMMARY

Object-oriented programming involves three fundamental concepts: abstract data types, inheritance, and dynamic binding. Object-oriented programming languages support the paradigm with classes, methods, objects, and message passing.

The discussion of object-oriented programming languages in this chapter revolves around seven design issues, exclusivity of objects, subclasses and subtypes, implementation and interface inheritance, type checking and polymorphism, single and multiple inheritance, dynamic binding, and explicit or implicit deallocation of objects.

Smalltalk is a pure object-oriented language—everything is an object and all computation is accomplished through message passing. Methods are constructed from expressions. An expression describes an object, which happens to be the value of the expression. Control structures in Smalltalk, like everything else, are constructed using objects and messages. Although they have a somewhat conventional appearance, their semantics is very different from that of corresponding structures in the imperative languages. In Smalltalk all subclasses are subtypes. All type checking and binding of messages to methods is dynamic and all inheritance is single. Smalltalk has no explicit deallocation operation.

C++ provides support for data abstraction, inheritance, and optional dynamic binding of messages to methods, along with all of the conventional features of C. This means that it has two distinct type systems. While Smalltalk's dynamic binding provides somewhat more programming flexibility than the hybrid language, C++, it is far less efficient. C++ provides multiple inheritance and explicit object deallocation. C++ includes a variety of access controls for the entities in classes, some of which prevent subclasses from being subtypes. Both constructor and destructor methods can be included in classes; both are implicitly called.

Java is not a hybrid language like C++; it is purely for object-oriented programming. All objects are allocated from the heap and are accessed through reference variables. There is no explicit object deallocation operation. The only subprograms are methods, and they can only be called through objects or classes. Only single inheritance is directly supported, although a kind of multiple inheritance is possible using interfaces. All binding of messages to methods is dynamic, except in the case of methods that cannot be overriden. In addition to classes, Java includes packages as a second encapsulation construct.

Ada 95 provides support for object-oriented programming through tagged types, which can use inheritance. Dynamic binding is possible by using classwide types. Derived types are extensions to parent types, unless they are defined in child library packages, in which case entities of the parent type can be eliminated in the derived type. Outside child library packages, all subclasses are subtypes.

Eiffel is a new object-oriented language in that it is not based on some previous language. It includes access controls for the entities in classes to restrict access to clients, subclasses, or both. Like Java, there is no explicit deallocation operation. Users can, but need not, define constructors and destructors in their classes. All bindings of messages to methods in Eiffel are dynamic.

REVIEW QUESTIONS

1. What are the three characteristic features of object-oriented languages?
2. What is the difference between a class variable and an instance variable?
3. What is an overriding method?
4. Describe a situation where dynamic binding is a great advantage over its absence.
5. What is a virtual method?
6. Describe briefly the seven design issues used in this chapter for object-oriented languages.
7. What is the message protocol of a method?
8. Why is it that classes of Smalltalk can respond to messages?
9. Explain the actions of the Smalltalk statement

   ```
   result <- first * second
   ```
10. What are the four parts of a Smalltalk class definition?
11. Explain how Smalltalk messages are bound to methods. When does this take place?
12. What type checking is done in Smalltalk? When does it take place?
13. What kind of inheritance does Smalltalk support?
14. What are the two primary effects that Smalltalk has had on computing?
15. What purpose does the Smalltalk pseudovariable **super** serve?
16. In essence, all Smalltalk variables are of a single type. What is that type?
17. How many parameters are there in a Smalltalk binary message?
18. Explain the precedence rules of Smalltalk expressions.
19. How can one force a Smalltalk block to be executed?
20. What purpose does the Smalltalk pseudovariable **self** serve?
21. From where can C++ objects be allocated?
22. How are C++ heap-allocated objects deallocated?
23. Are all C++ subclasses subtypes?
24. Under what circumstances is a C++ method call statically bound to a method?
25. What drawback is there to allowing designers to specify which methods can be statically bound?

26. Explain the difference between the two uses of **private** in C++.

27. What is a **friend** function in C++?

28. How is the type system of Java different from that of C++?

29. From where can Java objects be allocated?

30. How are Java objects deallocated?

31. Are all Java subclasses subtypes?

32. Under what circumstances is a Java method call statically bound to a method?

33. Are all Ada 95 subclasses subtypes?

34. How is a call to a subprogram in Ada 95 specified to be dynamically bound to a subprogram definition? When is this decision made?

35. What purpose does a creation clause have in Eiffel?

36. How is an Eiffel feature defined to be visible in subclasses but not clients?

37. What does the {none} qualifier do when it appears on an Eiffel feature?

38. How are Eiffel heap-allocated objects deallocated?

39. Under what circumstances is an Eiffel method call statically bound to a method?

40. How can an Eiffel subclass be defined not to be a subtype?

PROBLEM SET

1. Write the following Pascal loop structure in Smalltalk:

```
while count < 100 do
  begin
  sum := sum div (2 * count - 1);
  count := count + 1
  end
```

2. Write the following Pascal **for** loop in Smalltalk:

```
for index := 10 downto 1 do
  sum := sum + index
```

3. Write the following Pascal selection construct in Smalltalk:

```
if count < 10 then
  answer := 1
else
  begin
  answer := 0;
  count := 0
  end
```

4. Write the following C **while** loop structure in Smalltalk:

```
while (count < 100) {
  sum /= (2 * count - 1);
  count++;
  }
```

5. Write the following C **for** loop structure in Smalltalk:

```
for (index = 10; index > 0; index—)
  sum += index;
```

6. Write the following C selection construct in Smalltalk:

```
if (count < 10)
  answer = 1;
else
  answer = count = 0;
```

7. Write a Smalltalk instance method that accepts four integer values, where the first two are the numerator and denominator of a fraction and the last two likewise represent another fraction. Your method must return a two-element array object that represents the numerator and denominator of the product of the two given fractions.

8. Compare the dynamic binding of Eiffel, C++, Smalltalk, Ada 95, and Java.

9. Compare the class entity access controls of Eiffel, C++, Smalltalk, Ada 95, and Java.

10. Compare the single inheritance of Eiffel, C++, Smalltalk, Ada 95, and Java.

11. Compare the multiple inheritance of Eiffel and C++.

12. Compare the multiple inheritance of C++ with that provided by interfaces in Java.

12 Concurrency

Niklaus Wirth

Niklaus Wirth of ETH in Zurich has been continuously involved in language design since the mid-1960s. He left the ALGOL 68 design team in the mid-1960s to develop ALGOL-W. He also designed Euler and PL/360 in the 1960s. Since then he has been responsible for the developoment of the Pascal, Modula, Modula-2, and Oberon languages.

This chapter begins with descriptions of the various kinds of concurrency at the subprogram, or unit, level and at the statement level. Included in this introduction is a brief description of some common kinds of multiprocessor computer architectures. Next, we present a lengthy discussion on unit-level concurrency. We begin by describing the fundamental concepts that must be understood before discussing unit-level concurrency, including competition and cooperation synchronization. Next, the design issues for providing language support for concurrency are described. Then we present a detailed discussion, including program examples, of the three major approaches to language support for concurrency: semaphores, monitors, and message passing. A pseudocode example program is used to demonstrate how semaphores can be used. An example program in Concurrent Pascal is used to illustrate the use of monitors; for message passing, an Ada program is used. The Ada features that support concurrency are described in some detail. These include tasks, **entry** declarations, **accept** clauses, **select** clauses, guards, **delay** statements, and **terminate** statements. Following the Ada discussion is a brief introduction to the new language features of Ada 95 that support concurrency, including protected units and asynchronous message passing. The last example of language support for unit-level concurrency is that of Java. The last section of the chapter has a discussion of statement-level concurrency, including a short description of part of the language support provided for it in High-Performance FORTRAN.

12.1 Introduction

Concurrency is naturally divided into instruction level (executing two or more machine instructions simultaneously), statement level (executing two or more statements simultaneously), unit level (executing two or more subprogram units simultaneously), and program level (executing two or more programs simultaneously). Because no language issues are involved with them, we do not discuss instruction-level and program-level concurrency in this chapter. Concurrency at both the subprogram and the statement levels are discussed, with the focus on the subprogram level.

Concurrent execution of program units can occur either physically on separate processors or logically in some time-sliced fashion on a single-processor computer system. At first glance, this may appear to be a simple concept, but it presents a significant challenge to the programming language designer.

Concurrent control methods increase programming flexibility. They were originally invented to be used for particular problems faced in operating systems, but they can be used for a variety of other programming applications. For example, many software systems are designed to simulate actual physical systems, and many of these physical systems consist of multiple concurrent subsystems. For these applications, the more restricted form of subprogram control is inadequate.

Statement-level concurrency is quite different from concurrency at the unit level. From a language designer's point of view, statement-level concurrency is largely a matter of specifying how data should be distributed over multiple memories and which statements can be executed concurrently.

The intention of this chapter is to discuss the aspects of concurrency that are most relevant to language design issues rather than to present a definitive study of all of the issues of concurrency. That would clearly be inappropriate for a book on programming languages.

12.1.1 Multiprocessor Architectures

A large number of different computer architectures have more than one processor and can support some form of concurrent program execution. Before beginning to discuss kinds of concurrent execution of programs and statements, we briefly describe some of these architectures.

The first computers that had multiple processors actually had one general-purpose processor and one or more other processors that were used only for input and output operations. This allowed these computers, which appeared in the late 1950s, to concurrently execute one program while performing input or output for other programs. Because this kind of concurrency does not require language support, we will not consider it further.

By the early 1960s, there were machines that had multiple complete processors. These processors were used by the job scheduler of the operating system, which simply distributed separate jobs from a batch-job queue to the separate processors. Systems with this structure supported program-level concurrency.

In the mid-1960s, multiprocessor computers appeared that had several identical partial processors that were fed certain instructions from a single instruction stream. For example, some machines had two or more floating-point multipliers, while others had two or more complete floating-point arithmetic units. The compilers for these machines were required to determine which instructions could be executed concurrently and to schedule these instructions accordingly. Systems with this structure supported instruction-level concurrency.

There are now many different kinds of multiprocessor computers, the most common two categories of which are described in the following two paragraphs.

Computers that have multiple processors that execute the same instruction simultaneously, each on different data, are called Single-Instruction Multiple-Data (SIMD) architecture computers. In a SIMD computer, each processor has its own local memory. One processor controls the operation of the other processors. Because all of the processors, except the controller, execute the same instruction at the same time, no synchronization is required in the software. Perhaps the most widely used SIMD machines are a category of machines called vector processors. They have groups of registers that store the operands of a vector operation in which the same instruction is executed on the whole group of operands simultaneously. The kinds of programs that can most benefit from this architecture are common in scientific computation, an area of computing that is often the target of multiprocessor machines.

Computers that have multiple processors that operate independently but whose operations can be synchronized are called Multiple-Instruction Multiple-Data (MIMD) computers. Each processor in an MIMD computer executes its own instruction stream. MIMD computers can appear in two distinct configurations, distributed and shared memory systems. The distributed MIMD machines, in which each processor has its own memory, can be either built in a single box or distributed over a large area. The shared memory MIMD machines obviously must provide some means of synchronization to prevent memory access clashes. Even distributed MIMD machines require synchronization to operate together on single programs. MIMD computers, which are more expensive and more general than SIMD computers, clearly support unit-level concurrency.

12.1.2 Categories of Concurrency

There are two distinct categories of concurrent unit control. The most general category of concurrency is that in which, assuming that more than one processor is available, several program units from the same program literally execute simultaneously. This is **physical concurrency.** A slight relaxation of this concept of concurrency allows the programmer and the application software to assume that there are multiple processors providing actual concurrency when, in fact, the actual execution of programs is taking place in interleaved fashion on a single processor. This is **logical concurrency.** It is similar to the illusion of simultaneous execution that is provided to different users of a multiprogramming computer system. From the programmer's and language designer's points of view, logical concurrency is the same as physical concurrency. It is the language implementor's task to map the logical concurrency to the underlying hardware. Both logical and physical concurrency allow the concept of concurrency to be used as a program design methodology. For the remainder of this chapter, we will mean logical concurrency whenever we use the word concurrency without qualification.

One useful technique for visualizing the flow of execution through a program is to imagine a thread laid on the statements of the source text of the program. Every statement reached on a particular execution is covered by the thread representing that execution. Visually following the thread through the source program traces the execution flow through the executable version of the program. A **thread of control** in a program is the sequence of program points reached as control flows through the program.

Programs that have coroutines (see Chapter 8), though they are sometimes called quasi-concurrent, have a single thread of control. Programs executed with physical concurrency can have multiple threads of control. Each processor can execute one of the threads. Although logically concurrent program execution may actually have only a single thread of control, such programs can only be designed and analyzed by imagining them as having multiple threads of control. When a multithreaded program executes on a single processor machine, its threads are mapped onto a single thread. It becomes, in this case, a virtually multithreaded program.

Statement-level concurrency is a relatively simple concept. Loops that include statements that operate on array elements are unwound so the processing can be distributed over multiple processors. For example, a loop that executes 500 repetitions and includes a statement that operates on one of 500 array elements may be unwound so that each of ten different processors can simultaneously process 50 of the array elements.

12.1.3 Motivations for Studying Concurrency

There are at least two reasons to study concurrency. First and foremost, it provides a method of conceptualizing program solutions to problems. Many problem domains lend themselves naturally to concurrency in much the same way that recursion is a natural way to design the solution to some problems. Many programs are written to simulate physical entities and activities. In many cases, the system being simulated includes more than one entity, and the entities do whatever they do simultaneously—for example, aircraft flying in a control area, relay stations in a communications network, and the various machines in a manufacturing facility. To simulate such systems accurately with software, we need software that can deal with concurrency.

The second reason to discuss concurrency is that multiple processor computers are now being widely used, thus creating the need for software to make effective use of that hardware capability. Because of the importance of both statement-level and unit-level concurrency, facilities to provide them must be developed and included in contemporary programming languages.

12.2 Introduction to Subprogram-Level Concurrency

Before we can discuss language support for concurrency, we must introduce the underlying concepts of concurrency and the requirements for it to be useful. Then we can discuss the language design issues for languages that support concurrency.

12.2.1   Fundamental Concepts

A **task** is a unit of a program that can be in concurrent execution with other units of the same program. Each task in a program can provide one thread of control.

There are three characteristics of tasks that distinguish them from subprograms. First, a task may be implicitly started, whereas a subprogram must be explicitly called. Second, when a program unit invokes a task, it need not wait for the task to complete its execution before continuing its own. Lastly, when the execution of a task is completed, control may or may not return to the unit that started that execution.

A task can communicate with other tasks through shared nonlocal variables, through message passing, or through parameters. If a task does not communicate with or affect the execution of any other task in the program in any way, it is said to be **disjoint.** Because tasks often work together to create simulations or solve problems and therefore are not disjoint, they must use some form of communication to either synchronize their executions or share data or both.

Synchronization is a mechanism that controls the order in which tasks execute. Two kinds of synchronization are required when tasks share data, cooperation and competition. **Cooperation synchronization** is required between task A and task B when task A must wait for task B to complete some specific activity before task A can continue its execution. **Competition synchronization** is required between two tasks when both require the use of some resource that cannot be simultaneously used. Specifically, if task A needs to access shared data location x while task B is accessing x, task A must wait for task B to complete its processing of x, regardless of what that processing is. So, for cooperation synchronization, tasks may need to wait for the completion of specific processing upon which their correct operation depends, whereas for competition synchronization, tasks may need to wait for the completion of any other processing by any task currently occurring on specific shared data.

A simple form of cooperation synchronization can be illustrated by a common kind of problem called the producer-consumer problem. This problem originated in the development of operating systems, in which one program unit produces some data value or resource and another uses it. Produced data are usually placed in a storage buffer by the producing unit and removed from that buffer by the consuming unit. The sequence of stores to and removals from the buffer must be synchronized. The consumer unit must not be allowed to take data from the buffer if the buffer is empty. Likewise, the producer unit cannot be allowed to place new data in the buffer if the buffer is full. This is called the problem of cooperation synchronization because the users of the shared data structure must cooperate if the buffer is to be used correctly.

Competition synchronization prevents two tasks from accessing a shared data structure at exactly the same time—a situation that could destroy the integrity of that shared data. To provide competition synchronization, mutually exclusive access to the shared data must be guaranteed.

To clarify the competition problem, consider the following scenario: Suppose task A must add 1 to the shared integer variable TOTAL, which has an initial value of 3. Furthermore, suppose task B must multiply the value of TOTAL by 2. Each task accomplishes its operation on TOTAL by fetching the value of TOTAL, performing an arithmetic operation, and putting the new value back in TOTAL. Without competition synchronization, three different values could result from these operations. If task A completes its operation before task B begins, the value will be 8, which is assumed here to be correct. But if both A and B fetch the value of TOTAL before either task puts its new value back, the result will be incorrect. If A puts its value back first, the value of TOTAL will be 6. This case is shown in Figure 12.1. If B puts its value back first, the value of TOTAL will be 4. The importance of competition synchronization should now be clear.

One general method for providing mutually exclusive access to a shared resource is to consider the resource to be something that a task can possess and then allow only a single task to possess it at a time. To gain possession of a shared resource, a task must request it. When a task is finished with a shared resource that it possesses, it must relinquish that resource so that the resource can be made available to other tasks.

Three methods of providing for mutually exclusive access to a shared resource are semaphores, which are discussed in Section 12.3; monitors, which are discussed in Section 12.4; and message passing, which is discussed in Section 12.5.

Mechanisms for synchronization must be able to delay task execution. Synchronization imposes an order of execution on tasks that is enforced with these delays. To understand what happens to tasks through their life-

Figure 12.1
The need for competition synchronization

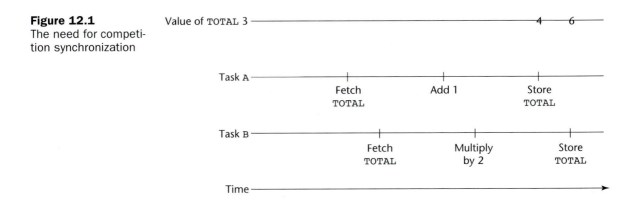

times, we must consider how task execution is controlled. Regardless of whether a machine has a single processor or more than one, there is always the possibility of there being more tasks than there are processors. A program called a **scheduler** manages the sharing of processors among the tasks. If there were never any interruptions and tasks all had the same priority, the scheduler could simply give each task a time slice, such as 0.1 seconds, and when a task's turn came, the scheduler could let it execute on a processor for that amount of time. Of course, there are several events that complicate this, for example delays for synchronization and waits for input or output operations.

Tasks can be in several different states, which are:

1. New: A task is in the new state when it has been created, but has not yet begun its execution.

2. Runnable or ready: A runnable task is ready to run, but is not currently running. It either has not been given processor time by the scheduler, or it had run previously but was blocked in one of the ways described in the paragraph 4 below. Tasks that are runnable are stored in a queue that is often called the **task ready queue.**

3. Running: A running task is one that is currently executing; that is, it has a processor and its code is being executed.

4. Blocked: A task that is blocked has been running, but that execution was interrupted by one of several different events, the most common of which is an input or output operation. Because input and output operations are much slower than program execution, a task that starts an input or output operation is blocked from using the processor while it waits until the input or output operation is completed. In addition to these kinds of blocking, some languages provide operations for the user program to specify that a task be blocked.

5. Dead: A dead task is no longer active in any sense. A task dies when its execution is completed. In some languages, a task can reach the dead state as a result of an explicit request by the user program, for example, the `stop` method in Java.

One important issue in task execution is the following: How is a ready task chosen to move to running state when the task currently running has become blocked or whose time slice has expired? Several different algorithms have been used for this choice, some based on specifiable priority levels. The algorithm that chooses is implemented in the scheduler.

Associated with the concurrent execution of tasks and the use of shared resources is the concept of liveness. In the environment of sequential programs, a program has the characteristic of **liveness** if it continues to execute, eventually leading to completion. In more general terms, liveness means that if some event—say program completion—is supposed to occur, it will occur, eventually. That is, progress is continually made. In the environment of concurrency and the use of shared resources, the liveness of a task can cease to exist, meaning that the program cannot continue and thus will never terminate.

For example, suppose task A and task B both need the shared resources X and Y to complete their work. Further suppose that task A gains possession of X and task B gains possession of Y. After some execution, task A needs resource Y to continue, so it requests Y but must wait until B releases it. Likewise, task B requests X but must wait until A releases it. Neither relinquishes the resource it possesses, and as a result, both lose their liveness, guaranteeing that execution of the program will never complete normally. This particular kind of loss of liveness is called **deadlock.** Deadlock is a serious threat to the reliability of a program, and therefore its avoidance demands serious consideration in both language and program design.

We are now ready to discuss some of the linguistic mechanisms for providing concurrent unit control.

12.2.2 Language Design for Concurrency

A number of languages have been designed to support concurrency, beginning with PL/I in the middle 1960s and including the contemporary languages, Ada 95 and Java.

12.2.3 Design Issues

The most important design issues for language support for concurrency have already been discussed at length: competition and cooperation synchronization. In addition, there are the issues of how and when tasks start and end executions, and how and when they are created.

The following is a summary of the primary design issues for language support for concurrency:

- How is cooperation synchronization provided?
- How is competition synchronization provided?
- How and when do tasks begin and end execution?
- Are tasks statically or dynamically created?

In addition to these, there are several design issues of secondary importance. Prominent among them is how to provide for task scheduling. However, for simplicity's sake, our discussion of concurrency is intentionally incomplete, and only the design issues listed above are discussed in this section.

The following sections discuss three alternative answers to the design issues for concurrency: semaphores, monitors, and message passing.

12.3 Semaphores

A semaphore is a very simple mechanism that can be used to provide synchronization of tasks. In the following paragraphs we describe semaphores and discuss how they can be used for this purpose.

12.3.1 Introduction

In an effort to provide for competition synchronization through mutually exclusive access to shared data structures, Edsger Dijkstra devised semaphores in 1965 (Dijkstra, 1968b). Semaphores can also be used to provide cooperation synchronization.

A semaphore is a data structure consisting of an integer and a queue that stores task descriptors. A task descriptor is a data structure that stores all of the relevant information about the execution state of a task. The concept of a semaphore is that, to provide limited access to a data structure, one places guards around the code that accesses the structure. A guard is a linguistic device that allows the guarded code to be executed only under a specified condition. A guard can be used to allow only one task to access a shared data structure at a time. A semaphore is an implementation of a guard. An integral part of a guard mechanism is a technique for ensuring that all attempted executions of the guarded code eventually take place. This is accomplished by having requests for access that occur when access cannot be granted be stored in the task descriptor queue, from which they are later allowed to leave and execute the guarded code. This is the reason a semaphore must have both a counter and a task descriptor queue.

The only two operations provided for semaphores were originally named P and V by Dijkstra, after the two Dutch words *passeren* (to pass) and *vrygeren* (to release) (Andrews and Schneider, 1983). We will refer to these as wait and release in the following discussion.

12.3.2 Cooperation Synchronization

Through much of this chapter, we use the example of a shared buffer to illustrate the different approaches to providing cooperation and competition synchronization. For cooperation synchronization, such a buffer must have some way of recording both the number of empty positions and the number of filled positions in the buffer. The counter component of a semaphore variable can be used for this purpose. One semaphore variable, say `emptyspots`, can be used to store the number of empty locations in a shared buffer, and another, say `fullspots`, can be used to store the number of filled locations in the buffer. The task queues of these two semaphores store tasks that have been blocked by the delay operation of the semaphore.

Our example buffer is designed as an abstract data type in which all data enters the buffer through the subprogram `DEPOSIT`, and all data leaves the buffer through the subprogram `FETCH`. Then the `DEPOSIT` subprogram only needs to check with the `emptyspots` semaphore to see if there are any empty positions. If there is at least one, it can go ahead with the `DEPOSIT`, which must include decrementing the counter of `emptyspots`. If the buffer is full, the caller to `DEPOSIT` must be made to wait in the `emptyspots` queue for an empty spot to become available. When the `DEPOSIT` is complete, the `DEPOSIT` subprogram increments the counter of the `fullspots` semaphore to indicate there is one more filled location in the buffer.

The `FETCH` subprogram has the opposite sequence of `DEPOSIT`. It checks the `fullspots` semaphore to see if the buffer contains at least one item. If it does, an item is removed and the `emptyspots` semaphore has its counter incremented by 1. If the buffer is empty, the calling process is put in the `fullspots` queue to wait until an item appears. When `FETCH` is finished, it must increment the counter of `emptyspots`.

The operations on semaphore types often are not direct—they are done through the wait and release subprograms. Therefore, the `DEPOSIT` operation just described is actually accomplished in part by calls to wait and release. Note that wait and release must be able to access the task-ready queue.

The wait subprogram is used to test the counter of a given semaphore variable. If the value is greater than zero, the caller can carry out its operation. In this case, the counter value of the semaphore variable is decremented to indicate there are now one fewer of whatever it counts. If the value of the counter is zero, the caller must be placed on the waiting queue of the semaphore variable and the processor must be given to some other ready task.

The release operation is used by a task to allow some other task to have one of whatever the counter of the specified semaphore variable counts. If the queue of the specified semaphore variable is empty, which means no task is waiting, release increments its counter (to indicate there is one more of whatever is being controlled that is now available). If one or more tasks are waiting, release moves one of them from the semaphore queue to the ready queue.

The following is a concise description of wait and release:

```
wait(aSemaphore)
if aSemaphore's counter > 0 then
    decrement aSemaphore's counter
```

    else
        put the caller in aSemaphore's queue
        attempt to transfer control to some ready task
          (If the task ready queue is empty, deadlock occurs)
    end

release(aSemaphore)
if aSemaphore's queue is empty {no task is waiting} **then**
    increment aSemaphore's counter
else
    put the calling task in the task ready queue
    transfer control to a task from aSemaphore's queue
end

We can now present an example program that implements cooperation synchronization for a shared buffer. In this case, the shared buffer stores integer values and is structured as a logically circular structure. It is designed for use by possibly multiple producer and consumer tasks.

The following code shows the definition of such producer and consumer tasks. Two semaphores are used to ensure against buffer underflow or overflow, thus providing cooperation synchronization. Assume that the buffer has length BUFLEN, and the routines that actually manipulate it already exist as FETCH and DEPOSIT. Accesses to the counter of a semaphore are specified by dot notation. For example, if fullspots is a semaphore, its counter is referenced by fullspots.count.

```
semaphore fullspots, emptyspots;
fullspots.count := 0;
emptyspots.count := BUFLEN;
task producer;
  loop
  -- produce VALUE --
  wait(emptyspots);     { wait for a space }
  DEPOSIT(VALUE);
  release(fullspots);   { increase filled spaces }
  end loop;
end producer;

task consumer;
  loop
  wait(fullspots);      { make sure it is not empty }
  FETCH(VALUE);
  release(emptyspots);  { increase empty spaces }
  -- consume VALUE --
  end loop;
end consumer;
```

The semaphore `fullspots` causes the `consumer` task to be queued to wait for a buffer entry if it is currently empty. The semaphore `emptyspots` causes the `producer` task to be queued to wait for an empty space in the buffer if it is currently full.

12.3.3 Competition Synchronization

Our buffer example does not provide competition synchronization. Access to the structure can be controlled with an additional semaphore. This semaphore need not count anything, but simply indicate with its counter whether the buffer is currently being used. The `wait` statement allows the access only if the semaphore's counter has the value 1, which indicates that shared buffer is not currently being accessed. If the semaphore's counter has a value of 0, there is a current access taking place, and the task is placed on the queue of the semaphore. Notice that the semaphore's counter must be initialized to 1. The queues of semaphores must always be initialized to empty.

A semaphore that only requires a binary-valued counter, like the one we use to provide competition synchronization, is called a **binary semaphore.**

The example code that follows illustrates the use of semaphores to provide both competition and cooperation synchronization for a concurrently accessed shared buffer.

The `access` semaphore is used to ensure mutually exclusive access to the buffer. Note again that there may be more than one producer and more than one consumer.

```
semaphore access, fullspots, emptyspots;
access.count := 1;
fullspots.count := 0;
emptyspots.count := BUFLEN;


task producer;
  loop
  -- produce VALUE --
  wait(emptyspots);      { wait for a space }
  wait(access);          { wait for access }
  DEPOSIT(VALUE);
  release(access);       { relinquish access }
  release(fullspots);    { increase filled spaces }
  end loop;
end producer;

task consumer;
  loop
  wait(fullspots);       { make sure it is not empty }
  wait(access);          { wait for access }
```

```
      FETCH(VALUE);
      release(access);      { relinquish access }
      release(emptyspots);  { increase empty spaces }
      -- consume VALUE --
   end loop
 end consumer;
```

A brief look at this example may lead one to believe there is a problem with it. Specifically, suppose that while a task is waiting at the `wait(access)` call in `consumer` another task takes the last value from the shared buffer. Fortunately, this cannot happen, because the `wait(fullspots)` reserves a value in the buffer for the task that calls it by decrementing the `fullspots` counter.

There is one crucial aspect of semaphores that thus far has not been discussed. Recall the earlier description of the problem of competition synchronization: Operations on shared data must not be overlapped. If a second operation can be begun while an earlier operation is still in progress, the shared data can become corrupted. A semaphore is itself a shared data object, so the operations on semaphores are also susceptible to the same problem. It is therefore essential that semaphore operations be uninterruptible. Many computers have uninterruptible instructions that were designed specifically for semaphore operations. If such instructions are not available, then using semaphores to provide competition synchronization is a serious problem with no simple solution.

PL/I was the first programming language to include concurrent tasks. It allowed user programs to execute any subprogram concurrently with the unit that called it. The mechanism for synchronization of these concurrent executions was, however, wholly inadequate. It consisted of only binary semaphores, which were called events, and the ability to detect when a task had completed its execution.

ALGOL 68, which allowed compound statement-level concurrency, included a semaphore data type named **sema**.

12.3.4 Evaluation

Using semaphores to provide cooperation synchronization creates an unsafe programming environment. There is no way to statically check for the correctness of their use, which depends on the semantics of the program in which they appear. In the buffer example, leaving the `wait(emptyspots)` statement out of the `producer` task would result in buffer overflow. Leaving the `wait(fullspots)` statement out of the `consumer` task would result in buffer underflow. Leaving out either of the releases would result in deadlock. These are cooperation synchronization failures.

The reliability problems that semaphores cause in providing cooperation synchronization also arise when using them for competition synchronization. Leaving out the `wait(access)` statement in either task can cause insecure access to the buffer. Leaving out the `release(access)` statement in either task results in deadlock. These are competition synchronization failures. Noting the danger in using semaphores, Per Brinch Hansen wrote "The semaphore is an elegant synchronization tool for an ideal programmer who never makes mistakes" (Brinch Hansen, 1973). Unfortunately, programmers of that kind are rare.

12.4 Monitors

One solution to some of the problems of semaphores in a concurrent environment is to encapsulate shared data structures with their operations and hide their representations—that is, make shared data structures abstract data types. This solution can provide competition synchronization without semaphores by transferring responsibility for synchronization to the run-time system.

12.4.1 Introduction

When the concepts of data abstraction were being formulated, the people involved in that effort applied the same concepts to shared data in concurrent programming environments to produce monitors. According to Per Brinch Hansen (Brinch Hansen, 1977, page xvi), Edsger Dijkstra suggested in 1971 that all synchronization operations on shared data be gathered into a single program unit. Brinch Hansen formalized this concept in the environment of operating systems (Brinch Hansen, 1973). The following year, Hoare named these structures monitors (Hoare, 1974).

The first programming language to incorporate monitors was Concurrent Pascal (Brinch Hansen, 1975). Modula (Wirth, 1977), CSP/k (Holt et al., 1978), and Mesa (Mitchell et al., 1979) also provide monitors. The following discussion of monitors is based on their incarnation in Concurrent Pascal.

Concurrent Pascal is Wirth's Pascal with three important kinds of constructs added: classes from SIMULA 67, processes (the Concurrent Pascal name for tasks), and monitors. Our concern here is with the features that support concurrent programming: processes and monitors.

A Concurrent Pascal process has a syntactic form similar to that of a procedure, but the semantics is quite different. All processes are types, so they are defined in **type** statements of the form

```
type process_name = process (formal parameters)
   -- local declarations --
   -- process body --
end
```

Because they are types, process definitions are merely templates for actual processes. Because variable declarations are used to create processes, processes can be created either statically or dynamically. Declaring a variable to be of a process type creates the code for the process but does nothing else. To cause the allocation of its local data and to begin its execution, an **init** statement with actual parameters must be used, such as

init process_variable_name (actual parameters)

After execution of the **init**, the process remains in the running state for the duration of the program, except when it is blocked.

The general form of Concurrent Pascal monitors is

type monitor_name = **monitor** (formal parameters)
  ---- declarations of shared variables ----
  ---- definitions of local procedures ----
  ---- definitions of exported procedures ----
  ---- initialization code ----
end

The exported procedures of a monitor are syntactically different from local procedures only in that they contain the reserved word **entry** in their **procedure** statements.

The **init** statement, with actual parameters, is used to create instances of monitors. This causes dynamic allocation of storage for the variables of the process and execution of the initialization code. The lifetime of monitor variables, except those in monitor procedures, begins with the **init** and terminates with the program. Their scope is restricted to the monitor itself. The exported procedures of a monitor can be called by either processes or procedures in other monitors.

12.4.2 Competition Synchronization

One of the most important features of monitors is that shared data is resident in the monitor rather than in any of the client units. Thus the programmer does not synchronize mutually exclusive access to shared data through the use of semaphores or other mechanisms. Because all accesses are resident in the monitor, the monitor implementation can be made to guarantee synchronized access by simply allowing only one access at a time. Calls to monitor procedures are implicitly queued if the monitor is busy at the time of the call.

12.4.3 Cooperation Synchronization

Although mutually exclusive access to shared data is intrinsic with a monitor, cooperation between processes is still the task of the programmer. In particular, the programmer must guarantee that a shared buffer does not experience underflow or overflow. For this purpose, Concurrent Pascal has a special data type, **queue**, and two operations on it, `delay` and `continue`. The **queue** type is a form of semaphore, and the two operations are related to the send and release semaphore operations. A variable of **queue** type stores processes that are waiting to use a shared data structure.

The `delay` operation takes a **queue** type variable as a parameter. Its action is to place the process that calls it in the specified queue and remove its exclusive access rights to monitor data structures. Thus the process that executes `delay` has its execution suspended. The monitor is then available to other processes. So `delay` differs from the wait semaphore operation because `delay` always blocks the caller.

The `continue` operation also takes a **queue** type parameter. Its action is to disconnect the process that calls it from the monitor, thus freeing the monitor to access by other processes; `continue` then examines the specified queue. If the queue contains a process, that process is removed and its execution, which had been suspended by a `delay` operation, is restarted. The `continue` operation differs from the release operation for semaphores because release always has some effect, whereas `continue` does nothing if the queue is empty.

A program containing four processes and a monitor that provides synchronized access to a concurrently shared buffer is shown in Figure 12.2.

Using the **queue** data type and the `delay` and `continue` operations, a monitor can be constructed that controls a shared buffer, thus providing both competition and cooperation synchronization. In the following example, a shared buffer is implemented as a logically circular list of 100 integers.

Figure 12.2
A program using a monitor to control access to a shared buffer

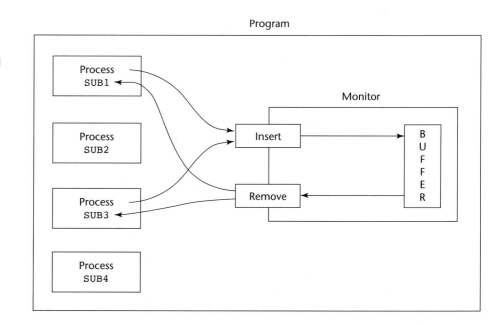

```
type databuf =
  monitor
    const bufsize = 100;
    var buf : array [1..bufsize] of integer;
        next_in,
        next_out : 1..bufsize;
        filled   : 0..bufsize;
        sender_q,
        receiver_q : queue;

  procedure entry deposit(item : integer);
    begin
    if filled = bufsize
      then delay(sender_q);
    buf[next_in] := item;
    next_in := (next_in mod bufsize) + 1;
    filled := filled + 1;
    continue(receiver_q)
    end;

  procedure entry fetch(var item : integer);
    begin
    if filled = 0
      then delay(receiver_q);
    item := buf[next_out];
    next_out := (next_out mod bufsize) + 1;
    filled := filled - 1;
    continue(sender_q)
    end;

  begin
  filled := 0;
  next_in := 1;
  next_out := 1
  end;
```

An instance of type `databuf` is an abstraction of a particular kind of buffer for storing integers. Besides storing integers, a `databuf` type buffer coordinates the activities of adding and removing its values by concurrent processes. The integrity of this buffer is guaranteed by the mechanisms used to construct it. It is protected against underflow and overflow, and concurrent processes using it cannot destructively interfere with each other.

An example of declarations for the processes that can use the `databuf` monitor is as follows:

```
type producer = process(buffer : databuf);
  var newvalue : integer;
  begin
  cycle
    -- produce newvalue --
    buffer.deposit(newvalue);
  end
  end;
```

```
type consumer = process(buffer : databuf);
  var stored_value : integer;
  begin
  cycle
    buffer.fetch(stored_value);
    -- consume stored_value --
  end
  end;
```

The **type** declarations of the monitor `databuf` and the two processes `producer` and `consumer` can be included in the declaration section of a program in which they are to be used, as in

```
-- type declarations --

var new_producer : producer;
    new_consumer : consumer;
    new_buffer   : databuf;
begin
init new_buffer, new_producer(new_buffer),
    new_consumer(new_buffer);
end;
```

This may appear a bit odd to the reader not familiar with concurrent programs, because it is not obvious how the program either begins or terminates. Our example program begins when the **init** is executed, creating a buffer and two processes, at which time the processes begin execution. Note that the **cycle** .. **end** in both the consumer and producer are infinite loops. They never end.

12.4.4 Evaluation

Monitors are a better way to provide competition synchronization than semaphores, primarily because of the problems of semaphores, as discussed in Section 12.3. The use of **queue** type variables to provide cooperation synchronization through `delay` and `continue` is, however, subject to the same problems as semaphores used in other languages for this purpose.

12.5 Message Passing

The monitor construct is a dependable and safe method for providing competition synchronization for shared data access in concurrent units that share a single memory. However, consider the problem of synchronizing the units in a distributed system, in which each processor has its own memory, rather than a single shared memory. Obviously, the monitor construct does not model this situation very naturally. However, synchronization in a distributed system can be achieved quite naturally with message passing.

12.5.1 Introduction

The first efforts to design languages that provide the capability for message passing among concurrent tasks were those of Brinch Hansen (1978) and Hoare (1978). The pioneer developers of message passing also developed a technique for handling the problem of what to do when multiple simultaneous requests were made by other tasks to communicate with a given task. It was decided that some form of nondeterminism was required to provide a kind of fairness in choosing which among those requests would be taken first. This fairness can be defined in various ways, but in general it means that all requesters are provided an equal chance of communicating with a given task. Nondeterministic constructs for statement-level control, called guarded commands, were introduced by Dijkstra (1975). (Guarded commands are discussed in Chapter 7.) Guarded commands are the basis of the construct designed for controlling message passing.

12.5.2 The Concept of Synchronous Message Passing

Message passing can be either synchronous or asynchronous. The asynchronous message passing of Ada 95 is described in Section 12.6. Here we describe synchronous message passing. The basic concept of synchronous message passing is that tasks are often busy and, when busy, are unwilling to be interrupted by other units. Suppose task A and task B are both in execution, and A wishes to send a message to B. Clearly, if B is busy, it is not desirable to allow another task to interrupt it. That would disrupt B's current processing. Furthermore, messages usually cause associated processing in the receiver, which may not be sensible if other processing is incomplete. The alternative is to provide a linguistic mechanism that allows a task to specify to other tasks when it is ready to receive messages. This is somewhat like an executive who instructs his or her secretary to hold all incoming calls until another activity, perhaps an important meeting, is completed. Later, the executive tells the secretary he or she is now willing to receive one of the callers who has been placed on hold.

A task can be designed so it can suspend its execution at some point, either because it is idle or because it needs information from another unit before it can continue. This is like a person who is waiting for an important call. In some cases, there is nothing else to do but sit and wait. In this situation, if task A wants to send a message to B, and B is willing to receive a message, the message can be transmitted. This actual transmission is called a **rendezvous.** Note that a rendezvous can occur only if both the sender and receiver want it to happen. The information of the message can be transmitted in either or both directions.

Both cooperation and competition synchronization of tasks can be conveniently handled with the message-passing model, as described in the following subsections.

12.5.3 The Ada 83 Message-Passing Model

The Ada design for tasks is partially based on the work of Brinch Hansen and Hoare in that message passing is the design basis and nondeterminism is used to choose among competing message-sending tasks.

The full Ada tasking model is complex, and the following discussion of it must be limited. The focus here will be on the Ada version of the synchronous message-passing mechanism.

Ada tasks can be more active than monitors. Monitors are passive entities that provide management services for the shared data they store. They provide their services, however, only when those services are requested. When used to manage shared data, Ada tasks can be thought of as managers that can reside with the resource they manage. They have several mechanisms, some deterministic and some nondeterministic, that allow them to choose among competing requests for access to their resources.

The form of Ada tasks is similar to that of Ada packages. There are two parts, a specification part and a body part, both with the same name. The interface of a task is its entry points, or locations where it can accept messages from other tasks. It is natural that these be listed in the specification part of a task. Because a rendezvous can involve an exchange of information, messages can have parameters; therefore, task entry points must also allow parameters, which must also be described in the specification part. In appearance, a task specification is very similar to the package specification for an abstract data type.

As an example of an Ada task specification, consider the following, which includes a single entry point named `ENTRY_1`, which has an in-mode parameter:

```
task TASK_EXAMPLE is
  entry ENTRY_1(ITEM : in INTEGER);
end TASK_EXAMPLE;
```

A task body must include some syntactic form of entry points that correspond to the **entry** clauses in that task's specification part. In Ada, these are specified by **accept** clauses, which are introduced by the **accept** reserved word. An **accept clause** is defined as the range of statements beginning with the **accept** reserved word and ending with the matching **end** reserved word. **accept** clauses are themselves relatively simple, but other constructs in which they can be embedded can make their semantics quite complex. A simple **accept** clause has the form

```
accept entry_name (formal parameters) do
  ...
end entry_name;
```

The **accept** name matches the name in an **entry** clause in the associated task specification part. The optional parameters provide the means of communicating data between the caller and the called task. The statements between the **do** and the **end** define the operations that take place during the rendezvous. These statements are together called the **accept clause body.** During the actual rendezvous, the sender task is suspended.

Ada tasks communicate with other tasks using the rendezvous mechanism. Whenever a task entry point, or **accept** clause, receives a message that it is not ready to accept, for whatever reason, the sender task must be suspended until the entry point in the receiver task is ready to accept the message. Of course, the entry point must also remember the sender tasks that have sent messages that were not accepted. For this purpose, each **accept** clause in a task has a queue associated with it. The queue records a list of other tasks that have attempted to communicate with the associated entry point.

The following is the skeletal body of the task whose specification was given above:

```
task body TASK_EXAMPLE is
  begin
  loop
    accept ENTRY_1(ITEM : in INTEGER) do
      ...
    end ENTRY_1;
  end loop;
  end TASK_EXAMPLE;
```

The **accept** clause of this task body is the implementation of the **entry** named ENTRY_1 in the task specification. If the execution of TASK_EXAMPLE begins and reaches the ENTRY_1 **accept** clause before any other task sends a message to ENTRY_1, TASK_EXAMPLE is suspended. If another task sends a message to ENTRY_1 while TASK_EXAMPLE is suspended at its **accept**, a rendezvous occurs and the **accept** clause body is executed. Then, because of the loop, execution proceeds to the **accept** again. If no additional calling task has sent a message to ENTRY_1, execution is again suspended to wait for the next message.

A rendezvous can occur in two basic ways in this simple example. First, the receiver task, TASK_EXAMPLE, can be waiting for another task to send a message to the ENTRY_1 entry. When the message is sent, the rendezvous occurs. This is the situation described above. Second, the receiver task can be busy with one rendezvous, or with some other processing not associated with a rendezvous, when another task attempts to send a message to the same entry. In that case, the sender is suspended until the receiver is free to accept that message in a rendezvous. If several messages

Figure 12.3
Two ways a rendezvous
with `TASK_EXAMPLE`
can occur

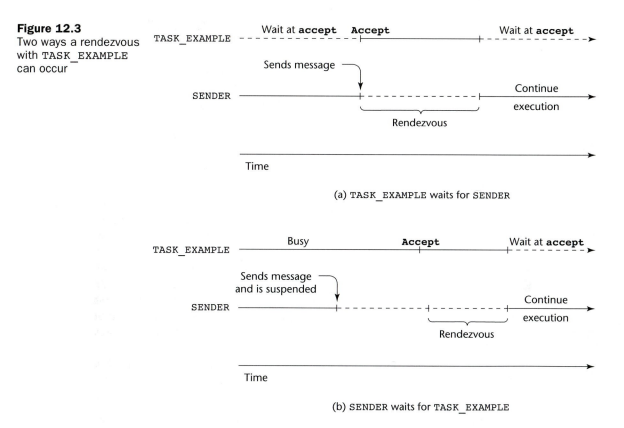

(a) `TASK_EXAMPLE` waits for `SENDER`

(b) `SENDER` waits for `TASK_EXAMPLE`

arrive while the receiver is busy, the senders are queued to wait their turn for a rendezvous.

The two rendezvous just described are illustrated with the time line diagrams in Figure 12.3.

Tasks need not have entry points. Such tasks are called **actor tasks** because they do not wait for a rendezvous in order to do useful work. Actor tasks can rendezvous with other tasks by sending them messages. In contrast to actor tasks, a task can have entry points but little or no code other than that associated with accepting messages, so it can only react to other tasks. Such a task is called a **server task.**

An Ada task that sends a message to another task must know the entry name in that task. However, the opposite is not true: A task entry need not know the name of the task from which it will accept messages. This asymmetry is in contrast to the design of the language known as CSP (Communicating Sequential Processes) (Hoare, 1978). In CSP, which also uses the message-passing model of concurrency, tasks accept messages only from explicitly named tasks. The disadvantage of this is that libraries of tasks cannot be built for general use.

The usual graphical method of describing a rendezvous in which task A sends a message to task B is shown in Figure 12.4.

Figure 12.4
Graphical representation of a rendezvous caused by a message sent from task A to task B

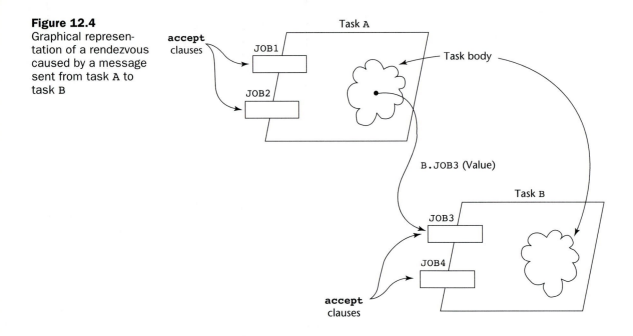

Ada tasks are types, and as such they can be either anonymous or named. An Ada task with a named type can be dynamically created using the **new** operator and referenced through a pointer. For example, consider the following:

```
task type BUFFER is
  entry DEPOSIT(VALUE : in INTEGER);
  entry FETCH(VALUE : out INTEGER);
end;
type BUF_PTR is access BUFFER;
...
BUF_PTR := new BUFFER;
```

Tasks are declared in the declaration part of a package, subprogram, or block. They begin executing at the same time as the statements in the code to which that declarative part is attached. For example, a task declared in a main program begins execution at the same time as the first statement in the code body of the main program. Task termination, which is a complex issue, is discussed later in this section.

Tasks may have any number of entries. The order in which the associated **accept** clauses appear in the task dictates the order in which messages can be accepted. If a task that has more than one entry point and requires them to be able to receive messages in any order, the task uses a **select** statement to enclose the entries, as in the following:

```
task body TASK_EXAMPLE is
  loop
    select
```

```
            accept ENTRY_1(formal parameters) do
              ...
            end ENTRY_1;
            ...
          or
            accept ENTRY_2(formal parameters) do
              ...
            end ENTRY_2;
            ...
          end select;
        end loop;
      end TASK_EXAMPLE;
```

In this task, there are two **accept** clauses, each of which has an associated queue. The action of the **select**, when it is executed, is to examine the queues associated with the two **accept** clauses. If one of the queues is empty but the other contains at least one waiting message, the **accept** clause associated with the waiting message has a rendezvous with the task that sent the first message that was received. If both **accept** clauses have empty queues, the **select** waits until one of the entries is called. If both **accept** clauses have nonempty queues, one of the **accept** clauses is nondeterministically chosen to have a rendezvous with one of its callers. The loop forces the **select** statement to be executed repeatedly, forever.

The **end** of the **accept** clause marks the end of the code that assigns or references the formal parameters of the **accept** clause. The code, if there is any, between an **accept** clause and the next **or** (or the **end select** if the **accept** clause is the last one) is called the **extended accept clause.** The extended **accept** clause is executed only after the associated (immediately preceding) **accept** clause is executed. This execution of the extended **accept** clause is not part of the rendezvous and can take place in parallel with the calling task. The sender is suspended during the rendezvous, but it is restarted (put back in the ready queue) when the end of the **accept** clause is reached. If an **accept** clause has no formal parameters, the **do-end** is not required, and the **accept** clause can consist entirely of an extended **accept** clause. Such an **accept** clause would be used exclusively for synchronization.

12.5.4 Cooperation Synchronization

Each **accept** clause can have a guard attached, in the form of a **when** clause, that can delay rendezvous. For example,

```
when not FULL(BUFFER) =>
  accept DEPOSIT(NEW_VALUE) do
```

An **accept** clause with a **when** clause can be either open or closed. If the Boolean expression of the **when** clause is currently true, that **accept** clause is called **open;** if the Boolean expression is false, the **accept** clause is called **closed.** An **accept** clause that does not have a guard is always open. An open **accept** clause is available for rendezvous; a closed **accept** clause cannot rendezvous.

Suppose there are several guarded **accept** clauses in a **select** clause. Such a **select** clause is usually placed in an infinite loop. The loop causes the **select** clause to be executed repeatedly, with each **when** clause evaluated on each repetition. Each repetition causes a list of open **accept** clauses to be constructed. If exactly one of the open clauses has a nonempty queue, a message from that queue is taken and a rendezvous takes place. If more than one of the open **accept** clauses have nonempty queues, one queue is chosen nondeterministically, a message is taken from that queue, and a rendezvous takes place. If the queues of all open clauses are empty, the task waits for a message to arrive at one of those **accept** clauses, at which time a rendezvous will occur. If a **select** is executed and every **accept** clause is closed, a run-time exception, or error, results. This possibility can be avoided either by making sure one of the **when** clauses is always true or by adding an **else** clause in the **select**. An **else** clause can include any sequence of statements, except an **accept** clause.

A **select** clause may have a special statement, **terminate**, that is selected only when it is open and no other **accept** clause is open. A **terminate** clause, when selected, means that the task is finished with its job but is not yet terminated. Task termination is discussed later in this section.

12.5.5 Competition Synchronization

The features described so far provide for cooperation synchronization and communication among tasks. We next discuss how mutually exclusive access to shared data structures can be enforced.

If access to a data structure is to be controlled by a task, then mutually exclusive access can be achieved by declaring the data structure within a task. The semantics of task execution usually guarantees mutually exclusive access to the structure, because only one **accept** clause in the task can be active at a given time. The only exceptions to this occur when tasks are nested in procedures or other tasks. For example, if a task that defines a shared data structure has a nested task, that nested task can also access the shared structure, which could destroy the integrity of the data. Thus, tasks that are meant to control access to a shared data structure should not define procedures or tasks.

The following is an example of an Ada task to provide synchronized access to a buffer. It is very similar in effect to our monitor example.

```
task BUF_TASK is
  entry DEPOSIT(ITEM : in INTEGER);
  entry FETCH(ITEM : out INTEGER);
end BUF_TASK;
```

```
task body BUF_TASK is
  BUFSIZE : constant INTEGER := 100;
  BUF    : array (1..BUFSIZE) of INTEGER;
  FILLED : INTEGER range 0..BUFSIZE := 0;
  NEXT_IN,
  NEXT_OUT : INTEGER range 1..BUFSIZE := 1;
  begin
  loop
    select
      when FILLED < BUFSIZE =>
        accept DEPOSIT(ITEM : in INTEGER) do
          BUF(NEXT_IN) := ITEM;
        end DEPOSIT;
        NEXT_IN := (NEXT_IN mod BUFSIZE) + 1;
        FILLED := FILLED + 1;
    or
      when FILLED > 0 =>
        accept FETCH(ITEM : out INTEGER) do
          ITEM := BUF(NEXT_OUT);
        end FETCH;
        NEXT_OUT := (NEXT_OUT mod BUFSIZE) + 1;
        FILLED := FILLED - 1;
      end select;
    end loop;
  end BUF_TASK;
```

In this example, both **accept** clauses are extended. These allow concurrent execution of BUF_TASK with the calling tasks.

The tasks for the producer and consumer that could use BUF_TASK have the following form:

```
task PRODUCER;
task CONSUMER;
task body PRODUCER is
  NEW_VALUE : INTEGER;
  begin
    loop
      -- produce NEW_VALUE --
      BUF_TASK.DEPOSIT(NEW_VALUE);
    end loop;
  end PRODUCER;

task body CONSUMER is
  STORED_VALUE : INTEGER;
  begin
    loop
      BUF_TASK.FETCH(STORED_VALUE);
      -- consume STORED_VALUE --
    end loop;
  end CONSUMER;
```

12.5.6   Task Termination

We now address the issue of task termination. We must first define task completion. The execution of a task is **completed** if control has reached the end of its code body. This may occur because an exception is raised for which there is no handler (Ada exception handling is described in Chapter 13). If a task has not created any other tasks, called dependents, it is terminated when its execution is completed. A task that has created dependent tasks is terminated when the execution of its code is completed and all of its dependents are terminated. A task may end its execution by waiting at an open **terminate** clause. In this case, the task is terminated only when its master (the block, subprogram, or task that created it) and all of the tasks that depend on that master have either completed or are waiting at an open **terminate** clause. In that case, all of these tasks are terminated simultaneously. A block or subprogram is not exited until all of its dependent tasks are terminated.

12.5.7   Priorities

Both named and anonymous types can be assigned priorities. This is done with a pragma, as in

```
pragma priority(expression);
```

The value of the expression specifies the relative priority for the task or task type definition in which it appears. The possible range of priority values is implementation dependent. The highest priority possible can be specified with the last attribute the `priority` type, which is defined in `System` (`System` is a predefined package). For example, the following specifies the highest priority in any implementation:

```
pragma priority(System.priority'last);
```

Priorities on Ada tasks apply only to tasks in the ready state. They are used to specify order to the scheduler's choice of which task to move to the running state next. If there are three tasks waiting at a particular **accept** clause and they have different priorities, those priorities does not affect which will rendezvous first.

12.5.8   Binary Semaphores

If access to a data structure is to be controlled and the data structure is not encapsulated in a task, another means must be used to provide mutually exclusive access. One way is to build a binary semaphore task to use with the task that references the data structure. Such a binary semaphore task could be defined as follows:

```
task BINARY_SEMAPHORE is
  entry WAIT;
  entry RELEASE;
end BINARY_SEMAPHORE;

task body BINARY_SEMAPHORE is
  begin
  loop
    accept WAIT;
    accept RELEASE;
  end loop;
  end BINARY_SEMAPHORE;
```

The purpose of this task is to guarantee that the WAIT and RELEASE operations occur alternatively.

The BINARY_SEMAPHORE task illustrates the simplifications that are possible when Ada messages are passed only for synchronization, rather than to also pass data. Specifically, notice the simple form of **accept** clauses that do not need bodies.

Use of the BINARY_SEMAPHORE task to provide mutually exclusive access to a shared data structure would take place exactly as with the use of semaphores in the example program in Section 12.3. Of course, this use of semaphores suffers all of the potential problems discussed there.

Like semaphores, monitors can be simulated with the Ada tasking capability. Tasks provide implicit mutual exclusive access, exactly as do monitors. So the Ada tasking model supports both semaphores and monitors.

12.5.9 Evaluation

In the absence of distributed processors with independent memories, the choice between monitors and message passing as means of providing competition synchronization is somewhat a matter of taste. Cooperation synchronization in message passing is less dependent than semaphores (which are required with monitors) on correct usage. Overall, therefore, message passing is slightly better, even in a shared memory environment.

For distributed systems, however, message passing is a better model for concurrency, because it naturally supports the concept of separate processes executing in parallel on separate processors.

12.6 Concurrency in Ada 95

One of the goals of the design of Ada 95 was to improve the capabilities of Ada 83 for specifying concurrency. The exclusive use of the Ada 83 message passing model for controlling access to shared data results in slow

execution because of the complexity of the rendezvous mechanism. To re-
lieve this situation, Ada 95 includes protected objects, which provide
more convenient and efficient access control for shared data. Ada 95 also
includes a method of providing asynchronous task communication. We
first discuss protected objects.

12.6.1 Protected Objects

In Ada 83, access to shared data is controlled by enclosing the data in a
task and allowing access only through task entries, which implicitly provide for competition synchronization. One problem with this method is
that it is difficult to implement the rendezvous mechanism efficiently. Ada
95 protected objects provide an alternative method of providing competition synchronization that need not involve rendezvous.

A protected object is not a task; it is more like a monitor. Protected objects can be accessed by either protected subprograms or by entries similar to those in tasks. The protected subprograms can either be protected
procedures, which provide mutually exclusive read-write access to the data
of the protected object, or protected functions, which provide concurrent
read-only access to that data. Within the body of a protected procedure, the
current instance of the enclosing protected unit is defined to be a variable;
within the body of a protected function, the current instance of the enclosing protected unit is defined to be a constant, which allows concurrent
read-only access.

Entry calls to a protected object provide synchronous communication
with one or more tasks using the same protected object. These entry calls
provide access similar to that provided to the data enclosed in a task.

The buffer problem that is solved with a task in the previous subsection can be more simply solved with a protected object.

```
protected BUFFER is
  entry DEPOSIT(ITEM : in INTEGER);
  entry FETCH(ITEM : out INTEGER);
private
  BUFSIZE : constant INTEGER := 100;
  BUF    : array (1..BUFSIZE) of INTEGER;
  FILLED : INTEGER range 0..BUFSIZE := 0;
  NEXT_IN,
  NEXT_OUT : INTEGER range 1..BUFSIZE := 1;
end BUFFER;

protected body BUFFER is
  accept DEPOSIT(ITEM : in INTEGER)
                 when FILLED < BUFSIZE is
    begin
    BUF(NEXT_IN) := ITEM;
    NEXT_IN := (NEXT_IN mod BUFSIZE) + 1;
```

```
      FILLED := FILLED + 1;
      end DEPOSIT;
   accept FETCH(ITEM : out INTEGER) when FILLED > 0 is
      begin
      ITEM := BUF(NEXT_OUT);
      NEXT_OUT := (NEXT_OUT mod BUFSIZE) + 1;
      FILLED := FILLED - 1;
      end FETCH;
 end BUFFER;
```

12.6.2 Asynchronous Messages

The other significant addition Ada 95 makes to the concurrency capabilities of Ada 83 is the ability for tasks to send asynchronous messages to other tasks. The rendezvous of Ada 83 is strictly synchronous; both the sender and the receiver must be ready for communication before they actually communicate through the rendezvous.

An Ada 95 task can have a special **select** clause, called an **asynchronous select**, which can react immediately to messages from other tasks. Such a clause can have either of two different triggering alternatives, an entry call or a **delay** statement. In addition to the triggering part, the asynchronous select clause has an abortable part, which could contain any sequence of Ada statements. The semantics of an asynchronous select clause is that it executes just one of its two parts. If the triggering event occurs (either the **entry** call is received or the **delay** timer terminates), it executes that part. Otherwise, it executes the abortable clause. The following two examples of asynchronous **select** clauses appear in the Ada 95 reference manual (AARM, 1995). In the first code segment, the abortable clause is executed repeatedly (because of the loop) until the call to `Terminal.Wait_For_Interrupt` is received. In the second code segment, the function called in the abortable clause executes for at least five seconds. If it is not finished by then, the **select** is exited.

```
      -- Main command loop for a command interpreter
   loop
     select
       Terminal.Wait_For_Interrupt;
       Put_Line("Interrupted");
     then abort
       -- This will be abandoned upon terminal interrupt
       Put_Line("-> ");
       Get_Line(Command, Last);
       Process_Command(Command (1..Last));
     end select;
   end loop;
   -- A time-limited calculation
   select
```

```
        delay 5.0;
        Put_Line("Calculation does not converge");
    then abort
        -- This calculation should finish in 5.0 seconds;
        --  if not, it is assumed to diverge.
        Horribly_Complicated_Recursive_Function(X, Y);
    end select;
```

12.7 Java Threads

The concurrent units in Java are objects that include a method named `run`, whose code can be in concurrent execution with other such methods and with the `main` method. There are two ways of defining a class whose objects can have concurrent methods. One of these is to define a subclass of the predefined class `Thread`, which provides support for the `run` method. This is often, but not always, an acceptable technique. Recall from Chapter 11 that Java does not support multiple inheritance. However, a class can inherit from a class and implement an interface, which is a kind of abstract class. Therefore, a class can inherit from its natural parent and implement the interface `Runnable`, which provides partial support for concurrency.

12.7.1 The Thread Class

The bare essentials of `Thread` are two methods named `run` and `start`. The `run` method is always overriden by subclasses of `Thread`. It is precisely the place where the code that defines what the thread does is put. The `start` method of `Thread` starts its object as a concurrent unit by calling its `run` method. The call to `start` is unusual in that control returns immediately to the caller, which then continues its execution, in parallel with the newly started `run` method.

When a Java application program (as opposed to an applet) begins execution, a new thread is created (in which the **main** method will run) and **main** is called. Therefore, all Java programs run in threads.

The `Thread` class is strange in that it is not the natural parent of any other classes. It provides some services for its subclasses, but it is not related in any natural way to their computational purposes. Nevertheless, `Thread` is the only class available to the programmer for creating concurrent Java programs.

It is difficult to give a precise description of how the Java scheduler works, because the different implementations (Solaris, Windows 95, etc.) currently do not schedule threads in exactly the same way. Typically, however, the scheduler gives equal-size time slices to each runnable thread in round-robin fashion, as long as all of these threads have the same priority.

The `Thread` class provides several methods for controlling the execution of `Thread` objects. The `yield` method, which takes no parameters, is a request from the running thread to voluntarily surrender the remainder of its time slice. The thread is immediately put in the task-ready queue, making it runnable. The scheduler then chooses the highest priority thread from the task-ready queue. If there are no other runnable threads with priority higher than the one that just yielded the processor, it may also be the next thread to get a time slice. `yield` is a static method, so it must be called with the name of the class as a prefix, rather than an object.

The `sleep` method has a single parameter, which is the integer number of milliseconds that the caller of `sleep` wants the thread to be blocked. After the specified number of milliseconds has passed, the thread will be put in the task-ready queue. Because there is no way to know how long a thread will be in the task-ready queue before it runs, the parameter to `sleep` is the minimum amount of time the thread will *not* be in execution. The `sleep` method can throw `InterruptedException`, which must be handled in the method that calls `sleep`. Exceptions are described in detail in Chapter 13.

The `suspend` method is used when the execution of a thread must be temporarily suspended, after which time it might be restarted. A variation of this kind of operation is now common in operating systems that are meant to be used by a wide variety of people. For example, when a Windows 95 user specifies that a file is to be saved and the directory already has a file with the name of the currently open file, the operating system asks the user to verify that the file is to be rewritten before that operation is done. In the context of threads, consider the process of a user asking the system to stop the execution of a particular thread. The method that is executed as a result of the user request (by selecting a button in a window, for example) can first suspend the thread that the user wants stopped, ask the user to verify, and then either stop or resume the thread. These operations are illustrated in the following code segment:

```java
Thread ballgame;
...
public void stopButton() {
  ballgame.suspend();
  if (askUser(
    "Do you really want to quit the ballgame? (y/n)"))
    ballgame.stop();
  else
    ballgame.resume();
}
```

The `askUser` method displays its parameter message and then reads the keyboard response of the user. If the response is **y** or **Y**, the method returns **true**; otherwise it returns **false**. The `stop` method kills a thread, moving it to the dead state. The `resume` method moves a thread from the blocked state to the task-ready queue.

12.7.2 Priorities

The priorities of threads need not all be the same. A thread's default priority is the same as the thread that created it. If **main** creates a thread, its default priority is the constant NORM_PRIORITY, which is usually 5. Thread defines two other priority constants, MAX_PRIORITY and MIN_PRIORITY, whose values are usually 10 and 1, respectively. The priority of a thread can be changed with the method setPriority. The new priority can be any of the predefined constants or any other number between MIN_PRIORITY and MAX_PRIORITY. The getPriority method returns the current priority of a thread.

When there are threads with different priorities, the scheduler's behavior is controlled by those priorities. When the executing thread is blocked or killed or the time slice for it expires, the scheduler chooses the thread from the task-ready queue that has the highest priority. A thread with lower priority will run only if one of higher priority is not in the task-ready queue when the opportunity arises.

12.7.3 Competition Synchronization

In Java, competition synchronization is achieved by specifying that the methods that access shared data are run completely before another method is executed on the same object. In other words, we can specify that once a particular method begins its execution, that execution will be completed before any other method begins its execution on the same object. Such methods place a lock on the object, which prevents other methods from executing on the object. This is specified on a method by adding the **synchronized** modifier to the method's definition, as in the following skeletal class definition:

```
class ManageBuf {
  private int [100] buf;
  ...
  public synchronized void deposit(int item) { ... }
  public synchronized int fetch() { ... }
  ...
}
```

The two methods defined in `ManageBuf` are both defined to be **synchronized**, which prevents them from interfering with each other while executing on the same object, even if they are called by separate threads.

In some cases, the number of statements that deal with the shared data structure is significantly less than the numbering of other statements in the method in which it resides. In these cases, it is better to synchronize the code segment that accesses or changes the shared data structure rather than the whole method. This can be done with a so-called synchronized statement, whose general form is:

```
synchronized(expression)
  statement
```

where the expression must evaluate to an object and the statement can be a single statement or a compound statement. The object is locked during execution of the statement or compound statement. So the statement or compound statement is executed exactly as if it were the body of a synchronized method.

An object that has synchronized methods defined for it must have a queue associated with it that stores the synchronized methods that have attempted to execute on it while it was being operated upon by another synchronized method. When a synchronized method completes its execution on an object, a method that is waiting in the object's waiting queue, if there is such a method, is put in the task-ready queue.

12.7.4 Cooperation Synchronization

Cooperation synchronization in Java is accomplished by using the `wait` and `notify` methods that are defined in `Object`, the root class of all Java classes. All classes except `Object` inherit these methods. The `wait` method is placed in a loop that tests the condition for legal access. If the condition is false, the thread is put in a queue to wait. The `notify` method is called to tell one waiting thread that the thing it was waiting for has happened.

`wait` and `notify` can only be called from within a synchronized method, because they use the lock placed on an object by such a method.

The `wait` method can throw `InterruptedException`, which is a descendant of `Exception`. Therefore, any code that calls `wait` must also catch `InterruptedException`. Assuming the condition for which we wait is called `theCondition`, the conventional way to use `wait` is as follows:

```
try {
  while (!theCondition)
    wait();
  -- Do whatever is needed after theCondition comes true
}
catch(InterruptedException myProblem) { ... }
```

The **try** clause defines the scope of exception handling and **catch** is the exception handler for the **try** clause.

The following program implements a circular queue for storing **int** values. It illustrates both cooperation and competition synchronization.

```
// Queue
// This class implements a circular queue for storing int
// values. It includes a constructor for allocating and
// initializing the queue to a specified size. It has
// synchronized methods for inserting values into and
// removing values from the queue.

class Queue {
  private int [] que;
  private int nextIn,
              nextOut,
              filled,
              queSize;

  public Queue(int size) {
    que = new int [size];
    filled = 0;
    nextIn = 1;
    nextOut = 1;
    queSize = size;
  }  //** end of Queue constructor

  public synchronized void deposit (int item) {
    try {
      while (filled == queSize)
        wait();
      que [nextIn] = item;
      nextIn = (nextIn % queSize) + 1;
      filled++;
      notify();
    }  //** end of try clause
    catch(InterruptedException e) {}
  }  //** end of deposit method

  public synchronized int fetch() {
    int item = 0;
    try {
      while (filled == 0)
        wait();
      item = que [nextOut];
      nextOut = (nextOut % queSize) + 1;
      filled--;
      notify();
    }  //** end of try clause
    catch(InterruptedException e) {}
    return item;
  }  //** end of fetch method
}  //** end of Queue class
```

Notice that the exception handler (**catch**) does nothing here.

Classes to define producer and consumer objects that could use the Queue class can be defined as:

```
class Producer extends Thread {
  private Queue buffer;
  public Producer(Queue que) {
    buffer = que;
  }
  public void run() {
    int new_item;
    while (true) {
      //-- Create a new_item
      buffer.deposit(new_item);
    }
  }
}

class Consumer extends Thread {
  private Queue buffer;
  public Consumer(Queue que) {
    buffer = que;
  }
  public void run() {
    int stored_item;
    while (true) {
      buffer.fetch(stored_item);
      //-- Consume the stored_item
    }
  }
}
```

The following code creates a Queue object, and a Producer and a Consumer object, both attached to the Queue object, and starts their execution:

```
Queue buff1 = new Queue(100);
Producer producer1 = new Producer(buff1);
Consumer consumer1 = new Consumer(buff1);
producer1.start();
consumer1.start();
```

If necessary, we could define one or both of the Producer and the Consumer as implementations of the Runnable interface rather than as subclasses of Thread. The only difference is in the first line, which would now appear as:

```
class Producer implements Runnable {
```

To create and run an object of such a class, it is still necessary to create a Thread object that is connected to the object. This is illustrated in the following code:

```
Producer producer1 = new Producer(buff1);
Thread producerThread = new Thread(producer1);
producerThread.start();
```

12.7.5 Evaluation

Java's support for concurrency is relatively simple but effective. Both monitors and semaphores can be constructed easily in Java.

12.8 Statement-Level Concurrency

In this section, we take a brief look at language design for statement-level concurrency. From the language design point of view, the objective of such designs is to provide a mechanism that the programmer can use to inform the compiler of ways it can map the program onto a multiprocessor architecture. Although ALGOL 68 included a semaphore type that was meant to deal with statement-level concurrency, we do not discuss that application of semaphores here.

In this section, we discuss only one collection of linguistic constructs from one language for statement-level concurrency. Furthermore, we will describe the constructs and their objectives in terms of SIMD architecture machines, although they were designed to be useful for a variety of architecture configurations.

The problem addressed by the language constructs we discuss is that of minimizing the communication required among processors and the memories of other processors. The assumption is that it is faster for a processor to access data in its own memory than that of some other processor. Well-designed compilers can do a great deal in this process, but much more can be done if the programmer is able to provide information to the compiler about the possible concurrency that could be used.

12.8.1 High-Performance FORTRAN

High-Performance FORTRAN (HPF) (ACM, 1993b) is a collection of extensions to FORTRAN 90 that are meant to allow programmers to specify information to the compiler to help it optimize the execution of programs on multiprocessor computers. HPF includes both new specification statements and intrinsic, or built-in, subprograms. This section discusses only some of the new statements.

The primary specification statements of HPF are for specifying the number of processors, the distribution of data over the memories of those processors, and the alignment of data with other data in terms of memory

placement. The HPF specification statements appear as special comments in a FORTRAN program. Each of them is introduced by the prefix !HPF$, where the ! is the character used to begin lines of comments in FORTRAN 90. This prefix makes them invisible to FORTRAN 90 compilers but easy to recognize for HPF compilers.

The **PROCESSORS** specification has the form:

```
!HPF$ PROCESSORS procs (n)
```

This statement is used to specify to the compiler the number of processors that can be used by the code generated for this program. This information is used in conjunction with other specifications to tell the compiler how data is to be distributed to the memories associated with the processors.

The **DISTRIBUTE** statement specifies what data is to be distributed and the kind of distribution that is to be used. Its form is

```
!HPF$ DISTRIBUTE (kind) ONTO procs :: identifier_list
```

In this statement, the kind can be either **BLOCK** or **CYCLIC**. The identifier list is the names of the array variables that are to be distributed. A variable that is specified to be **BLOCK** distributed is divided into *n* equal groups, where each group consists of contiguous collections of array elements evenly distributed over the memories of all the processors. For example, if an array with 500 elements named **LIST** is **BLOCK** distributed over five processors, the first 100 elements of **LIST** will be stored in the memory of the first processor, and so forth. A **CYCLIC** distribution specifies that individual elements of the array are cyclically stored in the memories of the processors. For example, if **LIST** is **CYCLIC** distributed, again over five processors, the first element of **LIST** will be stored in the memory of the first processor, the second element in the memory of the second processor, and so forth.

The form of the **ALIGN** statement is

```
ALIGN array1_element WITH array2_element
```

ALIGN is used to relate the distribution of one array with that of another. For example,

```
ALIGN list1(index) WITH list2(index+1)
```

specifies that the **index** element of **list1** is to be stored in the memory of the same processor as the **index+1** element of **list2**, for all values of index. The two array references in an **ALIGN** appear together in some statement of the program. Putting them in the same memory (which means the same processor) ensures that the references to them will be as close as possible.

Consider the following example code segment:

```
      REAL list_1 (1000), list_2 (1000)
      INTEGER list_3 (500), list_4 (501)
!HPF$ PROCESSORS proc (10)
```

```
!HPF$ DISTRIBUTE (BLOCK) ONTO procs :: list_1, list_2
!HPF$ ALIGN list_3 (index) WITH list_4 (index+1)
      ...
    list_1 (index) = list_2 (index)
    list_3 (index) = list_4 (index+1)
```

In each execution of the above assignment statements, the two referenced array elements will be stored in the memory of the same processor.

The HPF specification statements actually only provide information for the compiler that it may or may not use to optimize the code it produces. What the compiler actually does depends on its level of sophistication and the particular architecture of the target machine.

The FORALL statement specifies a collection of statements that may be executed concurrently. For example,

```
FORALL (index = 1:1000) list_1 (index) = list_2 (index)
```

specifies the assignment of the elements of list_2 to the corresponding elements of list_1. Conceptually, it specifies that the right side of all 1,000 assignments can be evaluated first, before any assignments take place. This is what permits concurrent execution of all of the assignment statements.

We have briefly discussed only a part of the capabilities of HPF. However, it should be enough to provide the reader with an idea of the kinds of language extensions that are useful for programming computers with possibly large numbers of processors.

SUMMARY

Concurrent execution can be at the subprogram, or unit, level or the statement level. We use the phrase physical concurrency when multiple processors are actually used to execute concurrent units. If concurrent units are executed on a single processor, we use the term logical concurrency. The underlying conceptual model of all concurrency can be referred to as logical concurrency.

Two of the primary facilities that concurrent languages must provide are mutually exclusive access to shared data structures (competition synchronization) and cooperation among tasks.

Semaphores can be used to provide both competition and cooperation synchronization among concurrent tasks. It is easy to use semaphores incorrectly, resulting in errors that cannot be detected by the compiler, linker, or run-time system.

Monitors are data abstractions that provide a natural way of allowing mutually exclusive access to data shared among tasks. They are included in several programming languages. Cooperation synchronization in languages with monitors must be provided with some form of semaphores.

Ada provides complex but effective constructs, based on the message-passing model, for concurrency. The basic concurrent units are tasks that communicate with each other through the rendezvous mechanism, which is synchronous message passing. A rendezvous is the action of a task accepting a message sent by another task. Ada includes both simple and complicated methods of controlling the occurrences of rendezvous among tasks.

Ada 95 includes additional capabilities for the support of concurrency, primarily protected objects, and asynchronous message passing.

Java provides concurrent units in a rather simple but effective way. Any class that either inherits from `Thread` or implements `Runnable` can override an inherited method named `run` and have that method's code executed concurrently with other such methods and with the main method. Competition synchronization is specified by defining methods that access shared data to be synchronized. Small sections of code can also be synchronized. Cooperation synchronization is accomplished by using the methods `wait` and `notify`.

High-Performance FORTRAN includes statements for specifying how data is to be distributed over the memory units connected to multiple processors. Also included are statements for specifying collections of statements that can be executed concurrently.

BIBLIOGRAPHIC NOTES

The general subject of concurrency is discussed at great length in Andrews and Schneider (1983), Holt et al. (1978), and Ben-Ari (1982).

The monitor concept is developed and its implementation in Concurrent Pascal is described by Brinch Hansen (1977).

The early development of the message-passing model of concurrent unit control is discussed by Hoare (1978) and Brinch Hansen (1978). An in-depth discussion of the development of the Ada tasking model can be found in Ichbiah et al. (1979). Ada 95 is described in detail in AARM (1995). High-Performance FORTRAN is described in ACM (1993b).

REVIEW QUESTIONS

1. What are the three levels of concurrency in programs?
2. What level of program concurrency is best supported by SIMD computers?
3. What level of program concurrency is best supported by MIMD computers?
4. What is the thread of control of a program?
5. Define *task*, *disjoint task*, *synchronization*, *competition* and *cooperation synchronization*, *liveness*, and *deadlock*.
6. What kind of tasks do not require any kind of synchronization?

7. What are the design issues for language support for concurrency?

8. Describe the actions of the wait and release operations for semaphores.

9. What is a binary semaphore? What is a counting semaphore?

10. What are the primary problems with using semaphores to provide synchronization?

11. What advantage do monitors have over semaphores?

12. Define *rendezvous*, **accept** *clause*, **entry** *clause*, *actor task*, *server task*, *extended* **accept** *clause*, *open* **accept** *clause*, *closed* **accept** *clause*, and *completed task*.

13. Which is more general, concurrency through monitors or concurrency through message passing?

14. Are Ada tasks created statically or dynamically?

15. What purpose does an extended **accept** clause serve?

16. How is cooperation synchronization provided for Ada tasks?

17. What is the advantage of protected objects in Ada 95 over tasks for providing access to shared data objects?

18. Describe the Ada 95 asynchronous **select** clause.

19. Specifically, what Java program unit can run concurrently with the main method in an application program?

20. What does the Java sleep method do?

21. What does the Java yield method do?

22. What are the two Java constructs that can be synchronized?

23. What Java methods are used to support cooperation synchronization?

24. Explain why Java includes the **Runnable** interface.

25. What is the objective of the specification statements of High-Performance FORTRAN?

26. What is the purpose of the **FORALL** statement of High-Performance FORTRAN?

PROBLEM SET

1. Explain clearly why competition synchronization is not a problem in a programming environment that has symmetric unit control but no concurrency.

2. What is the best action a system can take when deadlock is detected?

3. Write an Ada task to implement general semaphores.

4. Write an Ada task to manage a shared buffer such as the one in our example, but use the semaphore task from Problem 3.

5. Busy waiting is a method whereby a task waits for a given event by continuously checking for that event to occur. What is the main problem with this approach?

6. In the producer-consumer example of Section 12.3, suppose that we incorrectly replaced the `release(access)` in the consumer process with `wait(access)`. What would be the result of this error on execution of the system?

7. From a book on VAX assembly language programming, determine what instructions the VAX architecture includes to support the construction of semaphores.

8. From a book on assembly language programming for a computer that uses an Intel Pentium processor, determine what instructions are provided to support the construction of semaphores.

9. Suppose two tasks **A** and **B** must use the shared variable **BUF_SIZE**. Task **A** adds 2 to **BUF_SIZE**, and task **B** subtracts 1 from it. Assume that such arithmetic operations are done by the three-step process of fetching the current value, performing the arithmetic, and putting the new value back. In the absence of competition synchronization, what sequences of events are possible and what values result from these operations? Assume the initial value of **BUF_SIZE** is 6.

10. Compare the Java competition synchronization mechanism with that of Ada.

11. Compare the Java cooperation synchronization mechanism with that of Ada.

12. What happens if a monitor procedure calls another procedure in the same monitor?

13 Exception Handling

Edsger Dijkstra

Edsger Dijkstra, recipient of the ACM Turing Award in 1972, currently serves as Schlumberger Chair in Computer Sciences at the University of Texas-Austin. He was a member of the team that pioneered "The Multiprogramming System" which was the world's first operating system with concurrent processes. This structure made proofs of absence of the danger of deadlock and proofs of other correctness properties feasible. In 1976, Dijkstra authored the text "A Discipline of Programming."

This chapter first describes the fundamental concepts of exception handling, including hardware- and software-detectable exceptions, exception handlers, and the raising of exceptions. Then the design issues for exception handling are introduced and discussed, including the binding of exceptions to exception handlers, continuation, default handlers, and exception disabling. The remainder of the chapter describes and evaluates the exception-handling facilities of four programming languages: PL/I, Ada, C++, and Java.

13.1 Introduction to Exception Handling

Most computer hardware systems are capable of detecting certain run-time error conditions, such as floating-point overflow. Many programming languages are designed and implemented in such a way that the user program can neither detect nor attempt to deal with such errors. In these languages, the occurrence of such an error simply causes the program to be terminated and control to be transferred to the operating system. The typical operating system reaction to a run-time error is to print a diagnostic message, which may be very meaningful or highly cryptic, and then terminate the program.

In the case of input and output operations, however, the situation is sometimes different. For example, a FORTRAN READ statement can intercept input errors and end-of-file conditions, both of which are detected by the input device hardware. In both cases, the READ statement can specify the label of some statement in the user program that deals with the condition. In the case of the end-of-file, it is clear that the condition is not always to be considered an error. In most cases, it is nothing more than a signal that one kind of processing is completed and a new kind should begin. In spite of the obvious difference between end-of-file and events that are always errors, such as a failed input process, FORTRAN handles both situations with the same mechanism. Consider the following FORTRAN READ statement:

```
READ(UNIT=5, FMT=1000, ERR=100, END=999) WEIGHT
```

The ERR clause specifies that control is to be transferred to the statement labeled 100 if an error occurs in the read operation. The END clause specifies that control is to be transferred to the statement labeled 999 if the read operation encounters the end of the file. So FORTRAN uses simple branches for both input errors and end-of-file.

There is a category of serious errors that are not detectable by hardware but could be detected by code generated by the compiler. For example, array subscript range errors are almost never detected by hardware (there were a few computers that *did* detect subscript range errors in hardware), but they do lead to fatal errors that are often only noticed later in the program execution.

Detection of subscript range errors is sometimes required by the language design. For example, Pascal and Java compilers must generate code to check the correctness of every subscript expression. In C, subscript ranges are not checked because the cost of such checking was (and is) not believed to be worth the benefit of detecting such errors. In some compilers for some languages, subscript range checking can be selected if desired by the program or in the command that executes the compiler.

Many contemporary languages provide mechanisms that can take action when some hardware-detectable and certain software-detectable conditions occur. They also allow the programmer to define other unusual events and use the same mechanisms to deal with them when they arise. These mechanisms are collectively called exception handling.

Perhaps the most important reason some languages do not include exception handling is the complexity it adds to the language.

13.1.1 Basic Concepts

We term both the errors detected by hardware, such as disk read errors, and unusual conditions, such as end-of-file (which are also detected by hardware), as exceptions. We further extend the concept of an exception to include errors or unusual conditions that are software-detectable. Accordingly, we define **exception** to be any unusual event, erroneous or not, that is detectable either by hardware or software and that may require special processing.

The special processing that may be required by the detection of an exception is called **exception handling.** This processing is done by a code unit called an **exception handler.** An exception is **raised** when its associated event occurs. Exception handlers are usually different for different exception types. Detection of end-of-file nearly always requires some specific program action. But, clearly, that action would not also be appropriate for a floating-point overflow exception. In some other cases, the only action could be the generation of an error message and an orderly termination of the program.

In some situations, it may be desirable to ignore certain exceptions for a time. This would be done by disabling the exception. A disabled exception could be enabled again at a later time.

The absence of separate or specific exception-handling facilities in a language does not preclude the handling of user-defined, software-detected exceptions. Such an exception detected within a program unit is often handled by the unit's caller, or invoker. One possible design is to send an auxiliary parameter, which is used as a status variable. The status variable is assigned a value in the called unit according to the correctness and/or normalness of its computation. Immediately upon return from the called unit, the caller tests the status variable. If the value indicates that an exception has occurred, the handler, which may reside in the calling unit, can be enacted. Many of the C language library functions use a variant of this approach: The return values are used as error indicators.

Another possibility is to pass a label parameter to the subprogram. Of course, this is only possible in languages that allow labels to be used as parameters. Passing a label allows the called unit to return to a different point in the caller if an exception has occurred. As in the first alternative, the handler is often a segment of the calling unit's code. This is a common use of label parameters in FORTRAN.

A third possibility is to have the handler as a separate subprogram that is passed as a parameter to the called unit. In this case, the handler subprogram is provided by the caller, but the called unit calls the handler when an exception is raised. One problem with this approach is that one is required to send a handler subprogram with *every* call, whether it is desirable or not. Furthermore, to deal with several different kinds of exceptions, several different handler routines would need to be passed, complicating the code.

If it is desirable to handle an exception in the unit in which it is detected, the handler is simply a segment of code in that unit.

There are some definite advantages to having exception handling built into a language. First, without exception, handling the code required to detect error conditions can considerably clutter a program. For example, suppose a subprogram includes expressions that contain ten division operations, and every one could have a zero divisor. Without built-in exception handling, every one of these operations would need to be preceded by a selection construct to detect the possible division-by-zero error. The presence of exception handling in the language could permit the compiler to insert such checks in the code when requested by the program.

Another advantage of language support for exception handling results from exception propagation. Exception propagation allows an exception raised in one program unit to be handled in some other unit in its dynamic or static ancestry. This allows a single exception handler to be used for a large number of different program units. This reuse can result in significant savings in development cost and program size.

A language that supports exception handling encourages its users to consider all of the events that could occur during program execution and how they can be handled. This is far better than not considering such possibilities and simply hoping nothing will go wrong. This advantage is related to requiring a multiple selector construct to include actions for all possible values of the control expression, as is required by Ada.

Finally, there are programs in which dealing with non-erroneous but unusual situations can be simplified with exception handling, and without it program structure can become overly convoluted.

13.1.2   **Design Issues**

We now explore some of the design issues for an exception-handling system when it is part of a programming language. Such a system might allow both built-in and user-defined exceptions and exception handlers. Consider the following skeletal subprogram that includes an exception-handling mechanism:

```
void example() {
  ...
  average = sum / total;
  ...
  return;
/* Exception handlers */
  when zero_divide {
    average = 0;
    printf("Error—divisor (total) is zero\n");
  }
  ...
}   /** function example **/
```

The exception of division by zero is intercepted in the function, which transfers control to the appropriate handler, which is then executed.

The first design question for user-defined exception handlers is their form. This is, essentially, a choice between having handlers that are complete program units or handlers that are code segments. In the latter case, they may be embedded in the units that raise the exceptions they are to handle, as in the above example, or they may be embedded in a different unit, such as the unit that called the one in which the exception is raised.

If the handler is a separate unit and the language uses static scoping, it can be in the same scope as the code that can cause it to be raised. This simplifies communications between the two units. If the handler is a separate unit outside the scope of the unit that can raise its associated exception, communication can be through parameters.

Another important design issue for exception handling is how an exception occurrence is bound to an exception handler. This issue occurs on two different levels. On the unit level, there is the question of how the same exception being raised in different points in a unit can be bound to different handlers within the unit. For example, in the subprogram above, there is a handler for a division-by-zero exception that appears to be written to deal with an occurrence of division by zero in a particular statement (the one shown). But suppose the function includes several other expressions with division operators. For those operators, this handler is probably not appropriate. So, it should be possible to bind the exceptions that can be raised by particular statements to particular handlers, even though the same exception can be raised by many different statements.

At a higher level, the binding question arises when there is no exception handler local to the unit in which the exception is raised. In this case, the designer must decide whether to propagate the exception to some other unit and, if so, where. How this propagation takes place and how far it goes have an important impact on the writability of exception handlers. For example, if handlers must be local, then many handlers must be written, which complicates both the writing and reading of the program. On the other hand, if exceptions are propagated, a single handler might handle the same exception raised in several program units, which may require the handler to be more general than one would prefer.

Another important factor is whether the binding of exceptions to handlers is static or dynamic; that is, whether binding depends on the syntactic layout of the program or on its execution sequence. As it is in other language constructs, static binding of exceptions is easier to understand and implement than dynamic binding.

After an exception handler executes, either control can transfer to somewhere in the program outside of the handler code, or program execution can simply terminate. We term this the question of control continuation after handler execution, or simply **continuation.** Termination is obviously the simplest choice, and in many error exception conditions, it is the best. However, in other situations, particularly those associated with unusual but not erroneous events, the choice of continuing execution is best. In these cases, some conventions must be chosen to determine where execution should continue. It might be the statement that raised the exception, the statement after the statement that raised the exception, or possibly some other unit. The choice to return to the statement that raised the exception may seem like a good one, but in the case of an error exception, it is only useful if the handler somehow is able to modify the values or operations that caused the exception to be raised. Otherwise the exception will simply be reraised. The required modification for an error exception is often very difficult. Even when possible, however, it may not be a sound practice. It allows the program to remove the symptom of a problem without removing the cause.

The two issues of binding of exceptions to handlers and continuation are illustrated in Figure 13.1.

Another design issue is the following: If users are allowed to define exceptions, how are these exceptions specified? The usual answer is to require that they be declared in the specification parts of the program units in which they can be raised. The scope of a declared exception is usually the scope of the program unit that contains the declaration.

In the case where a language provides built-in exceptions, several other design issues follow. For example, should the language run-time system provide default handlers for the built-in exceptions, or should the user be required to write handlers for all exceptions? Another question is whether built-in exceptions can be raised explicitly by the user program. This can be convenient if there are software-detectable situations in which the user would like to use a built-in handler.

Figure 13.1
Exception handling
control flow

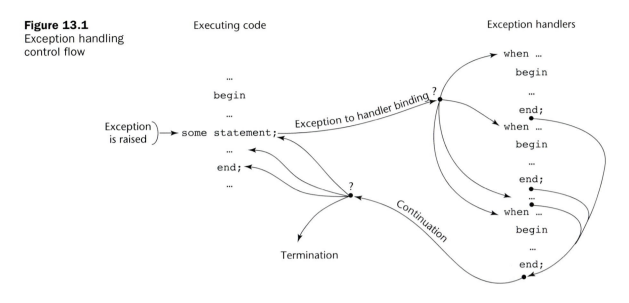

Another issue is whether hardware-detectable errors should be treated as exceptions that could be handled by user programs. If not, all exceptions obviously are software-detectable. A related question is whether there should be any built-in exceptions.

Finally, there is the question of whether exceptions, either built-in or user-defined, can be temporarily or permanently disabled. This question is somewhat philosophical, particularly in the case of built-in error conditions. For example, suppose a language has a built-in exception that is raised when a subscript range error occurs. Many believe that subscript range errors should always be detected, and therefore it should not be possible for the program to disable detection of these errors. Others argue that subscript range checking is too costly for production software, where, presumably, the code is sufficiently error-free that range errors should not occur.

The exception-handling design issues can be summarized as follows:

- How and where are exception handlers specified, and what is their scope?
- How is an exception occurrence bound to an exception handler?
- Where does execution continue, if at all, after an exception handler completes its execution? (This is the question of continuation.)
- How are user-defined exceptions specified?
- Should there be default exception handlers for programs that do not provide their own?
- Can built-in exceptions be explicitly raised?
- Are hardware-detectable errors treated as exceptions that may be handled?

- Are there any built-in exceptions?
- Should it be possible to disable exceptions?

13.1.3   History

PL/I (ANSI, 1976) pioneered the concept of allowing user programs to be directly involved in exception handling. The language allows the user to write exception handlers for a long list of language-defined exceptions. Furthermore, PL/I introduced the concept of user-defined exceptions, which allow programs to create software-detected exceptions. These exceptions use the same mechanisms that are used for the built-in exceptions.

Since PL/I was designed, a substantial amount of work has been done to design alternative methods of exception handling. In particular, CLU (Liskov et al., 1984), Mesa (Mitchell et al., 1979), Ada, COMMON LISP (Steele, 1984), ML (Milner et al., 1990), C++, Modula-3 (Cardelli et al., 1989), Eiffel, and Java include exception-handling facilities.

We are now prepared to examine the exception-handling facilities of four of these programming languages.

13.2 Exception Handling in PL/I

In still another pioneering effort, the designers of PL/I tackled the problem of providing users with the first linguistic mechanisms for exception handling. As was their style in other areas, they provided facilities that are very powerful and highly flexible. But, as with some other PL/I constructs, its exception-handling facilities are difficult to understand, implement, and correctly use.

PL/I provides built-in exceptions and allows users to define their own.

13.2.1   Exception Handlers

User-defined exception handlers have the form of executable code blocks. They can appear anywhere an executable statement can appear, and have the form

```
ON condition [SNAP]
   BEGIN;
   ...
   END;
```

where condition is the name of the associated exception. In place of the BEGIN-END block, the single keyword, SYSTEM can be used to specify that the system-supplied handler is to be used. The keyword SNAP, when included, specifies that the dynamic chain of the program at the time the exception was raised is to be printed when the exception occurs. This provides the traceback information that allows the programmer to determine how execution got to the point of the exception. Such information is an obvious aid to debugging.

The referencing environment of a PL/I exception handler is that of the code in which it is embedded. Because exception handlers do not have parameters, it is common to place handlers near the places where their exceptions are likely to be raised.

13.2.2 Binding Exceptions to Handlers

The binding of exceptions to handlers in PL/I is dynamic. The ON statement specifies the binding of an exception to an exception handler. Because it is executable, its position in the program has a critical impact on its effect. If ON were a declarative statement, there could be only one per exception per block. In fact, however, there can be more than one ON statement for a given exception, even within the same block. The ON binding stays in effect until either a new ON statement for the same exception is executed or the block in which it appears is exited.

13.2.3 Continuation

In PL/I, built-in exception handlers for different exceptions provide different continuation actions. For some exceptions, execution returns to the statement that caused the exception; other conditions cause program termination. User-defined handlers can cause control to go to any part of the program they wish after handling an exception, but there is no mechanism that provides the address of the statement that caused the exception, so it is often impossible to return to it. The choice between the two actions in system handlers was made on the basis of whether it was deemed possible for a handler to fix the cause of the problem and continue successfully. In some cases, such as some arithmetic errors, it was believed that successful continued processing was not possible. In other cases, such as the CONVERSION exception (for errors in converting strings to numerics), it was thought possible to recover, and thus control is returned to the statement that caused the exception after the handler completed its execution. The PL/I design for continuation is often confusing for program readers and writers alike.

13.2.4 Other Design Choices

User-defined exceptions are created in PL/I programs by using a simple declaration with the form

```
CONDITION exception_name
```

All built-in exceptions have built-in handlers. These handlers can be preempted by user-defined exception handlers. User-defined exceptions must be raised explicitly, which is done with a statement of the form

```
SIGNAL condition (exception_name)
```

Any condition can be explicitly raised with a `SIGNAL` statement, although the built-in exceptions are normally raised implicitly by hardware or software conditions. A `SIGNAL` of an exception that is currently disabled does nothing.

PL/I defines 22 built-in exceptions. These range from arithmetic errors, such as `ZERODIVIDE`, to programming errors, such as `SUBSCRIPTRANGE`. Built-in exceptions are divided into three categories: (1) those that are always enabled, (2) those that are enabled by default but can be disabled by user code, and (3) those that are disabled by default but can be enabled by user code.

The process of enabling and disabling conditions is accomplished by prefixing a statement, block, or procedure with the exception name or names, as in

```
(SUBSCRIPTRANGE, NOOVERFLOW):
  BEGIN;
  ...
  END;
```

In this case, the `SUBSCRIPTRANGE` exception is enabled and the `OVERFLOW` exception is disabled. (The default values for these are the opposite, `NOSUBSCRIPTRANGE` and `OVERFLOW`.) The prefix `NO` can be attached to any exception that is not permanently enabled (to disable it).

13.2.5 An Example

The following example program illustrates two simple but common uses of exception handlers in PL/I. The program computes and prints a distribution of input grades by using an array of counters. There are ten categories of grades (0–9, 10–19, ..., 90–100). The grades themselves are used to compute indexes into an array of counters, one for each grade category. Invalid input grades are detected by trapping indexing errors in the counter array. A grade of 100 is special in the computation of the grade distribution, because the categories all have ten possible grade values, except the highest, which has eleven (90, 91, ..., 100). (The fact that there are more possible A

grades than Bs or Cs is conclusive evidence of the generosity of teachers.)
The grade of 100 is also handled in the same exception handler that is used
for invalid input data.

```
GRADE_DISTRIBUTION: PROCEDURE OPTIONS (MAIN);
   DECLARE FREQ(1:10) FIXED INIT ((10) 0),
            NEW_GRADE FIXED,
            LIMIT_1 FIXED,
            LIMIT_2 FIXED,
            INDEX FIXED;
/* Exception Handlers */
   ON ENDFILE (SYSIN) GOTO FINISH;
   ON SUBSCRIPTRANGE
     BEGIN;
     IF NEW_GRADE = 100 THEN
       FREQ(10) = FREQ(10) + 1;
     ELSE
       DO;
       PUT LIST ('INPUT GRADE:' || NEW_GRADE ||
         'NOT IN RANGE') SKIP;
       GOTO INPUT_LOOP;
       END;
     END;
/* Main program body */
INPUT_LOOP:
  DO;
  GET LIST (NEW_GRADE);
  INDEX = NEW_GRADE / 10 + 1;
(SUBSCRIPTRANGE):
  FREQ(INDEX) = FREQ(INDEX) + 1;
  END INPUT_LOOP;

FINISH:
  PUT LIST ('LIMITS  FREQUENCY') SKIP(2);
  DO INDEX = 0 TO 9;
    LIMIT_1 = 10 * INDEX;
    LIMIT_2 = LIMIT_1 + 9;
    IF INDEX = 9 THEN
      LIMIT_2 = 100;
    PUT LIST (LIMIT_1, LIMIT_2, FREQ(INDEX+1));
  END;
END GRADE_DISTRIBUTION;
```

Three different events trigger exception handling in this program.
Among these three, only one is an error; the other two simply signal that
something special has happened. In one case, it is a grade of 100; in the
other, the end of the input data has been reached.

Notice that the handler for the SUBSCRIPTRANGE exception allows execution to continue for illegal grades, even though the built-in handler for
that exception, which the program overrides, would cause program termination.

13.2.6 Evaluation

PL/I offers a powerful facility for exception detection and handling. Its high level of flexibility, however, is not without cost. The primary example of this is the dynamic binding of exceptions to handlers, which causes a problem in writability and readability that is related to the problems of dynamic scoping. Indeed, it is the same problem: The scope of the exception handler is dynamic, so it is impossible to determine from a program listing which binding is in effect at any given point in the program. Because of dynamic binding, it is easy to have a handler unintentionally used for an exception that is in fact syntactically far from the exception and also completely inappropriate for that exception in that situation. For example, consider the following simple code segment:

```
(SUBSCRIPTRANGE):
  BEGIN;
  ...
  ON SUBSCRIPTRANGE
    BEGIN;
    PUT LIST('ERROR - BAD SUBSCRIPT IN ARRAY SUBSUM');
    GO TO FIXIT;
    END;
  ...
  ON SUBSCRIPTRANGE
    BEGIN;
    PUT LIST('ERROR - BAD SUBSCRIPT IN ARRAY BLK ');
    GO TO QUIT;
    END;
  ...
LABEL1:;
  ...
  BLK(I, J, K) = SUM;
  ...
  END;
```

If the code between the two handlers for the exception SUBSCRIPTRANGE happened to include a GO TO LABEL1, then the first handler would be executed if the exception was raised by the assignment to BLK. This would enact the wrong handler, causing at very least a good deal of confusion for the user (it would incorrectly state that the error was with the array SUBSUM rather than BLK).

Another serious problem is posed by the flexibility of the continuation rules of PL/I exceptions. They are difficult to implement, harmful to readability in the same way that the goto is, and also difficult to learn to use effectively.

Because PL/I's mechanisms for exception handling were thought to be too complex, they were not copied by other language designers. A more restricted model was proposed in 1975 by Goodenough (1975), in which exceptions are statically bound to exception handlers. An even more constrained model was designed into the CLU language in the mid-1970s (Liskov et al., 1984). Later languages based the design of their exception handling, at least in part, on that of CLU.

13.3 Exception Handling in Ada

Exception handling in Ada is a powerful tool for constructing more reliable software systems. It includes the good parts of the exception handling design of both PL/I and CLU.

13.3.1 Exception Handlers

Ada exception handlers are usually local to the code in which the exception can be raised. Because this provides them with the same referencing environment, parameters for handlers are not necessary and are not allowed.

Exception handlers have the general form

when exception_choice {| exception_choice} => statement_sequence

where the braces are metasymbols that mean that what they contain may be left out or repeated any number of times. The exception_choice has the form

exception_name | **others**

The exception name indicates the particular exception or exceptions that this handler is meant to handle. The statement sequence is the handler body. The reserved word **others** indicates that the handler is meant to handle any exceptions not named in any other local handler.

Exception handlers can be included in blocks or in the bodies of subprograms, packages, or tasks. Regardless of the block or unit in which they appear, handlers are gathered together in an **exception** clause, which must be placed at the end of the block or unit. For example, the usual form of an exception clause is shown in the following:

```
begin
-- the block or unit body --
exception
     when exception_name_1 = >
       -- first handler --
     when exception_name_2 = >
       -- second handler --
     -- other handlers --
end;
```

Any statement that is legitimate in the block or unit in which the handler appears is also legal in the handler.

13.3.2 Binding Exceptions to Handlers

When the block or unit that raises an exception includes a handler for that exception, the exception is statically bound to that handler. If an exception is raised in a block or unit that does not have a handler for that particular exception, the exception is propagated to some other block or unit. The way in which exceptions are propagated depends on the program entity in which the exception occurs.

When an exception is raised in a procedure, whether in the elaboration of its declarations or in the execution of its body, and the procedure has no handler for it, the exception is implicitly propagated to the calling program unit at the point of the call. This policy is reflective of the design philosophy that exception propagation should trace back through the control path (dynamic ancestors), not through static ancestors.

If the calling unit to which an exception has been propagated also has no handler for the exception, it is again propagated to that unit's caller. This continues, if necessary, to the main program. If an exception is propagated to the main program and a handler is still not found, the program is terminated.

In the realm of exception handling, an Ada block is considered to be a parameterless procedure that is "called" by its parent block when execution control reaches the block's first statement. When an exception is raised in a block, in either its declarations or executable statements, and the block has no handler for it, the exception is propagated to the next larger enclosing scope, which is the code that "called" it. The point to which the exception is propagated is just after the end of the block in which it occurred, which is its "return" point.

When an exception is raised in a package body and the package body has no handler for the exception, the exception is propagated to the declaration section of the unit containing the package declaration. If the package happens to be a library unit (which is separately compiled), the program is terminated.

If an exception occurs in a task body and the task contains a handler for the exception, that handler is executed and the task is marked as being completed. If the task does not have a handler for the exception, the task is simply marked as being completed; the exception is not propagated. The control mechanism of a task is too complex to lend itself to a reasonable and simple answer to the question of where its unhandled exceptions should be propagated.

Exceptions can also occur during the elaboration of the declarative sections of subprograms, blocks, packages, and tasks. For example, suppose that a function is called to initialize a variable in its declaration statement, as in the following:

```
procedure RIVER is
   CURRENT_FLOW : FLOAT := GET_FLOW;
   ...
begin
   ...
end RIVER;
```

Assume that GET_FLOW is a function with no parameters. If GET_FLOW raises and propagates an exception to its caller, the exception is reraised in this declaration. Storage allocation during declaration elaboration can also raise an exception.

When exceptions are raised during the declaration elaborations of procedures, packages, and blocks, those exceptions are propagated exactly as if the exception were raised in the associated code section. In the case of a task, the task is marked as being completed, no further elaboration takes place, and the built-in exception TASKING_ERROR is raised at the point of activation for the task.

13.3.3 Continuation

The block or unit that raises an exception, along with all units to which the exception was propagated but that did not handle it, is always terminated. Control never returns implicitly to the raising block or unit after the exception is handled. Control simply continues after the exception clause, which is always at the end of a block or unit. This causes an immediate return to a higher level of control.

When deciding where an execution would continue after exception handler execution was completed in a program unit, the Ada design team had little choice, because the requirements specification for Ada (Department of Defense, 1980a) clearly states that program units that raise exceptions cannot be continued or resumed. However, in the case of a block, a statement can be retried after it raises an exception and that exception is handled. For example, suppose a statement that can raise an exception and a handler for that exception are both enclosed in a block, which is itself enclosed in a loop. The following example code segment, which gets four integer values in the desired range from the keyboard, illustrates this kind of structure:

```
...
type AGE_TYPE is 0..125;
type AGE_LIST_TYPE is array (1..4) of AGE_TYPE;
package AGE_IO is new INTEGER_IO (AGE_TYPE);
use AGE_IO;
AGE_LIST : AGE_LIST_TYPE;
...
begin
for AGE_COUNT in 1..4 loop
   loop  -- loop for repetition when exceptions occur
```

```
EXCEPT_BLK:
   begin  -- compound to encapsulate exception handling
   PUT_LINE("Enter an integer in the range 0..125");
   GET(AGE_LIST(AGE_COUNT));
   exit;
   exception
     when DATA_ERROR =>  -- Input string is not a number
       PUT_LINE("Illegal numeric value");
       PUT_LINE("Please try again");
     when CONSTRAINT_ERROR =>  -- Input is < 0 or > 125
       PUT_LINE("Input number is out of range");
       PUT_LINE("Please try again");
   end EXCEPT_BLK;
 end loop;  -- end of the infinite loop to repeat input
              -- when there is an exception
end loop;  -- end of for AGE_COUNT in 1..4 loop
...
```

Control stays in the inner loop, which contains only the block, until a valid input number is received.

13.3.4 Other Design Choices

Ada includes five built-in exceptions,

```
CONSTRAINT_ERROR
NUMERIC_ERROR
PROGRAM_ERROR
STORAGE_ERROR
TASKING_ERROR
```

Each of these is actually a category of exceptions. For example, the exception CONSTRAINT_ERROR is raised when an array subscript is out of range, when there is a range error in a numeric variable that a range restriction, when a reference is made to a record field that is not present in a discriminated union, and in a few additional situations.

User-defined exceptions are defined with the following declaration form:

exception_name_list : **exception**

Such exceptions are treated exactly as built-in exceptions, except that they must be raised explicitly.

There are default handlers for the built-in exceptions, all of which result in program termination.

Exceptions are explicitly raised with the **raise** statement, which has the general form

raise [exception_name]

The only place a **raise** statement can appear without naming an exception is within an exception handler. In that case, it reraises the same exception that caused execution of the handler. This has the effect of propagating the exception according to the propagation rules stated previously. A **raise** in an exception handler is useful when one wishes to print an error message where an exception that is raised but handle the exception elsewhere.

An Ada pragma is a directive to the compiler. Certain run-time checks that are parts of the built-in exceptions can be disabled in Ada programs by use of the SUPPRESS pragma, the simple form of which is

pragma SUPPRESS(check_name)

The SUPPRESS **pragma** can only appear in declaration sections. When it appears, the specified check may be suspended in the associated block or program unit of which the declaration section is a part. Explicit raises are not affected by SUPPRESS. Although it is not required, most Ada compilers implement the SUPPRESS **pragma**.

Examples of checks that can be suppressed are the following. INDEX_CHECK and RANGE_CHECK specify two of the checks that are normally done in an Ada program. INDEX_CHECK refers to array subscript range checking. RANGE_CHECK refers to checking such things as the range of a value being assigned to a subtype variable. If either INDEX_CHECK or RANGE_CHECK is violated, CONSTRAINT_ERROR is raised. DIVISION_CHECK and OVERFLOW_CHECK are suppressible checks associated with NUMERIC_ERROR. The following **pragma** disables array subscript range checking:

pragma SUPPRESS(INDEX_CHECK);

There is an option of SUPPRESS that allows the named check to be further restricted to particular objects, types, subtypes, and program units.

13.3.5 An Example

The following example has the same intent and use of exception handling as the PL/I program shown earlier in this chapter. It produces a distribution of input grades by using an array of counters for ten grade categories. Illegal grades are detected by checking for invalid subscripts used in incrementing the selected counter.

```
with TEXT_IO; use TEXT_IO;
procedure GRADE_DISTRIBUTION is
  package INTEGER_TEXT_IO is new INTEGER_IO(INTEGER);
  use INTEGER_TEXT_IO;
  FREQ: array (1..10) of INTEGER := (others => 0);
  NEW_GRADE,
  INDEX,
```

```
      LIMIT_1,
      LIMIT_2 : INTEGER;
    begin
      loop
      GET(NEW_GRADE);
      INDEX := NEW_GRADE / 10 + 1;
        begin  -- A block for the CONSTRAINT_ERROR handler
        FREQ(INDEX) := FREQ(INDEX) + 1;
        exception
          when CONSTRAINT_ERROR =>
            if NEW_GRADE = 100 then
              FREQ(10) := FREQ(10) + 1;
            else
              PUT("ERROR -- new grade: ");
              PUT(NEW_GRADE);
              PUT(" is out of range");
              NEW_LINE;
            end if;
        end;  -- end of block for the CONSTRAINT_ERROR handler
      end loop;
    exception  -- This handler includes all final computations
      when END_OF_FILE =>
        PUT("Limits  Frequency");
        NEW_LINE; NEW_LINE;
        for INDEX in 0..9 loop
          LIMIT_1 := 10 * INDEX;
          LIMIT_2 := LIMIT_1 + 9;
          if INDEX = 9 then
            LIMIT_2 := 100;
          end if;
          PUT(LIMIT_1);
          PUT(LIMIT_2);
          PUT(FREQ(INDEX + 1));
          NEW_LINE;
        end loop;  -- for INDEX in 0..9 ...
  end GRADE_DISTRIBUTION;
```

Notice that the code to handle invalid input grades is in its own local block. This allows the program to continue after such exceptions are handled, as in our earlier example that reads values from the keyboard.

13.3.6 Evaluation

As is the case in some other language constructs, Ada's design of exception handling represents something of a consensus, at least at the time of its design (the late 1970s and early 1980s), of ideas on the subject. It is clearly a significant advance over the exception handling of PL/I. For some time,

Ada was the only widely used language that included exception handling. The exception handling in C++ and Java has now changed that.

13.4 Exception Handling in C++

The exception handling of C++ was accepted by the ANSI C++ standardization committee in 1990 and subsequently found its way into C++ implementations. The design is based in part on the exception handling of CLU, Ada, and ML.

13.4.1 Exception Handlers

In Section 13.3, we saw that Ada uses program units or blocks to specify the scope for exception handlers. C++ uses a special construct that is introduced with the reserved word **try** for this purpose. A **try** construct includes a compound statement called the **try** clause and a list of exception handlers. The compound statement defines the scope of the following handlers. The general form of this construct is

```
try {
//** Code that is expected to raise an exception
}
catch(formal parameter) {
//** A handler body
}
...
catch(formal parameter) {
//** A handler body
}
```

Each of the **catch** functions are exception handlers. A **catch** function can have only a single formal parameter, which is similar to a formal parameter in a function definition in C++, including the possibility of it being only an ellipsis (...). The formal parameter can be a naked type specifier, such as **float**, as in a function prototype. When information about the exception is to be passed to the handler, the parameter includes a type name and a variable name that is used for that purpose. For example, a user can define a class as an exception and include as many data members as are necessary. Otherwise the formal parameter can be just a type name, whose only purpose is to make the handler uniquely identifiable. A handler with an ellipsis formal parameter is the catch-all handler; it is enacted for any raised exception if no previous handler is chosen. The process by which thrown exceptions are connected to handlers is discussed in Section 13.4.2.

In C++, exception handlers can include any C++ code.

13.4.2 Binding Exceptions to Handlers

C++ exceptions are raised only by the explicit statement **throw**, whose general form is

> **throw** [expression];

The brackets are metasymbols used to specify that the expression is optional. A **throw** without an operand can only appear in a handler. When it appears there, it reraises the exception, which is then handled elsewhere. This is exactly like the Ada use of a **raise** statement without an exception name.

The word **throw** was chosen because both `signal` and `raise` are functions in the ANSI C standard library.

The type of the **throw** expression selects the particular handler, which of course must have a "matching" type formal parameter. In this case, matching means the following: A handler with a formal parameter of type `T`, **const** `T`, `T&` (a reference to an object of type `T`), or **const** `T&` matches a **throw** with an expression of type `T`. In the case where `T` is a class, a handler whose parameter is type `T` or any class that is an ancestor of `T` matches. There are more complicated situations in which a **throw** expression matches a formal parameter, but they will not be described here.

An exception raised in a **try** construct causes an immediate end to the execution of the code in that **try** construct. The search for a matching handler begins with the handlers that immediately follow the **try** construct. The matching process is done sequentially on the handlers until a match is found. This means that if any other match precedes an exactly matching handler, the exactly matching handler will not be used. If there is a **catch** with an ellipsis formal parameter, it will match any **throw**, so it is not useful to place such a **catch** anywhere but at the end of the list of handlers.

Exceptions are handled locally only if a match is found in a local handler. If no handler match is found locally, the exception is propagated to the caller of the function in which it was raised. If no matching handler is found in the program, the program is terminated.

13.4.3 Continuation

After a handler has completed its execution, control flows to the first statement following the **try** construct (the statement immediately after the last handler in the sequence of handlers of which it is an element). A handler may reraise an exception, using a **throw** without an expression, in which case that exception is propagated to the caller.

13.4.4 Other Design Choices

In terms of the design issues summarized in Section 13.1.2, the exception handling of C++ is simple. There are *only* user-defined exceptions, and they are not specified (though they might be declared as new classes). There are no default handlers, for system-detected exceptions cannot be handled. Exceptions cannot be disabled.

A C++ function can list the types of the exceptions (the types of the throw expressions) that it could raise. This is done by attaching the reserved word **throw**, followed by a parenthesized list of these types, to the function header. For example,

```
int fun() throw (int, char *) { ... }
```

specifies that the function **fun** could raise exceptions of type **int** and **char** * but no others. If the types in the **throw** clause are classes, then the function can throw any exception that is derived from the listed classes. If a function header has a **throw** clause and raises an exception that is not listed in the **throw** clause and is not derived from a class listed there, it causes a fatal error. The list of types in the list may be empty, meaning the function will not raise any exceptions. If there is no **throw** specification on the header, the function can raise any exception. The list is not part of the function's type.

When an exception terminates a **try** construct, all stack-dynamic and heap-dynamic variables that were allocated by code executed in the construct before the exception occurred are deallocated. Therefore, the handler can never access such variables.

13.4.5 An Example

The following example once again has the same intent and use of exception handling as the PL/I program shown in Section 13.2.5. It produces a distribution of input grades by using an array of counters for ten categories. Illegal grades are detected by checking for invalid subscripts used in incrementing the selected counter.

```
#include <iostream.h>
void main() {   //* Any exception can be raised
  int new_grade,
      index,
      limit_1,
      limit_2,
      freq[10] = {0,0,0,0,0,0,0,0,0,0};
  short int eof_condition;
  try {
    while (1) {
      if (!cin >> new_grade)  //* When cin detects eof,
```

```
        throw eof_condition;   //* raise eof_condition
    index = new_grade / 10;
    {try {
       if (index < 0 || index > 9)
         throw(new_grade);
       freq[index]++;
    }   //* end of inner try compound
    catch(int grade) {   //* Handler for index errors
      if (grade == 100)
        freq[9]++;
      else
        cout << "Error -- new grade: " << grade
             << " is out of range" << endl;
    }   //* end of catch(int grade)
  }   //* end of the block for the inner try-catch pair
}   //* end of while (1)
}   //* end of outer try compound
catch(short int) {   //** Handler for eof
  cout << "Limits   Frequency" << endl;
  for (index - 0; index < 10; index++) {
    limit_1 = 10 * index;
    limit_2 = limit_1 + 9;
    if (index == 9)
      limit_2 = 100;
    cout << limit_1 << limit_2 << freq[index] << endl;
  }   //* end of for (index == 9)
}   //* end of catch (short int)
}   //* end of main
```

This program is meant to illustrate the mechanics of C++ exception handling. However, both of the uses of exceptions in this example are better handled by other means. The end-of-file condition is easier to handle by simply controlling the **while** loop with the `cin` expression as the control expression. Furthermore, the index range exception is usually handled in C++ by overloading the indexing operation, which could then raise the exception, rather than the direct detection of the indexing operation with the selection construct used in our example.

13.4.6 Evaluation

In some ways the C++ exception-handling mechanism is similar to that of Ada: Binding exceptions to handlers is static, and unhandled exceptions are propagated to the function's caller. But in other ways the C++ design is quite different: There are no built-in hardware-detectable exceptions that can be handled by the user and exceptions are not named. This leads to the odd design that exceptions are connected to handlers through a parameter type in which the formal parameter could be absent. The type of the formal parameter of a handler determines the condition under which it is called but may have nothing whatever to do with the nature of the raised exception. Therefore, the use of predefined types certainly does not promote readability. It is much better to define classes with meaningful names in a meaningful hierarchy that can be used for defining exceptions.

13.5 Exception Handling in Java

In Chapter 12, the Java example program includes the use of exception handling with little explanation. This section describes the details of Java's exception handling capabilities.

Java's exception handling is based on that of C++, but it is designed to be more within the object-oriented language paradigm.

13.5.1 Classes of Exceptions

All Java exceptions are objects of classes that are descendants of the `Throwable` class. The Java system includes two system-defined exception classes that are subclasses of `Throwable`, `Error`, and `Exception`. The `Error` class and its descendants are related to errors that are thrown by the Java interpreter, such as running out of heap memory. These exceptions are never thrown by user programs, and they should never be handled there. There are two system-defined direct descendants of `Exception`, `RuntimeException` and `IOException`. As its name indicates, `IOException` is thrown when an error has occurred in an input or output operation, all of which are defined as methods in the various classes defined in the package `java.io`.

There are system-defined classes that are descendants of `RuntimeException`. In most cases, `RuntimeException` is thrown when a user program causes an error. For example, `ArrayIndexOutOfBoundsException`, which is defined in `java.util`, is a commonly thrown exception that descends from `RuntimeException`. Another commonly thrown exception that descends from `RuntimeException` is `NullPointerException`.

User programs can define their own exception classes. The convention in Java is that user-defined exceptions are subclasses of `Exception`.

13.5.2 Exception Handlers

The exception handlers of Java have the same form as those of C++, except the parameter of every **catch** must be present and its class must be a descendant of the predefined class, `Throwable`.

The syntax of the **try** construct in Java is exactly as that of C++.

13.5.3 Binding Exceptions to Handlers

Throwing an exception is quite simple. An instance of the exception class is given as the operand of the **throw** statement. For example, suppose we define an exception named `MyException` as

```
class MyException extends Exception {
  public MyException() {}
  public MyException(String message) {
    super (message);
  }
}
```

This exception can be thrown with

```
throw new MyException();
```

The creation of the instance of the exception for the **throw** could be done separately from the **throw** statement, as in

```
MyException myExceptionObject = new MyException();
...
throw myExceptionObject;
```

One of the two constructors we have included in our new class has no parameter and the other has a `String` object parameter that it sends to the superclass (`Exception`), which displays it. So our new exception could be thrown with

```
throw new MyException
    ("a message to specify the location of the error");
```

The binding of exceptions to handlers in Java is less complex than in C++. If an exception is thrown in the compound statement of a **try** construct, it is bound to the first handler (**catch** function) immediately following the **try** clause whose parameter is the same class as the thrown object, or an ancestor of it. If a matching handler is found, the **throw** is bound to it and it is executed.

Exceptions can be handled and then rethrown by including a **throw** statement without an operand at the end of the handler. The newly thrown exception will not be handled in the same **try** where it was originally thrown, so looping is not a concern. This rethrowing is usually done when some local action is useful, but further handling by an enclosing **try** clause or a caller is necessary. A **throw** statement in a handler could also throw some exception other than the one that transferred control to this handler; one particular exception could cause another to be thrown.

13.5.4 Continuation

When a handler is found in the sequence of handlers in a **try** construct, that handler is executed and program execution continues with the statement following the **try** construct. If none is found, the handlers of enclosing **try** constructs are searched, innermost first. If no handler is found in this process, the exception is propagated to the caller of the method. If the method call was in a **try** clause, the search for a handler continues in the attached collection of handlers in the clause. Propagation continues until the original caller is found, which, in the case of an application program, is main. If no matching handler is found anywhere, the program is terminated. In many cases, exception handlers include a **return** statement to terminate the method in which the exception occurred.

To ensure that exceptions that can be thrown in a **try** clause are always handled in a method, a special handler can be written that matches all exceptions that are derived from Exception simply by defining the handler with an Exception type parameter, as in

```
catch (Exception genericObject) {
   ...
}
```

Because a class name always matches itself or any ancestor class, any class derived from Exception matches Exception. Of course, such an exception handler should always be placed at the end of the list of handlers, for it will block the use of any handler that follows it in the **try** construct in which it appears. This is because the search for a matching handler is sequential, and the search ends when a match is found.

The object parameter to an exception handler is not entirely useless, as it may have appeared to be so far in this discussion. During program execution, the Java run-time system stores the class name of every object in the program. The method getClass can be used to get an object that stores the class name, which itself can be gotten with the getName method. So we can retrieve the name of the class of the actual parameter from the **throw** statement that caused the handler's execution. For the handler above, this is done with

```
genericObject.getClass().getName()
```

The message associated with the parameter object, which is created by the constructor, can be gotten with

```
genericObject.getMessage()
```

13.5.5 Other Design Choices

The **throws** clause of Java has the appearance and placement (in a program) that is similar to that of the **throw** specification of C++. However, the semantics of **throws** is completely different from that of the C++ **throw** clause.

The appearance of an exception class name in the **throws** clause of a Java method specifies that that exception class or any of its descendant exception classes can be thrown by the method. For example, when a method specifies that it can throw `IOException`, it means it can throw an `IOException` object or an object of any of its descendant classes, such as `EOFException`.

Exceptions of class `Error` and `RuntimeException` and their descendants are called **unchecked exceptions.** All other exceptions are called **checked exceptions.** Unchecked exceptions are never a concern of the compiler. However, the compiler ensures that all checked exceptions a method can throw are either listed in its **throws** clause or are handled in the method. The reason why exceptions of the classes `Error` and `RuntimeException` and their descendants are unchecked is that any method could throw them.

A method cannot declare more exceptions in its **throws** clause than the method it overrides, though it may declare fewer. So if a method has no **throws** clause, neither can any method that overrides it. A method can throw any exception listed in its **throws** clause, along with any of their descendant classes. A method that does not directly throw a particular exception, but calls another method that could throw that exception, must list the exception in its **throws** clause. This is the reason the `buildDist` method (in the example below), which uses the `readLine` method, must specify `IOException` in the **throws** clause of its header.

A method that calls a method that lists a particular checked exception in its **throws** clause has three alternatives for dealing with that exception: First, it can catch the exception and handle it. Second, it can catch the exception and throw an exception that is listed in its own **throws** clause. Third, it could declare the exception in its own **throws** clause and not handle it, which effectively propagates the exception to an enclosing **try** clause, if there is one, or to the method's caller if there is no enclosing **try** clause.

There are no default exception handlers, and it is not possible to disable exceptions.

13.5.6 An Example

Following is the Java class with the capabilities of the C++ program in Section 13.4:

```java
import java.io.*;

// The exception definition to deal with the end of data
class NegativeInputException extends Exception {
  public NegativeInputException() {
    System.out.println("End of input data reached");
  } //** end of constructor
} //** end of NegativeInputException class

class GradeDist {
```

```
int newGrade,
    index,
     limit_1,
     limit_2;
int [] freq = {0, 0, 0, 0, 0, 0, 0, 0, 0, 0};

void buildDist() throws IOException {
// Input: A list of integer values that represent
//         grades, followed by a negative number
// Output: A distribution of grades, as a percentage for
//          each of the categories 0-9, 10-19, ...,
//          10-100.
  DataInputStream in = new DataInputStream(System.in);
  try {
    while (true) {
      System.out.println("Please input a grade");
      newGrade = Integer.parseInt(in.readLine());
      if (newGrade < 0)
        throw new NegativeInputException();
      index = newGrade / 10;
      try {
        freq[index]++;
      } //** end of inner try clause
      catch(ArrayIndexOutOfBoundsException) {
        if (newGrade == 100)
          freq [9]++;
        else
          System.out.println("Error - new grade: " +
                             newGrade + " is out of range");
      } //** end of catch (ArrayIndex...
    } //** end of while (true) ...
  } //** end of outer try clause
  catch(NegativeInputException) {
    System.out.println ("\nLimits    Frequency\n");
    for (index = 0; index < 10; index++) {
      limit_1 = 10 * index;
      limit_2 = limit_1 + 9;
      if (index ==9)
        limit_2 = 100;
      System.out.println("" + limit_1 + " - " +
                        limit_2 + "       " + freq [index]);
    } //** end of for (index = 0; ...
  } //** end of catch (NegativeInputException ...
} //** end of method buildDist
```

The exception for a negative input, `NegativeInputException`, is defined in the program. Its constructor displays a message when an object of the class is created. Its handler produces the output of the method. The `ArrayIndexOutOfBoundsException` is predefined and is thrown by the interpreter. In both of these cases, the handler does not include an object name in its parameter. In neither case would a name serve any purpose. Note that all handlers get objects as parameters, but they are often not useful.

13.5.7 The `finally` Clause

There are some situations in which a process must be executed regardless of whether or not a **try** clause throws an exception and regardless of whether or not a thrown exception is caught in a method. One example of such a situation is a file that must be closed. Another is if the method has some external resource that must be freed in the method regardless of how the execution of the method terminates. The **finally** clause was designed for these kinds of needs. A **finally** clause is placed at the end of the list of handlers just after a **try** construct. In general, the whole construct looks like

```
try {
  ...
}
catch (...) {
  ...
}
... //** More handlers
finally {
}
```

The semantics of this construct is as follows: If the **try** clause throws no exceptions, the **finally** clause is executed before execution continues after the **try** construct. If the **try** clause throws an exception and it is caught by a following handler, the **finally** clause is executed after the handler completes its execution. If the **try** clause throws an exception but it is not caught by a handler following the **try** construct, the **finally** clause is executed before the exception is propagated.

A **try** construct with no exception handlers can be followed by a **finally** clause. This only makes sense, of course, if the compound statement has a **break**, **continue**, or **return** statement. Its purpose in these cases is the same as when it is used with exception handling. For example, we could have something like the following:

```
try {
  for (index = 0; index < 100; index++) {
    ...
    if (... ) {
      return;
    }  //** end of if
    ...
  }  //** end of for
}  //** end of try clause
```

```
finally {
    ...
}  //** end of try construct
```

The **finally** clause here will be executed, regardless of whether the **return** terminates the loop or it ends normally.

13.5.8   Evaluation

The Java mechanisms for exception handling are an improvement over the C++ version on which they are based.

First, a C++ program can throw any type defined in the program or by the system. In Java, only objects that are instances of **Throwable** or some class that descends from it can be thrown. This separates the objects that can be thrown from all of the other objects (and non-objects) that inhabit a program. What significance can be attached to an exception that causes an **int** value to be thrown?

Second, a C++ program unit that does not include a **throws** clause can throw any exception, which tells the reader nothing. A Java method that does not include a **throws** clause cannot throw any checked exception that it does not handle. Therefore, the reader of a Java method knows from its header what exceptions it could throw but does not handle.

Third, the addition of the **finally** clause is a great convenience in certain situations. It allows clean-up kinds of actions to take place regardless of how a compound statement terminated.

Finally, the Java run-time system implicitly throws a variety of exceptions, such as for array indices out of range and null reference variable accesses, which can be handled by any user program. A C++ program can handle only those exceptions that it explicitly throws.

Relative to the exception handling of Ada, Java's facilities are roughly comparable. The presence of the **throws** clause in a Java method is a good aid to readability, whereas Ada has no corresponding feature. Java is certainly closer to Ada than it is to C++ in one area, that of allowing programs to deal with system-detected exceptions.

SUMMARY

Exception handling has been incorporated into few widely used languages, although many experimental languages designed since the mid-1970s have had such facilities.

PL/I has powerful and flexible exception-handling capabilities, but there are a number of difficulties with the design. Overall, PL/I exception handling is sometimes too complex to be easily used and understood. The dynamic binding of exceptions to their handlers is one of the major causes of these problems.

Ada provides extensive exception-handling facilities and a small but comprehensive collection of built-in exceptions. Exceptions are statically bound to handlers. The handlers are attached to the program entities, although exceptions can be implicitly or explicitly propagated to other program entities if no local handler is available.

C++ exception handling uses static binding of exceptions to handlers. No built-in exceptions are included. Exceptions are bound to handlers by connecting the type of the expression in the **throw** statement to that of the formal parameter of the handler. Handlers all have the same name, **catch**.

Java exceptions are objects whose ancestry must trace back to some class that implements the interface **Throwable**. There are two categories of exceptions, checked and unchecked. Checked exceptions are a concern for the user program and the compiler. Unchecked exceptions can occur anywhere and are often ignored by user programs.

The Java **throws** clause of a method lists the checked exceptions that it could throw and does not handle. It must include exceptions that methods it calls could raise and propagate back to its caller.

The Java **finally** clause provides a mechanism for guaranteeing that some code will be executed regardless of how the execution of a **try** compound terminates.

BIBLIOGRAPHIC NOTES

One of the most important papers on exception handling that is not connected with a particular programming language is the work by Goodenough (1975). The problems with the PL/I design for exception handling are covered in MacLaren (1977). The CLU exception-handling design is clearly described by Liskov and Snyder (1979). Exception-handling facilities of the Ada language are described by Goos and Hartmanis (1983). Exception handling in C++ is described by Stroustrup (1991).

REVIEW QUESTIONS

1. Define *exception, exception handler, raising an exception, disabling an exception, continuation,* and *built-in exception.*

2. What are the design issues for exception handling?

3. What does it mean for an exception to be bound to an exception handler?

4. What is the problem with PL/I's binding of exceptions to handlers?

5. What are the possible frames for exceptions in Ada?

6. Where are unhandled exceptions propagated in Ada if raised in a subprogram? A block? A package body? A task?

7. Where does execution continue after an exception is handled in Ada?

8. How can an exception be explicitly raised in Ada?

9. How is a user-defined exception defined in Ada?

10. How can an exception be suppressed in Ada?

11. What is the name of all C++ exception handlers?

12. How can exceptions be explicitly raised in C++?

13. How are exceptions bound to handlers in C++?

14. How can an exception handler be written in C++ so that it handles any exception?

15. Where does execution control go when a C++ exception handler has completed its execution?

16. Does C++ include built-in exceptions?

17. What is the root class of all Java exception classes?

18. What is the parent class of most Java user-defined exception classes?

19. How can an exception handler be written in Java so that it handles any exception?

20. What is the difference between a C++ **throw** specification and a Java **throws** clause?

21. What is the difference between checked and unchecked exceptions in Java?

22. Can you disable a Java exception?

23. What is the purpose of the Java **finally** clause?

PROBLEM SET

1. What run-time errors or conditions, if any, can Pascal programs detect and handle?

2. From textbooks on the PL/I and Ada programming languages, look up the respective sets of built-in exceptions. Do a comparative evaluation of the two, considering both completeness and flexibility.

3. Write an Ada code segment that retries a call to a procedure, tape_read, that reads input from a tape drive and can raise the tape_read_error exception.

4. From *The Programming Language Ada Reference Manual* (Goos and Hartmanis, 1983), determine how exceptions that take place during rendezvous are handled.

5. From a textbook on COBOL, determine how exception handling is done in COBOL programs.

6. In languages without exception-handling facilities, it is common to have most subprograms include an "error" parameter, which can be set to some value representing "OK" or some other value representing "error in procedure." What advantage does a linguistic exception-handling facility like that of Ada have over this method?

7. In a language without exception-handling facilities, we could send an error-handling procedure as a parameter to each procedure that can detect errors that must be handled. What disadvantages are there to this method?

8. Compare the methods suggested in Problems 6 and 7. Which do you think is better and why?

9. Compare the exception-handling facilities of C++ with those of Ada. Which design, in your opinion, is the most flexible? Which makes it possible to write more reliable programs?

10. Suppose you are writing an Ada procedure that has three alternative methods for accomplishing its requirements. Write a skeletal version of this procedure so that if the first alternative raises any exception, the second is tried, and if the second alternative raises any exception, the third is executed. Write the code as if the three methods were procedures named **ALT1**, **ALT2**, and **ALT3**.

11. Write an Ada program that inputs a list of integer values in the range of –100 to 100 from the keyboard and computes the sum of the squares of the input values. This program must use exception handling to ensure that the input values are in range and are legal integers, to handle the error of the sum of the squares becoming larger than a standard **INTEGER** variable can store, and to detect end-of-file and use it to cause output of the result. In the case of overflow of the sum, an error message must be printed and the program terminated.

12. Write a C++ program for the specification of Problem 11.

13. Write a Java program for the specification of Problem 11.

14. Write a detailed comparison of the exception-handling capabilities of C++ and those of Java.

15. Consider the following Java skeletal program:

```java
class Big {
  int i;
  float f;
  void fun1() throws {int} {
    ...
    try {
      ...
      throw i;
      ...
      throw f;
      ...
    }
    catch(float) { ... }
    ...
  }
class Small {
  int j;
  float g;
  void fun2() throws {float} {
    ...
    try {
```

```
  ...
    try {
      Big.fun1();
      ...
      throw j;
      ...
      throw g;
      ...
    }
  catch(int) { ... }
  ...

}

catch(float) { ... }
}
```

In each of the four **throw** statements, where is the exception handled? Note that fun1 is called from fun2 in class Small.

14 Functional Programming Languages

John McCarthy

John McCarthy and Marvin Minsky formed MIT's Artificial Intelligence Project in 1958. In 1958–1959, McCarthy designed LISP, which became operational in 1959. McCarthy also served on the ALGOL design team.

This chapter introduces functional programming and some of the programming languages that have been designed for this approach to software development. Because these languages are based on mathematical functions, we begin by reviewing the fundamental ideas of these, including Church's lambda functional notation. Also included in this section is a brief discussion of functional forms and a few examples of the most common of these. Next, the idea of a functional programming language is introduced, followed by a look at the first functional language, LISP, and its list data structures and functional syntax, which is based on lambda notation. The next somewhat lengthy section is devoted to an introduction to Scheme, including some of its primitive functions, special forms, functional forms, and some examples of simple functions written in Scheme. We then briefly discuss some of the imperative features of Scheme. Next, we give short introductions to COMMON LISP, ML, and Haskell to show some different (from Scheme) design ideas for functional programming languages. A section follows that describes some of the applications of functional programming languages. Finally, we present a short comparison of functional and imperative languages.

14.1 Introduction

The first 13 chapters of this book have been concerned primarily with the imperative and object-oriented programming languages. With the exception of Smalltalk, the object-oriented languages we have discussed have had forms that are similar to the imperative languages. This chapter is the first to focus on a category of nonimperative languages.

The high degree of similarity among the imperative languages arises in part from one of the common bases of their design: the von Neumann architecture, as discussed in Chapter 1. We can think of the imperative languages collectively as a progression of developments to improve the basic model, which was FORTRAN I. All have been designed to make efficient use of von Neumann architecture computers. Although the imperative style of programming has been found acceptable by most programmers, its heavy reliance on the underlying architecture is thought by some to be an unnecessary restriction on the process of software development.

Other bases for language design exist, many of them oriented more to particular programming paradigms or methodologies than to efficient execution on a particular computer architecture. Thus far, however, the reduced efficiency in executing programs written in these languages has prevented them from becoming as popular as the imperative languages.

The functional programming paradigm, which is based on mathematical functions, is the design basis for one of the most important nonimperative styles of languages. This style of programming is supported by functional, or applicative, programming languages.

LISP began as a purely functional language, but it soon acquired some important imperative features that increased its execution efficiency. It is still the most important of the functional languages, at least in the sense that it is the only one that has achieved widespread use. Scheme is a small, static-scoped dialect of LISP. COMMON LISP is an amalgam of several early 1980s dialects of LISP. ML is a strongly typed functional language with more conventional syntax than LISP and Scheme. Haskell is partially based on ML but is a purely functional language.

The objective of this chapter is to introduce the concept, but not the process, of functional programming. We also will describe several ways in which a language can be designed to provide convenient facilities for functional programming. Our approach is to discuss mathematical functions and functional programming and then to introduce a subset of Scheme that is purely functional to illustrate the functional programming style. Sufficient material on Scheme is included to allow the reader to write some simple but interesting programs. It is difficult to acquire an actual feel for functional programming without some actual programming experience, so that is strongly encouraged.

14.2 Mathematical Functions

A mathematical function is a **mapping** of members of one set, called the **domain set,** to another set, called the **range set.** A function definition specifies the domain and range sets, either explicitly or implicitly, along with the mapping. The mapping is described by an expression or, in some cases, by a table. Functions are often applied to a particular element of the domain set. Note that the domain set may be the cross product of several sets. A function yields, or returns, an element of the range set.

One of the fundamental characteristics of mathematical functions is that the evaluation order of their mapping expressions is controlled by recursion and conditional expressions, rather than by the sequencing and iterative repetition that are common to the imperative programming languages.

Another important characteristic of mathematical functions is that, because they have no side effects, they always define the same value given the same set of arguments. Side effects in programming languages are connected to variables that model memory locations. A mathematical function defines a value, rather than specifying a sequence of operations on values in memory to produce a value. There are no variables in the sense of imperative languages, so there can be no side effects.

14.2.1 Simple Functions

Function definitions are often written as a function name, followed by a list of parameters in parentheses, followed by the mapping expression. For example,

cube(x) $\equiv x * x * x$, where x is a real number

In this definition the domain and range sets are the real numbers. The symbol $\equiv$ is used to mean "is defined as." The parameter, x, can represent any member of the domain set, but it is fixed to represent one specific element during evaluation of the function expression. This is how the parameters of mathematical functions differ from the variables in imperative languages.

Function applications are specified by pairing the function name with a particular element of the domain set. The range element is obtained by evaluating the function mapping expression with the domain element substituted for the occurrences of the parameter. For example, cube(2.0) yields the value 8.0. Once again, it is important to note that during evaluation, the mapping of a function contains no unbound parameters, where a bound parameter is a name for a particular value. Every occurrence of a parameter is bound to a value from the domain set and is considered a constant during evaluation.

Early theoretical work on functions separated the task of defining a function from that of naming the function. Lambda notation, as devised by Alonzo Church (Church, 1941), provides a method for defining nameless functions. A **lambda expression** specifies the parameter and the mapping of a function. The lambda expression is the function itself. For example, consider

$\lambda(x)x * x * x$

As stated above, before evaluation, a parameter represents any member of the domain set, but during evaluation it is bound to a particular member. When a lambda expression is evaluated for a given parameter, the expression is said to be applied to that parameter. The mechanics of such an application are the same as for any function evaluation. Application of the lambda expression above is denoted as in the following example:

$(\lambda(x)x * x * x)(2)$

which results in the value 8.

Lambda expressions, like other function definitions, can have more than one parameter.

14.2.2 Functional Forms

A higher-order function, or **functional form,** is one that either takes functions as parameters or yields a function as its result, or both. One common kind of functional form is **function composition,** which has two functional parameters and yields a function whose value is the first actual parameter function applied to the result of the second. Function composition is written as an expression, using ° as an operator, as in

$$h \equiv f \circ g$$

For example, if

$$f(x) \equiv x + 2$$
$$g(x) \equiv 3 * x$$

then h is defined as

$$h(x) \equiv f(g(x)), \text{ or } h(x) \equiv (3 * x) + 2$$

Construction is a functional form that takes a list of functions as parameters. When applied to an argument, a construction applies each of its functional parameters to that argument and collects the results in a list or sequence. A construction is syntactically denoted by placing the functions in brackets, as in [f, g]. Consider the following example:
Let

$$g(x) \equiv x * x$$
$$h(x) \equiv 2 * x$$
$$i(x) \equiv x / 2$$

then

$$[g, h, i](4) \text{ yields } (16, 8, 2)$$

Apply-to-all is a functional form that takes a single function as a parameter. If applied to a list of arguments, apply-to-all applies its functional parameter to each of the values in the list argument and collects the results in a list or sequence. Apply-to-all is denoted by α. Consider the following example:
Let

$$h(x) \equiv x * x$$

then

$$\alpha(h, (2, 3, 4)) \text{ yields } (4, 9, 16)$$

There are many other functional forms, but these examples should illustrate their characteristics.

14.3 **Fundamentals of Functional Programming Languages**

The objective of the design of a functional programming language is to mimic mathematical functions to the greatest extent possible. This results in an approach to problem solving that is fundamentally different from methods used with imperative languages. In an imperative language, an expression is evaluated and the result is stored in a memory location, which is represented as a variable in a program. This necessary attention to memory cells results in a relatively low-level programming methodology. A program in an assembly language often must also store the results of partial evaluations of expressions. For example, to evaluate

$$(x + y)/(a - b)$$

the value of $(x + y)$ is computed first. That value must then be stored while $(a - b)$ is evaluated. To help alleviate this problem, the compiler handles the storage of intermediate results of expression evaluations in high-level languages. The storage of intermediate results is still required, but the details are hidden from the programmer.

A purely functional programming language does not use variables or assignment statements. This frees the programmer from concerns about the memory cells of the computer on which the program is executed. Without variables, iterative constructs are not possible, for they are controlled by variables. Repetition must be done by recursion rather than by repetition. Programs are function definitions and function application specifications, and executions consist of evaluating the function applications. Without variables, the execution of a purely functional program has no state in the sense of operational and denotational semantics. The execution of a function always produces the same result when given the same parameters. This is called **referential transparency.** It makes the semantics of purely functional languages far simpler than the semantics of the imperative languages and the functional languages that include imperative features.

A functional language provides a set of primitive functions, a set of functional forms to construct complex functions from those primitive functions, a function application operation, and some structure or structures for representing data. These structures are used to represent the parameters and values computed by functions. A well-defined functional language requires only a small number of primitive functions.

Although functional languages are often implemented with interpreters, they can also be compiled.

Imperative languages usually provide only limited support for functional programming. Most, for example, include some kind of function definition and enactment facilities. The most serious drawback to using an imperative language to do functional programming is that functions in imperative languages have restrictions on the types of values that can be returned. In many languages, such as FORTRAN and Pascal, only scalar type values can be returned. More importantly, they cannot return a function. Such restrictions limit the kinds of functional forms that can be provided. Another serious problem with the functions of imperative languages is the possibility of functional side effects.

14.4 The First Functional Programming Language: LISP

A number of functional programming languages have been developed. The oldest and most widely used is LISP. Studying functional languages through LISP is somewhat akin to studying the imperative languages through FORTRAN: LISP was the first functional language, but some now believe that, although it has steadily evolved over the last 30 years, it no longer represents the latest design concepts for functional languages. In addition, with the exception of the first version, all LISP dialects include imperative language features, such as imperative-style variables, assignment statements, and iteration. (Imperative-style variables are used to name memory cells, whose values can change many times during program execution.) Despite this and their somewhat odd form, the descendants of the original LISP represent well the fundamental concepts of functional programming and are therefore worthy of study.

14.4.1 Data Types and Structures

There were only two types of data objects in the original LISP: atoms and lists. They are not types in the sense that imperative languages have types. In fact, the original LISP was a typeless language. Atoms, which have the form of identifiers, are the symbols of LISP. Numeric constants are also considered atoms.

Recall from Chapter 2 that LISP originally used lists as its data structure because they were thought to be an essential part of list processing. As it eventually developed, however, LISP rarely requires the operations of insertion and deletion.

Lists are specified by delimiting their elements within parentheses. The elements of simple lists are restricted to atoms, as in

    (A B C D)

Nested list structures are also specified by parentheses. For example, the list

    (A (B C) D (E (F G)))

is a list of four elements. The first is the atom A; the second is the sublist (B C); the third is the atom D; the fourth is the sublist (E (F G)), which has as its second element the sublist (F G).

Internally, lists are usually stored as single-linked list structures, in which each node has two pointers and represents an element. A node for an atom has its first pointer pointing to some representation of the atom, such as its symbol or numeric value. A node for a sublist element has its first pointer pointing to the first node of the sublist. In both cases, the second pointer of a node points to the next element of the list. A list is referenced by a pointer to its first element.

The internal representations of our two example lists are shown in Figure 14.1. Note that the elements of a list are shown horizontally. The last element of a list has no successor, so its link is NIL. Sublists are shown with the same structure.

14.4.2 The First LISP Interpreter

The original intent was to have a notation for LISP programs that would be as close to FORTRAN's as possible, with additions when necessary. This notation was called M-notation, for meta-notation. There was to be a compiler that would translate programs written in M-notation into semantically equivalent machine code programs for the IBM 704.

Early in the development of LISP, McCarthy decided to write a paper that would promote list processing as an approach to general symbolic processing. McCarthy believed that list processing could be used to study computability, which at the time was usually studied using Turing machines. McCarthy thought that the processing of symbolic lists was a more natural model of computation than Turing machines. One of the common requirements of the study of computation is that one must be able to prove certain computability characteristics of the whole class of whatever model of computation is being used. In the case of the Turing machine model,

Figure 14.1
Internal representation of two LISP lists

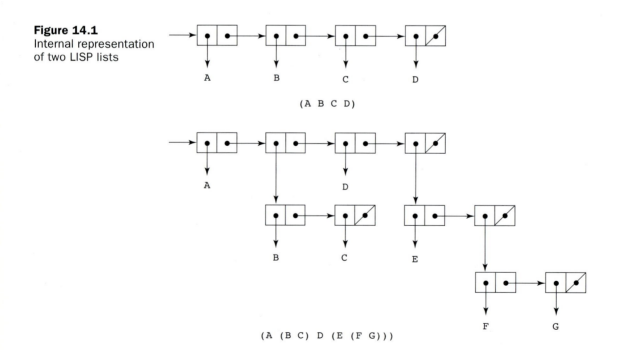

(A B C D)

(A (B C) D (E (F G)))

one can construct a universal Turing machine that can mimic the operations of any other Turing machine. From this concept came the idea of constructing a universal LISP function that could evaluate any other function in LISP.

The first requirement for the universal LISP function was a notation that allowed functions to be expressed in the same way data was expressed. The parenthesized list notation described in Section 14.4.1 had already been adopted for LISP data, so it was decided to invent conventions for function definitions and function calls that could also be expressed in list notation. Function calls were specified in a prefix list form called Cambridge Polish, as in the following:

(function_name   argument_1 ... argument_n)

For example, if + is a function that takes two numeric parameters,

(+ 5 7)

evaluates to 12.

The lambda notation described in Section 14.2.1 was chosen to specify function definitions. It had to be modified, however, to allow the binding of functions to names so that functions could be referenced by other functions and by themselves. This name binding was specified by a list consisting of the function name and a list containing the lambda expression, as in

(function_name (LAMBDA (arg_1 ... arg_n) expression))

If you have had no prior exposure to functional programming, it may seem odd to even consider a nameless function. However, nameless functions are sometimes useful in functional programming (as well as in mathematics). For example, consider a function whose action is to produce a function for immediate application to a parameter list. The produced function has no need for a name, for it is applied only at the point of its construction. Such an example is given in Section 14.5.6.

LISP functions specified in this new notation were called S-expressions, for symbolic expressions. Eventually, all LISP structures, both data and code, were called S-expressions. An S-expression can be either a list or an atom. We will often refer to S-expressions simply as expressions.

McCarthy successfully developed a universal function that could evaluate any other function. This function was named EVAL and was itself in the form of an expression. Two of the people in the AI Project, Stephen B. Russell and Daniel J. Edwards, noticed that an implementation of EVAL could serve as a LISP interpreter, and they promptly constructed such an implementation (McCarthy et al., 1965).

There were several important results of this quick, easy, and unexpected implementation. First, all early LISP systems copied EVAL and were therefore interpretive. Second, the definition of M-notation, which was the planned programming notation for LISP, was never completed or implemented, so S-expressions became LISP's only notation. The use of the same notation for data and code has important consequences, one of which will be discussed in Section 14.5.7. Third, much of the original language design was effectively frozen, keeping certain odd features in the language, such as the conditional expression form and the use of zero for both the null address and logical false.

Another feature of early LISP systems that was apparently accidental was the use of dynamic scoping. Functions were evaluated in the environments of their callers. No one at the time knew much about scoping, and it is doubtful that much thought was given to the choice. Dynamic scoping was used for most dialects of LISP before 1975. Contemporary dialects either use static scoping or allow the programmer to choose between static and dynamic scoping.

14.5 An Introduction to Scheme

In this section, we describe a part of Scheme (Dybvig, 1996). We have chosen Scheme because it is relatively simple, it is popular in colleges and universities, and Scheme interpreters are readily available for a wide variety of computers. The version of Scheme described in this section is Scheme 4.

14.5.1 Origins of Scheme

The Scheme language, which is a dialect of LISP, emerged from MIT in the mid-1970s (Sussman and Steele, 1975). It is characterized by its small size, its exclusive use of static scoping, and its treatment of functions as first-class entities. As first-class entities, Scheme functions can be the values of expressions and elements of lists, and they can be assigned to variables and passed as parameters. Early versions of LISP did not provide all of these capabilities.

As a small language with simple syntax and semantics, Scheme is well-suited to educational applications, such as courses in functional programming, and also general introductions to programming.

Note that most of the functions in the following sections that are written in Scheme would require only minor modifications to be made into LISP functions.

14.5.2 Primitive Functions

Names in Scheme can consist of letters, digits, and special characters except parentheses; they are case insensitive but must not begin with a digit.

The Scheme interpreter is a read-evaluate-write infinite loop. It repeatedly reads an expression typed by the user (in the form of a list), interprets the expression, and displays the resulting value. Literals evaluate to themselves. So, if you type a number to the interpreter, it simply displays the number. Expressions that are calls to primitive functions are evaluated in the following way: First, each of the parameter expressions is evaluated, in no particular order. Then the primitive function is applied to the parameter values, and the resulting value is displayed.

Scheme includes primitive functions for the basic arithmetic operations. These are +, −, *, and /, for add, subtract, multiply, and divide. * and + can have zero or more parameters. If * is given no parameters, it returns 1; if + is given no parameters, it returns 0. + adds all of its parameters together. * multiplies all its parameters together. / and − can have two or more parameters. In the case of subtraction, all but the first parameter are subtracted from the first. Division is similar to subtraction. Examples are as follows:

EXPRESSION	VALUE
42	42
(* 3 7)	21
(+ 5 7 8)	20
(- 5 6)	−1
(- 15 7 2)	6
(- 24 (* 4 3))	12

SQRT returns the square root of its numeric parameter, if the parameter's value is not negative.

The next Scheme primitive we describe is a utility function required by the nature of the Scheme function application operation, EVAL. EVAL is the basis of all function evaluation in Scheme, whether primitive or otherwise. It is called to handle the evaluate part of the read-evaluate-write action of the Scheme interpreter. When applied to a primitive function, EVAL first evaluates the parameters of the given function. This action is necessary when the actual parameters in a function call are themselves function calls, which is frequently the case. In some calls, however, the parameters are data elements, either atoms or lists, rather than function references. When a parameter is not a function reference, it obviously should not be evaluated.

For example, suppose we have a function that has two parameters, an atom and a list, whose purpose is to determine whether the given atom is in the given list. Neither the atom nor the list should be evaluated; they are literal data to be examined. To avoid evaluating a parameter, it is first given as a parameter to the primitive function QUOTE, which simply returns it without change. The following examples illustrate QUOTE:

(QUOTE A) returns A
(QUOTE (A B C)) returns (A B C)

In the remainder of this chapter, we will use the common abbreviation of the call to QUOTE, which is done by simply preceding the expressions to be quoted by an apostrophe symbol ('). Thus, instead of (QUOTE (A B)), we will use '(A B).

Computer programs manipulate data regardless of whether the language is imperative or functional. Because lists are the primary data structure of Scheme, the language must include primitives for manipulating lists. In particular, it must provide operations for selecting parts of a list, which in a sense dismantle the list, and at least one operation for constructing lists. Because the primary operations of functional languages are provided by functions, Scheme includes primitive functions for these operations.

There are two primitive list selectors in Scheme: CAR and CDR (pronounced "could-er"). The CAR function returns the first element of a given list. The following examples illustrate CAR:

```
(CAR '(A B C)) returns A
(CAR '((A B) C D)) returns (A B)
(CAR 'A) is an error (A is not a list)
(CAR '(A)) returns A
(CAR '()) is an error
```

The CDR function returns the remainder of a given list after its CAR is removed:

```
(CDR '(A B C)) returns (B C)
(CDR '((A B) C D)) returns (C D)
(CDR 'A) is an error
(CDR '(A)) returns ()
```

The names of the CAR and CDR functions are peculiar at best. The origin of these names lies in the first implementation of LISP, which was on an IBM 704 computer. The 704's memory words had two fields, named decrement and address, that were used in various operand addressing strategies. Each of these fields could store a machine memory address. The 704 also included two machine instructions, named CAR (contents of address register) and CDR (contents of decrement register), that extracted the associated fields. It was natural to use the two fields to store the two pointers of a list node so that a memory word could neatly store a node. Using these conventions, the CAR and CDR instructions of the 704 provided efficient list selectors. The names carried over into the primitives of all dialects of LISP.

CONS is the primitive list constructor. It builds a list from its two arguments, the first of which can be either an atom or a list; the second is usually a list. Its action is to insert its first parameter as the new CAR of its second parameter. Consider the following examples:

```
(CONS 'A '()) returns (A)
(CONS 'A '(B C)) returns (A B C)
```

```
(CONS '() '(A B)) returns (() A B)
(CONS '(A B) '(C D)) returns ((A B) C D)
```

The results of these CONS operations are shown in Figure 14.2. Note that CONS is, in a sense, the inverse of CAR and CDR. CAR and CDR take a list apart, and CONS constructs a new list from given list parts. The two parameters to CONS become the CAR and CDR of the new list. Thus, if lis is a list, then

```
(CONS (CAR lis) (CDR lis))
```

is the identity function.

LIST is a function that constructs lists from a variable number of parameters. It is a shorthand version of nested CONS functions, as illustrated in

```
(LIST 'apple 'orange 'grape)
```

which is equivalent to

```
(CONS 'apple (CONS 'orange (CONS 'grape '() )))
```

Figure 14.2
The result of several
CONS operations

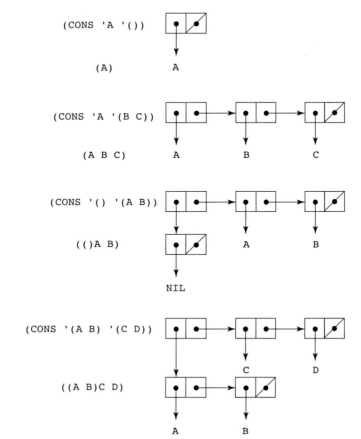

Three important predicate functions among Scheme's primitive functions are EQ?, NULL?, and LIST?. Notice that all predefined predicate functions have names that end with a question mark. A predicate function is one that returns a Boolean value (either true or false). In Scheme, the two Boolean values are #T and #F. The Scheme interpreter returns the empty list, ( ), instead of #F. Any non-null list returned by a predicate function is interpreted as #T.

The EQ? function takes two symbolic parameters. It returns #T if both parameters are atoms and the two are the same; otherwise, it returns ( ). Consider the following examples:

```
(EQ? 'A 'A) returns #T
(EQ? 'A 'B) returns ()
(EQ? 'A '(A B)) returns ()
(EQ? '(A B) '(A B)) returns () or #T
```

As the last case indicates, the result of comparing lists with EQ? is implementation dependent—some yield #T and some yield ( ). The reason for this difference is that EQ? is often implemented as a pointer comparison (do two given pointers point to the same place?), and two lists that are exactly the same are often not duplicated in memory. At the time the Scheme system creates a list, it checks to see if there is already such a list. If there is, the new list is nothing more than a new pointer to the existing list. In these cases, the two lists will be judged equal by EQ?. However, in some cases, it may be difficult to detect the presence of an identical list, in which case a new list is created. In this scenario, EQ? yields ( ).

Note that EQ? works for symbolic atoms but does not necessarily work for numeric atoms. Predicates for comparing numeric atoms follow. As discussed above, EQ? also does not work reliably for list parameters.

The LIST? predicate function returns #T if its single argument is a list and ( ) otherwise, as in the following examples:

```
(LIST? '(X Y)) returns #T
(LIST? 'X) returns ()
(LIST? '()) returns #T
```

The NULL? function tests its parameter to determine whether it is the empty list and returns #T if it is. Consider the following examples:

```
(NULL? '(A B)) returns ()
(NULL? '()) returns #T
(NULL? 'A) returns ()
(NULL? '(())) returns ()
```

The last case is ( ) because the parameter is not the empty list. Rather, it is a list containing a single element, an empty list.

Scheme includes a collection of predicate functions for numeric data. Among them are the following:

Function	*Meaning*
=	Equal
<>	Not equal
>	Greater than
<	Less than
>=	Greater than or equal to
<=	Less than or equal to
EVEN?	Is it an even number?
ODD?	Is it an odd number?
ZERO?	Is it zero?

It was stated earlier that EQ? works for symbolic atoms but not necessarily for numeric atoms. The = predicate works for numeric atoms but not symbolic atoms.

Sometimes it is convenient to be able to test two atoms for equality when it is not known whether they are symbolic or numeric. For this purpose, Scheme has a different predicate, EQV?, which works on both numeric and symbolic atoms. The primary reason to use EQ? or = rather than EQV? when it is possible is that EQ? and = are faster than EQV?.

Scheme includes a few simple output functions, such as

(DISPLAY expression)

and

(NEWLINE)

with the obvious semantics. Most output from Scheme programs, however, is the normal output from the interpreter, displaying results of applying EVAL to top-level functions.

Scheme parameters are passed by value, so regardless of what a function does to its parameters, the actual parameters are not affected.

14.5.3 Functions for Constructing Functions

As stated earlier, LISP-based languages use lambda notation in list form to define functions. For example, the lambda expression list

(LAMBDA (L) (CAR (CDR L)))

is a function that returns the second element of its given parameter, which must be a list. This function can be applied in the same way that named functions are: by placing it in the beginning of a list that contains the actual parameters. For example, we could have

((LAMBDA (L) (CAR (CDR L))) '(A B C))

which yields B. Notice that actual parameters to Scheme functions that are defined as parameters of the lambda expression are not quoted; an example is the parameter L in the call to CDR in the expression above. L is called a bound variable within the lambda expression. A bound variable never changes in the expression after being bound to an actual parameter value at the time the lambda expression is first called for evaluation.

The special form function DEFINE serves two fundamental needs of Scheme programming, to bind a name to a value and to bind a name to a lambda expression. The former use may sound like DEFINE can be used to create imperative language style variables. However, these name bindings create named constants, not variables.

DEFINE is called a special form because it is interpreted in a different way than the normal primitives like CAR and the arithmetic functions, as we shall soon see.

The simplest form of DEFINE is one used to bind a symbol to the value of an expression. This form is

```
(DEFINE symbol expression)
```

For example,

```
(DEFINE pi 3.14159)
(DEFINE two_pi (* 2 pi))
```

If these two expressions have been typed to the Scheme interpreter and then pi is typed, the number 3.14159 will be displayed; when two_pi is typed, 6.28318 will be displayed.

The DEFINE function can also be used to bind a lambda expression to a name. In this case, the lambda expression is abbreviated to remove the word *lambda*. In this form, DEFINE takes two lists as parameters. The first parameter is the prototype of a function call, with the function name followed by the formal parameters, all in a list. The second list is the expression to which the name is to be bound. The general form of such a DEFINE is

```
(DEFINE (function_name parameters)
    body
)
```

where the parameters are separated by spaces (not commas) and the body is a sequence of expressions in the form of lists.

The following example call to DEFINE binds the name square to the expression that follows it:

```
(DEFINE (square number) (* number number))
```

Once the interpreter evaluates this function, it can be used, as in

```
(square 5)
```

which displays 25.

The semantics of the special form DEFINE when used to define a function is as follows. The parameters part of the first parameter and the whole second parameter are considered together to be a lambda expression. The name in the first parameter is bound to this lambda expression.

To illustrate the difference between primitive functions and the DEFINE special form, consider

    (DEFINE x 10)

If DEFINE were a primitive function, EVAL's first action on this expression would be to evaluate the two parameters of DEFINE. If x was not already bound to a value, this would be an error.

As another example of a simple function, consider

    (DEFINE (second lst) (CAR (CDR lst)))

In this case, the name second is bound to the lambda expression

    ((LAMBDA (lst)(CAR (CDR lst)))

Once this function is evaluated, it can be used, as in

    (second '(A B C))

which returns B.

14.5.4 Control Flow

The control flow mechanisms of Scheme are modeled after those of mathematical functions. Control flow in mathematical function definitions is quite different from that in programs in imperative programming languages. Whereas functions in imperative languages are defined as collections of statements that may include several kinds of sequence control flow, mathematical functions do not have multiple statements and use only recursion and conditional expressions for evaluation flow. For example, the factorial function can be defined with these two operations as

$$f(n) \equiv \begin{cases} 1 \text{ if } n = 0 \\ \\ n * f(n-1) \text{ if } n > 0 \end{cases}$$

Note that a mathematical conditional expression is in the form of a list of pairs, each of which is a guarded expression. Each guarded expression consists of a predicate guard and an expression. The value of such a conditional expression is the value of the expression associated with the predicate that is true. Only one of the predicates is true for a given parameter or parameter list.

Scheme has two control structures, one for two-way selection and one for multiple selection. Both of these are special forms. The two-way selector, named IF, has three parameters: a predicate expression, a then_expression, and an else_expression. A call to IF has the form

    (IF predicate then_expression else_expression)

For example,

```
(DEFINE (factorial n)
  (IF (= n 0)
    1
    (* n (factorial (- n 1)))
))
```

Notice how closely the form of this function relates to that of the mathematical definition of factorial given above.

The Scheme multiple selector special form is named COND. COND is a slightly generalized version of the mathematical conditional expression; it allows more than one predicate to be true at the same time. Because different mathematical conditional expressions have different numbers of parameters, COND does not require a fixed number of actual parameters. Each parameter to COND is a pair of expressions in which the first is a predicate.

The general form of COND is

```
(COND
        (predicate_1 expression {expression})
        (predicate_2 expression {expression})
        ...
        (predicate_n expression {expression})
        (ELSE expression {expression})
)
```

In some implementations, ELSE is optional.

The semantics of COND is as follows: The predicates of the parameters are evaluated one at a time, in order from the first, until one evaluates to #T. The expressions that follow the first predicate that is found to be #T are then evaluated, and the value of the last is returned as the value of COND. Note that the atom #T could be used as a constant predicate in a COND, in which case #T's expressions are always evaluated and the value of the last is returned as COND's value. Of course, it only makes sense to use #T as the predicate of the last parameter of COND. The special predicate constant ELSE, which means the same as #T, is usually used in these situations.

If no parameter to COND has a predicate that evaluates to #T, COND returns ( ). Notice the similarity between a COND and the multiple selection statement with an "otherwise" clause at the end, such as an Ada **case** statement.

14.5.5 Example Scheme Functions

This section contains several examples of function definitions in Scheme. These programs solve simple list-processing problems.

Consider the problem of membership of a given atom in a given simple list. A simple list is one without sublists. If the function is named `member`, it could be used as follows:

```
(member 'B '(A B C)) returns #T
(member 'B '(A C D E)) returns ()
```

Thinking in terms of iteration, the membership problem is simply to compare the given atom and the individual elements of the given list, one at a time in some order, until either a match is found or there are no more elements in the list to be compared. A similar process can be accomplished using recursion. The function can compare the given atom with the CAR of the list. If they match, the value `#T` is returned. If they do not match, then the atom can only be found in the remainder of the list, so the function should call itself with the CDR of the list as the list parameter and return the result of this recursive call. In this process, there are two ways out of the recursion: Either the list is empty on some call and `()` is returned, or a match is found and `#T` is returned.

Altogether, there are three cases that must be handled in the function: an empty input list, a match between the atom and the CAR of the list, or a mismatch between the atom and the CAR of the list, which causes the recursive call. These three are exactly the three parameters to COND, with the last being the default case that is triggered by an ELSE predicate. The complete function follows:

```
(DEFINE (member atm lis)
  (COND
    ((NULL? lis) '())
    ((EQ? atm (CAR lis)) #T)
    (ELSE (member atm (CDR lis)))
))
```

This form is typical of simple Scheme list-processing functions. In such functions, the data in lists are processed one element at a time. The individual elements may be gotten by CAR, and the process is continued using recursion on the CDR of the list.

Notice that the null test must precede the equal test, because CAR of an empty list is an error.

As another example, consider the problem of determining whether two given lists are equal. If the two lists are simple, the solution is relatively easy, although some unfamiliar techniques are involved. A predicate function for comparing simple lists is shown here:

```
(DEFINE (equalsimp lis1 lis2)
  (COND
    ((NULL? lis1) (NULL? lis2))
    ((NULL? lis2) '())
    ((EQ? (CAR lis1) (CAR lis2))
```

```
            (equalsimp (CDR lis1) (CDR lis2)))
      (ELSE ' ())
  ))
```

The first case, which is handled by the first parameter to COND, is for when the first list parameter is the empty list. This can occur in an external call if the first list parameter is initially empty. Because a recursive call uses the CDRs of the two parameter lists as its parameters, the first list can be empty in such a call if the first list has had all of its elements removed by previous recursive calls. When the first list is empty, the second list must be checked to see if it is also empty. If so, they are equal (either initially or the CARs were equal on all previous recursive calls), and NULL? correctly returns #T. If the second list is not empty, it is larger than the first list and () should be returned, as it is by NULL?. Recall that any nonempty list that is returned by a predicate function is interpreted as #T.

The next case deals with the second list being empty when the first list is not. This situation occurs only when the first list is larger than the second. Only the second list must be tested, because the first case catches all instances of the first list being empty.

The third case is the recursive step that tests for equality between corresponding elements in the two lists. It does this by comparing the CARs of the two nonempty lists. If they are equal, then the two lists are equal up to this point, so recursion is used on the CDRs of both. This case fails when two unequal atoms are found. When this occurs, we obviously do not want to continue, so the default case, which is last, takes effect and causes the functional value to be () without further comparisons.

Note that equalsimp expects lists as parameters and does not operate correctly if either or both parameters are atoms.

The problem of comparing general lists is slightly more complex than this, because sublists must be traced completely in the comparison process. This is a situation where the power of recursion is uniquely appropriate, because the form of sublists is the same as that of the given lists. Any time the corresponding elements of the two given lists are lists, they are separated into their two parts, CAR and CDR, and recursion is used on them. This is a perfect example of the usefulness of the divide-and-conquer approach. If the corresponding elements of the two given lists are atoms, they can simply be compared using EQ?.

The definition of the complete function follows:

```
(DEFINE (equal lis1 lis2)
  (COND
    ((NOT (LIST? lis1)) (EQ? lis1 lis2))
    ((NOT (LIST? lis2)) ' ())
    ((NULL? lis1) (NULL? lis2))
    ((NULL? lis2)) '())
    ((equal (CAR lis1) (CAR lis2))
        (equal (CDR lis1) (CDR lis2)))
    (ELSE '())
  ))
```

The first two cases of the COND handle the situation where either of the parameters is an atom instead of a list. The third and fourth cases are for the situation where one or both lists are empty. These cases also prevent subsequent cases from attempting to take the CAR of an empty list. The fifth COND case is the most interesting. The predicate is a recursive call with the CARs of the lists as parameters. If this call returns #T, then recursion is used again on the CDRs of the lists. This allows the two lists to include sublists to any depth.

This definition of equal works on any pair of expressions, not just lists. equal is equivalent to the system predicate function EQUAL?. Note that EQUAL? should be used only when necessary (the forms of the actual parameters are not known), because it is much slower than EQ? and EQV?.

Another commonly needed list operation is that of constructing a new list that contains all of the elements of two given list arguments. This is usually implemented as a Scheme function named append. It can be constructed by repeated use of CONS to place the elements of the first list argument into the second list argument. To clarify the action of append, consider the following examples:

```
(append '(A B) '(C D R)) returns (A B C D R)
(append '((A B) C) '(D (E F))) returns ((A B) C D (E F))
```

The definition of append is

```
(DEFINE (append lis1 lis2)
  (COND
    ((NULL? lis1) lis2)
    (ELSE (CONS (CAR lis1) (append (CDR Lis1) lis2)))
))
```

Consider the following Scheme function, named guess, which uses the member function described in this section. Try to determine what it does before reading the description that follows it. Assume the parameters are simple lists.

```
(DEFINE (guess lis1 lis2)
  (COND
    ((NULL? lis1) '())
    ((member (CAR lis1) lis2)
            (CONS (CAR lis1) (guess (CDR lis1) lis2)))
    (ELSE (guess (CDR lis1) lis2))
))
```

The two parameters of guess are assumed to be simple lists. guess yields a simple list that contains the common elements of its two parameter lists. So if the parameter lists represent sets, guess computes a list that represents the intersection of those two sets.

LET is a function that allows names to be temporarily bound to the values of subexpressions. It is often used to factor out the common subexpressions from more complicated expressions. These names can then be used in the evaluation of another expression. Its general form is

```
(LET (
        (name_1 expression_1)
        (name_2 expression_2)
        . . .
        (name_n expression_n))
        body
)
```

The semantics of LET is that the first n expressions are evaluated and the resulting values are bound to their associated names. Then the expressions in the body are evaluated. The result of LET is the value of the last expression in its body. The following example illustrates the use of LET:

```
(DEFINE (quadratic_roots a b c)
  (LET (
    (root_part_over_2a
          (/ (SQRT (- (* b b) (* 4 a c))) (* 2 a)))
    (minus_b_over_2a (/ (- 0 b) (* 2 a)))
        )
  (DISPLAY (+ minus_b_over_2a root_part_over_2a))
  (NEWLINE)
  (DISPLAY (- minus_b_over_2a root_part_over_2a))
))
```

The DISPLAY function is convenient in quadratic_roots because we want this function to display its two results.

LET creates a new local static scope in much the same way as Ada's **declare**. New variables can be created, used, and then discarded when the end of the new scope is reached. The named components of LET are like assignment statements, but they can be used only in LET's new scope. Furthermore, they cannot be rebound to new values in LET.

LET is actually just shorthand for a LAMBDA expression. The following two expressions are equivalent:

```
(LET ((alpha 7))(* 5 alpha))
((LAMBDA (alpha) (* 5 alpha)) 7)
```

In the first expression, 7 is bound to alpha with LET; in the second, 7 is bound to alpha through the parameter of the LAMBDA expression

14.5.6 Functional Forms

This section describes two common mathematical functional forms that are provided by Scheme, composition and apply-to-all.

14.5.6.1 Functional Composition

Functional composition is the only primitive functional form provided by the original LISP. All subsequent LISP dialects, including Scheme, also provide it. Functional composition is the essence of how EVAL works. All non-quoted lists are interpreted to be function calls, which requires their parameters to be evaluated first. This applies recursively to the smallest list in any expression, which is precisely what functional composition means. The following examples illustrate function composition:

```
(CDR (CDR '(A B C))) returns (C)
(CAR (CAR '((A B) B C))) returns A
(CDR (CAR '((A B C) D))) returns (B C)
(NULL? (CAR '(() B C))) returns #T
(CONS (CAR '(A B)) (CDR '(A B))) returns (A B)
```

Notice that the function names in inner calls are not quoted because they must be evaluated rather than treated as literal data.

14.5.6.2 An Apply-to-All Functional Form

The most common functional forms provided in common functional programming languages are variations of mathematical apply-to-all functional forms. The simplest of these is mapcar, which has two parameters, a function and a list. mapcar applies the given function to each element of the given list, and it returns a list of the results of these applications. A Scheme definition of mapcar follows:

```
(DEFINE (mapcar fun lis)
  (COND
    ((NULL? lis) '())
    (ELSE (CONS (fun (CAR lis)) (mapcar fun (CDR lis))))
))
```

Note the simple form of mapcar, which expresses a complex functional form. This is testament to the great expressive power of Scheme.

As an example of the use of mapcar, suppose we want all of the elements of a list cubed. We can accomplish this with

```
(mapcar (LAMBDA (num) (* num num num)) '(3 4 2 6))
```

This call returns (27 64 8 216).

Note that in this example the first parameter to mapcar is a LAMBDA expression. When EVAL evaluates the LAMBDA expression, it constructs a function that has the same form as any predefined function except that it is nameless. In the expression above, this nameless function is immediately applied to each element of the parameter list and the results are returned in a list.

14.5.7 Functions That Build Code

The fact that programs and data have the same structure can be exploited in constructing programs. Because user programs can call the function EVAL, they can construct other programs and immediately evaluate them.

One of the simplest examples of this process involves numeric atoms. Most Scheme systems include a function for numeric atoms named +, which takes any number of numeric atoms as arguments and returns their sum. For example, (+ 3 7 10 2) returns 22.

Our problem is: Suppose that in a program we have a list of numeric atoms and need the sum. We cannot apply + directly on the list, because + can take only atomic parameters, not a list of numeric atoms. We could, of course, write a function that repeatedly adds the CAR of the list to the sum of its CDR, using recursion to go through the list. Such a function follows:

```
(DEFINE (adder lis)
  (COND
    ((NULL? lis) 0)
    (ELSE (+ (CAR lis) (adder (CDR lis))))
))
```

An alternative solution to the problem is to write a function that builds a call to + with the proper parameter forms. This can be done by using CONS to insert the atom + into the list of numbers. This new list can then be submitted to EVAL for evaluation, as in the following:

```
(DEFINE (adder lis)
  (COND
    ((NULL? lis) 0)
    (ELSE (EVAL (CONS '+ lis)))
))
```

Note that the plus function's name is quoted to prevent EVAL from evaluating it in the evaluation of CONS. As an example, consider that the call

```
(adder '(3 4 6))
```

causes adder to build the list

```
(+ 3 4 6)
```

The list is then submitted to EVAL, which invokes + and returns the result, 13.

In all earlier versions of Scheme, the EVAL function evaluates its expression in the outermost scope of the program. The latest version of Scheme, Scheme 4, requires a second parameter to EVAL that specifies the scope in which the expression is to be evaluated. For simplicity's sake, we left the scope parameter out of our example and we do not discuss scope names here.

14.5.8 Imperative Features of Scheme

Scheme, like other contemporary LISP dialects, includes several features that are borrowed from the imperative languages. For example, names can be bound to values, and those bindings can be changed later. This is done with the function SET!, as in the following:

```
(SET! pi 3.141593)
```

The `SET!` function returns the value it binds.

In a purely functional version of LISP, lists cannot be changed. They can be taken apart with `CAR` and `CDR`, but a given list cannot be changed, for that would require an imperative language feature—a side effect—of a function call. Scheme includes two functions that create such side effects, `SET-CAR!` and `SET-CDR!`. Consider the following examples:

```
(DEFINE lst (LIST 'A 'B))
(SET-CAR! lst 'C)
(SET-CDR! lst '(D))
```

The `SET-CAR!` changes the list bound to `lst` from `(A B)` to `(C B)`. The `SET-CDR!` changes the list `(C B)` to `(C D)`.

The imperative features of Scheme described above were put in Scheme for the sake of efficiency, but these strayings from functional programming also have their costs. Programs become harder to debug and maintain because of the possibility of aliasing and because side effects allow identical function calls to produce different results at different times. For example, consider the following:

```
(DEFINE count 0)
(DEFINE (inc_count number)
  (SET! count (+ count number))
)
```

Although the following two calls to `inc_count` are identical, they produce different results.

```
(inc_count 1)
0
(inc_count 1)
1
```

14.6 COMMON LISP

COMMON LISP (Steele, 1984) was created in an effort to combine the features of several early 1980s dialects of LISP, including Scheme, into a single language. Being a combination, it is a quite large and complex language. Its basis, however, is the original LISP, so its syntax, primitive functions, and fundamental nature come from that language.

Recognizing the occasional flexibility provided by dynamic scoping, as well as the simplicity of static scoping, COMMON LISP allows both. The default scoping for variables is static, but by declaring a variable to be "special," that variable becomes dynamically scoped.

The list of features of COMMON LISP is long: a large number of data types and structures, including such things as records, arrays, complex numbers, and character strings; powerful input and output operations; a form of packages for modularizing collections of functions and data, and also providing access control; the imperative features of Scheme—specifically functions that do what Scheme's SET!, SET-CAR!, and SET-CDR! do, plus more of its own.

COMMON LISP, along with most dialects of LISP except Scheme, includes a function named PROG that allows statement sequencing, as is common in imperative languages. Labels and the two functions, GO and RETURN, are included to provide iteration control. GO is used to transfer control to a label within the scope of PROG. RETURN is a means of exiting the PROG. The general form of PROG is

```
(PROG (local variables)
 expression_1
 ...
 expression_n
 )
```

The local variables are initialized to NIL, have the scope of the PROG, and exist only during execution of PROG. If there are global names that are the same as the locals, the globals are unaffected (and hidden) in PROG. Expressions in PROG that are atoms are treated as labels. GO transfers control to its parameter, which must be a label within the PROG expression list. RETURN has a parameter, which becomes the value of PROG.

Note that PROG is included in contemporary versions of LISP only to provide backward compatibility with older dialects. COMMON LISP has better constructs to provide the capabilities of PROG. For example, COMMON LISP has DOTIMES and DOLIST constructs for iteration and PROG1, PROG2, and PROGN for building sequences.

SETQ is the COMMON LISP function that corresponds to Scheme's SET!, and DEFUN is its version of DEFINE. Consider the following iterative version of the list membership function. The iterative version is followed by a recursive version similar to one that appeared in Section 14.5.5.

```
(DEFUN iterative_member (atm lst)
  (PROG ()
    loop_1
      (COND
        ((NULL lst) (RETURN NIL))
        ((EQUAL atm (CAR lst)) (RETURN T))
      )
    (SETQ lst (CDR lst))
    (GO loop_1)
))

(DEFUN recursive_member (atm lst)
  (COND
    ((NULL lst) NIL)
    ((EQUAL atm (CAR lst)) T)
    (T (recursive_member atm (CDR lst)))
))
```

Note that T is COMMON LISP's version of the Boolean value true, NIL is the Boolean false value, ATOM is a predicate that determines whether its parameter is an atom, and a null list is considered both a list and an atom.

As another example, consider the following iterative and recursive functions that compute the length of a list:

```
(DEFUN iterative_length (lst)
  (PROG (sum)
    (SETQ sum 0)
   again
    (COND
      ((ATOM lst (RETURN sum)))
    )
    (SETQ sum (+ 1 sum))
    (SETQ lst (CDR lst))
    (GO again)
))


(DEFUN recursive_length (lst)
  (COND
    ((NULL lst) 0)
    (T (+ 1 (recursive_length (CDR lst))))
  )
)
```

In a sense, Scheme and COMMON LISP are opposites. Scheme is far smaller and somewhat cleaner, in part because of its exclusive use of static scoping. COMMON LISP was meant to be a commercial language and has succeeded in being a widely used language for AI applications. Scheme, on the other hand, is more frequently used in college courses on functional programming. It is also more likely to be studied as a functional language because of its relatively small size. An important design criterion of COMMON LISP that caused it to be a very large language is the desire to make it compatible with several earlier dialects of LISP.

14.7 ML

ML (Milner et al., 1990) is a static-scoped functional programming language, like Scheme. It differs from LISP and its dialects, including Scheme, in a number of significant ways. It uses a syntax that is more similar to that of Pascal than that of LISP. It has type declarations, uses type inferencing, which means that variables need not be declared, and it is strongly typed. The type of every variable and expression can be determined at compile time. This is in stark contrast to Scheme, which is essentially typeless. ML has exception handling and a module facility for implementing abstract data types. A brief history of the development and primary features of ML is given in Chapter 2. Chapter 4 includes an introduction to the idea of type inferencing as it appears in ML.

In ML, names can be bound to values with value declaration statements of the form

```
val new_name = expression;
```

For example,

```
val distance = time * speed;
```

Do not get the idea that this statement is exactly like the assignment statements in the imperative languages, for it is not. The **val** statement binds a name to a value, but the name cannot be later rebound to a new value. Well, in a sense it can. Actually, if you do rebind a name with a second **val** statement, it causes a new entry in the environment that is not related to the previous version of the name. In fact, its type need not be the same. **val** statements do not have side effects. They simply add a name to the current environment and bind it to a value, like the LET special form of LISP. The normal use of **val** is in a **let** expression, whose general form is

```
let val new_name = expression_1 in expression_2 end
```

For example,

```
let
   val pi = 3.14159
in
   pi * radius * radius
end;
```

ML has lists and list operations, although their appearance is not like those of LISP. ML also has enumerated types, arrays, and tuples, which are records.

Function declarations in ML appear in the general form

```
fun function_name (formal_parameters) = function_body_expression;
```

For example,

```
fun square (x : int) = x * x;
```

Note that

```
fun square (x) = x * x;
```

is illegal, because the type of **x** cannot be determined by the compiler. So functions that use arithmetic operators cannot be polymorphic. The same is true for functions that use relational operators, except = and <>, and Boolean operators. However, functions that use only list operations, =, <>, and tuple operators (those for forming tuples and for component selection) can be polymorphic.

The ML selection control flow construct is actually a conditional expression with the form

```
if E then then_expression else else_expression
```

E must evaluate to a Boolean value. Only one of the two other expressions are evaluated.

There are no type coercions in ML; the types of the operands of an operator or assignment simply must match to avoid syntax errors.

14.8 Haskell

Haskell (Thompson, 1996) is similar to ML in that it uses a similar syntax, is static scoped, is strongly typed, and uses the same type inferencing method. It differs from ML in that it is purely functional; it has no variables and no assignment statement. In fact, it allows no side effects and includes no imperative features of any kind. This sets it apart from nearly all other programming languages. Two other characteristics set Haskell apart from ML. First, it uses a different evaluation technique called **lazy evaluation,** in which no subexpression is evaluated until its value is known to be required. Second, Haskell has a method of defining lists that allows infinite lists. These are called **list comprehensions.** Some of the features of Haskell originated in the language Miranda (Turner, 1986).

The code in this section is written in version 1.4 of Haskell.

Consider the following definition of the factorial function. Note that the syntax of function definition and function application is that the function's name is simply written next to the parameters.

```
fact 0 = 1
fact n = n * fact (n - 1)
```

This definition shows that function definitions may include more than one line, where the lines define versions of the function for different forms of actual parameters. The proper function expression value (right side) is chosen by pattern matching the actual parameters to the formal parameters. Formal parameters that are constants obviously match themselves in actual parameters. A name in a formal parameter pattern matches an actual parameter that is not matched in a constant pattern. The matched actual parameter value is then used as the name's value in the corresponding expression in the right side. The function defined above is partial, for it cannot define a value for negative parameters.

Using pattern matching, we can define a function for computing the nth Fibonacci number with the following:

```
fib 0 = 1
fib 1 = 1
fib (n + 2) = fib (n + 1) + fib n
```

Guards can be added to lines of a function definition to specify the circumstances under which the definition can be applied. For example,

```
fact n
  | n == 0 = 1
  | n > 0  = n * fact(n - 1)
```

This is a more precise definition of factorial than our previous one, for it restricts the range of actual parameter values to those for which it works. Pattern matching would of course fail in this use, for the parameter pattern is n for both value expressions. This form of a function definition is called a conditional expression.

An otherwise can appear as the last condition in a conditional expression, with the obvious semantics. For example,

```
fun n
  | n < 10    = 0
  | n > 100   = 2
  | otherwise = 1
```

Lists are written in brackets, as in

```
colors = ["blue", "green", "red", "yellow"]
```

Haskell includes a collection of list operators. For example, lists can be catenated with ++, : serves as an infix version of CONS, and .. is used to specify arithmetic series. For example,

```
5:[2, 7, 9]   results in [5, 2, 7, 9]
[1, 3..11]  results in [1, 3, 5, 7, 9, 11]
[1, 3, 5] ++ [2, 4, 6]  results in [1, 3, 5, 2, 4, 6]
```

Two examples of functions that operate on lists are

```
sum [] = 0
sum (a:x) = a + sum x

product [] = 1
product (a:x) = a * product x
```

In both of these, a:x specifies the list with a CAR, or head, as a and a CDR, or tail, as x. sum returns the sum of the elements of a given list. product returns the product of the elements of a given list. Both sum and product are standard Haskell functions.

Using product, a factorial function can be written in the simpler form

```
fact n = product [1..n]
```

The function length returns the number of elements in a given list. For example,

```
length(colors) returns 4
```

In Haskell, a **where** clause is similar to ML's **let** and **val**, except the bindings are given after the expression that uses them. For example, we could write

```
quadratic_root a b c =
     [minus_b_over_2a - root_part_over_2a,
      minus_b_over_2a + root_part_over_2a]
     where
       minus_b_over_2a = - b / (2.0 * a)
       root_part_over_2a =
                    sqrt(b ^ 2 - 4.0 * a * c) / (2.0 * a)
```

List comprehensions provide a method of describing lists that represent sets. The syntax of a list comprehension is the same as that often used to describe sets in mathematics, the general form of which is

[body | qualifiers]

For example,

[n * n * n | n ← [1..50]]

defines a list of the cubes of the numbers from 1 to 50. It is read as "a list of all n*n*n such that n is taken from the range of 1 to 50." In this case the qualifier is in the form of a **generator.** It generates the numbers from 1 to 50. In other cases, the qualifiers are in the form of Boolean expressions, in which case they are called **tests.** This notation can be used to describe algorithms for doing many things, such as finding permutations of lists and sorting lists. For example, consider the following function, which when given a number n returns a list of all its factors:

factors n = [i | i ← [1..n **div** 2], n **mod** i == 0]

Next, consider the conciseness of Haskell shown in the following implementation of the quicksort algorithm:

```
sort [] =  []
sort (a:x) = sort [b | b <- x, b ≤ a]
   ++ [a] ++
   sort [b | b ← x, b > a]
```

This definition of quicksort is significantly shorter than the same algorithm coded in an imperative language.

We now return to the topic of lazy evaluation. Recall that in Scheme the parameters to a function are fully evaluated before the function is called. Lazy evaluation means that parameters to functions are evaluated only when it is necessary to evaluate the function. So if a function has two parameters, but on a particular execution of the function the first parameter is not used, the actual parameter passed for that execution will not be evaluated. Furthermore, if only a part of an actual parameter must be evaluated for an execution of the function, the rest is left unevaluated. Finally, actual parameters are evaluated only once, if at all.

The fact that a language uses lazy evaluation opens up some interesting possibilities. One of these is defining infinite data structures. For example, consider the following:

```
positives = [0..]
evens = [2, 4..]
squares = [n * n | n ← [0..]]
```

Of course, no computer can actually represent all of the numbers of these lists, but that does not prevent their use if lazy evaluation is used. For example, if we wanted to know if a particular number was a perfect square, we could check the squares list with a membership function. Suppose we had a predicate function named `member` that determined whether a given list contained a given atom. Then we could use it as in

```
member squares 16
```

which would return `True`. The `squares` definition would be evaluated until the `16` was found. The `member` function would need to be carefully written. Specifically, if it were

```
member [] b = False
member (a:x) b = (a == b) || member x b
```

it would work correctly with squares only if the given number was a perfect square. If not, `squares` would keep generating squares forever, or until some memory limitation was reached, looking for the given number in the list. The following function performs the membership test of an ordered list, abandoning the search and returning `False` if a number greater than the searched-for number is found.

```
member2 (m:x) n
  | m < n      = member2 x n
  | m == n     = True
  | otherwise  = False
```

Lazy evaluation is not without its costs. It would certainly be surprising if such expressive power and flexibility came free. In this case, the cost is in a far more complicated semantics, which results in much slower speed of execution.

14.9 Applications of Functional Languages

Over the past 35 years in the history of high-level programming languages only a few functional languages have gained widespread use. Most prominent among these is LISP. In spite of its heavy use of the assignment statement, APL also is often considered a functional language, partly because of its functional forms.

APL has been used for a wide variety of applications, ranging from hardware description to management information systems. Because of the great difficulty in reading a typical APL program, its most natural place in contemporary computing is in the category of throwaway programming.

With its powerful collection of array operations, it is an excellent vehicle for quick but dirty solutions to problems involving many array manipulations.

LISP is a versatile and powerful language. For its first 15 years, it was thought of, mostly by nonusers, as a strange language that was very costly to use. Indeed, it was common in the 1960s and early 1970s to think of two categories of languages, one containing LISP and one with all of the other programming languages.

As described in this chapter, LISP was developed for symbolic computation and list-processing applications, which lie mainly in the AI realm of computing. In AI applications, LISP and its derivative languages are still the standard languages.

Within AI a number of areas have been developed, primarily through the use of LISP. Although other kinds of languages can be used—primarily logic programming languages—most existing expert systems, for example, were developed in LISP. LISP also dominates in the areas of knowledge representation, machine learning, natural language processing, intelligent training systems, and the modeling of speech and vision.

Outside AI, LISP has also been successful. For example, the EMACS text editor is written in LISP, as is the symbolic mathematics system, MAC-SYMA, which does symbolic calculus, among other things. The LISP machine is a personal computer whose entire systems software is written in LISP. LISP has also been successfully used to construct experimental systems in a variety of application areas.

Scheme is widely used to teach functional programming. It is also used in some universities to teach introductory programming courses. Use of ML and Haskell has been, for the most part, restricted to research laboratories and universities.

14.10 A Comparison of Functional and Imperative Languages

A brief discussion of the advantages—some widely accepted and some only widely conjectured—of functional programming and functional programming languages is now in order.

It is natural to compare functional programming with programming in imperative languages. Because imperative languages are based directly on the von Neumann architecture, programmers using them must deal with the management of variables and assignment of values to them. The results of this are increased efficiency of execution but laborious construction of programs. In a functional language, the programmer need not be concerned with variables, because memory cells need not be abstracted into the language. One result of this is decreased efficiency of execution. Another result, however, is a higher level of programming, which should require less labor than programming in an imperative language. Many believe that this is the case and that it is a definite advantage of functional programming.

Functional languages can have a very simple syntactic structure. The list structure of LISP is an example. The syntax of the imperative languages is much more complex. The semantics of functional languages can also be simple compared to that of the imperative languages.

Concurrent execution in the imperative languages is difficult to design and difficult to use. For example, consider the tasking model of Ada, in which cooperation among concurrent tasks is the responsibility of the programmer. Functional programs can be executed by first translating them into graphs. These graphs can then be executed through a graph reduction process, which can be done with a great deal of concurrency that was not specified by the programmer. The graph representation naturally exposes many opportunities for concurrent execution. Cooperation synchronization in this process is not the concern of the programmer. Further description of this process is beyond the scope of this book.

In an imperative language, the programmer must make a static division of the program into its concurrent parts, which are then written as tasks. This can be a complicated process. Programs in functional languages can be divided into concurrent parts dynamically by the execution system, making the process highly adaptable to the hardware on which it is running. Understanding concurrent programs in imperative languages is much more difficult.

SUMMARY

Mathematical functions are named or unnamed mappings that use only conditional expressions and recursion to control their evaluations. Complex functions can be built using functional forms, in which functions are used as parameters, returned values, or both.

Functional programming languages are modeled on mathematical functions. In their pure form, they do not use variables or assignment statements to produce results; rather they use functional applications, conditional expressions, and recursion for execution control, and functional forms to construct complex functions. LISP began as a purely functional language but soon had a number of imperative language features added in order to increase its efficiency and ease of use.

The first version of LISP grew out of the need for a list-processing language for AI applications. LISP is still the most widely used language for that area.

The first implementation of LISP was serendipitous: The original version of EVAL was developed solely to demonstrate that a universal LISP function could be written.

Because LISP data and LISP programs have the same form, it is possible to have a program build another program. The availability of EVAL allows such programs to be executed immediately.

Scheme is a relatively simple dialect of LISP that uses static scoping exclusively. Like LISP, Scheme's primary primitives include functions for constructing and dismantling lists, for conditional expressions, and simple predicates for numbers, symbols, and lists. Scheme includes some imperative operations, such as for changing an element of a given list.

COMMON LISP is a large LISP-based language that was designed to include most of the features of the LISP dialects of the early 1980s. It allows both static- and dynamic-scoped variables and includes many imperative features.

ML is a static-scoped and strongly typed functional programming language that uses a syntax that is more similar to Pascal than to LISP. It includes a type inferencing system and exception handling, and with ML it is possible to implement abstract data types.

Haskell is similar to ML, but it is purely functional; it has no variables and no assignment statement. All expressions in Haskell are evaluated using a lazy method. With its list comprehensions, Haskell allows programs to deal with infinite lists.

Although LISP's primary area of application is AI, it has been successfully used for a number of different areas of problem solving.

Although there may be advantages to purely functional languages over their imperative relatives, their lower efficiency of execution on von Neumann machines has prevented them from being considered by many as replacements.

BIBLIOGRAPHIC NOTES

The first published version of LISP can be found in McCarthy (1960). A widely used version from the mid-1960s until the late 1970s is described in McCarthy et al. (1965) and Weissman (1967). The somewhat standardized contemporary version, COMMON LISP, is described in Steele (1984). The Scheme language, along with some of its innovations and advantages, is discussed in Rees and Clinger (1986). Dybvig (1996) is a good source of information on programming in Scheme. ML is defined in Milner et al. (1990). Ullman (1994) is an excellent introductory textbook for ML. Programming in Haskell is introduced in Thompson (1996).

A rigorous discussion of functional programming in general can be found in Henderson (1980). The process of implementing functional languages through graph reduction is discussed in detail in Peyton Jones (1987).

REVIEW QUESTIONS

1. Define *functional form* and *referential transparency*.
2. What data types were part of the original LISP?
3. What is the difference between `EQ?`, `EQV?`, and `=`?

4. What are the differences between the evaluation method used for the Scheme special form, **DEFINE**, and that used for its primitive functions?

5. What are the two forms of **DEFINE**?

6. Describe the semantics of **COND**.

7. Describe the semantics of **LET**.

8. Why were imperative features added to most dialects of LISP?

9. In what ways are COMMON LISP and Scheme opposites?

10. What scoping rule is used in Scheme? In COMMON LISP? In ML? In Haskell?

11. What are three ways that ML is very different from Scheme?

12. What is type inferencing, as used in ML? (See Chapter 4.)

13. What are three features of Haskell that make it very different from Scheme?

14. What does lazy evaluation mean?

PROBLEM SET

1. Write a Scheme function that returns the reverse of its simple list parameter.

2. Write a Scheme predicate function that tests for the structural equality of two given lists. Two lists are structurally equal if they have the same list structure, although their atoms may be different.

3. Write a Scheme function that returns the union of two simple list parameters that represent sets.

4. Write a Scheme function with two parameters, an atom and a list, that returns the list with all occurrences, no matter how deep, of the given atom deleted. The returned list cannot contain anything in place of the deleted atoms.

5. Write a Scheme function that takes a list as a parameter and returns it with the second top-level element removed. If the given list does not have two elements, the function should return **( )**.

6. Read John Backus's paper on FP (Backus, 1978) and compare the features of Scheme discussed in this chapter with the corresponding features of FP.

7. Find definitions of the Scheme functions **EVAL** and **APPLY**, and explain their actions.

8. One of the most modern and complete programming environments for any language is the INTERLISP system for LISP, as described in "The INTERLISP Programming Environment," by Teitelmen and Masinter (*IEEE Computer*, Vol. 14, No. 4, April 1981). Read this article carefully and compare the difficulty of writing LISP programs on your system with that of using INTERLISP (assuming that you do not normally use INTERLISP).

9. Refer to a book on LISP programming and determine what arguments support the inclusion of the **PROG** feature in LISP.

10. A functional language could use some data structure other than the list. For example, it could use sequences of symbols. What primitives would such a language have in place of the **CAR**, **CDR**, and **CONS** primitives of Scheme?

11. What does the following Scheme function do?

```
(define (y s lis)
  (cond
    ((null? lis) '() )
    ((equal? s (car lis)) lis)
    (else (y s (cdr lis)))
))
```

12. What does the following Scheme function do?

```
(define (x lis)
  (cond
    ((null? lis) 0)
    ((not (list? (car lis)))
      (cond
        ((eq? (car lis) nil) (x (cdr lis)))
        (else (+ 1 (x (cdr lis))))))
    (else (+ (x (car lis)) (x (cdr lis))))
))
```

15 Logic Programming Languages

Robert Kowalski

Robert Kowalski of the University of Edinburgh is a researcher in artificial intelligence. Kowalski, along with Alain Colmerauer and Phillippe Roussel of the University of Aix-Marseille, developed the first logic programming language, Prolog.

The objectives of this chapter are to introduce the concepts of logic programming and logic programming languages, including a brief description of a subset of Prolog. We begin with an introduction to predicate calculus, which is the basis for logic programming languages. This is followed by a discussion of how predicate calculus can be used for automatic theorem proving systems. We then present a general overview of logic programming. Next, a lengthy section introduces the basics of the Prolog programming language, including arithmetic, list processing, and the use of a trace tool that can be used to help debug programs and also to illustrate how the Prolog system works. The last two sections describe some of the problems of Prolog as a logic language and some of the application areas in which Prolog has been used.

15.1 Introduction

Chapter 14 discusses the functional programming paradigm, which is significantly different from the software development methodologies used with the imperative languages. In this chapter, we describe another different programming methodology. In this case, the approach is to express programs in a form of symbolic logic and use a logical inferencing process to produce results. Logic programs are declarative rather than procedural, which means that only the specifications of the desired results are stated rather than detailed procedures for producing them.

Programming that uses a form of symbolic logic as a programming language is often called **logic programming,** and languages based on symbolic logic are called **logic programming languages,** or **declarative languages.** We have chosen to describe the logic programming language Prolog because it is the only widely used logic language.

The syntax of logic programming languages is remarkably different from that of the imperative and functional languages. The semantics of logic programs also bears little resemblance to that of imperative language programs. These observations should lead the reader to some curiosity about the nature of logic programming and declarative languages.

15.2 A Brief Introduction to Predicate Calculus

Before we can discuss logic programming, we must briefly investigate its basis, which is formal logic. This is not our first contact with formal logic in this book; it was used extensively in the axiomatic semantics described in Chapter 3.

A **proposition** can be thought of as a logical statement that may or may not be true. It consists of objects and the relationships of objects to each other. Formal logic was developed to provide a method for describing propositions, with the goal of allowing those formally stated propositions to be checked for validity.

Symbolic logic can be used for the three basic needs of formal logic: to express propositions, to express the relationships between propositions, and to describe how new propositions can be inferred from other propositions that are assumed to be true.

There is a close relationship between formal logic and mathematics. In fact, much of mathematics can be thought of in terms of logic. The fundamental axioms of number and set theory are the initial set of propositions, which are assumed to be true. Theorems are the additional propositions that can be inferred from the initial set.

The particular form of symbolic logic that is used for logic programming is called **predicate calculus.** In the following subsections, we present a brief look at predicate calculus. Our goal is to lay the groundwork for a discussion of logic programming and the logic programming language Prolog.

15.2.1　Propositions

The objects in logic programming propositions are represented by simple terms, which are either constants or variables. A constant is a symbol that represents an object. A variable is a symbol that can represent different objects at different times, although in a sense that is far closer to mathematics than the variables in an imperative programming language.

The simplest propositions, which are called **atomic propositions,** consist of compound terms. A **compound term** is one element of a mathematical relation, written in a form that has the appearance of mathematical function notation. Recall from Chapter 14 that a mathematical function is a mapping, which can be represented either as an expression or as a table or list of tuples. So compound terms are elements of the tabular definition of a function.

A compound term is composed of two parts: a **functor,** which is the function symbol that names the relation, and an ordered list of parameters. A compound term with a single parameter is a 1-tuple; one with two parameters is a 2-tuple, and so forth. For example, we might have the two propositions

　　man(jake)
　　like(bob, steak)

which state that {jake} is a 1-tuple in the relation named man, and that {bob, steak} is a 2-tuple in the relation named like. If we added the proposition

　　man(fred)

to the two propositions above, then the relation man would have two distinct elements, {jake} and {fred}. All of the simple terms in these propositions—man, jake, like, bob, and steak—are constants. Note that these propositions have no intrinsic semantics. They mean whatever we want them to mean. For example, the second example above may mean that bob likes steak, or that steak likes bob, or that bob is in some way similar to a steak.

Propositions can be stated in two modes: one in which the proposition is defined to be true, and one in which the truth of the proposition is something that is to be determined. In other words, propositions can be stated to be facts or queries. The example propositions above could be either.

Compound propositions have two or more atomic propositions, which are connected by logical connectors, or operators, in the same way compound logic expressions are constructed in imperative languages. The names, symbols, and meanings of the predicate calculus logical connectors are as follows:

Name	Symbol	Example	Meaning
negation	$\neg$	$\neg\,a$	not a
conjunction	$\cap$	$a \cap b$	a and b
disjunction	$\cup$	$a \cup b$	a or b
equivalence	$\equiv$	$a \equiv b$	a is equivalent to b
implication	$\supset$	$a \supset b$	a implies b
	$\subset$	$a \subset b$	b implies a

The following are examples of compound propositions:

$$a \cap b \supset c$$
$$a \cap \neg b \supset d$$

The operator $\neg$ has the highest precedence. The operators $\cap$, $\cup$, and $\equiv$ all have higher precedence than $\supset$ and $\subset$. So the second example above is equivalent to

$$(a \cap (\neg b)) \supset d$$

Variables can appear in propositions but only when introduced by special symbols called quantifiers. Predicate calculus includes two quantifiers, as described below, where X is a variable and P is a proposition:

Name	Example	Meaning
universal	$\forall XP$	For all X, P is true
existential	$\exists X.P$	There exists a value of X such that P is true

The period between X and P simply separates the variable from the proposition. For example, consider the following:

$$\forall X.(\text{woman}(X) \supset \text{human}(X))$$
$$\exists X.(\text{mother}(\text{mary}, X) \cap \text{male}(X))$$

The first of these propositions means that for any value of X, if X is a woman, then X is a human. The second means that there exists a value of X such that mary is the mother of X and X is a male; in other words, mary has a son. The scope of the universal and existential quantifiers is the atomic propositions to which they are attached. This scope can be extended using parentheses, as in the two compound propositions just described. So the universal and existential quantifiers have higher precedence than any of the operators.

15.2.2 Clausal Form

We are discussing predicate calculus because it is the basis for logic programming languages. As with other languages, logic languages are best in their simplest form, meaning redundancy should be minimized.

One problem with the predicate calculus as we have described it thus far is that there are too many different ways of stating propositions that have the same meaning; that is, there is a great deal of redundancy. This is not such a problem for logicians, but if predicate calculus is to be used in an automated (computerized) system, it is a serious problem. To simplify matters, a standard form for propositions is desirable. Clausal form, which is a relatively simple form of propositions, is one such standard form. Without loss of generality, all propositions can be expressed in clausal form. A proposition in clausal form has the following general syntax:

$$B_1 \cup B_2 \cup \ldots \cup Bn \subset A_1 \cap A_2 \cap \ldots \cap A_m$$

in which the As and Bs are terms. The meaning of this clausal form proposition is as follows: If all of the As are true, then at least one B is true. The primary characteristics of clausal form propositions are the following: Existential quantifiers are not required; universal quantifiers are implicit in the use of variables in the atomic propositions; and no operators other than conjunction and disjunction are required. Also, conjunction and disjunction need appear only in the order shown in the general clausal form: disjunction on the left side and conjunction on the right side. All predicate calculus propositions can be algorithmically converted to clausal form. Nilsson (1971) gives proof that this can be done and a simple conversion algorithm for doing it.

The right side of a clausal form proposition is called the **antecedent.** The left side is called the **consequent** because it is the consequence of the truth of the antecedent. As examples of clausal form propositions, consider the following:

likes(bob, trout) $\subset$ likes(bob, fish) $\cap$ fish(trout)
father(louis, al) $\cup$ father(louis, violet) $\subset$ father(al, bob) $\cap$ mother(violet, bob) $\cap$ grandfather(louis, bob)

The English version of the first of these states that if bob likes fish and a trout is a fish, then bob likes trout. The second states that if al is bob's father and violet is bob's mother and louis is bob's grandfather, then louis is either al's father or violet's father.

15.3 Predicate Calculus and Proving Theorems

Predicate calculus provides a method of expressing collections of propositions. One use of collections of propositions is to determine whether any interesting or useful facts can be inferred from them. This is exactly analogous to the work of mathematicians, who strive to discover new theorems that can be inferred from known axioms and theorems.

The early days of computer science (the 1950s and early 1960s) saw a great deal of interest in automating the theorem-proving process. One of the most significant breakthroughs in automatic theorem-proving was the discovery of the resolution principle by Alan Robinson at Syracuse University (Robinson, 1965).

Resolution is an inference rule that allows inferred propositions to be computed from given propositions, thus providing a method with potential application to automatic theorem proving. Resolution was devised to be applied to propositions in clausal form. The concept of resolution is the following: Suppose there are two propositions with the forms

$$P_1 \subset P_2$$
$$Q_1 \subset Q_2$$

Their meaning is that P_2 implies P_1 and Q_2 implies Q_1. Further suppose that P_1 is identical to Q_2, so that we could rename P_1 and Q_2 as T. Then, we could rewrite the two propositions as

$$T \subset P_2$$
$$Q_1 \subset T$$

Now, because P_2 implies T and T implies Q_1, it is logically obvious that P_2 implies Q_1, which we could write as

$$Q_1 \subset P_2$$

The process of inferring this proposition from the original two propositions is resolution.

As another example, consider the two propositions:

older(joanne, jake) $\subset$ mother(joanne, jake)
wiser(joanne, jake) $\subset$ older(joanne, jake)

From these propositions, the following proposition can be constructed using resolution:

wiser(joanne, jake) ⊂ mother(joanne, jake)

The mechanics of this resolution construction are simple: The terms of the left sides of the two propositions are ANDed together to make the left side of the new proposition. Then the same thing is done to get the right side of the new proposition. Next, the term that appears on both sides of the new proposition is removed from both sides. The process is exactly the same when the propositions have multiple terms on either or both sides. The left side of the new inferred proposition initially contains all of the terms of the left sides of the two given propositions. The new right side is similarly constructed. Then the term that appears in both sides of the new proposition is removed. For example, if we have

father(bob, jake) ∪ mother(bob, jake) ⊂ parent(bob, jake)

grandfather(bob, fred) ⊂ father(bob, jake) ∩ father(jake, fred)

resolution says that

mother(bob, jake) ∪ grandfather(bob, fred) ⊂
　　　　　　　　　parent(bob, jake) ∩ father(jake, fred)

which has all but one of the atomic propositions of both of the original propositions. The one atomic proposition that allowed the operation father(bob, jake) in the left side of the first and in the right side of the second is left out. In English, we would say

if:　　bob is the parent of jake implies that bob is either the father
　　　　　　　or mother of jake

and:　bob is the father of jake and jake is the father of fred implies
　　　　　　　that bob is the grandfather of fred

then:　*if* bob is the parent of jake and jake is the father of fred
　　　　　then: either bob is jake's mother or bob is fred's grandfather

Resolution is actually more complex than these simple examples illustrate. In particular, the presence of variables in propositions requires resolution to find values for those variables that allow the matching process to succeed. This process of determining useful values for variables is called **unification.** The temporary assigning of values to variables to allow unification is called **instantiation.**

It is common for the resolution process to instantiate a variable with a value, fail to complete the required matching, and then be required to backtrack and instantiate the variable with a different value. We will discuss unification and backtracking more extensively in the context of Prolog.

A critically important property of resolution is its ability to detect any inconsistency in a given set of propositions. This property allows resolution to be used to prove theorems, which can be done as follows: We can envision a theorem proof in terms of predicate calculus as a given set of pertinent propositions, with the negation of the theorem itself stated as a new proposition. The theorem is negated so that resolution can be used to prove the theorem by finding an inconsistency. This is proof by contradiction. Typically, the original propositions are called the **hypotheses,** and the negation of the theorem is called the **goal.**

Theoretically, this is a valid and useful process. The time required for resolution, however, can be a problem. Although resolution is a finite process when the set of propositions is finite, the time required to find an inconsistency in a large database of propositions may be huge.

Theorem proving is the basis for logic programming. Much of what is computed can be couched in the form of a list of given facts and relationships as hypotheses, and a goal to be inferred from the hypotheses, using resolution.

When propositions are used for resolution, only a restricted kind of clausal form can be used, which further simplifies the resolution process. The special kinds of propositions, called **Horn clauses,** can be in only two forms: They have either a single atomic proposition on the left side or an empty left side. [Horn clauses are named after Alfred Horn, who studied clauses in this form (Horn, 1951).] The left side of a clausal form proposition is sometimes called the head, and Horn clauses with left sides are called headed Horn clauses. Headed Horn clauses are used to state relationships, such as

likes(bob, trout) ⊂ likes(bob, fish) ∩ fish(trout)

Horn clauses with empty left sides, which are often used to state facts, are called headless Horn clauses. For example,

father(bob, jake)

Most, but not all, propositions can be stated as Horn clauses.

15.4 An Overview of Logic Programming

Languages used for logic programming are called declarative languages because programs written in them consist of declarations rather than assignments and control flow statements. These declarations are actually statements, or propositions, in symbolic logic.

One of the essential characteristics of logic programming languages is their semantics, which is called **declarative semantics.** The basic concept of this semantics is that there is a simple way to determine the meaning of each statement, and it does not depend on how the statement might be used to solve a problem. Declarative semantics is considerably simpler than the semantics of the imperative languages. For example, the meaning of a given proposition in a logic programming language can be concisely determined from the statement itself. In an imperative language, the semantics of a simple assignment statement requires examination of local declarations, knowledge of the scoping rules of the language, and possibly even examination of programs in other files just to determine the types of the variables in the assignment statement. Then, assuming the expression of the assignment contains variables, the execution of the program prior to the assignment statement must be traced to determine the values of those variables. The resulting action of the statement, then, depends on its run-time context. Comparing this with the simple examination of a single statement, with no need to consider textual context or execution sequences, it is clear that declarative semantics is far simpler than the semantics of imperative languages. Thus, declarative semantics is often stated as one of the advantages that declarative languages have over imperative languages (Hogger, 1984, pp. 240–241).

Programming in both imperative and functional languages is primarily procedural, which means that the programmer knows *what* is to be accomplished by a program and instructs the computer on exactly *how* the computation is to be done. In other words, the computer is treated as a simple device that obeys orders. Everything that is computed must have every detail of that computation spelled out. Some people believe that this is the essence of the difficulty of programming computers.

Programming in some kinds of nonimperative languages, and in particular in logic programming languages, is nonprocedural. Programs in such languages do not state exactly *how* a result is to be computed but rather describe the form of the result. The difference is that we assume the computer system can somehow determine *how* the result is to be gotten. What is needed to provide this capability for logic programming languages is a concise means of supplying the computer with both the relevant information and a method of inference for computing desirable results. Predicate calculus supplies the basic form of communication to the computer, and the proof method developed first by Robinson provides the inference technique.

An example commonly used to illustrate the difference between procedural and nonprocedural systems is the process of rearranging a list of data into some particular order, otherwise known as sorting. In a language like C++, sorting is done by explaining in a C++ program all of the details of some sorting algorithm to a computer that has a C++ compiler. The computer, after translating the C++ program into machine code or some interpretive intermediate code, follows the instructions and produces the sorted list.

In a nonprocedural language, it is necessary only to describe the characteristics of the sorted list: It is some permutation of the given list such that for each pair of adjacent elements, a given relationship holds between the two elements. To state this formally: Suppose the list to be sorted is in an array named list that has a subscript range $1...n$. The concept of sorting the elements of the given list, named old_list, and placing them in a separate array, named new_list, can then be expressed as follows:

sort(old_list, new_list) $\subset$ permute(old_list, new_list) $\cap$ sorted(new_list)
sorted(list) $\subset$ $\forall$j such that $1 \leq j < n$, list(j) $\leq$ list(j + 1)

where permute is a predicate that returns true if its second parameter array is a permutation of its first parameter array.

From this description, the nonprocedural language system could produce the sorted list. That makes nonprocedural programming sound like the mere production of concise software requirements specifications, which is a fair assessment. Unfortunately, however, it is not that simple. Logic programs that use only resolution face serious problems of machine efficiency. Furthermore, the best form of a logic language may not have yet been determined, and good methods of creating programs in logic programming languages for large problems have not yet been developed.

15.5 The Origins of Prolog

As was stated in Chapter 2, Alain Colmerauer and Phillippe Roussel at the University of Aix-Marseille, with some assistance from Robert Kowalski at the University of Edinburgh, developed the fundamental design of Prolog. Colmerauer and Roussel were interested in natural language processing and Kowalski was interested in automated theorem proving. The collaboration between the University of Aix-Marseille and the University of Edinburgh continued until the mid-1970s. Since then, research on the development and use of the language has progressed independently at those two locations, resulting in, among other things, two syntactically different dialects of Prolog.

The development of Prolog and other research efforts in logic programming received limited attention outside of Edinburgh and Marseille until the announcement in 1981 that the Japanese government was launching a large research project called the Fifth Generation Computing Systems (FGCS) (Fuchi, 1981; Moto-oka, 1981). One of the primary objectives of the project was to develop intelligent machines, and Prolog was chosen as the basis for this effort. The announcement of FGCS aroused in researchers and the governments of the United States and several European countries a sudden strong interest in artificial intelligence and logic programming.

15.6 The Basic Elements of Prolog

There are now a number of different dialects of Prolog. These can be grouped into several categories: those that grew from the Marseille group, those that came from the Edinburgh group, and a collection of dialects that have been developed for microcomputers, such as micro-Prolog, which is described by Clark and McCabe (1984). The syntactic forms of these are somewhat different. Rather than attempt to describe the syntax of several dialects of Prolog or some hybrid of them, we have chosen one particular, widely available dialect, which is the one developed at Edinburgh. This form of the language is sometimes called Edinburgh syntax. Its first implementation was on a DEC System-10 (Warren et al., 1979).

15.6.1 Terms

As with programs in other languages, Prolog programs consist of collections of statements. There are only a few kinds of statements in Prolog, but they can be complex. All Prolog statements are constructed from terms.

A Prolog **term** is a constant, a variable, or a structure. A constant is either an **atom** or an integer. Atoms are the symbolic values of Prolog and are similar to their counterparts in LISP. In particular, an atom is either a string of letters, digits, and underscores that begins with a lowercase letter or a string of any printable ASCII characters delimited by apostrophes.

A variable is any string of letters, digits, and underscores that begins with an uppercase letter. Variables are not bound to types by declarations. The binding of a value, and thus a type, to a variable is called an **instantiation.** Instantiation occurs only in the resolution process. A variable that has not been assigned a value is called uninstantiated. Instantiations last only as long as it takes to satisfy one complete goal, which involves the proof or disproof of one proposition. Prolog variables are only distant relatives, in terms of both semantics and use, to the variables in the imperative languages.

The last kind of term is called a structure. Structures represent the atomic propositions of predicate calculus, and their general form is the same:

> functor(parameter list)

The functor is any atom and is used to identify the structure. The parameter list can be any list of atoms, variables, or other structures. As discussed at length in the following section, structures are the means of specifying facts in Prolog. They can also be thought of as objects, in which case they allow facts to be stated in terms of several related atoms. In this sense, structures are relations, for they state relationships among terms. A structure is also a predicate when its context specifies it to be a query (question).

15.6.2 Fact Statements

Our discussion of Prolog statements begins with those statements used to construct the hypotheses, or database of assumed information—the statements from which new information can be inferred.

Prolog has two basic statement forms; these correspond to the headless and headed Horn clauses of predicate calculus. The simplest form of headless Horn clause in Prolog is a single structure, which is interpreted as an unconditional assertion, or fact. Logically, facts are simply propositions that are assumed to be true.

The following examples illustrate the kinds of facts one can have in a Prolog program. Notice that every Prolog statement is terminated by a period.

```
female(shelley).
male(bill).
female(mary).
male(jake).
father(bill, jake).
father(bill, shelley).
mother(mary, jake).
mother(mary, shelley).
```

These simple structures state certain facts about `jake`, `shelley`, `bill`, and `mary`. For example, the first states that `shelley` is a `female`. The last four connect their two parameters with a relationship that is named in the functor atom; for example, the fifth proposition might be interpreted to mean that `bill` is the `father` of `jake`. Note that these Prolog propositions, like those of predicate calculus, have no intrinsic semantics. They mean whatever the programmer wants them to mean. For example, the proposition

```
father(bill, jake).
```

could mean `bill` and `jake` have the same `father` or that `jake` is the `father` of `bill`. The most common and straightforward meaning, however, is that `bill` is the `father` of `jake`.

15.6.3 Rule Statements

The other basic form of Prolog statement for constructing the database corresponds to a headed Horn clause. This form can be related to a known theorem in mathematics from which a conclusion can be drawn if the set of given conditions is satisfied. The right side is the antecedent, or *if* part, and the left side is the consequent, or *then* part. If the antecedent of a Prolog statement is true, then the consequent of the statement must also be true. Because they are Horn clauses, the consequent of a Prolog statement is a single term, while the antecedent can be either a single term or a conjunction.

Conjunctions contain multiple terms that are separated by logical AND operations. In Prolog, the AND operation is implied. The structures that specify atomic propositions in a conjunction are separated by commas, so one could consider the commas to be AND operators. As an example of a conjunction, consider the following:

```
female (shelley), child (shelley).
```

The general form of the Prolog headed Horn clause statement is

```
consequence_1 :- antecedent_expression.
```

It is read as follows: "consequence_1 can be concluded if the antecedent expression is true or can be made to be true by some instantiation of its variables." For example,

```
ancestor(mary, shelley) :- mother(mary, shelley).
```

states that if `mary` is the `mother` of `shelley`, then `mary` is an `ancestor` of `shelley`. Headed Horn clauses are called **rules** because they state rules of implication between propositions.

As with clausal form propositions in predicate calculus, Prolog statements can use variables to generalize their meaning. Recall that variables in clausal form provide a kind of implied universal quantifier. The following demonstrates the use of variables in Prolog statements:

```
parent(X, Y) :- mother(X, Y).
parent(X, Y) :- father(X, Y).
grandparent(X, Z) :- parent(X, Y) , parent(Y, Z).
sibling(X, Y) :- mother(M, X) , mother(M, Y),
                 father(F, X) , father(F, Y).
```

These statements give rules of implication among some variables, or universal objects. In this case, the universal objects are `X`, `Y`, `Z`, `M`, and `F`. The first rule states that if there are instantiations of `X` and `Y` such that `mother(X, Y)` is true, then for those same instantiations of `X` and `Y`, `parent(X, Y)` is true.

15.6.4 Goal Statements

So far, we have described the Prolog statements for logical propositions, which are used to describe both known facts and rules that describe logical relationships among facts. These statements are the basis for the theorem-proving model. The theorem is in the form of a proposition that we want the system to either prove or disprove. In Prolog, these propositions are called goals, or queries. The syntactic form of Prolog goal statements is identical to that of headless Horn clauses. For example, we could have

```
man(fred).
```

to which the system will respond either **yes** or **no**. The answer **yes** means that the system has proved the goal was true under the given database of facts and relationships. The answer **no** means that either the goal was proved false or the system was simply unable to prove or disprove it.

Conjunctive propositions and propositions with variables are also legal goals. When variables are present, the system not only asserts the validity of the goal but also identifies the instantiations of the variables that make the goal true. For example,

```
father(X, mike).
```

can be asked. The system will then attempt, through unification, to find an instantiation of x that results in a true value for the goal.

Because goal statements and some nongoal statements have the same form (headless Horn clauses), a Prolog implementation must have some means of distinguishing between the two. Interactive Prolog implementations do this by simply having two modes, indicated by different interactive prompts: one for entering fact and rule statements and one for entering goals. The user can change the mode at any time.

15.6.5 The Inferencing Process of Prolog

This section examines Prolog resolution. Efficient use of Prolog requires that the programmer know precisely what the Prolog system does with his or her program.

Queries are called **goals.** When a goal is a compound proposition, each of the facts (structures) is called a **subgoal.** To prove that a goal is true, the inferencing process must find a chain of inference rules and/or facts in the database that connect the goal to one or more facts in the database. For example, if Q is the goal, then either Q must be found as a fact in the database or the inferencing process must find a fact P_1 and a sequence of propositions $P_2, P_3, ..., P_n$ such that P

$$P_2 :- P_1$$
$$P_3 :- P_2$$
$$...$$
$$Q :- Pn$$

Of course, the process can and often is complicated by compound right sides of rules and the presence of variables in rules. The process of finding the Ps, when they exist, is basically a comparison, or matching, of terms with each other.

Because the process of proving a subgoal is done through proposition-matching process, it is sometimes called matching. In some cases, proving a subgoal is called **satisfying** that subgoal.

Consider the following query:

```
man(bob).
```

This goal statement is the simplest kind. It is relatively easy for resolution to determine whether it is true or false: The pattern of this goal is compared with the facts and rules in the database. If the database includes the fact

```
man(bob).
```

the proof is trivial. If, however, the database contains the following fact and inference rule,

```
father(bob).
man(X) :- father(X).
```

Prolog would be required to find these two statements and use them to infer the truth of the goal. This would necessitate unification to instantiate x temporarily to bob.

Now consider the goal

```
man(X).
```

In this case, Prolog must match the goal against the propositions in the database. The first proposition that it finds that has the form of the goal, with any object as its parameter, will cause x to be instantiated with that object's value. x is then displayed as the result. If there is no proposition having the form of the goal, the system indicates, by saying no, that the goal cannot be satisfied.

There are two opposite approaches to attempting to match a given goal to a fact in the database. The system can begin with the facts and rules of the database and attempt to find a sequence of matches that lead to the goal. This approach is called bottom-up resolution, or **forward chaining.** The alternative is to begin with the goal and attempt to find a sequence of matching propositions that lead to some set of original facts in the database. This approach is called top-down resolution, or **backward chaining.** In general, backward chaining works well when there is a reasonably small set of candidate answers. The forward chaining approach is better when the number of possibly correct answers is large; in this situation, backward chaining would require a very large number of matches to get to an answer. Prolog implementations use backward chaining for resolution, presumably because its designers believed backward chaining was suitable for a larger class of problems than forward chaining.

Consider again the example query:

```
man(bob).
```

Assume the database contains

```
father(bob).
man(X) :- father(X).
```

Forward chaining would search for and find the first proposition. The goal is then inferred by matching the first proposition with the right side of the second rule (`father(X)`) through instantiation of x to bob and then matching the left side of the second proposition to the goal. Backward chaining would first match the goal with the left side of the second proposition (`man(X)`) through the instantiation of x to bob. As its last step, it would match the right side of the second proposition (now `father(bob)`) with the first proposition.

The next design question arises whenever the goal has more than one structure, as in our example above. The question then is whether the solution search is done depth first or breadth first. A **depth-first** search finds a complete sequence of propositions—a proof—for the first subgoal before working on the others. A **breadth-first** search works on all subgoals of a given goal in parallel. Prolog's designers chose the depth-first approach primarily because it can be done with fewer computer resources. The breadth-first approach is a parallel search that can take a large amount of memory.

The last feature of Prolog's resolution mechanism that must be discussed is backtracking. When a goal with multiple subgoals is being processed and the system fails to show the truth of one of the subgoals, the system abandons the subgoal it could not prove. Instead, the system reconsiders the previous subgoal, if there is one, and attempts to find an alternative solution to it. This backing up in the goal to the reconsideration of a previously proven subgoal is called **backtracking.** A new solution is found by beginning the search where the previous search for that subgoal stopped. Multiple solutions to a subgoal result from different instantiations of its variables. Backtracking can require a great deal of time and space because it may have to find all possible proofs to every subgoal. These subgoal proofs may not be organized to minimize the time required to find the one that will result in the final complete proof, which exacerbates the problem.

To solidify your understanding of backtracking, consider the following example. Assume that there is a set of facts and rules in a database and that Prolog has been presented with the following compound goal:

```
male(X), parent(X, shelley).
```

This goal asks whether there is an instantiation of X such that X is a male and X is a parent of shelley. Prolog first finds the first fact in the database with male as its functor. It then instantiates X to the parameter of the found fact, say mike. Then it attempts to prove that parent(mike, shelley) is true. If it fails, it backtracks to the first subgoal, male(X), and attempts to resatisfy it with some alternative instantiation of X. The resolution process may have to find every male in the database before it finds the one that is a parent of shelley. It definitely must find all males to prove that the goal cannot be satisfied. Note that our example goal might be processed more efficiently if the order of the two subgoals were reversed. Then, only after resolution had found a parent of shelley would it try to match that person with the male subgoal. This is more efficient if shelley has fewer parents than there are males in the database, which seems like a fair assumption. Section 15.7.1 discusses a method of limiting the backtracking done by a Prolog system.

Database searches in Prolog always proceed in the direction of first to last.

The following two subsections describe Prolog examples that further illustrate the resolution process.

15.6.6   Simple Arithmetic

Prolog supports integer variables and integer arithmetic. Originally, the arithmetic operators were functors, so that the sum of 7 and the variable x was formed with

```
+(7, X)
```

Prolog now allows a more abbreviated syntax for arithmetic with the **is** operator. This operator takes an arithmetic expression as its right operand and a variable as its left operand. All variables in the expression must already be instantiated, but the left-side variable cannot be previously instantiated. For example, in

```
A is B / 17 + C.
```

If B and C are instantiated but A is not, then this clause will cause A to be instantiated with the value of the expression. When this happens, the clause is satisfied. If either B or C is not instantiated or A is instantiated, the clause is not satisfied and no instantiation of A can take place. The semantics of an **is** proposition is considerably different from that of an assignment statement in an imperative language. This difference can lead to an interesting scenario. Because the **is** operator makes the clause in which it appears look like an assignment statement, a beginning Prolog programmer may be tempted to write a statement such as

```
Sum is Sum + Number.
```

which is never useful, or even legal, in Prolog. If Sum is not instantiated, the reference to it in the right side is undefined and the clause fails. If Sum is already instantiated, the clause fails because the left operand cannot have a current instantiation when **is** is evaluated. In either case, the instantiation of Sum to the new value will not take place. (If the value of Sum + Number is required, it can be bound to some new name.)

Prolog does not have assignment statements in the same sense as imperative languages. They are simply not needed in most of the programming for which Prolog was designed. The usefulness of assignment statements in imperative languages depends on the capability of the programmer to control the execution control flow of the code in which the assignment statement is embedded. Because this type of control is not always possible in Prolog, such statements are far less useful.

As a simple example of the use of numeric computation in Prolog, consider the following problem: Suppose we know the average speeds of several automobiles on a particular racetrack and the amount of time they are on the track. This basic information can be coded as facts, and the relationship between speed, time, and distance can be written as a rule, as in the following:

```
speed(ford, 100).
speed(chevy, 105).
```

```
speed(dodge, 95).
speed(volvo, 80).
time(ford, 20).
time(chevy, 21).
time(dodge, 24).
time(volvo, 24).
distance(X, Y) :- speed(X, Speed),
                  time(X, Time),
                  Y is Speed * Time.
```

Now, queries can request the distance traveled by a particular car. For example, the query

```
distance(chevy, Chevy_Distance).
```

instantiates `Chevy_Distance` with the value 2205. The first two clauses in the right side of the distance computation statement simply instantiate the variables `Speed` and `Time` with the corresponding values of the given automobile functor. After satisfying the goal, Prolog also displays the name `Chevy_Distance` and its value.

At this point it is instructive to take an operational look at how a Prolog system produces results. Prolog has a built-in structure named `trace` that displays the instantiations of values to variables at each step during the attempt to satisfy a given goal. `trace` is used to understand and debug Prolog programs. To understand `trace`, it is best to introduce a different model of the execution of Prolog programs, called the **tracing model.**

The tracing model describes Prolog execution in terms of four events: (1) call, which occurs at the beginning of an attempt to satisfy a goal, (2) exit, which occurs when a goal has been satisfied, (3) redo, which occurs when backtrack causes an attempt to resatisfy a goal, and (4) fail, which occurs when a goal fails. Call and exit can be related directly to the execution model of a subprogram in an imperative language if processes like `distance` are thought of as subprograms. The other two events are unique to logic programming systems. In the following trace example, the goal requires no redo or fail events.

The following is a trace of the computation of the value for `Chevy_Distance`:

```
trace.
distance(chevy, Chevy_Distance).

(1) 1 Call: distance(chevy, _0)?
(2) 2 Call: speed(chevy, _5)?
(2) 2 Exit: speed(chevy, 105)
(3) 2 Call: time(chevy, _6)?
(3) 2 Exit: time(chevy, 21)
(4) 2 Call: _0 is 105*21?
(4) 2 Exit: 2205 is 105*21
(1) 1 Exit: distance(chevy, 2205)

Chevy_Distance = 2205
```

Symbols in the trace that begin with the underscore character (_) are internal variables used to store instantiated values. The first column of the trace indicates the subgoal whose match is currently being attempted. For example, in the trace above, the first line with the indication (3) is an attempt to instantiate the temporary variable _6 with a `time` value for `chevy`, where `time` is the second term in the right side of the statement that describes the computation of `distance`. The second column indicates the call depth of the matching process. The third column indicates the current action.

To illustrate backtracking, consider the following example database and traced compound goal:

```
likes(jake, chocolate).
likes(jake, apricots).
likes(darcie, licorice).
likes(darcie, apricots).

trace.
likes(jake, X), likes(darcie, X).

(1) 1 Call: likes(jake, _0)?
(1) 1 Exit: likes(jake, chocolate)
(2) 1 Call: likes(darcie, chocolate)?
(2) 1 Fail: likes(darcie, chocolate)
(1) 1 Redo: likes(jake, _0)?
(1) 1 Exit: likes(jake, apricots)
(3) 1 Call: likes(darcie, apricots)?
(3) 1 Exit: likes(darcie, apricots)

X = apricots
```

One can think about Prolog computations graphically as follows: Consider each goal as a box with four ports—call, fail, exit, and redo. Control enters a goal in the forward direction through its call port. Control can also enter a goal from the reverse direction through its redo port. Control can also leave a goal in two ways: if the goal succeeded, control leaves through the exit port; if the goal failed, control leaves through the fail port. A model of the example above is shown in Figure 15.1. In this example, control flows through each subgoal twice. The second subgoal fails the first time, which forces a return through redo to the first subgoal.

Figure 15.1
Control flow model for the goal `likes (jake, X), likes (darcie, X)`

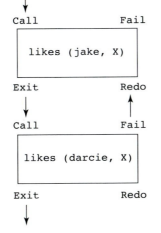

15.6.7 List Structures

So far, the only Prolog data structure we have discussed is the atomic proposition, which looks more like a function call than a data structure. Atomic propositions, which are also called structures, are actually a form of records. The other basic data structure supported is the list, which is similar to the list structure used by LISP. Lists are sequences of any number of elements, where the elements can be atoms, atomic propositions, or any other terms, including other lists.

Prolog uses a conventional syntax to specify lists. The list elements are separated by commas, and the entire list is delimited by square brackets, as in

```
[apple, prune, grape, kumquat]
```

The notation [ ] is used to denote the empty list. Instead of having explicit functions for constructing and dismantling lists, Prolog simply uses a special notation. [X | Y] denotes a list with head X and tail Y, where head and tail correspond to CAR and CDR in LISP. This is similar to the notation used in Haskell.

A list can be created with a simple structure, as in

```
new_list([apple, prune, grape, kumquat]).
```

which states that the constant list [apple, prune, grape, kumquat] is a new element of the relation named new_list (a name we just made up). This statement does not bind the list to a variable named new_list; rather, it does the kind of thing that the proposition

```
male(jake)
```

does. That is, it states that [apple, prune, grape, kumquat] is a new element of new_list. Therefore, we could have a second proposition with a list argument, such as

```
new_list([apricot, peach, pear])
```

In query mode, one of the elements of new_list can be dismantled into head and tail with

```
new_list([New_List_Head | New_List_Tail]).
```

If new_list has been set to have the two elements as above, this statement instantiates New_List_Head with the head of the first list element (in this case apple) and New_List_Tail with the tail of the list (or [prune, grape, kumquat]). If this were part of a compound goal and backtracking forced a new evaluation of it, New_List_Head and New_List_Tail would be reinstantiated to apricot and [peach, pear], respectively, because [apricot, peach, pear] is the next element of new_list.

The notation used to dismantle lists can also be used to create lists from given instantiated head and tail components, as in

```
[Element_1 | List_2]
```

If `Element_1` has been instantiated with `pickle` and `List_2` has been instantiated with `[peanut, prune, popcorn]`, the notation above will create, for this one reference, the list `[pickle, peanut, prune, popcorn]`.

As was stated above, the list notation that includes the | symbol is universal: It can specify either a list construction or a list dismantling. Note further that the following are equivalent:

```
[apricot, peach, pear | []]
[apricot, peach | [pear]]
[apricot | [peach, pear]]
```

When dealing with lists, certain basic operations are often required, such as those found in LISP. As an example of such operations in Prolog, we examine a definition of `append`, which is related to such a function in LISP. In this example, the differences and similarities between functional and declarative languages can be seen. We need not specify how Prolog is to construct a new list from the given lists; rather, we need only specify the characteristics of the new list in terms of the given lists.

In appearance, the Prolog definition of `append` is very similar to the LISP version, and a kind of recursion in resolution is used in a similar way to produce the new list. In the case of Prolog, the recursion is caused and controlled by the resolution process.

The first two parameters to the `append` operation in the following code are the two lists to be appended, and the third parameter is the resulting list:

```
append([], List, List).
append([Head | List_1], List_2, [Head | List_3]) :-
            append(List_1, List_2, List_3).
```

The first proposition specifies that when the empty list is appended to any other list, that other list is the result. This statement corresponds to the recursion-terminating step of the LISP `append` function. Note that the terminating proposition is placed before the recursion proposition. This is done because we know that Prolog will match the two propositions in order, starting with the first (because of its use of the depth-first order).

The second proposition specifies several characteristics of the new list. It corresponds to the recursion step in the LISP function. The left-side predicate states that the first element of the new list is the same as the first element of the first given list, because they are both named `Head`. Whenever `Head` is instantiated to a value, all occurrences of `Head` in the goal are, in effect, simultaneously instantiated to that value. The right side of the second statement specifies that the tail of the first given list (`List_1`) has the second given list (`List_2`) appended to it to form the tail (`List_3`) of the resulting list.

One way to read the second statement of `append` is as follows: Appending the list [Head | List_1] to any list List_2 produces the list [Head | List_3], but only if the list List_3 is formed by appending List_1 to List_2. In LISP, this would be

```
(CONS (CAR FIRST) (APPEND (CDR FIRST) SECOND))
```

In both the Prolog and LISP versions, the resulting list is not constructed until the recursion produces the terminating condition; in this case, the first list must become empty. Then the resulting list is built using the `append` function itself; the elements taken from the first list are added, in reverse order, to the second list. The reversing is done by the unraveling of the recursion.

To illustrate how the `append` process progresses, consider the following traced example:

```
trace.
append([bob, jo], [jake, darcie], Family).

(1) 1 Call: append([bob, jo], [jake, darcie], _10)?
(2) 2 Call: append([jo], [jake, darcie], _18)?
(3) 3 Call: append([], [jake, darcie], _25)?
(3) 3 Exit: append([], [jake, darcie], [jake, darcie])
(2) 2 Exit: append([jo], [jake, darcie], [jo, jake,
                    darcie])
(1) 1 Exit: append([bob, jo], [jake, darcie],
                    [bob, jo, jake, darcie])
Family = [bob, jo, jake, darcie]
yes
```

The first two calls, which represent subgoals, have List_1 nonempty, so they create the recursive calls from the right side of the second statement. The left side of the second statement effectively specifies the arguments for the recursive calls, or goals, thus dismantling the first list one element per step. When the first list becomes empty, in a call, or subgoal, the current instance of the right side of the second statement succeeds by matching the first statement. The effect of this is to return as the third parameter the value of the empty list appended to the second original parameter list. On successive exits, which represent successful matches, the elements that were removed from the first list are appended to the resulting list, Family. When the exit from the first goal is accomplished, the process is complete, and the resulting list is displayed.

The `append` propositions can also be used to create other list operations, such as the following, whose effect we invite the reader to determine. Note that `list_op_2` is meant to be used by providing a list as its first parameter and a variable as its second, and the result of `list_op_2` is the value to which the second parameter is instantiated.

```
list_op_2([], []).
list_op_2([Head | Tail], List) :- list_op_2(Tail, Result),
                                   append(Result, [Head], List).
```

As the reader may have been able to determine, `list_op_2` causes the Prolog system to instantiate its second parameter with a list that has the elements of the list of the first parameter, but in reverse order. For example, (`[apple, orange, grape], Q`) instantiates Q with the list `[grape, orange, apple]`.

Once again, although the LISP and Prolog languages are fundamentally different, similar operations can use similar approaches. In the case of the reverse operation, both the Prolog's `list_op_2` and LISP's `reverse` function include the recursion terminating condition, along with the basic process of appending the reversal of the CDR or tail of the list to the CAR or head of the list to create the result list.

The following is a trace of this process, now named `reverse`:

```
trace.
reverse([a, b, c], Q).

(1) 1 Call: reverse([a, b, c], _6)?
(2) 2 Call: reverse([b, c], _65636)?
(3) 3 Call: reverse([c], _65646)?
(4) 4 Call: reverse([], _65656)?
(4) 4 Exit: reverse([], [])
(5) 4 Call: append([], [c], _65646)?
(5) 4 Exit: append([], [c], [c])
(3) 3 Exit: reverse([c], [c])
(6) 3 Call: append([c], [b], _65636)?
(7) 4 Call: append([], [b], _25)?
(7) 4 Exit: append([], [b], [b])
(6) 3 Exit: append([c], [b], [c, b])
(2) 2 Exit: reverse([b, c], [c, b])
(8) 2 Call: append([c, b], [a], _6)?
(9) 3 Call: append([b], [a], _32)?
(10) 4 Call: append([], [a], _39)?
(10) 4 Exit: append([], [a], [a])
(9) 3 Exit: append([b], [a], [b, a])
(8) 2 Exit: append([c, b], [a], [c, b, a])
(1) 1 Exit: reverse([a, b, c], [c, b, a])

Q = [c, b, a]
```

Suppose we need to be able to determine whether a given symbol is in a given list. A straightforward Prolog description of this is

```
member(Element, [Element | _]).
member(Element, [_ | List]) :- member(Element, List).
```

The underscore indicates an "anonymous" variable; it is used to mean that we do not care what instantiation it might get from unification. The first statement above succeeds if `Element` is the head of the list, either initially or after several recursions through the second statement. The second statement succeeds if `Element` is in the tail of the list. Consider the following traced examples:

```
trace.
member(a, [b, c, d]).
(1) 1 Call: member(a, [b, c, d])?
(2) 2 Call: member(a, [c, d])?
(3) 3 Call: member(a, [d])?
(4) 4 Call: member(a, [])?
(4) 4 Fail: member(a, [])
(3) 3 Fail: member(a, [d])
(2) 2 Fail: member(a, [c, d])
(1) 1 Fail: member(a, [b, c, d])
no

member(a, [b, a, c]).
(1) 1 Call: member(a, [b, a, c])?
(2) 2 Call: member(a, [a, c])?
(2) 2 Exit: member(a, [a, c])
(1) 1 Exit: member(a, [b, a, c])
yes
```

15.7 Deficiencies of Prolog

Several problems arise in using Prolog as a logic programming language. Although it is a useful tool, it is neither a pure nor a perfect logic programming language.

15.7.1 Resolution Order Control

Prolog, for reasons of efficiency, allows the user to control the ordering of pattern matching during resolution. In a pure logic programming environment, the order of attempted matches that take place during resolution is nondeterministic, and all matches could be attempted concurrently. However, because Prolog always matches in the same order, starting at the beginning of the database and at the left end of a given goal, the user can profoundly affect efficiency by ordering the database statements to optimize a particular application. For example, if the user has knowledge that certain rules are much more likely to succeed than the others during a particular "execution," then the program can be made more efficient by placing those rules first in the database.

Slow program execution is not the only negative result of user-defined ordering in Prolog programs. It is very easy to write statements in forms that cause infinite loops and thus total program failure. For example, consider the following recursive statement form:

```
f(X, Y) :- f(Z, Y), g(X, Z).
```

Because of Prolog's left-to-right depth-first order of evaluation, regardless of the purpose of the statement, it will cause an infinite loop. As an example of this kind of statement, consider

```
ancestor(X, X).
ancestor(X, Y) :— ancestor(Z, Y), parent(X, Z).
```

In attempting to satisfy the first subgoal of the right side of the second proposition, Prolog instantiates z to make `ancestor` true. It then tries to satisfy this new subgoal, coming right back to the definition of `ancestor` and repeating the same process, leading to unending recursion.

This particular problem is identical to the problem a recursive descent parser has with left recursion in a grammar rule, as discussed in Chapter 3. As was the case with grammar rules in parsing, simply reversing the order of the terms in the right side of the proposition above eliminates the problem. The trouble with this is that a simple change of term ordering should not be crucial to the correctness of the program. After all, the lack of the need for programmer concern for control order is supposedly one of the advantages of logic programming.

In addition to allowing the user to control database and subgoal ordering, Prolog, in another concession to efficiency, allows some explicit control of backtracking. This is done with the cut operator, which is specified by an exclamation point (`!`). The cut operator is actually a goal, not an operator. As a goal, it always succeeds immediately, but it cannot be resatisfied through backtracking. Thus, a side effect of the cut is that subgoals to its left in a compound goal also cannot be resatisfied through backtracking. For example, in the goal

```
a, b, !, c, d.
```

if both a and b succeed but c fails, the whole goal fails. This goal would be used if it were known that whenever c fails, it is a waste of time to resatisfy b or a.

The purpose of the cut then is to allow the user to make programs more efficient by telling the system when it should not attempt to resatisfy subgoals that presumably could not result in a complete proof.

As an example of one use of the cut operator, consider the `member` rules from Section 15.6.7, which are repeated below:

```
member(Element, [Element | _]).
member(Element, [_ | List]) :- member(Element, List).
```

If the list argument to `member` represents a set, then it can be satisfied only once (sets contain no duplicate elements). Therefore, if `member` is used as a subgoal in a multiple subgoal goal statement, there can be a problem. The problem is that if `member` succeeds but the next subgoal fails, backtracking will attempt to resatisfy `member` by continuing a prior match. But because the list argument to `member` has only one copy of the element to begin with, `member` cannot possibly succeed again, which eventually causes the whole goal to fail, in spite of any additional attempts to resatisfy `member`. The solution to this inefficiency is to add a right side to the first statement of the `member` definition, with the cut operator as the sole element, as in

```
member(Element, [Element | _]) :- !.
```

Backtracking will not attempt to resatisfy `member` but instead will cause the entire subgoal to fail.

Cut is particularly useful in a programming strategy in Prolog called **generate and test.** In these programs, the goal consists of subgoals that generate potential solutions, which are then checked by later "test" subgoals. Rejected solutions require backtracking to "generator" subgoals, which generate new potential solutions. As an example of a generate and test program, consider the following, which appears in Clocksin and Mellish (1984):

```
divide(N1, N2, Result) :- is_integer(Result),
                          Product1 is Result * N2,
                          Product2 is (Result + 1) * N2,
                          Product1 =< N1, Product2 > N1, !.
```

This program performs integer division, using addition and multiplication. Because most Prolog systems provide division as an operator, this program is not actually useful, other than to illustrate a simple generate and test program.

The predicate `is_integer` succeeds as long as its parameter can be instantiated to some nonnegative integer. If its argument is not instantiated, `is_integer` instantiates it to the value 0. If the argument is instantiated to an integer, `is_integer` instantiates it to the next larger integer value.

So, in `divide`, `is_integer` is the generator subgoal. It generates elements of the sequence 0, 1, 2, ..., one each time it is satisfied. All of the others are the testing subgoals—they check to determine whether the value produced by `is_integer` is, in fact, the quotient of the first two parameters, `N1` and `N2`. The purpose of the cut as the last subgoal is simple: It prevents `divide` from ever trying to find an alternative solution once it has found *the* solution. Although `is_integer` can generate a huge number of candidates, only one is the solution, so the cut here prevents useless attempts to produce secondary solutions.

Use of the cut operator has been compared to the use of the goto in imperative languages (Van Emden, 1980). Although it is sometimes needed, it is possible to abuse it. Indeed, it is sometimes used to make logic programs have a control flow that is inspired by imperative programming styles.

The ability to tamper with control flow in a Prolog program is a deficiency because it is directly detrimental to one of the important advantages of logic programming—that programs do not specify how solutions are to be found. Rather, they simply specify what the solution should look like. This makes programs easier to write and easier to read. They are not cluttered with the details of how the solutions are to be determined and, in particular, the precise order in which the computations are done to produce the solution. So, while logic programming requires no control flow directions, Prolog programs frequently use them, mostly for the sake of efficiency.

15.7.2 The Closed World Assumption

The nature of Prolog's resolution sometimes creates misleading results. The only truths, as far as Prolog is concerned, are those that can be proved using its database. It has no knowledge of the world other than its database. Any query about which there is insufficient information in the database to prove absolutely is assumed to be false. Prolog can prove that a given goal is true, but it cannot prove that a given goal is false. It simply assumes that, because it cannot prove a goal true, the goal must be false. In essence, Prolog is a true/fail system, rather than a true/false system.

Actually, the closed world assumption should not be at all foreign to you—our judicial system operates the same way. Suspects are innocent until proven guilty. They need not be proven innocent. If a trial cannot prove a person guilty, he or she is considered innocent.

The problem of the closed world assumption is related to the negation problem, which is discussed in the following subsection.

15.7.3 The Negation Problem

Another problem with Prolog is its difficulty with negation. Consider the following database of two facts and a relationship:

```
parent(bill, jake).
parent(bill, shelley).
sibling(X, Y) :- (parent(M, X), parent(M, Y).
```

Now, suppose we typed the query

```
sibling(X, Y).
```

Prolog will respond with

```
X = jake
Y = jake
```

Thus Prolog "thinks" `jake` is a `sibling` of himself. This happens because the system first instantiates `M` with `bill` and `X` with `jake` to make the first subgoal, `parent(M, X)`, true. It then starts at the beginning of the database again to match the second subgoal, `parent(M, Y)`, and arrives at the instantiations of `M` with `bill` and `Y` with `jake`. Because the two subgoals are satisfied independently, with both matchings starting at the database's beginning, the response above appears. To avoid this, x must be specified to be a `sibling` of Y only if they have the same `parents` *and* they are not the same. Unfortunately, stating that they are not equal is not straightforward in Prolog, as we will discuss. The most exacting method would require adding a fact for every pair of atoms, stating that they were not the same. This can, of course, cause the database to become very large, for there is often far more negative information than positive information. For example, most people have 364 more unbirthdays than they have birthdays.

A simple alternative solution is to state in the goal that x must not be the same as Y, as in

```
sibling(X, Y) :- parent(M, X), parent(M, Y), not(X = Y).
```

In other situations, the solution is not so simple.

The Prolog `not` operator is satisfied in this case if resolution cannot satisfy the subgoal x = Y. Therefore, if the `not` succeeds, it does not necessarily mean that x is not equal to Y; rather, it means that resolution cannot prove from the database that x is the same as Y. Thus the Prolog `not` operator is not equivalent to a logical NOT operator, in which NOT means that its operand is provably true. This nonequivalency can lead to a problem if we happen to have a goal of the form

```
not(not(some_goal)).
```

which would be equivalent to

```
some_goal.
```

if Prolog's `not` operator were a true logical NOT operator. In some cases, however, they are not the same. For example, consider again the `member` rules:

```
member(Element, [Element | _]) :- !.
member(Element, [_ | List]) :- member(Element, List).
```

To discover one of the elements of a given list, we could use the goal

```
member(X, [mary, fred, barb]).
```

which would cause x to be instantiated with `mary`, which would then be printed. But if we used

```
not(not(member(X, [mary, fred, barb]))).
```

the following sequence of events would take place: First, the inner goal would succeed, instantiating x to `mary`. Then Prolog would attempt to satisfy the next goal:

```
not(member(X, [mary, fred, barb])).
```

This would fail because `member` succeeded. When this goal failed, x would be uninstantiated because Prolog always uninstantiates all variables in all goals that fail. Next, Prolog would attempt to satisfy the outer `not` goal, which would succeed, because its argument had failed. Finally, the result, which is X, would be printed. But X would not be currently instantiated, so the system would indicate that. Generally, uninstantiated variables are printed in the form of a string of digits preceded by an underscore. So the fact that Prolog's not is not equivalent to a logical NOT can be, at the very least, misleading.

The fundamental reason why logical NOT cannot be an integral part of Prolog is the form of the Horn clause:

$$A \; :\!- \; B_1 \cap B_2 \cap \; \cdots \; \cap B_n$$

If all the B propositions are true, it can be concluded that A is true. But regardless of the truth or falseness of any or all of the Bs, it cannot be concluded that A is false. From positive logic, one can only conclude positive logic. Thus the use of Horn clause form prevents any negative conclusions.

15.7.4 Intrinsic Limitations

A fundamental goal of logic programming, as stated in Section 15.4, is to provide nonprocedural programming; that is, a system by which programmers specify what a program is supposed to do but need not specify how that is to be accomplished. The example given there for sorting is rewritten here:

sort(old_list, new_list) $\subset$ permute(old_list, new_list) $\cap$ sorted(new_list)
sorted(list) $\subset$ $\forall$j such that $1 \leq j < n$, list(j) $\leq$ list(j + 1)

This can easily be written in Prolog. For example, the sorted subgoal can be expressed as

```
sorted ([]).
sorted ([x]).
sorted ([x, y | list]) :- x <= y, sorted ([y | list]).
```

The problem with the sort process above is that it has no idea of how to sort, other than simply to enumerate all permutations of the given list until it happens to create the one that has the list in sorted order—a very slow process, indeed.

So far, no one has discovered a process by which the description of a sorted list can be transformed into some efficient algorithm for sorting. Resolution is capable of many interesting things, but certainly not this. Therefore, a Prolog program that sorts a list must specify the details of how that sorting can be done, as is the case in an imperative or functional language.

Do all of these problems mean that logic programming should be abandoned? Absolutely not! As it is, it is capable of dealing with many useful applications. Furthermore, it is based on an intriguing concept, and is therefore interesting in and of itself. Finally, there is the possibility that some new inferencing technique will be developed that will allow a logic programming language system that requires only the what, and not the how, in its specification of programs.

15.8 Applications of Logic Programming

In this section, we briefly describe a few of the larger classes of present and potential applications of logic programming in general and Prolog in particular.

15.8.1 Relational Database Management Systems

Relational database management systems (RDBMSs) store data in the form of tables. Queries on such databases are often stated in relational calculus, which is a form of symbolic logic. The query languages of these systems are nonprocedural in the same sense that logic programming is nonprocedural. The user does not describe how to retrieve the answer; rather, he or she only describes the characteristics of the answer. The connection between logic programming and RDBMSs should be obvious. Simple tables of information can be described by Prolog structures, and relationships between tables can be conveniently and easily described by Prolog rules. The retrieval process is inherent in the resolution operation. The goal statements of Prolog provide the queries for the RDBMS. Logic programming is thus a natural match to the needs of implementing an RDBMS.

One of the advantages of using logic programming to implement an RDBMS is that only a single language is required. In a typical RDBMS, a database language includes statements for data definitions, data manipulation, and queries, all of which are embedded in a general-purpose programming language, such as COBOL. The general-purpose language is used for processing the data and input and output functions. All of these functions can be done in a logic programming language.

Another advantage of using logic programming to implement an RDBMS is that deductive capability is built in. Conventional RDBMSs cannot deduce anything from a database other than what is explicitly stored in them. They contain only facts, rather than facts *and* inference rules. The primary disadvantage of using logic programming for an RDBMS, compared with a conventional RDBMS, is that the logic programming implementation is slower. Logical inferences simply take longer than ordinary table look-up methods using imperative programming techniques.

15.8.2 Expert Systems

Expert systems are computer systems designed to emulate human expertise in some particular domain. They consist of a database of facts, an inferencing process, some heuristics about the domain, and some friendly human interface that makes the system appear much like an expert human consultant. In addition to their initial knowledge base, which is provided by a human expert, expert systems learn from the process of being used, so their databases must be capable of growing dynamically. Also, an expert system should include the capability of interrogating the user to get additional information when it determines that such information is needed.

One of the central problems for the designer of an expert system is dealing with the inevitable inconsistencies and incompleteness of the database. Logic programming appears to be well suited to deal with these problems. For example, default inference rules can help deal with the problem of incompleteness.

Prolog can and has been used to construct expert systems. It can easily fulfill the basic needs of expert systems, using resolution as the basis for query processing, using its ability to add facts and rules to provide the learning capability, and using its trace facility to inform the user of the "reasoning" behind a given result. Missing from Prolog is the automatic ability of the system to query the user for addition information when it is needed.

One of the most widely known uses of logic programming in expert systems is the expert system construction system known as APES, which is described in Sergot (1983) and Hammond (1983). The APES system includes a very flexible facility for gathering information from the user during expert system construction. It also includes a second interpreter for producing explanations to its answers to queries.

APES has been successfully used to produce several expert systems, including one for the rules of a government social benefits program and one for the British Nationality Act, which is the definitive source for rules of British citizenship.

15.8.3 Natural Language Processing

Certain kinds of natural language processing can be done with logic programming. In particular, natural language interfaces to computer software systems, such as intelligent databases, and other intelligent knowledge-based systems can be conveniently done with logic programming. For describing language syntax, forms of logic programming have been found to be equivalent to context-free grammars. Proof procedures in logic programming systems have been found to be equivalent to certain parsing strategies. In fact, backward chaining resolution can be used directly to parse sentences whose structures are described by context-free grammars. It has also been discovered that some kinds of semantics of natural languages can be made clear by modeling the languages with logic programming. In particular, research in logic-based semantics networks has shown that sets of sentences in natural languages can be expressed in clausal form (Deliyanni and Kowalski, 1979). Kowalski (1979) also discusses logic-based semantic networks.

15.8.4 Education

In the area of education, there have been extensive experiments in teaching children as young as seven how to use the logic programming language micro-Prolog (Ennals, 1980). Researchers claim a number of advantages in teaching Prolog to young people. First, it is possible to introduce computing using this approach. It also has the side effect of teaching logic, which can result in clearer thinking and expression. This can help students in learning a variety of subjects, such as solving equations in mathematics, dealing with grammars for natural languages, and understanding the rules and order of the physical world.

The experiments in teaching logic programming to the very young have produced the interesting result that it is easier to teach logic programming to a beginner than to a programmer with a significant amount of experience in an imperative language.

15.9 Conclusions

Many believe that Prolog is, at least at this point, still a grand experiment. It has a number of proponents, however, as many other languages have had. Some of these believe it can be at least a part of the solution to the software crisis, in which the imperative languages currently in use simply cannot cope with the problems that need to be solved by computers (Cuadrado and Cuadrado, 1985).

Some of the reasons why adherents believe that Prolog is better than imperative languages are the following, as originally stated by Jacques Cohen (1985), one of Prolog's boosters:

- Because Prolog is based on logic, Prolog programs are likely to be more logically organized and written, which should lead to fewer errors and less maintenance.

- Prolog processing is naturally parallel, making Prolog interpreters particularly able to take advantage of multiple-processor machines.

- Because of the conciseness of Prolog programs, development time is decreased, making it a good tool for prototyping.

Of course, there are people who do not agree. Many computer scientists are skeptical of Prolog's usefulness outside a few small areas of artificial intelligence. Some believe Prolog will replace LISP as the main language of artificial intelligence, although that is certainly not clear at this time. Warren et al. (1977) has made a comparison of the two languages.

SUMMARY

Symbolic logic provides the basis for logic programming and logic programming languages. The approach of logic programming is to use as a database a collection of facts and rules that state relationships between facts, and to use an automatic inferencing process to check the validity of new propositions, assuming the facts and rules of the database are true. This approach is the one developed for automatic theorem proving.

Prolog is the most widely used logic programming language. The origins of logic programming lie in Robinson's development of the resolution rule for logical inference. Prolog was developed primarily by Colmeraur and Roussel at Marseille, with some help from Kowalski at Edinburgh.

Logic programs should be nonprocedural, which means that the characteristics of the solution are given but the complete process of getting the solution is not.

Prolog statements are facts, rules, or goals. Most are made up of structures, which are atomic propositions, and logic operators, although arithmetic expressions are also allowed.

Resolution is the primary activity of a Prolog interpreter. This process, which uses backtracking extensively, involves mainly pattern matching among propositions. When variables are involved, they can be instantiated to values to provide matches. This instantiation process is called unification.

There are a number of problems with the current state of logic programming. For reasons of efficiency, and even to avoid infinite loops, programmers must sometimes state control flow information in their programs. Also, there are the problems of the closed world assumption and negation.

Logic programming has been used in a number of different areas, primarily in relational database systems, expert systems, and natural language processing.

BIBLIOGRAPHIC NOTES

The Prolog language is described in several books. Edinburgh's form of the language is covered in Clocksin and Mellish (1997). The microcomputer implementation is described in Clark and McCabe (1984).

Hogger (1984) is an excellent book on the general area of logic programming. It is the source of the material in this chapter's section on logic programming applications.

1. What are the three primary uses of symbolic logic in formal logic?
2. What are the two parts of a compound term?
3. What is the general form of a proposition in clausal form?
4. Give general (not rigorous) definitions of *resolution* and *unification*.
5. What are the forms of Horn clauses?
6. What is the basic concept of declarative semantics?
7. What are the three forms of a Prolog term?
8. What is the syntactic form and usage of fact and rule statements in Prolog?
9. Explain the two approaches to matching goals to facts in a database.
10. Explain the difference between a depth-first and a breadth-first search when discussing how multiple goals are satisfied.
11. Explain how backtracking works in Prolog.
12. Explain what is wrong with the Prolog statement K **is** K + 1.
13. What are the two ways a Prolog programmer can control the order of pattern matching during resolution?
14. Explain the generate and test programming strategy in Prolog.
15. Explain the closed world assumption used by Prolog. Why is this a limitation?
16. Explain the negation problem with Prolog. Why is this a limitation?
17. Explain the connection between automatic theorem proving and Prolog's inferencing process.
18. Explain the difference between procedural and nonprocedural languages.
19. Explain why Prolog systems must do backtracking.
20. What is the relationship between resolution and unification in Prolog?

1. Compare the concept of data typing in Ada with that of Prolog.
2. Describe how a multiple-processor machine could be used to implement resolution. Could Prolog, as currently defined, use this method?
3. Write a Prolog description of your family tree (based only on facts) going back to your grandparents and including all descendants. Be sure to include all relationships.
4. Write a set of rules for family relationships, including all relationships from grandparents through two generations. Now add these to the facts of Problem 3, and eliminate as many of the facts as you can.
5. Write a Prolog program that succeeds if the intersection of two given list parameters is empty.

6. Write a Prolog program that returns a list containing the union of the elements of two given lists.

7. Write a Prolog program that returns the last element of a given list.

8. Explain two ways in which the list processing capabilities of Scheme and Prolog are similar.

9. In what way are the list processing capabilities of Scheme and Prolog different?

Bibliography

AARM. (1995) *Annotated Ada Reference Manual*. International Standard, ISO/IEC 8652: 1995, Version 6.0. December 21, 1994. Intermetrics, Cambridge, MA.

ACM. (1979) "Part A: Preliminary Ada Reference Manual" and "Part B: Rationale for the Design of the Ada Programming Language." *SIGPLAN Notices*, Vol. 14, No. 6.

ACM. (1993a) History of Programming Language Conference Proceedings. *ACM SIGPLAN Notices*, Vol. 28, No. 3, March.

ACM. (1993b) "High Performance FORTRAN Language Specification Part 1." FORTRAN Forum, Vol. 12, No. 4.

Aho, A.V., R. Sethi, and J.D. Ullman. (1986) *Compilers: Principles, Techniques, and Tools*. Addison-Wesley, Reading, MA.

Aho, A.V., B.W. Kernighan, and P.J. Weinberger. (1988) *The AWK Programming Language*. Addison-Wesley, Reading, MA.

Ambler, A.L., D.I. Good, J.C. Browne, W.F. Burger, R.M. Cohen, C.G. Hoch, and R.E. Wells. (1977) "Gypsy: A Language for Specification and Implementation of Verifiable Programs." Proceedings of the ACM Conference on Language Design for Reliable Software. *ACM SIGPLAN Notices*, Vol. 12, No. 3, pp. 1–10.

Andrews, G.R., and F.B. Schneider. (1983) "Concepts and Notations for Concurrent Programming." *ACM Computing Surveys*, Vol. 15, No. 1, pp. 3–43.

ANSI. (1976) *American National Standard Programming Language PL/I*. ANSI X3.53–1976. American National Standards Institute, New York.

ANSI. (1978a) *American National Standard Programming Language FORTRAN*. ANSI X3.9–1978. American National Standards Institute, New York.

ANSI. (1978b) *American National Standard Programming Language Minimal BASIC*. ANSI X3.60–1978. American National Standards Institute, New York.

ANSI. (1985) *American National Standard Programming Language COBOL*. ANSI X3.23–1985. American National Standards Institute, New York.

ANSI. (1989) *American National Standard Programming Language C*. ANSI X3.159–1989. American National Standards Institute, New York.

ANSI. (1992) *American National Standard Programming Language FORTRAN 90*. ANSI X3.198–1992. American National Standards Institute, New York.

Arden, B.W., B.A. Galler, and R.M. Graham. (1961) "MAD at Michigan." *Datamation*, Vol. 7, No. 12, pp. 27–28.

Backus, J. (1954) "The IBM 701 Speedcoding System." *J. ACM*, Vol. 1, pp. 4–6.

Backus, J. (1959) "The Syntax and Semantics of the Proposed International Algebraic Language of the Zurich ACM-GAMM Conference." *Proceedings International Conference on Information Processing*. UNESCO, Paris, pp. 125–132.

Backus, J. (1978) "Can Programming Be Liberated from the von Neumann Style? A Functional Style and Its Algebra of Programs." *Commun. ACM*, Vol. 21, No. 8, pp. 613–641.

Backus, J., F.L. Bauer, J. Green, C. Katz, J. McCarthy, P. Naur, A.J. Perlis, H. Rutishauser, K. Samelson, B. Vauquois, J.H. Wegstein, A. van Wijngaarden, and M. Woodger. (1962) "Revised Report on the Algorithmic Language ALGOL 60." *Commun. ACM*, Vol. 6, No. 1, pp. 1–17.

Ben-Ari, M. (1982) *Principles of Concurrent Programming*. Prentice-Hall, Englewood Cliffs, NJ.

Birtwistle, G.M., O.-J. Dahl, B. Myhrhaug, and K. Nygaard. (1973) *Simula BEGIN*. Van Nostrand Reinhold, New York.

Bobrow, D.G., L. DeMichiel, R. Gabriel, S. Keene, G. Kiczales, and D. Moon. (1988) "Common Lisp Object System Specification X3J13 Document 88-002R." *ACM SIGPLAN Notices*, Vol. 17, No. 6, pp. 216–229.

Bodwin, J.M., L. Bradley, K. Kanda, D. Litle, and U.F. Pleban. (1982) "Experience with an Experimental Compiler Generator Based on Denotational Semantics." *ACM SIGPLAN Notices*, Vol. 17, No. 6, pp. 216–229.

Bohm, C., and G. Jacopini. (1966) "Flow Diagrams, Turing Machines, and Languages with Only Two Formation Rules." *Commun. ACM*, Vol. 9, No. 5, pp. 366–371.

Bolsky, M., and D. Korn. (1995) *The New KornShell Command and Programming Language*. Prentice-Hall, Englewood Cliffs, NJ.

Booch. G. (1987) *Software Engineering with Ada*. 2nd ed., Benjamin/Cummings, Redwood City, CA.

Bradley, J.C. (1989) *QuickBASIC and QBASIC Using Modular Structures*. W.C. Brown, Dubuque, IA.

Brinch Hansen, P. (1973) *Operating System Principles*. Prentice-Hall, Englewood Cliffs, NJ.

Brinch Hansen, P. (1975) "The Programming Language Concurrent-Pascal." *IEEE Transactions on Software Engineering*, Vol. 1, No. 2, pp. 199–207.

Brinch Hansen, P. (1977) *The Architecture of Concurrent Programs*. Prentice-Hall, Englewood Cliffs, NJ.

Brinch Hansen, P. (1978) "Distributed Processes: a Concurrent Programming Concept." *Commun. ACM*, Vol. 21, No. 11, pp. 934–941.

Cardelli, L., J. Donahue, L. Glassman, M. Jordan, B. Kalsow, and G. Nelson. (1989) Modula-3 Report (revised). Digital System Research Center, Palo Alto, CA.

Chambers, C., and D. Ungar. (1991) "Making Pure Object-Oriented Languages Practical." *SIGPLAN Notices*, Vol. 26, No. 1, pp. 1–15.

Chomsky, N. (1956) "Three Models for the Description of Language." *IRE Transactions on Information Theory*, Vol. 2, No. 3, pp. 113–124.

Chomsky, N. (1959) "On Certain Formal Properties of Grammars." *Information and Control*, Vol. 2, No. 2, pp. 137–167.

Church, A. (1941) *Annals of Mathematics Studies. Volume 6: Calculi of Lambda Conversion*. Princeton Univ. Press, Princeton, NJ. Reprinted by Klaus Reprint Corporation, New York, 1965.

Clark, K.L., and F.G. McCabe. (1984) *Micro-PROLOG: Programming in Logic*. Prentice-Hall, Englewood Cliffs, NJ.

Clarke, L.A., J.C. Wileden, and A.L. Wolf. (1980) "Nesting in Ada Is for the Birds." *ACM SIGPLAN Notices*, Vol. 15, No. 11, pp. 139–145.

Cleaveland, J.C. (1986) *An Introduction to Data Types*. Addison-Wesley, Reading, MA.

Cleaveland, J.C., and R.C. Uzgalis. (1976) *Grammars for Programming Languages: What Every Programmer Should Know About Grammar*. American Elsevier, New York.

Clocksin, W.F., and C.S. Mellish. (1997) *Programming in Prolog,* 4e. Springer-Verlag, New York.

Cohen, J. (1981) "Garbage Collection of Linked Data Structures." *ACM Computing Surveys*, Vol. 13, No. 3, pp. 341–368.

Cohen, J. (1985) "Describing Prolog by Its Implementation and Computation." *Commun. ACM*, Vol. 28, No. 12, pp. 1311–1324.

Conway, M.E. (1963). "Design of a Separable Transition-Diagram Compiler." *Commun. ACM*, Vol. 6, No. 7, pp. 396–408.

Conway, R., and R. Constable. (1976) "PL/CS—A Disciplined Subset of PL/I." Technical Report TR76/293. Department of Computer Science, Cornell University, Ithaca, NY.

Cornell University. (1977) PL/C User's Guide, Release 7.6. Department of Computer Science, Cornell University, Ithaca, NY.

Correa, N. (1992) "Empty Categories, Chain Binding, and Parsing." pp. 83–121, *Principle-Based Parsing*. eEds. R.C. Berwick, S.P. Abney, and C. Tenny., Kluwer Academic Publishers, Boston.

Cuadrado, C.Y., and J.L. Cuadrado. (1985) "Prolog Goes to Work." *BYTE*, August 1985, pp. 151–158.

Dahl, O.-J., E.W. Dijkstra, and C.A.R. Hoare. (1972) *Structured Programming*. Academic Press, New York.

Dahl, O.-J., and K. Nygaard. (1967) "SIMULA 67 Common Base Proposal." Norwegian Computing Center Document, Oslo.

Deliyanni, A., and R.A. Kowalski. (1979) "Logic and Semantic Networks." *Commun. ACM*, Vol. 22, No. 3, pp 184–192.

Department of Defense. (1960) "COBOL, Initial Specifications for a Common Business Oriented Language."

Department of Defense. (1961) "COBOL—1961, Revised Specifications for a Common Business Oriented Language."

Department of Defense. (1962) "COBOL—1961 EXTENDED, Extended Specifications for a Common Business Oriented Language."

Department of Defense. (1975a) "Requirements for High Order Programming Languages, STRAWMAN." July.

Department of Defense. (1975b) "Requirements for High Order Programming Languages, WOODENMAN." August.

Department of Defense. (1976) "Requirements for High Order Programming Languages, TINMAN." June.

Department of Defense. (1977) "Requirements for High Order Programming Languages, IRONMAN." January.

Department of Defense. (1978) "Requirements for High Order Programming Languages, STEELMAN." June.

Department of Defense. (1980a) "Requirements for High Order Programming Languages, STONEMAN." February.

Department of Defense. (1980b) "Requirements for the Programming Environment for the Common High Order Language, STONEMAN."

Department of Defense. (1990) "Ada 9X Requirements." Office of the Under Secretary of Defense for Acquisition, Washington, DC.

Deutsch, L.P., and D.G. Bobrow. (1976) "An Efficient Incremental Automatic Garbage Collector." *Commun. ACM*, Vol. 11, No. 3, pp. 522–526.

Dijkstra, E.W. (1968a) "Goto Statement Considered Harmful." *Commun. ACM*, Vol. 11, No. 3, pp. 147–149.

Dijkstra, E.W. (1968b) "Cooperating Sequential Processes." In *Programming Languages*, F. Genuys (ed.). Academic Press, New York, pp. 43–112.

Dijkstra, E.W. (1972) "The Humble Programmer." *Commun. ACM*, Vol. 15, No. 10, pp. 859–866.

Dijkstra, E.W. (1975). "Guarded Commands, Nondeterminacy, and Formal Derivation of Programs." *Commun. ACM*, Vol. 18, No. 8, pp. 453–457.

Dijkstra, E.W. (1976). *A Discipline of Programming*. Prentice Hall, Englewood Cliffs, NJ.

Dybvig, R.K. (1996) *The Scheme Programming Language* 2e. Prentice Hall PTR, Upper Saddle River, NJ, 248 pages.

Ellis, M.A., and B. Stroustrup (1990) *The Annotated C++ Reference Manual*. Addison-Wesley, Reading, MA.

Ennals, J.R. (1980) "Logic as a Computer Language for Children." Logic Programming Research Reports. Theory of Computing Research Group, Department of Computing, Imperial College of Science and Technology, London.

Farber, D.J., R.E. Griswold, and F.P. Polansky. (1964) "SNOBOL, a String Manipulation Language." *J. ACM*, Vol 11, No. 1, pp. 21–30.

Farrow, R. (1982) "LINGUIST 86: Yet Another Translator Writing System Based on Attribute Grammars." *ACM SIGPLAN Notices*, Vol. 17, No. 6, pp. 160–171.

Feuer, A., and N. Gehani. (1982) "A Comparison of the Programming Languages C and Pascal." *ACM Computing Surveys*, Vol. 14, No. 1, pp. 73–92.

Fischer, C.N., G.F. Johnson, J. Mauney, A. Pal, and D.L. Stock. (1984) "The Poe Language-Based Editor Project." *ACM SIGPLAN Notices*, Vol. 19, No. 5, pp. 21–29.

Fischer, C.N., and R.J. LeBlanc. (1977) "UW-Pascal Reference Manual." Madison Academic Computing Center, Madison, WI.

Fischer, C.N., and R.J. LeBlanc. (1980) "Implementation of Runtime Diagnostics in Pascal." *IEEE Transactions on Software Engineering*, SE-6, No. 4, pp. 313–319.

Fischer, C.N., and R.J. LeBlanc. (1988) *Crafting a Compiler*. Benjamin/Cummings, Menlo Park, CA.

Floyd, R.W. (1967) "Assigning Meanings to Programs." *Proceedings Symposium Applied Mathematics, in Mathematical Aspects of Computer Science*, ed. J.T. Schwartz. American Mathematical Society, Providence, RI.

Frege, G. (1892) "Über Sinn und Bedeutung." *Zeitschrift für Philosophie und Philosophisches Kritik*, Vol. 100, pp. 25–50.

Friedl, J.E.F. (1997) *Mastering Regular Expressions*. O'Reilly Publ. Co., Sabastopol, CA.

Friedman, D.P., and D.S. Wise. (1979) "Reference Counting's Ability to Collect Cycles Is Not Insurmountable." *Information Processing Letters*, Vol. 8, No. 1, pp. 41–45.

Fuchi, K. (1981) "Aiming for Knowledge Information Processing Systems." *Proceedings of the International Conference on Fifth Generation Computing Systems*. Japan Information Processing Development Center, Tokyo. Republished (1982) by North-Holland Publishing, Amsterdam.

Gehani, N. (1983) *Ada: An Advanced Introduction*. Prentice-Hall, Englewood Cliffs, NJ.

Ghezzi, C., and M. Jazayeri. (1987) *Programming Language Concepts*. 2d ed. Wiley, New York.

Gilman, L., and A.J. Rose. (1976) *APL: An Interactive Approach*. 2d ed. J. Wiley, New York.

Goldberg, A., and D. Robson. (1983) *Smalltalk-80: The Language and Its Implementation*. Addison-Wesley, Reading, MA.

Goodenough, J.B. (1975) "Exception Handling: Issues and Proposed Notation." *Commun. ACM*, Vol. 18, No. 12, pp. 683–696.

Goos, G., and J. Hartmanis (eds.). (1983) *The Programming Language Ada Reference Manual*. American National Standards Institute. ANSI/MIL-STD-1815A–1983. Lecture Notes in Computer Science 155. Springer-Verlag, New York.

Gordon, M. (1979) *The Denotational Description of Programming Languages, An Introduction*. Springer-Verlag, Berlin–New York.

Gosling, J., B. Joy, and G. Steele. (1996) *The Java Language Specification*. Addison-Wesley, Reading, MA.

Gries, D. (1981) *The Science of Programming*. Springer-Verlag, New York.

Griswold, R.E., and M.T. Griswold. (1983) *The ICON Programming Language*. Prentice-Hall, Englewood Cliffs, NJ.

Griswold, R.E., F. Poage, and I.P. Polonsky. (1971) *The SNOBOL 4 Programming Language*. 2d ed. Prentice-Hall, Englewood Cliffs, NJ.

Hammond, P. (1983) APES: A User Manual. Department of Computing Report 82/9. Imperial College of Science and Technology, London.

Henderson, P. (1980) *Functional Programming: Application and Implementation*. Prentice-Hall, Englewood Cliffs, NJ.

Hoare, C.A.R. (1969) "An Axiomatic Basis of Computer Programming." *Commun. ACM*, Vol. 12, No. 10, pp. 576–580.

Hoare, C.A.R. (1972) "Proof of Correctness of Data Representations." *Acta Informatica*, Vol. 1, pp. 271–281.

Hoare, C.A.R. (1973) "Hints on Programming Language Design." *Proceedings ACM SIGACT/SIGPLAN Conference on Principles of Programming Languages.* Also published as Technical Report STAN-CS-73-403, Stanford University Computer Science Department.

Hoare, C.A.R. (1974) "Monitors: An Operating System Structuring Concept." *Commun. ACM*, Vol. 17, No. 10, pp. 549–557.

Hoare, C.A.R. (1978) "Communicating Sequential Processes." *Commun. ACM*, Vol. 21, No. 8, pp. 666–677.

Hoare, C.A.R. (1981) "The Emperor's Old Clothes." *Commun. ACM*, Vol. 24, No. 2, pp. 75–83.

Hoare, C.A.R., and N. Wirth. (1973) "An Axiomatic Definition of the Programming Language Pascal." *Acta Informatica*. Vol. 2, pp. 335–355.

Hogger, C.J. (1984) *Introduction to Logic Programming*. Academic Press, London.

Holt, R.C., G.S. Graham, E.D. Lazowska, and M.A. Scott. (1978) *Structured Concurrent Programming with Operating Systems Applications*. Addison-Wesley, Reading, MA.

Horn, A. (1951) "On Sentences Which Are True of Direct Unions of Algebras." *J. Symbolic Logic*, Vol. 16, pp. 14–21.

Hudak, P. and J. Fasel. (1992) "A Gentle Introduction to Haskell,"", ACM SIG-PLAN Notices, 27(5), May 1992, pp. T1–T53.

Huskey, H.K., R. Love, and N. Wirth. (1963) "A Syntactic Description of BC NELIAC." *Commun. ACM*, Vol. 6, No. 7, pp. 367–375.

IBM. (1954) "Preliminary Report, Specifications for the IBM Mathematical FORmula TRANslating System, FORTRAN." IBM Corporation, New York.

IBM. (1956) "Programmer's Reference Manual, The FORTRAN Automatic Coding System for the IBM 704 EDPM." IBM Corporation, New York.

IBM. (1964) "The New Programming Language." IBM UK Laboratories.

Ichbiah, J.D., J.C. Heliard, O. Roubine, J.G.P. Barnes, B. Krieg-Brueckner, and B.A. Wichmann. (1979) "Rationale for the Design of the Ada Programming Language." *ACM SIGPLAN Notices*, Vol. 14, No. 6, Part B.

IEEE. (1985) "Binary Floating-Point Arithmetic." IEEE Standard 754, IEEE, New York.

Ingerman, P.Z. (1967). "Panini-Backus Form Suggested." *Commun. ACM*, Vol. 10, No. 3, p. 137.

Intermetrics. (1993) Programming Language Ada, Draft, Version 4.0. Cambridge, MA.

ISO. (1982) *Specification for Programming Language Pascal*. ISO7185–1982. International Organization for Standardization, Geneva, Switzerland.

Iverson, K.E. (1962) *A Programming Language*. John Wiley, New York.

Jensen, K., and N. Wirth. (1974) *Pascal Users Manual and Report*. Springer-Verlag, Berlin.

Johnson, S.C. (1975) "Yacc—Yet Another Compiler Compiler." Computing Science Report 32. A.T.& T. Bell Laboratories, Murray Hill, NJ.

Jones, N.D. (ed.) (1980) *Semantic-Directed Compiler Generation*. Lecture Notes in Computer Science, Vol. 94. Springer-Verlag, Heidelberg, FRG.

Kay, A. (1969) The Reactive Engine. Ph.D. Thesis. University of Utah, September.

Kernighan, B.W., and R. Pike. (1984) *The UNIX Programming Environment*. Prentice-Hall, Englewood Cliffs, NJ.

Kernighan, B.W., and D.M. Ritchie. (1978) *The C Programming Language*. Prentice-Hall, Englewood Cliffs, NJ.

Knuth, D.E. (1967) "The Remaining Trouble Spots in ALGOL 60." *Commun. ACM*, Vol. 10, No. 10, pp. 611–618.

Knuth, D.E. (1968a) "Semantics of Context-Free Languages." *Mathematical Systems Theory*, Vol. 2, No. 2, pp. 127–146.

Knuth, D.E. (1968b) *The Art of Computer Programming*, Vol. I. 2d ed. Addison-Wesley, Reading, MA.

Knuth, D.E. (1974) "Structured Programming with GOTO Statements." *ACM Computing Surveys*, Vol. 6, No. 4, pp. 261–301.

Knuth, D.E. (1981) *The Art of Computer Programming*, Vol. II. 2d ed. Addison-Wesley, Reading, MA.

Knuth, D.E., and Luis Trabb Pardo. (1977) "Early Development of Programming Languages." In *Encyclopedia of Computer Science and Technology*, Vol. 7. Dekker, New York, pp. 419–493.

Kowalski, R.A. (1979) *Logic for Problem Solving*. Artificial Intelligence Series, Vol. 7. Elsevier-North Holland, New York.

Lampson, B.W. (1983) "A Description of the Cedar Language." Tech. Report CSL-83-15. Xerox Palo Alto Research Center, December.

Lampson, B.W., J.J. Horning, R.L. London, J.G. Mitchell, and G.J. Popek. (1977) "Report on the Programming Language Euclid." *ACM SIGPLAN Notices*, Vol. 12, No. 2. (Revised Report, XEROX PARC Technical Report CSL78-2.)

Laning, J.H., Jr., and N. Zierler. (1954) "A Program for Translation of Mathematical Equations for Whirlwind I." Engineering memorandum E-364. Instrumentation Laboratory, Massachusetts Institute of Technology, Cambridge, MA.

Ledgard, H. (1984) *The American Pascal Standard*. Springer-Verlag, New York.

Ledgard, H.F., and M. Marcotty. (1975) "A Genealogy of Control Structures." *Commun. ACM*, Vol. 18, No. 11, pp. 629–639.

Liskov, B., and A. Snyder. (1979) "Exception Handling in CLU." *IEEE Transactions on Software Engineering*, Vol. SE-5, No. 6, pp. 546–558.

Lomet, D. (1975) "Scheme for Invalidating References to Freed Storage." *IBM J. of Research and Development*, Vol. 19, pp. 26–35.

MacLaren, M.D. (1977) "Exception Handling in PL/I." *ACM SIGPLAN Notices*, Vol. 12, No. 3, pp. 101–104.

Marcotty, M., H.F. Ledgard, and G.V. Bochmann. (1976) "A Sampler of Formal Definitions." *ACM Computing Surveys*, Vol. 8, No. 2, pp. 191–276.

Mather, D.G. and S.V. Waite (eds.). (1971) *BASIC*. 6th ed. University Press of New England, Hanover, NH.

McCarthy, J. (1960) "Recursive Functions of Symbolic Expressions and Their Computation by Machine, Part I." *Commun. ACM*, Vol. 3, No. 4, pp. 184–195.

McCarthy, J., P.W. Abrahams, D.J. Edwards, T.P. Hart, and M. Levin. (1965) *LISP 1.5 Programmer's Manual*. 2d ed. MIT Press, Cambridge, MA.

McCracken, D. (1970) "Whither APL." *Datamation*, Sept. 15, pp. 53–57.

Meyer, B. (1992) *Eiffel the Language*. Prentice-Hall, Englewood Cliffs, NJ.

Microsoft. (1991) *Microsoft Visual Basic Language Reference*. Document DB20664-0491, Redmond, WA.

Milner, R., M. Tofte, and R. Harper. (1990) *The Definition of Standard ML*. MIT Press, Cambridge, MA.

Milos, D., U. Pleban, and G. Loegel. (1984) "Direct Implementation of Compiler Specifications." *ACM Principles of Programming Languages 1984*, pp. 196–202.

Mitchell, J.G., W. Maybury, and R. Sweet. (1979) *Mesa Language Manual*, Version 5.0, CSL-79-3. Xerox Research Center, Palo Alto, CA.

Mössenbock, H. (1993) *Object-Oriented Programming in Oberon-2*. Springer-Verlag, New York.

Moto-oka, T. (1981) "Challenge for Knowledge Information Processing Systems." *Proceedings of the International Conference on Fifth Generation Computing Systems*. Japan Information Processing Development Center, Tokyo. Republished (1982) by North-Holland Publishing, Amsterdam.

Naur, P. (ed.) (1960) "Report on the Algorithmic Language ALGOL 60." *Commun. ACM*, Vol. 3, No. 5, pp. 299–314.

Newell, A., and H.A. Simon. (1956) "The Logic Theory Machine—A Complex Information Processing System." *IRE Transactions on Information Theory*, Vol. IT-2, No. 3, pp. 61–79.

Newell, A., and F.M. Tonge. (1960) "An Introduction to Information Processing Language V." *Commun. ACM*, Vol. 3, No. 4, pp. 205–211.

Nilsson, N.J. (1971) *Problem Solving Methods in Artificial Intelligence*. McGraw-Hill, New York.

Osterhout, J.K. (1994) *Tcl and the Tk Toolkit*. Addison-Wesley, Reading, MA.

Pagan, F.G. (1981) *Formal Specifications of Programming Languages*. Prentice-Hall, Englewood Cliffs, NJ.

Papert, S. (1980) *MindStorms: Children, Computers and Powerful Ideas*. Basic Books, New York.

Perlis, A., and K. Samelson. (1958) "Preliminary Report—International Algebraic Language." *Commun. ACM*, Vol. 1, No. 12, pp. 8–22.

Peyton Jones, S.L. (1987) *The Implementation of Functional Programming Languages*. Prentice-Hall, Englewood Cliffs, NJ.

Polivka, R.P., and S. Pakin. (1975) *APL: The Language and Its Usage*. Prentice-Hall, Englewood Cliffs, NJ.

Pratt, T.W. (1984) *Programming Languages: Design and Implementation*. 2d ed. Prentice-Hall, Englewood Cliffs, NJ.

Rees, J., and W. Clinger. (1986) "Revised Report on the Algorithmic Language Scheme." *ACM SIGPLAN Notices*, Vol. 21, No. 12, pp. 37–79.

Remington-Rand. (1952) "UNIVAC Short Code." Unpublished collection of dittoed notes. Preface by A.B. Tonik, dated October 25, 1955 (1 p.); Preface by J.R. Logan, undated but apparently from 1952 (1 p.); Preliminary exposition, 1952? (22 pp., where in which pp. 20–22 appear to be a later replacement); Short code supplementary information, topic one (7 pp.); Addenda #1, 2, 3, 4 (9 pp.).

Richards, M. (1969) "BCPL: A Tool for Compiler Writing and Systems Programming." *Proc. AFIPS SJCC*, Vol. 34, pp. 557–566.

Robinson, J.A. (1965) "A Machine-Oriented Logic Based on the Resolution Principle." *Journal of the ACM*, Vol. 12, pp. 23–41.

Roussel. P. (1975) "PROLOG: Manual de Reference et D'utilisation." Research Report. Artificial Intelligence Group, Univ. of Aix-Marseille, Luming, France.

Rovner, P. (1986) "Extending Modula-2 to Build Large, Integrated Systems." *IEEE Software*, Vol. 3, No. 6, November.

Rubin, F. (1987) "'GOTO Statement Considered Harmful' considered harmful" (letter to editor). *Commun. ACM*, Vol. 30, No. 3, pp. 195–196.

Rutishauser, H. (1967) *Description of ALGOL 60*. Springer-Verlag, New York.

Sammet, J.E. (1969) *Programming Languages: History and Fundamentals*. Prentice-Hall, Englewood Cliffs, NJ.

Sammet, J.E. (1976) "Roster of Programming Languages for 1974–75." *Commun. ACM*, Vol. 19, No. 12, pp. 655–669.

Schorr, H., and W. Waite. (1967) "An Efficient Machine Independent Procedure for Garbage Collection in Various List Structures." *Commun. ACM*, Vol. 10, No. 8, pp. 501–506.

Scott, D.S., and C. Strachey. (1971) "Towards a Mathematical Semantics for Computer Language." *Proceedings, Symposium on Computers and Automation*, ed. J. Fox. Polytechnic Institute of Brooklyn Press, New York, pp. 19–46.

Sebesta, R.W. (1991) *VAX Structured Assembly Language Programming* 2e. Benjamin/Cummings Publ. Co., Redwood City, CA.

Sergot, M.J. (1983) "A Query-the-User Facility for Logic Programming." In *Integrated Interactive Computer Systems*, eds. P. Degano and E. Sandewall. North-Holland Publishing, Amsterdam.

Sewry, D.A. (1984b) "Modula-2 and the Monitor Concept." *ACM SIGPLAN Notices*, Vol. 19, No. 11, pp. 33–41.

Shaw, C.J. (1963) "A Specification of JOVIAL." *Commun. ACM*, Vol. 6, No. 12, pp. 721–736.

Sommerville, I. (1992) *Software Engineering*. 4th ed., Addison-Wesley, Reading, MA.

Steele, G.L., Jr. (1984) *Common LISP*. Digital Press, Burlington, MA.

Stoy, J.E. (1977) *Denotational Semantics: The Scott-Strachey Approach to Programming Language Semantics*. MIT Press, Cambridge, MA.

Stroustrup, B. (1983) "Adding Classes to C: An Exercise in Language Evolution." Software—Practice and Experience, Vol. 13, pp. 139–161.

Stroustrup, B. (1984) "Data Abstraction in C." *AT & T Bell Laboratories Technical Journal*, Vol. 63, No. 8.

Stroustrup, B. (1986) *The C++ Programming Language*. Addison-Wesley, Reading, MA.

Stroustrup, B. (1988) "What Is Object-Oriented Programming?" *IEEE Software*, May 1988, pp. 10–20.

Stroustrup, B. (1991) *The C++ Programming Language*. 2d ed. Addison-Wesley, Reading, MA.

Sussman, G.J., and G.L. Steele, Jr. (1975) "Scheme: An Interpreter for Extended Lambda Calculus." MIT AI Memo No. 349 (December, 1975).

Suzuki, N. (1982) "Analysis of Pointer 'Rotation'." *Commun. ACM*, Vol. 25, No. 5, pp. 330–335.

Tanenbaum, A.S. (1978) "A Comparison of Pascal and ALGOL 68." *Computer Journal*, Vol. 21, pp. 316–323.

Tanenbaum, A.S. (1990) *Structured Computer Organization*. 3d ed. Prentice-Hall, Englewood Cliffs, NJ.

Tanenbaum, A.S., Y. Langsam, and M.J. Augenstein (1990) *Data Structures Using C*. Prentice-Hall, Englewood Cliffs, NJ.

Taylor, W., L. Turner, and R. Waychoff. (1961) "A Syntactic Chart of ALGOL 60." *Commun. ACM*, Vol. 4, p. 393.

Teitelbaum, T., and T. Reps. (1981) "The Cornell Program Synthesizer: A Syntax-Directed Programming Environment." *Commun. ACM*, Vol. 24, No. 9, pp. 563–573.

Teitelman, W. (1975) *INTERLISP Reference Manual*. Xerox Palo Alto Research Center, Palo Alto, CA.

Thompson, S. (1996) *Haskell: The Craft of Functional Programming*. Addison-Wesley, Reading, MA, 500 pages.

Turner, D. (1986) "An Overview of Miranda." *ACM SIGPLAN Notices*, Vol. 21, No. 12, pp. 158–166.

Turner, D. (1990) (ed.) *Research Topics in Functional Programming*. Addison-Wesley, Reading, MA.

Ullman, J.D. (1994) *Elements of ML Programming*. Prentice-Hall, Englewood Cliffs, NJ.

Van Emden, M.H. (1980) "McDermott on Prolog: A Rejoinder." *SIGART Newsletter*, No. 72, August, pp. 19–20.

van Wijngaarden, A. B.J. Mailloux, J.E.L. Peck, and C.H.A. Koster. (1969) "Report on the Algorithmic Language ALGOL 68." *Numerische Mathematik*, Vol. 14, No. 2, pp. 79–218.

Wall, L., T. Christiansen, and R.L. Schwartz. (1996) *Programming perl, 2e*. O'Reilly & Associates, Sebastopol, CA.

Warren, D.H.D., L.M. Pereira, and F.C.N. Pereira. (1977) "Prolog: The Language and Its Implementation Compared to LISP." *ACM SIGPLAN Notices*, Vol. 12, No. 8, and *ACM SIGART Newsletter*, Vol. 6, No. 4.

Warren, D.H.D., L.M. Pereira, and F.C.N. Pereira. (1979) "User's Guide to DEC System-10 Prolog." Occasional Paper 15. Department of Artificial Intelligence, Univ. of Edinburgh, Scotland.

Watt, D.A. (1979) "An Extended Attribute Grammar for Pascal." *ACM SIGPLAN Notices*, Vol. 14, No. 2, pp. 60–74.

Wegner, P. (1972) "The Vienna Definition Language." *ACM Computing Surveys*, Vol. 4, No. 1, pp. 5–63.

Weissman, C. (1967) *LISP 1.5 Primer*. Dickenson Press, Belmont, CA.

Welsh, J., M.J. Sneeringer, and C.A.R. Hoare. (1977) "Ambiguities and Insecurities in Pascal." *Software—Practice and Experience*, Vol. 7, No. 6, pp. 685–696.

Wexelblat, R.L. (ed.). (1981) *History of Programming Languages*. Academic Press, New York.

Wheeler, D.J. (1950) "Programme Organization and Initial Orders for the EDSAC." *Proc. R. Soc. London*, Ser. A, Vol. 202, pp. 573–589.

Wilkes, M.V. (1952) "Pure and Applied Programming." In *Proceedings of the ACM National Conference*, Vol. 2. Toronto, pp. 121–124.

Wilkes, M.V., D.J. Wheeler, and S. Gill. (1951) *The Preparation of Programs for an Electronic Digital Computer, with Special Reference to the EDSAC and the Use of a Library of Subroutines*. Addison-Wesley, Reading, MA.

Wilkes, M.V., D.J. Wheeler, and S. Gill (1957) *The Preparation of Programs for an Electronic Digital Computer*. 2d ed. Addison-Wesley, Reading, MA.

Wirth, N. (1971) "The Programming Language Pascal." *Acta Informatica*, Vol. 1, No. 1, pp. 35–63.

Wirth, N. (1973) *Systematic Programming: An Introduction*. Prentice-Hall, Englewood Cliffs, NJ.

Wirth, N. (1975) "On the Design of Programming Languages." *Information Processing 74* (Proceedings of IFIP Congress 74), North Holland, Amsterdam, pp. 386–393.

Wirth, N. (1977) "Modula: A Language for Modular Multi-Programming." *Software—Practice and Experience*, Vol. 7, pp. 3–35.

Wirth, N. (1985) *Programming in Modula-2*. 3d ed. Springer-Verlag, New York.

Wirth, N. (1988) "The Programming Language Oberon." *Software—Practice and Experience*, Vol. 18, No. 7, pp. 671–690.

Wirth, N., and C.A.R. Hoare. (1966) "A Contribution to the Development of ALGOL." *Commun. ACM*, Vol. 9, No. 6, pp. 413–431.

Wulf, W.A., D.B. Russell, and A.N. Habermann. (1971) "BLISS: A Language for Systems Programming." *Commun. ACM*, Vol. 14, No. 12, pp. 780–790.

Zuse, K. (1972) "Der Plankalkül." Manuscript prepared in 1945, published in *Berichte der Gesellschaft für Mathematik und Datenverarbeitung*, No. 63 (Bonn, 1972); Part 3, 285 pp. English translation of all but pp. 176–196 in No. 106 (Bonn, 1976), pp. 42–244.

Index

J